EDEN Annual Conference 2024

Learning in the Age of AI: Towards Imaginative Futures

Full Papers

Graz, Austria
16 - 18 June 2024

Editors:

Josep M. Duart
Elena Trepule

ISBN: 979-8-3313-0344-0

Printed from e-media with permission by:

Curran Associates, Inc.
57 Morehouse Lane
Red Hook, NY 12571

Some format issues inherent in the e-media version may also appear in this print version.

European Distance and E-Learning Network (EDEN)
Budapest University of Technology & Economics
H-1111 Budapest, Egry J. u.1.
Hungary

secretariat@eden-online.org

Additional copies of this publication are available from:

Curran Associates, Inc.
57 Morehouse Lane
Red Hook, NY 12571 USA
Phone: 845-758-0400
Fax: 845-758-2633
Email: curran@proceedings.com
Web: www.proceedings.com

TABLE OF CONTENTS

The Tokenization Problem: Understanding Generative AI's Computational Language Bias

Marijana Asprovska[1], Nathan Hunter[2]

[1] University of Glasgow, United Kingdom; marijanaasprovska@gmail.com
[2] United Kingdom, nathan@chatgpttrainings.com

Correspondence: Marijana Asprovska: marijanaasprovska@gmail.com

Abstract:

The revolutionary potential of ChatGPT raises a critical question: Revolutionary for whom? This paper examines potential inequalities in how ChatGPT "tokenizes" texts across different languages. Translated 3,000-5,000 character passages in 108 languages were analyzed using OpenAI's tokenizer. English was treated as the baseline, with a "token multiplier" calculated for each language. The analysis revealed English was over 13 times more efficient than some languages. Key findings showed while the pre-training dataset size and character counts have nuanced roles, the alphabet used and the prevalence of special characters significantly impact efficiency. These discrepancies have real-world implications regarding usage costs and model limitations across languages. Thus, consciously addressing the tokenization imbalance is critical for ensuring equitable access to AI systems across diverse languages.

Keywords: ChatGPT; tokenization; language efficiency; language bias.

Introduction

The revolutionary rise of ChatGPT has sparked immense curiosity about the capabilities of generative AI. Since its launch in November 2022, ChatGPT has seen explosive user growth, surpassing major platforms like Spotify and Instagram to become the fastest adopted app in history (Buchholz, 2023; Wodecki, 2023). The promise of transformative productivity and learning gains with ChatGPT has captivated public interest. Surveys show widespread adoption, with 89% of American workers utilizing AI tools (Checkr.com, 2023) and students leveraging ChatGPT for tutoring support (Intelligent.com, 2023).

However, as the hype builds around ChatGPT's potential, a critical question arises: Who stands to benefit the most from this AI revolution? Evidence suggests significant inequality. While 80% of leaders use AI regularly, only 20% of frontline workers do so, with less training support (Beauchene et al., 2023). More pressingly, non-native English speakers face greater barriers fully capitalizing on ChatGPT, with higher plagiarism accusations (Liang et al., 2023) and weaker performance across languages (Lai et al., 2023).

This paper investigates a core technological factor potentially driving language inequality in ChatGPT – imbalances in how texts are tokenized across languages. We introduce the notion of "tokenization efficiency" ("efficiency" for short) relative to English and systematically analyze 108 languages using OpenAI's tokenizer. We define tokenization efficiency as how many tokens are needed for a particular text. Our goal is twofold: (1) uncover what factors, like dataset size, alphabet, and special characters, significantly impact efficiency, and (2) quantify the inequality between languages in the tokenization process, which impacts cost of use, cost of training, context window size, and output size.

The role of tokens in Large Language Models

As a Large Language Model (LLM), ChatGPT's architecture is based on the transformer model – a neural network architecture that learns context by tracking relationships in sequential data (e.g. words in a sentence)

(Vaswani et al., 2017). It means ChatGPT generates coherent text through techniques of next-word prediction and language modelling. Fundamental to the transformer are tokens, which make up the basic computational units the model processes to represent pieces of text. For instance, as Figure 1 shows, the sentence "The cat sat on the mat" is broken into tokens i.e. tokenized in the following way: "The", "cat", "sat", "on", "the", "mat". Each token is converted into a number allowing the model to analyze the words sequentially and understand the relationships to one another in order to determine the meaning.

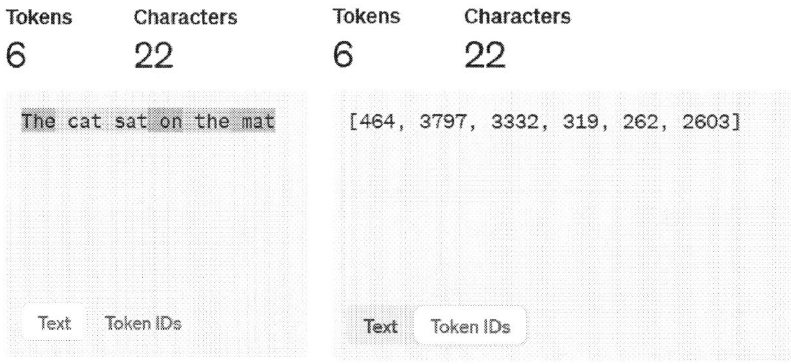

Figure 1: Token breakdown of a sentence using OpenAI's Tokenizer (https://platform.openai.com/tokenizer)

In English, most words are related to a single token, while others could have two or more tokens to express the word. An efficient tokenization process is one where fewer tokens are needed to represent the set of words given. Language A could be considered less efficient in tokenization than language B if more tokens are needed to represent language A than needed for language B.

LLMs have a limit on how much information they can process while predicting the next word. This limit is called "context window". The context window is measured in tokens, not words. The number of tokens used correlates to the computational power needed, which in turn impacts the cost of usage. Each token processed requires computing resources, so more tokens mean greater resource requirements. Companies like OpenAI incur these costs when running transformer models, and charge usage fees based on tokens to cover expenses. For example, OpenAI prices access to the GPT-4 32k model at $0.06 per 1,000 tokens used for a context window of 32,000 tokens (OpenAI, n.d.). Since the context window is measured in tokens, a language requiring more tokens than another for the same content will have higher real-world usage costs. Additionally, with a fixed context window limit, fewer words of a less efficient language can be processed by the model.

Research methods

The principal goal of this research was to compare how different languages are tokenized in ChatGPT. To conduct a comprehensive and unbiased analysis, a robust and systematic methodology was devised, detailed in the sections below.

Text selection

Four distinct types of text were selected to ensure wide coverage of language usage: an excerpt from a news article (sourced from The Guardian), a chapter from a children's book (Peter Pan), an excerpt from a school book (The Art of Ancient Egypt), and an excerpt from a philosophical book (The Second Sex). Each text was between 3,000 and 5,000 characters in length in English, providing a diverse range of linguistic complexity and stylistic variations.

Translation

Each selected text was translated into 108 languages using Google Translate. A recent study by Aiken (2019) found that while some variability exists, Google Translate provides relatively consistent translation accuracy across a wide range of languages. Using Google Translate also helps control for potential inconsistencies in translation quality and style that could skew results if human translators were used.

Tokenization

After translating the texts, OpenAI's tokenizer (https://platform.openai.com/tokenizer) was used to break down the translated text into tokens. When given a text in any language, the tokenizer calculates the number of tokens the text will be broken up into. Each of the four translated texts from the 108 languages were given to the tokenizer, and the total token count was recorded.

Data analysis

This paper introduces a "token multiplier of English" as the main comparative measure. Since the objective of this paper is to quantify the differences in tokenization costs between languages, using metrics like "words to 1000 tokens" or "characters to 1000 tokens" wouldn't have been suitable. For instance, while the Hawaiian translation of our first text consisted of 700 words, the Hebrew version of the same text contained only 361 words. Using such metrics could have obscured the token efficiency differences between languages in our findings due to differences in word or character count. Our chosen methodology required comparing texts with equivalent meanings and determining the discrepancies in token counts for each. English token efficiency serves as the reference point for comparing the token efficiency of other languages. For instance, if an English text has 100 tokens, and another language requires 200 tokens, then the latter language would have a "token multiplier of English" value of 2. On the other hand, if the translation requires only 50 tokens, its token multiplier would be 0.5.[1]

Findings

This research has four hypothesis for predicting which factors would influence the inequality in tokenization across languages:

1. The higher the number of characters in a text, the more tokens the text will use.
2. The size of the pre-training dataset influences the efficiency of the tokenization process.
3. Languages with Latin-based alphabets have more efficient tokenization.
4. Languages using Latin-based alphabets with a higher frequency of special characters have less efficient tokenization.

Figure 2 displays the tokenization efficiency per language as compared to English for the 108 languages analyzed, based on the four chosen texts. The results show English outperforming all other languages in terms of tokenization efficiency, with the least efficient languages being over 13 times less efficient when parsed into tokens.

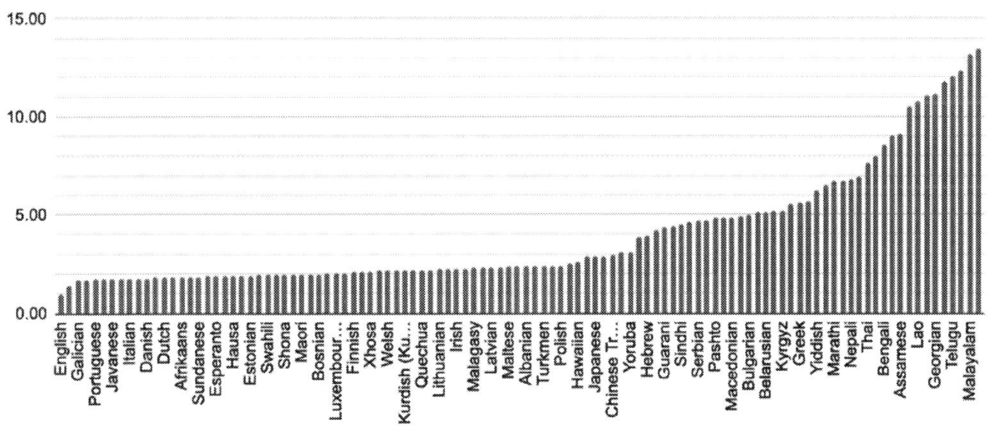

Figure 2: Tokenization efficiency per language[2]

[1] All texts, translations, tokenization processes, and statistical data are available in the appendix of this paper.

[2] Due to legibility constraints, not all languages could be displayed on this initial chart. A comprehensive account of the data collected for all languages is available in the appendix.

Hypothesis 1: The higher the number of characters in a text, the more tokens the text will use

Although many languages have been identified as having similar efficiency levels when spoken, as pointed out in a study by Coupé et al. (2019), the data revealed considerable discrepancies in the number of characters used in Google Translate's output.

The relationship between the average number of characters and the number of tokens used for different languages is shown in Figure 3. The relationship between the two is not consistently proportional across the different languages, making it evident that the number of characters in a text is not heavily defining the efficiency of the language. For example, Georgian uses fewer characters than English does, yet it is still 11 times less efficient than English itself.

To probe this relationship further, the correlation coefficient between the average number of characters used and the number of tokens produced was calculated. The analysis resulted in a correlation coefficient of -0.057, signifying a negligible correlation. This suggests that the proficiency of a language in converting meaning into characters does not substantially impact the tokenization process. Therefore, there is almost no relationship between the number of characters and the number of tokens when comparing texts that have been literally translated.

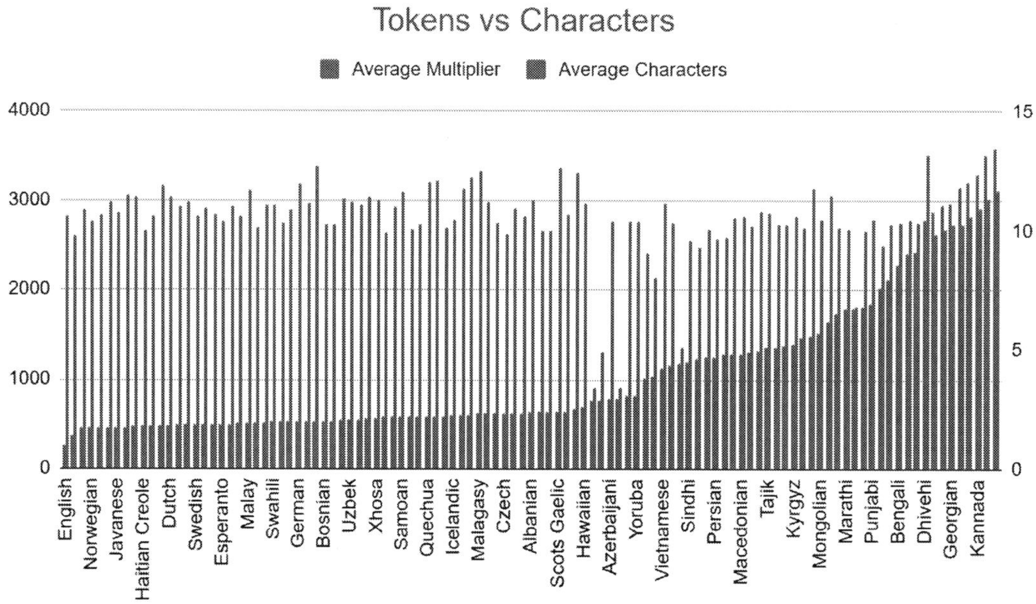

Figure 2: The relationship between the average number of characters and tokens for different languages

Hypothesis 2: The size of the pre-training dataset influences the efficiency of the tokenization process

OpenAI has not explicitly revealed the precise sources of the data used in their pre-training datasets. Nevertheless, Hypothesis 2 postulates that there might be a correlation between the size of the pre-training dataset for a specific language and ChatGPT's capability to effectively tokenize the text. As OpenAI (2023a) suggests in their FAQ, "The models are optimized for use in English, but many of them are robust enough to generate good results for a variety of languages". Since it is unfeasible to obtain a breakdown of ChatGPT's pre-training dataset by language, as OpenAI does not share that data publicly, a similar approach to Lai and colleagues (2023) was adopted. Hence, the data of this research was compared against the language breakdown of the Common Crawl corpus – a frequently used dataset for pre-training LLMs. It shall be noted that languages are represented in the Common Crawl corpus unevenly. The distribution of text across languages typically reflects the linguistic diversity of the internet and the prevalence of specific languages online. The comparison is shown in Figure 4.

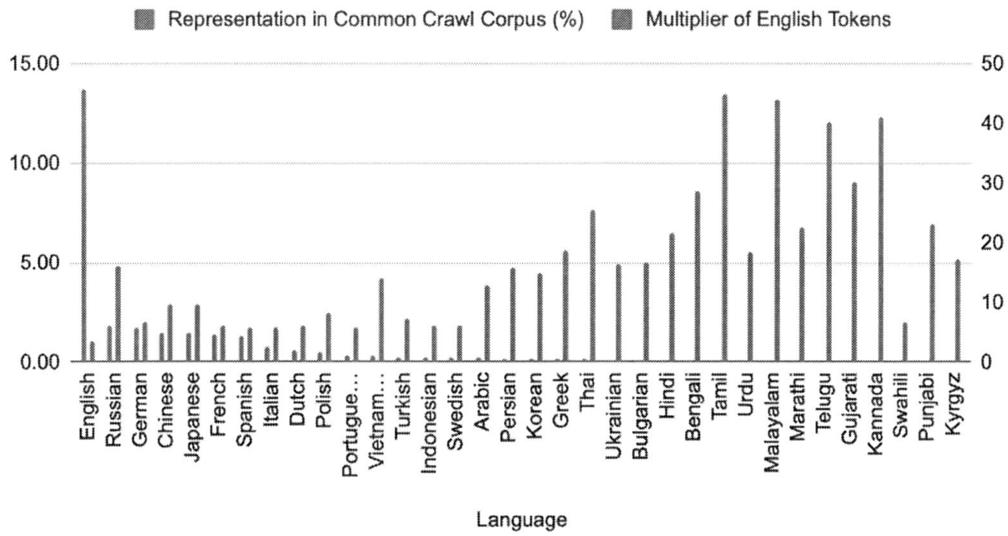

Figure 4: Comparison between the data of the research and the representation of different languages in the Common Crawl corpus

The correlation calculations resulted in a coefficient of -0.312, which indicates a rather low significance in this regard. The languages that proved most efficient in terms of tokenization were Latin, Galician, and Norwegian – languages that are perhaps not typically expected to be OpenAI's priority for their pre-training dataset. Conversely, while Russian is the second most dominant language in the Common Crawl corpus, its efficiency is almost three times less than that of Norwegian. Such results show an exceedingly weak relationship between the size of the pre-training dataset and the number of tokens different languages use for the same amount of characters.

Hypothesis 3: Languages with Latin-based alphabets have more efficient tokenization

Out of the 108 languages compared, 66 of them use Latin-based alphabets while the top 61 most efficient languages in terms of tokenization also use a Latin-based alphabet. It is plausible that ChatGPT's competence in efficiently tokenizing words in one language could enhance its performance in another language that shares a similar alphabet. This could potentially account for why Latin proves so efficient in tokenization.

Table 1: Analyzed alphabets and their standard deviations of tokenization performance

	Arabic alphabet	**Cyrillic alphabet**	**Devanagari alphabet**	**Latin alphabet**	**All alphabets**
Standard deviation	0.51	0.29	0.12	0.51	3.01

Table 1 shows the alphabets analyzed in this paper. Among the languages analyzed, four distinct alphabets were used by three or more languages. Upon examining the standard deviation of tokenization performance within any given alphabet, deviations as low as 0.12, 0.29, and 0.51 were found. This suggests that the efficiency of tokenization for languages within the same alphabet family is relatively consistent. Meanwhile, the standard deviation considering tokenization performance across all languages and alphabets was 3.01. This indicates a higher variability in tokenization efficiency across languages with different alphabets. A detailed view is offered in Figure 5.

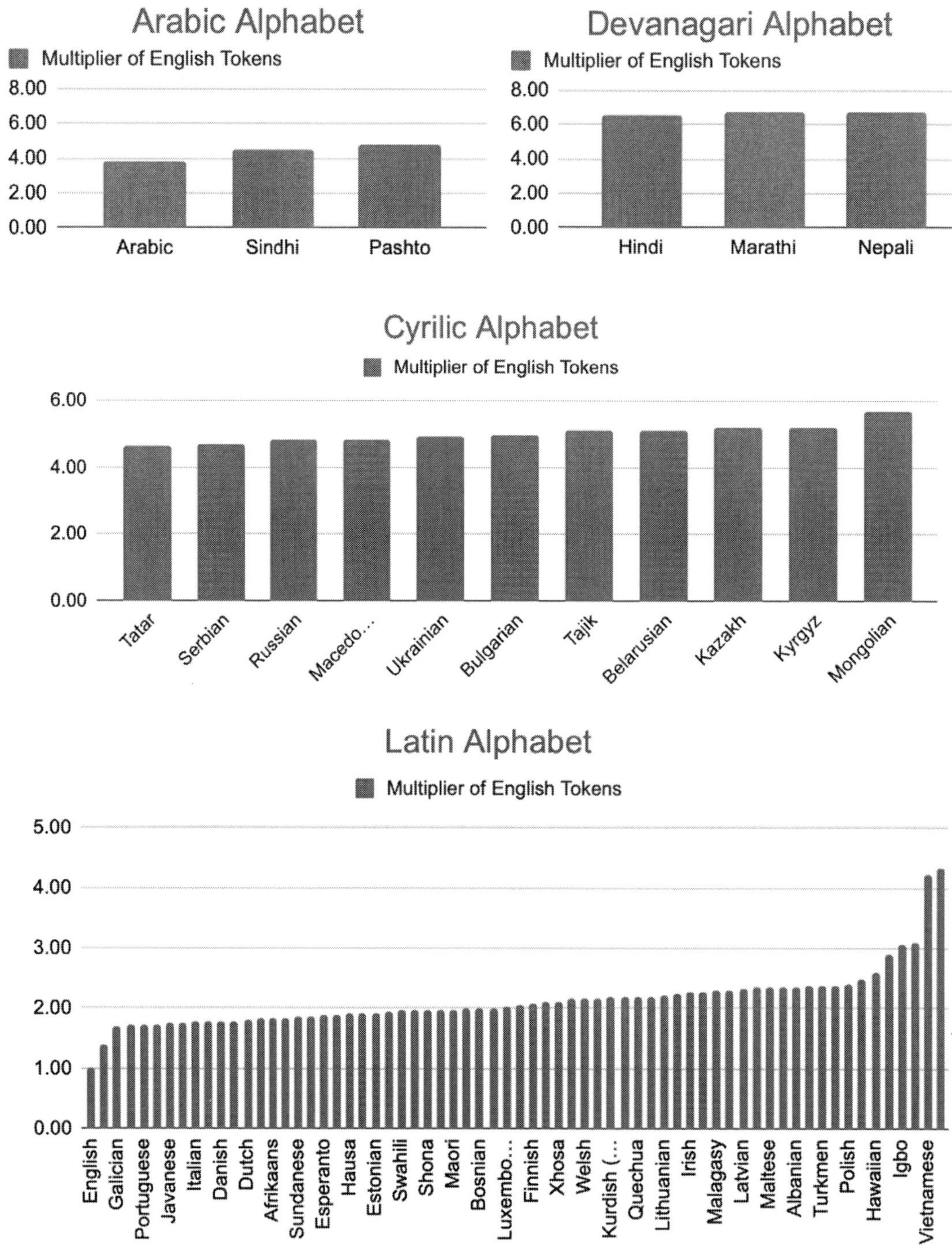

Figure 5: Tokenization efficiency by different alphabet

However, even with this level of analysis, when looking at the Latin alphabet chart in Figure 5, it can be seen that there is a substantial amount of unexplained variance that extends beyond the influence of the alphabet itself. This implies that, while the alphabet used by a language does play a role in its tokenization efficiency, there are likely other significant factors at play too.

Hypothesis 4: Languages using Latin-based alphabets with a higher frequency of special characters have less efficient tokenization

In the tokenization process ChatGPT tends to break words containing special characters into a higher number of tokens in comparison to words devoid of these characters. As an illustrative example shown in Figure 6, the word "resume" is broken down in two tokens: "res" and "ume". However, "résumé", which contains special characters, is further fragmented into four tokens: "r", "é", "sum", and "é". This phenomenon leads to speculation about whether the prevalence of special characters in some languages using Latin-based alphabets could influence the efficiency of tokenization.

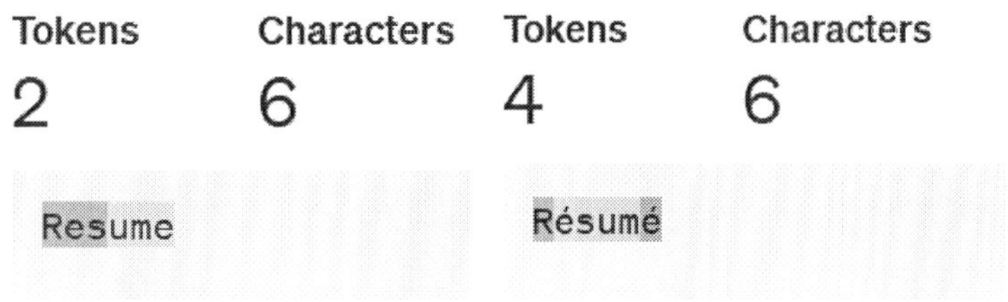

Figure 6: Tokenization process for words with and without special characters (Source: OpenAI's tokenizer)

To test this hypothesis, the average number of special characters present within the texts in languages using Latin-based alphabet was compared to the "multiplier of English tokens". The aim was to discern if the presence of special characters had any meaningful impact on tokenization efficiency within Latin-based alphabets.

The correlation coefficient calculated was 0.677, a figure that implies a moderate to strong positive correlation. This suggests that languages using Latin-based alphabets with a higher frequency of special characters tend to have less efficient tokenization, as the special characters lead to the generation of more tokens for the same meaning. The detailed overview is shown in Figure 7 below.

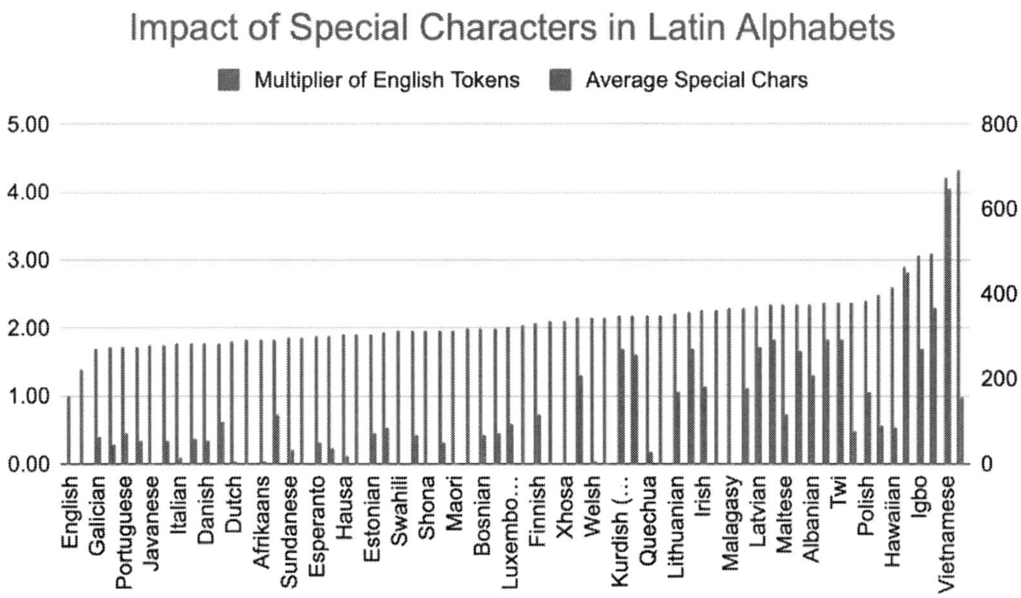

Figure 7: Number of special characters per language with a Latin-based alphabet

This finding not only helps to explain the discrepancies in tokenization efficiency among Latin-based languages but also provides insight into why Latin itself is particularly efficient. With Latin being devoid of special characters, its tokenization process is streamlined, resulting in superior efficiency. Consequently, special characters within Latin-based alphabets emerge as a significant factor influencing tokenization efficiency.

Implications and real-world consequences

The differences in tokenization efficiency identified in this paper could have real-world consequences in terms of creating barriers to entry into the generative AI world and thus driving social inequalities. This section discusses two potential consequences: context limits and higher usage costs.

Context limits

At the moment of writing, the GPT-3.5 model can consider up to 16,000 tokens in the recent context. However, the number of words that these 16,000 tokens represent can vary greatly depending on the language. In English, for example, this context window can encapsulate about 12,000 words, providing enough space to feed into an entire scholarly article or a lengthy conversation. However, for languages that have less efficient tokenization, the same number of tokens may only represent a much shorter piece of text, making the final task results less accurate and effective. Table 2 illustrates an example of the word limit the ChatGPT-3.5 model has in different languages, given its current limit of tokens.

Table 2: Some languages and their context limit of words

	English	Spanish	Arabic	Hindi	Korean	Armenian
Context limit of words	12,125	7,328	2,921	2,077	1,736	1,231

Due to the context window, a user attempting to interact with ChatGPT in a language that is tokenized less efficiently will find that the model "forgets" earlier parts of the conversation or text more quickly. This reduces the potential applications of such models in certain languages, limiting the depth of text analysis and conversation that can be performed which then impacts the quality of task performance. Such implications raise the question of Whose productivity will generative AI tools like ChatGPT boost? It appears to be that English speakers have the advantage to benefit from the productivity gains associated with AI, but speakers of less token-efficient languages are not set off for the same revolutionized way of work unless they speak a more token-efficient language. Even then, AI-powered tools tend to be discriminative for non-native English speakers (Liang et al., 2023). Such a narrative could incentivize the usage of the English language in non-international environments too, on account of the local language.

Higher usage costs

Consider a scenario where a development team is building an educational app to offer free tutoring to underprivileged children. They opt to use GPT models to power the tutoring service, which requires paying for Application Programming Interface (API) usage. In this made-up scenario, let us assume that in English, the weekly cost of using the API per student is about $2. Based on the findings of the average token multiplier compared to English presented in this paper, Table 3 shows a comparison of the usage costs with a few other languages.

Table 3: Scenario-based comparison of weekly costs for certain languages

	English	French	Ukrainian	Thai	Tamil
Weekly cost	$2	$4	$10	$15	$27

Such a significant cost differential could influence the choice of language for developers. Consider a team in Mumbai, India, weighing up the benefits of using Marathi, Hindi, or English for their app. Given the stark differences in usage costs, the developers might choose English, despite it not being the native language for many of their intended users. The cost differential, therefore, not only impacts the affordability of such applications but could also impinge upon their cultural accessibility and inclusivity.

The disparity in tokenization efficiency across different languages, therefore, has concrete implications in real-world applications, both in terms of functionality and cost-effectiveness. Addressing these imbalances is not only a matter of technical refinement but also of ensuring equitable access and opportunities in the era of AI-powered applications.

Possible solutions

Wider context windows for Large Language Models

One of the potential solutions to the tokenization challenge involves expanding the context window to such an extent that variations between languages become negligible in real-world applications. This necessitates a shift in the research focus. Rather than creating models that are well-adapted to English or any single language, models that are proficient in understanding the diversity of all human languages should be developed.

However, this push for a broader context window comes with its own set of challenges. As the context window scales up, simultaneous work on lowering the cost per token is needed. This means a conscious strive to enhance efficiency and make this technological revolution inclusive, cost-effective, and accessible for all languages. The aim should not just be about enhancing the language model's performance, but also about shaping a research paradigm that promotes inclusivity and equality in the language technology space.

Targeted pre-training datasets

Another promising avenue to tackle the tokenization challenge lies in the creation of targeted pre-training datasets. This paper uncovers an intriguing pattern: an expansive pre-training dataset in English surprisingly benefited other languages that share a similar alphabet. This phenomenon opens the door to a potential solution. Thus, it is to be proposed that by significantly enhancing the pre-training datasets for a specific language from each of the Cyrillic, Devanagari, and Arabic scripts, it could potentially impart the benefits to a host of languages that use the same alphabet.

This targeted approach is not just about scaling up the size of the datasets. It is about smartly directing the resources toward training sets that will have a broader impact. This line of thinking presents a compelling case for the conscious and strategic allocation of resources in language model training, with the ultimate aim of creating a more inclusive digital language landscape.

Study limitations and recommendations for further research

This research, aimed at gaining a deeper understanding of tokenization efficiency across a broad spectrum of languages, does encompass a few crucial limitations which need to be addressed. Initially, the research is done using OpenAI's tokenizer of GPT-3 as the only available model of the tokenizer at the moment of the data analysis. However, at the time of publishing GPT-3.5 and GPT-4 tokenizers were made available too, which might present different figures and values in the tokenization.

Another point to note is that the general public has no specific insight into the exact language breakdown in OpenAI's pre-training dataset, a key factor that could affect this analysis. This paper used the Common Crawl corpus as a stand-in due to its wide linguistic representation, but the actual distribution within the pre-training dataset may differ. The discrepancies between these datasets might significantly influence tokenization efficiency. An additional constraint involves the usage of Google Translate for handling data across 108 languages. The quality of Google Translate's service can be inconsistent across languages, with digitally under-represented languages often receiving less accurate translations.

Finally, the chosen focus primarily on languages using Latin alphabets may have unintentionally limited the depth of the investigation. While the Latin script's global prevalence makes a practical choice, this concentration could potentially miss interesting insights from languages with different writing systems. Future work may aim to include a more diverse range of scripts for a comprehensive understanding of global tokenization efficiency.

Conclusion

This paper was designed to evaluate the efficiency of tokenization in ChatGPT across 108 languages, using English as a reference point. The findings revealed significant performance differences, with English surpassing all other languages, and the least efficient languages lagging behind by a factor of 13. Further examination revealed that while the number of characters and the size of the pre-training dataset play a subtle role, the alphabet used and the frequency of special characters significantly affect efficiency. Languages using Latin scripts demonstrated superior performance, whereas those incorporating a higher number of special characters showed noticeably reduced efficiency.

These disparities in tokenization have two crucial real-world consequences. First, they generate inherent computational cost differences, with the use of less efficient languages leading to higher expenses. Second, they pose limitations on the context window size. For languages that are tokenized less efficiently, the same number of tokens allows for far less textual content. This confines the model's capacity for tasks that require broader context, putting certain languages at a disadvantage.

Despite providing valuable insights, this research has some limitations. Relying on Google Translate may introduce translation inconsistencies, and the primary focus on Latin alphabets precludes analysis of other globally prevalent writing systems. Future studies could usefully delve into these aspects in more detail.

Going forward, consciously addressing these tokenization imbalances will be critical in ensuring equitable access to the benefits of generative AI across a diverse array of languages and user groups. Implementing broader context windows and targeted pre-training dataset are two promising strategies for promoting more inclusive language modeling. As AI continues to develop, maintaining the accessibility and empowerment of technology for all must be an unwavering priority. This paper underscores key areas to guide both technical and ethical progress in this direction.

References

Aiken, M.W. (2019). An updated evaluation of Google translate accuracy. Studies in Linguistics and Literature. http://www.scholink.org/ojs/index.php/sll/article/view/2180/2299

Beauchene, V., De Bellefonds, N., Duranton, S., & Mills, S. (2023). AI at work: What people are saying. BCG Global. https://www.bcg.com/publications/2023/what-people-are-saying-about-ai-at-work

Buchholz, K. (2023, January 24). ChatGPT sprints to one million users. Statista Infographics. https://www.statista.com/chart/29174/time-to-one-million-users/

Coupé, C., Oh, Y. S., Dediu, D., & Pellegrino, F. (2019). Different languages, similar encoding efficiency: Comparable information rates across the human communicative niche. Science Advances, 5(9). https://doi.org/10.1126/sciadv.aaw2594

Eleti, A., Harris, J., & Kilpatrick, L. (2023, June 13). Function calling and other API updates. openai.com. Retrieved June 22, 2023, from https://openai.com/blog/function-calling-and-other-api-updates

Howard, J., & Ruder, S. (2018). Universal language model fine-tuning for text classification. https://doi.org/10.18653/v1/p18-1031

Insights from American workers: A survey on AI in the workplace. (2023, May 24). Checkr.com. Retrieved June 16, 2023, from https://checkr.com/resources/articles/ai-workplace-survey-2023

Lai, V. D., Ngo, N. T., Veyseh, A. P. B., Man, H., Dernoncourt, F., Bui, T., & Nguyen, T. H. (2023). ChatGPT beyond English: Towards a comprehensive evaluation of large language models in multilingual learning. arXiv (Cornell University). https://doi.org/10.48550/arxiv.2304.05613

Liang, W., Yuksekgonul, M., Mao, Y., Wu, E., & Zou, J. (2023). GPT detectors are biased against non-native English writers. arXiv (Cornell University). https://doi.org/10.48550/arxiv.2304.02819

Marr, B. (2023, May 19). A short history of ChatGPT: How we got to where we are today. Forbes. https://www.forbes.com/sites/bernardmarr/2023/05/19/a-short-history-of-chatgpt-how-we-got-to-where-we-are-today/

New survey finds students are replacing human tutors with ChatGPT. (2023, June 9). Intelligent. Retrieved June 16, 2023, from https://www.intelligent.com/new-survey-finds-students-are-replacing-human-tutors-with-chatgpt/

OpenAI. (2023). GPT-4 technical report. arXiv (Cornell University). https://doi.org/10.48550/arxiv.2303.08774

OpenAI. (2023a). How do I use the OpenAI API in different languages? OpenAI Help Center. Retrieved June 24, 2023, from https://help.openai.com/en/articles/6742369-how-do-i-use-the-openai-api-in-different-languages

OpenAI. (n.d.). Pricing. https://openai.com. https://openai.com/pricing

Peters, M. J., Neumann, M. E., Iyyer, M., Gardner, M., Clark, C. M., Lee, K., & Zettlemoyer, L. (2018). Deep contextualized word representations. https://doi.org/10.18653/v1/n18-1202

Schulman, J., Wolski, F., Dhariwal, P., Radford, A., & Klimov, O. (2017). proximal policy optimization algorithms. ArXiv. https://arxiv.org/pdf/1707.06347.pdf

Solaiman, I., Brundage, M., Clark, J., Askell, A., Herbert-Voss, A., Wu, J., Radford, A., Krueger, G., Kim, J. W., Kreps, S., McCain, M., Newhouse, A., Blazakis, J., McGuffie, K., & Wang, J. (2019). Release strategies and the social impacts of language models. ArXiv. https://arxiv.org/ftp/arxiv/papers/1908/1908.09203.pdf

Thoppilan, R., De Freitas, D., Hall, J., Shazeer, N., Kulshreshtha, A., Cheng, H., Jin, A., Bos, T., Baker, L., Du, Y., Li, Y., Lee, H., Zheng, H. S., Ghafouri, A., Menegali, M., Huang, Y., Krikun, M., Lepikhin, D., Qin, J., . . . Le, Q. (2022). LaMDA: Language Models for Dialog Applications. ArXiv. https://arxiv.org/abs/2201.08239

Uszkoreit, J. (2017, August 31). Transformer: A novel neural network architecture for language understanding. https://research.google/. Retrieved May 28, 2023, from https://ai.googleblog.com/2017/08/transformer-novel-neural-network.html

Vaswani, A., Shazeer, N., Parmar, N., Uszkoreit, J., Jones, L., Gomez, A. N., Kaiser, L., & Polosukhin, I. (2017). Attention is all you need. In arXiv (Cornell University) (Vol. 30, pp. 5998–6008). Cornell University. https://arxiv.org/pdf/1706.03762v5

Williams, R. (2023, July 13). ChatGPT can turn bad writers into better ones. https://www.technologyreview.com/. Retrieved July 17, 2023, from https://www.technologyreview.com/2023/07/13/1076199/chatgpt-can-turn-bad-writers-into-better-ones/?utm_source=www.theneurondaily.com&utm_medium=newsletter&utm_campaign=4-ai-use-cases

Wodecki, B. (2023). UBS: ChatGPT may be the fastest growing app of all time. AI Business. https://aibusiness.com/nlp/ubs-chatgpt-is-the-fastest-growing-app-of-all-time

Yu, L., Simig, D., Flaherty, C., Aghajanyan, A., Zettlemoyer, L., & Lewis, M. (2023). MEGABYTE: Predicting million-byte sequences with multiscale transformers. ArXiv. https://doi.org/10.48550/arXiv.2305.07185

Appendix

The texts used, the word and token counts, as well as other computations used are summarised and presented here.

Is artificial intelligence an opportunity for inclusive education? A case study in a fully online university

José Israel Reyes[1], Julio Meneses[2]

[1] eLearning Innovation Center (eLinC), Universitat Oberta de Catalunya, Barcelona, Spain; jreyesrey@uoc.edu
[2] Faculty of Psychology and Education Sciences; eLearning Innovation Center (eLinC), Universitat Oberta de Catalunya, Barcelona, Spain; jmenesesn@uoc.edu

Correspondence: José Israel Reyes: jreyesrey@uoc.edu

Abstract:

Artificial intelligence in education has emerged as an opportunity to facilitate teaching and learning, especially in learning environments mediated by technology, such as online higher education. Despite its growing prominence, there is a lack of empirical research analysing how artificial intelligence affects inclusive education. Therefore, this study aims to analyse the perspectives and viewpoints of online course designers on leveraging these technologies to promote equal participation for all learners. Twelve professors participated in semi-structured interviews that were subsequently analysed through thematic analysis. The findings encompass two main themes. On one hand, the use of artificial intelligence in education as a tool for inclusive education within a human-centric pedagogy. Participants are cautious about using artificial intelligence to replace human work but recognise its potential contribution to facilitate content accessibility and comprehension. On the other, the adoption of a new approach for learning and assessment based on reflection and metacognition. Our participants' strategies include modifying some assessment practices when designing their courses for enabling learners to compare artificial intelligence creations, although they also highlight the lack of knowledge on using these technologies. Therefore, shifting to an assessment approach based on strengthening metacognition, reflection, and critical thinking skills emerges as a means to promote learners' inclusion supported by artificial intelligence. Our study also emphasises the importance of promoting artificial intelligence literacy for both professors and learners to effectively incorporate these technologies in the educational processes.

Keywords: Artificial intelligence, online higher education, inclusive education, educational technology, learners with disability.

Introduction

Artificial intelligence in education (AIEd) has disrupted the educational processes, highlighting an existent gap between professors and technology. Research about AIEd focuses on learning and teaching practices such as personalised learning, assessment, prediction and profiling, and tutoring (Tang et al., 2023; Zawacki-Richter et al., 2019). It is important to differentiate artificial intelligence (AI) and AIEd. AI is an umbrella term that includes a broad range of technologies and methods including machine learning, algorithms, data mining, natural language processing, deep learning, and artificial neural networks (Bond et al., 2024). AIEd, on the other hand, specifically applies these technologies and methods for educational purposes in areas such as instruction, learning, evaluation, and decision-making processes (del Gobbo et al., 2023). In online higher education, AIEd is often used to create suitable learning environments, learning and course recommendations, prediction models, and behaviour detection (Chen et al., 2020; Narimani & Barberà, 2024). Regarding learning and assessment, AIE technologies offer valuable support through resource recommendations, automatic assessment, prediction of learners' performance and satisfaction, and improvement of students' learning experience (Ouyang et al., 2022).

AIEd has the potential to assist both professors and learners in their educational duties. Some investigations suggest the promise for a dual teaching model in which educators utilise AIEd to accomplish bureaucratic and routinary duties while increasing efforts to personalise the learners' experience (Meron & Araci, 2023; Pedró et al., 2019). There are still some challenges for effectively leveraging AIEd in the classrooms, despite the integration of these technologies into higher education over the past three decades (Zawacki-Richter et al.,

2019). Apart from pedagogical uses, there are also concerns with ethical considerations such as the risk of compromising learners' privacy and replacing human work with AI (Bond et al., 2024). Institutions and professors also see AI as a source of increasing learners' plagiarism. For instance, the presence of technologies such as chatbots, could cause greater problems of deception and copying practices among students (Ivanov, 2023). The inaccuracy of the information given by AIEd tools also causes some preoccupation, so learners are exposed to learn wrong or incomplete concepts and procedures (Meron & Araci, 2023).

The application of AIEd encompasses various paradigms, offering diverse perspectives on its integration within online higher education. Ouyang and Jaio (2021) define three key paradigms that underpin AIEd in this context: AI-directed, learner-as-recipient; AI-supported, learner-as-collaborator; and AI-empowered, learner-as-leader. In the AI-directed paradigm, AI assumes a directive role, guiding and directing the learning process, whereas in the other two, learners are protagonists of their learning. So, the AI-supported paradigm shifts the focus towards collaborative learning environments, wherein AI technologies support learners' capabilities as collaborators in the educational process. Finally, in the AI-empowered paradigm, AI technologies empower learners to take on leadership roles in their educational journey. The last two paradigms emphasise learners taking control of their learning. In any case, institutions and faculty should consider that educational methods in the era of AIEd require a shift towards more dynamic, interactive, and learner-centred pedagogies (Walter, 2024).

Using AIEd may cause inequalities and exclusion for marginalised communities as organisations such as the United Nations have warned (Pedró et al., 2019). Nowadays, the intersection between AIEd and disability has only been studied in the early educational levels, focussing on assistive perspectives (Knox et al., 2019; Toyokawa et al., 2023). Although research on employing AIEd for inclusion is lacking in higher education, a substantial body of literature has addressed learning personalisation as one of the most promising roles of AI in online universities (Ouyang et al., 2022; Tang et al., 2023). Personalising learning for learners belonging to marginalised communities through automated technologies has emerged as a real opportunity. However, adopting these technologies entails using a significant amount of personal information from learners, which may pose risks to their security and data protection if suitable protocols are not carefully applied. Furthermore, the main goal of inclusive education is not only providing individualised learning experiences but fair and equitable opportunities to all. That is, promoting the active participation of everyone in the social life (Knox et al., 2019). Taking these issues into account, this paper aims to provide an understanding of how to leverage AIEd to promote inclusion in online higher education beyond automation, assistance, and profiling.

This study is part of a broader project aimed at exploring professors' experiences in designing inclusive online courses. The investigation has been conducted in a Spanish fully online and asynchronous university with a learner-based educational model. In this institution, a group of professors design the courses including learning resources, learning activities, and assessment. So, we have incorporated their experiences and reflections on incorporating AIEd for inclusive purposes while designing online learning and assessment activities.

The following research questions guided our research:

What are the experiences of course designers with incorporating AIEd for inclusive purposes in online higher education?

How can course designers leverage AIEd to make online higher education suitable for everyone?

Methodology

This is an exploratory qualitative research based on a case study. This research design is suitable for delving deeply into a phenomenon by thoroughly exploring a particular context (Yin, 2012). The data has been collected via semi-structured interviews with 12 online course designers. Participants were recruited by inviting them directly through the institutional email and then contacting the ones interested in the study. All respondents were informed of the research project and its objectives, their rights, and the conditions of their participation through informed consent. Next, we used thematic analysis (Braun & Clarke, 2006) to analyse the collected information with the assistance of Atlas.ti software.

Findings

We have identified two main themes in this study: professors' learning strategies based on AIEd and their insights on using it as a tool for inclusive education within a human-centric pedagogy and the adoption of a new approach for learning and assessment that includes developing all learners' critical thinking and metacognitive skills. These themes are shaped by narratives and recurring aspects that explain the current practices incorporated in participants' courses, their reflections on how to incorporate AIEd for inclusive purposes in the curricular design, as well as the challenges it currently entails. Table 1 synthesises participants' overall narratives, which are discussed throughout the Findings section.

Table 1: Participants' narratives about inclusive education based on AIEd.

Narratives	Current applications	Future lines of work	Challenges
AIEd as a tool	Facilitates professors' and learners' task development. Improves content accessibility and reading comprehension.	Professors could use AIEd to enhance all learners' academic achievements. Learners should use AIEd to improve their understanding and critical thinking.	Risk of dependency and getting incomplete information.
Literacy	Professors lack knowledge about AIEd for inclusive education. Learners need training on using AIEd adequately.	Professors need adequate knowledge to incorporate AIEd in inclusive course design. Learners should learn how and when using AIEd.	Marginalised learners remain invisible. Inexistence of training policies and protocols.
Assessment approach	Learning strategies based on comparing and appraising AI-created outcomes.	Learners should utilise AIEd to enhance their reflexive and critical-based skills.	Difficulties in distinguishing AI-based and human-based outcomes.

The human-centric pedagogy: AIEd is just an auxiliary tool for inclusive education.

The role of AI in inclusive online courses should be auxiliary rather than replacing professors' involvement. Our participants consider that AI technologies offer a prominent contribution to the learning of all students, but they also emphasise the importance of supervision by professors to prevent inconsistencies and to incorporate reflection, creativity, and empathy. P12 commented: "For me, it's just another tool and it will never replace something as fundamental and human as comprehension, the ability to reflect... That's where you have your role as an expert". While these technologies may improve learners' learning possibilities, human mediation remains essential: "It could be an aid, but not a substitute for either professors or learners" (P5).

AIEd technologies such as Chatbots can help learners with accessing and comprehending learning content. Our participants are aware that accessibility is the primary barrier preventing full inclusion of learners with disabilities in online learning environments. Therefore, incorporating support mechanisms based on AI could help to enhance learners' interaction with learning contents. P1 reflected:

> It is important to be able to adapt and incorporate this type of tools. Thinking on people who may have specific educational needs, it [AIEd] may also provide great solutions. For instance, if we create learning materials in a single format, they can use these tools to convert them [learning materials] into a more convenient format.

Participants also reflect on the importance of defining a clear strategy that orientates on deciding when and where AIEd can be used. For instance, employing specific tools to improve reading comprehension emerges as a good opportunity for enhancing accessibility. However, professors should also ensure that learners develop learning competencies by themselves. Accordingly, P8 commented: "I would distinguish between different levels of reading for different types of texts. For some cases, i.e. great literature texts, yes –I myself use it– and for others like critical thinking-based texts, no".

Therefore, participants' perceptions on using AI to support learners with disabilities are ambivalent. On the one hand, there are concerns about learners' dependency on these technologies, as well as on getting incomplete information or inconsistencies of some topics. "The problem with artificial intelligence is the illusion that you are learning. [Students] believe they have completed the activity and that it is done correctly." (P10). And, on the other hand, participants show their willingness to orientate learners on using it properly. "It's probably better to advise students to try reading the text first and then summarise it with ChatGPT if they find difficulties. However, it's important to caution them to be careful, sometimes it may miss things or give you wrong answers" (P9).

Learners with disabilities remain invisible from both AIEd and institutions' policies. In some participants' views, these technologies nowadays are more focused on meeting the needs of majorities, creating an exclusion of minorities with different needs such as those with disabilities. Yet, institutions are not especially concerned on addressing this gap. P3 conveyed: "The main issues regarding the use of artificial intelligence are sustainability and academic rigour, but inclusivity is handled more like an anecdote".

A new approach to evaluating learners focusing on metacognition and reflection.

The use of AI as a tool for inclusive education should start with both learners' and professors' literacy. Our participants highlight a lack of knowledge and preparation on how to use AIEd for supporting and assessing learning from an inclusive perspective. "We need to know how [to use AIEd]. What do we tell learners with a specific need about using AI tools? How does it help them and how should they leverage what it is offering to them?" (P12). Some participants have proactively begun exploring the potential of this technology, driven by their awareness of the opportunities it offers for enhancing students' learning: "I am training myself in AI, and for me, it's quite useful to supporting students... it can be a tool that assists you on that matter" (P1).

Professors' knowledge of using AIEd has to be transferred to learners as well, so students can use it in a way that positively impacts their learning and skills. Learners' literacy on AI should be focused on learning-to-learn strategies so that they are able to "formulate questions and create prompts that teach and give them what they really need and can be useful to them" (P11).

The incorporation of AIEd involves professors to revolutionise their teaching and assessment methods. Our participants consider that the integration of these technologies should shift the focus of learning and evaluation processes toward developing learners' metacognitive skills. P7 commented: "AIEd has allowed us or forced us –or both– to rethink a little bit how questions [within assessment activities] are formulated". Given the importance of developing marginalised learners' autonomy, assessment should be designed for learners to demonstrate the achievement of competencies in a way that AI has a secondary role: "What we shouldn't do is evaluate only what AI can already provide, that is, we need to push it a little further" P3.

Beyond using AIEd for creating new learning outcomes, learners' activity should focus on reflecting, comparing, and apprising the ones created by these technologies. Another alternative is leveraging these tools to make online learning more interactive, as P5 exemplified:

> Using it [AIEd] in contexts where you could assess certain competencies –not only regarding students with difficulties, but with all students– which are now very difficult to evaluate. For example, activities in which students simulate certain things and artificial intelligence takes on the other role.

Discussion and conclusion

The results of this study give us an understanding of course designers' perspectives on effectively incorporating AIEd to promote the inclusivity of online higher education. Three main arguments have emerged from the analysis. First, these technologies serve as a significant means of support to favour the engagement of diverse learners in online higher education, particularly on accessibility, interactivity, and reading comprehension. Second, there is an important need to enhance professors' and learners' literacy in integrating AIEd while designing learning and assessment activities, thus levering all the advantages it could grant for teaching and learning. And third, professors must shift their learning and assessment strategies toward more reflexive and critical thinking-based paradigms to benefit the entire student body.

AIEd is an emergent topic. Therefore, the near future interventions should focus on training both professors and learners on how to take profit of it to promote learners' holistic development. As the existing literature suggests, there are multiple initiatives based on supporting learners from a generalised approach on topics such as personalisation, tutoring, and resource recommendation (Bond et al., 2024; Tang et al., 2023; Zawacki-Richter et al., 2019). However, knowledge circulates primarily among professionals in informatics and computational sciences and it is not adequately transferred to other disciplines (Toyokawa et al., 2023).

The need to advise learners on learning-to-learn strategies is now more crucial than ever (Walter, 2024). There is a need to boost literacy programmes aimed at preparing both professors to apply AIEd in curricular design for inclusive purposes and learners to enhance their learning possibilities. Our results suggest that professors are more concerned on learners' development than on cheating practices, which is quite positive for promoting the application of inclusive pedagogies based on AIEd. As observed by Knox et al. (2019) and Walter (2024), there is a significant opportunity to transform educational processes towards student-centred innovative practices that enable both personalised learning and collective integration for everyone. In this regard, it is important to focus AIEd-based learning strategies on social constructivism (learner-as-collaborator) and connectivism (learner-as-leader) paradigms (Ouyang & Jiao, 2021).

Marginalised learners such as those with disabilities remain unnoticed both by institutions and AIEd technology designers. UNESCO warns of the risk of creating inequalities if access to AIEd technologies becomes challenging for certain communities of learners (Pedró et al., 2019). That is, supporting this group of learners is essential to ensure they take profit of this tools for their learning. The available evidence indicates that the few initiatives aimed at addressing this gap have been ran within the earliest educational levels and focused mainly on an individualised approach, rather than emphasising the inclusion of all learners in the educational processes (Knox et al., 2019; Toyokawa et al., 2023).

Conclusion

The emergence of AIEd has brought significant changes to online higher education, requiring faculty to adapt their teaching and assessment methods. While current practices predominantly emphasise personalisation, it is crucial to recognise that these technologies can extend beyond individualised learning. The incorporation of these tools in the educational processes has the potential to contribute to other areas such as improving accessibility and fostering autonomy and metacognition. It also contributes to liberating professors from administrative tasks, enabling them more time to provide quality feedback to students. Therefore, adopting these technologies will help online universities to promote learning opportunities for everyone. In this regard, professor need support to effectively apply AIEd benefits towards enhancing the involvement of marginalised communities in the learning processes. Ultimately, the use of these technologies should focus on enhancing accessibility, comprehension, and text production, as well as on interacting, collaborating, and developing critical thinking skills for all learners.

Acknowledgements

We thank the participants for sharing their experiences, as well as the Vice-Rector for Teaching and Learning and the Deans of each university's Faculty for their support.

Funding Information

This research has been funded by Fundació per a la Universitat Oberta de Catalunya.

References

Bond, M., Khosravi, H., De Laat, M., Bergdahl, N., Negrea, V., Oxley, E., Pham, P., Chong, S. W., & Siemens, G. (2024). A meta systematic review of artificial intelligence in higher education: A call for increased ethics, collaboration, and rigour. International Journal of Educational Technology in Higher Education, 21(1), 4. https://doi.org/10.1186/s41239-023-00436-z

Braun, V., & Clarke, V. (2006). Using thematic analysis in psychology. Qualitative Research in Psychology, 3(2), 77–101. https://doi.org/10.1191/1478088706qp063oa

Chen, X., Xie, H., & Hwang, G.-J. (2020). A multi-perspective study on Artificial Intelligence in Education: Grants, conferences, journals, software tools, institutions, and researchers. Computers and Education: Artificial Intelligence, 1, 100005. https://doi.org/10.1016/j.caeai.2020.100005

del Gobbo, E., Guarino, A., Cafarelli, B., Grilli, L., & Limone, P. (2023). Automatic evaluation of open-ended questions for online learning. A systematic mapping. Studies in Educational Evaluation, 77, 101258. https://doi.org/10.1016/j.stueduc.2023.101258

Ivanov, S. (2023). The dark side of artificial intelligence in higher education. The Service Industries Journal, 43(15–16), 1055–1082. https://doi.org/10.1080/02642069.2023.2258799

Knox, J., Wang, Y., & Gallagher, M. (2019). Introduction: AI, Inclusion, and 'Everyone Learning Everything'. In J. Knox, Y. Wang, & M. Gallagher (Eds.), Artificial Intelligence and Inclusive Education: Speculative Futures and Emerging Practices (pp. 1–13). Springer. https://doi.org/10.1007/978-981-13-8161-4_1

Meron, Y., & Araci, Y. T. (2023). Artificial intelligence in design education: Evaluating ChatGPT as a virtual colleague for post-graduate course development. Design Science, 9, e30. https://doi.org/10.1017/dsj.2023.28

Narimani, A., & Barberà, E. (2024). Extracting Course Features and Learner Profiling for Course Recommendation Systems: A Comprehensive Literature Review. The International Review of Research in Open and Distributed Learning, 25(1), 197–225. https://doi.org/10.19173/irrodl.v25i1.7419

Ouyang, F., & Jiao, P. (2021). Artificial intelligence in education: The three paradigms. Computers and Education: Artificial Intelligence, 2, 100020. https://doi.org/10.1016/j.caeai.2021.100020

Ouyang, F., Zheng, L., & Jiao, P. (2022). Artificial intelligence in online higher education: A systematic review of empirical research from 2011 to 2020. Education and Information Technologies, 27(6), 7893–7925. https://doi.org/10.1007/s10639-022-10925-9

Pedró, F., Subosa, M., Rivas, A., & Valverde, P. (2019). Artificial intelligence in education: Challenges and opportunities for sustainable development (Programme and Meeting Document ED-2019/WS/8; Working Papers on Education Policy, pp. 1–46). UNESCO. https://unesdoc.unesco.org/ark:/48223/pf0000366994

Tang, K.-Y., Chang, C.-Y., & Hwang, G.-J. (2023). Trends in artificial intelligence-supported e-learning: A systematic review and co-citation network analysis (1998–2019). Interactive Learning Environments, 31(4), 2134–2152. https://doi.org/10.1080/10494820.2021.1875001

Toyokawa, Y., Horikoshi, I., Majumdar, R., & Ogata, H. (2023). Challenges and opportunities of AI in inclusive education: A case study of data-enhanced active reading in Japan. Smart Learning Environments, 10(1), 67. https://doi.org/10.1186/s40561-023-00286-2

Walter, Y. (2024). Embracing the future of Artificial Intelligence in the classroom: The relevance of AI literacy, prompt engineering, and critical thinking in modern education. International Journal of Educational Technology in Higher Education, 21(1), 15. https://doi.org/10.1186/s41239-024-00448-3

Yin, R. K. (2012). Applications of case study research (3rd ed.). SAGE.

Zawacki-Richter, O., Marín, V. I., Bond, M., & Gouverneur, F. (2019). Systematic review of research on artificial intelligence applications in higher education – where are the educators? International Journal of Educational Technology in Higher Education, 16(1), 39. https://doi.org/10.1186/s41239-019-0171-0

A proposal for the incorporation of AI in producing images for educational content at UNAM

Jorge Leon-Martinez[1], Edith Tapia-Rangel[2]

[1] Coordination of Open University and Digital Education, National Autonomous University of Mexico, Mexico; jorge_leon@cuaieed.unam.mx
[2] Coordination of Open University and Digital Education, National Autonomous University of Mexico, Mexico; edith_tapia@cuaieed.unam.mx

Correspondence: Jorge LEON-MARTINEZ: jorge_leon@cuaieed.unam.mx

Abstract:

After many years of development, artificial intelligence (AI) is beginning to permeate with greater intensity in our daily activities, including the educational field. This paper presents a proposal for the use of Generative AI (GAI) for the creation of images that accompany the educational content developed by teachers at the National Autonomous University of Mexico (UNAM) in collaboration with the Coordination of Open University and Digital Education (CUAED). This proposal seeks to bring teachers closer to using these new tools through a comprehensive approach that does not only focus on using the tool.

Keywords: digital education content development process, Generative Artificial Intelligence, image creation, teacher training, open educational resources, distance education

Introduction

Advances in artificial intelligence in recent months have permeated practically all areas of society, including the educational field. Based on the above, a proposal is presented, applied to the content development process of the CUAED, an UNAM entity that supports non-face-to-face education.

From this process, the activity of illustrating educational content with images was chosen in a first selection, to make use of artificial intelligence in the generation of content, considering the difficulty that teachers face in finding the desired images.

Based on these considerations, a proposal is presented to train teachers in basic elements of artificial intelligence, copyright of products derived from artificial intelligence, prompt engineering and incorporation of images in repositories. With these elements the teacher will be able to start working with AI to generate their images.

Organizational framework - UNAM

The Coordination of Open University and Digital Education (CUAED) is an academic-administrative entity of the UNAM that supports academic institutions in developing digital educational content for face-to-face, distance, continuing education, and open educational resources. For this purpose, it employs a development process consisting of 5 stages: Project profile, Content analysis, Pedagogical advice and style correction, Visual communication and integration, and Evaluation and updating.

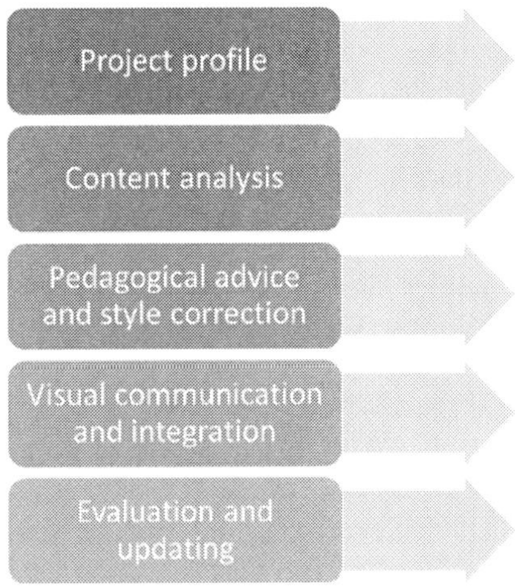

Figure 1: Development process. Stages in the development process. Own elaboration.

In the stage called Project Profile, both the academic entity and CUAED carry out a definition of the project in terms of management and legal aspects; the design of the educational event in terms of pedagogical aspects, visual communication, and style correction; training of teachers in copyright matters so that they can subsequently write the contents in a zero version.

The Content Analysis stage begins with verifying two phases: the pedagogical aspect of the academic programs, their representation in the instructional scripts, the unification of criteria in the pedagogical advisory team, and the visual aspect, where different graphic proposals are developed for the project. Subsequently, the pedagogical advisory area analyzes the thematic structure of the contents and academic programs to weigh the workload and adjust the learning objectives, among other things. In contrast, the visual communication area adjusts the approved graphic interface. Finally, the project management area prepares a Work Plan proposal where time and communication commitments between the parties are established; and the final graphic interface is approved.

The third stage, Pedagogical assessment and style correction, consists of two phases. The pedagogical advice phase is carried out directly between the pedagogical advisor and the expert teacher. During this phase, the didactic planning of the academic event is elaborated; basic and complementary materials are reviewed and defined; content is structured; and learning and evaluation activities are developed and fine-tuned. For the treatment of the content, the pedagogical advisor submits the multimedia resources catalog to the expert teacher for consideration, and together, they search for images according to what the teacher wishes to represent in the content. If finding suitable images is impossible, the instructional script requests the creation of a new and original image based on a textual description. This description is the one that the visual communicator will follow in the next stage to generate the image. As the process progresses, the pedagogical advisor integrates all this information into the instructional script. In the end, the script is released until it has the approval of the expert teacher and is sent to the proofreading area. In the next phase, called Style Correction, a spelling, syntax, writing, and general style review of the instructional script and all the accompanying documents is carried out. These observations are submitted to the expert teacher, who can accept or reject them. Once the specialist teacher approves the instructional script, it is sent to the Design and Visual Communication area.

The visual communication and integration stage consists of three phases. The first, known as Integration, is carried out by the design and visual communication area, which organizes the final scripts and materials received to plan the timing. This phase includes integrating the contents in the different formats requested, developing multimedia resources, and publishing the educational event on the platform. The Review against screen phase takes place in the Pedagogical Consulting area, which reviews all the elements integrated into the platform against the instructional script sent. Finally, in the correction phase, Visual Communication corrects the observations sent and sends them to Pedagogical Consultancy for further Review. This cycle ends when Asesoría pedagógica accepts that all corrections have been applied and proceeds to the release of the academic event.

The academic entities carry out this stage, which means evaluating and updating the designed resources. Through evaluation tools, they identify the educational event's strengths and weaknesses for improvement.

Theoretical framework

Returning to the activities of the Pedagogical advice and style correction stage, it is possible to identify an area of opportunity in the activity of "searching for images according to what the teacher wishes to represent in the content," especially when the image does not appear, and the teacher requests "the creation of a new and original image based on a textual description." With Generative Artificial Intelligence, it is now possible to create images with particular characteristics that can be done by the teachers themselves, working on it until it is what they require. The following sections support this idea.

Images in educational content

Why are images so important in educational content? There is a famous saying that a picture is worth a thousand words, and today, in this society where multimedia publications abound, it is more valid than ever. This is perhaps because of the very nature of human cognition, which draws mental images in our imagination when we read a text in such a way that they help us understand or enjoy reading more (Zhang, Zhang, Zhang, Zhang, & So, 2023, p. 1).

Educational content is no exception, as Rodriguez (2008) points out "Educational content has relied on the value of the image to illustrate the text" (p. 156).

The use of images for educational content must adhere to appropriate pedagogical strategies that, in practice, give meaning and significance to students, allowing them "the collective and interactive construction of knowledge, emphasizing that the skills developed and the conceptualizations learned through these strategies are easy to remember and possible to recreate" (Guillén, 2020, p. 2). Likewise, multimedia educational contents that enable learning, attend to specific principles related to the "combination and articulation of written texts, oral narratives, images, and graphic resources." (Coll, Engel, and Bustos, 2008, p. 257)

This construction of contents is transcendent for the construction of the student alone and for contrasting and negotiating them with his peers and his teacher (Coll, Engel, and Bustos, 2008, p. 259).

In this way, educational contents illustrated with images provide knowledge and information through visualization, promoting the understanding and retention of contents that, in some cases, are difficult to transmit verbally or textually and inviting the student to reflect, analyze, and relate new concepts or previous with elements of everyday life. (Guillén, 2020, p.5)

These are some of the mechanisms that explain the potential of educational content with visual supports:

1. They help memory processes by allowing us to expand working memory, create permanent files, share memories, etc.
2. They decrease the extent of cognitive effort needed to solve equivalent problems.
3. They stimulate or activate specific mental processes intrinsically, determining patterns of cognitive behavior and the way the mind works.
4. They enable the creation of certain inferences about the represented world. (Coll, Engel and Bustos, 2008, pp. 259-260)

Artificial Intelligence in Education

Information and communication technologies are a field that never stops advancing and is constantly evolving. One of its goals is to reach human intelligence through what is known today as artificial intelligence. Artificial intelligence is the culmination of innovations and developments in computers, computer-related technologies, machines, and information and communication technologies, which give computers the ability to perform human-like functions." (Chen, Chen and Lin, 2020, p. 75265) In recent years, artificial intelligence has reached a level of development that makes its use possible by the general population.

Thanks to AI's affordability, multiple social and productive sectors have adopted AI tools within their processes, and the education sector has not been the exception.

In the education sector, AI can support the functions of classroom management (grading and student feedback, personalizing learning plans, providing information to teachers for decision-making), teaching (proposing personalized content, enabling instruction beyond the classroom, adapting instruction per student); and learning (identifying and addressing student learning defenses promptly, predicting student academic trajectory, identifying learning status for timely intervention). (Chen, Chen and Lin, 2020, p. 75272).

Daily, more AI technologies are incorporated in educational settings, such as student and school assessment (adaptive learning method and personalized learning approach, academic analytics); grading and evaluation (image recognition, computer vision, prediction system); personalized intelligent teaching (Bayesian knowledge interference data mining, intelligent teaching systems, learning analytics); brilliant school (facial recognition, voice recognition, virtual labs, augmented reality, virtual reality, hearing and sensing technologies); and remote online and mobile education (edge computing, personalized virtual assistants, real-time analytics). (Chen, Chen and Lin, 2020, p. 75268).

AI has also been used for "curriculum, content, and instruction development" (Chen, Chen, & Lin, 2020, p. 75269-75270), which constitute an educational event, together with teaching, assessment, and communication.

Content generation with Artificial Intelligence

Digital content production (including educational content) has gone through three stages. In the first stage, content was generated by professional teams, which guaranteed its high quality but had the disadvantage of a long and challenging production cycle. The second stage introduced more accessible and affordable user tools for content creation, reducing production times and costs and leading to greater user participation. Still, this content could have been of higher quality due to the different levels and capabilities of the users. The third stage is AI-generated content, which overcomes the obstacles of the first two modes: the first concerning time and the second concerning quality. (Wu, Gan, Chen, Wan, & Lin, 2023, pp. 2-3) Recently, AI content generation tools have become more powerful, such that it is already possible to visualize the potential they have to "revolutionize the way we retrieve and consume information." (Bie et al., 2023, p. 1).

As technological advances progress, these tools will be able to generate high-quality content that will gradually become indistinguishable from content generated by human writers, designers, and artists.

AI-generated content can be classified into the following types (Wu, Gan, Chen, Wan, & Lin, 2023):

- Text generation. These tools consider the generation of structured writing (data driven), creative writing (personalized and original), and dialog writing (for interacting with users such as chatbots).
- Image generation. AI makes it possible to generate and edit images with few visual skills and knowledge, attending to specific requirements that the image must meet, even creating 3D models from 2D images
- Audio generation. AI technologies for audio generation have two aspects: the first one generates voice from text, i.e., text input is converted into spoken speech and is currently mature enough to achieve natural voice fluency while still improving to reach emotional levels in spoken language; the other aspect in audio generation has to do with voice cloning, which, from an audio recording, reproduces the voice for a new speech input, which is useful mainly in dubbing.
- Video generation. As in the image generation tools, the text inputs are used to generate the video at the frame level and, later, through AI, to organize the frames into videos.

Images with Artificial Intelligence

AI for image generation from text uses various advanced and complex techniques, such as machine learning, generative adversarial networks and diffusion models, and attention-based recurrent neural networks, among others, to use preexisting knowledge, learned semantic representations, and training with huge textual databases (Ali, Tang, Connolly, 2024, p. 88) (Singh, 2023, p. 1).

Specifically, text-to-image generation comprises all those computational methods that can convert "human-written textual descriptions, such as keywords or phrases, into visually represented concepts that have the same semantic meaning as the text." (Osama, 2023, p. 5)

The design of a tool for generating images from text descriptions is not a trivial task, so it has become a relevant milestone in the evolution of artificial intelligence, providing new horizons for creative expression, design, and multimedia content creation, visibly decreasing the gap that exists between the images produced by the best visual artists and artificial intelligence. (Zhang, Zhang, Zhang, Zhang and So, 2023, p. 1) (Bie, et. al., 2023, p. 1)

The generation of images with text has proven valuable due to several situations. One is that it allows design experts to approach a wider variety of concepts from new angles, which could offer novel solutions to challenging problems (Osama, 2023). It reduces the time and cost of producing high-quality images, allowing content to be created quickly, economically, and competently (Singh, 2023, p. 1). It also allows users to generate the required image with the level of accuracy they want and with the necessary adjustments and corrections in a concise space, allowing the rapid exploration of different concepts and ideas (Noel, 2024, p. 2).

These situations, and others, have provided image generation systems with text that have applications in marketing, education, entertainment, and other productive sectors.

For example, in education, they can create visual elements to improve the learning experience, as discussed in the "Images in educational content" section. The following proposal is presented based on the combination of these two elements.

Implementation proposal

One of the ways to introduce the use of AI tools with UNAM teachers is through the support of image-to-text generation tools. This would support the development process of digital educational content, specifically during pedagogical consulting when teachers need help finding the visual representations that best fit the content they want to illustrate on the Internet or image banks. Therefore, we propose using these tools to allow them to obtain good-quality images without needing experts in the design and creation of images.

To train teachers to generate images with IAG, the following work path is proposed:

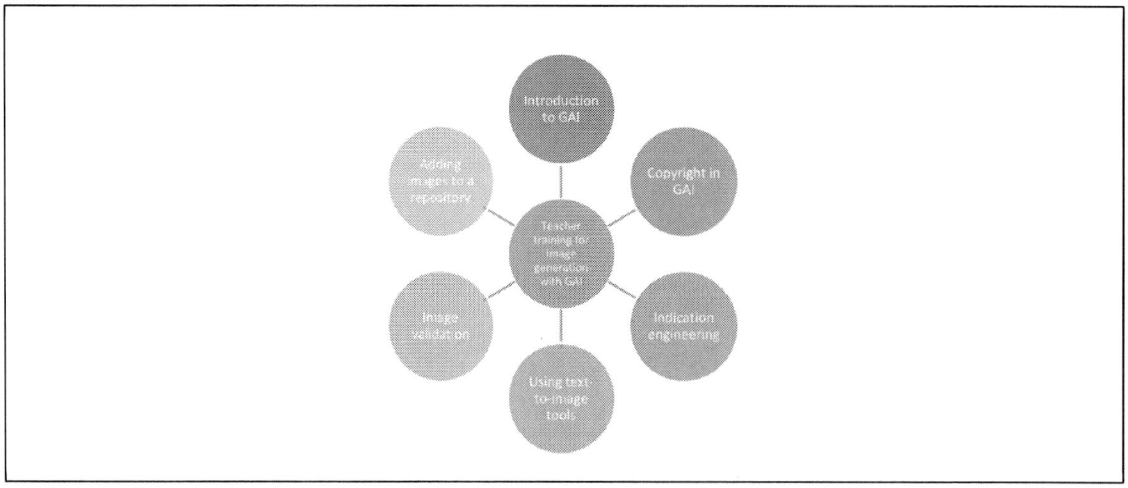

Figure 2: Teacher training. Scheme of teacher training for image generation with GAI. Own elaboration.

- Introduction to Generative Artificial Intelligence
  - Recognize the different milestones that mark the evolution of Artificial Intelligence
  - Identify the main characteristics of Generative Artificial Intelligence
  - Recognize the mechanism used by Generative Artificial Intelligence to generate images from text
- Copyright in Generative Artificial Intelligence products
  - Recognize the copyright regulations that apply to Generative Artificial Intelligence products
- Prompt Engineering (Oppenlaender, 2003). In the tools for generating images from text, the text called prompts, which are the premises on which the image will be built, is critical. This aspect has become so crucial in these tools that the term "prompt engineering" is already used to refer to it. Prompt engineering is an emerging area of research in human-computer interaction (HCI) that is concerned with formulating input request for deep generative models and, from a broader perspective, how humans can effectively interact with artificial intelligence. It is, therefore, essential for teachers to be familiar with these terms, and to this end, the following aspects are proposed to be worked on:
  - Consider features involved in the structural analysis of an iconic message
  - Establish that the text input prompts must be provided in a clear and specific format for text-generated images to be effective
  - Images can be enhanced by adding keywords and key phrases to the text input prompts. These phrases are known as prompt modifiers. By adding a cue modifier to a text input, one seeks to direct the tool in generating an image in specific directions, thus modifying the resulting image
  - Identify that the process to achieve the desired image is iterative and experimental. Prompt engineering is not intuitive and will require extensive experimentation and trial and error.
  - Identify and visit online databases of prompts and prompt modifiers with resulting products.
  - Use of text-to-image tools
    - Locate with the teachers the AI tools to generate images from text by searching the Internet for the most recent ones.
    - Choose four tools and perform image production exercises by applying the same prompts to the chosen tools.
    - In all cases, refine the images with modifiers to observe the resulting images. Retain the final text entries and images.
  - Image validation (Singh, 2023)
    - Validate that the image corresponds to what is expected.
    - Review and analyze the balance between visual quality and processing time.
    - Verify that the content produced is associated with social or public norms to avoid misinterpreting or misrepresenting the message.
- Incorporating images into a repository
  - Introduction to metadata
  - Generation of the metadata file
  - Submission for repository integration

Conclusions

Developing and implementing a training program for creating images integrated into developing digital educational content through IAG at UNAM represents a strategic opportunity to enrich this process and prepare teachers for the challenges and opportunities of the digital future.

The adoption or appropriation of technologies such as AGI by UNAM faculty has the potential to transform teaching and learning and enrich educational content with innovative and personalized visual material. This can improve students' comprehension and retention of information, especially in complex concepts or topics.

Creating engaging digital educational content through IAG can help address different educational topics and support inclusion and equity at the university level. The content developed can be shared, benefiting a broader academic community.

The proposed training program for creating images through the IAG seeks not only to improve the digital skills of UNAM teachers with these tools but also to promote a culture of innovation and adaptability in the face of emerging technologies. This is essential in a world where technological skills are constantly evolving.

By implementing this program, UNAM reaffirms its commitment to educational innovation and teacher training, contributing to the advancement of knowledge and educational practice and setting standards for other universities nationwide.

References

Ali, R., Tang, O.Y., Connolly, I,D, et al. (2024). Demographic Representation in 3 Leading Artificial Intelligence Text-to-Image Generators. JAMA Surgery, 159(1), 87-95. : 10.1001/jamasurg.2023.5695

Bie, F., Yang, Y., Zhou, Z., Ghanem, A., Zhang, M., Yao, Z., Wu, X., Holmes, C., Golnari, P., Clifton, D.A., He, Y., Tao, D., León, S. (2023). RenAIssance: A Survey into AI Text-to-Image Generation in the Era of Large Model. https://arxiv.org/pdf/2309.00810.pdf.

Chen L., Chen P., Lin, Z. (2020). Artificial Intelligence in Education: A Review. IEEE Access, 8(1), 75264-75278. Retrieved from https://ieeexplore.ieee.org/document/9069875.

Guillen, G. (2020). La pedagogía de la imagen como forma de promover el aprendizaje significativo dentro del aula. Revista Docentes 2.0, 9(1), 96-108. https://doi.org/10.37843/rted.v9i1.90.

Noel, G.P.J.C. (2024). La pedagogía de la imagen como forma de promover el aprendizaje significativo dentro del aula. Anat. Sci. Educ. 2024, 00, 1-5. https://doi.org/10.1002/ase.2336.

Oppenlaender, J. (2023). A taxonomy of prompt modifiers for text-to-image generation. Behaviour & Information Technology, Nov, 1-14. DOI: 10.1080/0144929X.2023.2286532.

Osama N. (2023). Artificial intelligence's effects on design process creativity: "A study on used A.I. Text-to-Image in architecture". Journal of Building Engineering, 80(2023), 107999. Retrieved from https://www.sciencedirect.com/science/article/pii/S2352710223021794.

Coll, C., Engel, A., Bustos, A. (2008). Los entornos virtuales de aprendizaje basados en la representación visual del conocimiento. In Coll, C. y Monereo, C. (Ed.), Psicología de la Educación Virtual. Aprender y enseñar con las Tecnologías de la Información y la comunicación (pp. 253–273). Morata.

Rodríguez, J.L. (2008). La presentación y organización de los contenidos virtuales: Lenguajes y formatos de representación. In Coll, C. y Monereo, C. (Ed.), Psicología de la Educación Virtual. Aprender y enseñar con las Tecnologías de la Información y la comunicación (pp. 153–173). Morata.

Singh, A. (2023, Nov). A Survey of AI Text-to-Image and AI Text-to-Video Generators. Paper presented at the 4th International Conference on Artificial Intelligence, Robotics and Control, Cairo, Egypt. https://arxiv.org/abs/2311.06329.

Wu, J., Gan, W., Chen, Z., Wan, S. & Lin, H. (March 26, 2023). AI-Generated Content (AIGC): A Survey. https://arxiv.org/abs/2304.06632.

Zhang, C., Zhang, C., Zhang, M., So, I. (April 2, 2023). Text-to-image Diffusion Models in Generative AI: A Survey. https://arxiv.org/abs/2303.07909.

United Nations Education Scientific and Cultural Organization (2019). How Can Artificial Intelligence Enhance Education?. https://www.unesco.org/en/articles/how-can-artificial-intelligence-enhance-education.

Revolution, evolution, or regression – the transformation of assessments through times of pandemic and AI

Stylianos Hatzipanagos[1], Linda Amrane-Cooper[2], Alan Tait [3]

[1] Centre for Online and Distance Education, University of London, United Kingdom; hatzips@gmail.com
[2] Centre for Online and Distance Education, University of London, United Kingdom; linda.amrane-cooper@london.ac.uk
[3] Centre for Online and Distance Education, University of London, United Kingdom; alan.tait@open.ac.uk

Correspondence: Stylianos Hatzipanagos: hatzips@gmail.com

Abstract:

In this paper we will discuss the tensions between, revolution, evolution and regression that are shaping assessment practice in higher education. The two major influences on shaping assessment in higher education in recent years have been: (1) the pandemic that pressurised universities to embrace online practice, sometimes temporarily. When the post pandemic pushback restored 'tried and tested' face to face practices in exam centres and traditional assessment spaces (e.g. labs), it revealed the potential for adopting online tools and practices and the value of enhancing digital competences for staff and students; and (2) Artificial Intelligence (AI) as a disruptor, which since the autumn of 2022 continues to influence approaches and attitudes to assessment. Institutional concerns for impact on reputation and the focus on integrity and student conduct is shaping the assessment landscape as are the technological and pedagogical opportunities and risks presented by proctoring software and generative AI. We claim that elements of revolution, evolution and regression can be traced in the developing landscape of assessment redesign and technology mediated assessment.

The paper will synthesise the outcomes of two projects, at the Centre for Online and Distance Education, University of London: (a) the longitudinal evaluation of assessment practises between 2020 and 2023 and (b) a project that looked at perceptions of academic integrity in the current climate of AI threats and opportunities.

Keywords: Digital learning futures, assessment in higher education, academic integrity, redesigning assessment

Introduction

Assessment practice has been subjected to a series of transformations since 2020. The two major disrupting forces were the pandemic and Artificial Intelligence (AI). The former pressurised universities to embrace online practice, sometimes only temporarily. However, even when the post pandemic pushback restored tried and tested face to face opportunities in exam centres and traditional assessment spaces (e.g. labs), the potential of adopting online tools and practices and the value of enhancing digital competences for staff and students was revealed. The latter (AI), since the autumn of 2022, continues to transform approaches and attitudes to assessment. Both disruptors brought integrity and student conduct into renewed focus. Beyond the moral panic of educational practitioners, institutional concerns for impact on reputation, the emergent technology is shaping the assessment landscape through mainly (a) a requirement for proctoring of assessments, through technology or human invigilation and (b) redesign of assessments or a combination of both.

This paper will explore the ways in which the tensions and synergies between the two drivers, AI and the pandemic, are shaping assessment practice in higher education, and we suggest that these developments can be charted through the notion of revolution, evolution, and regression.

Background

Online assessment is more vulnerable to academic offences, and most of the research done on this topic, is based on that assumption. Yet, there are some experts, that believe that this is not the case. For instance, Adzima (2020), argues that online assessment provides the same opportunities to commit an academic offence as in face-to-face learning environment, and that the main difference is on whether there is technology in place to deter or detect such behaviours. Individual factors relate to the students' characteristics, such as gender, nationality, age, intellectual capacity, social pressure. Within this context, academic misconduct is linked to international students' lack of sufficient knowledge of the English language (Parnther, 2022). Others argue that the transition to HE can generate the lack of confidence needed, and therefore, young students engaged in higher levels of academic dishonesty behaviour compared with older students (Surahman, 2022). International students may demonstrate cultural differences or academic unpreparedness and understanding of higher education policies, which could enhance the likelihood of committing an academic offence (Parnther 2022). As far as online learning is concerned, students might feel unable to seek support from providers, which might lead students to commit academic offences. Student behaviour is key to mitigate any form of academic misconduct, as it will be dealt in the following sections.

Our claim is that the recent period in higher education assessment practice was governed by three paradigms:

(a) Revolution: this related to radical changes in assessment practice. For instance, A characteristic of this revolution was the required and rapid move to online timed assessments, replacing examination hall pen and paper practice in response to pandemic lockdowns. Pre-pandemic this often was the case in institutions that needed to expand or modernise.

(b) Evolution: the evolution represented a slower development of assessment practices, under the influence of developing technology, updating processes and practices and learning from the experiences of previous assessment rounds.

(c) Regression: the paradigm describes a return to more traditional practices after attempts to modernise or embrace technology. A characteristic example of this is the return to traditional exam centres after the pandemic for many providers, due to challenges with quality assurance.

Methodology

In both initiatives, (a) the longitudinal evaluation of assessment practises between 2020 and 2023 and (b) the project that explored perceptions of academic integrity, we used a variety of tools to capture the views of the key stakeholders.

For the longitudinal evaluation the main instruments of investigation were:

1. A survey sent out to students
2. Interviews with a subset of respondents of the survey to explore further survey findings.
3. A survey with a target audience of examiners
4. A survey with a target audience of the recognised teaching centres at the University of London (UoL).
5. Interviews with a selection of Programme Directors

For the academic integrity project, we used

1. An investigation of contemporary commercial solutions
2. Interviews with Programme Directors from University of London and federated university programmes, other UK and international institutions that employ technologies and tools to support academic integrity and
3. Interviews with staff with responsibilities in assessment.

Findings

For the fourth year since the outbreak of the Covid-19 pandemic in 2020, an evaluation was conducted of the 2023 examinations for international programmes in UoL and federated universities. There was broad continuity in methodology (Amrane-Cooper et al, 2023a), with focus on student behaviours, student sentiment, student outcomes and operational issues. Following the evolution of the assessment practices at UoL between 2020 and 2022, in 2023 attention was also paid to the use of the digital assessment systems provided by the Inspera assessment system, and to the advent of generative AI and its implications for teaching, learning and assessment, and in particular academic integrity.

There was broad continuity in terms of student, examiner, and academic programme director attitudes. The sense of emergency from the initial year of Covid-19 lockdown in 2020 which revolutionised the delivery of assessment subsided into an evolutionary path of quality enhancement in terms of assessment design and management. In particular, the use of laptops rather than handwritten scripts was now accepted practice, and the Inspera assessment system that was in pilot mode in 2022 was largely accepted by students, examiners, programme teams and Recognised Teaching Centres.

It is noteworthy that academic integrity issues were significantly better controlled in 2023, and the number of assessment offence cases has fallen to below pre-pandemic 2019 levels. However, the number of cases where action was taken remains higher than in 2019, at 407 as against 97. There are a complex range of factors at play in the downward trend of assessment offences. Online proctoring was used in some cases that contributed to the reduction of misconduct, with varied student feedback.

It is gratifying to note that communications from UoL and federated institutions appeared to be better co-ordinated, in that there is a reduction in the number of complaints, but the improvement of quality and timeliness continue to have prominence.

Interviews with Programme Directors and related staff reveal that there was a significant process of reform of design of assessment, which may also have contributed to the enhancement of academic integrity. There were approaches to address over-assessment by placing emphasis on sustained engagement in assessment during the course of study, resulting in using examinations differently.

2023 was also the year in which generative AI made its first major impact on higher education, and particularly the high profile ChatGPT application. Feedback from students was clear that they were aware of ChatGPT, and that the majority regarded it as an opportunity to enhance learning, although a minority were more concerned about the threat to academic integrity, as were examiners. which Generative AI had been used illegitimately in assessments is complex.

UoL case study

The longitudinal evaluation between 2020 and 2023 of online assessment at UoL and its partner universities in global programmes have evidenced the importance of understanding and managing academic integrity from equal perspectives of security and assessment design.

Pre-pandemic in UoL online and distance provision followed a traditional model of pen and paper fixed-time examinations in local exam halls, a model in place world-wide since 1858. With students distributed in up to 190 countries, an extensive network of over 600 independently quality-assured examination centres across the globe was in place. Going into lockdown in March 2020, UoL was preparing to distribute up to 110,000 paper examinations that summer. That spring saw a revolution in the approach taken to assessment: moving all examinations to an online format distributed through the virtual learning platforms. Programme teams and administrative staff worked around the clock to facilitate online assessments for over 35,000 students in 23 time zones. Previously fixed time, generally closed book examinations, moved online but were also transformed into open-world examinations in a variety of different formats. For example, examinations taken over seven days or four-hour examinations that could be taken at any point in 24 hours (Amrane-Cooper et al, 2023b).

The following two summers (2021, 2022), saw an evolution of approaches, with the introduction, for some students, of an enterprise platform that offered enhanced security features such as video and sound recording and the option to lock-down browsers. Detailed discussions with regulators in many countries in the University operates, with the student voice group, with other institutions and with our academic programme teams led to many changes in our examination designs and delivery modes: our online assessment practice was evolving.

By summer 2023 concerns over academic integrity became more urgent and in May and June 2023 UoL provided their first return to exam hall assessment for some students. No longer pen and paper based, computer facilitated assessment were in place, but students were moved back into assessment centres with human invigilation as part of the experience. For summer 2024, in a highly AI influenced world, the majority of the UoL students being assessed at that point will attend local examination centres for their fixed time examinations. To what extent can this be framed as regression or evolution, or does it represent elements of both?

Discussion

Our findings point to a higher education assessment landscape that combines elements of revolution, evolution, and regression paradigms. We examined our findings from the two projects outlined above, within the framework of these paradigms (see Table 1).

Revolution	Access to assessment – more students taking exams and students with additional needs undertaking assessment;
	The use of laptops instead of handwritten scripts as accepted enhanced practice;
	Perceptions amongst stakeholders that academic integrity issues are better controlled through (1) proctoring and the assessment platform, (2) assessment design and (3) academic integrity resources for students;
	Generative AI applications are transfiguring many aspects of learning and teaching, including assessment. Staff, and to a lesser degree students, are widely aware of generative AI in applications such as ChatGPT, and its incorporation into teaching and assessment in ways that both protect academic integrity and develop important skills for students will be a priority for the foreseeable future;
	Building a culture of trust with students is central to the practice of learning and teaching, driven by the challenges to assessment over the last 4 years.
Evolution:	A reduced number of cases of academic offences. The effectiveness of tools used to assure academic integrity, particularly bespoke assessment platforms, with features such as lockdown browsers and proctoring services in the online space, continue to present challenges;
	Changing perceptions of integrity under the influence of recent developments;
	Redesigning assessment as a core foundation to support academic integrity.
Regression	Integrity wise, staff awareness and greater knowledge of generative AI affordances do not necessarily lead to staff confidently identifying academic offences committed using AI;
	Assessment policy lags behind developments and has not kept up with changes and threats to academic integrity;
	Evidence of institutional communication strategies that aimed to ensure that students were kept informed of relevant issues, however little evidence that student views have been collected over the recent period to support dialogue about academic integrity.

Table 1. Examples of revolution, evolution and regression.

Conclusions

The paper explored the notion of revolution, evolution, and regression as drivers of assessment practice, examining the tensions and synergies between them that are shaping assessment practice in higher education. Our data seem to offer a way forward to a range of provisional conclusions, provisional because there is little consensus but rather, considerable concern, about how learning, teaching and assessment are going to be reconfigured because of generative AI.

Firstly, the concerns are substantially common to both campus-based and online and distance modes. This appears to be a space where the digital and AI revolutions drive innovation across all modes of a higher education. It is true that students in the online mode are unlikely to demand a return to presential modes, and indeed our research reveals how valued is the possibility to sit assessment events at home due to the diminution of cost and fatigue of travel to examination centres, and indeed in some countries the avoidance of risk, especially to women. Further, the advantages to students with disability are clear.

We have also uncovered practice that seeks to build a culture of trust with students as central to the practice of learning and teaching, driven by the challenges to assessment over the last 4 years. This is in sharp distinction to the core framing assumption that students cheat and will always seek to cheat, and that the primary institutional responsibility is to put effort into systems both conventional and technologically innovative such as online proctoring. While the latter may be necessary, some academic programme leaders have argued that the culture of trust is a core outcome of studentship, important for personal, community and professional lives. Such an approach embeds the development of respect for the student and for academic practice into training in academic integrity which is now widely developed in the sector. This can complement but not replace the policing of student behaviour.

We are concerned about the workload for academic and professional staff cohorts as we all seek to understand how generative AI can be developed to support learning, teaching, and assessment, rather than be excluded or seen primarily as a threat. There appears to be little understanding of the scale of investment needed in terms of assessment redesign that is central to the most positive outcomes of the impact of generative AI. We have evidence that such redesign is very positively reported in some programmes, in, rebalancing continuous assessment, both formative and summative, with final summative assessment. However there appears to be little in terms of institutional policy at this stage, which is lagging behind the reality of changing practice. Redesigning can fruitfully go further into rethinking the learning outcomes we need from our programmes of study, as well as the skills and knowledge represented there, and the ways in which they can be demonstrated by learners.

Finally, it seems clear that emerging practice is going to need to balance demands for both the protection of public reputation of qualifications and institutions through the policing of academic integrity with the more developmental commitment to education as a broad training in humanistic values. It is only honest to recognise that these two dimensions are at times perceived to be in tension, and senior management may impose a strong preference for the former over the latter. We prefer to see a creative tension, necessary at all times but at present due to the emerging understandings of how generative AI is going to impact teaching, learning and assessment. That tension should be the focus of continuing research, in order that the higher education sector can offer the best example of reflective practice and continuing quality enhancement. The last word should go to the acknowledgment that our students will continue to live in worlds that are vastly different in resources and opportunities, and these are likely to be exacerbated by AI in the immediate future. We in the higher education sector will have to continue to seek to manage those inequalities as they impact on educational outcomes, as we have done over the last 30 years of the digital revolution.

References

Adzima, K. (2020) 'Examining Online Cheating in Higher Education Using Traditional Classroom Cheating as a guide'. The Electronic Journal of e-Learning, 18(6), pp. 476-493. DOI: 10.34190/JEL.18.6.002.

Amrane-Cooper L., Hatzipanagos S. and Tait A. (2023a) Silver linings: rethinking assessment pedagogy under the pandemic. European Journal of Open, Distance and E-Learning, Vol.25 (Issue 1), pp. 93-103. https://doi.org/10.2478/eurodl-2023-0007

Amrane-Cooper, L. Baume, D., Hatzipanagos, S. Hughes G, Tait A. (2023b) Taking assessment online – systems, issues and practices: a case study'. In 'Online and Distance Education for a Connected World,' UCL Press, London 2023.

Parnther, C (2022) International Students and Academic Misconduct: Considering Culture, Community, and Context. Journal of College and Character, 23:1, 60-75. DOI: 10.1080/2194587X.2021.2017978

Surahman, E., & Wang, T.-H. (2022). Academic dishonesty and trustworthy assessment in online learning: A systematic literature review. Journal of Computer Assisted Learning, 38(6), 1535– 1553. https://doi.org/10.1111/jcal.12708

Technology Enhanced Assessment in Higher Education

Giedrė Tamoliūnė[1], Airina Volungevičienė[2], Estela Daukšienė[3], Elena Trepulė[4], Rimantė Čepauskienė[5], Indrė Oleškevičienė[6]

[1] Vytautas Magnus University, Lithuania; giedre.tamoliune@vdu.lt
[2] Vytautas Magnus University, Lithuania; airina.volungeviciene@vdu.lt
[3] Vytautas Magnus University, Lithuania; estela.dauksiene@vdu.lt
[4] Vytautas Magnus University, Lithuania; elena.trepule@vdu.lt
[5] Vytautas Magnus University, Lithuania; rimante.cepauskiene@vdu.lt
[6] Vytautas Magnus University, Lithuania; indre.oleskeviciene@vdu.lt

Correspondence: Giedrė Tamoliūnė, giedre.tamoliune@vdu.lt

Abstract:

Research indicates that assessment of learning and assessment of learning outcomes are the biggest challenges that teachers in higher education (HE) face. Traditional assessment practices do not work when learning and teaching is supported with technologies, which is inevitable in HE today. Teachers lack digital competence in designing assessment strategies and applying digital technologies for assessment of learning process and learning outcomes. DIGI-PROF project aims to address these challenges by introducing innovative learning and teaching practices that promote transparent technology enhanced assessment for online learning. This paper seeks to identify how teachers have progressed with application of digital technologies to support technology enhanced assessment of learning process and learning outcomes. The research revealed which technologies teachers apply for technology enhanced assessment of learning process (voice/video/text communication channels, file-sharing services, emails, and online quizzes), and how teachers use these technologies to facilitate learning process (providing feedback, applying technologies for peer assessment, and monitoring of students' learning). The study opened perspectives for further investigation on the use of learning analytics data to monitor and track students' learning progress.

Keywords: technology enhanced assessment, higher education, assessment of learning process, assessment of learning outcomes

Introduction

In a technology enhanced learning (TEL) environment, assessment differs from traditional face-to-face settings, necessitating pedagogical decisions that ensure effective and engaging student learning experiences (Alavi et al., 2021) as well as supporting learning process and learning outcomes. Communication from the Commission to the European Parliament, the Council, the European Economic and Social Committee, and the Committee of the Regions on achieving the European Education Area by 2025 (Communication, September 30, 2020) emphasized the need for Higher Education Institutions (HEI) to collaboratively build resilient and future-looking education systems by creating new ways of learning, teaching and assessment, and new education practices that are essential in the digital era.

Designing and implementing technology enhanced assessment strategies in online learning is one of the biggest challenges that HE teachers face. The traditional assessment practices are not effective when teaching and learning is supported with technologies, and, therefore, cause challenges for HEIs and teachers. Also, research shows that teachers express the absence of competencies, especially those related to the evaluation of educational practice (Basilotta-Gomez-Pablos et al., 2022) and technology enhanced assessment following the DigCompEdu framework (Santos et al., 2021).

The DIGI-PROF project addresses these challenges by creating innovative learning and teaching practices that lead to a transparent online learning assessment. The project results suggest training materials for developing teachers' digital competencies in assessment (following the DigCompEdu framework) to be able to design transparent assessment strategies in online courses, leading to the recognition of learning outcomes with micro-credentials. The training resources also allow teachers to develop competencies to monitor, support, and engage students in online learning through evidence-based solutions, using learning analytics data for timely and efficient feedback and support.

This study aims to identify how teachers have progressed with application of digital technologies to support technology enhanced assessment of learning process and learning outcomes.

Theoretical background

The process of designing assessments should be based on the understanding of the implications of adopting or integrating assessment of, for, or as learning approaches (Moreira et al., 2022), which typically refer to the ongoing "formative assessment" and the final "summative assessment". According to Hutchings (1992), the formative assessment can be seen as an assessment behind the outcomes, claiming that "the promise of assessment-mandated or otherwise-is improved student learning, and improvement requires attention not only to results but also to how results occur. Assessment behind outcomes means looking more carefully at the process and conditions that lead to the learning we care about..." (Hutchings, 1992, 6). Transparent assessment in online learning is very important due to the unique challenges and dynamics of a VLE. As noted by Moreira et al. (2022), despite the focus, purpose, and format of the assessment, assessment tasks and assignments should be fully aligned with the intended learning outcomes and assessment criteria that will be used. This approach of transparent assessment seeks to promote fairness, accountability, and understanding among students, teachers, and the assessment process itself. In this case, information regarding how assessments are conducted, what criteria are used, and how results are interpreted should be accessible to all parties involved. Some of the main aspects specific to transparent assessment in online learning could be clearly defined assessment criteria, feedback, and clear expectations communicated to learners, including criteria for evaluation, deadlines, and topics. In short, – transparent assessment refers to the clear explanations and clarifications of how the alignment among key course parameters, i.e., learning outcomes, methods, and assessment strategy, is ensured. Equally, it is important to ensure that students are introduced to the requirements for technology use, explaining what tools or platforms are used in the course to ensure students are comfortable with the technology and understand how to use it effectively for assessment purposes and monitoring and self-reflection of the learning process. The European Digital Education Plan highlights that "digital technology, when deployed skilfully and effectively by educators, can fully support the agenda of high quality and inclusive education and training for all learners" (EU, 2020, p. 1).

Another essential aspect of technology enhanced assessment in online learning is data monitoring and continuous analysis of students' learning progress based on the data informed by learning analytics (LA). LA can be defined as "a tool for assessment, interpretation, and analysis of learner-generated data in the online learning environment, in order to make the learning and teaching process more efficient by the teacher on interventions needed to advise or consult learners in due time to enhance their academic success" (Volungevičienė et al., 2021, p. 12).

Formative assessment fosters a culture of continuous improvement by collecting students' feedback and fostering their metacognition about their assessment and learning experiences. This may help refine and improve assessment practices over time. Also, assessment interventions designed at different stages of the study period help teachers monitor students' learning by enhancing it and supporting metacognitive, social, and emotional skills.

The aspects mentioned above are also represented in the DigCompEdu framework (2017), which, next to providing guidelines for developing technology-enhanced assessment strategies, highlights the importance of analysing evidence and using digital technologies to deliver timely feedback to support students in their learning process. In this research, we covered aspects of all three elements of the assessment – assessment strategies, analysing evidence and feedback and planning (Fig. 1).

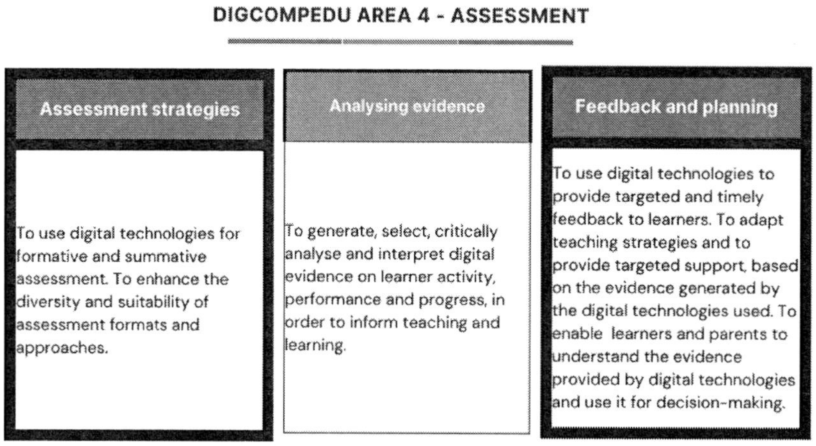

Figure 1: Area 4 – Assessment. DigCompEdu Framework (Redecker, 2017).

Assessment of student's learning process is one of the areas that digitally competent educators should be able to plan and design. Here, the focus of assessment activities and digital technologies is transferred from learning outcomes to a more periodic and frequent assessment that supports learning and fosters self-reflection. This assessment supports frequent feedback, focusing not only on evaluations of activities but also on their general performance and behavior. At the same time, by monitoring students learning, interactions, participation, and the evaluation of activities, teachers may help and support students in their performance and learning.

Research methodology

The online survey was designed using a theoretical framework presented earlier and a methodological framework that followed three phases: design, implementation, and evaluation (see Fig. 2).

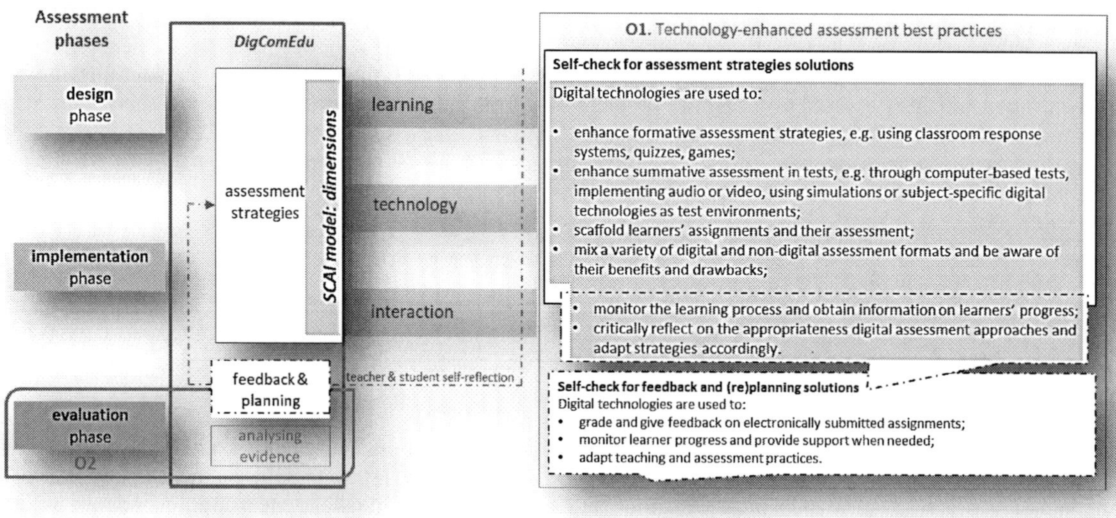

Figure 2: Methodological framework (Moreira, et al., 2022).

Research context. The research has been conducted as part of the Erasmus+ project DIGI-PROF, which aims to support HE teachers and HE institutions to design and implement transparent assessment for online learning and recognition of learning outcomes by proposing methodology, guidelines, practical tools, and training material to develop their digital competences. The survey aimed to identify HE teacher concerns and challenges while designing assessment strategies for online learning by recognizing how the three areas of digital assessment competencies described in the Digital Competences Framework for Educators (DigCompEdu Framework) are reflected by HE teachers-practitioners.

Research participants. Participants of the research were HE teachers who used digital technologies to enhance teaching and learning and assess students' learning and/or learning outcomes.

Research instrument. The questionnaire was developed during the DIGI-PROF project on the basis of the DigCompEdu Framework: Area of Digital Assessment. It consists of 55 statements, divided into three blocks of questions: Demographics, Digital assessment competence self-evaluation, and Using digital assessment tools.

Data collection and analysis. The online questionnaire was distributed among teachers in HEIs in different countries from 7 March 2022 to 5 April 2022 via professional networks, HEIs' intranets, and social networks by all project partner institutions. A descriptive data analysis was used to summarize and describe the primary characteristics of the data set. Also, in this paper, the focus is on the results representing the use of digital technologies to assess the student's learning process, leaving the use of digital technologies to assess students' learning outcomes/results out of the scope of this paper.

Research results

Demographics

Respondents' age varied from 28 to 75 years, with experience teaching in a TEL environment varying from 1 to 35 years and experience assessing students' learning online varying from 1 to 25+ years. Respondents' distribution by gender: 61% females, 37% males, and 2% preferred not to say.

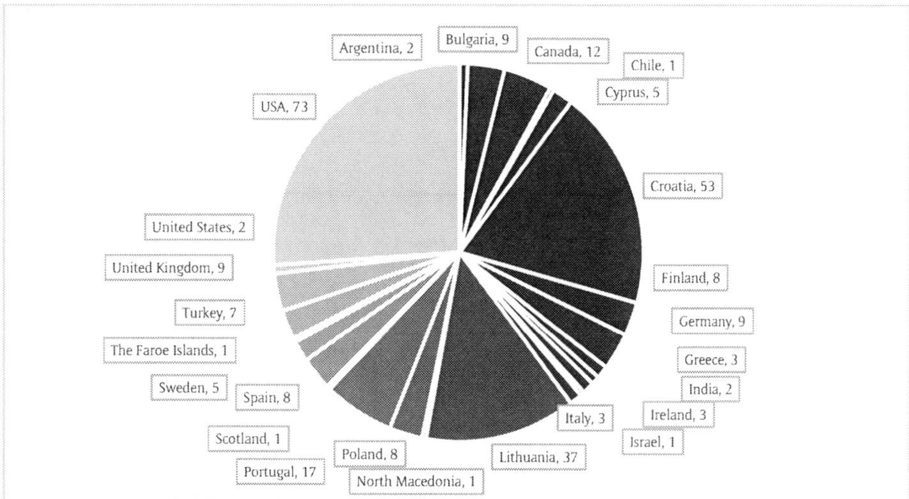

Figure 3: Respondents' distribution by country.

The use of digital technologies for assessment

A total of 293 responses were received: 283 research participants confirmed using digital technologies for assessment. The study discloses the frequency of the use of digital technologies for assessment (see Fig. 4).

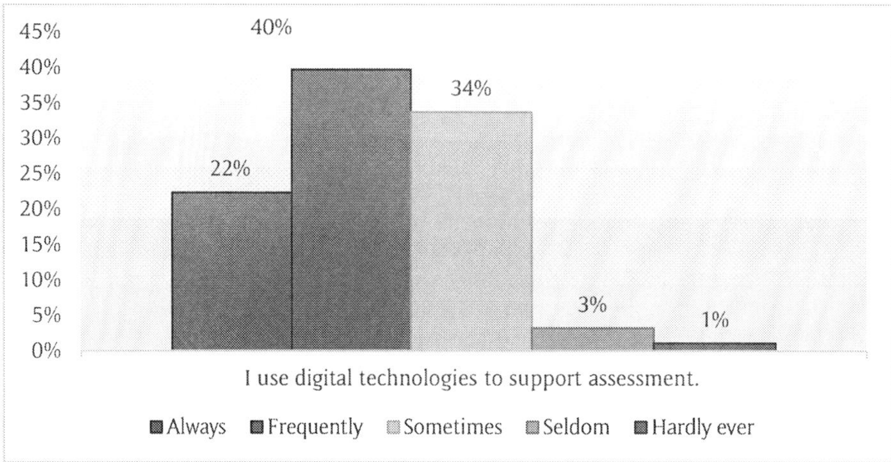

Figure 4: The frequency of using digital technologies to support assessment strategies.

The study discloses that respondents use digital technologies always or frequently for both assessment of students' learning process (61%), and assessment of students' learning outcomes/results (60%). Also, more than 30% of respondents responded that they sometimes use digital technologies for assessment (see Fig. 5).

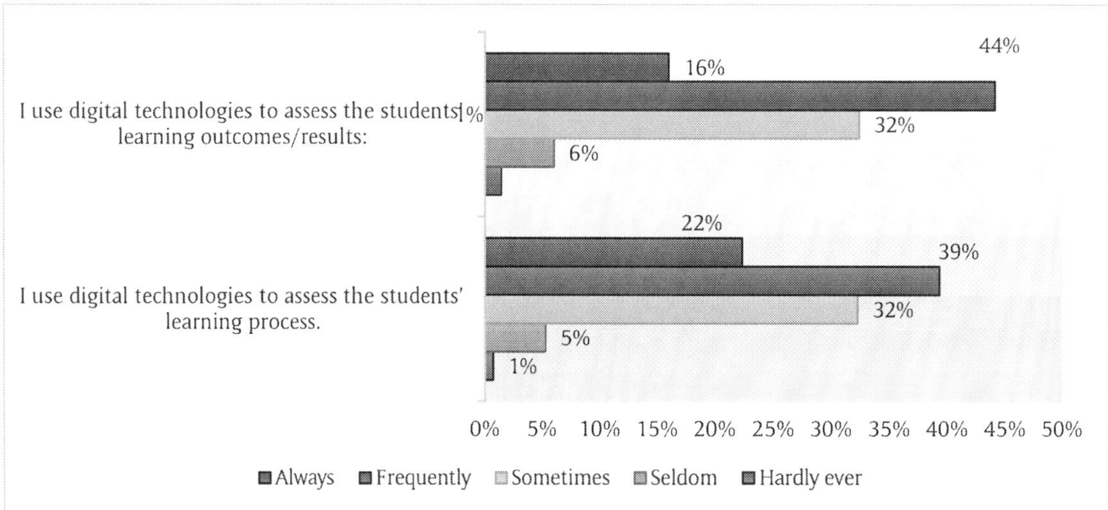

Figure 5: The use of digital technologies to support assessment, students' learning process, and students' learning outcomes/results.

At the same, only a small number of participants used digital technologies hardly ever or seldom to assess students' learning process (6%), and to assess students' learning outcomes/results (7%). This data gives a general overview of the fact that using digital technologies for assessment is quite a common practice when looking at areas of digital assessment defined in the DigCompEdu framework. Therefore, analysing and identifying the main tools used in this process is necessary for improving assessment practices.

The use of digital technologies to assess the student's learning process.

According to the survey results, most respondents use e-mails (44%), hosting and file-sharing services (40%), and voice/video/text communication channels (39%) always and frequently to assess students' learning process. At the same time, social networks, image-sharing channels, podcasts, game-based apps, and blogs are hardly ever used for assessing the learning process (see Fig. 6).

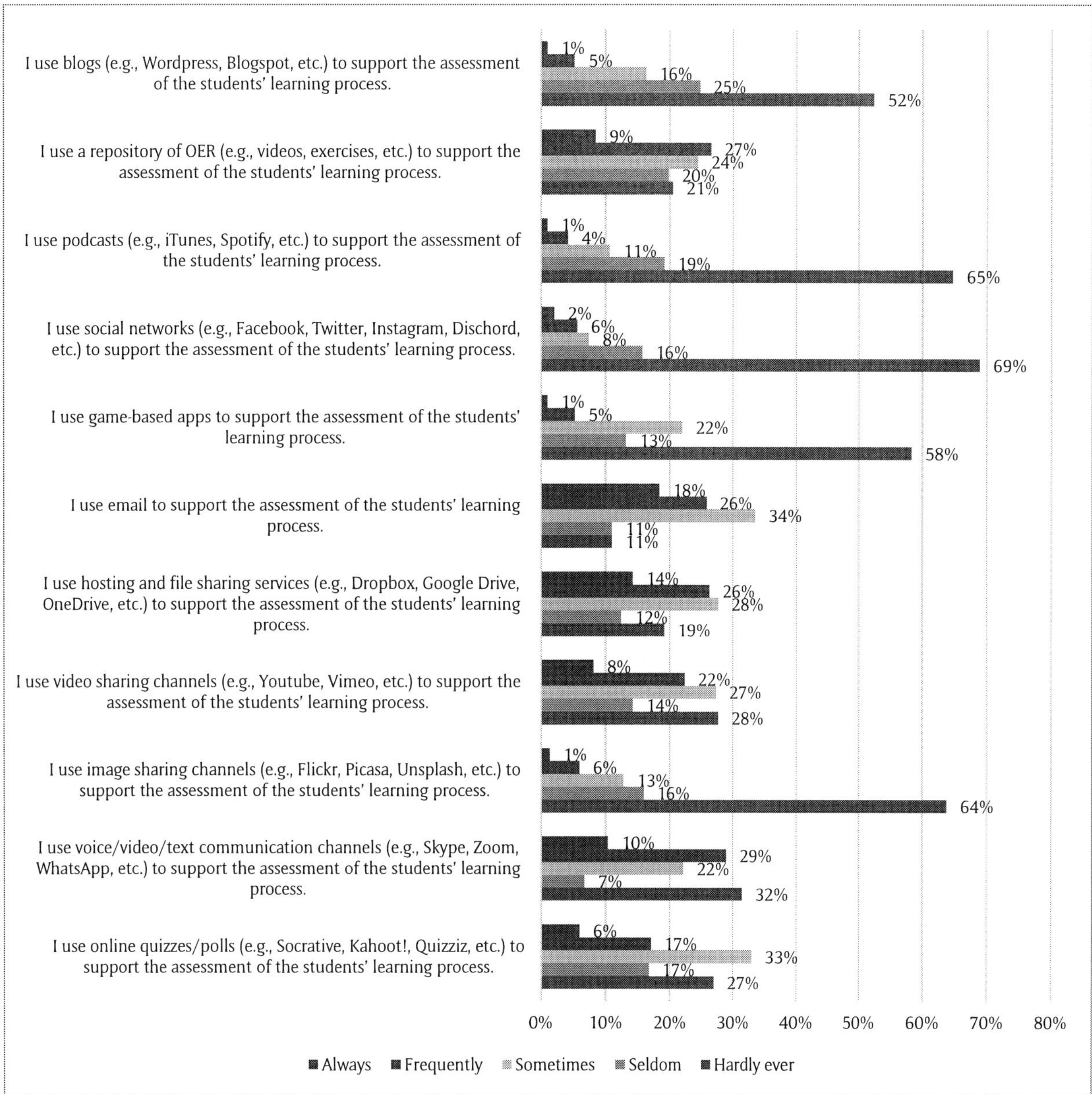

Figure 6: The use of digital technologies to assess students' learning process.

It is worth noting that the number of respondents using some digital technologies, for example, video-sharing channels (30%), is similar to those who use the same technology hardly ever (28%). The same is true for voice/video/ text communication channels: 29% respondents use these frequently, while 32% respondents use them hardly ever.

The use of digital tools to support students' learning process.

As discussed in the theoretical section, assessing students' learning process involves not just determining what technologies teachers use but also why and what they use them for. Results reveal that 58% of respondents use digital tools always and frequently to provide timely feedback to students, 39% use digital tools to support the peer review process, however 30% of respondents hardly ever use digital tools to support self-reflection (Fig. 7).

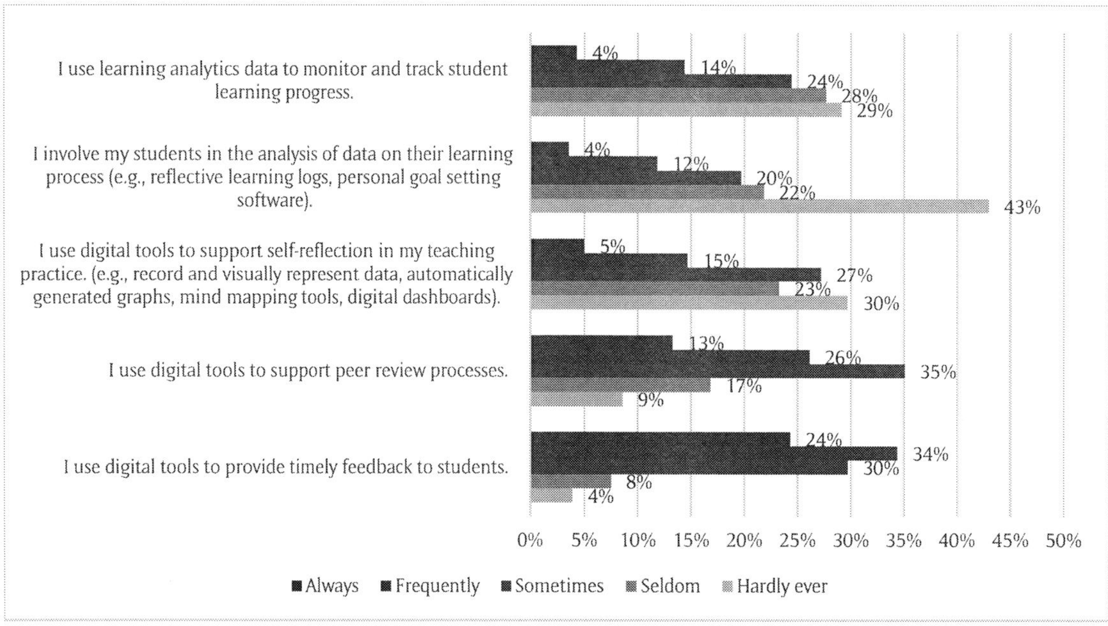

Figure 7: The use of digital technologies to support the learning process.

Study revealed that 43% of participants hardly ever involve students in analysing data of their learning process, and hardly ever (29%) or seldom (28%) use learning analytics data to monitor and track students' learning progress. These results may lead to a presumption that while teachers are absent from the digital competence to analyse digital evidence, they may find it difficult to involve students in analysing data on their learning process. As a result, this may contribute to the results of national surveys showing that student monitoring, engagement, and support may cause significant challenges for HE teachers when referring to the transparent assessment in online learning.

Conclusions

This study identified how HE teachers have progressed with application of digital technologies to support technology enhanced assessment of learning process and learning outcomes by disclosing which technologies teachers apply for technology enhanced assessment of learning process in their practice most frequently. Mostly used digital technologies are voice/video/text communication channels, file-sharing services, emails, and online quizzes, while technologies like podcasts or image sharing channels are used hardly ever. Given that a significant proportion of the responses to the statements were relatively evenly distributed between those teachers who always and frequently use particular digital technologies, like video/audio/text channels, and those who use the same technologies hardly ever, there is a need to encourage teachers to share their practices in designing technology enhanced assessment strategies. Also, teachers should be encouraged to collaboratively experiment and test new models of technology-enhanced assessment for online learning, that are didactically correct, are concise and integral with new modalities of online learning design, lead to a transparent assessment and bring value to students. The research results demonstrated that most frequently teachers facilitate learning process by using digital tools to provide timely feedback and support peer review process. However, it is noted that even though a significant number of research participants use digital technologies for the technology enhanced assessment, teachers seldom or hardly ever to monitor students' learning and involve students in the analysis of data on their learning process.

DIGI-PROF project seeks to address the aspects mentioned by establishing new innovative teaching and learning practices applying the DigCompEdu framework to develop digital competencies of teachers and HE institutions, to support digital capabilities of HEIs and create digitally enabled collaboration among HE teachers and students through formal study programs leading to micro-credentials. Finally, within the project framework, HE teachers and HE institutions will establish new scenarios for HE international collaboration, designing new courses for bachelor study programs with transparent assessment, efficient student support taught by digitally competent professors in a virtual and blended study mode, and leading to micro-credentials.

Research results led to the development of a training material "Designing transparent assessment strategies for online learning in HE" (Moreira et al., 2022) that supports the development of HE teachers' digital assessment competence by introducing how to:

- develop assessment strategies in a VLE;
- select proper technologies to support the assessment purpose best;
- involve students in digitally supported assessment;
- create evidence-based assessment;
- assess learning outcomes in a VLE, and define/apply assessment criteria;
- use tests in digital assessment to assess knowledge, skills, and values/responsibilities;
- design and apply peer assessment in a VLE;
- and use digital tools to provide timely feedback to students.

The training material, as well as other resources created within the DIGI-PROF project, is available on the project website at https://eden-europe.eu/digi-prof/.

Finally, results of this study opened perspectives for further investigation on the use of learning analytics data to monitor and track students' learning progress.

Competing interests

The authors have no competing interests to declare.

Funding Information

This research is being supported by the Erasmus+ Programme of the European Union project "Transparent assessment for online learning by digitally competent professors", No. 2021-1-LT01-KA220-HED-000031154.

References

Basilotta-Gomez-Pablos, V., Matarranz, M., Casado-Aranda,L.-A., and Otto, A. (2022). Teachers' digital competencies in higher education: A systematic literature review. International Journal of Educational Technology in Higher Education, 19(8). https://doi.org/10.1186/s41239-021-00312-8

European Union (2020). Digital Education Action Plan 2021-2027. https://education.ec.europa.eu/sites/default/files/document-library-docs/deap-communication-sept2020_en.pdf

Fernández-Olaskoaga, L., Guitert Catasús, M., Romeu Fontanillas, T., Cerro Martínez, J.P. (2023). Learning Analytics: A View on the Design and Assessment of Asynchronous Online Discussions for Better Teaching Performance. Educ. Sci., 13, 1064. https://doi.org/10.3390/educsci13101064

Memarian, B. and Doleck, T. (2024). A review of assessment for learning with artificial intelligence. Computers in Human Behavior: Artificial Humans, 2(1). https://doi.org/10.1016/j.chbah.2023.100040

Moreira A., Balula A., Costa N., Vasconcelos S., Neto T., Volungeviciene A., Greenspon R. (2022) Designing transparent assessment strategies for online learning in HE. DigiProf project training material. https://teacamp.vdu.lt/course/index.php?categoryid=15

National Forum for the Enhancement of Teaching and Learning in Higher Education. (March, 2017). Assessment of/for/as learning. Retrieved 25th February, 2022 from https://www.teachingandlearning.ie/our-priorities/student-success/assessment-of-for-as-learning/#1540351973453-cdd138e4-2d65

Redecker, C. (2017). European Framework for the Digital Competence of Educators: DigCompEdu. Punie, Y. (ed). EUR 28775 EN. Publications Office of the European Union, Luxembourg. JRC107466. https://doi.org/10.2760/159770

Santos, C., Pedro, N., and Mattar, J. (2021). Digital competence of higher education professors: Analysis of academic and institutional factors. Obra Digital, 21, 69-92. https://doi.org/10.25029/od.2021.311.21

Volungevičienė, A. (2021). Learning Analytics: a Metacognitive Tool to Engage Students. Sciendo. https://doi.org/10.2478/9788366675643

The changing role of educators in the age of artificial intelligence: Molding minds at the digital dawn

Rena Alasgarova[1], Jeyhun Rzayev[2]

[1]The Modern Educational Complex Named in Honour of Heydar Aliyev, Azerbaijan; rena.alasgarova@mtk.edu.az
[2]School of Education, ADA University, Azerbaijan; jrzayev@ada.edu.az

Correspondence: Rena Alasgarova: rena.alasgarova@mtk.edu.az

Abstract

This study investigates the impact of artificial intelligence (AI) on the roles and practices of educators and outlines the professional development needs in the era of AI. Employing qualitative interviews with 75 teachers across 15 schools in Azerbaijan, the research explores the integration of AI into education. It leverages the Technological Pedagogical Content Knowledge (TPACK) framework to examine the convergence of technology, pedagogy, and content expertise in teaching. Findings reveal that while AI has the potential to enhance personalized learning, its adoption poses significant challenges, including teacher burnout, ethical concerns, and the need for professional development programs. The study highlights the importance of practical training to enable educators to effectively integrate AI into teaching. Limitations include context specificity and potential biases in self-reporting. Future research should assess the long-term educational impacts of AI and expand to various educational settings for a broader perspective.

Keywords: AI, education, training, professional development

Introduction

Everlasting changes in technologies, which have recently been very rapid, have impacted presumably all spheres of human activity. Education has been facing relevant changes in the way teachers teach and learners learn. Starting many decades ago with the introduction of computers into the classroom and later the internet, followed up by mobile devices, such changes are inevitable, and educators, as well any other educational stakeholders, need to keep up the pace with the modern world.

The ubiquitous presence of artificial intelligence (AI) has made the lives of many students easier. So, it is supposed to do for their teachers. But has it? Navigating through classroom management, content delivery, staff meetings, lesson observations, curriculum, lesson plans, and other paperwork has been adding to already unstable life-work balance of the teacher. Atop comes a variety of free or almost-free AI platforms students use for their assignments. With this trend, teachers and educators need to add one more role to their duties and responsibilities to make AI a friend rather than a foe. This increases the necessity of introducing professional development programs and training that will equip teachers with relevant skills and reduce emotional and physical burnout (Schleicher, 2018).

The incorporation of AI into education requires a thorough reassessment of teaching methods and a deep comprehension of the convergence of technology, pedagogy, and content expertise. The Technological Pedagogical Content Knowledge (TPACK) framework helps to clarify the relationship between three essential areas of teacher expertise: content (C), pedagogy (P), and technology (T). As long as it has the ability to direct the professional development requirements and preferred support mechanisms for educators in the era of AI, the TPACK framework, which Mishra and Koehler developed in 2006, is significant to this study. It offers a solid theoretical foundation that helps teachers successfully incorporate technology into their teaching methods.

The focus of this research was on exploring the expanding role of teachers and educators in the context of AI adoption in education. This study investigated the systems of support and professional development that teachers require to successfully incorporate AI tools into their lesson plans. Hence, the study was guided by two research questions: (1) How does the integration of AI in education impact the role and practices of teachers? and (2) What are the professional development needs and preferred support mechanisms for educators in the AI era?

To investigate the research questions, this study utilized a qualitative research design, employing in-depth interviews with teachers from both private and public schools in Azerbaijan. The research attempted to include a broad spectrum of viewpoints and instructional environments by choosing a varied set of educators as participants. The data gathering procedure prioritized the comprehension of teachers' initial responses to AI, their approaches to incorporating AI tools into teaching methodologies, and their perceived requirements for professional growth.

Technological Pedagogical Content Knowledge (TPACK)

Mishra and Koehler (2006) proposed the TPACK framework, which outlines the knowledge that teachers need to have in order to effectively incorporate technology into their instructional practices. The three main categories of knowledge identified are Content Knowledge (CK), Pedagogical Knowledge (PK), and Technological Knowledge (TK). The interaction between these forms of knowledge gives rise to three distinct areas of expertise: Pedagogical Content Knowledge (PCK), Technological Content Knowledge (TCK), and Technological Pedagogical Knowledge (TPK). TPACK provides the holistic understanding of how to integrate content, pedagogy, and technology effectively in educational settings required for effective education using technology, as it encompasses all three main knowledge domains (Figure 1).

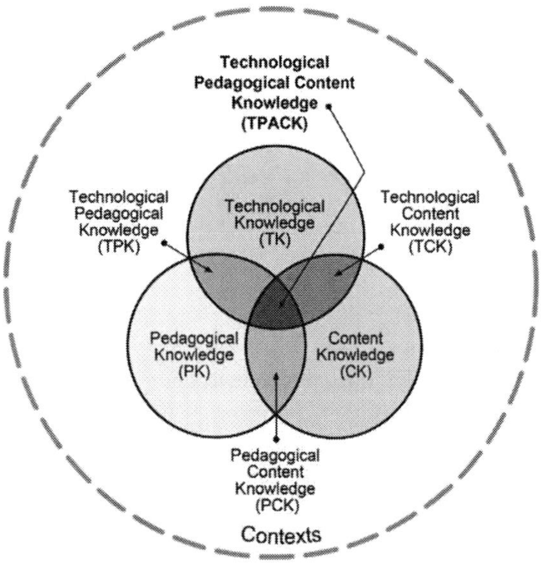

Figure 1: Technological Pedagogical Content Knowledge. Reproduced by permission of the publisher, © 2012 by tpack.org

The TPACK framework suggests that teachers go beyond traditional methods and gain a thorough understanding of AI technologies (TK) in the era of AI. It is recommended that this information be applied pedagogically (TPK) to enhance learning outcomes in certain subject areas (TCK). Educators should become adept at selecting and applying AI tools that align with learning objectives, modifying their techniques to fully leverage the individualization and customization capabilities of AI platforms, and critically evaluating the impact of AI on the academic performance of students (Koehler et al., 2013). Professional development programs targeted at strengthening the TPACK of educators should prioritize the development of transdisciplinary abilities, practical experience with AI tools, and reflective practice that analyzes the practical and ethical implications of incorporating AI in education.

Challenges of teaching in an AI-rich context

Although AI offers numerous advantages for active learning, its integration into education poses significant challenges for teachers. Lack of understanding and skill among teachers in incorporating AI tools into teaching methods might lead to inefficient use of innovative technologies. The digital divide relates to discrepancies in technological connectivity between educational institutions and communities, which may intensify educational inequities for disadvantaged students (Selwyn, 2019).

AI in education transforms the role of the teacher from being a provider of knowledge to becoming a facilitator of learning. Educators must explore novel approaches to incorporating AI tools into immersive learning environments (Nemorin et al., 2022). With this, it is crucial that professional development and assistance prioritize the ethical utilization of AI, employ efficient educational approaches, and foster the cultivation of critical thinking and digital literacy abilities in students (Holmes et al., 2019). These factors collectively aggravate teacher burnout, highlighting a pressing need for structured support systems that tackle the difficulties of integrating AI into education.

Methodology

With an emphasis on the professional development and support systems required for successful AI integration into teaching practices, the goal of this research was to examine how teachers and educators are growing in the context of integrating AI into education. A qualitative study technique was used to examine the experiences, attitudes, and actions of in-service teachers, considering the complex nature of this study. Qualitative research is especially well-suited for examining phenomena in their natural environments since it gives researchers a thorough grasp of the situations and people involved (Creswell and Poth, 2017). This approach allowed for an in-depth exploration of the perceptions and challenges educators face in the digital transformation of teaching, areas that quantitative methods might not fully capture due to their structured and numerical nature.

The main study method used to enable a thorough knowledge of individual instructors' experiences with AI in the classroom was in-depth interviews. In-depth interviews, according to Brinkmann and Kvale (2015), provide a special way for researchers to interact with participants one-on-one and encourage them to express their feelings, thoughts, and insights in their own words. The validity and reliability of the research tool were enhanced through the review of interview questions by two experts in the field of educational technology and qualitative research methods. This expert review helped ensure that the questions were clear, relevant, and capable of eliciting the desired information from participants.

Research findings and discussion

The data collected from in-depth interviews with teachers at Azerbaijani public and private schools was carefully examined using a thematic analysis approach in accordance with the principles outlined by Braun and Clarke (2006). Thematic analysis enables a comprehensive and adaptable analysis of the dataset, facilitating the exploration of patterns occurring when incorporating AI into the teaching and learning process. With the permission of the State Agency for Preschool and General Education, the study focused on 75 teachers from 15 schools in Azerbaijan. This approval ensured the participation of a diverse group of educators, enhancing the representativeness of the sample. To ensure research ethics, all participants were provided with consent forms that detailed the purpose and procedures of the study and their rights as participants. This process adhered to ethical guidelines for research with human subjects, ensuring that participants were informed, and consent was obtained in line with ethical standards in educational research (Creswell & Creswell, 2022).

The interview questions covered understanding the emotional and cognitive response to and practical examples of AI integration in teaching, challenges in the use of AI and strategies to mitigate these obstacles, gaps in current training and support systems, evaluation of the effects of AI on student outcomes, and perspectives on future trends. The transcribed interviews were analyzed to retrieve initial concepts.

The evaluation of the key concepts demonstrated the relationships between the ideas behind the teachers' understanding and attitudes towards the integration of AI into a teaching and learning environment (Figure 2). As reported by the majority of teachers, the process of successful integration of AI into the classroom equally involves all educational stakeholders, as integration needs to commence with the relevant changes in educational policies and be continued by constant support in the classrooms by teachers and at home by parents and/or caretakers (Selwyn, 2019). The alternations in policies need to reflect the establishment of professional development programs for teachers (Darling-Hammond et al., 2017). This is necessitated by the lack of awareness about AI platforms as a whole and their use in an educational context in particular among the majority of the interviewed teachers. Some teachers have also commented on their growing concerns about the impact of AI use on learning outcomes, specifically the decline in creativity and critical thinking skills, as well as the increased opportunities for plagiarism, which in the long run can have a negative impact on motivation. "The internet has already been keeping the doors for cheating ajar; AI has flung it wide open," responded one of the teachers. However, the interviewed teachers, though doubtful about future integration of AI into a learning process, embraced the idea of the inevitability of this process and reported the necessity of training programs that would be focused on practical application of AI and ethical issues that may follow: "The question now is not WHY, but HOW.".

Another concern that has been raised by many of the participants is the emotional well-being of teachers and the level of burnout and stress they encounter in the classrooms and beyond (Schleicher, 2018). The community is said to have recently increased their demands on teachers, and with the number of responsibilities and duties contemporary educators are dealing with now, extra challenges build up to emotional and nervous breakdowns (Greenberg et al., 2016). Hence, systems of support and professional development in the AI domain should aim at tailoring ways to make AI a useful classroom tool.

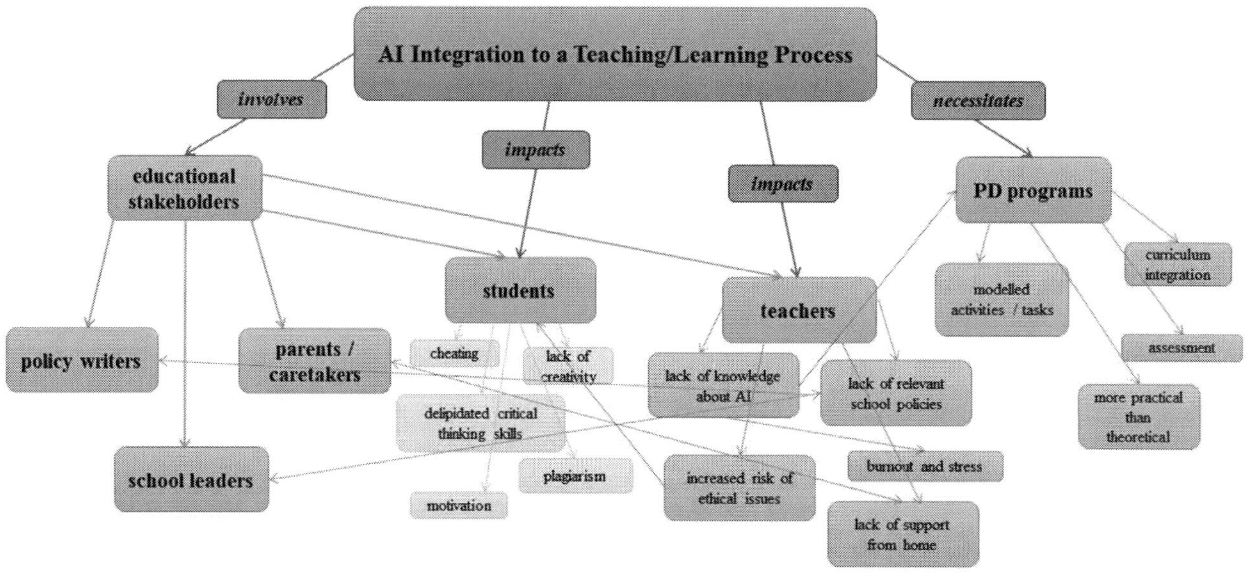

Figure 2: Concept map: AI Integration to a teaching and learning process.

After re-evaluating the key concepts, initial codes were generated by marking ideas and potential themes directly on the transcripts via MAXQDA, a qualitative data analysis software that facilitated the organization and categorization of the data. Each piece of data was coded systematically, ensuring consistency and comprehensiveness in the further identification of themes.

The analysis of the initial codes and frequency of mentions of these codes in interviews (Table 1) demonstrated the attitudes and concerns of the in-service teachers towards AI and its impact on the quality of a learning process. For the time being, without the support of policy writers and school leadership teams and a lack of relevant AI training, teachers have reservations about the successful and "painless" integration of such platforms into school curricula. Nevertheless, the teachers tend to accept the fact that students will be using AI, whether teachers are professionally trained to utilize these tools or not: "We can't avoid artificial intelligence entering our lives as we can't prevent progress from happening. We were once used to be suspicious about calculators too." Four codes that emerged from the analysis of the concepts stood out as some of the most frequently referred to: teacher burnout, desire for practical PD programs, ethical and privacy concerns, and impact on the learning process.

Table 1: Initial codes and frequency of instances.

Initial codes	Number of instances
Awareness of AI	102
Misuse of AI	93
Burnout	301
Desire for practical PD programs	269
Skepticism towards AI integration	103
Potential of AI as a learning tool	98
Ethical and privacy concerns	234
Future orientation and adaptability	72
Impact on learning process	211

Following the initial coding, codes were collated into potential themes. This involved a process of grouping all relevant coded data extracts and organizing these into thematic clusters. The themes were then reviewed and refined to ensure they accurately represented the dataset. Once the themes were defined and refined, the next step involved developing a thematic map of the analysis. This map provided a visual representation of the relationships between themes, offering insights into how different aspects of teachers' experiences and perceptions of integrating AI into education interconnect (Figure 3).

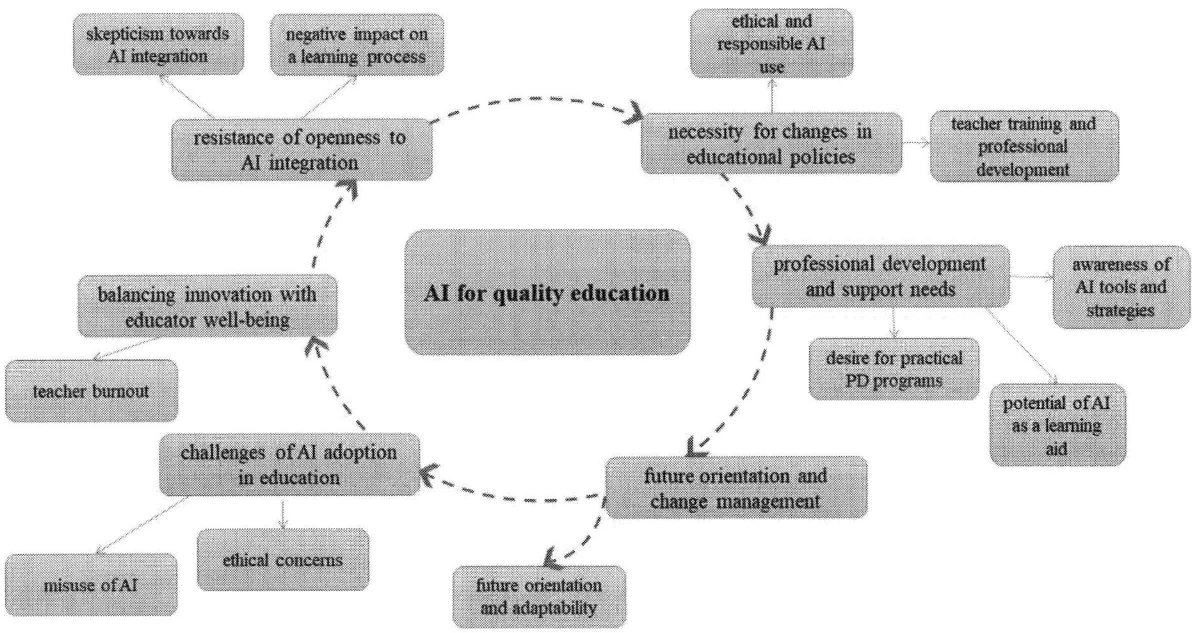

Figure 3: Thematic map.

The evaluation of the insights shared by the teachers derived AI for quality education as an overarching theme. The connection between the themes constitutes a cycle involving the teachers' perceptions and required steps to lead towards the intended results – future orientation and adaptability of AI for quality education. Challenges of AI adoption in education, such as misuse of AI tools both by teachers and students and rising ethical concerns, lead to the incapability of some teachers to balance innovation with educator well-being, i.e., decreased levels of stress and burnout. This might hinder the process of effective and efficient employment of AI in educational settings, as such integration faces resistance of openness to AI integration. The teachers feel unconfident and skeptical about the use of AI in classrooms and comment on how AI can negatively impact the learning process, making students indolent in their studying habits and eventually demotivated. These challenges condition the necessity for changes in educational policies that reflect the ethical and responsible use of AI, and teacher training and professional development. To reduce teacher burnout and meet teachers' lacks and needs, professional development and support need to be tailored to raise teachers' awareness of AI tools and strategies and provide practical guidelines for using AI as a learning aid. Given the taken measures are successful, future orientation and change management will contribute to the integration of AI into the learning environment. As long as the gaps are still observed, the process will continue for reevaluation of professional development support and policies until the desired outcome is achieved.

During the AI era, educators require a diverse range of professional development opportunities and support mechanisms. These should focus on effectively incorporating technology into teaching methods and subject knowledge. This is represented by the expanded Technological Pedagogical Content Knowledge (TPACK) framework (Figure 4). This comprehensive framework highlights the necessity for educators to receive training not only in the technical aspects of AI, referred to as Technological Knowledge (TK), but also in pedagogically sound methods of applying AI to teaching, known as Technological Pedagogical Knowledge (TPK), and aligning it with specific subject matter, known as Technological Content Knowledge (TCK) (Mishra & Koehler, 2006).

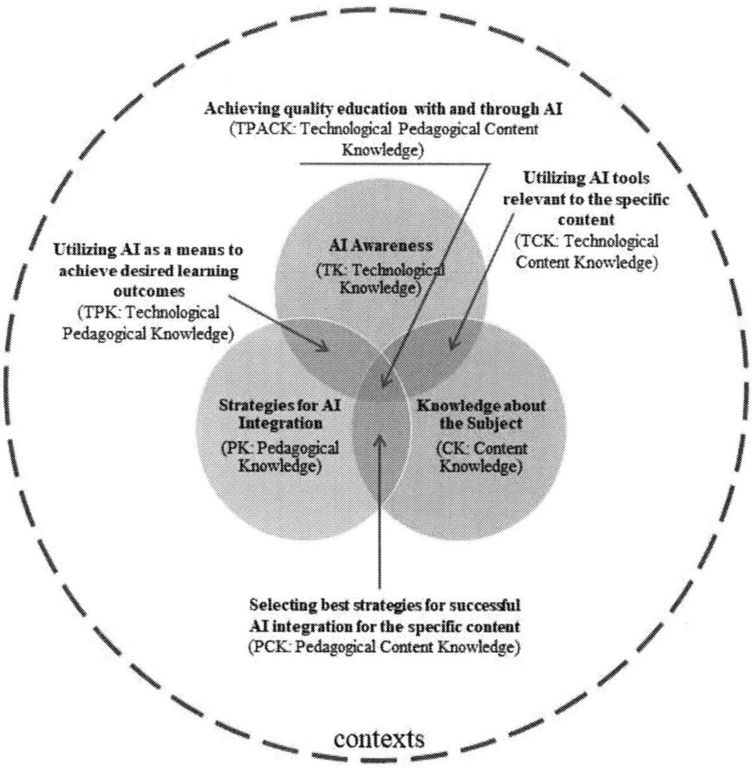

Figure 4. AI integration to education through TPACK framework.

Therefore, it is crucial to provide professional development programs that aim to improve teachers' TPACK, enabling them to effectively navigate the intricacies of AI technologies and resources. Educators necessitate experiential instruction that encompasses tangible illustrations of how AI might be employed to individualize learning and evaluate student achievement. An equally significant aspect is the enhancement of educators' ability to determine the most suitable AI tools for their teaching goals and to customize these tools to various classroom environments (Harris et al., 2010).

Support systems should encompass more than sporadic workshops and should incorporate continuous mentoring, peer collaboration, and the opportunity to engage with a community of practice. This community should cultivate an environment that promotes collaborative learning, enabling educators to communicate their experiences, resources, and ideas for the integration of AI (Archambault & Barnett, 2010). In addition, it is vital for educators to have access to technical support teams that can provide assistance in the deployment and resolution of issues with AI technologies.

Educators also require emotional and psychological assistance to effectively navigate the shift towards AI-enhanced teaching, in addition to the skills-based and community support systems. This assistance should recognize the augmented workload and probable stress that arise from the implementation of new technology and offer measures to uphold the well-being of teachers (Schleicher, 2018). Ergo, the primary goal of professional development and support mechanisms should be to enable instructors to utilize AI as a valuable tool to improve instruction and student learning, rather than as a source of stress that worsens burnout. By integrating these programs with the TPACK framework, educators can enhance their ability to effectively utilize the advantages of AI in a manner that is pedagogically sound, tailored to specific subjects, and ethically conscious.

Conclusion

As AI becomes more prevalent, educators must adapt from traditional teaching methods to more facilitative roles, guiding students through AI-enhanced learning experiences (Selwyn, 2019). This study emphasizes the transformative impact of AI on education, which requires a fundamental change in the roles and methods of educators. Although the incorporation of AI offers a hopeful future for individualized and effective education, it also presents significant challenges that must not be disregarded.

This shift necessitates professional development programs that address ethical considerations and the potential impacts of AI on student learning outcomes. These programs should equip teachers with the knowledge and skills to integrate AI tools into their curricula while fostering critical thinking and creativity among students (Nemorin et al., 2022).

Ethical and privacy concerns, particularly those related to data use and the potential for AI to perpetuate biases, must be addressed in professional development programs (Eubanks, 2018). Teachers must be prepared to address and mitigate potential ethical issues arising from AI integration. Additionally, the integration of AI has a significant impact on teacher burnout, as the introduction of AI technologies adds complexity to their roles (Schleicher, 2018). Professional development programs should provide strategies for managing this transition, providing teachers with mechanisms to cope with burnout and stress effectively.

The study acknowledges certain limitations. While the qualitative approach provides deep insights, the findings may not be universally applicable beyond the specific context of Azerbaijani schools. Additionally, the reliance on self-reported data may introduce biases, as participants could potentially provide socially desirable responses or reflect on their experiences in ways that align with perceived expectations.

Future research should explore the long-term effects of AI integration on educational outcomes and teacher well-being and the development of more scalable professional development models. It should also extend to diverse educational contexts to formulate a more global understanding of the impact of AI on education. The necessity for ongoing dialogue between educators, policymakers, and AI technologists is paramount to ensuring the ethical, fair, and effective deployment of AI in classrooms worldwide.

References

Archambault, L. M., & Barnett, J. H. (2010). Revisiting technological pedagogical content knowledge: Exploring the TPACK framework. Computers & Education, 55(4), 1656–1662. https://doi.org/10.1016/j.compedu.2010.07.009

Brinkmann, S., & Kvale, S. (2015). Interviews: Learning the craft of qualitative research interviewing. Sage.

Creswell, J. W., & Creswell, J. D. (2022). Research design: Qualitative, quantitative, and mixed methods approaches (6th ed.). Sage.

Creswell, J. W., & Poth, C. N. (2017). Qualitative inquiry and research design: Choosing among five approaches (4th ed.). Sage.

Darling-Hammond, L., Hyler, M., & Gardner, M. (2017). Effective teacher professional development. Learning Policy Institute. https://doi.org/10.54300/122.311

Eubanks, V. (2018). Automating inequality: How high-tech tools profile, police, and punish the poor. St. Martin's Publishing Group.

Greenberg, M. T., Brown, J. L., & Abenavoli, R. M. (2016, September). Teacher stress and health. Edna Bennett Pierce Prevention Research Center. https://www.rwjf.org/en/library/research/2016/07/teacher-stress-and-health.html

Harris, J., Mishra, P., & Koehler, M. (2009). Teachers' technological pedagogical content knowledge and learning activity types. Journal of Research on Technology in Education, 41(4), 393–416. https://doi.org/10.1080/15391523.2009.10782536

Holmes, W., Bialik, M., & Fadel, C. (2019). Artificial Intelligence in Education: Promises and implications for teaching and learning. The Center for Curriculum Redesign.

Mishra, P., & Koehler, M. J. (2006). Technological Pedagogical Content Knowledge: A Framework for Teacher Knowledge. Teachers College Record, 108(6), 1017-1054. https://doi.org/10.1111/j.1467-9620.2006.00684.x

Nemorin, S., Vlachidis, A., Ayerakwa, H. M., & Andriotis, P. (2022). Ai hyped? A horizon scan of discourse on Artificial Intelligence in Education (AIED) and development. Learning, Media and Technology, 48(1), 38–51. https://doi.org/10.1080/17439884.2022.2095568

Schleicher, A. (2018). World class. Strong Performers and Successful Reformers in Education. https://doi.org/10.1787/9789264300002-en

Selwyn, N. (2019). Should robots replace teachers?: Ai and the Future of Education. Polity Press.

An institutional AI digital assistant: what do distance learners expect and value?

Bart Rienties[1], Christothea Herodotou[1], Felipe Tessarolo[1], John Domingue[2], Subby Duttaroy[3], Denise Whitelock[1]

[1] Institute of Education Technology, The Open University, UK; bart.rienties@open.ac.uk
[2] Knowledge Media Institute, The Open University, UK; john.domingue@open.ac.uk
[3] Business Development Unit, The Open University, UK; subby.duttaroy@open.ac.uk

Correspondence: Bart Rienties: bart.rienties@open.ac.uk

Abstract:
The rapid evolution of Generative AI (Gen AI) and its integration into higher education necessitates a critical evaluation of teaching and learning practices. Many students already use publicly available AI digital assistants (p-AIDA) like ChatGPT for academic purposes. However, there are concerns around the use of such p-AIDA tools, in particular in terms of data privacy, academic integrity, Intellectual Property (IP), and the impact on the quality of education. Therefore, this mixed methods study explored the perspectives from 10 distance learning students on whether the development of an institutional AI Digital Assistant (i-AIDA) might mitigate some of these concerns. By comparing i-AIDA with p-AIDA our research underscores the potential benefits and limitations of in-house Gen AI tools in enhancing learning experiences without compromising academic integrity, IP or privacy.

Keywords: Artificial Intelligence, Digital Assistant, public vs institutional AI, Student expectations, mixed method, distance learning, chatbots.

Introduction

With the rapid evolution of Generative AI (Gen AI:Kasneci et al., 2023; Strzelecki, 2023; Yan et al., 2023) and applications like ChatGPT, higher education institutions are required to critically review their teaching and learning practice. Emerging statistics show that more than half (53%) of UK students consult AI for marked work (Freeman, 2024). Such studies indicate that whether (or not) HEIs want their students to use Gen AI, in practice most students use Gen AI while studying.

There is enthusiasm in terms of using Gen AI in teaching and learning (Darvishi et al., 2024; Kasneci et al., 2023). For example, in our first Design-Based Research (DBR) study with 10 Open University students (Rienties et al., 2024) we illustrated that all students agreed about the potential usefulness of receiving Gen AI support while studying. Reported benefits included real-time assistance and query resolution, support for academic tasks, personalisation and accessibility, and emotional and social support.

At the same time, there are several scholars who are worried about Gen AI tools in terms of what the long-term impact might be on the quality of assessment and feedback, and the role of the educator (Hamilton et al., 2023). Furthermore, there is some emerging evidence that students, educators, and senior management are worried about what happens to their data and intellectual property (IP) when using publicly available Gen AI tools like ChatGPT (Bozkurt & Sharma, 2023). Indeed, students expressed concerns around ethical and social implications of implementing Gen AI, data privacy and data use, and academic integrity and misuse (Rienties et al., 2024).

One way to potentially address some of these concerns is for institutions to create their own institutional AI Digital Assistant (i-AIDA) using the concept of a "walled garden". This would allow students and educators to securely use, trust, and share their data and IP (e.g., course materials, assessments, marking criteria), thereby potentially limiting prior concerns regarding the quality of i-AIDA responses and related privacy issues. At the same time, given the speed of developments of ChatGPT and the breadth of data it can access, one could wonder whether institutions should even consider investing money in developing their own Gen AI approaches. Alternatively, institutions could have their own 'tuned' models based on their own materials. These models could be smaller than the generic versions and run on their own machines or own cloud space. Therefore, we developed a DBR approach to explore the affordances and limitations of developing an i-AIDA as opposed to using a publicly available AIDA (p-AIDA) by asking students about their perspectives given that many students actively use ChatGPT. In this follow-up study from Rienties et al. (2024) we specifically aimed to explore the following research question: What are the students' perspectives of i-AIDA relative to using a p-AIDA?

Methods

Setting and participants

This study was conducted at The Open University (OU), the largest distance learning university in Europe. As described previously by Rienties et al. (2024), students were demonstrated a possible i-AIDA at the start of their interview (see Figure 1), after which a range of semi-structured questions were raised. In the second stage, students completed an online quantitative survey constructed based upon their interview data. In total 10 participants (six female and four male) joined one of the online interviews, from STEM (n=5), business (n=2, education (n=2), and arts/social sciences (n=1). Most of them were working while studying and had diverse educational backgrounds (See Rienties et al. (2024).

Figure 1 Screenshot of possible institutional AI Digital Assistant

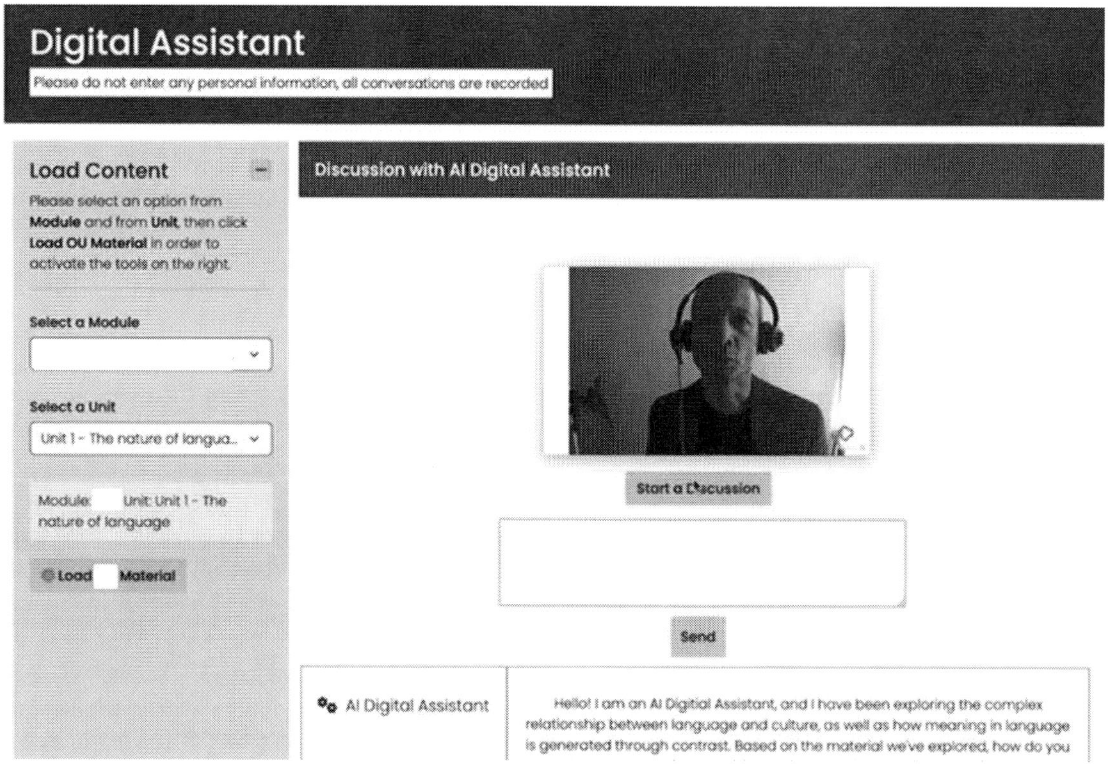

Instruments

Online interviews: A five-minute recording of a possible i-AIDA was screenshared including three potential examples (e.g., automatic feedback on a set of open assessment quizzes of a particular unit in a module, AI generated flash cards for revision, i-AIDA responding in real-time to student academic questions). The primary reason for sharing this demo i-AIDA was to allow participants to activate any prior knowledge or experience with AI, and if participants had no experience with AI to prompt some initial thoughts and ideas of how an i-AIDA might support their studies.

Online follow-up survey: Interview results were shar with study's participants aiming to gather feedback on whether (or not) results resonated with them. Eight out of ten participants responded to this follow-up survey.

Procedure

Following Morgan (2023) we initially used emergent thematic analysis within ChatGPT4 to generate separate analyses for each of the interview questions. These themes were sense-checked, and subsequently coded independently by two authors (FT, BR) as positive, mixed or negative sentiments. This research received Human Ethics Research Approval (HREC/2023-0183-4).

Results

Nine of ten participants indicated that an i-AIDA would be useful for their studies, while one participant could see it being used by students with support needs. In Table 1 eight themes were identified by participants that would either favour an in-house development of such an i-AIDA relative to a p-AIDA like ChatGPT, or perhaps hamper such an in-house development.

Table 1 Positive/mixed/negative sentiments towards i-AIDA (per participant) relative to p-AIDA

Theme	Positive	Mixed	Negative
Personalisation and Relevance: provide personalised responses, tailored to my academic needs and context, differentiating it from generic AI tools	6	0	1
Accuracy and Specificity: based upon institutional curated content that not only provides relevant answers but also directs students to specific institutional resources for further learning	6	0	1
Language and Accessibility: multi-lingual and accessible, catering to a diverse student body	5	0	0
24/7 Accessibility and Immediate Feedback: available round-the-clock for immediate feedback and support in their academic setting.	4	0	1
User Experience and Interface Design: easy of use, user-friendly, and integrated (e.g., in the OU module website)	2	0	0
Future Orientation and Career Planning: provide guidance for future modules and career planning	2	0	0
Academic Integrity and Plagiarism: potential misuse of AI for completing assignments, potential plagiarism, and academic integrity	0	1	2
Data Privacy and Ethical Use: how student data and inputs to the AI are used, stored, and potentially shared, emphasising the need for transparency and consent	0	1	1

Note: Not all participants contributed to each and every theme during the interviews.

Two themes were specifically addressed by at least six participants: personalisation and relevance, and accuracy and specificity. As explained:

> I think one positive to having a specific [i-AIDA] would be that the information you're getting from it would be pertinent to what you're studying as opposed to random answers. (I05, 34:10)

In terms of accuracy and specificity, participants indicated that i-AIDA should be based upon the OU's academic materials and approaches rather than generic materials used by ChatGPT.

> Specific to our Institution is a very important point, because it seems more protective of the students, and therefore I think that's of more value. I think that may be a key thing. It's like a sort of enclosed AI rather than something that's just out there for anyone or anything. (I02, 41:08)

> What I think should be different than public available tools such as Open AI. Open AI is kind of based on everything; I do not want this [i-AIDA] to be based on everything. I want [i-AIDA] to be based on academic sources ... it is an academic AI. (I03, 34:50)

Five participants were positive about an i-AIDA in terms of language and accessibility.

> Multi language provision is a very good use actually. Especially with the OU being so diverse and I think this is a real key aspect, [...] this is something that could probably be done quite easy. (I08: 38:02)

I03 argued that it would also allow for a broader range of academic resources to be included.

> Very often I feel academic publications kind of forget papers that are outside of the group United States/Europe. There are some really amazing papers in Portuguese that are not being used just because they're in Portuguese. Using these also to feed the AI, I think is more important even than multiple language provision. (I03, 38:45)

In terms of 24/7 Accessibility and Immediate Feedback, I05 suggested that responses from AI should be based upon what she was studying in her course.

> Because I do agree with the 24/7 availability. The instant feedback and I like the tailored if it can produce tailored responses based on the OU material because the course that I'm doing is OU material, it's not outside sources. So, like the other AI are no use to me because it might pull from different websites. (I09, 55:17)

I09 indicated that she wanted the i-AIDA to provide discipline specific suggestions on academic questions she might have, but not giving the answers to assignments.

> As long as it is that walled garden idea, because you've seen all the other AI sites just because people are uploading their essays on to them doesn't mean the essays are any good. The information that I would want from this kind of service is information by OU that I can use, and I don't want OU to write an assignment for me, I want to be able to ask questions and get to know my subject more, but what I wouldn't like is you can go on loads sites and people upload nonsense. I don't want someone else's garbage. (I09, 45:26)

Two participants saw i-AIDA as potentially helpful in providing guidance for future modules and career planning, suggesting a broader application beyond immediate academic assistance.

> I'm finding the careers emails that are coming through very useful because I am looking for a career change. That sort of thing would be good. (I05, 39:37)

Finally, participants indicated that a main benefit of having the i-AIDA integrated in the OU infrastructure would be a more seamless user experience and interface design:

> Having it embedding into the OU website so it's easily accessible for everyone. If we're directing students off somewhere else, that could increase the feeling of this OU tool, is it slightly external tool? Where is my data going? I think it needs to be embedded [in] the module websites or the OU website.

Nonetheless, three participants raised concerns about how to maintain academic integrity, and how i-AIDA could be used for plagiarism checks, ensuring originality in student work:

> The other thing I wonder about is the capacity in relation to plagiarism, because this would be a really good tool for plagiarism checking. How a student doesn't then get accused of plagiarism? (I02, 42:27)

Finally, two participants were worried about data privacy and ethical use.

> The AI would just learn what certain academics and stuff thinks the best writing style and philosophy [are]? And it would refine that just in the same way that if the OU just used stuff from the staff and the students to develop this AI, how is that not going to be biased? (I10, 44:58)

In order to sense check participants' own and peer answers, in the follow-up survey participants reflected on the results from interviews with participants. Six out of eight thought that an i-AIDA would be easy to use based upon what was demoed, while five out of eight indicated that they would use an i-AIDA frequently if it would be available to them. Perhaps because of the walled garden approach suggested during the interviews, only two participants were worried that their data would be shared by others, or used for external sources, such as training a p-AIDA like ChatGPT.

Discussion

Many higher education institutions across the globe are grappling with the question of whether (or not) to use a publicly available AI digital assistant (p-AIDA) like ChatGPT in their teaching and learning, and whether to develop their own unique institutional approach (i-AIDA). In this mixed methods study, we demonstrated a possible i-AIDA to ten distance learners at OU with detailed interviews and a follow-up online survey. We explored what students' perspectives were if OU would develop an i-AIDA using licensed and approved material relative to just using a p-AIDA such as ChatGPT.

Our study indicates that students have nuanced perspectives on the role of Gen AI in academic support and integrity. This study illustrates consensus amongst most students about the utility of Gen AI in potentially enhancing their learning experiences, with particular emphasis on personalized and accessible education when these are embedded in their specific learning journeys. However, it simultaneously underscores the critical concerns surrounding academic integrity, data privacy, and the potential depersonalization of education through generalised AI solutions.

The positive reception of an i-AIDA by all but two participants, tailored to specific students' academic needs and contexts, suggests a strong preference for AI tools like i-AIDA that respect the unique learning journeys that students partake in. This aligns with the desire for a "walled garden" approach, which promises improved data security and relevance of study content and context, addressing some of the concerns around more generic p-AIDA tools like ChatGPT.

Perhaps a new feature of this study was the explicit desire for personalisation and relevance, combined with accuracy and specificity. This went above and beyond whether an AIDA would hallucinate (or not), and indicated that students wanted that an (i)AIDA would know where they are in their studies, what potentially the next steps might be, and how to get there. Another new feature was the desire for an i-AIDA to include multiple languages and have accessibility features. As the OU attracts a diverse range of students from various cultural and socio-economic backgrounds, this might have been more pronounced relative to other studies. Finally, students indicated that the user experience and interface design of i-AIDA should be easy to use, user-friendly, and integrated into the learning platform and modules that students were studying, rather than a stand-alone tool.

Nonetheless, while students might want such an i-AIDA, whether the educators at the OU and senior management would agree would depend on the feasibility and cost-effectiveness of developing such bespoke solutions, especially given the rapid advancement and broad accessibility of p-AIDAs. This study contributes to the ongoing discourse on whether (or not) institutions should use p-AIDA or i-AIDA in their curriculum, advocating for a cautious yet proactive approach to discuss such approach with relevant stakeholders.

Limitations and future research

A limitation of this study was the relatively small sample size. However, we reached saturation in terms of the themes that emerged after eight participants. Furthermore, given the validation of the subsequent results in stage two by the participants, there was consensus amongst most participants in terms of the expected services and potential concerns of an i-AIDA relative to a p-AIDA. In future research, in line with DBR principles we would like to explore how initial prototypes of i-AIDA are perceived by both students, educators, and managers. This approach will aid us as we develop inclusive and transparent mechanisms and policies with all stakeholders involved to ensure that a future i-AIDA approach is appropriate for the diverse range of students at the OU.

Acknowledgements

We are grateful for the support from all those students who participated in this research.

References

Bozkurt, A., & Sharma, R. C. (2023). Challenging the status quo and exploring the new boundaries in the age of algorithms: Reimagining the role of generative AI in distance education and online learning. Asian Journal of Distance Education, 18(1), 1-8.

Darvishi, A., Khosravi, H., Sadiq, S., Gašević, D., & Siemens, G. (2024). Impact of AI assistance on student agency. Computers & Education, 210, 104967. https://doi.org/https://doi.org/10.1016/j.compedu.2023.104967

Freeman, J. (2024). Provide or punish? Students' views on generative AI in higher education. https://www.hepi.ac.uk/wp-content/uploads/2024/01/HEPI-Policy-Note-51.pdf

Hamilton, A., Wiliam, D., & Hattie, J. (2023). The Future of AI in Education: 13 Things We Can Do to Minimize the Damage. https://doi.org/10.35542/osf.io/372vr

Kasneci, E., Sessler, K., Küchemann, S., Bannert, M., Dementieva, D., Fischer, F., Gasser, U., Groh, G., Günnemann, S., Hüllermeier, E., Krusche, S., Kutyniok, G., Michaeli, T., Nerdel, C., Pfeffer, J., Poquet, O., Sailer, M., Schmidt, A., Seidel, T., Stadler, M., Weller, J., Kuhn, J., & Kasneci, G. (2023). ChatGPT for good? On opportunities and challenges of large language models for education. Learning and Individual Differences, 103, 102274. https://doi.org/https://doi.org/10.1016/j.lindif.2023.102274

Morgan, D. L. (2023). Exploring the Use of Artificial Intelligence for Qualitative Data Analysis: The Case of ChatGPT. International Journal of Qualitative Methods, 22, 16094069231211248. https://doi.org/10.1177/16094069231211248

Rienties, B., Domingue, J., Duttaroy, S., Herodotou, C., Tessarolo, F., & Whitelock, D. (2024). What distance learning students want from an AI Digital Assistant. Distance Education, 1-17. https://doi.org/10.1080/01587919.2024.2338717

Strzelecki, A. (2023). To use or not to use ChatGPT in higher education? A study of students' acceptance and use of technology. Interactive Learning Environments, 1-14. https://doi.org/10.1080/10494820.2023.2209881

Yan, L., Sha, L., Zhao, L., Li, Y., Martinez-Maldonado, R., Chen, G., Li, X., Jin, Y., & Gašević, D. (2023). Practical and ethical challenges of large language models in education: A systematic scoping review. British Journal of Educational Technology, n/a(n/a). https://doi.org/https://doi.org/10.1111/bjet.13370

The Democratisation of AI in, for and through Education: A Position Paper

Paul Prinsloo[1], Mohammad Khalil[2]

[1] Department of Business Management, University of South Africa, South Africa; prinsp@unisa.ac.za
[2] SLATE: Centre for the Science of Learning & Technology, University of Bergen, Norway; mohammad.khalil@uib.no

Correspondence: Paul Prinsloo: prinsp@unisa.ac.za

Abstract:

Amid the many claims surrounding the operationalisation of Artificial Intelligence (AI) in education, is the claim that AI can democratise education - referring to, inter alia, increasing access to equitable, high-quality lifelong learning opportunities for all. There is, however, also the claim that education should play an integral role in democratising AI. While the role of AI in democratising education is well-documented, the role of education in democratising AI is less clear. In this opinion paper, we briefly map the issues at stake in democratising education through AI, before focusing on claims on the role to democratise AI in, through and for education. We conclude this position paper with a number of pointers to inform policy, curricula and teaching practice.

Keywords: Artificial Intelligence (AI), democratising, education

Introduction

While literature about the impact of Artificial Intelligence (AI) on and in education, precedes the launch of ChatGPT at the end of 2022, research on the impact of AI on and in education has increased exponentially. There is (almost) not any aspect of teaching and learning, and education in general, that will remain unaffected by AI as AI is changing admissions (Slimi & Carballido, 2023), student support through chatbots (EL Azhari et al., 2023), assessment (Crompton & Burke, 2023), teacher workloads (Maphosa & Maphosa, 2023), pedagogy and how students learn (Jackson, 2024), students' competencies and teacher competencies (Baena-Rojas et al., 2023), and so forth.

One of the claims about AI in the context of education is that AI will democratise knowledge and, per se education (Ozsevim, 2023). In a recently published position paper, Bulathwela et al. (2024) maps the potential of AI to democratise education but also point to a number of perils. The authors position their paper against the background of the reality that despite the fact that education is a human right, access to equitable education is still for millions of children, an unrealised dream. To build and maintain "a sustainable, large-scale and inclusive AI in the Education ecosystem that facilitates equitable, high-quality lifelong learning opportunities for all", the authors propose a number of "pillars" including, but not limited to targeting finance to "those left behind", the sharing of expertise and resources, applying universal design, as well as collecting "data on and for exclusion with attention and respect" (p. 8). Other authors exploring the democratisation of education through AI include, but are not limited to Kamalov et al. (2023), Kucirkova and Leaton Gray (2023), and a McKinsey and Company (2019) report in which they report on an interview with Sal Khan, founder of the Khan Academy.

While democratising education through AI may be linked to democratising AI in, through and for education, it is however, not clear what is meant by the democratisation of AI (e.g. Rao, 2020; Seeger, 2023), and how it will play out in the context of education. The purpose of this position paper is therefore to map elements of the claims and research about the democratisation of AI in, through and for education.

The paper unfolds as follows: We firstly map the background to democratising AI in, through and for education by referring to literature outside of scholarly articles - an informative article published in Medium by Rao (2023), a United Kingdom parliamentary briefing (Big Innovation Centre 2023), overviews of the notion of democratising AI (outside the context of education) by Seger (2023) and Seger et al. (2023). We acknowledge that this selection of literature is highly selective, but for the purposes of providing a backdrop to this position paper we consider it to be justified (see the discussion on our methodological approach to this position paper later).

A brief background to the notion of democratising AI in, through and for education

Already in 2020, Rao warned that the democratisation of AI is a "double-edged sword". Democratisation refers to more people having access to "the raw materials of knowledge, tools, and data required to build an AI system" and the fact that Google, Microsoft and Amazon "released premade, drag-and-drop or no-code AI tools that allow people to integrate AI into applications without needing to know how to build machine learning models." While access to the use and benefits of AI often dominates the discussions about the democratisation of AI, Rao (2023) points to the democratisation of AI referring to a range of aspects, e.g access to data (the democratisation of data visualisation and generation), the democratisation of storage and computing (data ingestion, storage and infrastructure), algorithms (the use, development and sharing of machine learning and deep learning algorithms), model development (end-to-end model development, training and deployment), as well as democratising the AI marketplace (the use, exchange, monetisation of data, algorithms models and outcomes).

Rao (2020) furthermore emphasises that it is important to know who you democratise for - "casual users, power users, and specialist developers." Data visualisation can, for example, benefit all three groups of users while the democratisation of model development should be focused on specialist developers. Rao also points to three potential benefits of the democratisation of AI namely (1) "reduces entry barriers for individuals as well as organisations to start experimenting with AI"; (2) "reduces the overall cost of building AI solutions"; (3) "increasing the speed of adoption of AI in the academic and business world: (italics in the original). Rao also answers the question of how to democratise - and he proposes four essential elements namely (1) access (plus training); (2) use (and governance); (3) control (and IP rights); and (4) own (and making open/increasing access).

A UK Parliamentary Brief titled "Democratising Artificial Intelligence: Generative AI as a Catalyst for Change in Education" by the Big Innovation Centre (2023) highlights "the opportunities of AI to enable personalised, adaptive learning at scale, democratise access to high-quality instruction, and augment human teachers" (p. 12; italics added). Rose Luckin (in Big Innovation Centre, 2023) states that "AI could be a huge force for bringing greater equality. I still believe if we can democratise AI, we can democratise Education, and if we can really democratise Education, then we bring about equality" (p. 26; italics added). Luckin further states that the democratisation of AI and the transformation of education are linked - "we could democratise AI and through doing that, we could transform Education, and we could do it with positive impact" (in Big Innovation Centre, 2023, p. 27). (This links back to the position paper by Bulathwela et al., 2024 referred to earlier).

Just as no-one should be denied access to education (a human right), Louis Halpern (in Big Innovation Centre, 2023) states that no one should be denied access to AI - "you've got to have the freedom to interact with your AI in your own way, with your own words, with your hand motions, with your pictures, with any way that you choose to communicate yourself" (p. 29). Halpern further states that "While democratising access to AI models holds potential to allow more universal benefiting from Generative technologies, [he] insists that appropriate statutory data rights and protections must be enshrined in policy to prevent exacerbating existing inequalities" (in Big Innovation Centre, 2023, p. 17). In ensuring that "historically marginalised communities also experience Generative AI's advantages by guaranteeing data dignity", legislation would be essential - "by codifying fairness principles into law we can help guarantee that Generative models do not ultimately undermine social progress by departing from democratic values" (in Big Innovation Centre, 2023, p. 17).

Seger (2023) distinguishes between democratising the use of AI, its development, its benefits and the governance of AI. Seger (2023) further states that "Democracy is not about giving every individual the power to do whatever they would like. Rather, it involves introducing processes to facilitate the representation of diverse and often conflicting beliefs, opinions, and values into decisions about how people and their actions are governed." Seger et al (2023) summarise the use of the phrase "democratising AI" as referring to "(1) the democratisation of AI use, (2) the democratisation of AI development, (3) the democratisation of AI profits, and (4) the democratisation of AI governance" (p. 1).

With the above as background, the next section explains our methodological approach in arriving at our position in this position paper.

Methodological approach

Position papers normally do not present a formal methodology. Yet, this does not mean that authors did not have an approach to formulate their 'position'. The purpose of a position paper is to present a thesis to an audience based on an examination of evidence, and presented to convince readers that the argument is worthy of serious consideration and adds value to our understanding of a phenomenon. An example of a position paper in the context of AI and education (AIED) is by Hwang et al. (2020) where the authors "propose a framework to show the considerations of implementing AIED in different learning and teaching settings." The authors define the value proposition of a position paper as follows: "Position papers aim to present an arguable opinion, a new idea, an innovative pedagogical/system model, or a new conceptual framework about the research topics of this journal. Although a position paper does have to include data that supports the proposed opinion, its arguments and ideas must be logically valid and convincing" (Hwang et al., 2020, p. 4).

In the case of this paper, we were curious about what exactly is meant by the phrase "the democratisation of AI '' or, alternatively, "democratising AI", both phrases in the context of education. Initially we did a search on two databases, namely Web of Science and Scopus - but in both cases, found only two scholarly, peer-reviewed articles with the search string "democratising Artificial Intelligence" OR "democratizing Artificial Intelligence" OR the "democratisation of AI" OR the "democratization of AI" AND education. On 5 February 2024 we used Hartzing's Publish or Perish using the same search string and downloaded the first 500 records (excluding patents and citations). In total between the three databases (WoS, Scopus and Google Scholar using Hartzing's Publish or Perish) we downloaded 184 records, excluded 9 duplicates (including the two found on WoS and Scopus) and we were left with 176. The 176 sources were exported using Excel. Books, book chapters, reports, editorials, theses, and working papers were excluded - a total of 44 records, leaving 132 journal articles and conference papers. A further 6 records were excluded due to not having access through both institutional libraries of the authors. The reviewers worked through the remaining 128 records using a code book looking for the exact phrases as indicated in the search string. Only five (5) articles/conference presentations were found to address the "democratisation of AI'' or "democratising AI" in the context of education and are listed below:

- Coeckelbergh, M. (2023). Democracy, epistemic agency, and AI: political epistemology in times of artificial intelligence. AI and Ethics, 3(4), 1341-1350
- Jurayev, S. B. (2023). Leveraging Artificial Intelligence in education: A comprehensive analysis. Innovative Development in Educational Activities, 2(13), 257-261.
- Khan, S., Morales, A., & Plale, B. (2023). Democratisation is a process, not a destination: Operationalizing ethics and democratisation in a cyberinfrastructure for AI project. Proceedings of the EAI 2nd International Conference on AI for People, Democratizing AI.
- Stamboliev, E. (2023). Proposing a Postcritical AI Literacy: Why We Should Worry Less about Algorithmic Transparency and More about Citizen Empowerment. Media Theory, 7(1), 202-232.
- Sundberg, L., & Holmström, J. (2024). Teaching Tip: Using No-code AI to Teach Machine Learning in Higher Education. Journal of Information Systems Education, 35(1).

In order to formulate our position, we will briefly summarise the five papers and the evidence that provide regarding the democratisation of AI for and through education before formulating our position.

Analysis

Coeckelbergh's (2023) main argument is structured around three linked concepts namely democracy, AI and epistemic agency resulting in the question "do citizens have sufficient epistemic agency in the light of AI?" (p. 1342). The notion of 'epistemic agency' refers to the extent individuals have control over their beliefs and "how these beliefs are formed and revised" (p. 1342), under which/whose influences. Without epistemic agency, individuals' democratic agency is weakened, if not subverted. While Coeckelbergh (2023) acknowledges that epistemic agency was always vulnerable to being shaped by dominant information flows, recent advances in AI increasingly result in individuals mistrusting and doubting their own epistemic capacities and overall, have even less control over the formation of their knowledge. "When ultimately only AI knows the truth, then those who control AI also control the truth and thereby the citizens. Once the epistemic agency of citizens is eroded in this manner, there is no longer a ground for democracy" (p. 1345). Individuals' epistemic agency is eroded by "filter" and "epistemic bubbles" formed and controlled by recommender algorithms, sabotaging an individual's epistemic agency. A crucial strategy for safeguarding individuals' epistemic agency is education.

Jurayev (2023), maps the role of AI in the digital transformation of today's organisations, and points to the need for the democratisation of AI "making it accessible to a wider range of people. No-code AI platforms allow individuals, regardless of their technical background, to build and deploy AI models with minimal coding" (p. 258). This, according to Jurayev (2023) will help to "increase the number of people who can participate in the AI deployment process, resulting in the inclusion of more diverse perspectives and ideas" (p. 259). The author concludes that mainstreaming no-code AI platforms will "save time and resources, by avoiding the need to hire expensive data scientists or developers to build AI models" (p. 259). Jurayev (2023) does not, however, explicitly discuss the democratisation of AI in and for education and concludes his article with a general discussion on the challenges and opportunities for AI in education.

Khan et al. (2023) state that "democratisation might seem less ambiguous than normative principles like fairness, owing to its roots in political and socio-economic development, but when applied as a goal of artificial intelligence, the clarity of the term seems to evaporate" (p. 1). These authors state that "democratisation has not been well theorised in AI literature, much less studied in situ" (pp. 1-2). The main gist of the article is to "discuss [...] operational issues at the intersection of AI ethics, democratisation, and cyberinfrastructure" (p. 2) and the authors only refer in passing to the effect of the democratisation of AI in education, training, and knowledge transfer "if different cultures and ideas are represented in computing, resulting systems are more intelligent and more democratic" (p. 6), referring to the intersection of AI and social action proposed by (Gill, 1988).

Stamboliev (2023), in the context of media literacy education, firstly argues that democratising AI implies making it more accessible and explainable, thereby depoliticising "transparency into a remedy for algorithmic opacity, treating transparency as artificially stripped of its ideological meanings" (p. 201). As such transparency in AI is "presented as an antidote to ideology" with the consequence that "it makes us focus too much on algorithmic opacity, rather than explaining the wider power of AI" (p. 201). Secondly, Stamboliev (2023) argues that focusing on transparency "hinders us from having debates on who holds the power around AI's explanations, application or critique" (p. 201; italics added). As such, the author proposes a "post-critical AI literacy to strengthen debates on access, empowerment, and resistance" (p. 201; italics in the original).

Democratising AI, according to Stamboliev (2023) "aims to increase the transparency and accessibility of AI and algorithms through reorganised and simplified models, texts, and visualisations" in "the fight against the rise of AI opacity" (p. 2020). Lacking in the focus on transparency, is focusing on AI's "computational features" while forgetting that "AI is all about ideology and power" (p. 2020). Stamboliev (2023) illustrates the danger of focusing only on transparency in pointing to OpenAI's chatbots which

> seem very accessible and democratised, but their algorithmic underbelly is deceptive in terms of sources, algorithmic instructions, reinforcement strategies, and ideology; hence, chatbots are opaque on various levels not making their algorithmic opacity less of a problem, but not the only problem (p. 204).

Depoliticising AI does not make AI less opaque "but less accessible" in the sense that it "keeps us from having more conversations about how to equip individuals with more accessible, critical, and inclusive AI literacies" (p. 204). In proposing a 'post-critical' critique, Stamboliev (2023) is not anti-critique, or beyond critique but the approach allows for the unpacking of "additional sensibilities that fall short" in critical approaches of AI. We therefore need to discuss democratising "access to AI as power, not as algorithm" (p. 206; italics in the original). [See Stamboliev's (2023) discussion of explainability and transparency]. Except for the fact that focusing on explainability and transparency, presents AI as a technical problem to solve, "making algorithms transparent is an ideological choice on what to conceal and what to reveal" (p. 209). By making AI transparent, does not reveal the motifs and effects of AI as power.

Making AI transparent and explainable, also does not allow those affected by AI to, necessarily, understand the implications, and to take action. Transparent AI will not, necessarily, allow those impacted by AI to intervene and stop its impact. In order to do that, one has to understand AI not as algorithm, but as networks of power. Developing technological and instrumental digital competence, does not automatically empower citizens to understand AI as "an ideologically charged process" (p. 219). Citizens [and students] should understand AI's "design, purpose and effects" (p. 220). Democratising AI in, for, and through education should also result in "stronger resistance alliances between journalists, grassroots activists, academics, and the general public" (p. 221). Democratising AI means teaching "the complexity of AI in its breadth, [including] media studies, social and political sciences and involve them in shaping AI literacy, which means to look beyond data and computer sciences hegemonizing this discourse" (p. 221-222). The issue at stake is not only to understand AI but to understand "society's needs" (p. 222).

In the last article in the corpus, Sundberg and Holmström (2024) propose that low-code AI could democratise the adoption of AI "systems and stimulate their multidisciplinary use" (p. 3) specifically considering students from/with non-technical backgrounds. Low-code AI, or "AI as service" "are easy-to-use and affordable forms of AI, and they guide users through the process of developing and deploying AI models, with no need to learn all about the intricacies associated with complex algorithms" (p. 2). The authors report on a course where 19 students from business and administration, computer science, and behavioural sciences attended. The authors conclude that it is possible to include no-code AI in their courses and introduce students to using no-code AI in "effective and responsible ways" (p. 9).

Our position

As is clear from this brief review of documents, we agree with Khan et al. (2023) that the democratisation of AI in, through and for education is under-theorised and there is scant published research evidence outside of the low-code research by Sundberg and Holmström (2024) and Jurayev (2023) of successful efforts to democratise AI in, through and for education. There is furthermore evidence that democratising AI, as presented by, for example, Khan et al, (2023), and Halpern (in Big Innovation Centre, 2023) is foreseen to be achieved by increasing the involvement of populations, genders and groups of individuals who are currently not involved but affected by AI. Increasing the participation of individuals to AI as service as well as increase the diversity of the participating individuals may be part of the initial democratisation of AI in, for and through education, but it only addresses two elements of the democratisation of AI as proposed by Rao (2023) namely access to the use, development and sharing of machine learning and deep learning algorithms, as well as data visualisation and generation. Such steps do not address the other aspects proposed by Rao namely access to storage and computing (data ingestion, storage and infrastructure), model development (end-to-end model development, training and deployment), as well as democratising the AI marketplace (the use, exchange, monetisation of data, algorithms models and outcomes).

Even when all the elements of the democratisation of AI as suggested by Rao (2023), Seger (2023) and Seger et al (2023) are achieved, it would still fall short of the proposals put forth by Coeckelbergh (2023) and Stamboliev (2023) who point to the need to think deeper and more critically about what democratisation of AI in, through and for education should look like, for example increasing students epistemic agency (Coeckelbergh, 2023) and understanding AI not as algorithm but as networks of power (Stamboliev, 2023).

Conclusion

While the democratisation of AI in, for and through education is linked to the notion of the democratisation of education through AI, in this position paper we presented evidence that the democratisation of AI in, for and through AI is under-theorised and under-researched. Current efforts to increase participation in AI through education through AI-as-service (low-code applications) and widening the diversity of participants, current thinking and practices have barely scraped the surface. If we do not address AI as networks of power (Stamboliev, 2023), increase (1) access (plus training); (2) use (and governance); (3) control (and IP rights); and (4) own (and making open/increasing access)(Rao, 2023) and capacitating students' to defend and realise their epistemic agency (Coeckelbergh, 2023), then the democratisation of AI in, for and through education will remain a dream deferred.

References

Big Innovation Centre. (2023). Democratising Artificial Intelligence: Generative AI as a Catalyst for Change in Education. Parliamentary Brief. Retrieved from https://biginnovationcentre.com/wp-content/uploads/2023/11/Parliamentary-Brief-Generative-AI-Education.pdf

Bulathwela, S., Pérez-Ortiz, M., Holloway, C., Cukurova, M., & Shawe-Taylor, J. (2024). Artificial Intelligence Alone Will Not Democratise Education: On Educational Inequality, Techno-Solutionism and Inclusive Tools. Sustainability, 16(2), 781. https://doi.org/10.3390/su16020781.

Coeckelbergh, M. (2023). Democracy, epistemic agency, and AI: political epistemology in times of artificial intelligence. AI and Ethics, 3(4), 1341-1350. https://doi.org/10.1007/s43681-022-00239-4

Crompton, H., & Burke, D. (2023). Artificial intelligence in higher education: the state of the field. International Journal of Educational Technology in Higher Education, 20(1), 1-22. https://doi.org/10.1186/s41239-023-00392-8.

Baena-Rojas, J., Castillo-Martínez, I., Mendez-Garduño, J., Suárez-Brito, P., & López-Caudana, E. (2023). Information communication technologies, artificial intelligence, and social robotics: a complex-thinking vector in higher education?. Journal of Social Studies Education Research, 14(2), 21-50.

EL Azhari, K., Hilal, I., Daoudi, N., & Ajhoun, R. (2023). SMART chatbots in the E-learning domain: A systematic literature review. International Journal of Interactive Mobile Technologies, 17(15), 4-37. https://doi.org/10.3991/ijim.v17i15.40315

Hwang, G. J., Xie, H., Wah, B. W., & Gašević, D. (2020). Vision, challenges, roles and research issues of Artificial Intelligence in Education. Computers and Education: Artificial Intelligence, 1, 100001.

Indigenous AI. (2020). Position Paper. https:// www. indigenous- ai. net/ posit ion- paper/

Jackson, E. A. (2024). The Evolution of Artificial Intelligence: A Theoretical Review of its Impact on Teaching and Learning in the Digital Age. ECONSTOR. http://hdl.handle.net/10419/280893

Jurayev, S. B. (2023). Leveraging Artificial Intelligence in education: A comprehensive analysis. Innovative Development in Educational Activities, 2(13), 257-261.

Kamalov, F., Santandreu Calonge, D., & Gurrib, I. (2023). New era of artificial intelligence in education: Towards a sustainable multifaceted revolution. Sustainability, 15(16), 12451. https://doi.org/10.3390/su151612451

Khan, S., Morales, A., & Plale, B. (2023). Democratisation is a process, not a destination: Operationalizing ethics and democratisation in a cyberinfrastructure for AI project. Proceedings of the EAI 2nd International

Conference on AI for People, Democratising AI. Retrieved from https://icicle.osu.edu/media/document/2023-11-01/democracratization-process_a-case-study_caip-2023_khanmoralesplale.pdf

Kucirkova, N., & Leaton Gray, S. (2023). Beyond Personalization: Embracing Democratic Learning Within Artificially Intelligent Systems. Educational Theory, 73(4), 469-489. https://doi.org/10.1111/edth.12590

Maphosa, V., & Maphosa, M. (2023). Artificial intelligence in higher education: a bibliometric analysis and topic modeling approach. Applied Artificial Intelligence, 37(1), 2261730. https://doi.org/10.1080/08839514.2023.2261730.

McKinsey & Company. (2019). Beyond the Industrial Revolution education model: Sal Khan on training and skills in the 21st century. Retrieved from https://www.mckinsey.com/featured-insights/future-of-work/beyond-the-industrial-revolution-education-model-sal-khan-on-training-and-skills-in-the-21st-century#/

Ozsevim, I (2023). Andrew Ng: Deepening and democratising learning. Retrieved from https://aimagazine.com/articles/andrew-ng-deepening-and-democratising-learning

Rao, A.S. (2020). Democratisation of AI. A double-edged sword. Medium. Retrieved from https://towardsdatascience.com/democratization-of-ai-de155f0616b5

Seger, E. (2023). What Do We Mean When We Talk About "AI Democratisation"? Centre for Governance of AI. Retrieved from https://www.governance.ai/post/what-do-we-mean-when-we-talk-about-ai-democratisation

Seger, E., Ovadya, A., Siddarth, D., Garfinkel, B., & Dafoe, A. (2023). Democratising AI: Multiple meanings, goals, and methods. In Proceedings of the 2023 AAAI/ACM Conference on AI, Ethics, and Society (pp. 715-722).

Slimi, Z., & Carballido, B. V. (2023). Navigating the Ethical Challenges of Artificial Intelligence in Higher Education: An Analysis of Seven Global AI Ethics Policies. TEM Journal, 12(2), 590-602. DOI: 10.18421/TEM122-02

Stamboliev, E. (2023). Proposing a Postcritical AI Literacy: Why We Should Worry Less about Algorithmic Transparency and More about Citizen Empowerment. Media Theory, 7(1), 202-232.

Sundberg, L., & Holmström, J. (2024). Teaching Tip: Using No-code AI to Teach Machine Learning in Higher Education. Journal of Information Systems Education, 35(1).

Cracking the AIEd code: Dialogic-relational academic advising

Jan Petrus Bosman[1], Wim van Petegem[2], Tinne de Laet[3], Nompilo Tshuma[4],

[1] Centre for Learning Technologies, Stellenbosch University, South Africa; jpbosman@sun.ac.za
[2] Faculty of Engineering Technology, KU Leuven, Belgium; wim.vanpetegem@kuleuven.be
[3] Faculty of Engineering Science, KU Leuven, Belgium; tinne.delaet@kuleuven.be
[4] Faculty of Education, Stellenbosch University, South Africa; ntshuma@sun.ac.za

Correspondence: Jan Petrus Bosman: jpbosman@sun.ac.za

Abstract:

To contribute to cracking the theoretical AI in education code, interviews with academic advisors at a European university were analysed using a dialogic-relational translation device to develop a sociomaterial framework for building EdTech and AIEd theory. The four personas (Consultant, Coach, Counsellor, Collaborator) emerging from the data analysis represent the mental models of academic advisors regarding using technology in their practice. These personas could be used to understand the underlying dynamic of the academic advising practice, for developing personalised training, or to design future human-centred AI-infused academic advising systems. The dialogic-relational framework could also be adapted to create translation devices to analyse and build EdTech and AIEd theory regarding other educational teaching-learning-assessment practices.

Keywords: Academic advising, Educational technology, AI in education, Sociomaterialism, Dialogic-relational framework; Mental models; Personas

Background: Cracking the AI in education code[1]?

If we want to move towards imaginative higher educational futures in the age of AI, we need to build a solid theoretical foundation for our digitally supported teaching-learning-assessment practices. Otherwise, we will continue the overhyped, non-reproducible "snake oil" myths of much of the current AI research (Kapoor & Narayanan, 2022). To build a practical theory for AI in education (AIEd), we need to start by understanding the theory of educational technology (EdTech), which is also known for often being built upon myths and for appropriating "the useful inventions of the business and leisure industries" (Laurillard, 2012, p.2). The "knowledge blindness" regarding the theoretical foundations of educational technology is not new and has been documented extensively (Howard & Maton, 2011; Jones & Czerniewicz, 2011; and Oliver, 2013). Despite the general paucity of theorising in the field, there is a growing body of knowledge around the theoretical practices of EdTech[2]. This research will hopefully contribute to building the theoretical foundations for understanding EdTech and, more specifically, AIEd practices.

The premise of the study is that the higher education practice of academic advising is a teaching-learning-assessment field (Steele, 2016) that incorporates EdTech research (Pasquini & Steele, 2016) and provides valuable opportunities for empirical inquiry. The use of academic advising descriptive- and predictive machine learning-enabled analytics dashboards has been studied extensively over the last decade (Gutiérrez et al., 2020) and contributes potential important building blocks for cracking the EdTech and AIEd code.

Rupert and Major's recent book, The theory of educational technology (Wegerif & Major, 2024) contributes to building EdTech theory by suggesting a dialogic foundation for educational design. Apart from describing how

[1] The idea of cracking the code of how Artificial Intelligence works in education is inspired by Wayne Hugo's book, Cracking the code to educational analysis (Hugo, 2013) in which he, drawing on Bernstein, develops a coding system for understanding the phenomenon of education.

[2] E.g., Laurillard (2002) proposes a conversational framework; Mehlenbacher (2010) gives a critical review on instructional design and technology; Waghid et al. (2016) describes EdTech as a democratic process; (Waghid et al., 2016) and Bosman and Strydom (2021) theorises blended learning as a practical knowledge.

technology can open up dialogic space, they venture into the realm of AIEd and show how a dialogic approach might unlock our understanding of how GenAI might "work" in educational contexts, offering "the potential to prepare learners more effectively for the next level of education: dialogue with the Infinite Other" (Wegerif & Major 2024, p.140).

Dialogic educational theory opens up the possibility of understanding the use of EdTech and AIEd in academic advising practices (especially regarding current machine-learning dashboards or emerging GenAI-type systems in the form of conversational agents or advising chatbots). The use of dialogic theory in the academic advising field, in general, is sparse (Colgan, 2016; Yamashita & Mynard, 2015), and the specific focus on the dialogic educational use of technology (EdTech or AIEd) in academic advising is to our understanding novel. For this study we will show the results of applying dialogic theory to academic advising with technology perspectives. We call this the Dialogic Relations (DR).

We also suggest that the solid dialogic EdTech foundation of Rupert and Major (2024) could possibly be extended to include another theoretical angle, namely technological relationality. By relationality, we mean the sociomaterial insight that it is possible (and maybe critical) to see the material aspects of our educational practice, and especially digital technology, as actors in the social (dialogic) and material (technology) building of assemblages of meaning and "refuse to separate the human dimensions of educational practices from their material dimensions, and rather focus on the relational composition of these practices" (Decuypere & Simons, 2016, p.27). We call these Technologic Relations (TR). The study shows how DR and TR can be analysed separately, as well as what happens when the two approaches are combined to provide a useful and interesting analytical lens for understanding and developing EdTech and AIEd practices.

To describe the underlying dynamics of AI in education (AIEd), we, therefore, build on these recent dialogical theories of educational technology and a sociomaterial relational understanding and provide an empirical European university analysis of how academic advisors understand and use AI-infused advising dashboards and other advising technologies. This dialogic-relational analysis of interview data is presented as a potential reproducible framework with which also to crack the code(s) of other AIEd contexts that seek to provide learner-centric care through digital spaces.

Dialogic-relational translation device to develop academic advising personas

A translation device builds on Basil Bernstein's notion of external languages of description and provides "an alternative to the false dichotomy of either imposing theory on data or miraculously deriving theories from data" (Maton & Chen, 2016, p.29). Table 1 represents a translation device for connecting the theory of Dialogic Relations and Technologic Relations with the interview data of this particular object of study (academic advising with technology). It is structured so that "when read from left to right, it translates theory into data, and when read from right to left it translates data into theory" thereby making the basis of the analysis more explicit (Maton & Chen, 2016, p.43,47).

The idea of developing the sociomaterial concepts of Dialogic Relations (DR) and Technologic Relations (TR) are derived from Legitimation Code Theory (LCT) (Maton, 2014) where translation devices that make visible the invisible dynamics of how different dimensions of knowledge and knowing are legitimised have proven to be a powerful methodology for understanding the knowledge practices of different domains. We have developed a translation device based on a sociomaterial approach to studying academic advisors' mental models in terms of academic advising and the role of technology in the practice.

Sociomaterialism provides analytical approaches in the sense that they "refuse to separate the human dimensions of educational practices from their material dimensions" (Decuypere & Simons 2016, p.27). Developing a sociomaterial framework for studying academic advising with technology includes combining the level of Dialogic Relations (DR - the social) with the level of Technologic Relations (TR - the material).

In Dialogic Relations (DR), the idea is that "making meaning requires that there are always different voices in dialogue together. To be more dialogic, therefore, is to be more open to others and to otherness." This is over and against the powerful illusion of monologism that "there is only one true perspective and that every apparent difference can be reduced to this one true perspective" (Wegerif, 2021, p.172).

Technologic relations (TR) homes in on the level of relationality and relational thinking over and against representational thinking. In relational thinking, "anything might potentially relate with anything else, and this without assuming a priori differences between different actors", whereas representational thinking "differentiates between humans, human knowledge and the natural world as it is" (Decuypere & Simons, 2016, p.30).

Applied to academic advising with technology, one could posit the following external language of description in terms of Dialogic Relations (DR) and Technologic Relations (TR):

- Stronger Dialogic Relations (DR+) implies that academic advising is seen as a more dialogical, open-ended conversation in which the student has agency in determining the session's outcome. Weaker Dialogic Relations (DR-) sees academic advising as more monologic, where the advisor holds the agency to dispense advice, making the session outcome more structured and predictable.

- Regarding material relationality, stronger Technologic Relations (TR+) indicate a higher degree of relational thinking and view advising technology as an important actor or collaborator in the advising process. Weaker Technologic relations (TR-) indicate a more representational view of advising technology, meaning that it views advising technologies as separate tools in the human-focused act of advising.

Coding the qualitative interview data (n=19) in terms of DR+, DR-, TR+ and TR- opens a way to make the invisible visible. It is suggested as a way to describe and code the mental models that academic advisors hold regarding how advising technologies intersect (TR) with their view of academic advising (DR). There are many separate DR and TR coding instances in the data which will be analysed in a future study. In this paper, however, we focus on the results where DR and TR co-exist in the data. These instances are coded as DR/TR, and there are four simplified combinations, namely, DR-/TR-; DR+/TR-; DR-/TR+, and DR+/TR+. We posit that these four ensuing dynamic coding combinations can be utilised to construct academic advising with technology personas. Personas are potentially powerful concepts that are utilised in design thinking processes to understand and adapt to the users of a process or system (Dahiya & Kumar, 2018).

In Table 1 we unpack the four personas as a translation device that enables the movement from theory (the persona and code) to practice (the persona description with an example from the data).

Table 1: Translation Device for Dialogic-Relational Academic Advising Personas

Persona	Code	Description of persona	Example from data
Consultant	DR-/TR-	The Consultant has a weak dialogic view of academic advising coupled with a weak relationality with technology. This persona is advisor-centred and views technology merely as a tool. The student has lesser agency, and there is a low level of trust in emerging advising technologies.	I definitely see a role for more potential for the use of AI in advising especially when it when it comes about making information available, or accessible or transparent. I think we can do much more there than we do now. Especially in our complex institution ... (KIR03)
Counsellor	DR+/TR-	The Counsellor views advising as a highly dialogic process, but the relationality to technology in the process is still weak. This persona is student-centred and uses technology mostly to drive students to human advising interaction. Students have more agency, but emerging technology is not fully trusted as a partner in the process.	And I think that's maybe a good example of how I use all the technology is I use it as a sort of first navigational tool ready, and I'll look at it I'll use it, but I'll use it as a starting point to start a conversation, right because I always end up trying to have a conversation and by I tend not to use the structure of technology that I'm using ... (KAA35)
Coach	DR-/TR+	The Coach has a positive relationality with technology while leaning towards a weak dialogic view of the advising practice. This persona is	... it could be on a top sport level, it could be very data driven, you know, and because the power of your stroke is yes, that has so much miles or the

		advisor-centred and uses technology to track and gain insights on students' development. Students have less agency while technological trust to reveal insights through data is high.	ball is taking. And that's really wonderful input as long as there is a coach besides the computer besides the machine, that helping to understand the conclusions helping to understand yeah, what you're doing ... (KAA57)
Collaborator	DR+/TR +	The Collaborator combines a strong dialogic advising approach with a positive technologic relationality into a collaborative practice. This persona is student-centred and trusts in emerging technology to provide advisor and student data-based insights. Students have strong agency coupled with high technological trust to the point of a partnership between student, advisor and technology.	... these dashboards are made to reflect to make students reflect about their study situation specifically after an exam period. And one of the dashboards is used by a counsellor, and he can bring in data into a counselling session to stimulate reflection and action with the students ... (KIR02)

Results after coding with the Dialogic-Relational lens

Coding of the interview data using the Dialogic-Relational lens as developed in the translation device above (Table 1) emerged interesting results, as can be seen in Table 2. With regards to all 19 interview voices together, the Consultant persona is the most prevalent with 26 of the 60 codes (43%), followed by Counsellor (16 of 60 - 27%), Collaborator (11 of 60 - 18%) and Coach (7 of 60 -12%).

Table 2: Results of coded qualitative interview data according to personas (n=19)

Voices	**Consultant DR-TR-**	**Counsellor DR+TR-**	**Coach DR-TR+**	**Collaborator DR+TR+**
All voices (n=19)	**43%** (26/60)	27% (16/60)	12% (7/60)	18% (11/60)

Visually mapping the same data in Table 2 on a cartesian plane shows the overall distribution of the personas (Fig. 1).

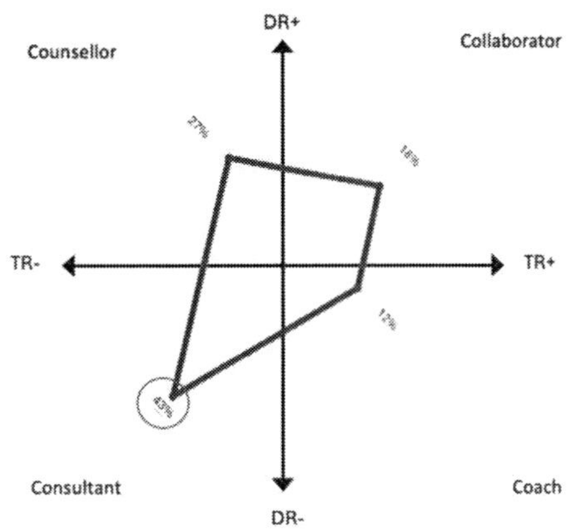

Fig. 1 Persona mapping: All voices combined (n=19)

When disaggregating the codes on DR and TR separately (Table 3), we find that the overall Dialogic relations of the combined grouping dataset seem to lean slightly towards weaker DR (DR- codes are 55%) and clearly inhabit weaker Technological relations (TR- codes are 70%).

Table 3: Results of coded qualitative interview data disaggregated by DR and TR (n=19)

Voices	**Strong Dialogic relations (DR+)**	**Weak Dialogic relations (DR-)**	**Strong Technologic relations (TR+)**	**Weak Technologic relations (TR-)**
All voices (n=19)	55%	45%	30%	70%

The translation device provides an analytical lens through which one can describe the mental models of academic advisors in the form of four personas. In this study we showed a first high-level analysis of the whole population of interviewed academic advisors. Although we do not report it here, it is expected that when we disaggregate the population into different groupings (e.g., central- and faculty-based advisors), the analysis will show code clashes and matches. The other interesting observation is that some individuals show more than one persona which might indicate that mental models might be fluid. This indicates a complex and dynamic reality regarding understanding how academic advising with technology works. It also reminds us that using the personas for designing future systems should keep in mind that they cannot be viewed simplistically and that human advisors still have their own agency to inhabit and utilise different personas when using technology for academic advising.

A limitation of this study is that there was no differentiating analysis of current advising technology (like descriptive dashboards) and emerging AI-infused technology (like advisor chatbots). It would be interesting to see if the mental models as represented by the four personas differ when advisors talk about known systems as opposed to future unknown advising technology systems. These ideas will be followed up with more detailed analyses in future studies.

Conclusions and implications

This novel study of the academic advising with technology mental models of academic advisors at a European university shows that a sociomaterial Dialogic-Relational analytic framework has the potential to crack the code of educational technology as well as AI in education.

With regards to academic advising, which is an educational field related to teaching-learning-assessment, a Dialogic-Relational analytical framework that was developed by creating a translation device on a sociomaterial theoretical foundation, shows promise as a way to analyse the practice of academic advising with technology. The translation device shows the possibility of four academic advising with technology personas (Consultant, Coach, Counsellor, and Collaborator). These personas are codified representations of the merged mental models of academic advisors in terms of their dialogical and relational views of academic advising with technology.

The academic advising personas could be used to design or critique future AI-infused academic advising technology systems. The idea of building a dialogical digital academic advisor twin to serve as the core of a human-centrically designed academic advisor chatbot (Bosman et al., 2022) or co-pilot for students to collaborate with as they successfully navigate their academic journeys, could potentially be served by integrating these four personas.

We hope this study will spark similar studies regarding more mainline higher educational teaching-learning-assessment practices. To use the Dialogic-Relational framework to study, for example, Generative AI in higher education teaching or how AI-infused learning analytics dashboards are used for student success, new translation devices must be developed for each particular object of study. It is our contention, however, that there will probably be strong overlaps in terms of mental model personas of university teachers' use of technology with the four personas of academic advising with technology. The persona names will probably change to be more relevant to the practice (like, e.g., Lecturer, Facilitator, Tutor or Collaborator). Still, the underlying sociomaterial codes will probably be similar and possibly even comparable.

References

Bosman, J. P., & Strydom, S. (2021). Building the knowledge base of blended learning: Implications for educational technology and academic development. In C. Winberg, S. McKenna, & K. Wilmot (Eds.), Building Knowledge In Higher Education: Enhancing teaching and learning with Legitimation Code Theory (pp. 198–219). Routledge. https://doi.org/10.4324/9781003028215-12

Bosman, J. P., Van Petegem, W., De Laet, T., & Tshuma, N. (2022). Edubots as academic advisers: A speculative social science fiction thought-experiment. In Dortmund International Research Conference 2022 Proceedings (Issue July, pp. 90–97). Fachhochschule Dortmund. https://irc.go-study-europe.de/wp-content/uploads/2022/10/IRC-2022_Proceedings_Web.pdf

Dahiya, A., & Kumar, J. (2018). How empathizing with persona helps in design thinking: An experimental study with novice designers. Conference: IADIS International Conference Interfaces and Human Computer Interaction 2018, 2018-July, 35–42.

Decuypere, M., & Simons, M. (2016). On the critical potential of sociomaterial approaches in education. Teor. Educ., 28(1), 25–44.

Gutiérrez, F., Seipp, K., Ochoa, X., Chiluiza, K., De Laet, T., & Verbert, K. (2020). LADA: A learning analytics dashboard for academic advising. Computers in Human Behavior, 107(February 2018), 105826. https://doi.org/10.1016/j.chb.2018.12.004

Howard, S., & Maton, K. (2011). Theorising knowledge practices: a missing piece of the educational technology puzzle. Research in Learning Technology, 19(3), 191–206. https://doi.org/10.3402/rlt.v19i3.17109

Hugo, W. (2013). Cracking the code to educational analysis. Pearson Education South Africa.

Jones, C., & Czerniewicz, L. (2011). Theory in learning technology. Research in Learning Technology, 19(3), 173–177. https://doi.org/10.3402/rlt.v19i3.17107

Kapoor, S., & Narayanan, A. (2022). AI snake oil - a sneak peek into the book: What makes AI click, what makes it snake oil, and how to tell the difference. https://www.aisnakeoil.com/p/a-sneak-peak-into-the-book

Laurillard, D. (2002). Rethinking university teaching: A conversational framework for the effective use of learning technologies. (2nd ed.). RoutledgeFalmer.

Laurillard, D. (2012). Teaching as a design science: Building pedagogical patterns for lerning and technology. Routledge.

Maton, K. (2014). Knowledge and Knowers: Towards a realist sociology of education. Routledge.

Maton, K., & Chen, R. T.-H. (2016). LCT in qualitative research: Creating a translation device for studying constructivist pedagogy. In K. Maton, S. Hood, & S. Shay (Eds.), Knowledge-building: Educational studies in Legitimation Code Theory (pp. 27–48). Routledge.

Oliver, M. (2013). Learning technology: Theorising the tools we study. British Journal of Educational Technology, 44(1), 31–43. https://doi.org/10.1111/j.1467-8535.2011.01283.x

Pasquini, L. A., & Steele, G. E. (2016). Technology in academic advising: Perceptions and practices in higher education. NACADA Technology in Advising Commission, February, 1–20.

Steele, G. E. (2016). Technology and academic advising. Beyond Foundations: Developing as a Master Academic Advisor, 305–326.

Waghid, Y., Waghid, F., & Waghid, Z. (2016). Educational technology and pedagogic encounters: Democratic education in potentiality. Sense Publishers.

Wegerif, R. (2021). A dialogic approach to education for democratic values illustrated with an empirical study of the effect of Internet-mediated dialogue across cultural differences. In P. Iyer & I. Bhattacharjee (Eds.), Moral and Political Discourses in Philosophy of Education (pp. 170–180). Routledge India.

Wegerif, R., & Major, L. (2024). The theory of educational technology: Towards a dialogic foundation for design. Routkledge.

Digital object-based learning for people with ASD: a training experience within heritage education contexts

Maria Rosaria Re[1], Mara Valente[2]

[1]Dept. History, Heritage, Education and Society, Tor Vergata University of Rome, Italy, maria.rosaria.re@uniroma2.it
[2] Dept. Education, University of Roma Tre, Italy, mara.valente@uniroma3.it

Correspondence: Maria Rosaria Re, maria.rosaria.re@uniroma2.it

Abstract:

The paper aims at presenting a training experience for future educators carried out during the academic year 2022/2023 on the use of Digital Object-Based Learning (OBL) for people with Autism Spectrum Disorders. Three different webinars, designed within the Erasmus+ Spektrum project, have been realised with a focus on the design, implementation, and evaluation of personalised museum educational experiences to foster social inclusion and wellbeing within people with specific educational needs through Object-based learning (OBL). As stated by the literature in the field, hands-on learning within heritage education contexts can really enhance people's interest in and understanding of a topic/subject and develop important transverse skills, thus promoting cultural participation of users at risk of social exclusion. During the webinars, specific models for planning learning sessions with ASD people were presented, together with wellbeing and empathy assessment tools to be used within museum context. The training experience ended with a digital OBL session, where museum educators were asked to collaboratively analyse, interpret, and evaluate digitised museum objects. More than 90 in-training educators, from different Italian and Spanish institutions, attended the webinars: results from a final assessment survey are presented in order to highlight strengths and weaknesses of the training experience, the soft and hard skills most promoted and the educational needs of the participants, trying to identify challenges and potential transformations within digital heritage education context.

Keywords: OBL, educators, training, heritage, ASD, digital learning.

Research context: the Spektrum project

The main focus of the SPEKTRUM project (Erasmus+ Youth. Action 2 - Strategic Partnerships) is to enhance the accessibility of the cultural heritage, especially the museums offer, to the young with autism spectrum disorders and their families. The project involves cultural organisations and research centres from Poland, Great Britain, Italy, Spain, and Belgium, partners with rich and long-standing experience in working with people with Autism Spectrum Disorders (ASD):

- the National Museum in Krakow (Coordinator)
- Roma Tre University – Centre for Museum Studies
- FARO. Vlaams steunpunt voor cultureel erfgoed
- UNED - Universidad Nacional de Educación a Distancia
- Outside In Pathways

The SPEKTRUM project partnership collaborates with cultural institutions and research centres from the UK, Italy, Spain and Belgium in order to develop a strategy to make museums more autism-friendly.

Over the course of the project, the Consortium worked to develop practical tools for museums to help the institution to be more open to people with ASD and their families. In particular, within the project, the Roma Tre University research team was in charge of realising, with the contribution of all partners, the "Spektrum Educational Toolkit" (available at https://media.mnk.pl/images/upload/pliki/spektrum/MNK-SPEKTRUM_EduToolkit_EN.pdf), an open educational resource (OER) designed for anyone with an interest in museum / heritage education. It focuses on a specific aspect of museum education work, namely the choice and application of learning methodologies and techniques for a specific target group: people with Autistic Spectrum Disorders (ASD). The document is meant to be a practical tool, which not only gives essential information in terms of educational planning, but also contains useful hyperlinks to research carried out in the field. The overall aim of the Spektrum Educational Toolkit is to improve museum professionals' awareness about ASD, in order to make museums and exhibitions more autism-friendly. Moreover, it explains how 5 non-conventional learning methodologies can be used within heritage education contexts: Creative artwork; Digital Storytelling; Object-based Learning; Digital Learning; Music in museums and exhibitions.

Considering the educational needs of educators, in particular those working in the heritage context, to improve their digital skills (ICOM 2020, UNESCO, 2020), the research group of the University of Roma Tre realised in the academic year 2022-2023, as part of the Spektrum project, specific online training webinars for educators aimed at deepening their knowledge of learning methodologies more related to digital learning contexts, such as object-based learning.

Object-based learning and digital learning context: an overview

Object-based learning (OBL) is an educational methodology that involves the integration of (museum) objects (documents, artworks, materials, etc.) into the learning setting. It consists of carefully studying an object by means of observation and tactile activity. Starting from a socio-constructivist approach, OBL allows learners to develop knowledge and understanding through tactile manipulation of artistic objects, or their reproduction by means of 3D printing, promoting observations on the shape of the object, comparisons with other objects, discussions on its function and a real exploratory investigation of the object itself.

In the last two decades, especially in Anglo-Saxon education, OBL is known and used as an important resource for learning from secondary school pupils to adults (Durbin, Morris & Wilkinson, 1990; Wiley, 2000; Paris, 2002; Lane & Wallace 2007). Psychosocial evidence indicates that the intrinsic, physical and material properties of objects can trigger memories, projections, sensory, emotional, and cognitive associations which enable participants to tap into issues of identity, meaning and belonging (Baumeister 1991; Frogett et al 2011; Chatterjee & Noble 2013; Chatterjee & Hannan 2016), providing users a direct link with a topic or the 'past' (van Veldhuizen, 2017). The experience of manipulating objects and, in particular, art objects allows learners to enter into close connection with the object itself, to identify with it, and to create their own meanings associated with it. Moreover, OBL improves academic skills, social interaction, and independent functioning (Baranek, 2002); it sharpens analytical ability; stimulates a research mindset, provokes questions (van Veldhuizen, 2017).

From research carried out in the museum field with visitors from different educational levels, OBL can be effective in promoting Critical thinking skills: where logistical and other kind of problems do not allow direct handling of the museum object, technology can be used to create a digital communication between the student and the object itself (Poce, 2018: 25). The use of OBL in totally digital contexts is particularly effective where hands-on learning cannot be used:

- due to conservation problems (the object is in a state of preservation that prevents direct manipulation);
- due to physical problems (the object is far from the place where the experience is realised or the user is unable to reach the place where the experience is realised);
- by learners with special educational needs (e.g. users with ASD and hypersensitivity may prefer an initial digital approach to the object).

The use of innovative technological instrumentation for the realisation of heritage experiences through OBL is particularly effective with a view to the social and cultural inclusion of all categories of users, especially for users with cognitive and sensory disabilities, children and the elderly. It stimulates the creation of stories, thus also encouraging the practice of storytelling, and in particular, in individuals with ASD it also encourages communication through the use of drawing, another means of communication.

Training experiences for educators within heritage education context

Before the diffusion of the Covid-19 pandemic, the training paths designed for educators working in the heritage field, such as museum educators, attached little importance to the use of the new digital technologies, to entrepreneurship promotion and to the development of transversal and digital skills (Poce, 2020; European Commission, 2016). Indeed, both recent graduates and workers, especially adult professionals, lack significant skills (OECD, 2022) for their future careers. Consequently, heritage educators have fewer opportunities to improve their professional development and add new forms of digital expression to their work (European Commission, 2018). However, the use of web and mobile tools and of social media has become increasingly popular in the field of heritage education, especially since 2020. In fact, the impact that the Covid-19 pandemic has had in accelerating the digital shift in the cultural and creative environment has been massive (NEMO, 2020; ICOM, 2020; UNESCO, 2020) and, simultaneously, it has brought about a growth in professional training experiences in this domain (NEMO, 2021). In this professional context, it is essential to stimulate Critical thinking and Creativity skills, in addition to merely Digital skills, in order to allow professionals to work in a critical and informed way whenever they use, create and assess digital tools e objects. In fact, since digital equipment develops as rapidly as the technical expertise of those who have to master these devices, it is crucial to know how to critically analyse contexts and virtual environments. It is also essential to know how to create new solutions, how to conceive and test in new contexts. All these actions are of critical importance to development and innovation (Carretero, Vuorikari & Punie, 2017).

Moreover, the research carried out in the education sector has produced wide literature on the different functions that museums have gradually performed in terms of learning spaces, of places for public social and cultural development (Tlili, 2015), of opportunities for inclusion (Falk & Dierking, 2018; UNESCO, 2021); and for promoting health and well-being (Chatterjee & Noble, 2013; Fancourt & Finn, 2019). All these functions, which represent a continuous and everyday challenge for museums, especially if related to the great variety of museums' users and their educational needs, require wide and varied training for professional educators. As Piazza and Rizzari (2022) highlights, if "museums are to be considered as active agents in today's learning societies, then museum educators – the professionals in charge of designing and facilitating interactions with users – perform a crucial task" (N.d.T.). Designing educational experiences aimed at training future museum educators must always rely on the importance of this role.

Research questions and methodology

Taking the above assumptions into consideration, the following research questions were defined:

- Can familiarity with digital OBL improve educators' perceived levels of professional competence?
- What types of soft skills can be promoted in educators participating in training activities on the use of digital OBL for users with ASD in heritage education contexts?

Three 2-hours webinars entitled "Innovative learning methodologies for people with ASD: Object-based learning, storytelling and well-being in museum context" have been realised from October to December 2022. The webinars were addressed to future educators, attending different BA degrees, MA degrees or postgraduate courses in the field of science education, digital education and heritage education.

The objectives of the training experience were to:

- be familiar with the main features of the OBL learning methodology, especially in museum education contexts for users with ASD;
- reflect on how OBL can promote well-being in museum educational contexts;
- understand which other learning methodologies can be used with OBL to improve its effectiveness in educational terms;
- reflect on the educational needs of users with ASD in museum contexts and how to use OBL to meet these needs;
- participate in a digital OBL session using digitised museum artworks.

After a more theoretical part on the use of OBL for heritage education experiences, specific models for planning learning sessions with ASD people were presented (CAST, 2018), together with well-being (Thomson & Chatterjee, 2014) and empathy (BES-A) assessment tools to be used within museum context. The training experience ended with a digital OBL session, where educators were asked to collaboratively analyse, interpret, and evaluate digitised museum objects, with the following activities:

1. Step 1: Digital OBL session. I SEE-I THINK-I WONDER activity on digitised 3D museum objects
2. Step 2: the researcher reveals the real identity of the object, its date, function;

3. Step 3: the participants try to identify with the object itself and give voice to it through oral or written narration, drawings.

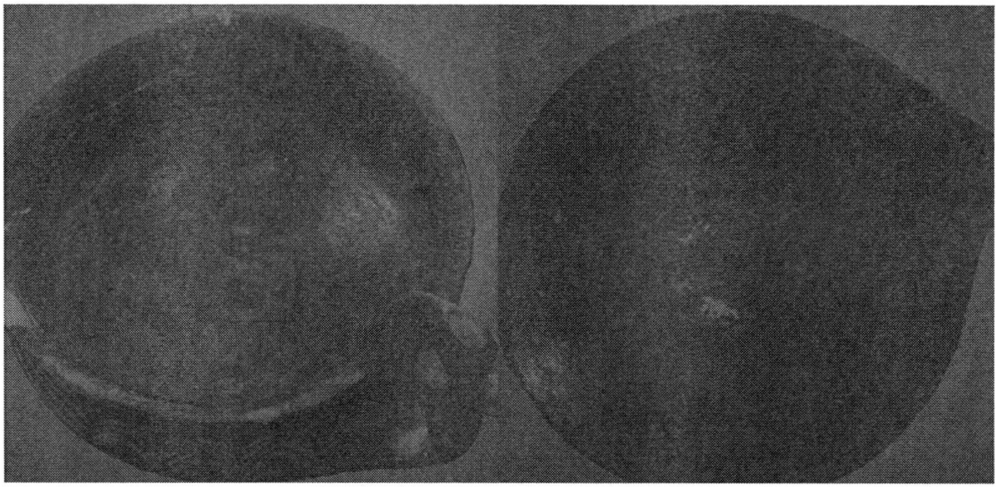

Figure 1: The 3D objects used during the I SEE - I THINK - I WONDER activity of digital OBL session

The training experience was evaluated by participants through the use of an ad-hoc assessment survey, composed of 16 items (closed, open-ended questions and Likert scale) divided into 4 main sections (see Table 1).

Table 1: Final assessment survey structure

Section	No. questions	Indicators
1	6	Socio-anagraphic information
2	8	Evaluation of the training experiences in terms of: quality of the webinar; kowledge acquired; skills sollicited; strenghts and weaknesses.
3	1	Evaluation of the training experience in term of emotional wellbeing
4	1	Possible OBL effect on learning experience.

Main findings of the survey

All the 93 participants in the training activities responded to the final assessment survey (M=7; F=85; 1=not declared).The average age is twenty-three years old; 83 respondents are Italian and 10 are Spanish. The group appears to be quite homogeneous in terms of profession; in fact, the majority (N=75) are students of the bachelor's degree in Education; only 4 are museum educators, 5 are teachers, and 9 have different professional backgrounds.

Respondents were asked to evaluate the quality of the workshop content using a 5-point Likert scale (1: minimum quality - 5: maximum quality). The indicator that received the highest score is the one related to Adherence to the content and objectives of the workshop program (Fig.2); 31 respondents assigned the maximum score (5), and 35 indicated 4: the content covered during the workshop was found to be very consistent with the expectations and purposes previously stated by the researchers.

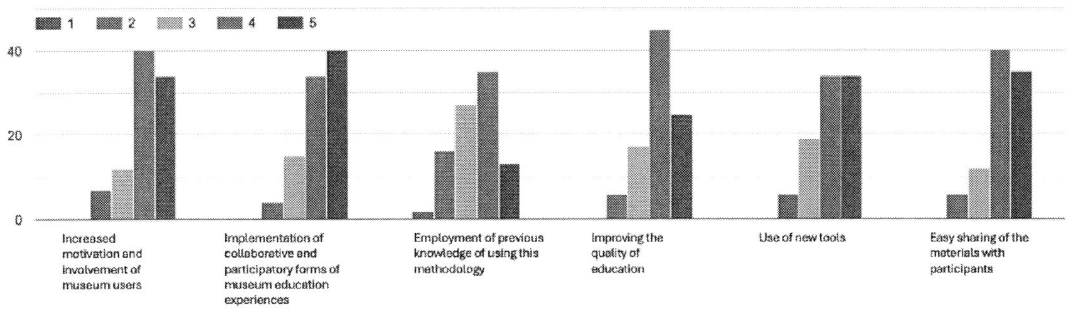

Figure 2: Evaluate the quality of the workshop content in terms of (1: lowest quality - 5: highest quality)

Two other indicators, related to the Clarity of the language and the Difficulty of the exercises, are considered qualitatively very adequate, respecting the expectations of the respondents. The indicator related to the language used in the workshop obtained 26 respondents assigning five points, 35 giving four points, 23 selecting 3, 9 assigning 2 points, and no respondent giving 1 point.

The indicator that receives the lowest score is the one related to Ease of understanding (mean= 3,5). This result is probably associated with respondents experiencing OBL activities using technological devices for the first time, which may not have favoured an immediate understanding of the learning activities to be carried out.

Afterward, respondents were asked to express opinions about the knowledge acquired, indicating their level of agreement or disagreement with specific indicators. Respondents were fairly unanimous that the learning process was gradual (N=78) and that the workshop largely met their expectations (N=74). However, the indicator related to the assumption that some information is self-evident and not adequately explained received non-univocal evaluations: 30 respondents agreed with this statement, 30 preferred not to say, and 33 completely disagreed. The indicator that received the highest number of disagreement responses is the Understanding of what needs to be done (N=37), confirming the data acquired through the previous item.

As regards the self-evaluation of the soft skills most solicited during the webinar (Fig.3), using a 5-point Likert scale (1: no incentive - 5: maximum incentive), respondents indicate Creativity as the most significantly enhanced skill (Mean= 4.6 , with 37 respondents assigning 5 points and 37 giving 4 points).

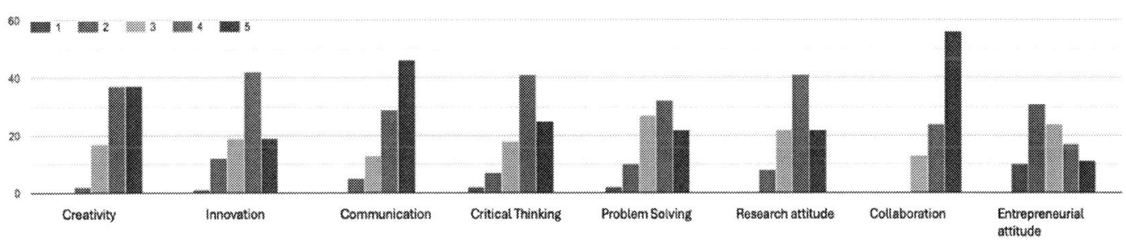

Figure 3: Self-Evaluate the acquired skills, indicating which of them were fostered by the workshop (1: no incentive - 5: maximum incentive)

Also Collaboration obtained good rates (mean= 4.5): 56 participants assigned 5 points and 24 respondents 4 points. Participation in the webinar activities and the exchange of opinions between colleagues also led the respondents to perceive Communication as highly implemented (mean= 4.2), together with Critical Thinking (mean= 3.9). The soft skill that was self-evaluated as least solicited was Entrepreneurship (mean= 2.9).

As regards the overall evaluation of the training activity, the average score assigned by participants, on a scale from 1 to 10, is 7.5 points (mode= 8; std. dv.= 1.1).

Moreover, participants were asked to assess to what extent, on a Likert scale from 1 to 5 (1: no incentive - 5: maximum incentive), the use of the OBL methodology promoted certain learning activities or aspects (Fig.4).

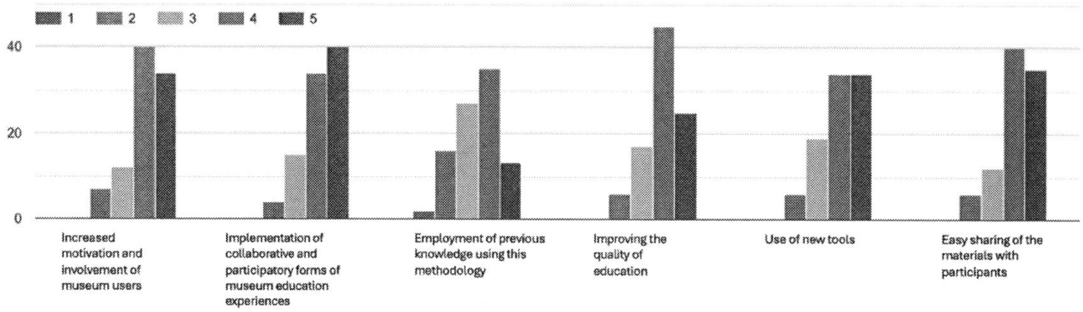

Figure 4: According to you, how influenced the use of object-based learning [always about this specific activity] (1: no incentive - 5: maximum incentive)

According to the data acquired, the most promoted learning experience is the Increase of motivation and involvement within museum users through the use of OBL: 34 respondents have assigned the maximum score (5), 39 indicated 4 points. Also the indicator related to the Implementation of collaborative and participatory museum education experiences received very positive scores (mean= 4.2). In line with other data, knowledge of the OBL and hands-on methodology was not widespread among all webinar participants before the training activity: this can be seen from the scores assigned to the Use of prior knowledge of this methodology indicator (mean=3.4).

Exploring the correlations existing between the skills solicited within the activities and learning through the OBL methodology, positive correlations are shown between Creativity and Increased motivation and involvement of museum users (r= ,434 p=.000). Creativity is also found to be significantly correlated with the indicator related to the Improvement of the quality of education inherent in the OBL activity carried out (r= ,443 p=.000). Innovation skill, also, results positively correlated with the use of new technological tools used in carrying out OBL activities (r= ,450 p= ,000). Moreover, Critical Thinking skills appears to be significantly correlated with the indicator related to the implementation of collaborative and participatory forms of museum education experiences fostered by the activity of learning through objects (r= ,499 p=.000) and the indicator related to facilitated sharing of materials with participants (r= 597 p=.000). Lastly, Collaboration is also positively correlated with the implementation of collaborative and participatory forms of museum education experiences solicited by OBL activity (r= ,453 p=.000).

Emerging correlations between implemented skills and specific attitudes fostered by participation in OBL activity confirm what the topic-specific literature states: learning through objects improves academic skills, social interaction, and independent functioning (Baranek, 2002). It sharpens analytical ability; stimulates a research mindset; provokes questions (van Veldhuizen et al., 2017).

Interesting findings also emerge from the open-ended question where respondents were asked to express whether and how participating in the training activity and experiencing the OBL methodology had positive effects on their well-being. Except for 4 participants who did not perceive any particularly positive effects, the remaining 89 all expressed favourable views on the matter, and the most frequent responses highlighted the perception of beneficial effects from collaborating with colleagues in carrying out the activity to having had the opportunity to exchange different points of view, underlying a solicitation in Critical thinking and Collaboration skills, in line with the literature in the field.

To assess the reliability of the proposed items constituting the questionnaire, Cronbach's alpha was calculated, which stands at a value of ,897 confirming a high internal consistency of the items based on the average inter-element correlation.

Conclusion

The design and implementation of the "Innovative learning methodologies for people with ASD: Object-based learning, storytelling and well-being in museum context" training activity responds to the education system's twofold need to train educational professionals capable of managing the pedagogical complexity of the museum context for the design of educational interventions effective for users with ASD, and to promote in (future) educators soft and professional skills. In fact, the overall purpose of the training activity is to illustrate the use of OBL within digital heritage learning contexts for promoting cultural inclusion, well-being and autism-friendly education practices.

From the data analysis, some positive considerations can be highlighted: firstly, the training experience can be considered generally positive: the good results on the overall evaluation of the webinars and their specific features show that the design of the training experience was generally well appreciated by participants.

Secondly, in response to one of the two research questions posed, different soft skills were solicited during the proposed activities: in fact, participants self-assessed an improvement in levels of Creativity above all, but also of Collaboration, Communication and Critical thinking, all results absolutely in line with research in the field. Despite the fact that, contrary to many studies, the training experience was carried out entirely online, the OBL methodology is perceived as effective in terms of improving a few soft skills. In particular, data on Critical Thinking skills promotion confirm what is argued in the literature in the field regarding physical or virtual OBL efficacy to promote processes of active engagement of learners in heritage education activities.

Furthermore, knowledge of the OBL methodology is perceived by participants as promoting specific professional skills, such as designing participatory education experiences, also in museum contexts, and supporting learners' good level of well-being, especially the social one.

Despite the fact that the results of the educational experience cannot be generalised due to obvious methodological choices, the data collected indicate possible future developments, such as the possibility of expanding the training activity with more specific content and meetings on OBL, including in-presence activities, so as to make clear the differences between physical and digital OBL experiences; using validated tools for the assessment of soft, hard skills (eg. digital skills) and well-being of participants; providing specific sessions on ASD-related content.

Acknowledgements

Maria Rosaria Re wrote the paragraphs 2, 3, 4 and 6; Mara Valente wrote the paragraphs 1 and 5.

Funding Information

Part of the activities described within the paper have been realised within the Erasmus+ KA205 project "Spektrum" 2019-3-PL01-KA205-077866.

References

Baranek, G. (2002). Efficacy of sensory and motor interventions for children with autism. Journal of Autism and Developmental Disorders, 32(5), 397-422, doi: 10.1023lA: lO2O541906O63.

Baumeister, R. F. (1991). Meanings of life. Guilford Press.

Commission européenne, Centre commun de recherche, Brande, L., Carretero, S., Vuorikari, R., et al. (2016). DigComp 2.0: the digital competence framework for citizens, Publications Office https://data.europa.eu/doi/10.2791/11517

CAST (2018). UDL and the learning brain. Wakefield, MA: Author. Retrieved from http://www.cast.org/products-services/resources/2018/udl-learning-brain-neuroscience

Chatterjee, H., & Noble, G. (2013). Museums, Health and Well-Being (1st ed.). Routledge.

Chatterjee, H.J., & Hannan, L. (2015). Engaging the Senses: Object-Based Learning in Higher Education (1st ed.). Routledge.

Durbin, G., Morris, S., Wilkinson, S. (1990). Learning from objects: A teachers guide. English.

European Commission (2017). Europe's Digital Progress Report EDPR 2017. https://ec.europa.eu/digital-single-market/en/news/europes-digital-progress-report-2017.

European Commission (2018). Digital Education Action Plan. https://eur- lex.europa.eu/legal-content/EN/TXT/?uri=COM:2018:22:FIN.

Falk, J.H., & Dierking, L.D. (2018). Learning from museums. Rowman & Littlefield.

Fancourt, D., Finn, S. (2019). What is the evidence on the role of the arts in improving health and well-being? A scoping review. Copenhagen: WHO Regional Office for Europe.

Froggett, L., Farrier, A., Poursanidou, K., Hacking, S. & Sagan, O. (2011) Who Cares? Museums, Health and Wellbeing Research Project. University of Central Lancashire.

ICOM (2020). Museums, museum professionals and COVID-19, ICOM report. https://icom.museum/wp-content/uploads/2020/05/Report-Museums-and-COVID-19.pdf

Lane, J., & Wallace, A. (2007). Hands On: Learning from Objects and Paintings. A Teacher's Guide. Scottish Museums Council.

NEMO (2020). Survey on the impact of the COVID-19 situation on museums in Europe Final Report. https://www.ne-mo.org/fileadmin/Dateien/public/NEMO_documents/NEMO_COVID19_Report_12.05.2020.pdf

NEMO (2021). Digital learning and education in museums. Innovative approaches and insights. https://www.ne-mo.org/fileadmin/Dateien/public/Publications/NEMO_Working_Group_LEM_Report_Digital_Learning_and_Education_in_Museums_12.2022.pdf

OECD (2022). Education at a Glance: OECD Indicators. OECD Publishing. https://www.oecd-ilibrary.org/docserver/3197152b-en.pdf?expires=1710500890&id=id&accname=guest&checksum=3CC3616C0E4443461857C8434EB354EF

Paris, S.G. (2002). Perspectives on Object –Centred Learning in Museums. Routledge.

Piazza, R., & Rizzari, S. (2022). The professional profile of the museum educator today: opportunities and challenges. Pedagogia oggi, 20(2), 42-49. https://doi.org/10.7346/PO-022022-05

Poce, A. (2018). Il patrimonio culturale per lo sviluppo delle competenze nella scuola primaria. Cultural Heritage and the Development of XXI Century Skills in Primary education. FrancoAngeli.

Poce, A. (2020). Education research in museum settings: methodologies, tools and functions / La ricerca empirica al museo: metodologie, strumenti e funzioni. Edizioni Scientifiche Italiane.

Thomson, Linda & Chatterjee, Helen. (2014). Assessing well-being outcomes for arts and heritage activities: Development of a Museum Well-being Measures toolkit. Journal of Applied Arts & Health. 5. 10.1386/jaah.5.1.29_1.

Tlili, A. (2015). In Search of Museum Professional Knowledge Base: Mapping the professional knowledge debate onto museum work. Educational Philosophy and Theory, 48(11), 1100-1122 10.1080/00131857.2015.1091284

UNESCO (2020). Museum Around the Word. In the Face of COVID 19, UNESCO report. https://unesdoc.unesco.org/ark:/48223/pf0000373530.

UNESCO (2021). Global education monitoring report, 2021/2: non-state actors in education: who chooses? who loses? unesdoc.unesco.org/in/rest/annotationSVC/DownloadWatermarkedAttachment/attach_import_94abd750-8c78-4505-b35f-81c0e635ac18?_=379875eng.pdf&to=586&from=1

Van Veldhuizen, A. (2017). Education Toolkit: methods & techniques from museum and heritage education. Liesbeth Tonckens and Gundy van Dijk.

Wiley, D.A., a cura di (2000). The instructional use of learning objects. Indiana Association for Instructional Technology and Association for Educational Communications and Technology.

N-TUTORR: Addressing Artificial Intelligence as one element of the transformation of Ireland's technological higher education sector

Sharon Flynn[1], Sean O'Reilly[2], Caroline O'Neill[3]

[1] Technological Higher Education Association, Ireland; sharon.flynn@thea.ie
[2] Technological Higher Education Association, Ireland; sean.oreilly@thea.ie
[3] Technological Higher Education Association, Ireland; caroline.oneill@thea.ie

Correspondence: Sean O'Reilly: sean.oreilly@thea.ie

Abstract:

A major transformation programme is underway across seven technological higher education institutions in Ireland. Investment of €40m #NextGenerationEU funding enables a programme to empower learners, to enhance staff capabilities, to improve the digital infrastructure, and to ensure long-lasting sustainable impact. Designed and implemented by significant collaboration of partner institutions, the programme explicitly adopts a holistic approach with inter-related work streams and work packages. The programme is underpinned by the six core themes of academic integrity, digital transformation, education for sustainability, employability, equality diversity & inclusion, universal design for learning. This comprehensive structure enables focus on key issues, emerging topics, and ensuring sustainable enhancement of learning, teaching and assessment across the technological sector. Multiple elements of the programme provided opportunities to reflect on the role of artificial intelligence, ranging from the perspective of challenges associated with academic integrity to the wider potential to be exploited to support and enhance learning and teaching. Students play an active role in considering these issues through focussed projects in partnership with staff and by acting as student champions to ensure that students' perspectives inform related discussions. Staff development opportunities have focussed on artificial intelligence and specific training is in place for senior institutional leaders. Active cooperation with the National Academic Integrity Network, which is facilitated by the national external quality agency, has led to complementary focussed activities. A national practitioners' network is being established to examine the impact of generative AI on higher education. Many of these structures could be replicated in other institutions or groups of institutions. While there are many examples of programme activities addressing important or topical issues, this paper particularly focuses on themes relating to the 2024 EDEN conference.

Keywords: student empowerment, staff capabilities, digital infrastructure, artificial intelligence, academic integrity, sustainable impact

Context: A digital transformation programme for a rapidly evolving sector

A major transformation initiative, the National Technological University Transformation for Recovery and Resilience programme, known as N-TUTORR, is underway in Ireland's technological higher education sector. Funded by the EU Recovery and Resilience Facility, #NextGenerationEU, €40m is being invested in seven higher education institutions between 2022 and 2024 to transform learning, teaching and assessment. Designed from the "bottom up" by a unique collaboration of the partners, the overall programme is explicitly informed by evidence. A sector-wide project coordinated by the Irish National Forum for the Enhancement of Teaching and Learning in Higher Education, "Next Steps for Teaching and Learning: Moving Forward Together", addressed key lessons for higher education from the period of public health restrictions associated with the pandemic. The national survey of student engagement (StudentSurvey.ie) deployed specific additional questions to capture students' experiences during this period as well as their overall experiences of higher education. A key report from the Technological Universities Research Network explicitly states the importance of state-of-the-art digital infrastructure and ICT provisions for the rapidly changing technological sector. Rapid change is a feature of the sector. State-funded higher education institutions, known as institutes of technology, evolved from Regional Technical Colleges which were established mainly in the 1970s. In 2018, there were fourteen institutes of technology geographically dispersed across the country. In 2022, this had evolved into five technological universities and two institutes of technology. A rigorous process with international evaluation panels, underpinned by legislation, enabled this change. The N-TUTORR programme is one of the investments supporting the establishment and continued development of this 'new' sector. The programme has four main work streams. These are:

1. Transform the Student Experience through Learner Empowerment

2. Transform Learning, Teaching and Assessment by Developing Staff Capabilities

3. Enable Digital Ecosystems to transform Learning, Teaching and Assessment

4. Securing Progress and Sustaining Impact

The programme was designed to foster collaboration and to deliver benefits to all partner institutions while recognising institutional autonomy, varied starting points, and differing aspirations.

The eight programme partners are comprised of the seven institutions and the sectoral representative body which hosts the programme management office. They are:

- Atlantic Technological University
- Dundalk Institute of Technology
- Institute of Art, Design and Technology, Dun Laoghaire
- Munster Technological University
- South East Technological University
- Technological University Dublin
- Technological University of the Shannon
- Technological Higher Education Association

Providing a forum in which to reflect on the role of artificial intelligence

The overall programme is designed to empower learners; to develop the capabilities of all staff (academic and professional, managerial, services and support); and to enhance the digital ecosystems to enable the former. The fourth work stream explicitly adopts a more forward-looking perspective, seeking to embed and secure change by maximising opportunities for sharing across and within institutions, and by widely disseminating the key learning points from the variety of related projects. Six core themes underpin the programme. These are academic integrity, digital transformation, education for sustainability, employability, equality diversity & inclusion, universal design for learning. The holistic nature of the overall programme and the clear linkages between each work stream provide multiple opportunities for students and staff to reflect on the opportunities and challenges associated with artificial intelligence and other emerging issues. Building on experiences from the pandemic-related period of emergency remote teaching, a clear focus sought to take a more planned and structured approach to address hybrid and hyflex learning, teaching and assessment.

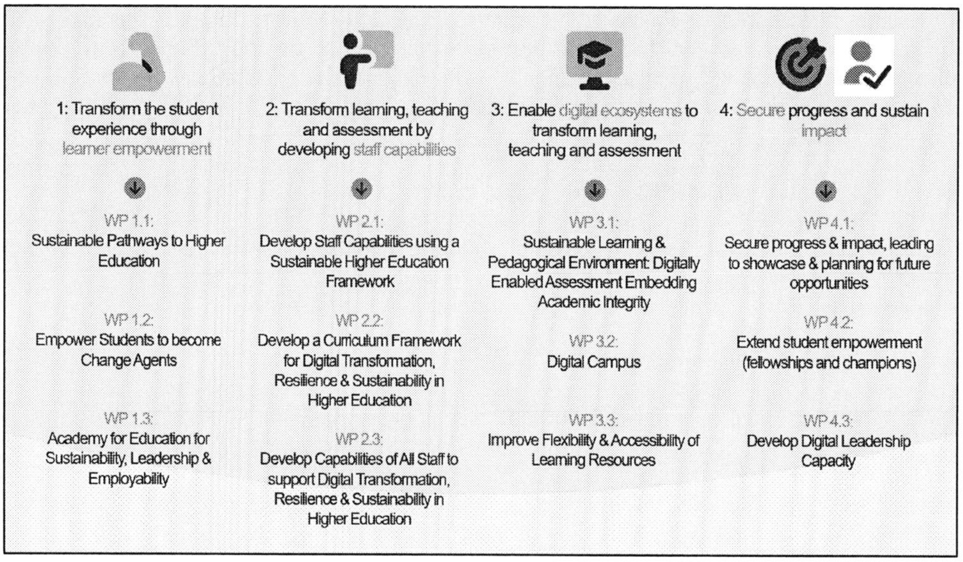

Figure 1: N-TUTORR has four work streams, each of which consists of three work packages. (Overview created by Programme Management Office.)

Student empowerment is explicitly and deliberately placed as the first work stream. Key parts of the student empowerment stream are Student Fellowship projects and Student Champions. These initiatives provide an explicit role for students to contribute to core themes in a meaningful way. 130 Fellowship projects were funded across the seven partner institutions. These involve students and staff working together to address issues of their own choice under one (or more) of the six core themes. 12 Fellowship projects chose to deal with issues around academic integrity and assessment. Examples include a "student-led approach towards finding solutions to the emergence of essay mills and AI technology in academic writing"; and a "student-led initiative to stress test the academic integrity of 3rd level course work using AI". In addition, 100 student champions were appointed to different but related roles in order to contribute to a range of institutional, sectoral and national initiatives. For example, student champions from across partners formed the entire panel for an online masterclass exploring academic integrity and assessment. The effectiveness and success of these elements of empowering learners has led to the extension of these particular initiatives beyond May 2024 until December 2024 when the current funding stream ceases.

Stream two focuses on developing staff capabilities. Masterclasses form one distinct part of this work stream. Masterclasses take place monthly, are scheduled at lunchtime to optimise attendance, and each event focusses on one of the core themes. For example, one of the masterclasses explored the role of artificial intelligence in higher education and how it can be embraced to support academic integrity and assessment. Development of a curriculum framework which embeds the six core themes is another central element of enhancing staff capabilities. This curriculum framework, and the associated set of graduate capabilities for sustainable and resilient higher education, are aligned to institutional gender action plans and the national Climate Action Plan. This sectoral framework acts as guidance to each partner institution to inform institutional policies and processes. Specific training opportunities are also in place for senior institutional staff. Among other topics, these include an online training session on "understanding Artificial Intelligence and considering the opportunities for GenAI" beyond solely the academic integrity perspective.

The third work stream, 'enhancing the digital ecosystem', has included a focus on digitally enabled examination / assessment and embedding academic integrity. It has also enabled significant investment in enhanced and flexible learning spaces under the theme of 'digital campus'. Consideration of open educational resources led to a consensus that resources relating to digital media production were a shared aspect for priority enhancement for all partner institutions. Other enhancements, adopted to varying extents by institutions in the context of their own priorities, include: additional functionality for virtual learning environments; virtual laboratory systems; varied software and hardware additions to enhance programme delivery.

The fourth work stream, Securing Progress and Sustaining Impact, focusses on embedding the transformative change and practices achieved to date and on developing digital leadership to enhance the capacity of partner institutions to plan for and manage future developments. This involves development of network structures to facilitate increased horizon scanning to identify emerging issues and trends, in addition to the establishment and development of a network of practitioners and experts across the technological sector that examines the impact of Generative AI (GenAI) on higher education, again beyond the implications solely for Academic Integrity.

The multiple strands of activity have led to active cooperation between the N-TUTORR programme and the National Academic Integrity Network (NAIN) which is facilitated by the national qualifications and quality agency, Quality and Qualifications Ireland (QQI). This has extended knowledge and appreciation of the cooperation into international contexts such as the Global Academic Integrity Network (GAIN) in additional to specific cooperation with the Australian Tertiary Education Quality and Standards Agency (TEQSA). A joint N-TUTORR / NAIN Working Group is in place, identifying some key areas with a specific focus on GenAI. This includes the roll out of a number of tools identified to assist with the threats to assessment and curating a multi-functional Repository which will be available for the GenAI Network to assist with sharing best practices, thus enabling consistency across the sector.

The concept of Student Champions has recently been extended to explore the potential impact of GenAI with a group of students with disabilities and / or learning differences. This project, with the project team drawn from students across all seven partner institutions, aims to create and maintain a repository of recommended AI tools which have been evaluated, and potentially ethically adapted, by students for students. The final resources, including support materials created by students, will be made available to all partner institutions.

There are multiple other examples of programme activities and initiatives addressing important or topical issues. This paper particularly focuses on themes relating to the 2024 EDEN conference.

Conclusion

The N-TUTORR transformation programme represents significant investment in Ireland's technological higher education institutions. It was designed, and is being implemented, by major collaboration from partner organisations and seeks to recognise the holistic and interconnected nature of learning, teaching and assessment in higher education. This structured design enabled developments in artificial intelligence to be addressed by programme activities using planned fora, networks and events. Many of these structures could be replicated in other institutions and / or groups of institutions where there is a desire to do so. As such, initiatives to empower students, to provide targeted development opportunities for staff, and to work collaboratively, contribute to higher education taking a leading role in determining how society can engage in meaningful, ethical use of artificial intelligence tools and services.

Funding information

The N-TUTORR programme is funded from Ireland's National Recovery and Resilience Plan (NRRP) Technological Universities Education and Training Reforms Programme. The Recovery and Resilience Facility is funded by the European Union and represents the largest component of #NextGenerationEU.

References

Global Academic Integrity Network website, www.globalacademicintegrity.network

National Forum for the Enhancement of Teaching and Learning, "Next Steps for Teaching and Learning: Moving Forward Together", https://www.teachingandlearning.ie/VITAL/nextsteps/#!/inav

National Academic Integrity Network (NAIN), https://www.qqi.ie/what-we-do/engagement-insights-and-knowledge-sharing/national-academic-integrity-network

N-TUTORR programme website, www.transforminglearning.ie

StudentSurvey.ie (Irish Survey of Student Engagement) Interim Results Bulletin 2021, https://studentsurvey.ie/reports/studentsurveyie-interim-results-bulletin-2021

Technological Universities: Connectedness and Collaboration through Connectivity (October 2019). Report of the Technological Universities Research Network to the Department of Education and Skills. https://hea.ie/technological_universities/tu-research-network-turn/

Tertiary Education Quality and Standards Agency (TEQSA), https://www.teqsa.gov.au/guides-resources/higher-education-good-practice-hub

How to Better Qualify ICT Graduates to Support Digital Education: A contribution from CALOHEE Tuning project qualifications framework

António Moreira Teixeira[1], Daiva Vitkutė-Adžgauskienė[2], Veerle Ongenae[3], Enzo Mingozzi[4], Christian-Andreas Schumann[5], Rafael Pastor Vargas[6]

[1] Laboratório de Educação a Distância e eLearning, Universidade Aberta, Portugal; Antonio.Teixeira@uab.pt
[2] Vytautas Magnus University, Lithuania; daiva.vitkute@vdu.lt
[3] Ghent University, Belgium; veerle.ongenae@ugent.be
[4] University of Pisa, Italy; enzo.mingozzi@unipi.it
[5] West Saxon University of Applied Sciences of Zwickau, Germany; christian.schumann@fh-zwickau.de
[6] Spanish Open University for Distance Education [UNED], Spain; rpastor@scc.uned.es

Correspondence: António Moreira Teixeira: Antonio.Teixeira@uab.pt

Abstract:

The Information and Communications Technology subject area is a broad multidisciplinary field of academic research and professional practice covering many topics ranging from electronics to system and network administration, to software development, cyber security, VR, AR, IoT and AI. Due to its nature, it cooperates closely with diverse areas, most notably eLearning and digital education. As contemporary educational institutions undergo a digital transformation, by which its processes are reengineered to take most of the possibilities offered by the emerging technologies, the contribution of the ICT field has become transversal and consequently of critical importance. The term ICT which refers to this wide multidisciplinary field differentiates from IT, which applies specifically to the management and use of computer systems to store, retrieve, transmit, and manipulate data. The continuous expansion of the field to new territories of practice such as education is requiring additional knowledge, skills and wider competences acquisition. In addition, high volatility of the job market creates the need for very adaptable professional profiles. As a result, there is a pressure from the job market for shorter and more job-oriented programmes, but also for competence frameworks which may serve as references for quality higher education and training. In this paper we present the Tuning Quality Reference Framework (QRF) for ICT which was developed as part of the CALOHEE Erasmus+ funded project. A multidisciplinary team with experts from 12 different countries (Portugal, Lithuania, Germany, Italy, Spain, Austria, Belgium, Greece, Turkey, Finland, Ireland and Romania) took part in the task. The QRF is built in a way to flexibly address all the mentioned complexity and continuously emerging new requirements including educational institutions and non-formal education organisations. The approach used also supports innovation in learning, teaching and assessment practices in ICT degrees, fostering open and digital education.

Keywords: ICT, eLearning, Digital Education; Open Education; Technology-Enhanced Learning; Qualifications Framework

Introduction

The Information and Communications Technology (ICT) subject area is a broad multidisciplinary field of academic research and professional practice covering many topics ranging from electronics to system and network administration, to software development, cyber security, VR, AR, IoT and AI. Due to its nature, it cooperates closely with diverse areas, most notably eLearning and digital education (Tikhonenko & Pereira, 2019). As contemporary educational institutions undergo a digital transformation, by which its processes are reengineered to take most of the possibilities offered by the emerging technologies, the contribution of the ICT field has become transversal and consequently of critical importance.

The term ICT which refers to this wide multidisciplinary field differentiates from IT, which applies specifically to the management and use of computer systems to store, retrieve, transmit, and manipulate data. The goals of ICT technologies are to improve the ways of creating, processing, and sharing data and information, as thus to improve human abilities in different areas of activity, including education. There is no single, universal definition of ICT, as the field is constantly evolving with increasing emphasis on interdisciplinarity. Consequently, the demand for degrees in ICT is expanding rapidly, even if it fails to keep up with the needs of the job market and in particular educational institution's needs. It is estimated that over three hundred and fifty thousand new students enrol each year in Informatics bachelor's programs in Europe, as the total number of enrolled students exceeds one million (Tikhonenko & Pereira, 2019). The corresponding estimated figure for students enrolled in master's programs in the field is over two hundred thousand (Tikhonenko & Pereira, 2019). Regarding graduations, around one hundred and sixty thousand students graduate each year in Informatics bachelor's programs and over sixty thousand in master's (Tikhonenko & Pereira, 2019).

The Qualifications Reference Framework for the Degrees in ICT[1] designed by the CALOHEE Tuning project and published as the Tuning Guidelines and Reference Points 2023 for the Design and Delivery of Degree Programmes in Information and Communication Technology - ICT (Teixeira et al., 2024) was produced to better support higher education institutions in the design and delivery process of programmes. It was prepared by a multidisciplinary team of experts from 12 HEI representing many different European countries (Portugal, Lithuania, Germany, Italy, Spain, Austria, Belgium, Greece, Turkey, Finland, Ireland and Romania). It addresses main ICT competences, characteristic of different Computer Science Disciplines, as defined in IEEE/ACM Reference Curricula documents: Computer Science, Computer Engineering, IS, IT, Software Engineering (ACM & IEEE, 2020). In this paper, we present the QRF for ICT and discuss its main features.

In ICT, three paradigms - theory, modelling and design - are equally important and fundamental. Information theory deals with those objects and their relationships whose relevance is determined by modelling and design. Modelling deals with the correspondence of theoretical objects and relationships to the real world. Design realises model-checked objects and relationships. In ICT, these paradigms are closely related, mutually conditioning and do not exist without each other. These paradigms are distinct because they are represented by different areas of expertise. Apart from the complex and dynamical landscape of computing knowledge, as well as the multidisciplinary nature of ICT, non-ICT issues dealing with social, political, economic, and environmental concerns, as ethical issues, have become of great importance.

The continuous expansion of the field to new territories of practice is requiring additional knowledge, skills and wider competences acquisition. High volatility of the job market creates the need for very adaptable professional profiles. There is a pressure from the job market for shorter and more job-oriented programmes. The QRF for ICT is built in a way to flexibly address all this complexity and continuously emerging new requirements including educational institutions and non-formal education organisations.

The Tuning-CALOHEE model

The QRF for ICT is intended to serve as an international reference point for the academic discipline in the European Higher Education Area (EHEA), representing the current situation in such a fast-changing societal environment. The QRF applies the Tuning methodology for (re-) designing, developing, implementing and evaluating study programmes for each of the Bologna cycles. Originally validated in 2007-2008, developments have followed since. The latest version in which the QRF for ICT is based can be found in Measuring and Comparing Achievements of Learning Outcomes in Higher Education in Europe (CALOHEE) projects (2018-2023)[2].

The Tuning methodology is based on the student-centred and active learning approaches it has promoted from the start (Lokhoff et al, 2010). Graduates need to have obtained as the outcome of their learning process the optimum set of competences required to execute their future professional tasks and take on their expected roles in society. As part of their education graduates should have developed levels of critical thinking and awareness that foster civic, social, environmental and cultural engagement. Recognition is given to current and possible future developments and issues.

The Tuning reference points ensure study programmes are comparable, compatible and transparent. They are expressed in terms of learning outcomes and competences. Competences represent a dynamic combination of cognitive and meta-cognitive skills, knowledge and understanding, interpersonal, intellectual and practical skills, and ethical values. Some competences are subject area related (specific to a subject area), others are generic (relevant for many or all in degree programmes). According to the Tuning model, subject specific competences and generic competences or general academic skills should be developed together. The Tuning model values the 'dimensions' approach. They contribute to structure a particular sector or subject area and make its basic characteristics more transparent. The use of the learning outcomes and competences approach

[1] https://www.tuning-calohex.eu/information-and-communication-technology

[2] Measuring and Comparing Achievements of Learning Outcomes in Higher Education in Europe (CALOHEE). https://www.calohee.eu/

implies changes regarding the teaching, learning and assessment methods. But also, it has implications in how quality enhancement can play a critical role in the process of conceiving and reviewing study programmes.

Level Cycle Descriptors: Competences and Learning Outcomes (EQF Levels 6 and 7)

When designing the QRF for ICT, we aimed at defining a meta-profile of an ICT professional based on five critical dimensions upon which the relevant competences are organised in order to build the profile of a successful ICT graduate in the contemporary knowledge society. The five dimensions mentioned above are the following:

Dimension 1: **Knowledge and understanding.**
Dimension 2: **Design, development, and management of processes of ICT systems and related processes.**
Dimension 3: **Informed decision making and learner ethics.**
Dimension 4: **Communication and collaboration.**
Dimension 5: **Professional life-long learning and continuous personal development.**

The ICT meta-profile categorises, structures, and organises competences into recognisable clusters, illustrating inter-relations among the different aspects of the desired graduate profile. Each dimension is defined by a set of associated competences, attributed to knowledge, skill and autonomy and responsibility (wider competences) competence categories. The following international qualification frameworks were used as reference: the EQF for Lifelong Learning (European Commission, 2008), the Dublin Descriptors, and the ACM and IEEE Computing Curricula 2020 (CC2020) (ACM & IEEE, 2020).

The complete description of the Qualifications Reference Framework for Bachelor's degrees in ICT (EQF level 6) is presented in Tables 1-5 below. A similar approach was used for Master's degrees (EQF level 7), which is not presented in full but only discussed in this paper due to word limits.

Table 1. Dimension 1: Knowledge and Understanding

(Sub)descriptor	Knowledge	Skills	Autonomy and Responsibility (Wider Competences)
L6_1. Level descriptor Knowledge and understanding	Demonstrate current understanding of core knowledge related to ICT.	Evidence the ability to contextualise, integrate and compare knowledge which is fundamental for ICT correctly applying the related terminology.	Manifest the ability to use, share and contribute to ICT-related knowledge and understanding in professional and societal settings.
Subset 1 L6_1.1 **STEM**	Demonstrate knowledge in mathematics, physics and other STEM fields which are core to ICT.	Evidence the ability to contextualise, integrate and compare STEM knowledge in solving ICT-specific problems.	Manifest the ability to identify, describe and aggregate STEM methodological knowledge required to solve problems in the ICT field.
Subset 2 L6_1.2 **ICT-related methodological-operational knowledge**	Demonstrate specialised methodological-operational knowledge in ICT systems in order to be able to design, develop and implement them.	Evidence the ability to contextualise, integrate and compare knowledge in order to design, implement and operate computer systems and networks.	Manifest the ability to acquire, prepare and critically assess specific methodological-operational knowledge in ICT to identify, formulate and solve application problems, configure and manage ICT systems of different complexity.
Subset 3 L6_1.3 **Legal aspects and organisational frameworks**	Demonstrate understanding of legal aspects and institutional frameworks of diverse types of organisations, alongside ICT-related regulations.	Evidence the ability to apply knowledge of business processes and corresponding IS in ICT professional contexts.	Manifest the ability to implement a digital strategy for a project or an organisation, being capable of starting an operation in an inclusive and sustainable manner.

Table 2. Dimension 2: Design, Development and Management of ICT Systems and related processes

(Sub)descriptor	Knowledge	Skills	Autonomy and Responsibility (Wider Competences)
L6_2. Level descriptor Design, development and management of ICT systems and related processes	Demonstrate current knowledge and understanding of the generic and ICT-related skills required to operate successfully in diversified contexts.	Evidence the ability to apply ICT-related and generic skills, which facilitate the development of critical thinking and evidence-based arguments and solving ICT related and societal problems.	Manifest an evidence-informed approach to managing technical/professional projects and activities, applying effectively ICT and societal related knowledge and skills, taking initiative, showing responsibility and leadership.
Subset 1 L6_2.1 **Methods and techniques in ICT**	Demonstrate knowledge and understanding of design and implementation of ICT systems, considering the ethical use of data and information technologies.	Evidence the ability to apply knowledge for analysing, designing, implementing, testing, maintaining and integrating ICT systems in companies and other organisations.	Manifest the ability to use appropriate methods and techniques in a target-oriented way to effectively address ICT problems.
Subset 2 L6_2.2 **Management of ICT processes**	Demonstrate knowledge of the different aspects involved in processes of ICT systems and applications development.	Evidence the ability to manage ICT processes and solve related problems.	Manifest the ability to manage ICT solutions autonomously and responsibly.
Subset 3 L6_2.3 **Transformational impact of ICT**	Demonstrate understanding of the transformational impact and implications of ICT in society, communities and work environments.	Evidence the ability to design and manage ICT solutions and systems which contribute to the needs and expectations of societies, communities, work environments, and individuals.	Manifest the ability to exercise initiative and acknowledge accountability for the executed ICT tasks.

Table 3. Dimension 3: Informed Decision making and Work Ethics

(Sub)descriptor	Knowledge	Skills	Autonomy and Responsibility (Wider Competences)
L6_3. Level descriptor Informed decision making and work ethics	Demonstrate current knowledge and understanding of relevant theoretical frameworks, concepts and methodologies and/or practices to gather, evaluate and interpret ICT related and societal information, in an ethical, inclusive and sustainable manner.	Evidence the ability to apply appropriate theories, concepts, methodologies and/or practices and ICT related and generic skills and competences to analyse, synthesise, and make informed judgments while considering relevant social, cultural, scientific and ethical issues and challenges.	Manifest the ability to evaluate ICT and societal challenges and problems and to reflect on relevant knowledge in order to contribute to ethical decision-making, finding individual and collaborative ways to move forward, ensuring participation and inclusion.
Subset 1 L6_3.1 **Reciprocal interactions between ICT and society**	Demonstrate comprehensive understanding of the reciprocal interactions between ICT and society.	Evidence the ability to apply comprehensive understanding of the reciprocal interactions between ICT and society to planning and managing of ICT projects.	Manifest the ability to identify appropriate and relevant inclusive, sustainable and ethical approaches to responsively manage work contexts in the ICT subject area and interdisciplinary contexts.
Subset 2 L6_3.2 **Professional,**	Demonstrate awareness of the key aspects of professional, ethical and	Evidence the ability to make decisions and informed judgements on	Demonstrate knowledge of the norms, regulations and codes of ICT practice, and

ethical and social responsibilities	social responsibilities linked to management of ICT activities, in particular decision-making and judgement formulation, namely the roles and dynamics of collaboration.	issues related to ICT, exercising professional, ethical and social responsibilities.	reflects on professional, ethical and social responsibilities in taking decisions and formulating judgments, valuing diversity.
Subset 3 L6_3.3 **Methodologies for ethically collecting and interpreting data**	Demonstrate comprehensive understanding of methodologies for gathering, evaluating and interpreting data.	Evidence the ability to apply ethical principles of good practice to the retrieval, storage, analysis, management and transformation of data.	Manifest the ability to identify collaborative and proficient ways to interpret and transform data for addressing relevant societal and community challenges.

Table 4. Dimension 4: Communication and Collaboration

(Sub)descriptor	Knowledge	Skills	Autonomy and Responsibility (Wider Competences)
L6_4. Level descriptor Communication and collaboration	Demonstrate current knowledge and understanding of the appropriate means, skills, attitudes, approaches and strategies to effectively communicate and collaborate, sharing ideas, challenges and solutions related to ICT for a variety of audiences.	Evidence effective communication of different types of information, expressing ideas, problems, challenges and possible solutions by applying technical and non-technical strategies, means and skills tailoring them to a variety of audiences including ICT specialists.	Manifest the ability to communicate effectively in predictable and unpredictable workplace and/or societal situations by listening to others and making convincing arguments in order to reach a common understanding of topics and activities involved.
Subset 1 L6_4.1 **Communication methods, tools and strategies**	Demonstrate current knowledge and understanding of existing and emerging innovative communication methods, tools, strategies, and their limitations.	Evidence the ability to communicate information and express ideas, problems and solutions effectively, clearly and unambiguously, orally and in writing, including English or another relevant foreign language.	Manifest the ability to identify and justify appropriate and relevant communication and collaboration methods, tools, and strategies, both established and innovative ones.
Subset 2 L6_4.2 **ICT-related terminology**	Demonstrate current knowledge of the scientific and discipline-specific technical terminology in the ICT field, namely in international contexts.	Evidence the ability to describe activities and communicate their results to ICT specialist and non-specialist audiences in national and international contexts using appropriate communication, strategies, methods and tools.	Manifest the ability to communicate effectively in multicultural and multilingual environments, using evidence, to non-experts, peers and professionals about the application of ICT and its ethical and social impact.
Subset 3 L6_4.3 **Team Management**	Demonstrate current knowledge and understanding of responsibilities and methods to manage teams that may be composed of different disciplines and levels.	Evidence the ability to collaborate or cooperate effectively in national and international work contexts as leader or member of teams that may be composed of different disciplines and levels, contributing to meet deliverable, schedule and budget requirements.	Manifest the ability to identify and implement an appropriate strategy to lead a small or medium complexity project in the ICT-related field, applying inclusive and ethical principles of conduct.

Table 5. Dimension 5: Professional Lifelong Learning and Continuous Personal Development

(Sub)descriptor	Knowledge	Skills	Autonomy and Responsibility (Wider Competences)
L6_5. Level descriptor Professional lifelong learning and continuous personal development	Demonstrate knowledge and understanding of the learning process and methods required for self-directed continuous learning and development in a variety of formats and settings.	Evidence learning skills and appropriate strategies to advance the continuous learning and development of self and others in order to reflect on, update, and upgrade knowledge, skill and competencies in ICT, and societal developments.	Manifest motivation and initiative to organise, manage, and evaluate learning and development activities for oneself and others in order to continually update and upgrade ICT related knowledge, skills, competences, taking into account societal developments.
Subset 1 L6_5.1 **Professional self-assessment**	Demonstrate knowledge and understanding of self-assessment methods needed for personal development.	Evidence the ability to continuously evaluate personal knowledge and skills.	Manifest the ability to conduct continuous self-assessing of own professional competences.
Subset 2 L6_5.2 **Autonomous learning**	Demonstrate knowledge and understanding of learning methods needed for personal development.	Evidence the ability to organise one's own study and/or learning process, using different kinds of learning methods and materials.	Manifest the ability to identify and justify appropriate learning strategies and methods in independent lifelong learning.
Subset 3 L6_5.3 **Continuous personal development**	Demonstrate advanced knowledge and understanding of learning methods necessary to follow developments in ICT subject area and within broader or multidisciplinary and societal contexts.	Evidence the ability to follow new developments in the ICT-related field, search for relevant information and seek appropriate support.	Manifest the ability to undertake further studies in emerging technologies in ICT also within trans- or multidisciplinary contexts.

The first dimension of the ICT QRF for EQF level 6 concerns knowledge and understanding as indicated in level descriptor 6.1. In this context, subset 6.1.1 highlights the importance of Mathematics, Physics, and other STEM as foundational knowledge in the field of ICT. However, given the broad spectrum of the field, as described in the previous sections, subset 6.1.2 also indicates the contribution of operational knowledge which is relevant for ICT. In fact, it is expected that a graduate in this field can acquire and mobilise knowledge competences to design, implement and operate computer systems and networks. For that purpose, a graduate should be able to critically assess specific methodological-operational knowledge to solve problems and configure and manage systems.

As a graduate in ICT typically operates in diverse work environments given the broad nature of the field, this QRF adds competences related to ability to understand the organisation, strategy and policies of institutions and business companies. In fact, a graduate in ICT should be also prepared to start and manage a project in a given organisation or a startup company.

These competences are also included the ICT QRF for EQF level 7. The main difference is the level of knowledge required, which at the Master level should be of an advanced and more specialised nature. Also, the problems related to ICT systems configuration and management which postgraduates are expected to solve should be of higher complexity. At both levels 6 and 7 attention was given to ensuring that graduates and postgraduates in ICT clearly understand the importance of designing inclusive and sustainable processes in ICT.

The second dimension of the QRF for ICT concerning EQF level 6 is related to the design, development and management of ICT systems and related processes. Here, subset 6.2.1 ensures that graduates can apply appropriate methods and techniques at the different phases of integration of ICT systems in companies and other organisations. At the same time, it also emphasises the need for graduates to be prepared to consider all aspects related to the ethical use of data and IT in these processes. This is an increasingly relevant topic in contemporary ICT work environments.

Following up on the need to ensure the integrity of graduates, subset 6.2.2 includes competencies which highlight their capacity to demonstrate autonomy and responsibility when managing ICT solutions. In the same direction, subset 6.2.3 focuses on the need for graduates to be aware of the transformational impact of ICT and to be able to address the concrete needs of people and organisations.

At the EQF level 7, the QRF for ICT adds to these competences a higher degree of complexity. This involves application of advanced and highly specialised knowledge as well as evidence-informed skills in the design, development and management of ICT systems and related processes in multi-dimensional and differentiated work and societal settings. Also, the ICT QRF for EQF level 7 adds innovation, entrepreneurship dimension, research, accountability and leadership dimensions to the graduate capacity to manage complex technical and content related activities, effective ICT solutions and applications.

The third dimension of the ICT QRF for EQF level 6 deals with informed decision making and work ethics. This is another emerging major concern when taking into consideration the expanding landscape of the ICT field of practice. In fact, the rise of Data Science has changed the perception of ICT resulting in an increased relevance of ethics. ICT is being recognised as the main knowledge centre in the digital transformation of society (Di Nitto et al., 2019). As such, subset 6.3.1 addresses the reciprocity of interaction between ICT and society. This subset highlights how graduates should be prepared to identify and apply inclusive, sustainable, and ethical approaches to planning and managing ICT-related tasks considering the interdisciplinary contexts in which they are expected to operate. The preparation of graduates to operate in such complex environments is also addressed by the competences included on subset 6.3.2. It focuses on the need for graduates to understand the norms, regulations and codes ruling the professional practice in ICT. However, the competences are formulated in a way to stress an autonomous, ethical, and socially responsible conduct by graduates. This focus on ethical responsibility is reinforced in subset 6.3.3 which concerns the capacity of graduates to identify and apply the best methodologies and practices to manage data.

On the ICT QRF for EQF Level 7, the competences of informed decision making, work ethics, understanding of norms, regulations and codes as well data management level are augmented. This is achieved by strengthening the capacity of graduates to reflect on new specialised knowledge and skills, as well as on professional, ethical and social responsibilities in taking decisions and formulating judgments. The ICT QRF for EQF level 7 tries to ensure that graduates can identify relevant inclusive and sustainable approaches as well as understand the value of diversity in their activities.

The fourth dimension of the ICT QRF for EQF level 6 concerns communication and collaboration. Again, the increasingly multinational and multicultural nature of work environments in ICT stresses the importance of communication. As such, subset 6.4.1 includes competences related to communication tools and strategies, including the ability to express in English or another relevant foreign language, as subset 6.4.2 focusses on the capacity to address effectively diverse and multicultural environments, including the knowledge of ICT-related terminology. Finally, subset 6.4.3 is related to collaboration competences, highlighting the capacity of graduates to lead and conduct simple or medium complex tasks in multidisciplinary and/or multinational teams.

The ICT QRF for EQF Level 7 strengthens and broadens the communication and collaboration competences, adding the capacity to communicate proficiently, to employ different sophisticated communication strategies, media, means and skills, to lead complex projects in ICT-related field.

The fifth and final dimension of the ICT QRF for EQF level 6 concerns an ever more important aspect of current and future ICT practice which is professional lifelong learning and continuous personal development. Subset 6.5.1 addresses the need for graduates to be able to continuously assess their own professional competences bearing in mind how their own work trajectory is evolving and technologies also changing. On subset 6.5.2 the QRF highlights the capability of graduates to organise and conduct autonomous informal or non-formal learning activities and on section 6.5.3 to pursue further studies, namely more advanced levels of qualifications.

At the EQF Level 7, the competences of professional lifelong learning and continuous personal development included in the QRF for ICT are broadened by adding the capacity to demonstrate advanced knowledge and understanding of the learning process and methods. In addition, postgraduates are expected to manifest continuous personal and professional development in individual, team-based and societal settings.

Learning, teaching and assessment innovation in ICT degrees

ICT as a subject or course of study has a very complex content and interdisciplinary context. Therefore, the challenges of transferring knowledge and skills in this area are very high. In terms of learning theory and didactics, several theories, methods, concepts and tools are used in combination to ensure the optimisation of teaching and learning processes, including assessment, both physically and digitally. This means that the transfer of knowledge and skills is based on multidimensional, hybrid models and concepts, which is also reflected in the forms of assessment. ICT cannot be regarded primarily as a technical study, but as preparation for a highly effective social practice. Accordingly, the learning activities required of students are extremely diverse.

Evidence collected by the CALOHEE project shows that European higher education institutions make use of almost every conceivable type of learning activity. However, the focus of the intellectual and social activities must always lie with the students if higher-level learning outcomes are to be achieved. The decisive consequence of this is that consumable learning situations such as lectures and presentations are beginning to be minimised in favour of active, product- and solution-oriented and creativity-based forms of learning. In fact, the dissemination of technology-enhanced learning is allowing to overcome most possible economic and organisational restrictions.

For students and teachers in the field of ICT, connectivism is becoming increasingly important alongside traditional learning theory perspectives of constructivism. Professionals who are ICT-affine and highly qualified in the field of ICT have a low entry threshold for networked and thus hybrid learning and teaching as a combination of formal and informal learning. At the same time, attempts are being made to optimise the variety of options through models of hybridization to ensure the best possible teaching and learning success. ICT professionals are predestined for this per se.

The guiding principle is that teaching concentrates on creating situations in which students can acquire knowledge, develop skills and build up complex competencies with a high level of cognitive and social participation. Teaching ICT in European higher education institutions is nowadays clearly less about providing information and increasingly more about organising opportunities for constructing knowledge and personal development. Confrontation with open questions, problems and tasks are therefore the means of choice - especially if they do not take place in the lecture hall, but in authentic environments such as companies or organisations.

Accordingly, assessment must also meet the challenges of the field. The first consequence of this is the need to apply practically all known forms of assessment, exploring the affordances of digital tools. Intended learning outcomes, learning activities, teaching methods and forms of assessment must harmonise if the best possible result is to be achieved (constructive alignment). For this reason, it is not possible to provide more detailed information on which assessment would be appropriate when. These decisions can only be made by the curriculum planners in close consultation with the lecturers. However, the principle is generally valid: the higher ranking the learning outcomes, the more complex the tasks to be completed must be within a range from a one-day task to a multi-semester project.

Conclusions

In such a rapidly evolving field as ICT, it is of the utmost importance that degree programs not only be academically sound but also relevant. For that, they must be adaptable and responsive to the dynamic nature of the ICT field, remaining updated with society and industry trends, tools, and emerging technologies. This relevance is vital for ensuring the credibility and reputation of degrees and HEI both at national and international level.

By aligning qualifications with European industry as well as digital education institutions and other organisations needs and standards, the QRF for ICT ensures graduates possess skills relevant in a rapidly evolving ICT landscape, enhancing employability across the continent. They aid in the development and review of curricula, ensuring that programs cover essential knowledge, skills, and competencies required in the ICT field today. By using these frameworks as a guide for accreditation processes, European HEI may ensure that their programs meet established standards, as the ones set by EQANIE (Equanie, 2015), and are recognized as reputable and valuable by relevant accrediting bodies.

We recognise the fact that HE students increasingly tend to follow complex trajectories. These trajectories include changing courses, taking breaks, combining subject areas, or moving between different courses or modalities (distance, hybrid and face-to-face). HEI must adapt their policies to this emerging phenomenon. As such, this QRF enables the creation of clear pathways for lifelong learning, allowing professionals to upskill, reskill, or pursue further education in ICT based on standardised levels and qualifications.

We believe that the QRF for ICT contributes to ensure that HE degrees meet defined standards, align with societal needs, facilitate international recognition, and promote ongoing learning in a rapidly evolving field such as this one. They may serve as a roadmap for HEI across Europe to deliver high-quality education and for students to acquire valuable skills and knowledge. In recent years, quality assurance bodies have been setting quality standards for the accreditation of HE provision which share many similar elements. Accordingly, the QRF for ICT can be used as a set of directrices for quality assurance national and international bodies, as EQANIE, in their reviewing processes on ICT-related programs given the specific nature of these frameworks. The same may apply to professional associations who issue standards for the ICT field of practice and the practitioners.

Acknowledgements

The authors wish to acknowledge the contribution of the additional members of the Special Interest Group Gottfried Csanyi, TU Wien [Technische Universität Wien], Austria; Sevgi Özkan Yildirim, Middle East Technical University, Turkey; Costas Tsolakidis, University of the Aegean, Greece; Antti Piironen, Helsinki Metropolia University of Applied Sciences, Finland; Ángeles Sanchez-Elvira Paniagua, Spanish Open University for Distance Education [UNED], Spain; Mark Brown, Dublin City University, Ireland; and Alexandru Luca, Students' League of the Faculty of Automatics and Computers, Timisoara Polytechnic University, Romania, who co-authored the Tuning Quality Reference Framework (QRF) for ICT.

Funding Information

The research presented in this paper was carried out in the framework of CALOHEE, an Erasmus+ project funded by the European Commission (609767-EPP-1-2019-1- ES-EPPKA2-CBHE-JP). This publication reflects the views only of the authors.

References

ACM & IEEE (2020). ACM and IEEE Computing Curricula 2020 (CC2020). https://www.acm.org/binaries/content/assets/education/curricula-recommendations/cc2020.pdf

Di Nitto, E., Eisenbach, S., García Fernández, I. & Gröller, E. (2019). The Wide Role of Informatics at Universities. Informatics Europe Report. Zurich: Informatics Europe. https://www.informatics-europe.org/component/phocadownload/category/9-publications.html?download=171:the-wide-role-of-informatics-at-universities-summary

European Commission (2008). The European Qualifications Framework for Lifelong Learning (EQF), Luxembourg: Office for Official Publications of the European Communities. https://europa.eu/europass/system/files/2020-05/EQF-Archives-EN.pdf

Equanie (2015). Euro-Inf Framework Standards and Accreditation Criteria for Informatics Programmes New Programme Outcomes. https://eqanie.eu/wp-content/uploads/2019/09/Euro-Inf_New_Programme_Outcomes_for_Accreditation_2015-10-12.pdf

Lokhoff, J., Wegewijs, B., Durkin, K., Wagenaar, R., Gonzalez, J., Isaacs, A.K., Donà dalle Rose, L.F., Gobbi, M. (2010). A Tuning Guide to Formulating Degree Programme Profiles: Including Programme Competences and Programme Learning Outcomes. CoRe2 Project. Bilbao, Groningen and The Hague: University of Deusto Press. https://tuningacademy.org/wp-content/uploads/2014/02/A-Guide-to-Formulating-DPP_EN.pdf

Teixeira, A., Vitkutė-Adžgauskienė, D., Ongenae, V., Mingozzi, E., Schumann, C.-A., Csanyi, G., Özkan Yildirim, S., Pastor Vargas, R., Sanchez Elvira, A., Costas, T., Piironen, A., Brown, M., & Luca, A. (2024). TUNING Guidelines and Reference Points for the Design and Delivery of Degree Programmes in Information and Communication Technology. University of Groningen: International Tuning Academy. https://www.calohee.eu/

Tikhonenko, S. & Pereira, C. (2019) Informatics Education in Europe: Institutions, Degrees, Students, Positions, Salaries — Key Data 2013-2018. Informatics Europe Report. Zurich: Informatics Europe. https://www.informatics-europe.org/component/phocadownload/category/9-publications.html?download=172:informatics-education-europe-data-2013-2018-summary

Systematic penetration of future higher education systems with AI

Christian Andreas Schumann[1], Emelie Schwill[2], Isabell Mrotzek[3]

[1] West Saxon University of Applied Sciences of Zwickau, Germany; christian-andreas.schumann@t-online.de
[2] West Saxon University of Applied Sciences of Zwickau, Germany; emelie.schwill@fh-zwickau.de
[3] West Saxon University of Applied Sciences of Zwickau, Germany; isabell.mrotzek@fh-zwickau.de

Correspondence: Christian Andreas Schumann: christian-andreas.schumann@t-online.de

Abstract:

Back in 2018, the Declaration on Cooperation for AI laid the foundations for increasing the technological and industrial capacities and acceptance of AI, overcoming the socio-economic challenges of transforming labour markets and modernising education, and ensuring an appropriate legal and ethical framework. (Nicholas & del Castillo 2023)
The systematic penetration of AI into the education systems of universities follows this intention. In order to achieve the ambitious goals of extensive AI use, the stakeholders in higher education must be empowered to develop and implement holistic AI concepts. From the possible options for using AI in higher education, the application possibilities are derived in a targeted manner, whereby the variety of possibilities makes it necessary to adapt general models to the specific situation of a university. A case study is used to explain the step-by-step development and introduction of a chatbot as part of a holistic concept for the use of AI at universities. Finally, the insights gained so far on the opportunities and risks of AI applications in higher education are discussed.

Keywords: AI in Higher Education, AI Penetration, Systemic Use of AI, Chatbots in University, Opportunities and Risks

Enabling holistic use of AI at universities

Stanford University's 2023 AI Index Report on measuring trends in AI shows that AI applications are increasingly characterised by holistic approaches and systematic procedures as well as cross-national and cross-sector collaborations. (Maslej 2023)

Human intelligence manifests itself in the ability to perceive (see, hear, feel, etc.), learn, know, think, communicate (speak, write, etc.) and act. Artificial intelligence can map and reproduce parts of these human abilities via functional equivalents. This results in a map of AI, from which the overlaps between natural and artificial intelligence can be seen. (Humm, Buxmann & Schmidt 2022)

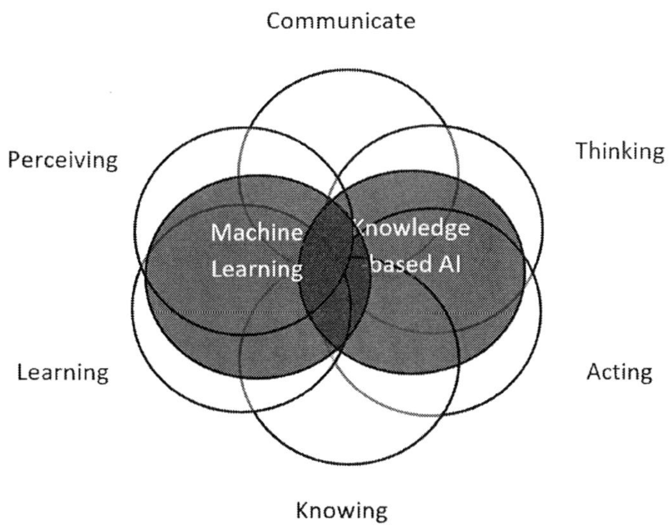

Figure 1: Map of AI (adapted from Humm, Buxmann & Schmidt 2022)

Based on these functional equivalents of human capabilities and AI services, it is possible to derive how AI should be defined in relation to human intelligence. Artificial intelligence is therefore a technology that enables computers and machines to simulate human intelligence and problem-solving skills. AI can take on tasks that would otherwise require human intelligence or intervention. (IBM 2024)

Depending on the extent to which AI functionalities match human capabilities, a distinction is made between levels of artificial intelligence in the narrower sense, general artificial intelligence and artificial superintelligence.

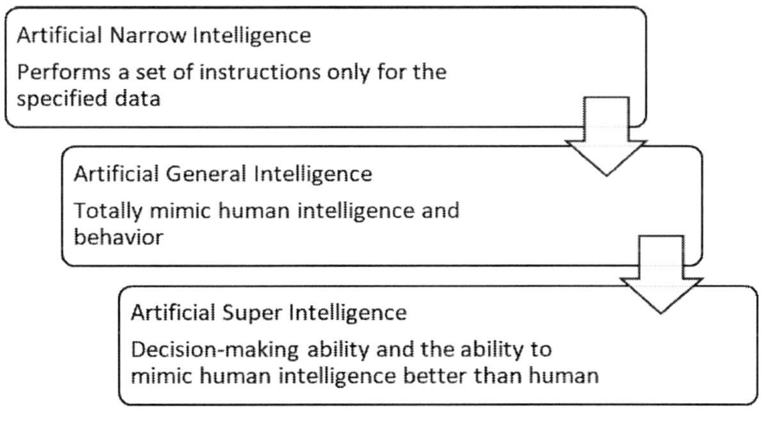

Figure 2: Stages of Artifical Intelliegence (according to Wadekar 2019)

Although artificial intelligence is at the centre of change, human action is required to enable systems to facilitate the use of AI. The process of enabling change is therefore primarily based on human expertise and therefore natural intelligence as the basis for change management. The ability to think and act holistically when using AI universities therefore requires a general understanding and commitment in the organisation that the change must be implemented. In addition, an effective leading coalition must be formed to develop a vision and strategy for the project, which is then communicated accordingly. Empowerment includes removing obstacles and empowering employees. In short, the willingness to change must be complemented by the ability to change. [Kotter: Leading the Change]

The holistic approach requires that all stakeholders involved in higher education are empowered to integrate AI into the complex higher education system and support the change. Stakeholder theory states that the role of managers is to foster co-operative relationships with stakeholders by balancing their interests. [Freeman RE, Harrison JS, Wicks AC, et al. (2010) Stakeholder Theory: The State of the Art. New York: Cambridge University Press].

To find out which groups of stakeholders need to be considered, the system boundaries need to be defined. Universities are seen as ecosystems that use dynamic capabilities frame working to develop human capital, advance technology, and transfer knowledge. During digitalisation, the systems become distributed, adaptive, and openly socio technical. Based on concepts of digitally enabled ecosystems, the groups of stakeholders for AI-enabled higher education systems can also be derived: Satellites, Complementors, Suppliers, and Strategic partners. (Lanzolla & Markides 2022)

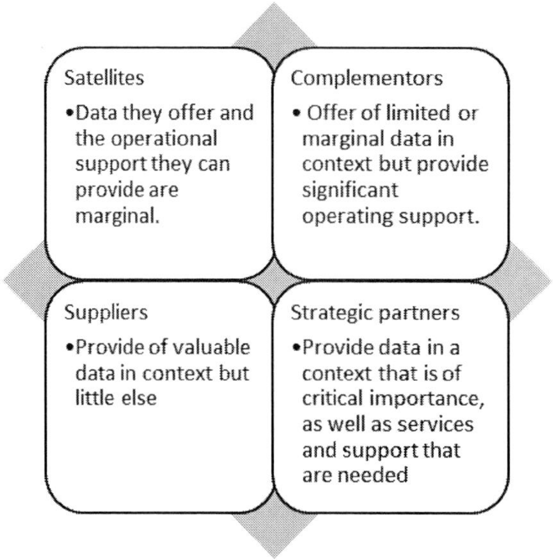

Figure 3: Partners in Digital Age (according to Lanzolla & Markides 2022)

To make the complexity of introducing AI at universities manageable, the holistic approach of all stakeholder groups should be taken as a starting point, but the focus should initially be on the strategic partners. Empowerment includes:

- Understanding all university processes in their mutual interaction
- Recognising the sub-processes suitable for AI applications
- Developing a holistic AI strategy for the university
- Step-by-step planning, development and introduction of AI solutions
- Integration of the partial solutions in line with the holistic strategy
- Transfer to operational business
- Maintenance and care as well as expansion

If the appropriate skills are in place, the willingness and ability to change can be balanced and the task can be tackled.

Development stages of the use of AI in higher education

Analysing the state of development of AI application in organisations in general and universities in particular is the prerequisite for a systematic and professional approach to planning, developing, and shaping the further transformation to AI-affine and AI-based university educational institutions. If the specific development status of the university is misjudged, failure is inevitable. The associated change in mindset usually has an inhibiting effect on the further results-orientated application of AI because the common sense of urgency and trust in the management's ability to lead, in its own performance and in the technology, itself are lost.

The development status of the AI application can be determined and presented using corresponding, special maturity models for individual organisational units. Maturity models contain methods for assessing and classifying organisations, systems, processes, and other components according to objective characteristics. They are used to determine the development status of systems or organisations and thus to initiate targeted measures for improvement. The models make it possible to define the maturity level of systems, including employees, processes, or functions, etc. and to select the appropriate approach for their further development.

In a matrix, the relationship between the features that can be used to characterise the maturity level and the maturity levels themselves can be established in two dimensions. According to the KI-MM approach, which forms the basis for further considerations, a distinction is made between:

- Characteristics: Ethical, equitable and responsible use; Strategy and resources; Organisation; Technological requirements; Data; Performance and application.
- Maturity levels: Initial, Engaged, Defined, Managed and Optimised.

Determining the maturity level using this model makes it possible to optimise the starting point, considering the characteristics of the relevant features and the existing level of AI application in the organisation. Specific actions and activities can be entered in each field in the matrix that is created during the categorisation to document the classification in a reliable manner. (Bloedorn, Kotras, Schwartz & et.al. 2022)

Application options for AI in the university

Knowledge transfer is a central task and core process for educational institutions such as universities. It requires appropriate knowledge management. Combining artificial intelligence and knowledge management means creating a partnership between humans and AI or between natural and artificial intelligence. The generation and management of knowledge are centred on people per se. (Davenport, T. & Prusak, L. 1998)

AI will therefore work most effectively with knowledge management when it is used in a complementary way, creating a collaborative intelligence in which natural and artificial intelligence reinforce each other with their complementary strengths. (Paschen, Wilson & Ferreira 2020)

Artificial and natural intelligence enter a symbiosis in which both sides take on coordinated roles.

Artificial Intelligence Roles	**Natural Intelligence Roles**
Personal Intelligence Assistants	Personal Knowledge Management
Specialised Intelligence	General Intelligence
Codification of Knowledge	Collaboration of Knowledge
Know-How and Know-What	Know-Why

Figure 4: Roles of Artificial and Human Intelligence in Combined Systems (according to Jarrahi, Askay, Eshraghi & Smith 2023)

According to Jarrahi, Askay, Eshraghi & Smith (2023), the integration of AI into knowledge management processes opens a variety of options for improving knowledge transfer:

Knowledge creation - Fostering predictive analytics via self-learning, analytical capacities, recognizing previously unknown patterns, sifting through organizational data and discovering relationships, developing new declarative knowledge.

Knowledge storing and retrieving - Harvesting, classifying, organizing, storing, and retrieving explicit knowledge, analyzing and filtering multiple channels of content and communication, facilitating knowledge reuse by teams and individuals.

Knowledge sharing - Connecting people working on the same issues by fostering weak ties and know-who, facilitating collaborative intelligence and shared organizational memory, generating a comprehensive perspective on knowledge sources and bottlenecks, creating more coordinated, connected systems across organizational silos.

Knowledge application - Enhancing situated knowledge application by searching and preparing knowledge sources, offering more natural and intuitive system interfaces (e.g., voice-based assistants), promoting equitable access to knowledge without fear of reprisal or social cost.

Interestingly, all these effects can be at least partially demonstrated in the realisation of a specific project for the complex application of AI at universities. In concrete terms, embedding AI in the university's knowledge and IT systems means, for example:

- Generation of new knowledge through additional predictive analyses using self-learning capabilities including recognition of new patterns, inspection of university data and relationships and documentation of new declarative knowledge.

- Classification organisations Storage of knowledge about processes from orientation, specialisation and learning pathway levels during AI enhancement, whereby different content from the planning of study programmes, learning pathway design, model development and deployment as well as university administration from different structural units is brought together and processed to facilitate reuse by individuals or groups of individuals.

- Strengthening interdisciplinary and cross-disciplinary collaboration between people from different organisational units to develop collaborative intelligence and a shared knowledge base during AI deployment. Abandon organisational and content-related silo thinking by creating coordinated and networked systems that can comprehensively access different existing sources of knowledge.

- Opening the application of knowledge to all member groups of the university and external partners through transparent access to existing knowledge sources, including the provision of appropriate system interfaces between humans and computers as well as between the individual information systems, thus enabling equal access to knowledge.

Necessary prerequisites for this include the creation of interdisciplinary teams, the development of all data and knowledge sources at the university, the linking of existing knowledge of an explicit and implicit nature, process reengineering including the fixing of symbiosis points for humans and AI, the permanent transfer of knowledge in the project group and in the university for AI application including the corresponding qualification levels, transparency and equal rights for all stakeholders in the change process in the course of AI utilisation.

Case study - Models for the gradual introduction of a chatbot as part of an AI solution

A case study on the gradual introduction of a chatbot as part of bundles of measures from the orientation, specialisation and learning pathway levels during AI expansion will be used as an example to demonstrate the system and procedure for setting up AI-supported orientation and administrative processes at universities. A prerequisite for each individual measure is the existence of an overall strategy from which the individual measure can be derived. Otherwise, there is a great risk that individual and co-ordinated isolated solutions will emerge which, although beneficial for themselves, will not benefit the entire university system.

In addition to ensuring the management and human-centred empowerment of the members of a university, the planning and implementation of a specific AI project depends on a development and implementation strategy. A strategy for AI includes a plan for how AI applications can be integrated into the university so that the university's general development goals can be announced and supported. The AI strategy includes steps on how to achieve effective utilisation and increased efficiency for the educational institution. (Matthew 2023)

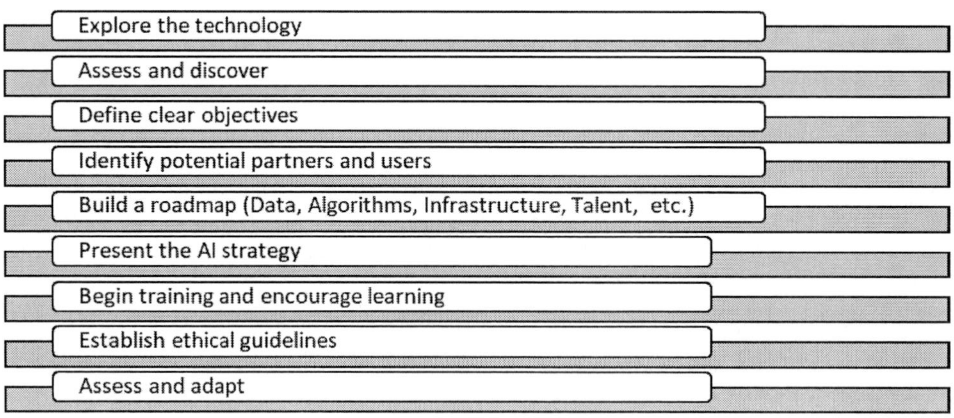

Figure 5: Steps for building a successful AI strategy (based on Matthew 2023)

When it comes to the provision of a special application such as a chatbot, for example, there should be a concept for the development of an AI system that also defines the steps in which the system development should take place. (Javaid 2024)

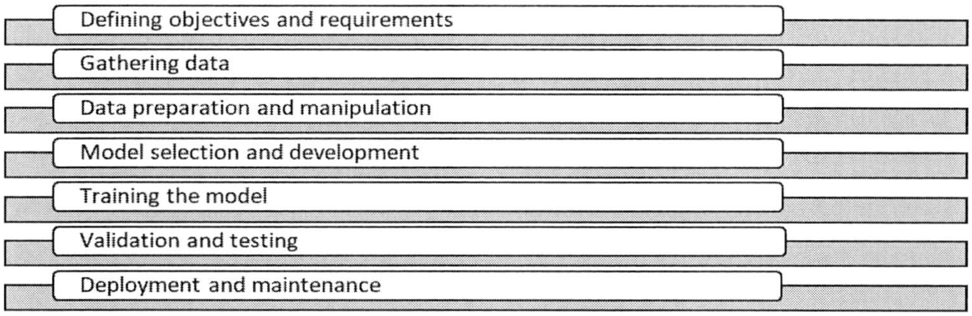

Figure 6: Steps to Developing AI Systems in 2024 (based on Javaid 2024)

The general process model for the use of AI at universities, which includes chatbot development and ultimately results in a concrete system implementation, is therefore divided into main phases.

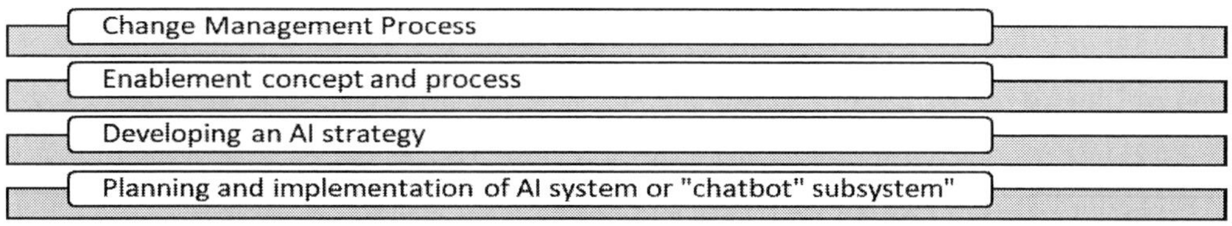

Figure 7: Main phases of the development of AI applications such as Chatbots

The strategies, models and concepts that form the basis for the development and use of a chatbot to support information, orientation and decision-making in study and administrative processes are equally suitable for other partial solutions or the overall solution for the use of AI at universities.

Opportunities and risks of using AI at universities

AI projects and applications are subject to a life cycle just like all other products and services. Lifecycle models base on a fundamental concept in systems or software engineering and development. They define the stages that a system or product has to pass through from its creation to its realisation or shutdown.

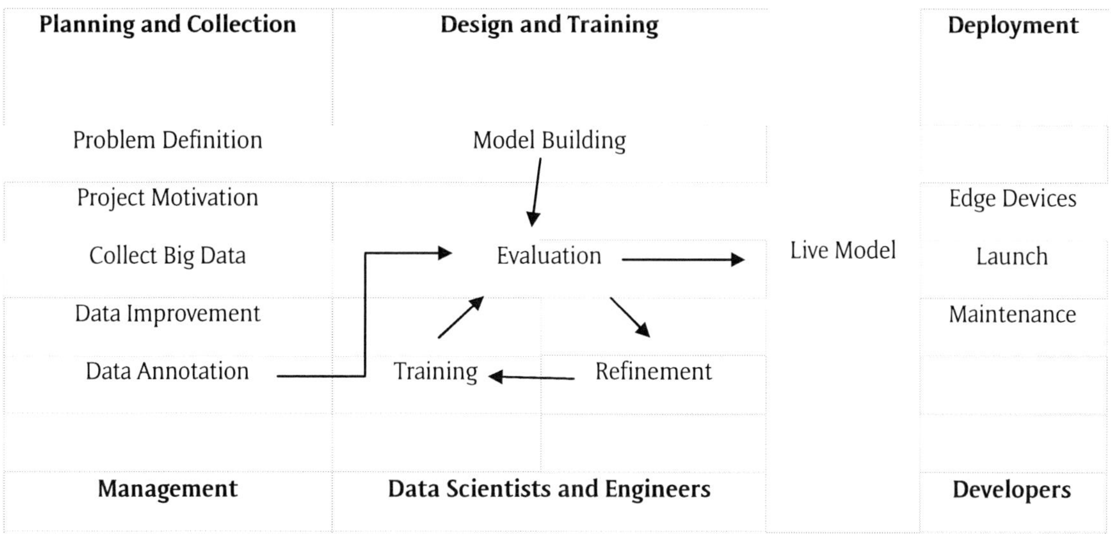

Figure 8: Lifecycle of an Artificial Intelligence Project (according to Sydorenko 2020)

Based on the three-stage life cycle model, which includes planning and data collection, design and training as well as deployment, general and specific opportunities and risks become clear, which result primarily from the degree of novelty of the development, the complexity of the task and the long-term impact over the entire life cycle. To date, the following insights have been gained as examples in an ongoing project on AI applications at universities:

Opportunities

- Improving performance and service quality.
- Systematic development of data and knowledge sources.
- Symbiosis of artificial and natural intelligence.
- Achieving unique selling points compared to competitors.
- Better information, orientation and decision support for stakeholders.
- Revision and streamlining of administrative and study processes.
- Greater structure and improved efficiency using AI.
- Increase in IT understanding and AI qualifications.
- Increased interdisciplinarity and teamwork.

Risks

- Excessive demands on administrative and teaching staff.
- Fragmentary implementation of the solution and lack of integration.
- Falsification of data and knowledge in transfer processes, for example in interfaces.
- Use of data with insufficient quality and informative value.
- Insufficient or incorrect training of AI solutions and therefore unreliable statements.
- Management errors and therefore marginal results.
- Bottlenecks in personnel and budget.

The further structured preparation of opportunities and risks, strengths and weaknesses in the form of a swot analysis will take place as the project progresses and more extensive experience and findings are gained.

Summary

AI will permeate educational institutions such as universities. Depending on the institution, different stages of development have been reached, which means that there are currently many different levels of maturity in the use of AI at universities. Each university must strategically determine its own organisation-specific path in terms of scope and time horizon. However, if this path is to be successful, a holistic approach and systematic procedure are required. It is important that educational institutions address the issue quickly so that they are not left behind in terms of content, methodology, pedagogy and technology.

This paper presents key requirements and aspects of the use of AI at universities from the experience of theoretical preparation and practical implementation in a relatively complex approach. The progress of knowledge takes place virtually daily in terms of method, content, structure, process, learning theory and practice. Because the project on which all of this is based has a certain pioneering role, the knowledge gained, and experience gained should be made accessible to a wide range of interested parties in the spirit of open science. In addition, the developments are so new that a discussion of the knowledge gained and the procedure in the community will be helpful and expedient for all sides.

References

Bloedorn, E., Kotras, D., Schwartz, P. et.al. (2022) The MITRE AI Maturity Model and Organizational Assessment Tool Guide: A Path to Successful AI Adoption. MITRE. https://www.mitre.org/sites/default/files/2023-11/PR-22-1879-MITRE-AI-Maturity-Model-and-Organizational-Assessment-Tool-Guide.pdf

Davenport, T., & Prusak, L. (1998). Working knowledge: How organizations manage what they know. Boston, MA: Harvard Business Press.

Humm, G., Buxmann, P., Schmidt, J.C. (2022). Grundlagen und Anwendungen von KI. Künstliche Intelligenz in der Forschung, Volume 48, pp 13-42. https://link.springer.com/chapter/10.1007/978-3-662-63449-3_2

IBM (2024). What is artificial intelligence (AI)? https://www.ibm.com/topics/artificial-intelligence

Jarrahi, M.H., Askay, D., Eshraghi, A., Smith. P. (2023) Artificial intelligence and knowledge management: A partnership between human and AI. Business Horizons 66. 87-99.

Javaid, S. (2024). 7 Steps to Developing AI Systems in 2024. AIMultiple. https://research.aimultiple.com/developing-ai/

Lanzolla, G., Markides. C. (2022). How to Choose the Right Ecosystem Partners for Your Business. Harvard Business Review. Digital Articles.

Matthew, F. (2023). How to build a successful AI strategy. IBM. https://www.ibm.com/blog/artificial-intelligence-strategy/

Nestor Maslej, Loredana Fattorini, Erik Brynjolfsson, John Etchemendy, Katrina Ligett, Terah Lyons, James Manyika, Helen Ngo, Juan Carlos Niebles, Vanessa Parli, Yoav Shoham, Russell Wald, Jack Clark, and Raymond Perrault, "The AI Index 2023 Annual Report," AI Index Steering Committee, Institute for Human-Centered AI, Stanford University, Stanford, CA, April 2023. https://aiindex.stanford.edu/wp-content/uploads/2023/04/HAI_AI-Index-Report_2023.pdf

Nicholas, L., del Castillo. J. (2023) The EU Policy and Legislative Framework on Artificial Intelligence. Report. EPF European Patients Forum. https://www.eu-patient.eu/globalassets/report-ai-0812---del-castillo-and-nicholas.pdf

Paschen, J., Wilson, M., & Ferreira, J. J. (2020). Collaborative intelligence: How human and AI create value along the B2B sales funnel. Business Horizons, 63(3), 403-414.

Sydorenko, I. (2020). The Lifecycle of an AI Project in 2020: A Detailed Breakdown. Label Your Data. https://labelyourdata.com/articles/lifecycle-of-an-ai-project-stages-breakdown

Wadekar, S. (2019). Stages of Artificial Intelligence. Cloud x Lab. https://cloudxlab.com/blog/stages-of-artificial-intelligence/

The impact of issuing micro-credentials for a higher education institution

Estela Daukšienė[1], Rimantė Čepauskienė[2], Airina Volungevičienė[3], Giedrė Tamoliūnė[4], Elena Trepulė[5], Daiva Urmonienė[6]

[1] Education Academy, Vytautas Magnus University, Lithuania; estela.dauksiene@vdu.lt
[2] Education Academy, Vytautas Magnus University, Lithuania; rimante.cepauskiene@vdu.lt
[3] Education Academy, Vytautas Magnus University, Lithuania; airina.volungeviciene@vdu.lt
[4] Education Academy, Vytautas Magnus University, Lithuania; giedre.tamoliune@vdu.lt
[5] Education Academy, Vytautas Magnus University, Lithuania; elena.trepule@vdu.lt
[6] Education Academy, Vytautas Magnus University, Lithuania; daiva.urmoniene@vdu.lt

Correspondence: Estela Daukšienė: estela.dauksiene@vdu.lt

Abstract:

Higher education institutions lead in innovation application and test various technology-enhanced solutions to correspond to student and labour market needs, foster and analyse innovative scenarios, and their impact on teaching and learning processes. There is a limited number of shared good practices that discuss technologies used for the issuance of micro-credentials, and this paper aims to reveal the higher education practice of testing some virtual infrastructures for issuing micro-credentials for students attending non-formal university courses. This research experimented with and tested VLE Moodle and Europass EDC infrastructures to issue micro-credentials. It was found that both Moodle VLE and Europass EDC infrastructure can be used to issue micro-credentials. Europass EDC infrastructure is more end-user friendly, while Moodle collects data during the learning process and can automatically transfer results to the micro-credential. However, both virtual infrastructures have some drawbacks, which may be fixed in the future.

Keywords: micro-credentials, higher education, preparation and issuance process, case study, Moodle, Europass Digital Credentials

The European Approach to Micro-credentials

Micro-credentials are defined in various ways across research papers, "depending on who is using the term and in what context."(Brown & Nic-Giolla-Mhichil, 2022, p.940) The research reported in this paper followed the definition outlined in the EU Council Recommendations (2022, p.13), which defined micro-credentials as "the record of the learning outcomes that a learner has acquired following a small volume of learning." The latter document also indicated some of the most common features of a micro-credential that were also met in different scientific publications. These various characteristics of a micro-credential in higher education may refer to shorter learning opportunities, finalised with a badge, certificate, or digital credential (Commonwealth of Learning et al., 2019; Oliver, 2019), focused on the development of specific skills (European Commission, 2020a; Maina et al., 2022) and/or finalised with assessment or assessed against transparent standards (Council of the European Union, 2021; Oliver, 2019); owned by learners (Pirkkalainen et al., 2023), recognised by employers or academic institutions Tamoliune et al., 2023), creating possibilities for stackability of credits (European Union et al., 2020) to a broader qualification (Sargent et al., 2023).

Brown and Nic-Giolla-Mhichil's (2022) research showed that European institutions focused on micro-credentials due to mainly "increased flexibility for learning, the promotion of life-long learning and employability" (p.949). However, testing innovations using different technological solutions and triggering change was also among the most popular attractors. The research of Pirkkalainen et al. (2023) highlighted that technological aspects were ranked as one of the five significant enablers of micro-credentials, also underlining the need for connections between commercial employment platforms and European educational institutions. However, the research on technologies or platforms used to issue micro-credentials is limited.

Selvaratnam (2023) points out that virtual infrastructures bring more accuracy to the credentialing process. Most HEIs use virtual learning environments (further VLE) in the study process to deliver educational content, manage assessments, and track learner progress. In the context of micro-credentials, VLE plays a vital role in hosting the courses or modules, tracking learners' completion of required activities or assessments, and generating evidence of learning that can be used to issue micro-credentials. Some VLE platforms offer integrations with digital badging systems, allowing institutions to automatically issue badges to learners upon completion of specified criteria within the VLE environment; others seek the issuance of digital certificates, which may represent the reached learning outcomes but also come with this supporting metadata.

Though some research emphasises that courses finalised with micro-credentials may be a space for teacher pedagogical experimentations, not contradicting this idea, this research accentuates that teacher proper use of technologies in the teaching and learning process is of high importance to log evidence, represented in a micro-credential. Acknowledging the limited practices in HEIs to issue micro-credentials and the rapid development of technological solutions, the **paper aims** to reveal the higher education practice of testing some virtual infrastructures for issuing micro-credentials for students attending non-formal courses.

A case study of preparing and issuing micro-credentials

To reach the research aim, a higher education institution's virtual learning platform and European digital credential infrastructure were selected for the experimentation and issue of micro-credentials. The research was implemented in the frame of a nationally-funded research project and sought to describe the process of issuance of micro-credentials by higher education institutions. The institution researchers selected five online courses for non-formal students for this experimentation. As the research aims to reveal the practice of testing technological solutions, the discussion on pedagogical changes while adapting courses and their implementation are not described here.

Preparing to issue micro-credentials in SMART Moodle VLE

A digital micro-credentials issuing infrastructure must be selected and set up within the institution to issue micro-credentials. In the case of Vytautas Magnus University, the Moodle virtual learning environment (further SMART Moodle VLE) has been chosen because this platform is used in formal and non-formal university studies.

First, the chosen VLE was technically adapted for the digital micro-credential issuance process. The SMART Moodle VLE has been updated with additional data fields such as learning mode, format, duration, language, contact hours, and course/program duration in days, weeks, months, etc. A micro-credential template as a digital certificate has also been developed and added to the platform.

Second, the course developers and lecturers had to enter the course learning outcomes and additional details and set the activities for learner assessment. Each course in the SMART Moodle VLE was set to track learner progress and issue a digital certificate—a micro-credential after the successful course completion, finalised with the teacher-assessed tasks.

All students and lecturers created accounts in the SMART Moodle virtual learning environment for testing. The user profiles were checked to ensure they had filled in all the details, as they would be automatically transferred to the micro-credential. This step may be skipped if an institution's selected platform uses data from users from different systems. The selected SMART Moodle VLE was an infrastructure created for testing and was not a regular university VLE.

The preparation for the issuance of micro-credentials using VLE may be summarised in the following steps:

1. Add additional data fields that micro-credential requires.
2. Create the courses and fill in the additional course data fields.
3. Create the micro-credential template.
4. Add course learning outcomes, learning, teaching materials, and activities; enable progress monitoring; set up an assessment strategy; and set the conditions for the course's completion.

5. Update and finalise a micro-credential (adapted to the course) template, adjusting selections according to:

   - type of assessment selected;
   - learning outcomes layout revised;
   - checked the display of information.

The process of issuance of micro-credentials in VMU SMART Moodle

The testing of the courses that were prepared to be finalised with micro-credentials took place between March and May 2023. The test was carried out with 66 students of non-formal studies enrolled in one or two courses out of the five tested. The learning was organised in groups and supervised by the lecturers. One of the course topics had to be micro-credentials, as the information on micro-credentials was new to all students. Lecturers had to present what they are, their value for learners, and how to use the micro-credentials in the near future.

The learning process started in March, and the final assignments were due by the end of May. Micro-credentials were issued between May and June after students had successfully completed their course learning (e.g., by completing the required assignments or passing the final test). Fig. 1 illustrates the key activities to be carried out by the individuals involved in a micro-credential issuance process - the system administrator, the course tutor/curriculum developer/teacher, and the learner/student.

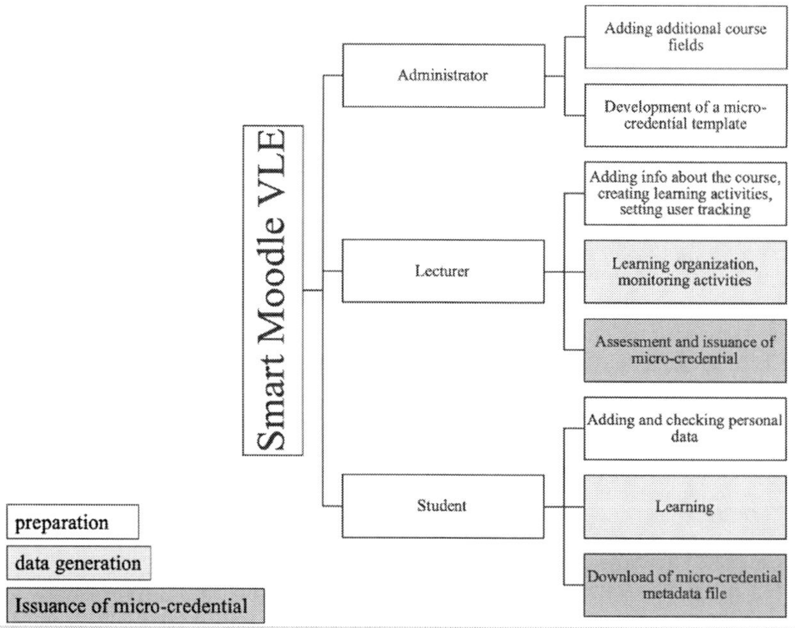

Figure 1: The participants and their main activities while preparing and issuing the digital micro-credentials in SMART Moodle VLE (created by authors)

Once the testing started, learners studied the materials of the chosen course, completed assignments or tests and monitored their progress. At the end of the learning process, learners who had successfully completed the courses were issued micro-credentials in the SMART Moodle environment. They received a digital certificate and a jason-type file, which included metadata generated by Moodle during the learning in the course. Micro-credentials were automatically generated for students according to the conditions set for successfully completing each course. Still, the learner had to download the micro-credential certificate and its data file manually.

Testing the digital micro-credentialing process resulted in 52 micro-credentials issued in the SMART Moodle VLE. During the testing of micro-credential issuance in SMART Moodle VLE, it was found that a micro-credential can be issued from the Moodle virtual learning environment. It collects and represents data from the learning process. However, the received result (a digital certificate as a micro-credential) is not (yet) compatible with other EU systems (which are constantly being updated), and the review of the issued micro-credential is rather complicated for the new user. Therefore, the institution also chose to test the issuance of micro-credentials through the Europass European Digital Credentials for Learning (hereafter Europass EDC) infrastructure.

Preparation and testing process of issuance of micro-credential in Europass EDC

The micro-credential issuance process in the Europass EDC infrastructure is broken down into three steps: (1) checking the functioning of the e-stamp, (2) entering the learning program descriptions, and (3) submitting the learner data. The first step is mandatory, while steps 2 and 3 are optional.

A qualified e-Seal is required to issue a micro-credential via the Europass EDC. It is a digital document security measure issued only to the institution's legal (or legally authorised) persons to certify digital documents' authenticity, validity, and integrity. What type of e-Seal, how to get it, and how to start using it is not described here as it is very country and institution-related. It is only worth mentioning that each country has its own trusted service providers, which list is available publicly.

To use the institution's e-Seal in the Europass EDC infrastructure, the open-source software NexU needs to be installed and run. This application allows you to check that the e-Seal is working correctly and that the settings have been appropriately selected.

As the data formats that can be automatically extracted from the Moodle environment are not currently available in the Europass EDC infrastructure, it has been chosen to test the issuance of micro-credentials as described in second step - by entering the information about the courses and the learners into Europass EDC. While SMART Moodle VLE is a learning environment, Europass EDC is an infrastructure for issuing digital micro-credentials rather than for the organisation of the learning process. Thus, the data generated in Moodle had to be manually entered into Europass EDC infrastructure.

This was a crucial but time-consuming step. The micro-credential template contains a number of elements that are entered separately for each course. If the course description includes the main information about the course (such as title, length, volume or learning, ECTS, learning outcomes, assignments, assessment strategy, etc.), this can be manually transferred from the course description; if not - information from the institution's VLE or other systems may be used. It is recommended that either a course teacher assists in entering this information in Europass EDC or provides coherent information (including the assessment strategy), indicating all necessary entries and the text supporting the achievements in the digital certificate to be received by the learner. The Europass EDC elements can be aggregated in several languages. It is recommended that micro-credentials be created by deciding which language the micro-credential will be issued and then adding another language if necessary.

During the testing of the micro-credential issuance process, the same courses and student data were used to issue micro-credentials. The same students received micro-credentials from the SMART Moodle VLE and the Europass EDC infrastructure. As this was the duplicating process, the researchers decided not to fill in all necessary entries from the learning process, limiting it only to the primary information (course title, student name, learning outcomes, and grades; ECTS, and the key assignments leading to course completion, also explaining their requirements and grading scales). It should be noted that the person who describes courses in Europass EDC infrastructure has to be present when entering learner data and sealing the micro-credentials, as the data is entered via individual login. The person authorised to e-seal micro-credentials can preview the information and data they are about to e-seal. Thus, internal institutional procedures should describe when micro-credentials may be issued, who is responsible for providing course information for whom what is to be reflected on the micro-credential, and who can e-seal the micro-credential.

Fig.2 shows the micro-credential, which was created, validated with e-Seal (sealed), and sent to the learner by email. The deposited micro-credential also means that a Europass account (where micro-credentials are temporarily deposited) was created and available until the learner chooses to move it elsewhere (see Figure 2). When the Europass EDC issues a micro-credential, an automatic account is created for each recipient, which remains active for a year unless the user starts using it.

When the micro-credential earner receives an email, some guidance information and links are provided next to the digital certificate displayed in the email. Following those links, the learner can view the issued credential with its metadata and create a Europass profile, where the received micro-credentials may be stored and shared with potential employers upon the need. Suppose a learner already has a Europass profile, and the micro-credential was issued using the same email indicated in the account. In that case, the micro-credential will be automatically added to their Europass profile. Suppose a learner already has a Europass profile, but the micro-credential was issued using a different email than the one associated with Europass. In that case, they may manually download the micro-credential and upload it to their profile. Issuing micro-credentials using Europass EDC creates the possibility for a learner to decide which achievements they want to share, with whom, and when.

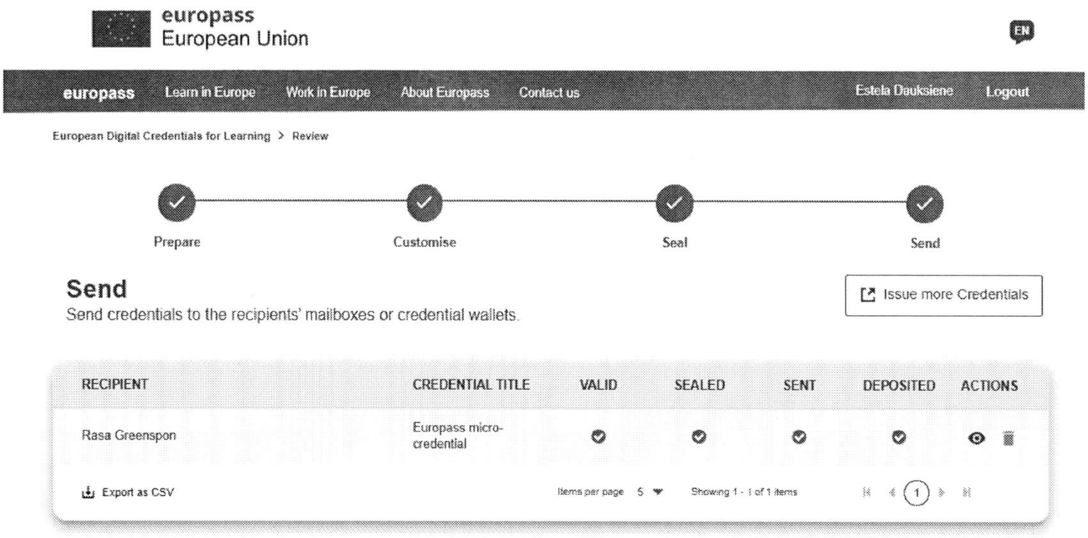

Figure 2: Successfully issued and sent to the learner micro-credential via Europass EDC.

The institution that issues micro-credentials using the Europass EDC infrastructure needs to have the registry, as the issued micro-credentials are not visible anywhere after they are sealed and sent to the earners.

Conclusions

Different educational providers, including higher education institutions, may issue micro-credentials. They provide evidence on the recorded learning outcomes of a learner who has successfully finished a small volume of learning. The research on different applications, impacts, and benefits of micro-credentials has increased in recent years. However, a limited number of shared good practices focus on virtual infrastructures and technologies used to issue micro-credentials, though the technological aspects were mentioned among the main drivers of micro-credentialing in different research.

This research reveals higher education institution's experimentation and testing of VLE Moodle and Europass EDC infrastructures to issue micro-credentials. It was found that although Moodle VLE collects more data during the learning process and can be used to issue micro-credentials, it has some drawbacks. First, the issued micro-credentials are not easily sharable and user-friendly as they lack compatibility with other systems. Second, they cannot be deleted from the platform they have been issued as their validity may not be checked later if the data was deleted. Micro-credential issuance using Europass EDC infrastructure is much more user-friendly for the learner or earner; however (at the moment of writing still), it requires lots of time of preparation for issuance - describing each course, assignment, achievement, etc., and this info cannot be transferable to other people's (who would like to take over the micro-credential issuance) Europass accounts. However, these challenges may be overcome with rapid technological developments and the hope for system compatibility and accessible data transferability.

Funding Information

The research was implemented during the project "Digital Micro-credentials in Higher Education," which received funding from the European Regional Development Fund (project No 13.1.1-LMT-K-718-05-0003) under a grant agreement with the Research Council of Lithuania (LMTLT). The project is funded as the European Union's response to the COVID-19 pandemic.

References

Brown, M., & Nic-Giolla-Mhichil, M. (2022). Unboxing micro-credentials: An inside, upside and downside view (Descifrando las microcredenciales: En qué consisten, ventajas e inconvenientes). Culture and Education, 34(4), 938–973. https://doi.org/10.1080/11356405.2022.2102293

Commonwealth of Learning, Rossiter, D., & Tynan, B. (2019). Designing & Implementing Micro-Credentials: A Guide for Practitioners (pp. 1–12). Commonwealth of Learning. https://oasis.col.org/server/api/core/bitstreams/770ff842-9a5e-424b-a253-0757fa539086/content

Council of the European Union. (2021). A European approach to micro-credentials: Brochure. https://education.ec.europa.eu/sites/default/files/2022-01/micro-credentials%20brochure%20updated.pdf

Council of the European Union. (2022). Proposal for a Council Recommendation on a European approach to micro-credentials for lifelong learning and employability (2021/0402(NLE), 9237/22; pp. 1–34). Council of the European Union. https://data.consilium.europa.eu/doc/document/ST-9237-2022-INIT/en/pdf

European Commission. (2020a). European Skills Agenda. Brussels: European Commission. https://ec.europa.eu/social/main.jsp?catId=1223&langId=en

European Union, Futures, H. S., Andersen, T., & Larsen, K. N. (2020). A European approach to micro-credentials: Output of the micro-credentials higher education consultation group: Final report (DOI: 10.2766/30863; pp. 1–36). Publications Office of the European Union. https://data.europa.eu/doi/10.2766/30863

Maina, M. F., Guàrdia Ortiz, L., Mancini, F., & Martinez Melo, M. (2022). A micro-credentialing methodology for improved recognition of HE employability skills. International Journal of Educational Technology in Higher Education, 19(1), 10. https://doi.org/10.1186/s41239-021-00315-5

McGreal, R., & Olcott, D. (2022). A strategic reset: Micro-credentials for higher education leaders. Smart Learning Environments, 9(1), 9. https://doi.org/10.1186/s40561-022-00190-1

Pirkkalainen, H., Sood, I., Padron Napoles, C., Kukkonen, A., & Camilleri, A. (2023). How might micro-credentials influence institutions and empower learners in higher education? Educational Research, 65(1), 40–63. https://doi.org/10.1080/00131881.2022.2157302

Sargent, J., Rienties, B., Leigh-Anne Perryman, & FitzGerald, E. (2023). Investigating the Views and Use of Stackable Microcredentials within a Postgraduate Certificate in Academic Practice. Journal of Interactive Media in Education. https://doi.org/10.5334/jime.805

Selvaratnam, R. (2023). Micro-credentialing Models and Practice. In M. D. Sankey, H. Huijser, & R. Fitzgerald (Eds.), Technology-Enhanced Learning and the Virtual University (pp. 451–464). Springer Nature Singapore. https://doi.org/10.1007/978-981-99-4170-4_23

Tamoliunė, G., Greenspon, R., Teresevičienė, M., Volungevičienė, A., Trepulė, E., & Daukšienė, E. (2023). Exploring the potential of micro-credentials: A systematic literature review. Frontiers in Education, 7. https://doi.org/10.3389/feduc.2022.1006811

Mini-Courses for Open Digital Competences for Educators

Diana Andone[1], Dimitra Vinatsella[2], Sofia Mougiakou[3], Demetrios Sampson[4], Sandra Kučina Softić[5], Tona Radobolja[6], Ana Zemljak Pećina[7], Vlad Mihaescu[8], Andrei Ternauciuc[9], Marc Gener Camins[10], Ester Tomàs Viñas[11], Anna Krassa[12]

[1] Politehnica University of Timisoara, Romania; diana.andone@upt.ro
[2] University of Piraeus, Greece; dvinatsella@gmail.com
[3] University of Piraeus, Greece; mougiakou@gmail.com
[4] University of Piraeus, Greece; sampson@unipi.gr
[5] University of Zagreb University Computing Centre, Croatia; sskucina@srce.hr
[6] University of Zagreb University Computing Centre, Croatia; Tona.Radobolja@srce.hr
[7] University of Zagreb University Computing Centre, Croatia; Tona.Radobolja@srce.hr
[8] Politehnica University of Timisoara, Romania; vlad.mihaescu@upt.ro
[9] Politehnica University of Timisoara, Romania; andrei.ternauciuc@upt.ro
[10] Department of Education, Generalitat de Catalunya, Catalonia, Spain; mgener2@xtec.cat
[11] Department of Education, Generalitat de Catalunya, Catalonia, Spain; etomas1@xtec.cat
[12] Moodle, Spain; anna@moodle.com

Correspondence: Diana Andone: diana.andone@upt.ro

Abstract:
The concept of Digital Competences for Educators is very important within European educational policies. Recent definitions of DigCompEdu are provided in a scientifically sound framework describing what it means for educators to be digitally competent DigCompEdu: European Framework for the Digital Competence of Educators and in the EU DEAP (Digital Education Action Plan 2021-2027 Resetting Education and Training for the Digital Age) defined in Sep 2020. This paper presents the results of the OpenDigCompEdu Erasmus+ project to accelerate the digital competences of educators in school education from Spain, Romania, Croatia, Greece and Norway towards the sustainable adoption of more online and blended approaches in education through the use of open educational technologies and open education principles. The paper presents the development of 5 micro-courses, all related to the development of digital education competences and to be offered online and in a blended format in Moodle Academy.

Keywords: Open Digital Competences, Moodle, school education, micro certificates

Introduction

Today, it is necessary to implement changes in the ways and methods of teaching and learning not only in the school education system, but at all levels of education. Digital technologies can enrich the learning experience, bring new and innovative teaching and learning opportunities, improve the quality of the educational process and better achieve learning outcomes (Williamson, 2016). A teacher is facing a great challenge, he/she is expected to be competent in using new technologies, to be able to apply them to the educational process and to introduce new teaching methods. They are expected, practically overnight, to have all the knowledge and competences needed to take on the new role of mentor, coordinator and facilitator of the educational process (Martin et al., 2021). Although many teachers have been using digital technologies to some extent before the pandemic the education model was dominantly classroom teaching. During the pandemic, teachers have moved to online teaching and learning overnight which did not enable them to prepare classes for an online environment but only to transfer classroom teaching to online (emergency remote teaching). During this time, teachers have gained significant experience in the use of digital technologies but, they are still insecure in their use (Softić et al., 2022). They lack an open course or education program that will give them the knowledge and tools but mainly the practices and support to become aware of which digital competencies they have and which they lack.

During the COVID-19 pandemic period, all the Ministries of Education have invested in enhancing the technical infrastructure of public schools both in terms of online teaching and learning management systems (such as Moodle) (Gaebel, M. et al., 2021). Within this context, the next step is to develop and provide online professional development initiatives that will target the further development of digital competences for educators, including school leaders, as well as the development of a flexible on-demand accreditation mechanism ideally based on micro-credentials and recognition of prior learning.

The OpenDigCompEdu project serves as a complementary activity to national initiatives providing the common European perspective to develop a European Digital Education Content Framework and a step forward in defining the criteria of a European Digital Skills Certificate (EDSC), both core priorities of EU DEAP 2020 (EU, 2020).

The concept of Digital Competences for Educators is critical within European educational policies. Recent definitions of DigCompEdu are provided in a scientifically sound framework describing what it means for educators to be digitally competent DigCompEdu: European Framework for the Digital Competence of Educators (Carretero Gomez et al., 2017) and in the EU DEAP (Digital Education Action Plan 2021-2027 Resetting Education and Training for the Digital Age, 2020) defined in Sep 2020. The JRC Science group have researched and published the Policy Approaches to Open Education, Case Studies from 28 EU States (OpenEdu Policies) (Inamorato et al., 2018) and the subsequent Policy recommendations on open education in Europe. Going open is a process for all involved: institutions, learners and teachers, as well as technological groups creating open education technologies (Open EdTech) (Brown, 2021). It depends on creating both digital and non-digital opportunities to make education more collaborative, transparent, and inclusive. Open education needs support from policies, technological development, and pedagogical approaches, via a multi-stakeholder approach, that can act systemically to create the change to further advance it in schools and create an "open education ecosystem" (Giovannella et al., 2015).

The shortage of digital skills in Europe reported in "European Digital Progress Report EDPR" (2019) of the European Commission: 45% of Europeans have insufficient or no digital skills. Based on the Digital Economy and Society Index (DESI) index of 2020, the countries partners in this project, Romania and Greece, are almost the last two with the lowest score on DESI, Croatia is in the lower half and Spain is just above the EU average score. The DigiTal education at School in Europe analyse Eurydice (2019), indicates that digital education in primary and secondary schools in Europe is at the lowest for the whole education system, even if the majority of European education policy makers have explicitly included learning outcomes related to all five digital competence areas and provision of continuing professional development (CPD) in the area of digital education. The further analysis realised by EC in the summer of 2020 in the consultation phase for the Digital Education Action Plan (DEAP) reveals that the intake of the digital competences for educators (DigCompEdu, 2017) is very low in the participating countries (except Norway) and especially in primary and secondary education.

For Spain, some of the main needs of the Department of Education of Catalonia in terms of improving the digital skills of teachers are: to provide mechanisms for searching on the multiple existing OERs, based on criteria such as curricular objectives, formats and teaching methodology; facilitate direct communication and collaboration between teachers with common interests, as well as direct communication of the institution with teachers; develop new tools for authoring educational resources in various formats, focusing on simplicity, usability and adequacy to educational objectives; create new training materials (courses) and improve the quality of existing ones, making more active use of video, mobile apps, interactive applications and new formats.

In recent years, the options for inclusion of open education principles and opportunities for more inclusion have increased, most notably through the advent of MOOCs and the use of OERs, Open Credentials and OEPs at all levels of education. A relevant example is open training materials for teachers developed in the EDUCRED project in Romania, dedicated to professors for schooling children ages 11-15, which will be taken into account, even if they are in Romanian. Many schools use digital equipment and strategies to open up their educational methodologies and to increase the digitalisation of education. But several of these resources and practices are either in English or in national languages and they are not validated or integrated outside of a small group of schools or communities of practice formed based on regions or subjects taught. We seek to address this need in this project and mainly with the results R1 and R2 of the project.

In Greece, improving digital skills is crucial in the face of digital transformation of the economy and society. In 2019, only 51% of Greeks aged 16-74 appeared to have at least basic digital skills, putting Greece well below the EU average (58%). At 1.8%, Greece has the lowest share of information and communications technology specialists in total employment in the EU (EU average: 3.9%). This is partly due to outward migration, as the share of graduates in this field is comparable to the EU average.

Croatian digital skills levels are low. In 2017, the percentage of 16-74-year-olds who have reported having basic or above-basic overall digital skills was the second lowest in the EU (41%, as compared with an EU average of 57%). The proportion of people regularly using the internet is among the lowest in the EU (73%, as compared with the EU average of 83%). The digital skills of young people aged 16-19 are slightly better than the EU average, but they dropped significantly between 2016 (70%) and 2017 (59%).

In Romania, although there is a national project on the training of teachers' digital skills, "Relevant curriculum, education open to all" (C.R.E.D.), aimed at training 55,000 teachers (by 2022) to use OERs and for the change of their teaching approach, there is a major shortage of digital skills professionals at the level of teachers in the pre-university education system. These skills are not just about using the computer in teaching, but about a certain type of teaching-learning strategy, the development of open educational resources, a certain attitude towards technology and so on.

OpenDigCompEdu project

This paper presents the partial results of the OpenDigCompEdu Erasmus+ project to accelerate the digital competences of educators in school education from Spain, Romania, Croatia, Greece and Norway towards the sustainable adoption of more online and blended approaches in education through the use of open educational technologies and open education principles. This is built on the momentum created by the pandemic which showed the importance of both digital competences and existing OERs and OEP (Rako & Softic, 2020) that can create this vision with the support of Open EdTech.

This comes as a necessary capacity at individual, organisational, and institutional levels to withstand emergencies like Covid19 and to enhance their digital readiness, resilience and capacity. Under this endeavour, the project will deepen the role of the digital transformation and the necessary adoption of innovative blended approaches, and target the development of key competences to the educators within the open education framework. The new OpenDigCompEdu educators will be open, digital enablers of change and innovation in their countries and regions with new profiles of educators that keep in front the digital content, technologies and practices and mix their in-field competencies with pedagogical values adopting open education.

The project was developed based on several goals and principles shared by all partners:

1. To enhance awareness of the need for a digital education ecosystem in European schools.
2. To devise and validate cross-country the profiles of digitally competent and confident educators within open education.
3. To enhance the uptake of open education, open education practices, resources and open digital tools for delivering competence-based teaching.

4. To create and validate an understanding of the sustainability in education through open education within the Framework for open and digital competences for educators.
5. To improve the achievement and recognition of digital competences for education through eportfolio and formal learning by introducing OpenDigCompEdu e-portfolio and OpenDigCompEdu MOOC courses for educators.
6. To introduce microcredentials and open badges in open digital competences for school education in the partner countries.
7. To enhance collaboration between educators, learners, school leaders, school institutions with education providers, universities, and companies developing open digital tools.

Addressing digital transformation through the development of digital readiness, resilience and capacity: At the core of OpenDigCompEdu stays the aim to support the digital transformation of school educators and school institutions. All of our project objectives support this, but mainly we plan to increase the shift towards an inclusive, sustainable and integrated within the education community, digital education with the uptake of open education, open education practices, resources and open digital tools.

Open education, open educational technologies, open educational resources, open education principles are here for almost two decades but are mainly used sporadically, by digital innovators or by higher education and have not emerged in mainstream school education. But in the last year, open education has proved its impact. Romania, Croatia, Greece and Spain's educational system have just realised the importance of these educational principles and the value of using open tools for a more efficient and cost-effective delivery of mainstream education.

This project focuses on using an innovative learning method in creating 5 courses on emergent topics (Open Digital Education Ecosystem, Learn Moodle Basics, Teaching with Open Digital Tools, New Assessment Models, OpenEdTech for Sustainability, Diversity & Inclusion, Climate Change in Education), structured in 3 learning paths dedicated to teachers, instructional designers and school leaders and administrators, and validate all of them as a micro-credential. The project also addresses the validation of the DigCompEdu through open education.

Guiding this project are the core beliefs of the DigCompEdu that the focus is not on technical skills. Instead, the Conceptual Framework, e-portfolio, courses aim to identify methods, models and training on how open digital technologies can be used to enhance and innovate education in schools. We used the Digital Competence Framework for Educators (DigCompEdu) grid, SELFIE and self-assessment tool as a starting point. We will not try to redefine SELFIE or the SELFIE methods for institutions and teachers, but we will try to enrich those from the open education and open educational technologies perspective. Education in 2020 has proven how important are these competences in modern education and those educators who had, even a minimum of digital skills have supported better their learners and institutions that have invested in digital interfaces before the pandemic times, have managed to provide a good and quality education and keep their learn engaged.

Significant results for OpenDigCompEdu:

1. Conceptual Framework for the application of digital competences for educators
2. Open digital skills Syllabus of 6 courses - Learn Moodle Basics, Teaching with Open Digital Tools, New Assessment Models, Open Digital Education Eco-system, Diversity & Inclusion in Education, Climate Change in Education
3. OpenEduComp training program Open Digital competences for Educators - 6 courses
4. Regional Capacity building and formation for school educators
5. Open Digital competences for Educators Micro-credentials

Courses Development

To validate this, the partners have developed 5 courses using the framework of the Moodle ABCtoLD method. ABC Learning Design (Young & Perović, 2016) is an engaging, fast workshop to help teaching teams co-develop module and programme designs for blended and online learning (Young & Perović, 2016). Individuals and teams can use the following six learning types to identify opportunities for online active learning and help prioritise changes and have been used and implemented in online course development, tested by several universities worldwide (Andone et al., 2020). The courses of Open Digital Education Ecosystem, Learn Moodle Basics, Teaching with Open Digital Tools, Assessment in Online Environment, OpenEdTech for Sustainability, Diversity & Inclusion and Climate Change in Education are small, online, multimedia-rich courses developed with study cases from all partners, interactive online activities and using existing OERs.

The partners have developed, validated and tested the first version of the design guidelines for Open Digital Competences. The Online ABC Learning Design was adapted, modelled to fit the target group's needs and successfully implemented this year by all partners. All partners took part in Co-Create Courses with ABC Learning Design webinars and several guides were developed on adapting the structure. Results achieved: ABC Learning Design templates, Guidelines - ABC learning types and Moodle, Moodle Academy - Template - ABC learning design planner, Template - ABC Learning Design Storyboard, Moodle Academy Course Builder, and Co-Create Courses with ABC Learning Design course in Moodle Academy, available to all.

The partners developed jointly the curricula and syllabus and agreed on the following structure and topics:

6 courses on the following topics, 1 course = 1 ECTS, i.e. 25 hours of learners' workload:

- Learn Moodle Basics (Moodle for School Teachers, Moodle ABC LD) lead Moodle
- Teaching with Open Digital tools (Tools for instructional models, Delivery of virtual classrooms, Development of digital open educational resources) lead UPT, Romania
- Assessment in Online Environment (Assess your Learners, Exploring Glossaries, Assignments, Forums Creating Quality Quiz Questions) lead SRCE, Croatia
- Open Digital Education Eco-system (Opening Up Education, Open Licenses, Open Content (Open Educational Resources), Open Technology, Open Data in Education, Introduction to Moodle.Net) lead UNIPI, Greece
- Diversity & Inclusion in Education (Include your Learners, Engage your Learners, Support your Learners, Accessibility) lead ISJ Timis, Romania
- Climate Change in Education (Environment topics course, Sustainability, circular economy, principles of renewable energy, green with examples and ideas) lead GENCAT, Spain

The curricula and syllabus were published online on a template, evaluated during Open Education Week Workshops in 2023 by school teachers.

The development of the educational materials, module by module, following Online ABC Learning Design was run by each partner with the technical support of the Moodle team. Some of the deadlines for materials development and video recordings were changed and adapted during the year, as instead of March 2023 for development of courses in English, following the Course Development template, was achieved by June 2023. At this moment all courses are integrated into Moodle Academy's online platform (Moodle, 2024), the registration process and format agreed upon between partners and courses are prepared for piloting in English.

The courses are integrated into Moodle Academy, and they are created following the European microcredential principles, to be independent, stackable and certify and validate the school educators' digital competences. The courses are now developed in English and enter the pilot phase for the content evaluation, the course framework and their delivery in Moodle Academy. Further results of the evaluation performed in 5 countries will be presented.

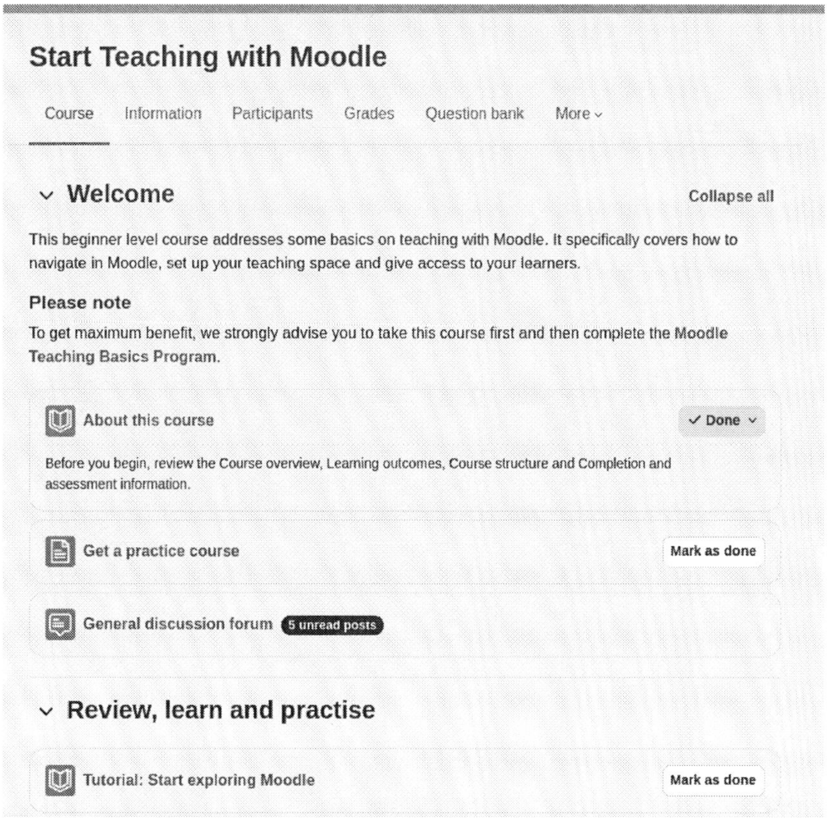

Figure 1: Caption from Moodle Academy of the Start Teaching with Moodle module, part of the Learn Moodle Basics course.

Courses Development in Greece

To validate the field of Open Education, the Greek partner University of Piraeus has developed the course "Open Digital Education Eco-system", presenting the Fundamentals of the Open Digital Education Eco-system in the school context and how the rapidly evolving field of open education can become a key success factor for teaching and learning. It aims to support the development of core competences for harnessing the power of and making best use of open education policies and practices.

The course consists of 6 Modules. The first module is called Opening Up Education and presents the main dimensions of open education. The second module refers to Open Licenses and their principles. The third is about Open Content and Open Educational Resources (OERs). Module number 4 discusses the basics of Open Technology. The 5th Module introduces the concept of Open Data and how to achieve impact in teaching, learning and assessment. It also discusses issues related to key Ethical Principles. The last module, National Content, presents existing national initiatives and case studies.

Each module includes Pre-check and Post-Check Multiple Choice Questions at the beginning and the end of each module. It also includes Quick check MCQs at the end of the topics/subtopics of each module, as well as Task Activities and a Checklist (of Statements) at the end of each module.

The course includes 16 originally produced graphics and 11 original videos, as well as 40 existing graphics and 25 existing videos. There are 22 pre-check MCQs, 135 quick check MCQs, and 60 post-checks. It also includes 33 task activities and 39 checklist statements.

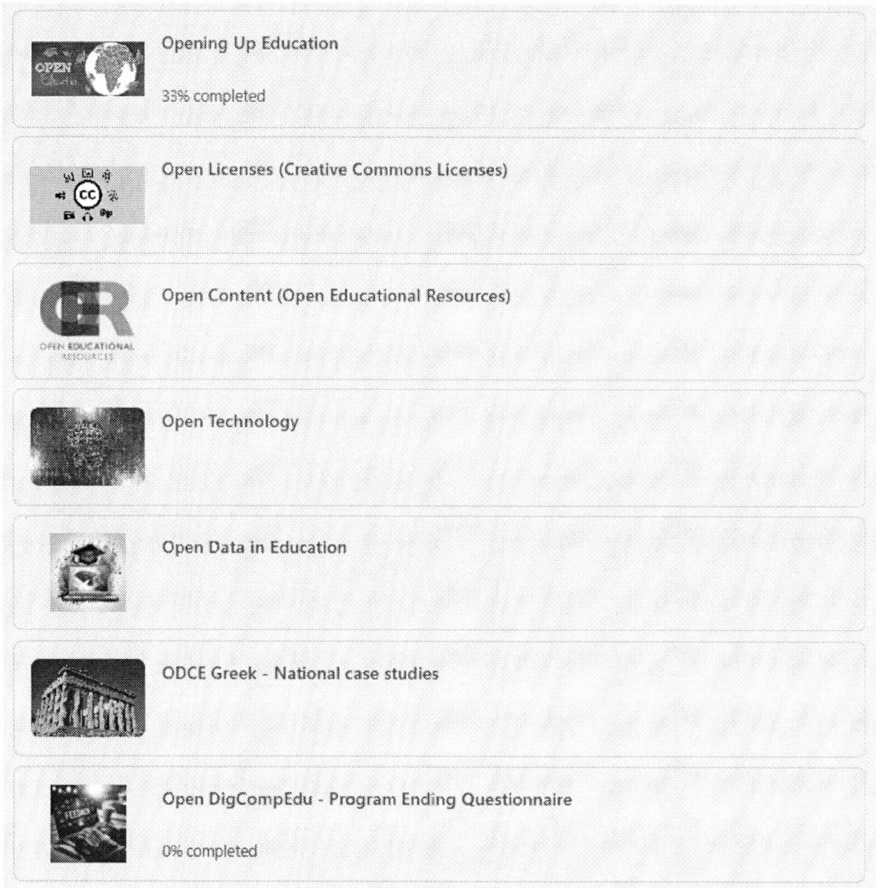

Figure 2: Overview of the main page of the Open Digital Education Eco-system course in MOODLE ACADEMY, consisting of the 6 Courses and the Program Ending Questionnaire.

Upon completing each module, learners earn the **OpenDigCompEdu/Moodle Academy badge** for the specific module.

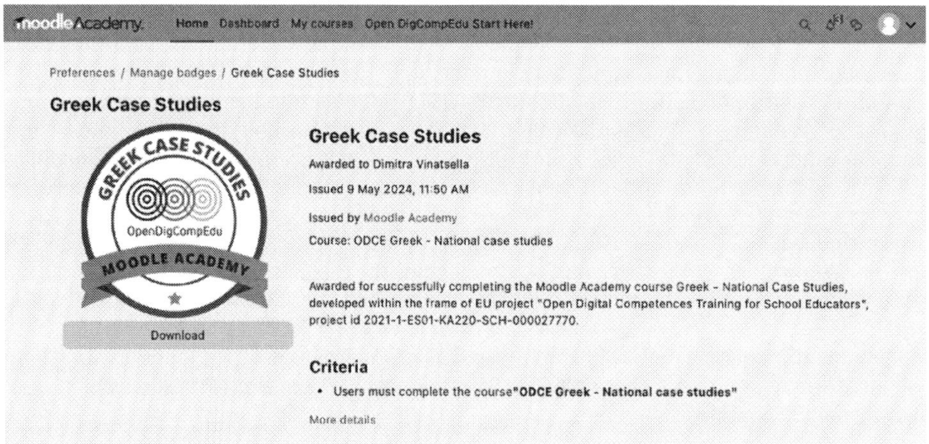

Figure 3: Example of an OpenDigCompEdu/Moodle Academy Badge

After completing all six modules and submitting the Program Ending Questionnaire a Certificate of Completion is automatically generated. The certificate includes a link and a QR Code to verify its validity in Moodle Academy.

Figure 4: ODCE 4 - Open Digital Education Ecosystem Certificate of Completion

Courses Development in Croatia

To validate assessment models, the University Computing Centre designed a course titled "Assessment in Online Environment". The aim was to provide participants with information and knowledge about which possibilities in Moodle they can use for formative and summative assessment in an online environment. The course provides many guidelines about the use of assessment activities as well as practical examples of use. The Interactive Gradebook Guide in Moodle will be very interesting to participants as they can download to their computer and use it whenever they need to. Interactive Guide enables them to use it whenever they need some information on score/grade usage in Moodle, and as it is interactive it enables them to open only the descriptions they want or to open it all and print it. The Guide also consists as well of examples of grading and the use of IF conditions in calculating grades.

The course consists of the following modules: Assess Your Learner, Assessment: Exploring Forums, Assessment: Exploring Assignments, Creating Quality Quiz Questions, Exploring Quizzes, Exploring Lessons, Exploring Workshop and Formative and Summative Assessment. At the beginning of the course, participants have a course pre-check to see what they know about assessment already respectively to self-evaluate their knowledge and to be able to see where to focus in the course or to better understand their perception on the possibilities of online assessment. Another quiz is at the end of the course to help participants to consolidate everything they learnt. They can take the quiz as often as they like, but they must achieve a minimum 80% pass grade. Upon completion of the quiz, they will receive a Moodle Academy badge.

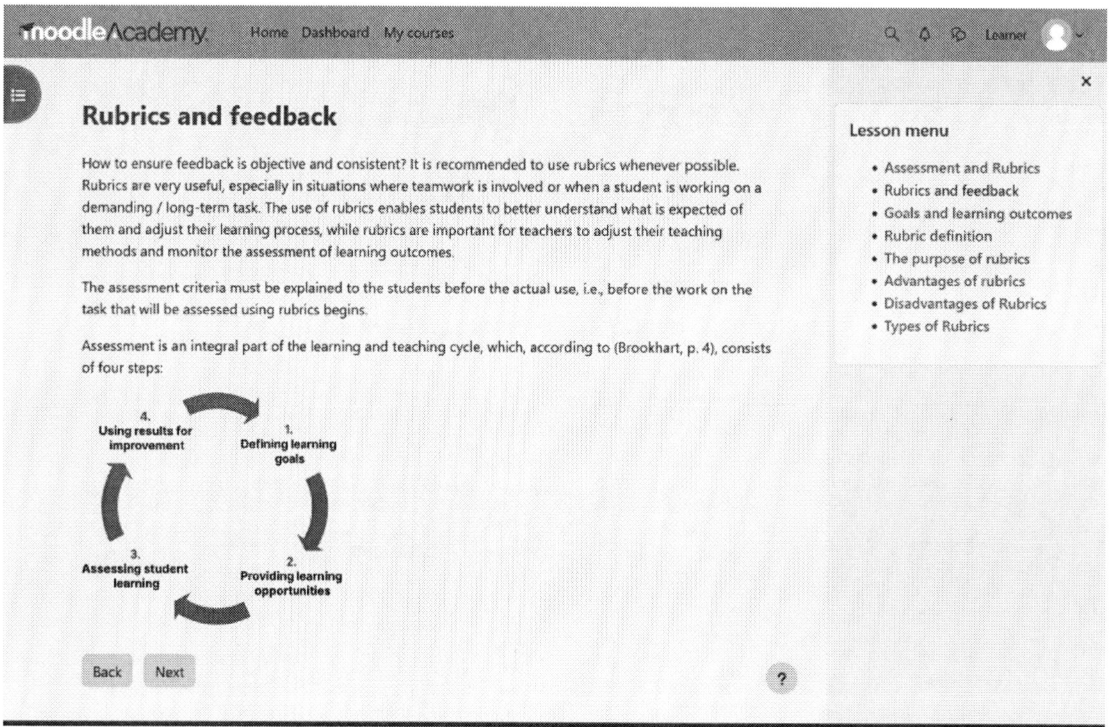

Figure 5: Caption from Moodle Academy on one of the modules in the course Assessment in Online Environment

Courses Development in Romania

To validate this, the Romanian partners Politehnica University of Timisoara and Timis County School Inspectorate have developed 2 courses - Teaching with Open Digital Tools, and the course OpenEdTech for Sustainability, Diversity & Inclusion.

We divided the Teaching with Open Digital Tools course in different sections, each of them ending with a quiz to test knowledge on the covered topics. In Introduction to Open Digital Tools we will explore open digital tools and their significance in education. We begin by defining open digital tools and then delve into open-source software (OSS). Examples of active OSS communities, such as GitHub and the Moodle Community, will be highlighted to illustrate the collaborative nature of these tools.

In Open Digital Tools for Teaching Systems, we focus on digital tools designed for teaching systems, particularly learning management systems (LMS). We will examine various LMS platforms, starting with Moodle, its functionalities, and the Moodle community. Other platforms such as Sakai, Atutor, Ilia, and Linux-based RedHat will receive brief mentions. Additionally, we will explore Blackboard, Google Classroom, and OpenEdX. The concept of Massive Open Online Courses (MOOCs) and the role of Open Educational Resources (OER) and OER Commons in education will also be discussed.

The section Open Digital Tools for Teaching Communication addresses digital tools that facilitate teaching communication. We will cover video conferencing and virtual classroom solutions such as Big Blue Button and Edumeet. The communication tools within Moodle, including Forum, Chat, Message, and Blog, will be discussed in detail. Other tools like Jupyter Notebook, Microsoft Whiteboard, Skype, Webex, Zoom, and Teams will be briefly mentioned. Strategies to engage learners using these tools will be provided.

Finally, in the section Open Digital Tools for Teaching Creation, we explore tools for creating educational content. We will discuss the principles of creating OERs and introduce interactive tools like H5P. Various office tools, including LibreOffice and Microsoft Forms, will be covered. Blogging platforms such as WordPress and collaborative tools within Moodle, like Choice and Wiki, will be discussed. We will also explore graphic design tools like GIMP, presentation tools like Prezi, and multimedia tools for audio and video creation, including Audacity, Openshot, OBS, and VLC media player. Evaluation tools like Kahoot and media management platforms like Kaltura will be examined. Ideas for engaging learners through content creation will be shared.

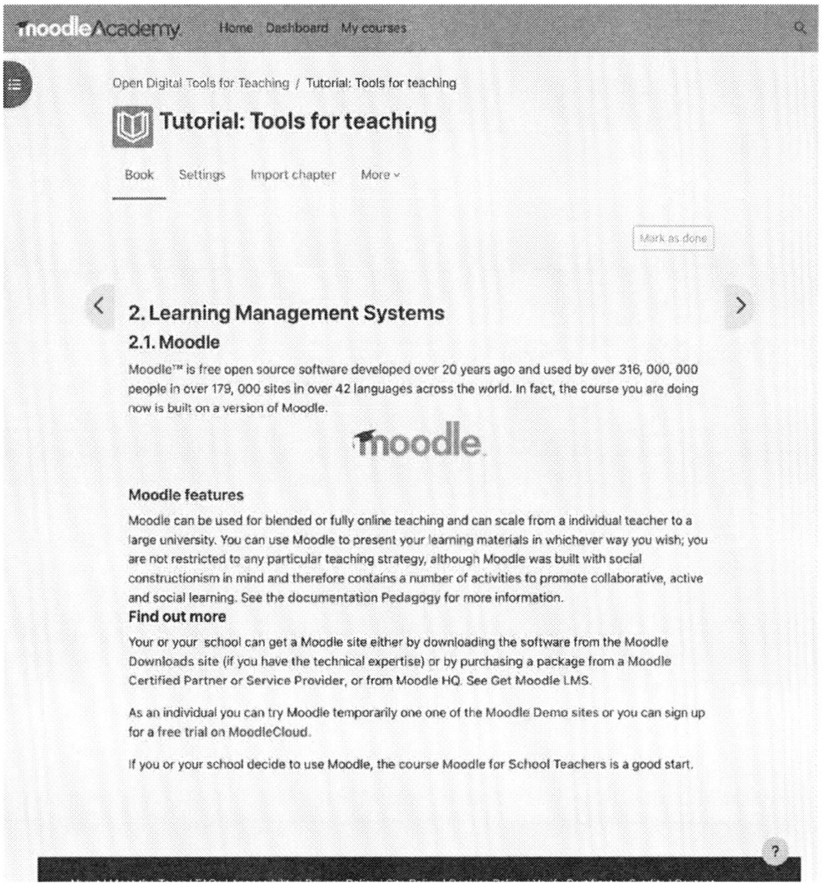

Figure 6: Caption from Moodle Academy on one of the modules in the course Teaching with Open Digital Tools

The course has been designed following the principles of ABC Learning Design. This is an engaging, fast workshop to help teaching teams co-develop module and programme designs for blended and online learning. Individuals and teams can use the following six learning types to identify opportunities for online active learning and help prioritise changes. The method divides learning tools in 6 categories of learning types: Acquisition, Collaboration, Discussion, Investigation, Practice and Production.

Some of the OERs used in this course have been created in other European projects: Acadigia[1] (analysed in detail by Ternauciuc et al, 2022), DigiCulture[2] (analysed in detail in several publications such as Andone et al 2020 and 2022) and ABC2VLE[3] (analysed in detail in Andone et al, 2020).

Courses Development in Spain

To validate this, the GENCAT partner has developed the course "Climate Change in Education". This course aims to provide teachers with the tools, knowledge, and digital skills necessary to effectively teach climate change in the classroom and help students understand the importance of this issue and the role they can play in addressing it.

[1] https://acadigia.eu/
[2] https://digiculture.eu/en/
[3] https://abc-ld.org/abctovle/abc-to-vle-partners/

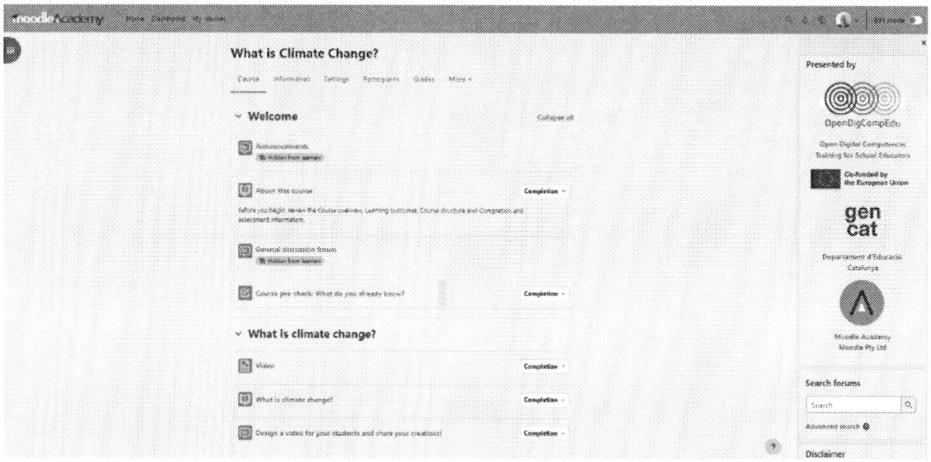

Figure 7: Caption from Moodle Academy on one of the modules in the course Climate Change in Education

It consists of five modules:

- Welcome and prior knowledge. Climate change is a topic that has gained significant attention in recent years and is now widely recognised as one of the most pressing issues facing the world today.
- What is Climate Change? It is essential that we educate future generations about the causes and impacts of climate change, and what they can do to help mitigate its effects.
- How can we educate about Climate Change? As educators, it is important to teach our students about possible actions and empower them to make a positive impact.
- School activities against Climate Change. We have a responsibility to prepare our students to understand and address the challenges of climate change.
- Evaluation of knowledge about Climate Change. More and more people are becoming aware of the issue and are taking action to reduce their carbon footprint.

Several Open Educational Resources (OER) will be provided throughout the course to support your learning, such as Impact Lab and Clic Zone.

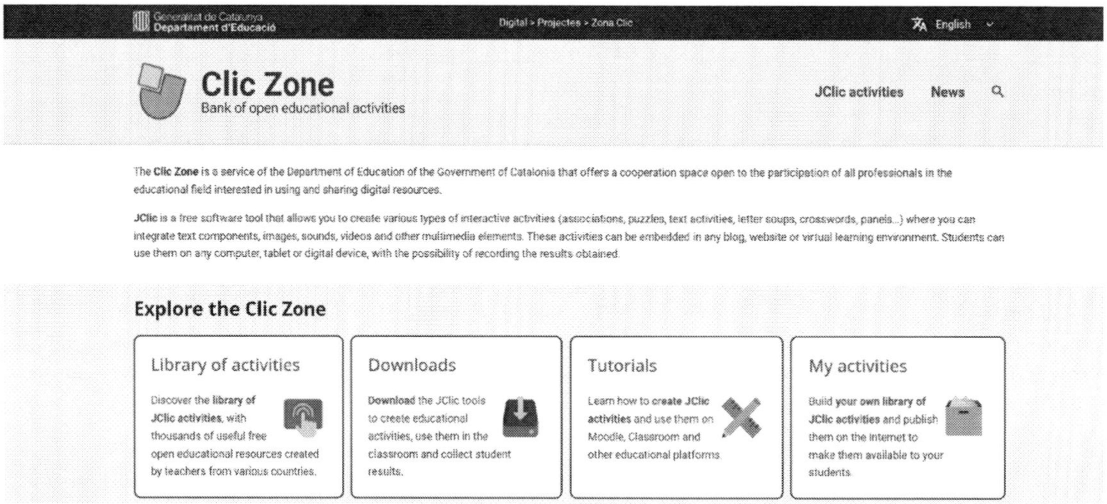

Figure 8: Caption from Moodle Academy on one of the modules in the course Climate Change in Education

Conclusions

As an Erasmus+ project, OpenDigCompEdu aligns with the open access requirement for project materials, and it was achieved through:

Online platforms - the project uses the Moodle Academy (moodle.academy), a learning centre for the global Moodle community. The training program developed by the project, based on the DigCompEdu framework, is available on this platform for free access for educators worldwide.

Project website - the OpenDigCompEdu project created a dedicated project website (https://opedigcompedu.eu) where project information, resources and deliverables are available to everyone. This ensures open access to project-related materials.

OERs - the project developed several OERs to support educators in enhancing their digital competences and will be developed, all will be freely available to the public, at the end of the project.

The project's five courses are now piloted, and further results will be presented in future publications.

Acknowledgements

The "Open Digital Competencies Training for School Educators" Erasmus+ Strategic Partnership project (2021-1-ES01-KA220-SCH-000027770) has been co-funded with support from the European Commission.

References

Andone, D., Mihaescu, V., & Vasiu, R. (2020). ABCTOVLE - ABC-LD Course Design Experiences for Blended and Online Education. 3, 142–149. https://doi.org/10.12753/2066-026X-20-188

Andone, D., Ternauciuc, A, Vasiu, R., Vlad Mihaescu, Silviu Vert, "Digiculture – The Development of Open Education Learning for Digital Skills Training", European Distance and E-Learning Network (EDEN) Proceedings, 22-24 June 2020, Timisoara, Romania, pp. 354-363, ISSN 2707-2819, DOI: 10.38069/edenconf-2020-ac0033

Andone, V. Mihaescu, A. Ternauciuc, S. Vert, R. Vasiu and M. Mocofan, "DigiCulture – courses for enhancing digital competences," 2021 IEEE Global Engineering Education Conference (EDUCON), 21-23 April 2021, Vienna Austria, pp. 1056-1060, doi: 10.1109/EDUCON46332.2021.9453911, WOS:000689064100157, ISBN 978-1-7281-8478-4, ISSN 2165-9567

ANDONE, D., MIHAESCU, V. and VASIU, R., 2020. ABCTOVLE-ABC-LD COURSE DESIGN EXPERIENCES FOR BLENDED AND ONLINE EDUCATION. eLearning & Software for Education, 3.

Brown, M. (2021). What are the Main Trends in Online Learning? A Helicopter View of Possible Futures. Asian Journal of Distance Education, 16(2), Article 2. http://www.asianjde.com/ojs/index.php/AsianJDE/article/view/605

Carretero Gomez, S., Vuorikari, R., & Punie, Y. (2017). DigComp 2.1: The Digital Competence Framework for Citizens with eight proficiency levels and examples of use (JRC106281) [EUR - Scientific and Technical Research Reports]. Publications Office of the European Union. https://doi.org/10.2760/38842 (online)

Digital Education Action Plan 2021-2027 Resetting education and training for the digital age, (2020) (testimony of European Commission). https://eur-lex.europa.eu/legal-content/EN/TXT/?uri=CELEX:52020DC0624

Gaebel, Michael, Zhang, Therese, Stoeber, H., & Morrisroe, A. (2021). Digitally enhanced learning and teaching in European higher education institutions (p. 68). European University Association. https://eua.eu/downloads/publications/digi-he%20survey%20report.pdf

Giovannella, C., Andone, D., Dascalu, M., Popescu, E., Rehm, M., & Roccasalva, G. (2015). Smartness of Learning Ecosystems and its bottom-up emergence in six European Campuses. IxD&A, 27, 79–92.

Inamorato, D. S. A., Nascimbeni, F., Bacsich, P., Atenas, J., Aceto, S., Burgos, D., & Punie, Y. (2018, January 4). Policy Approaches to Open Education—Case Studies from 28 EU Member States (OpenEdu Policies). JRC Publications Repository. https://doi.org/10.2760/283135

Martin, F., Kumar, S., & She, L. (2021). Examining Higher Education Instructor Perceptions of Roles and Competencies in Online Teaching. Online Learning, 25(4), 267–295. https://eric.ed.gov/?id=EJ1334524

Punie, Y., editor(s), Redecker, C., European Framework for the Digital Competence of Educators: DigCompEdu, EUR 28775 EN, Publications Office of the European Union, Luxembourg, 2017, ISBN 978-92-79-73718-3 (print),978-92-79-73494-6 (pdf), doi:10.2760/178382 (print),10.2760/159770 (online), JRC107466

Rako, S., & Softic, S. K. (2020). DEVELOPMENT AND USAGE OF OPEN EDUCATIONAL RESOURCES AMONG TEACHERS. EDULEARN20 Proceedings, 3849–3854. https://doi.org/10.21125/edulearn.2020.1053

Softić, S. K., Lasić-Lazić, J., & Tropša, V. (2022). THE EFFECT OF PANDEMIC ON THE TEACHERS' PERCEPTION OF TEACHING AND LEARNING IN ONLINE ENVIRONMENT. EDULEARN22 Proceedings, 8531–8537. https://doi.org/10.21125/edulearn.2022.2028

Ternauciuc, A., Andone, D., Wall, P. J., Araujo, M. S., & Arnaldo, R. M. (2022). ANALYSING DIGITAL TOOLS FOR TECHNICAL UNIVERSITIES. Towards Smart and Inclusive Learning Ecosystem, 7.

Williamson, B. (2016). Digital education governance: An introduction. European Educational Research Journal, 15(1), 3–13. https://doi.org/10.1177/1474904115616630

Young, C., & Perović, N. (2016). Rapid and Creative Course Design: As Easy as ABC? Procedia - Social and Behavioral Sciences, 228, 390–395. https://doi.org/10.1016/j.sbspro.2016.07.058

Revolutionising classrooms with AI: Educators' insights on transformative opportunities and challenges

Geesje van den Berg[1]

[1]Department of Curriculum and Instructional Studies, University of South Africa, South Africa; vdberg@unisa.ac.za

Correspondence: Geesje van den Berg: vdberg@unisa.ac.za

Abstract:

This paper examines the transformation opportunities of AI in education, focusing on its benefits and challenges from the perspectives of educators. The research methodology involves a qualitative study with practising educators who were students enrolled in a master's program in education at an open distance education university in South Africa. Data collection is conducted through an online discussion forum. The paper concludes that while AI offers exciting transformative opportunities such as personalised learning and effective education, it should be used wisely, complementing traditional teaching methods. It emphasises addressing biases, overuse, plagiarism, and data privacy issues. The study emphasises the need for more information on educator's use and perceptions to pave the way for AI to complement educators and, in so doing, benefit all educators and students equally.

Keywords: generative AI; benefits; challenges; education; transformation.

Introduction

Artificial intelligence (AI) refers to advanced computing systems that process the ability to perform tasks traditionally requiring human intelligence. These systems can learn, adapt, correct, synthesise and use large amounts of text to carry out complex tasks. The progress of AI has resulted in various advancements and innovations that education has greatly benefited from, as it serves as a crucial element of both societal growth and individual development. Integrating AI in education transforms how students learn, educators teach, and institutions function. It revolutionises the educational landscape by personalising learning experiences, delivering real-time personal feedback, bridging gaps, and encouraging a more inclusive and effective learning environment (Kamalov et al., 2023). AI has the ability to personalise learning through algorithms that dynamically adapt to individual students' needs.

The recent release of several generative AI models, such as ChatGPT, Pilot, and Bard, has marked a turning point in people's perceptions of AI. With the arrival of ChatGPT, everyone has become aware of the legitimacy and viability of AI. ChatGPT, which is the main tool used in the context of this research, is designed to be highly intelligent, intuitive, and capable of responding to complex requests in a human-like manner (OpenAI, 2024). It is changing how we interact with technology and paving the way for a new era of intelligent conversational AI (Bozkurt, 2023; Ray, 2023). This cutting-edge artificial intelligence chatbot uses deep learning techniques and has been trained on many online texts (Kung et al., 2023; OpenAI, 2024). However, as Baidoo-Anu and Owusu Ansah (2023) argue, the use of ChatGPT in education is substantial but should not be seen as a replacement for human educators. Although much has been written on the benefits and challenges ChatGPT may hold for education, most of the research involves literature reviews (e.g. Bozkurt, 2023; Grassini, 2023; Baidoo-Anu & Ansah, 2023), and not much empirical research on how educators see and use these tools has been published. Therefore, this paper reflects on GenAI in education from the perspectives of those at its heart – the educators. It not only presents their perspectives on the diverse benefits and challenges of GenAI but emphasises the necessity for a balanced, ethical, and informed approach to harnessing generativeAI's capabilities. The aim is to pave the way for GenAI to complement educators and, in so doing, benefit all educators and students equally

Literature review

Benefits of AI in education

One of the main benefits is that AI tools can analyse individual student performance and adapt learning materials to meet the unique needs of each student. This personalised approach helps students learn independently, addressing their strengths and weaknesses. Personalised learning systems have shown potential to improve teaching and learning (Akgun & Greenhow, 2022). Additionally, the provision of lesson content is a crucial aspect of education, and AI can play an important role in improving and supporting this process. AI systems can help create educational content, including lesson plans, presentations, and learning materials that benefit educators (Van den Berg & Du Plessis, 2023). Furthermore, AI applications can assist students in language learning by providing speech recognition, language translation, and grammar correction (McCombs & Valenzuela, 2020). Furthermore, AI can actively involve students and educators in learning through interactive learning platforms powered by AI to engage students in dynamic and stimulating educational experiences (Tlili et al., 2023). AI can provide instant personalised feedback on student responses helping them understand concepts more effectively and correcting misunderstandings promptly. What also comes as an added advantage is that AI saves educators time by automating routine tasks and improves the accessibility of knowledge and information for a diverse and global student population (Bozkurt, 2023). However, along with the unexpected benefits, there are also challenges that cannot be overlooked.

Challenges of AI in education

Several challenges need to be acknowledged, such as the risks of academic misconduct, bias, the dissemination of false information, and inadequate assessment design, which can hinder the development of essential graduate skills and promote superficial learning (Ray, 2023; Sullivan et al., 2023). Additional challenges and complexity include the risk of cheating and plagiarism, the ethical and social implications of using AI, and the need to adapt curriculum and assessment methods to the new technology (Tlili et al., 2023). Furthermore, human touch and empathy may be lacking in purely automated interaction systems as AI lacks emotional intelligence, making it difficult to understand or respond appropriately to human emotions (Bozkurt, 2023).

Methodology

An interpretative paradigm was adopted to understand the participants' perspectives and interpret the meaning they derived from their contexts (Kivunja & Kuyini, 2017). Participants had a unique context, as all of them were educators who were actively teaching while simultaneously pursuing a structured Master of Education program at an open distance learning university in South Africa. This unique combination of roles called for an exploratory case study design involving an examination of various viewpoints within a specific context (Yin, 2009) and provided a foundation for further research.

The research instrument was an online discussion forum for one of the four taught modules of a structured master programme. The forum was hosted on the university's learning management system, providing an interactive space for students to engage in academic discourse and exchange ideas with the lecturer and fellow students. Students had to participate in a discussion forum after every two study units. Four questions were posted, specifically designed to test their understanding and application of the knowledge and theory learnt in the study units. The students' year mark was influenced by participation, which had certain guidelines to follow. The discussion forum was set up to hide other students' posts until the first response was received.

As part of a study unit on artificial intelligence in education, students had to answer the following two questions were posted:

1. Do you use generative artificial intelligence tools in your teaching/training?
2. Share the most important benefits and challenges of using AI tools in your context.

Data analysis was done using a thematic approach (Braun & Clarke, 2012). Research ethics is a crucial aspect of any research study as it protects the rights and interests of all involved in the research process. In this research study, ethical clearance and permission were obtained from the institution where the study was conducted. Additionally, all participants gave their consent to use their data. Trustworthiness in qualitative research relates to a set of principles that ensure quality, underpinning both rigour in the research process and confidence in the findings (Lincoln & Guba, 1985). To ensure trustworthiness, this study considered measures of credibility, transferability, dependability, and confirmability, as described by Lincoln and Guba (1985).

Findings and discussion

Context and participant information

All participants were registered in a structured master's in education programme. The module used for this research was about technology integration in open-distance learning. Fourteen students were enrolled in this module; however, one student did not participate in this discussion. Also, three students indicated that they did not use AI. Their responses were excluded as the research focussed on participants who actively used AI tools for teaching.

Participants were not made aware of the study until after their discussions to avoid influencing their responses. Because of the group's diversity, it was ideal for indicating how educators on different levels use AI in their teaching. Interestingly, there was no significant difference between the different levels or genders.

Table 1: Participant information

Participants	**Gender**	**Teaching role**
E1	F	Primary school teacher
E2	F	Lecturer in public higher education
E3	F	Primary school teacher
E4	M	Lecturer in public higher education
E5	M	Trainer in the public sector
E6	M	Lecturer in the technical and vocational education and training sector
E7	F	Lecturer in private higher education
E8	F	Lecturer in private higher education
E9	F	Lecturer in public higher education
E10	F	Lecturer in public higher education

Themes and sub-themes

From the findings, themes and subthemes emerged, as indicated below.

Table 2: Themes and sub-themes

Themes	**Sub-themes**
Benefits	Individualised, 24/7 guidance and support Provision of lesson content Simplification of language Active involvement Immediate feedback Time-saving Accessibility of knowledge and information
Challenges	Bias Decrease in human interaction and the lack of emotional intelligence Inaccurate information Overuse of AI Plagiarism

	Data privacy and security

Benefits

Participants shared insightful feedback on how AI benefits them in their teaching.

The first sub-theme refers to the fact that AI tools could offer both educators and their students personalised support that was always available, which was seen as one of the major benefits.

As an example, a participant stated:

> AI can offer individualised guidance by adjusting to each student's particular learning preferences and speed. Chatbots can instantly provide individualised feedback on tasks and queries, assisting my students in quickly correcting their errors. (E1)

This comment highlights the potential advantage of individualised support that is always available, which can significantly reduce the burden on educators, allowing them to concentrate on other crucial aspects, such as teaching and social interaction (Grassini, 2023).

Another participant (E2) added that because AI tools were available round the clock, they could seek help or clarification at any time. Because AI tools focus on individual needs rather than following a one-size-fits-all approach, it moves the focus away from the educator to the student. It, therefore, can empower students to take more control over their learning.

The second sub-theme refers to the potential of generative AI tools to provide lesson content. They have the potential to gather information on a wide range of topics and customise worksheets, activities, and assessment tasks to the specific needs of a class or individual students (Van den berg & Du Plessis, 2023).

Most comments focussed on AI's ability to address students' individual needs. For example:

> AI systems like ChatGPT can be trained to comprehend each student's unique learning style and preferences, resulting in lesson plans and learning opportunities that are suited to each student's requirements. (E6)

Participants' responses highlight an important trend in education: the use of generative AI tools to customise and enhance lesson plans. This significant advancement will transform the way educators teach and students learn.

The third sub-theme was about AI's capacity to simplify language, which is crucial for education in cases where students have language challenges or are taught in another language than their home language. Generative AI tools to simplify language can greatly impact students' comprehension and, ultimately, their outcomes.

As an example, a participant stated:

> Generative AI tools can make complex concepts more accessible to students, particularly those who may struggle with language comprehension or have diverse linguistic backgrounds. I often ask my students to use ChatGPT to simplify content if they struggle. (E2)

Generative AI tools can lead to active involvement as another benefit, the fourth sub-theme. The interactive nature between humans and machines has been mentioned by various authors (e.g. Bozkurt, 2023; Grassini, 2023), and holds huge potential as it can provide personalised responses, immediate access to information, and tutoring, leading to a more equitable education system.

For example, a participant stated:

> AI serves as an interactive tool due to the speed with which it provides solutions to questions or problems I present to it. (E9)

Another participant mentioned the motivational nature of active involvement in AI:

> Learners can also be actively involved in their learning by asking questions to AI and be kept motivated to learn. (E4)

This comment confirms that AI tools can boost motivation because they make learning more accessible, engaging and aligned with students' specific needs.

The fifth sub-theme refers to the potential of generative AI tools to save time. This emerged as a strong sub-theme, as most participants mentioned it.

Participants shared the following:

> It saves time and effort when I prepare tasks for learners because ChatGPT has information on different topics. (E3)
>
> I save time by using AI tools to create general writing pieces, such as supportive text for teaching, support for students, test questions and quizzes, rubrics, tips, and suggestions. (E8)

Saving time for tasks that AI cannot perform can allow teachers more teaching time and improve teaching quality.

The final sub-theme was about the capability of generative AI tools to provide **access to information.**

Participants shared the following:

> Easy access to information. I do not have to consult many resources or read different textbooks to get the necessary information. (E3)
>
> In my context, the benefits of using AI tools are that they can serve as an information searching tool. It can provide a basis for facilitators and students to conduct further research on any subject. While it is widely acknowledged that simply copying and pasting information from AI tools is unacceptable, the information it provides can be used as a springing board that directs one to other sources and ideas. (E10)

The above responses highlight the ability of generative AI tools to sift numerous resources, enabling educators to obtain relevant information from one source quickly. This can be particularly beneficial in educational settings where time and access to information are challenging.

The second theme dealt with challenges when using generative AI tools.

Challenges

Several challenges were raised on the discussion forum, which led to several sub-themes.

The first sub-theme related to the fact that AI tools can provide biased information. This implies that information must be approached with caution and cross-checked with other sources (Tlili et al., 2023).

As an example, a participant said:

> I am aware of ethical concerns regarding the use of AI, including potential biases in the training data that can lead to biased or discriminatory responses. (E3)

In this regard, Grassini (2023) confirms that generative AI tools use vast amounts of data to learn and generate content. This data may not always be objective, affecting the generated content's accuracy and fairness.

The second sub-theme was about the challenge of a decrease in human interaction and the lack of emotional intelligence. In this regard, Baidoo and Anu (2023:56) confirm that generative AI models cannot replicate the same level of human interaction as a real educator:

For example, a participant stated:

> A heavy dependence on AI in the classroom can result in less human interaction, which is crucial for social and emotional growth. Also, AI lacks emotions and empathy, which are critical for offering pupils emotional assistance. (E1)

According to Bozkurt (2023), current generative AI tools lack emotional intelligence, which can negatively affect their ability to provide personalised support.

The third sub-theme referred to the provision of inaccurate information, which is, according to ChatGPT itself, a reality, as it indicated that because of reasons such as training data limitations, lack of real-time data, misinterpretation of queries, the complexity and ambiguity of language and its generative nature, it could produce false information (OpenAI, 2024). However, as Grassini (2023) predicts, false information might be mitigated in future.

As examples of their responses, participants said:

> So far, I've discovered that if you don't know your material or subject, ChatGPT can mislead the facilitator (E5)

> One should also check that there is no overreliance on the tool to create assessments. If you ask Chat GPT to create questions on a certain level of Bloom's taxonomy, it does so, but you still have to check for accuracy and correctness (E8)

Disseminating false information can hinder the development of essential graduate skills and promote superficial learning; therefore, information must be checked for accuracy.

The fourth sub-theme referred to the overuse of generative AI tools. Interestingly, eight participants indicated this as a significant challenge.

The following example serves as participants' responses:

> Overusing AI tools may make students dependent on technology for learning, impacting their capacity for critical thought and problem-solving. There's a risk that students may use these tools as a crutch rather than developing independent learning abilities. Some end up being too lazy to search for information. (E1)

The risk of plagiarism led to the fifth sub-theme. Using someone else's work without proper acknowledgement indeed raises serious questions about the academic integrity of the educational system. Tlili et al. (2023) confirm that it is easy to copy and paste information provided by generative AI tools without referencing, which leads to plagiarism and may breed laziness among students. What makes the situation even more complicated is that AI detection tools often struggle to identify cases of plagiarism (Grassini, 2023).

Adding to the complexity of plagiarism was a comment from a school teacher, stating that students might copy information provided by generative AI tools on their mobile phones and write it down in class as their own:

> Plagiarism is a challenge, as I fear that my learners might be using AI tools for copying since they are allowed to bring phones to school. There is no mechanism put in place to check plagiarism on written content (E3)

Another participant implied that educators, in general, were aware of this challenge:

> I think my concern is the same as everyone else's concerns, of which the most important one is plagiarism (E8)

The last sub-theme relates to ethics and revolves around the critical issue of data privacy and security. When ChatGPT was questioned about the origin of the data it provides, it indicated that it extracts data from various sources, including websites, open books, and other educational resources from its pre-existing knowledge base, real-time data it has been trained on, along with information provided by ChatGPT users (OpenAI, 2024). This means that in an educational context, educator and student data is at risk of being used for misuse, calling for an urgent need to address data privacy and security concerns.

For example, a participant stated:

The usage of AI chatbots raises serious ethical concerns since it may lead to the gathering and use of student data without the student's knowledge or consent. (E6)

Implications and concluding remarks

This paper reported on students' perceptions of the benefits and challenges of generative AI tools in their respective educational contexts. Based on an interpretative paradigm, an exploratory case study design was used to analyse data from responses on a discussion forum. The empirical research provides a complex picture and has pertinent implications. On the one hand, AI tools can lead to more personalised, efficient, and accessible learning experiences. They can adapt to individual learning styles, simplify concepts, and provide information quickly and efficiently. This can transform educational practices, making them more student-centred. However, on the other hand, AI tools come with significant challenges. Biases in AI can lead to unfair and incorrect information and overuse, and they can diminish essential human interactions and emotional connections. The risk of misinformation, plagiarism, and data security issues cannot be overlooked. While the benefits and challenges educators share in this study offer exciting possibilities for making education more personal and effective, they should be used wisely, complementing rather than replacing traditional teaching and learning. Educators and policymakers need to address the challenges, particularly in areas of bias, overuse, plagiarism, and data privacy, to fully harness its potential in education.

While the study provides important insights, its scope is limited by the small number of participants and the specific context in which it was conducted. It is possible that if a different sample had been used, the findings could have been different. Additionally, the study relied on a single instrument to collect data. As a result, more empirical research with the same and different groups and instruments will lead to a deeper understanding of how generative AI tools can benefit all its users equally, ultimately leading to improved learning outcomes

References

Akgun, S., & Greenhow, C. (2022). Artificial intelligence in education: Addressing ethical challenges in K-12 settings. AI and Ethics, 2(3), 431–440. DOI: 10.1007/s43681-021-00096-7

Baidoo-Anu, D., Owusu Ansah, L. 2023. Education in the era of generative artificial intelligence (AI): Understanding the potential benefits of ChatGPT in promoting teaching and learning. Journal of AI, 7(1): 52-62. http://dx.doi.org/10.2139/ssrn.4337484

Bozkurt, A. (2023). Unleashing the potential of generative AI, conversational agents and chatbots in educational praxis: A systematic review and bibliometric analysis of GenAI in education. Open Praxis, 15(4), pp. 261–270. DOI:10.55982/openpraxis.15.4.609

Braun, V., & Clarke, V. (2012). Thematic analysis. In H. Cooper, P. M. Camic, D. L. Long, A. T. Panter, D. Rindskopf, & K. J. Sher (Eds.), APA handbook of research methods in psychology, Vol. 2. Research designs: Quantitative, qualitative, neuropsychological, and biological (pp. 57–71). American Psychological Association. https://doi.org/10.1037/13620-004

Grassini, S. (2023). Shaping the future of education: Exploring the potential and consequences of AI and ChatGPT in Educational Settings. Education Sciences, 13, 692. https://doi.org/10.3390/educsci13070692

Kamalov, F.; Santandreu Calonge, D.; Gurrib, I. (2023). New era of artificial intelligence in education: Towards a sustainable multifaceted revolution. Sustainability, 15,12451. https://doi.org/10.3390/su151612451

Kivunja, C., & Kuyini, A. B. (2017). Understanding and applying research paradigms in educational contexts. International Journal of Higher Education, 6(5), 26-41. DOI:10.5430/IJHE.V6N5P26

Kung, T.H., Cheatham, M., Medenilla, A., Sillos, C., De Leon, L., Elepaño, C., et al. (2023) Performance of ChatGPT on USMLE: Potential for AI-assisted medical education using large language models. PLOS Digit Health 2(2): e0000198. https://doi.org/10.1371/journal.pdig.0000198

McCombs, M., & Valenzuela, S. (2020). Setting the agenda: Mass media and public opinion. John Wiley & Sons.

Lincoln, Y.S. & Guba, E.G. (1985). Naturalistic Enquiry. Newbury Park: CA: Sage.

OpenAI. (2024). ChatGPT (4) [Large language model]. https://chat.openai.com

Tlili, A., Shehata, B., Adarkwah, M. A., Bozkurt, A., Hickey, D. T., Huang, R., & Agyemang, B. (2023). What if the devil is my guardian angel: ChatGPT as a case study of using chatbots in education. Smart Learning Environments, 10(1), 15.

Ray, P.P. (2023). ChatGPT: A comprehensive review on background, applications, key challenges, bias, ethics, limitations and future scope. Internet of Things and Cyber-Physical Systems, 3, 121-154. https://doi.org/10.1016/j.iotcps.2023.04.003

Sullivan, M., Kelly, A., & McLaughlan, P. (2023). ChatGPT in higher education: Considerations for academic integrity and student learning. Journal of Applied Learning & Teaching, 6(1), 1–10. https://doi.org/10.37074/jalt.2023.6.1.17

Van den Berg, G.,& Du Plessis, E. 2023. ChatGPT and generative AI: possibilities for its contribution to lesson planning, critical thinking and openness in teacher education. Educational Sciences, 13, 998. https://doi.org/10.3390/educsci13100998

Yin, R.K., (2009). Case study research: Design and methods (Vol. 5). Sage, London.

How Phenomenon-Based Learning May Contribute to Counteract Disinformation: A Case Presentation from Austrian Secondary Schools

Michael Reicho[1]

[1] Institute of Education Research and Teacher Education, University of Graz, Austria; michael.reicho@uni-graz.at

Correspondence: Michael Reicho: michael.reicho@uni-graz.at

Abstract:

The distribution of disinformation in online environments poses an increasing risk for pupils to be confronted with manipulated content. As a pedagogical strategy for schools, phenomenon-based learning (PhBL) is said to train a variety of required digital competences. This article aims to describe PhBL as practical teaching intervention to address disinformation in secondary schools. PhBL is a cross-curricular and subject-unspecific teaching intervention with a suggested duration of 8-12 teaching lessons and an appropriate age starting from 12/13 years. This investigation included that teacher organized project-oriented activities. The evaluation comprised semi-structured interviews with pupils (n=36) and their teachers (n=8) as well as video-based classroom observations in six classes with 107 pupils. The findings indicate that this teaching approach supported pupils to compare information sources, evaluate credibility indicators, and act criticaly as online consumers. After the intervention pupils said that they felt more sceptical of online and social media information.

Keywords: Disinformation, Phenomenon-Based Learning, Multiliteracy, Secondary School, Teacher Education, Fake News

Introduction

A number of recent developments around the world have highlighted that fake news is one of the biggest threats facing the world today. Easy access to online technologies makes young people particularly vulnerable to disinformation, so it is important to equip them with the skills and confidence to identify manipulated content (Skipper et al., 2023). In relation to education, the key principle for addressing disinformation is to encourage and develop critical thinking and engagement through and in education (Carr et al., 2020). A recent study has highlighted that possessing information literacy significantly increases the likelihood of identifying disinformation (Jones-Jang et al., 2021).

We therefore need an awareness-raising of digital competences already at a young age in schools (Loveless & Williamson, 2013). Phenomenon-based learning (PhBL) is said to train a variety of digital competences that are required to counteract fake news (Lonka et al., 2018; Kangas & Rasi, 2021). I therefore investigated PhBL with pupils and teachers in Austria to see how open project teaching and learning based on PhBL principles trains critical media literacy and how it raises awareness against disinformation, leading to the following research question: What effect has 'phenomenon-based learning' on building critical media literacy to counteract fake news?

Understanding Fake News

Fake news are frequently defined as "fabricated information that mimics news media content in form but not in organisational process or intent" (Lazer et al., 2018, 1094) or as information, "that is intentionally and verifiably false, and could mislead readers" (Allcott & Gentzkow, 2017, 213). Other researchers have expanded the narrowly defined understanding with "poor journalism, political propaganda, and misleading forms of advertising and sponsored content" (Nielsen & Graves, 2017, 1). Since fake news has become a buzzword to delegitimize opponents, scholars have begun to use the term disinformation instead (Egelhofer et al., 2020). Researchers differentiate between misinformation, disinformation, misleading information or malinformation:

Misinformation is the distribution of false information without any intention to cause harm. Disinformation is the deliberate circulation of false information with the intention of causing harm. Malinformation occurs when genuine information is spread in order to cause harm, often by information that should remain private but enters the public discourse (Wardle & Derakhshan, 2017). Roozenbeek and van der Linden (2022) summarise misleading information as not necessarily being factually incorrect, but instead may misrepresent facts, ignore relevant context or contain a logical fallacy. Disinformation is often characterised by an extensive, uncontrolled or even systemic dissemination (Bradshaw, 2021), in many cases originating from populist groups (Hameleers & de Vreese, 2021) and frequently founded on rumours, prejudice, stereotypes, and fear, and is used as a tool for manipulation, persuasion and deception (Carr et al., 2020).

Digital Youth: Between digital native and digital naïve

Young people's media use behaviour is often portrayed in contradictory ways. On one hand, children are often viewed as vulnerable and in need of protection. On the other hand, they are depicted as pioneers who are active, competent, and seem to have an almost natural talent for media use (Hagen, 2003). Although young people have integrated social media into their daily routines, evidence suggests that the term 'digital natives', which implies that all young people are competent in the use of digital information, is a myth (Bennett et al., 2008). The assumption that young people are inherently tech-savvy is often based on their exposure to digital technologies from a young age. However, access to technology alone does not fully determine the nature of young people's technological skills (Loos et al, 2018).

These statements are supported from an Austrian study, showing that half of the 11-17-years old pass on news on current topics unchecked and 53% feel that checking information sources is a hassle. In everyday life, it is often found that the most common strategy for dealing with disinformation is to ignore it (57 %). 70% of young people find it challenging to determine the validity of information found on the internet. Nearly half of the respondents are frequently uncertain about the accuracy of online information. Additionally, 62% of Austrian youth are unaware of any fact-checking websites (saferinternet.at, 2023).

Teaching and Learning against Disinformation

Many scholars argue that education is an effective way to counter disinformation (McDougall et al., 2019; Herrero-Diz et al., 2020). Westheimer (2018) pointed out three ideas that should be taken up by educators: (1) Teach students to ask questions rather than avoid controversial issues and to understand that there is no single truth. (2) Familiarise them with different perspectives to ensure they do not believe their own reality is universally valid. (3) Encourage global connections and civic engagement. For this reason, pupils need to learn critical media literacies to be aware of disinformation.

As this paper does not aim to discuss the various definitions of critical media literacies, it will refer to the concept of multiliteracy. Multiliteracy is an "umbrella term encompassing concepts such as media literacy, visual literacy and advertising literacy" (Kangas & Rasi, 2021, p.3). Multiliteracy is the ability to use various tools to produce, combine, acquire, modify, understand, present, and evaluate information in different contexts, ways, and situations. Teaching multiliteracy at school aims to enable pupils to use digital technologies for self-expression and interaction, while also learning to operate responsibly in the use, production, and sharing of content in different formats (Kangas & Rasi, 2021).

Phenomenon-Based Learning to strengthen Multiliteracy

Following these thoughts, phenomenon-based learning (PhBL) seems to address these theoretical demands and to train multiliteracies. Phenomenon-based learning refers to cross-curricular learning activities in exploring a real-life phenomenon from multiple perspectives in different disciplines. According to PhBL, learners should seek information independently, compare and evaluate sources of information. Teachers are seen as expert coaches that encourage their pupils. PhBL involves teachers working together to define their project and then guiding pupils through independent group work in which they explore online sources, produce reports and present their findings. The process includes checkpoints for discussion, use of digital tools and reflection on learning outcomes compared to initial goals (Lonka, 2018; Kangas & Rasi, 2021).

Other scholars agree to these key aspects, as for example described by Leu et al. (2013): (1) define important questions (2) locate online information, (3) critically analyse and evaluate online information (4) synthesise online information and (5) writing to communicate or distribute online information (Leu et al., 2013). These considerations are also closely linked to the social media information literacy (SMIL) concept (Bühler et al., 2020).

Methods and Sample

This article describes phenomenon-based learning as practical teaching intervention to address disinformation in secondary schools in Austria. In a previous step we revised this teaching intervention with expert interviews (n=19) to adapt it to Austrian secondary schools adding the focus of disinformation (Fasching & Schubatzky, 2022).

I conducted video-based and written classroom observations of 6 classes in 17 teaching lessons with a total of 8 teachers and 107 pupils. After the project I conducted qualitative semi-structured interviews with 36 secondary school pupils aged 12 to 18 years. At the same time, I also conducted semi-structured (online) interviews with 8 teachers aged 26-45 years with a range of 2 to 20 years of teaching experience (Helfferich, 2014). I evaluated the interviews and classroom observations with a content analysis with inductive categories (Mayring, 2014). The implementation took place in May and June 2023 with three different schools in Styria.

Results and Findings

This section describes the main findings from the evaluation and feedback from pupils and teachers. Other details of this research are published elsewhere.

Opportunities and Challenges during Implementation

After the project, the teachers described phenomenon-based learning (PhBL) as a meaningful teaching intervention. PhBL seemed to train multiliteracy and to raise awareness to disinformation. The teachers noted that both they and the pupils enjoyed the independent work and in-depth discussions, which are "not always possible in regular classes" (T1). Some teachers said that they "would definitely recommend it to colleagues" (T7) and in general "are always looking for approaches to keep pupils motivated over a longer period of time" (T2). Phenomenon-based learning is a "sustainable approach that should be repeated" (T8).

Regarding the motivation of the pupils, the teachers reported at the beginning of the project a level of scepticism among the pupils. "It was difficult for them to find their way into the work" (T4). By the end, "pupils were more motivated compared to regular lessons" (T4). Most of the pupils confirmed their teacher's impression, stating that they were more motivated and therefore more productive because they were able to choose topics based on their own interests.

The teachers' biggest challenge was to slip into an unfamiliar 'passive' role as expert coaches and "to take themselves back and let pupils work" (T6). It seems important that teachers learn to trust their pupils - "believe in the pupils, give them freedom and they will surprise you with impressive results" (T8) and even rather weak pupils can "develop and you see qualities that you wouldn't otherwise notice" (T8). The observations showed that the most important tasks of the teachers were to explain how to evaluate information sources, to introduce (new) tools and to answer questions. During the phases of independent work, teachers also had more time for detailed feedback and for coaching pupils according to their individual needs.

Many pupils valued the freedom to be creative and the contrast to normal lessons. The pupils emphasised that it is good when "pupils are taught to make their own decisions" (P9). At the same time, finding and narrowing down the topics was a major challenge for the pupils. Many pupils said that they were a bit uncertain about the choice of topics and the scope of the results at the beginning. Teachers report that pupils are not experienced in being asked about their personal interests during class. As one teacher put it: "As teachers, we may sometimes provide answers to questions that do not interest our pupils. This can result in a situation where only one person speaks, and in the worst case, no one listens. However, this threat can be reduced through projects like this" (T2).

Working independently in small groups had a positive impact on most pupils as they were able to assist each other. The "project is perfect to practise working independently" and for many the collaborative "work in small groups is a support" (T4). However, task division was not always efficient and sometimes tasks overlapped. In general, pupils enjoyed the free management of time without pressure. "It is more fun and you memorise more when you work independently" (P1). Pupils admitted that they did other things during the lesson, but in return some of them met in their free time to work on the reports. During project days, pupils also enjoyed the individual organisation of breaks. When they were "in the flow", they "didn't take a break" (P11). In the teachers' perception, pupils' project planning was one of the biggest challenges. One teacher stated, that "some pupils are fully structured, some don't even know what day it is" (T6). Although they were asked to do so, not every group created a time plan.

Critical Source Analysis

According to the interviewed teachers, pupils displayed varying skills of multiliteracy. Some pupils seemed to operate indiscriminate and used the first available website they found, while others compared different sources. Especially the age group 16-18 seemed more practiced in evaluating online information, while the 12–13-year-olds were often overwhelmed with simple search tasks. "The boys didn't know how to use Google" (T1), commented one teacher.

During the observations, some pupils demonstrated high critical source analysis competences when they considered the reputation of a site. Well-known organisations, NGOs or media companies were considered as trustworthy. Some of the pupils even used Google Scholar to search for scientific sources. When they were evaluating information sources they paid attention to grammar mistakes, to dubious advertisements, to the date or the legal imprint of websites. Blogs or Wikipedia were typically not considered trustworthy. Occasionally, advanced search skills were observed, such as searching in different languages or searching for sources via references of good texts.

But many pupils showed a lack of critical source analysis skills since they often argued to base trustworthiness on the layout and design of a website. The observations highlighted that pupils often conducted superficial searches, relying on image information or featured snippets without actually reading the page. Pupils chose sources because they provided short and simple texts on their topics. In general, there seemed to be a difficulty in the distinction between objective and interest-driven content. One pupil even claimed that the first Google search result is always accurate, demonstrating reliance on the Google algorithm. Additionally, some pupils came across statistics that they could not explain when asked.

Teachers found that during the research phase, pupils faced challenges but also learned a lot. They encouraged pupils to use social media platforms like TikTok and Instagram for information gathering. However, pupils struggled to find reliable information on these platforms. They encountered low-quality content, often conflicting with reputable sources or solely based on opinions. Despite using social media for entertainment, pupils generally distrusted information found there, a significant aspect influencing their critical evaluation of sources.

Of particular concern was the use of artificial intelligence (e.g. ChatGPT) as trustworthy sources. When asked, one pupil said that ChatGPT was very trustworthy as she had never had a bad experience with it. In Google you have to read so much, ChatGPT sums it up well, according to the pupil. However, I also discovered some positive examples of artificial intelligence, as one group utilized an AI image generator to avoid violating copyrights. Another group used AI text-to-speech to add a voice-over to an explanatory video.

In summary, pupils mentioned the following indicators for selecting sources: Comparison of websites, inappropriate advertising on website, naming of authors, structure and layout of the site, contact details or imprint available as well as the level of reputation of the medium (e.g., public service media or international NGOs). Exercising these indicators is a very important learning experience to become aware of disinformation.

In connection to disinformation, the young people said that they felt more critical in analysing information sources after the project activity and that they would be more careful from now on navigating online information (including outside school tasks). We should "not always believe everything that is written on the internet" (P4) and we "should pay attention to good sources" (P9). "With a project like this, you are prepared for life, it supports you" (P11), were some of the statements they made.

Using Digital Tools

Becoming aware of disinformation, the process of acquiring multiliteracy skills includes the use of (new) digital tools that help to detect disinformation (Kangas & Rasi, 2021). At the beginning of the project, pupils were reluctant to use new and unfamiliar digital tools. According to them, this was also due to the perceived extra workload, and the difficulty to estimate the time needed to learn about those tools. With encouragement from their teachers, most of the pupils tried out new tools. Working with digital media "is important for our future" (P11).

Teaching Reflection

Teachers evaluated the preparation and post-processing time as very similar compared to regular lessons. Other teachers think that the project was even less time-consuming. "I would have imagined the project to be more time-consuming" (T7). Only the feedback during the lessons and especially for the digital presentations at the end, afforded more time of the teachers. Teachers had difficulties in grading the creative digital reports because the range of pupils' outputs was very diverse.

The eight teachers felt that project-based PhBL teaching is suitable for working with curriculum content and helps to deepen content already covered or to start with a new topic. Topics that had current relevance, in combination with language subjects (e.g., migration or climate change) were reported to be particularly suited. This is because it trains text comprehension, reading skills, and language and presentation skills, teachers said.

Suggestions for Future Implementations

The interviewed teachers offered suggestions to improve future PhBL projects. These include showing examples of other results for inspiration, providing more support in narrowing down and identifying topics, allowing sufficient time for final presentations to celebrate results, specifying a minimum number of sources for the digital report, finding a team of 2-3 teachers to combine several professional perspectives, and starting to work with digital tools earlier for faster groups. The teachers propose a grading system consisting of four codes and school marks ranging from 1-5 for the following areas: content, structure, creativity, and expression/grammar/spelling. These marks could be combined to give an overall grade. To improve the quality of the work, the pupils wish to have more time to prepare the topics thoroughly for future projects.

The teachers felt that phenomenon-based learning was appropriate and doable for pupils aged 12-13 and no problem for the older pupils. Teachers thought that PhBL can be used even for pupils younger than 12, if the scope is reduced, if simpler tools are employed, topics are made easier, and sources are suggested. However, the maturity of the pupils is more important than their age, teachers said.

The chosen duration of the activities lasting 8 to 12 lessons seemed a suitable period for all teachers. Here, both the division into two project days or the division of the lessons into one month worked very well. The teachers chose a suitable time for the project when there was no schoolwork, holidays or tests.

Discussion and Conclusion

Coming back to the proposed research question, the findings show that phenomenon-based learning (PhBL) seems a practical teaching intervention to raise awareness against disinformation in secondary schools because the implementation supported training pupils to compare information sources, evaluate credibility indicators, act as critical consumers of online information, and use digital tools to communicate results (Lonka et al., 2018). In the project, pupils showed varying levels of critical source evaluation, with some considering reputable sources and using advanced search techniques, while others relied on superficial criteria like website design. Many struggled to distinguish between objective and biased content, often trusting sources based on simplicity or Google rankings.

Working independently in small groups enhanced pupils' mutual learning through reflective discussions about sources and tools (Bühler et al., 2020). Pupils reported increased motivation due to the ability to choose topics based on their own interests. Teachers were able to provide individualised support as expert coaches. With PhBL, teachers were able to work with content from the curriculum, either deepening material or to work with new content. PhBL is a cross-curricular intervention and is suitable for most school subject. The invested time for teachers was similar to regular lessons.

Suggestions and Outlook

These findings suggest that teachers and pupils need time and practice for cross-curricular and open project teaching (Lonka et al., 2018). Teachers suggest an appropriate starting age of 12 to 13 years - depending on the maturity of the class. For future implementations, teachers suggest working with best practice examples to inspire pupils (and other teachers). Ongoing research could focus on how to implement PhBL in curricula in Austria. Further, it seems promising to implement and evaluate PhBL in other countries, including outside developed countries. Future research could explore the possibilities of combining subject-specific interventions (such as inoculation or debunking) and subject-unspecific approaches such as PhBL. Another area for further research is the inclusion of older target groups, such as adults or senior citizens.

References

Allcott, H., & Gentzkow, M. (2017). Social media and fake news in the 2016 election. Journal of economic perspectives, 31(2), 211-236. :10.1257/jep.31.2.211

Bennett, S., Maton, K. and Kervin, L. (2008), "The 'digital natives' debate: a critical review of the evidence", British Journal of Educational Technology, Vol. 39 No. 5, pp. 775-786. :10.1111/j.1467-8535.2007.00793.x

Bradshaw, S., Bailey, H., & Howard, P. N. (2021). Industrialized disinformation: 2020 global inventory of organized social media manipulation. Computational Propaganda Research Project.

Bühler, J., Murawski, M., Darvish, M., & Bick, M. (2020). Developing a Model to Measure Fake News Detection Literacy of Social Media Users. Disinformation, Misinformation, and Fake News in Social Media: Emerging Research Challenges and Opportunities, 213-227. :10.1007/978-3-030-42699-6_11

Carr, P. R., Cuervo Sanchez, S. L., & Daros, M. A. (2020). Citizen engagement in the contemporary era of fake news: hegemonic distraction or control of the social media context?. Postdigital Science and Education, 2(1), 39-60. :10.1007/s42438-019-00052-z

Egelhofer, J. L., Aaldering, L., Eberl, J. M., Galyga, S., & Lecheler, S. (2020). From novelty to normalization? How journalists use the term "fake news" in their reporting. Journalism Studies, 21(10), 1323-1343. :10.1080/1461670X.2020.1745667

Fasching, M., & Schubatzky, T. (2022). Beyond truth: Teaching digital competences in secondary school against disinformation: Experts' views on practical teaching frameworks for basic digital education in Austria. Medienimpulse, 60(3), 1-65. :10.21243/mi-03-22-19

Hagen, I. (2003). 'A Life without Media? Boring!' About the Significance of Media in Children and Young People's Life, in Lundby, K. (ed.) Flow or Seduction. Stories about ICT. Oslo: Gyldendal Akademisk, 197-224.

Hameleers, M., & de Vreese, C. (2021). Perceived mis-and disinformation in a post-factual information setting: a conceptualisation and evidence from ten European countries. In The Routledge Companion to Media Disinformation and Populism. 366-375. Routledge.

Helfferich, C. (2014). Leitfaden- und Experteninterviews. In: Baur, N. & Blasius, J. (Eds.), Handbuch Methoden der empirischen Sozialforschung (pp. 559–574). Springer.

Herrero-Diz, P., Conde-Jiménez, J., & Reyes de Cózar, S. (2020). Teens' motivations to spread fake news on WhatsApp. Social Media+ Society, 6(3). :10.1177/2056305120942879

Jones-Jang, S. M., Mortensen, T., & Liu, J. (2021). Does media literacy help identification of fake news? Information literacy helps, but other literacies don't. American behavioral scientist, 65(2), 371-388. :10.1177/0002764219869406

Kangas, M., & Rasi, P. (2021). Phenomenon-based learning of multiliteracy in a Finnish upper secondary school. Media Practice and Education, 22(4), 342-359. :10.1080/25741136.2021.1977769

Lazer, D. M., Baum, M. A., Benkler, Y., Berinsky, A. J., Greenhill, K. M., Menczer, F., ... & Zittrain, J. L. (2018). The science of fake news. Science, 359(6380), 1094-1096. :10.1126/science.aao2998

Leu, D. J., Forzani, E., Burlingame, C., Kulikowich, J., Sedransk, N., Coiro, J., & Kennedy, C. (2013). The new literacies of online research and comprehension: Assessing and preparing students for the 21st century with Common Core State Standards. Quality reading instruction in the age of Common Core Standards, 219-236.

Lonka, K., Makkonen, J., Berg, M., Talvio, M., Maksniemi, E., Kruskopf, M., ... & Westling, S. K. (2018). Phenomenal learning from Finland. Edita.

Loos, E., Ivan, L., & Leu, D. (2018). "Save the Pacific Northwest tree octopus": a hoax revisited. Or: How vulnerable are school children to fake news?. Information and Learning Science.

Loveless, A., & Williamson, B. (2013). Shaping Society, Technology and Learning Identity. In: Loveless A & Williamson B (eds.) Learning Identities in a Digital Age: Rethinking creativity, education and technology. Changing Times in Education. London: Routledge, pp. 7-30.

Mayring, P. (2014). Qualitative content analysis: theoretical foundation, basic procedures and software solution.

McDougall, J., Brites, M. J., Couto, M. J., & Lucas, C. (2019). Digital literacy, fake news and education [Alfabetización digital, fake news y educación]. Cultura y Educación, 31(2), 203– 212. :10.1080/11356405.2019.1603632

Nielsen, R., & Graves, L. (2017). "News you don't believe": Audience perspectives on fake news. In Reuters Institute for the Study of Jounalism (Reuters Institute for the Study of Journalism Factsheets). Reuters Institute for the Study of Jounalism.

Roozenbeek, J., & Van Der Linden, S. (2022). How to combat health misinformation: A psychological approach. American journal of health promotion, 36(3), 569-575. :10.1177/08901171211070958

Saferinternet.at (2023): Jugendliche im Fake News Dilemma, Institut für Jugendkulturforschung und Kulturvermittlung; Retrieved from https://www.saferinternet.at/news-detail/jugendliche-im-fake-news-dilemma

Skipper, Y., Jolley, D., & Reddington, J. (2023). 'But wait, that isn't real': A proof-of-concept study evaluating 'Project Real', a co-created intervention that helps young people to spot fake news online. British Journal of Developmental Psychology, 41(4), 371-384. :10.1111/bjdp.12456

Wardle, C., & Derakhshan, H. (2017). Information disorder: Toward an interdisciplinary framework for research and policymaking.

Westheimer, J. (2018). Democratic goals for education in the digital age. Teaching Citizenship in the Digital Area. Education Canada, 23-27.

The Effect of Progress Indicators on Students' Engagement, Learning Experience and Final Grade

Marko Matus[1], Ivana Ružić[2], Igor Balaban[3]

[1] University of Zagreb, Faculty of Organization and Informatics Varazdin, Croatia; marko.matus@foi.hr
[2] University of Zagreb, Faculty of Organization and Informatics Varazdin Croatia; First Primary School Cakovec, Croatia; ivana.ruzic@skole.hr
[3] University of Zagreb, Faculty of Organization and Informatics Varazdin, Croatia; igor.balaban@foi.hr

Correspondence: Marko Matus; marko.matus@foi.hr

Abstract:

Student analytics dashboards are identified as a tool to bridge the gap in interaction between students and teachers, as well as to help students more efficiently monitor their own progress. This research aims to explore the connections between progress tracking of students' work in the course, their learning experience, engagement, and final grades. In total, 77 students in a blended course covering economics and informatics were involved in the study. Progress through course materials was tracked using conditional activities, and students' progress was measured using self-assessment quizzes and badges. Results indicated a strong positive correlation between progress indicators and engagement, as well as between progress indicators and learning experience. A small correlation was found between progress indicators and final course grades.

Keywords: Progress indicators, Learning analytics dashboard, Engagement, Learning experience

Introduction

The pervasive influence of high technological advancements and digitalization extends across all sectors, including higher education. Recent years have witnessed a substantial surge in online courses, marking a shift from traditional to contemporary educational methods. This shift aligns with the evolving trend in education, where students increasingly seek the flexibility to learn anytime, anywhere, unrestricted by the traditional constraints of face-to-face education (Naranjo et al., 2019).

In the pursuit of enhancing the learning experience through information gathering and data analysis, learning analytics dashboards have emerged. These dashboards empower educators and students to make informed decisions based on the gathered information (Jivet et al., 2018). By integrating data from diverse sources such as student grades, tests, surveys, forums, and interactions through digital learning platforms, learning analytics dashboards effectively collect, analyse, and visualize learning data (Ming & Kee, 2021). It is believed that such a visual aspect not only aims to enhance understanding and interpretation but also positively impacts student motivation. Pedagogically, these dashboards contribute to identifying comprehension levels, diagnosing knowledge gaps, and tailoring teaching to individual student needs and specific conceptual/skill areas. According to Ming&Kee (2021), they provide a continuous evidence base for future lesson planning, but they can also provide predictions on students' course completion based on their current contributions to learning outcomes (Susnjak et al., 2022). Educators can utilize learning analytics dashboards to monitor students' progress over time, tracking access to learning materials, time spent in digital learning environments, and goal achievement.

This paper aims to examine the relationship between the learning analytics dashboard containing progress indicators for the course and (1) student engagement, (2) learning experience and (3) the final grade.

Progress indicators in learning analytics dashboards

The student analytics dashboard is a set of unique displays that aggregate multiple indicators in the learning process and/or in the context of one or more visualizations (Safsouf et al., 2022). It serves the fundamental purpose of delineating students' learning trends. Nonetheless, furnishing these dashboards to students serves multiple aims: fostering their social consciousness by facilitating comparisons with peers, enhancing self-awareness, altering learning approaches, and ultimately bolstering their motivation to learn (Park & Jo, 2019). Learning analytics dashboards have the potential to evolve into efficient learning support tools, delivering teaching and learning-related feedback as well as process-oriented feedback more effectively. Park & Jo (2019) showed that there are several prerequisites for a learning analytics dashboard to be successful: the effective design of the visual information, sufficient usability of the interface, understandable organization of the information, perceived usefulness, and the fulfilment of facilitated behavioural changes.

In this paper, we focus on dashboards that reflect progress indicators and are oriented towards personalized tracking of each individual student's progress (Jayashanka et al., 2022), enabling teachers to identify areas requiring interventions or tailored support more easily. Using dashboards, two information displays are possible: one for students and one for teachers. The teacher view provides a broader overview of the progress and engagement of all students within their course (Safsouf et al., 2022). The student view provides insights into their individual progress, behaviour, and contribution to the educational process. Students can track their overall progress through several interfaces, such as specific lessons to see what percentage of the content they have completed, assessment interfaces to view their knowledge assessment results, and interfaces that display upcoming important events such as deadlines or tests (Safsouf et al., 2022).

Progress indicators and engagement

Universities must prioritize elements that enhance online learning outcomes, thereby augmenting student satisfaction and engagement levels (Prabowo et al., 2022). To create an effective educational environment, learners must be involved and engaged in the learning process. Engagement is defined as the passion to participate in and accomplish the assigned learning activities (Rojas-López et al., 2019). Many studies show that the use of advanced technologies as a teaching strategy increases the engagement of learners.

Additionally, previous research findings suggest that successful online student engagement is shaped by various psychosocial factors, including peer community, an engaging online teacher, and students' confidence or self-efficacy. Structural factors such as workload and course design also play significant roles in influencing engagement. Essential skills for online student success include effective time management and organizational abilities, enabling students to manage their workload effectively (Farrell & Brunton, 2020). In that sense, progress indicators are expected to significantly aid in such a process. Moreover, enabling tracking of academic assignments and activities conducted in the online setting ought to foster peer collaboration and elevate student engagement, thereby enhancing the overall learning experience for students (Gamagee et al., 2022). Ramaswami et al. (2023) confirmed in their research a significant uptick in student engagement with learning technologies and online course resources immediately after using the dashboard. Concurrently, the findings demonstrated that the dashboard heightened respondents' levels of learning motivation, while the innovative insights derived from predictive and prescriptive analytics proved advantageous to their learning.

Progress indicators and learning experience

Wang & Han (2020) demonstrated that incorporating progress indicators into Learning Analytics Dashboards (LADs) enhances students' learning effectiveness. The utilization of these dashboards allows students, especially those with limited prior knowledge, to comprehensively understand their learning progress and avail additional opportunities for improving their learning efficiency.

Reading the information presented in learning analytics dashboards can pose a challenge, particularly as learners may prioritize specific indicators, leading to potential confusion over time. Park et al. (2022) stress the importance of designers and instructors providing supplementary or alternative resources that closely align with learners' needs, such as guidance on actions to take when maximum attempts are exceeded. Additionally, it is crucial to assess how learners perceive the various learning indicators displayed on their dashboards, as these perceptions may vary based on individual learning goals.

The findings from Valle et al.'s (2021) study indicate that learning analytics dashboards significantly alleviate students' interpretation anxiety and impact intrinsic goal orientation, depending on their initial levels of intrinsic goal orientation. The dashboard effectively reduced anxiety levels for students who began the course with higher anxiety levels. Thematic analysis revealed that students adopting a performance-avoidance goal orientation approach exhibited elevated anxiety levels, irrespective of the learning analytics dashboards used.

Research objectives

Literature review revealed that progress indicators can assist students in regulating their own learning within the course more easily and effectively. Therefore, this study focuses on how students perceive the use of progress indicators for self-monitoring within the Moodle Learning Management System, as well as how these indicators help students to be more engaged and have better learning experiences.

The main aim of this research is to identify correlations between students' monitoring of their own progress indicators (PI) and (1) their engagement (E); (2) their learning experience (LE), and (3) their final grades (FG).

Methods

Participants and Data Collection

The interdisciplinary course named "Business Informatics" spans topics in both economics and informatics and attracted a total of 112 part-time students during the 2023–2024 academic year in 2 Dislocated Centers (DC). The course was delivered in a blended format, consisting of synchronous and asynchronous components.

Each domain of knowledge (7 in total) within the course was supported by supplementary asynchronous resources for online classes. The topics covered in each domain of knowledge were divided into a series of Moodle's lesson activities. Students' progress through the lessons belonging to each domain of knowledge was managed using conditional activities to prohibit students from accessing additional aspects of the knowledge domain until they had demonstrated the necessary mastery of the earlier elements. Achieving a sufficient percentage of correct answers to the control questions at the end of a previous lesson was a requirement for accessing the subsequent lesson, and obtaining sufficient success in all the domain's lessons was a requirement for accessing the self-assessment quizzes. There was one final self-assessment quiz at the end of each domain of knowledge, without limitations to the number of attempts. Students were also awarded a badge for each final self-assessment completed with at least 75% success, demonstrating the achievement of the required level of mastery within that domain of knowledge.

In addition to self-assessments, official online flash tests, two midterms and the final exam were also required. Flash tests were used as a quick recap after every two to three synchronous classes. New tests were created for each official flash/midterm/exam session within the same Moodle course. Only the results of the official tests, conducted within a controlled environment, counted towards the final grade.

Progress indicators were implemented in LMS to enable students to track their progress according to each badge or the final self-assessment at the end of every knowledge domain. In total, 7 progress indicators were shown to students in the LA dashboard. Additionally, students' progress was visually represented by colour-coded indicators: green indicated that a student had met or exceeded the minimum requirements, red signified completion with a result below the required threshold, and blue colour indicated that the test had not been attempted.

Instrument

To assess the targeted constructs, an online survey was created and distributed to the participants upon completion of the course. The survey captured three targeted constructs: Engagement, Learning Experience, and Progress Indicators. The Engagement construct consisted of 4 items adopted from Kubischa (2024), while Learning Experience in the survey included 4 items from Ashby et al. (2011). The 4 Progress Indicator items were created based on the survey by Park & Jo (2015). Each item required students to indicate their level of agreement or disagreement on a Likert scale ranging from 1 - "strongly disagree" to 5 - "strongly agree".

Among the 112 students enrolled in the course, 77 of them completed the survey. Once the validity and reliability of the measurement instrument were confirmed, the final set of items was presented in Table 1.

Table 1: List of items in the measurement instrument

Engagement (E) (obtained from Kubischta, 2014)
E1: I respect the rules defined within the course.
E2: I complete tasks assigned within the course on time, such as self-assessments and assignments.
E3: I study at home even when there is no quiz.
E4: If I don't understand a concept while we're learning it in class, I make sure to figure it out.
Learning experience (LE) (obtained from Ashby et al, 2011):
LE1: I have managed to master the material (lessons and self-assessments) within the given deadlines.
LE2: The teaching materials are well connected to the activities in the course (lectures, exercises, self-assessments, quizzes).
LE3: Information about what and when to study was readily available.
LE4: The grading criteria for the course are clearly defined and known from the beginning.
Progress indicators (PI) (according to Park & Jo, 2015)
PI1: I often look at the flash test/badge progress indicators to track my progress.
PI2: I find the progress monitoring indicators in this course useful.
PI3: I believe that my points on the mid-term/final-exam are in line with the progress indicators.
PI4: I would like to be able to compare my progress with other students.

Results

Before interpreting the results, it was necessary to examine the validity of the measurement instrument, as presented in Table 2 for a sample of 77 participants. Initially, a Confirmatory Factor Analysis (CFA) was carried out, and items falling below the 0.6 threshold (Gefen & Straub, 2005) were removed to ensure the instrument scales' validity reached satisfactory levels. Following the completion of CFA, all metrics shown in Table 2 (CA - Cronbach's Alpha, AVE - Average Variance Extracted, CR - Composite Reliability) demonstrated the acceptable validity and reliability of the newly developed instrument.

Table 2: Construct reliability and validity

	CA	CR	AVE
Engagement	0.792	0.865	0.617
Learning experience	0.843	0.895	0.682
Progress indicators	0.720	0.825	0.546

In the next step, the correlations are calculated (see Table 3), interpreted according to Pallant (2007), and further analysed later in this paper. The correlation coefficients shown in Table 3 demonstrate a strong correlation between Progress Indicators and Engagement, and between Progress Indicators and Learning Experience. However, a small correlation was found between Progress Indicators and Final Grades

Table 3: Correlation coefficients between the main constructs

	r values	p values
Progress indicators -> Engagement	0.514**	0,000
Progress indicators -> Final grades	0.28*	0,014
Progress indicators -> Learning experience	0.684**	0,000

* statistically significant at p<0.05, ** statistically significant at p<0.01

In the end, we approached the analysis of each individual construct.

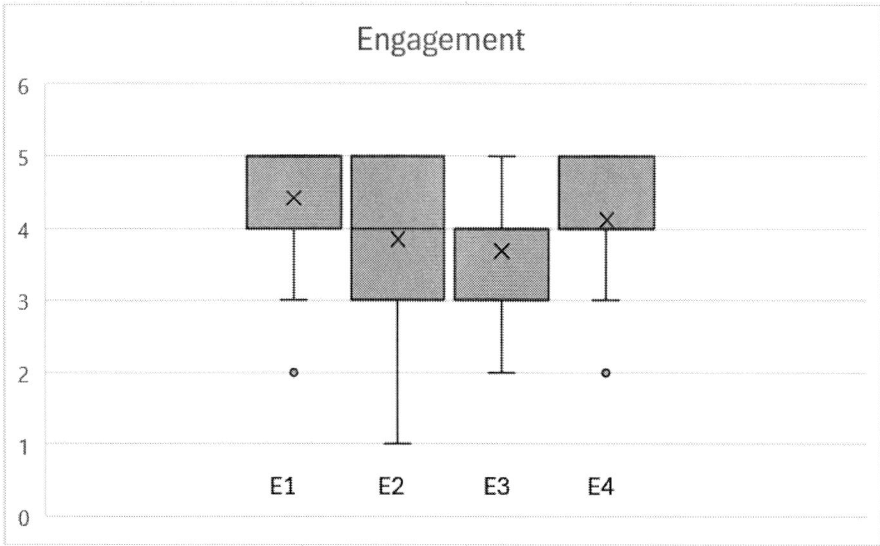

Figure 1: Distribution of answers for the "Engagement" construct (E1: median=5, mean=4.41; E2: median=4, mean=3.84; E3: median=4, mean=3.68; E4: median=4, mean=4.11)

The "Engagement" data in the Figure 1 box plot shows that the median values of items range from 4 to 5. We can observe that responses to all items are dispersed, except for E1 and E4. Regarding item 1, it can be concluded that students gravitate towards response 5 ("fully agree"), indicating a high level of respect for the rules within the course. Responses to item E4 tend towards response 4 ("Agree") (q1 = 4, q3= 5, with 50% of responses between 4 and 5, closer to the lower limit), suggesting that students work independently to understand concepts not covered in class. Similar trends are seen in responses to item E3, where students' responses fall between 3 and 4. However, it is evident that some have learned at home where there was no quiz, while others have not. Responses to E2 are dispersed (q1=3, q3=5, with 50% of answers between 3 and 5) but tend towards response 4 (indicating completion of tasks assigned within the course on time, such as self-assessments, assignments, and the like).

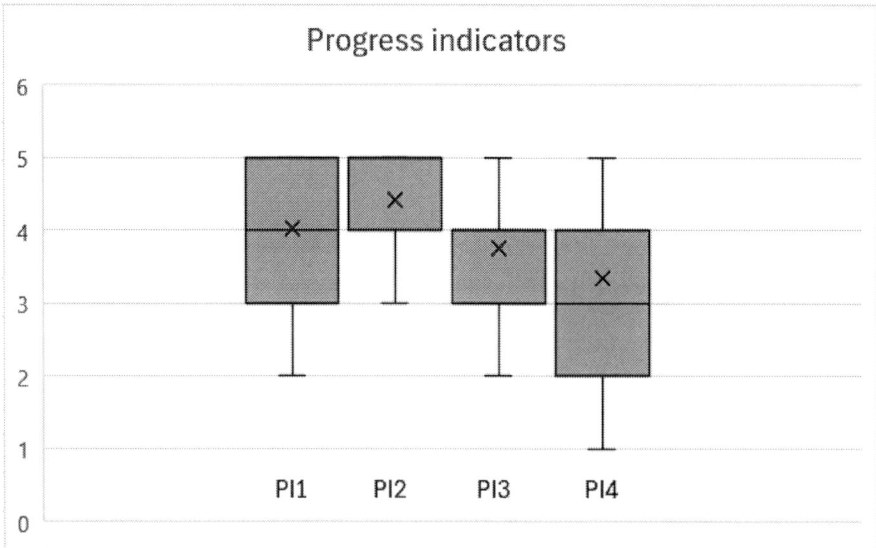

Figure 2. Distribution of answers for the "Progress indicators" construct (PI1: median=4, mean=4.02; PI2: median=5, mean=4.42; PI3: median=5, mean=3.80; PI4: median=3, mean=3.38)

For "Progress Indicators," mean values range between 3.08 (lowest) and 4.42 (highest). Regarding the first item, the median value is 4, and the mean value is 4.02, indicating that students generally agree (rating 4 out of 5 on the scale) that they often look at the flash test/badges progress indicators to track their progress (q1=3, q3=5, with 50% of responses falling between 3 and 5). The second item, which assesses: "I find the progress monitoring indicators in this course useful," has a very high median (5) and mean (4.42), aligning with response 5 ("totally agree"). PI3 aligns with response 4 (median = 5, mean = 3.80, q1 = 3, q3 = 4), indicating that students agree that their points on the mid-term/final exam are consistent with the progress monitoring indicators. For PI4, student responses are somewhat dispersed (q1=2, q3=4, with 50% of responses falling between 2 and 4), and responses range between 3 (neither agree nor disagree) and 4 (agree) for the item: "I would like to be able to compare my progress with other students."

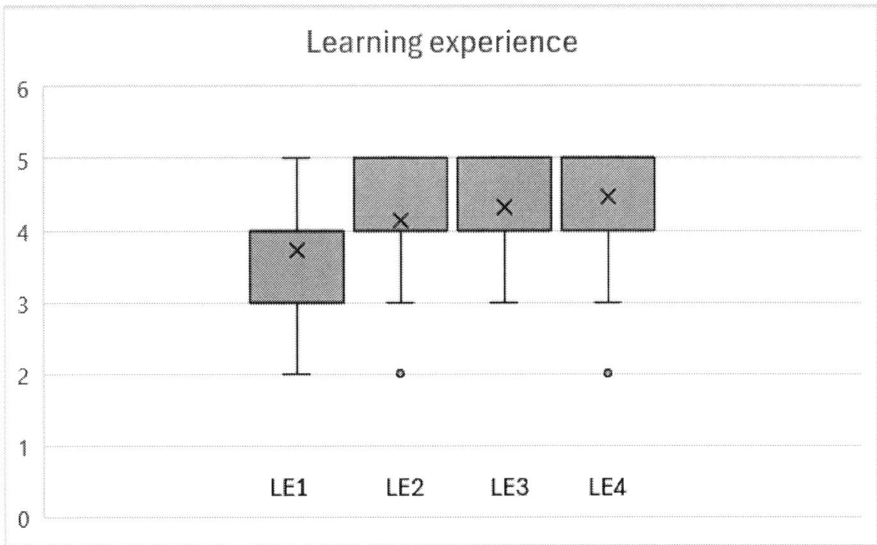

Figure 3. Distribution of answers for the "Learning experience" construct (LE1: median=4, mean=3.71; LE2: median=4, mean=4.14; LE3: median=4, mean=4.32; LE4: median=5, mean=4.47)

The "Learning Experience" data presented in Figure 3 box plot show that the median values of items range from 3.71 up to 4.47. It can be noticed that responses for item LE1 are somewhat more dispersed than for other items. This suggests that students neither agree nor disagree (answer no. 3) that they could manage to master the material (lessons and self-assessments) within the given deadlines. For other items related to the Learning Experience, it can be concluded that 50% of responses fall between responses 4 and 5, indicating that students generally agree with items LE2, LE3, and LE4.

Conclusion

This research focused on investigating how progress indicators can influence the engagement, final grade, and learning experience of students. A research instrument was developed to assess how students perceive their engagement within the course, the utilization of progress indicators, and their overall learning experience. At the end of the semester, final grades were also collected.

A total of 77 students participated in the survey. Results showed that progress indicators have a strong influence on student engagement and learning experience within the course. A small correlation was found between progress indicators and final grades. This paper demonstrates that progress indicators can positively influence learning experiences through their incorporation into Learning Analytics Dashboards (LADs), as already indicated by Wang & Han (2020). Additionally, it was confirmed that progress indicators can play a significant role in increasing students' engagement, aligning with the study of Ramaswami et al. (2023), who verified a notable increase in student engagement with learning technologies and online course materials following their interaction with the dashboard. Therefore, we can confirm that tracking students' progress using progress indicators can boost their engagement and experience due to the clarity of tasks yet to be completed compared to those already accomplished.

This approach combines subjective data, such as students' perceptions with objective data, such as students grades with and adequate sample to interpret the findings with confidence. However, this research only explored a limited set of factors and did not consider other factors that might have strong influence on student success (e.g. student motivation, satisfaction, etc.). Besides investigating the role of different factors in this process, future research could also strive to investigate the impact of learning experience and engagement on students' final scores. It would be beneficial to explore whether these factors play a mediating role in the correlation between progress indicators and students' final course grades, and in what manner.

References

Ashby, A., Richardson, J. T., & Woodley, A. (2011). National student feedback surveys in distance education: an investigation at the UK Open University. Open Learning: The Journal of Open, Distance and e-Learning, 26(1), 5-25.

Farrell, O., & Brunton, J. (2020). A balancing act: A window into online student engagement experiences. International Journal of Educational Technology in Higher Education, 17(1), 25.

Gamage, K. A., Gamage, A., & Dehideniya, S. C. (2022). Online and hybrid teaching and learning: Enhance effective student engagement and experience. Education Sciences, 12(10), 651.

Jayashanka, R., Hettiarachchi, E., & Hewagamage, K. P. (2022). Technology Enhanced Learning Analytics Dashboard in Higher Education. Electronic Journal of e-Learning, 20(2), 151-170.

Jivet, I., Scheffel, M., Specht, M., & Drachsler, H. (2018, March). License to evaluate: Preparing learning analytics dashboards for educational practice. In Proceedings of the 8th international conference on learning analytics and knowledge (pp. 31-40).

Kubischta, F. (2014). Engagement and Motivation: Questioning students on study-motivation, engagement and study strategies.

Ming, M. W. C., & Kee, C. S. (2021). Maximising Students' Learning Through Learning Analytics.

Naranjo, D. M., Prieto, J. R., Moltó, G., & Calatrava, A. (2019). A visual dashboard to track learning analytics for educational cloud computing. Sensors, 19(13), 2952.

Pallant, J. (2007). A step-by-step guide to data analysis using SPSS for windows version 15. SPSS Survival manual, 3.

Park, E., Ifenthaler, D., & Clariana, R. B. (2023). Adaptive or adapted to: Sequence and reflexive thematic analysis to understand learners' self-regulated learning in an adaptive learning analytics dashboard. British Journal of Educational Technology, 54(1), 98-125.

Park, Y., & Jo, I. H. (2015). Development of the learning analytics dashboard to support students' learning performance. Journal of Universal Computer Science, 21(1), 110.

Park, Y., & Jo, I. H. (2019). Factors that affect the success of learning analytics dashboards. Educational Technology Research and Development, 67(6), 1547-1571.

Prabowo, H., Ikhsan, R. B., & Yuniarty, Y. (2022, November). Student performance in online learning higher education: a preliminary research. In Frontiers in Education (Vol. 7, p. 916721). Frontiers.

Ramaswami, G., Susnjak, T., & Mathrani, A. (2023). Effectiveness of a Learning Analytics Dashboard for Increasing Student Engagement Levels. Journal of Learning Analytics, 10(3), 115-134.

Rojas-López, A., Rincón-Flores, E. G., Mena, J., García-Peñalvo, F. J., & Ramírez-Montoya, M. S. (2019). Engagement in the course of programming in higher education through the use of gamification. Universal Access in the Information Society, 18(3), 583-597.

Safsouf, Y., Mansouri, K., & Poirier, F. (2022, March). Understand the influence of learning analytics dashboards on learner self-regulation and academic success. In 2022 IEEE Global Engineering Education Conference (EDUCON) (pp. 1044-1047). IEEE.

Susnjak, T., Ramaswami, G. S., & Mathrani, A. (2022). Learning analytics dashboard: a tool for providing actionable insights to learners. International Journal of Educational Technology in Higher Education, 19(1), 12.

Valle, N., Antonenko, P., Valle, D., Sommer, M., Huggins-Manley, A. C., Dawson, K., ... & Baiser, B. (2021). Predict or describe? How learning analytics dashboard design influences motivation and statistics anxiety in an online statistics course. Educational Technology Research and Development, 69(3), 1405-1431.

Wang, D., & Han, H. (2021). Applying learning analytics dashboards based on process-oriented feedback to improve students' learning effectiveness. Journal of Computer Assisted Learning, 37(2), 487-499.

Human experts and Generative AI interaction: From real-world and real-life language learning diary-research app to a diary-learning app

Orit Ezra[1], Anat Cohen[1], Dror Shany[2]

[1] Tel Aviv University, Israel; oezra1@gmail.com
[1] Tel Aviv University, Israel; anatco@tauex.tau.ac.il
[2] Tel-Hai College, Israel; drorsha@m.telhai.ac.il

Correspondence: Orit Ezra: oezra1@gmail.com

Abstract:

Generative AI (GenAI) could be beneficial for instructional designers, expediting the design of educational mobile apps. One needed app, currently absent, is a digital diary for second and foreign-language learners to record their outside-classroom activities. Given the research and learning merits of keeping such diaries, a diary-research app (Langy) was previously developed to measure learners' real-life (RL) and real-world (RW) language learning. This study aims to provide design guidelines to transform this app into a learning app based on the interaction with ChatGPT during this design process and examine the human-machine interaction. The prompt submitted to ChatGPT4 described the diary-research app and asked for suggestions on how to transform it into a diary-learning app. ChatGPT produced 14 suggestions, upon which the researchers deliberated. The mutually created design suggestions emerging from this reciprocal interaction provide a blueprint for the new diary-learning app, adding a new purpose of promoting RL and RW learning (in addition to measuring) and relevant features such as goal settings, gaming rewards, and reflective prompts. Three processes were revealed during the complementary human-machine interaction: 1. ChatGPT's offered generic suggestions, which the researchers adapted to more specific app requirements. 2. The researchers linked between the ChatGPT's suggestions and added theoretical grounds. 3. The researchers, in some cases, altered or completely negated the ChatGPT's suggestions. This study contributes to the research field of language-learning diaries. Moreover, it contributes to our understanding of how GenAI can be used as an instructional designer to assist in the design of educational mobile apps.

Keywords: GenAI, language-learning diaries, contextualized language learning, mobile app development, human-machine interaction

Introduction

Since the massive penetration of Generative AI (GenAI) tools in late 2022, researchers and education practitioners have started considering the potential usages of these tools (Petrovska et al., 2024). One potential is using GenAI for designing and developing digital environments such as educational mobile apps (Mariani & Dwivedi, 2024), which design and development is a long process that requires time and human expertise (Champeny et al., 2004). GenAI, using large language models (LLM), can access big data and analyze it (Fütterer et al., 2023), which is difficult for human experts and likely to become a prolonged process (Cohen et al., 2021). Therefore, instructional designers tasked with designing educational apps could benefit from using GenAI.

Diaries and journals are considered valuable for recording occasions of outside-classroom language learning shortly after the event (Reinders & Benson, 2017) and reveal aspects of the language learning experience which is challenging to attain by other means (Curtis & Bailey, 2009). Diaries have mostly been used in second or foreign language learning studies as a research tool to collect information in order to investigate outside-classroom learning processes (e.g., Benson et al., 2018; García-Amaya, 2017; Ranta & Meckelborg, 2013). Diaries could also be useful in boosting learners' involvement and autonomy (Krishnan & Hoon, 2002).

However, as best we know, only a few studies (e.g., Litzler, 2014) have used diaries as a learning tool for the learners' and teachers' needs.

Moreover, neither of the previously used digital diaries in language-learning studies (Benson et al., 2018; García-Amaya, 2017; Ranta & Meckelborg, 2013) was a mobile diary application dedicated to language learning. Therefore, a diary-research mobile app called Langy, which is dedicated to language learning, was recently developed for the purposes of collecting data about outside-classroom real-world (RW) and real-life (RL) contextualized language learning (Ezra et al., 2022). In light of diaries' potential for becoming learning tools as well, the authors nowadays seek to transform the Langy diary-research app into a diary-learning app by drawing assistance from GenAI in designing the upgraded mobile app.

Langy – the mobile diary-research app

The purpose of the current diary-research app is to collect data to measure the learners' RL and RW learning, which is prominent for language learners. RL learning is related to the learner's life activities; RW is related to the learner's place. The learners who record their events using the Learner Diary module screens are guided using open or closed questions about aspects of the language, RL/RW context (such as activities and place information), mobile materials, and feelings. This input is required in order to measure five aspects of the learners' RL and RW learning that are key to students' learning development (Figure 1).

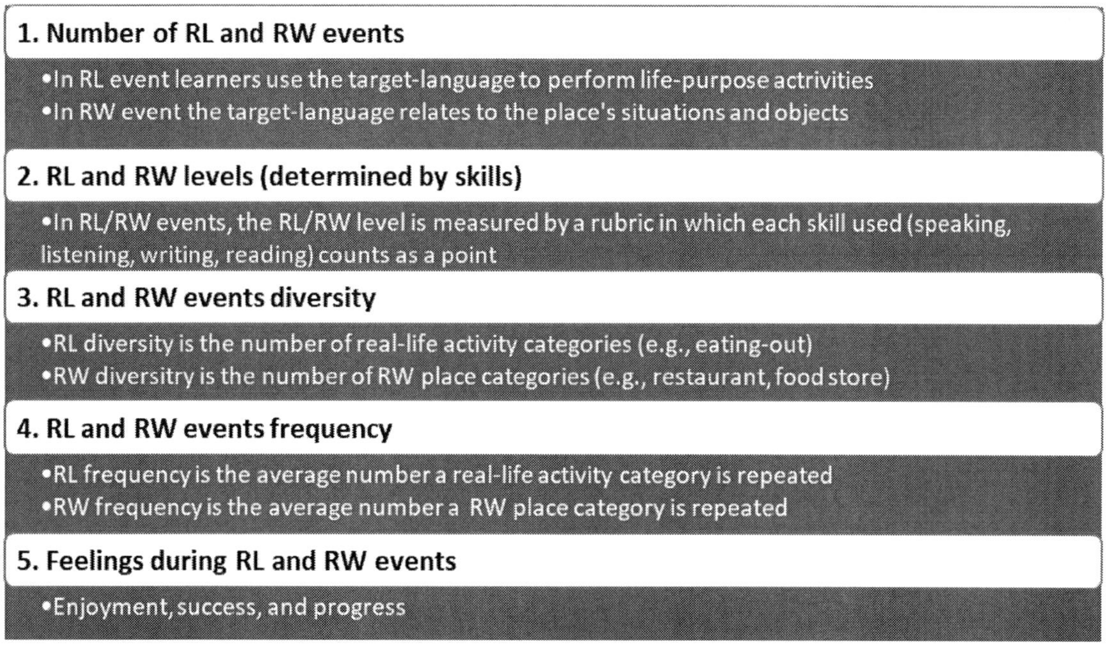

Figure 1: The five aspects of the learners' RL and RW learning

Figure 2.1 shows the Opening screen used by Chinese learners in Taiwan. Here, learners select a mobile or non-mobile event (in a mobile event, the learner uses a mobile device to help learn, practice, or use the target language). Figure 2.2 shows the first screen in both event types, the General Event Details screen, where the learner records the event's day, place, and title.

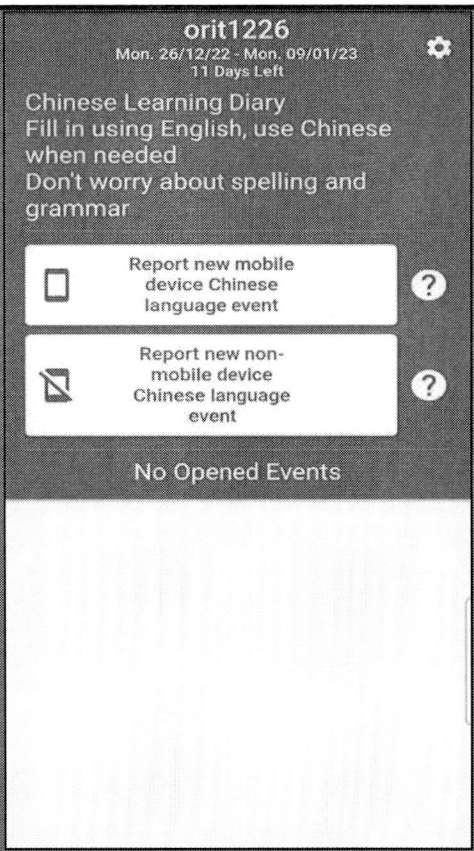

Figure 2.1: Opening screen

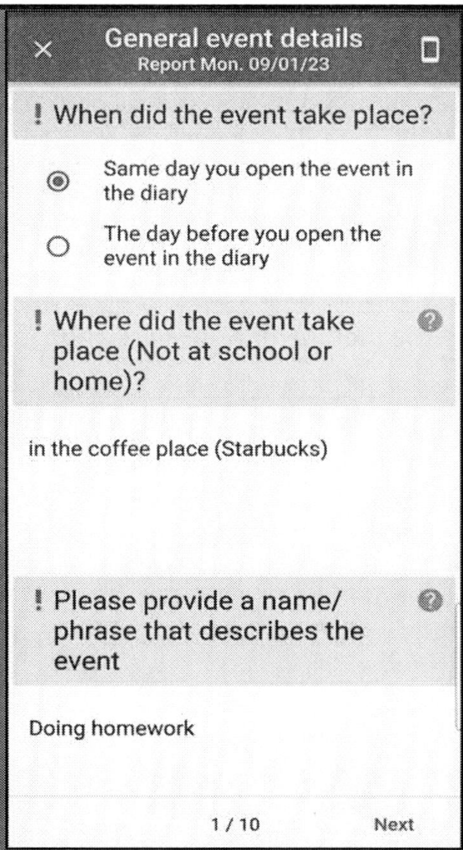

Figure 2.2: General Event Details screen

The Opening screen's titles and buttons, as well as the event screens' questions, are all configurable for other languages and research needs using JSON files. Figure 3 illustrates the flow of questions answered for each event through the screens.

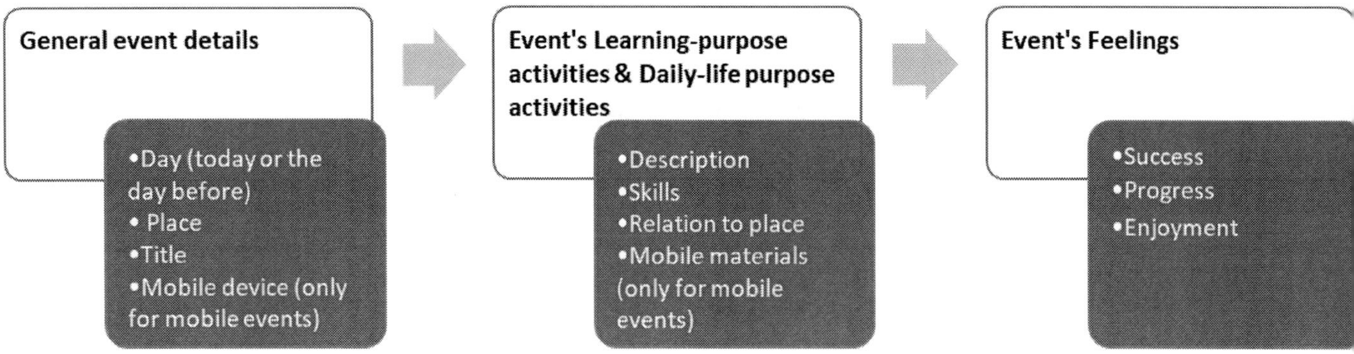

Figure 3: Flow of questions answered for events

The Admin Monitor module enables the researchers to track learners' progress and analyze the data by using the Track Learners' Activity screen (Figure 4) and the Learners' Submitted Events report.

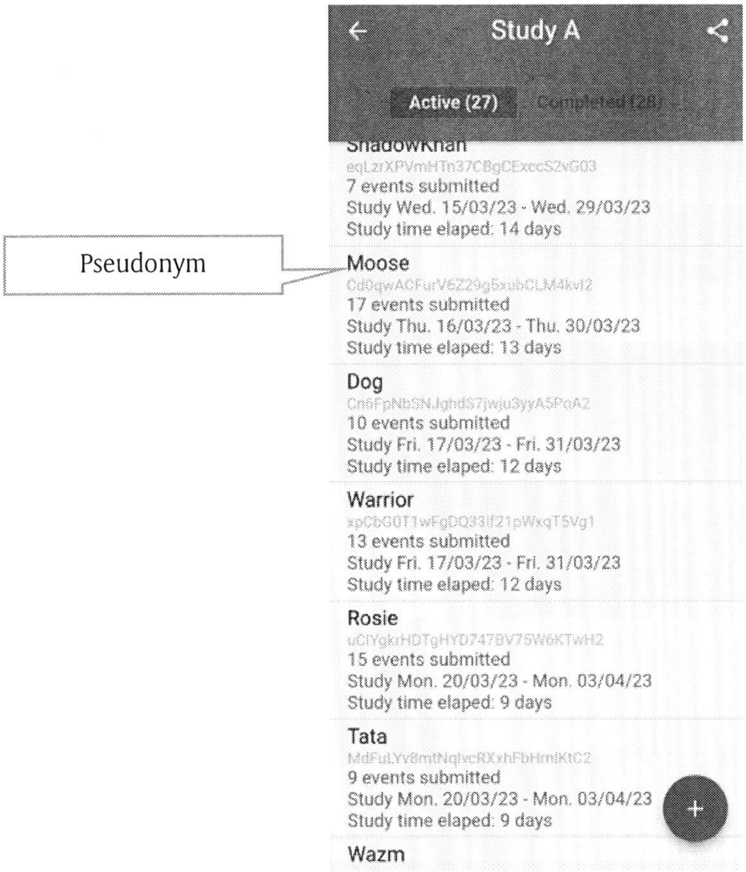

Figure 4: Track Learners' Activity screen

The study

In light of the lack of a dedicated diary-learning mobile app for language learners and teachers and the GenAI potential for expediting design and development, the researchers harnessed ChatGPT as an instructional designer to assist in the transformation process of the Langy RL/RW diary-research app into a diary-learning app. This study's purpose is twofold: to provide design guidelines for transforming the diary-research app into a diary-learning app for language learners and to examine the human-machine interaction as manifested in the researchers' interaction with ChatGPT during this design process. To this aim, this study targets to address the following question: What design suggestions are provided by ChatGPT for transforming a research-oriented RL/RW language-learning diary app into a diary-learning app? How can human experts act on these suggestions to design the new diary-learning app?

This study contributes to the research field of language-learning diaries by promoting a diary mobile app for research and learning. The insights about the human-machine interaction between the researchers and ChatGPT contribute to our understanding of how GenAI can be used as an instructional designer to assist in the design of educational mobile apps.

Method

ChatGPT4 was asked on December 17, 2023, to provide suggestions on how to transform the diary-research app into a diary-learning app using the following prompt:

> We developed a diary for language learners that collects their real-world and real-life learning activities outside the class. We collect the following information on each learning event: the date, the place, the title, used mobile device apps and website, a detailed description of the event, the language learning skills which were used in this event, an explanation of whether the learning was

related to the place, and feelings during this event including the feelings of progress and success. In addition, we can see in real-time how many events the learners are doing and we can export the data to Excel file. We now want to transform this diary into a powerful learning tool for our learners. Please give suggestion how to do it.

Using qualitative methodology, the researchers deliberated the ChatGPT's suggestions and integrated their complementary input. During deliberations, the researchers considered additional supporting literature and the five aspects of the app discussed above (Figure 1). The researchers are scholars in the field of educational technology (first and second authors) and cognitive psychology (third author).

Finding

ChatGPT, working in the capacity of the instructional designer, produced 14 suggestions. The 14 human-machine synthesized design suggestions are described below. Each suggestion starts with the ChatGPT point, followed by the expert team's reconstructed design point.

ChatGPT suggestion 1

"Personalized Learning Recommendations:

Use the data collected to provide personalized recommendations for each learner. Analyze their past activities, preferences, and progress to suggest future learning events or resources. For instance, if a learner frequently uses a particular app or website, the diary could recommend similar resources."

It would be beneficial to provide personalized recommendations based on learners' past events. Specifically, employing the adaptive learning principles (Aleven et al., 2016), learners should be recommended on the next RL activities and RW places, according to their previous events, with the intention of gradually increasing their number of RL and RW events, their diversity, and frequency. Low-activity learners should be encouraged to increase event numbers gradually, and high-activity learners to maintain their event numbers. Learners should also be directed to slightly different RL activities and RW places while not deserting previous activities and places. Thus diversifying the learning but smartly ensuring that the learner is suggested with RL activities and RW places relevant to them while maintaining frequency. Finally, the app should promote skills usage. For example, if learners dominantly use speaking and listening while visiting restaurants, a reading menu recommendation should be provided.

ChatGPT suggestion 2

"Gamification Elements:

Introduce gamification to make learning more engaging. This could include earning points, badges, or rewards for completing certain activities or reaching milestones. Leaderboards can also encourage friendly competition among learners."

Learners could receive individual benefits such as points accumulated based on reaching millstones of a number of RL and RW events, diversity, and frequency. However, we believe friendly competitions and leaderboards should be optional. Thus, learners who join the competition can receive benefits in light of their competitive achievements ranked against other contestants' achievements in the number of RL and RW events, their diversity, and their frequency. The app can also provide tips based on leaders' RL activities and RW places.

ChatGPT suggestion 3

"Interactive Feedback System:

Implement a system where learners can receive immediate feedback on their progress. This could be through automated analysis of their inputs or periodic reviews from language tutors."

The app should provide automated input analyses to facilitate personalized recommendations to learners (suggestion one); language teachers should provide periodic reviews. Teachers can see RL and RW categories among whole class students or for individual learners and can guide towards popular or non-popular RL activities and RW places. This could also increase the total RL and RW event numbers. Teachers can also guide towards using new skills in popular categories (e.g., reading a menu in a restaurant). Teachers should also use the students' reported feelings in personal student-teacher interactions since these could improve learners' feelings (LoCasale-Crouch et al., 2018).

ChatGPT suggestion 4
"Integration with Other Learning Tools:
Ensure the diary can seamlessly integrate with popular language learning apps and platforms. This will allow for a more cohesive learning experience, as learners can easily transfer data between different tools."

Langy should integrate with popular language learning apps such as electronic dictionaries and flashcards. These apps, which normally support decontextualized vocabulary learning, could then provide, for example, words related to specific RL and RW categories and spaced repetition (Edge et al., 2011) that is based on the diversity and/or frequency of RL and RW categories. Language exchange apps could also be enriched with data from Langy. Learners could be prompted to discuss issues related to popular and non-popular RL and RW categories or connect with people based on mutual or complimentary RL activities and RW places. By integrating Langy – an app primarily working on learners' procedural language knowledge (DeKeyser, 2015) related to their RL and RW learning – with these apps that promote declarative language knowledge, a cohesive and comprehensive learning process is supported. Langy could also benefit from integrating with generic apps (Reinders & Pegrum, 2016) such as WhatsApp or calendars.

ChatGPT suggestion 5
"Social Interaction Features:
Add features that allow learners to interact with each other. This could be through forums, chat rooms, or study groups. Peer support and discussion can be very beneficial for language learning."

Peer support, manifested by the social interaction features (forums, chat rooms, or study groups), reflects a wider pedagogy of social learning that is highly emphasized in second language learning (Mitchell et al., 2012). However, previous studies have shown that learners do not utilize enough of these outlets for learning (Cohen et al., 2019). They might prefer using dedicated language exchange apps or generic apps such as WhatsApp, as discussed above (suggestion four). Thus, Langy could expand an individual diary learning experience into a social diary-based language learning.

ChatGPT suggestion 6
"Customizable Learning Paths:
Allow learners to set their own goals and create customizable learning paths. The diary could then track their progress towards these goals and offer guidance on what steps to take next."

Setting personal goals is widely adapted in learning apps. The goal-setting theory (Locke & Latham, 2012) is a relevant motivational theory in this respect. Langy requires a mechanism that encourages learners to update their goals frequently. Learners should be prompted to set goals for a number of RL/RW events, skills for RL/RW events, and diversity and frequency of RL activities and RW places in these events. Langy's explicit goals accord with the goal-setting theory that encourages goals' specificity (Dörnyei & Ushioda, 2011). The diary could track the learner's progress toward these goals, enabling a customizable learning path by providing subsequent guidance for learners. This enriches suggestion one, as personalized recommendations are provided based on learners' past events and desired goals. It would also be beneficial to assist learners in actively tracking their progress toward achieving goals using visual presentations, as discussed in suggestion 7.

ChatGPT suggestion 7
"Visual Progress Tracking:
Enhance the diary with visual tools like graphs and progress bars to help learners visualize their language development over time."

Visual tracking of learning progress is common in various educational technologies. In Langy, this could be utilized to reflect the learners' progress in the five app aspects within a selected timeframe. Thus, graphs and bars would present changes in RL/RW events' numbers, skills employed, diversity, frequency, and feelings. Learners opting to participate in friendly competitions and leaderboards, as discussed in suggestion two, would visually track their progress in the app aspects comparatively. Suggestion six above mandates visual progress tracking tools for encouraging learners to meet their goals. Finally, visual tracking tools such as dashboards could also leverage teachers' capabilities to assist in periodic reviews (suggestion three).

ChatGPT suggestion 8
"Reflective Prompts:
Incorporate prompts that encourage learners to reflect on their experiences. This can deepen their understanding and help them recognize areas for improvement."

Abundant literature supports the use of reflective prompts to deepen learning and identify areas for improvement. We are particularly interested in reflection guidance using reflective question prompts, as endorsed by various studies concerning reflection guidance in computing systems (Fessl et al., 2017). We suggest daily reflective question prompts such as: Have you already recorded RW/RL events? How many RL/RW events did you do? Did you use the target language in a new RW place? Did you repeat some RL activity using the target language? Did you use multiple skills in your RL/RW events? Did your feelings improve while using the target language in RL/RW events?

ChatGPT suggestion 9
"Multimedia Support:
Enable learners to add multimedia elements to their entries, such as audio recordings or videos. This can make the diary more interactive and aid in practicing different language skills."

Indeed, learners should be able to add multimedia to aid in learning. First, since diary entries in the target language could promote language learning, it would be beneficial to use multimedia to maximize skills usage while reporting events. Second, using multimedia, learners could record the particular things they wish to remember about their events to enrich post-event learning and skills practice.

ChatGPT suggestion 10
"Offline Accessibility:
Ensure that the diary can be accessed and used even when learners are offline. This makes it more convenient and ensures that learning can continue without interruption."

Working offline is worthy of consideration, but it is contingent on technical limitations such as synchronization.

ChatGPT suggestion 11
"Machine Learning Insights:
Use machine learning algorithms to analyze the collected data and provide insights on learning patterns, common challenges, and effective strategies."

We endorse machine-learning insights. Specifically, actual event patterns can demonstrate learners' mal-learning sequences related to time, such as doing RL/RW events in too-spaced intervals. These patterns could be used to promote personal recommendations (suggestion one) and enrich the (externally provided) spaced repetition (suggestion four). Event-recording patterns, such as the proximity to the actual event time, could also be used for personal recommendations (suggestion one) to guide learners toward a more reliable diary-recording process.

ChatGPT suggestion 12
"Exportable Custom Reports:
Allow learners to generate custom reports from their diary entries, which they can use for self-assessment or share with tutors for further guidance."

Exportable reports build on feedback on progress (suggestion three). Exportable reports will be considered for learners and teachers alike to enhance their shared learning-teaching experience.

ChatGPT suggestion 13
"Language Exchange Programs:
Facilitate language exchange partnerships among users of different native languages to practice speaking and understanding real conversational language."

Facilitating language exchange was previously advocated through suggestions four and five that distinctly noted why and how Langy and language exchange apps could benefit from integrating. Thus, we prefer Langy remains an individual app that forwards its unique data to other language exchange apps.

ChatGPT suggestion 14
"Regular Updates and Improvements:
Continuously update the diary with new features, resources, and content based on user feedback and evolving language learning methodologies."

We are currently analyzing the feedback from 87 learners of Chinese as a second language who used the diary-research app in Taiwan. Once the diary-learning app is in use, periodic surveys and focus groups will become routine outlets advising on regular updates and improvements.

Discussion and conclusions

This study's purpose is twofold: to provide design guidelines for transforming the Langy diary-research app into a diary-learning app for language learners, and to examine the human-machine interaction as manifested in the experts' interaction with GenAI during this design process. The interaction between the ChatGPT4 and the three researchers resulted in 14 suggestions representing the fusion of their instructional design knowledge.

These initial design guidelines for Langy constitute the inception of a diary-learning app for language learners. It will advance the existing diary-research app by expanding its purpose and providing relevant features. The app's original narrower research purpose of sole detection of learner's RL and RW contextualized language learning grows with an additional purpose of promoting the learners' RL/RW learning. Langy is promoting contextualized RL/RW learning, which is mostly undealt in common language-learning apps (Ravenscraft, 2019). It can do so by harnessing various features, such as adaptive learning, gaming rewards, optional friendly competition and leaderboards, goal setting, tools and visual artifacts such as dashboards and reports for teachers and learners, reflective prompts, multimedia entries, and machine-learning insights. The contextualized RL/RW learning promoted in Langy will be complemented by integrating with dedicated or generic mobile apps (Reinders & Pegrum, 2016), such as dictionaries, flashcards, language exchange, and generic messaging services. Thus, the RL/RW learning is augmented with an enveloping, dedicated, pedagogical, and social learning layer. Implementing these features, Langy could become a more dynamic, interactive, and personalized tool, greatly enhancing the language learning experience (OpenAI, 2023). Notably, this paper presents 14 fused suggestions according to the ChatGPT's output. Additional instructional design ideas would likely be considered. Future studies should explore these based on additional literature and surveys with learners.

A reciprocal human-machine interaction with contributions from both sides is exhibited, displaying the experts' usage of the ChatGPT's suggestions as a basis for constructing new design suggestions. Three noticeable points were found to characterize this complementary human-machine interaction manifested in the reciprocal correspondence between the researchers and GenAI. First, ChatGPT generated general suggestions that could apply to any educational technology. The researchers adapted these generic suggestions to the specific app aspects, such as RL/RW diversity and frequency, according to their comprehensive familiarity with the app and their own knowledge of the literature. Future interaction could look further into each suggestion by telling ChatGPT the experts' response and providing more information on the app aspects of learners' RL/RW learning. Indeed, for GenAI to work optimally, the researchers would need to interrogate GenAI in steps, using an iterative process whereby the initial generated output can be further refined by more granular interrogation from which the final output can be produced (Svendsen & Garvey, 2023). Second, the researchers added links among the various suggestions and supplied additional theoretical grounds for them. Third, the researchers did not take ChatGPT's suggestions for granted and critically altered them or even negated them altogether. This study shows how GenAI can assist educational technology practitioners in designing a learning app by employing the human-machine corporation in which the different stakeholders learn from each other's affordances (Cohen et al., 2021).

Acknowledgements

We thank the Israel Polak Program for Excellence at Tel Aviv University in Israel who helped us fund this research.

References

Aleven, V., McLaughlin, E. A., Glenn, R. A., & Koedinger, K. R. (2016). Instruction based on adaptive learning technologies. In R. E. Mayer & P. A. Alexander (Eds.), Handbook of research on learning and instruction, second edition (pp. 522–559). Routledge. 10.4324/9781315736419-33/instruction-based-adaptive-learning-technologies-vincent-aleven-elizabeth-mcl-au-ghlin

Benson, P., Chappell, P., & Yates, L. (2018). A day in the life: Mapping international students' language learning environments in multilingual Sydney. Australian Journal of Applied Linguistics, 1(1), 20–32. https://doi.org/10.29140/ajal.v1n1.21

Champeny, L., Borgman, C. L., Leazer, G. H., Gilliland-Swetland, A. J., Millwood, K. A., D'Avolio, L., Finley, J. R., Smart, L. J., Mautone, P. D., Mayer, R. E., & Johnson, R. A. (2004). Developing a digital learning environment: An evaluation of design and implementation processes. Proceedings of the 4th ACM/IEEE-CS Joint Conference on Digital Libraries, 37-46. https://doi.org/10.1145/996350.996361

Cohen, A., Ezra, O., Hershkovitz, A., Tzayada, O., Tabach, M., Levy, B., Segal, A., & Gal, K. (2021). Personalizing mathematical content in educational applets repository: human teacher versus machine-based considerations. Educational Technology Research and Development, 69(3), 1505–1528. https://doi.org/10.1007/s11423-021-10002-x

Cohen, A., Shimony, U., Nachmias, R., & Soffer, T. (2019). Active learners' characterization in MOOC forums and their generated knowledge. *British Journal of Educational Technology*, *50*(1), 177–198. https://doi.org/10.1111/bjet.12670

Curtis, A., & Bailey, K. (2009). Diary studies. OnCUE Journal, 3(1), 67–85.

DeKeyser, R. (2015). Skill acquisition theory. In B. VanPatten & J. Williams (Eds.), Theories in second language acquisition: An introduction (second edition) (pp. 94–112). Routledge. https://doi.org/10.4324/9780203628942

Dörnyei, Z., & Ushioda, E. (2011). Teaching and researching motivation. Routledge. https://doi.org/10.4324/9781315833750

Edge, D., Searle, E., Chiu, K., Zhao, J., & Landay, J. A. (2011). MicroMandarin: mobile language learning in context. Proceedings of the SIGCHI Conference on Human Factors in Computing Systems, 3169–3178.

Ezra, O., Cohen, A., & Shany, D. (2022). A mobile diary application as an instrument for collecting real-world and real-life contextualized language learning. In J. Colpaert, Y. Wang, & G. Stockwell (Eds.), *Proceedings of the XXIst International CALL Research Conference* (pp. 137–145). Castledown. https://doi.org/10.29140/9781914291050

Fessl, A., Blunk, O., Prilla, M., & Pammer, V. (2017). The known universe of reflection guidance: A literature review. International Journal of Technology Enhanced Learning, 9(2–3), 103–125. https://doi.org/10.1504/IJTEL.2017.084491

Fütterer, T., Fischer, C., Alekseeva, A., Chen, X., Tate, T., Warschauer, M., & Gerjets, P. (2023). ChatGPT in education: Global reactions to AI innovations. Research Square. https://doi.org/10.21203/rs.3.rs-2840105/v1

García-Amaya, L. (2017). Detailing L1 and L2 use in study-abroad research: Data from the daily linguistic questionnaire. System, 71(2017), 60–72. http://dx.doi.org/10.1016/J.SYSTEM.2017.09.023

Krishnan, L. A., & Hoon, L. H. (2002). Diaries: Listening to 'voices' from the multicultural classroom. ELT Journal, 56(3), 227–239. https://doi.org/10.1093/ELT/56.3.227

Litzler, M. F. (2014). Independent study logs: Guiding and encouraging students in the process of language learning. Journal of Language Teaching and Research, 5(5), 994–998. https://doi.org/10.4304/jltr.5.5.994-998

LoCasale-Crouch, J., Jamil, F., Pianta, R. C., Rudasill, K. M., & DeCoster, J. (2018). Observed quality and consistency of fifth graders' teacher–student interactions: Associations with feelings, engagement, and performance in School. Sage Open, 8(3). https://doi.org/10.1177/2158244018794774

Locke, E. A., & Latham, G. P. (2012). Goal setting theory, 1990. In E. A. Locke & G. P. Latham (Eds.), New developments in goal setting and task performance (pp. 3–15). Routledge. https://doi.org/10.4324/9780203082744

Mariani, M., & Dwivedi, Y. K. (2024). Generative artificial intelligence in innovation management: A preview of future research developments. Journal of Business Research, 175. https://doi.org/10.1016/j.jbusres.2024.114542

Mitchell, R., Myles, F., & Marsden, E. (2012). Second language learning theories (third edition). Routledge. https://doi.org/10.4324/9780203770795

OpenAI. (2023). ChatGPT (Dec 17 version) [Large language model]. https://chat.openai.com/chat

Petrovska, O., Clift, L., Moller, F., & Pearsall, R. (2024). Incorporating Generative AI into software development education. Proceedings of the 8th Conference on Computing Education Practice, 37-40. https://doi.org/10.1145/3633053.3633057

Ranta, L., & Meckelborg, A. (2013). How much exposure to English do international graduate students really get? Measuring language use in a naturalistic setting. The Canadian Modern Language Review, 69(1), 1–33. http://dx.doi.org/10.3138/cmlr.987

Ravenscraft, E. (2019). 500 days of Duolingo: What you can (and can't) learn from a language app. The New York Times. https://www.nytimes.com/2019/05/04/smarter-living/500-days-of-duolingo-what-you-can-and-cant-learn-from-a-language-app.html

Reinders, H., & Benson, P. (2017). Research agenda: Language learning beyond the classroom. Language Teaching, 50(4), 561–578. https://doi.org/10.1017/S0261444817000192

Reinders, H., & Pegrum, M. (2016). Supporting language learning on the move. An evaluative framework for mobile language learning resources. In B. Tomlinson (Ed.), SLA research and materials development for language learning (pp. 219–231). Routledge. https://doi.org/10.4324/9781315749082

Svendsen, A., & Garvey, B. (2023). An outline for an interrogative/prompt library to help improve output quality from Generative-AI datasets (A white paper). Analytic Research Consortium. http://dx.doi.org/10.2139/ssrn.4495319

Integrating Artificial Intelligence in Vocational and Adult Education: A Supplement to the DigCompEdu Framework

George Bekiaridis[1], Graham Attwell[2]

[1] Active Citizens Partnership, Greece; george.bekiaridis@gmail.com
[2] Pontydysgu, Spain; grahamattwell@gmail.com

Correspondence: George Bekiaridis: george.bekiaridis@gmail.com

Abstract:

The AI Pioneers project, funded by the European Union, represents a significant initiative aimed at integrating Artificial Intelligence (AI) into the landscape of adult education and Vocational Education and Training (VET). Through a comprehensive methodology comprising of literature reviews, surveys, and interviews conducted with a wide range of educators and stakeholders, the project has identified key AI competencies that are essential for educators. These competencies align with the six areas of the DigCompEdu framework, including Professional Engagement, Digital Resources, Teaching and Learning, Assessment, Empowering Learners, and Facilitating Learners' Digital Competence.

The AI Pioneers project's main findings highlight the need for educators to develop skills in data literacy, computational thinking, ethical considerations of AI use, and the integration of AI tools into educational practices. By supplementing the DigCompEdu framework with AI-specific competencies, the project contributes to the continuing professional development of teachers and trainers, ensuring they are well-prepared for the the challenges and opportunities presented by AI in education. This initiative not only enhances educators' digital competencies but also plays a crucial role in preparing students for a future where AI is ubiquitous, thereby shaping the future of educational practices and outcomes.

Keywords: Artificial Intelligence, Educational Technology, Professional Development, DigCompEdu Framework, Vocational Education and Training, Digital Competence

Introduction

The advent of Artificial Intelligence (AI), in particular Generative AI, has precipitated a transformative shift across various sectors, including education. This shift is not merely technological but fundamentally alters how educational content is delivered, experienced, and assessed. Specifically, in the realms of adult education and Vocational Education and Training (VET), the integration of AI promises to enhance the educational experience, making learning more personalized, accessible, and aligned with the evolving needs of the workforce (see, for example, OECD, 2023). The pressing need for AI integration in these sectors stems from several factors, including the rapid pace of technological change, the increasing complexity of the global job market, and the necessity for continuous, lifelong learning. Adult and vocational learners, who often seek to upskill or reskill for new employment opportunities, stand to benefit from AI in education that can offer tailored learning experiences, flexible access to content, and immediate feedback.

The AI Pioneers project funded by the European Union Erasmus+ programme and involving a consortium of educational and research institutions, aims to systematically integrate AI in adult and vocational education. Its objectives are multifaceted: to map out the current landscape of AI in education, identify the specific competences educators need to effectively leverage AI, and develop a comprehensive framework to guide the integration of AI across educational practices. This initiative recognizes that educators' preparedness to use AI is as crucial as the technology itself. By focusing on building AI competences among teachers and trainers, the AI Pioneers project seeks to ensure that the benefits of AI can be fully realized in enhancing learning outcomes, fostering innovative teaching practices, and preparing students for a future in which AI is ubiquitous (Attwell, Bekiaridis & Deitmer, 2023).

This paper reports the initial findings and recommendations of the AI Pioneers project, particularly its supplement to the DigCompEdu framework, which outlines the essential skills and competences educators need in relation to AI in education.

The paper is structured to guide the reader through a comprehensive examination of AI integration in adult and vocational education. It begins with an Introduction that underscores the growing use of AI i in education and training and outlines the objectives of the AI Pioneers project. Following this, the Background section offers an overview of the DigCompEdu framework, its relevance to educators' digital competencies, and the potential transformative impact of AI on educational paradigms. The methodology section elucidates the research approach adopted in the AI Pioneers project, detailing the utilisation of literature reviews, surveys, and interviews to gain insights into AI's current status and potential in education. The section on findings explores the insights derived from the project, emphasizing the perceived benefits, challenges, and requisite AI competences for educators. In the following discussion, the implications of these findings for integrating AI into teaching, learning, and assessment practices in adult and vocational education are analysed. Finally, the conclusion and recommendations section summarises the paper's main points and offers actionable steps for educators, policymakers, and institutions to effectively embrace AI in education.

By exploring the AI Pioneers project and its contributions to the field, this paper aims to shed light on the role of AI in shaping the future of education, with a particular focus on adult education and vocational education and training. Through this analysis, we seek to contribute to the ongoing dialogue on how best to harness the potential of AI in enhancing educational outcomes and preparing learners for the challenges and opportunities of the digital age.

Background

The Digital Competence Framework for Educators (DigCompEdu) is an initiative by the European Union aimed at identifying and delineating the digital competences educators require to foster effective teaching and learning in the digital age. Launched to address the growing integration of digital technologies in educational environments, DigCompEdu offers a structured model that outlines 22 competencies across six areas: Professional Engagement, Digital Resources, Teaching and Learning, Assessment, Empowering Learners, and Facilitating Learners' Digital Competence. This comprehensive framework serves not only as a guide for educators seeking to enhance their digital skills but also as a benchmark for curriculum development and professional training programs in educational institutions across Europe and beyond. Its relevance lies in the recognition of the pivotal role that digital literacy and competences play in modern education, providing educators with a roadmap to integrate technology into their teaching practices thoughtfully and effectively (European Commission, 2017).

The impact of Artificial Intelligence (AI) on education introduces a new dimension to the DigCompEdu framework's relevance. AI technologies, from machine learning algorithms to natural language processing tools, are reshaping the educational landscape by enabling personalised learning, automating administrative tasks, and providing insights into student performance that were previously unattainable. These advances promise to make education more accessible, customized, and efficient. However, they also necessitate a new set of competences among educators, to understand how to integrate AI into their pedagogical strategies, make informed decisions based on AI-generated data, and navigate the ethical implications of using AI in educational settings.

The emerging need for AI competences among educators is twofold. Firstly, educators must be adept at leveraging AI tools to enhance teaching and learning processes. This includes using AI to personalize learning experiences, automate assessment and feedback, and create dynamic, interactive educational content. Secondly, educators have a critical role in preparing students for a future where AI is an integral part of daily life and work. This requires teaching students not only about the functionalities and applications of AI but also fostering critical thinking skills to evaluate the ethical and societal impacts of AI technologies.

In response to these developments, the DigCompEdu framework's integration of AI competences is important. By extending the framework to include AI-specific skills, educators are provided with a clear and structured approach to acquiring the knowledge and abilities needed to effectively utilise AI in educational contexts. This adaptation ensures that the DigCompEdu framework remains relevant and responsive to the evolving digital landscape, empowering educators to lead the way in harnessing the transformative potential of AI for the benefit of learners across all sectors of education.

Methodology

We employed a comprehensive research methodology to explore the integration of Artificial Intelligence (AI) in adult education and Vocational Education and Training (VET), focusing on identifying essential AI competencies for educators. This methodology was designed to gather in-depth insights and data from a variety of sources, ensuring a holistic understanding of the current landscape and the future potential of AI in education.

Literature Review: We undertook a literature review to establish a foundational understanding of the subject. This review encompassed academic journals, conference proceedings, policy reports, and other scholarly publications related to AI in education as well as newsletters and grey literature. The aim was to identify existing AI competences, understand how AI is currently being used in educational settings, and highlight gaps in knowledge and practice. This stage was crucial for framing the subsequent empirical research phases and ensuring that the project was grounded in the latest academic and practical insights.

Surveys: Following the literature review, the project team developed and distributed surveys to a diverse group of educators and trainers across the European Union. The survey was designed to capture quantitative and qualitative data on educators' perceptions, experiences, and challenges with AI in educational contexts. Questions ranged from general awareness and usage of AI tools to specific competences required to effectively implement AI in teaching and learning processes. The survey phase enabled the collection of broad-based data from the field, reflecting the current state of AI integration in education.

Interviews :To complement the survey data and gain deeper insights, the project conducted semi-structured interviews with key stakeholders, including educational policymakers, AI technology developers, academic experts, and practicing educators. These interviews were tailored to explore nuanced perspectives on the ethical, technical, and pedagogical aspects of AI in education. Participants were selected based on their expertise and experience, providing valuable qualitative data that enriched the findings from the literature review and surveys.

Data Collection and Analysis: Data collection was planned and executed, to gain a robust and representative sample. The analysis process involved both quantitative and qualitative methods. Quantitative data from surveys were analysed using statistical software to identify trends, correlations, and significant patterns. Qualitative data from interviews and open-ended survey responses were subjected to thematic analysis to uncover deeper insights into participants' experiences and viewpoints.

Overall, our methodology was designed to be comprehensive, inclusive, and reflective of the complexities involved in integrating AI into educational practices. By combining a literature review, surveys, and interviews, the project succeeded in capturing a multifaceted view of AI competences needed by educators, thereby contributing recommendations to the DigCompEdu framework.

Findings

Our research has unearthed insights into the integration of Artificial Intelligence (AI) in the educational domain, particularly within adult education and Vocational Education and Training (VET). The findings offer a nuanced understanding of the benefits, challenges, and AI competences necessary for educators to navigate this transformative landscape effectively (Attwell and Bekiaridis, 2024).

One of the most compelling revelations from the project is the benefits that AI integration brings to educational settings, but also the challenges. Educators and stakeholders identified personalised learning as a prime advantage, where AI's data-driven insights enable the tailoring of educational content to meet individual learner needs and preferences. This personalisation is seen as a key to enhancing student engagement and improving learning outcomes. Moreover, AI's ability to automate administrative tasks and assessments was highlighted, offering educators more time to focus on pedagogical strategies and student interaction. Additionally, AI tools facilitate innovative teaching methodologies, such as simulation-based learning and interactive games, enriching the learning experience and making complex concepts more accessible.

Despite the optimistic view on AI's role in education, the project also illuminated several challenges. A significant concern among educators revolves around the lack of preparedness and technical expertise to effectively utilise AI tools. This gap underscores the need for comprehensive professional development programmes tailored to building AI competences. Furthermore, ethical considerations, including data privacy, algorithmic bias, and equity in access to AI technologies, emerged as critical issues. These challenges highlight the importance of developing responsible and inclusive AI integration strategies that address potential biases and ensure equitable learning opportunities for all learners.

The project identified a core set of AI competences that educators need to effectively harness the benefits of AI while mitigating its challenges. Data literacy emerges as a fundamental competence, equipping educators with the skills to understand, interpret, and utilise data generated by AI tools. Computational thinking and an understanding of AI principles are also essential, enabling educators to critically evaluate AI tools and integrate them into their teaching practices. Moreover, ethical considerations in AI use are paramount, necessitating competences in navigating the moral implications of AI technologies in education. Educators also need skills in curriculum integration, allowing them to seamlessly incorporate AI tools into lesson plans and learning activities.

These findings underscore the transformative potential of AI in education, highlighting both the opportunities and obstacles in its integration. The identified competences form a foundation for teachers and trainers, guiding professional development initiatives and ensuring that the educational workforce is prepared to meet the demands of an AI-driven future.

Discussion

The findings from the AI Pioneers project, detailing the benefits, challenges, and essential AI competences for educators, provide a comprehensive overview of the current landscape and future direction of AI integration in adult and vocational education. These insights have significant implications for teaching, learning, and assessment practices, necessitating a discussion on how they can be effectively addressed and leveraged to enhance educational outcomes.

Implications for Teaching Practices

The potential of AI to personalise learning experiences by tailoring content to individual learner needs presents a paradigm shift in teaching methodologies. This requires a shift from a one-size-fits-all approach to a more learner-centered model. This transition requires not only technical proficiency in AI tools but also a pedagogical shift towards facilitating learning rather than direct instruction. Educators need to be able to integrate AI-driven insights into their teaching strategies, identifying individual learning paths, and adjusting teaching methods accordingly. Moreover, the use of AI to automate administrative tasks implies that educators can redirect their focus towards higher-order teaching activities, such as critical thinking, creative problem-solving, and interpersonal skills development.

Implications for Learning Experiences

AI's ability to provide dynamic, interactive learning materials and environments signifies a move towards more engaging and effective learning experiences. Learners can benefit from AI-driven simulations, games, and virtual labs, which make complex concepts more accessible and learning more experiential. However, this also places an onus on learners to develop digital literacy and critical thinking skills, enabling them to navigate AI-enhanced learning environments effectively. Additionally, the continuous feedback and assessment capabilities of AI tools can support the extension of formative assessment and encourage self-directed learning and resilience in the face of challenges.

Implications for Assessment Practices

AI-driven assessment tools offer the possibility of more efficient and unbiased evaluations of learner performance. The integration of AI into assessment practices can lead to more formative, continuous feedback mechanisms, enabling learners to receive timely insights into their progress and areas for improvement. However, this also raises ethical considerations regarding data privacy and the potential for AI bias, necessitating transparent, inclusive policies and practices. Educators must be equipped to critically evaluate the reliability and fairness of AI-driven assessments, ensuring that they complement rather than replace human judgment.

Overarching Implications

The integration of AI in adult education and vocational education and training underscores the need for a comprehensive strategy that encompasses policy development, professional development and training, infrastructure investment, and ethical guidelines. The development of AI competences among educators, fostering an environment that supports continuous learning and adaptation, should be a priority. Moreover, ethical considerations must be at the forefront of AI integration efforts, ensuring that AI tools are used responsibly, equitably, and in a manner that respects learner privacy and autonomy.

The AI Pioneers project highlights the transformative potential of AI in enhancing adult and vocational education. However, realizing this potential requires concerted efforts from educators, policymakers, and the wider educational community to address the challenges and leverage the opportunities presented by AI. By doing so, they can ensure that teaching, learning, and assessment practices evolve in ways that meet the needs of learners in an increasingly digital and AI-driven world.

Conclusion and Recommendations

The DigCompEdu Supplement illuminates the transformative potential of integrating Artificial Intelligence (AI) into adult and vocational education, highlighting the dual nature of AI as both a facilitator of personalized, efficient learning experiences and a challenge due to the technical, ethical, and accessibility concerns it raises. The Supplement underscores the necessity for educators to develop specific AI competences, including data literacy, computational thinking, and an understanding of ethical implications, to harness AI's benefits fully while mitigating its risks.

For the future of educational practices, our findings indicate a shift towards more learner-centered, adaptive, and engaging educational environments, empowered by AI technologies. To navigate this shift effectively, the following recommendations are offered:

For Educators: Engage in continuous professional development focused on AI competences. Experiment with AI tools within the classroom and workplace to enhance personalization and engagement in learning experiences.

For Policymakers: Develop and implement policies that support the ethical use of AI in education, ensuring data privacy and equity in access to AI-enhanced learning. Invest in infrastructure and professional development programs to facilitate AI integration.

For Institutions: Foster a culture of innovation and continuous learning around AI technologies. Provide resources and support for educators to experiment with and implement AI tools in their teaching and assessment practices.

Areas for further research and development include exploring effective strategies for integrating AI in diverse learning contexts, assessing the long-term impact of AI on learning outcomes, and developing frameworks for addressing ethical concerns in AI-driven education. By focusing on these areas, the educational community can ensure that the integration of AI into education not only enhances learning experiences but also aligns with broader societal values and goals.

References

Attwell, G. & Bekiaridis, G. (2024) Supplement to the DigCompEDU Framework Introduction to AI in Education, https://www.researchgate.net/publication/377117053_Supplement_to_the_DigCompEDU_Framework_Introduction_to_AI_in_Education

Attwell, G., Bekiaridis, G., Deitmer, L. (2023) AI Pioneers: Developing a Community of Practice for Artificial Intelligence (AI) and Vocational Education and Training, paper presented at 5th Crossing Boundaries Conference, Kaunas, Lithuania, https://www.researchgate.net/publication/371416736_AI_Pioneers_Developing_a_Community_of_Practice_for_Artificial_Intelligence_AI_and_Vocational_Education_and_Training

European Commission, Joint Research Centre, Redecker, C., Punie, Y. (2017) European framework for the digital competence of educators – DigCompEdu, Punie, Y.(editor), Publications Office, https://data.europa.eu/doi/10.2760/159770

OECD (2023), Building Future-Ready Vocational Education and Training Systems, OECD Reviews of Vocational Education and Training, OECD Publishing, Paris, https://doi.org/10.1787/28551a79-en.

Acknowledgments

The project "AI Pioneers – AI and the Future of Education" has been funded with the support of the European Commission within the framework of Erasmus+ programme call Partnerships for Innovation - Forward Looking Projects (ERASMUS-EDU-2022-PI-FORWARD). Project results are available at https://aipioneers.org/

How do Technical Vocational School Teachers Deal with Artificial Intelligence in the Classroom? An Attempt to Analyze AI Use at German VET Schools

Ludger Deitmer[1], Iven Dersch[2], Lisa Meyne[3], Christine Siemer[4]

[1]Institute Technology and Education (ITB), University of Bremen, Germany; deitmer@uni-bremen.de
[2] Institute Technology and Education (ITB), University of Bremen, Germany; idersch@uni-bremen.de
[3] Institute Technology and Education (ITB), University of Bremen, Germany; lmeyne@uni-bremen.de
[4] Institute Technology and Education (ITB), University of Bremen, Germany; chsiemer@uni-bremen.de

Correspondence: Ludger Deitmer: deitmer@uni-bremen.de

Abstract
This paper examines how selected vocational schools in Germany are dealing with the integration of artificial intelligence into the school context and how vocational school teachers and their students are undertaking initial attempts and projects to integrate various technologies and AI into teaching practice. The focus here is primarily on the concrete practical teaching level in vocational schools, so that the content and methods of teaching by vocational school teachers and the concrete technological applications are considered. The first pilot applications of AI systems at vocational schools are the focus of interest, so that a selection of 5 AI-committed schools are presented in this article (predominantly automation and robotic projects). The investigation took place as part of the Erasmus+ project AI Pioneers, which consists of an international consortium working to establish a VET network with regard to the integration of AI in educational settings.

Keywords: Artificial Intelligence in Education, AI in Vocational Education and Training, German VET Schools, AI Pioneers

Introduction

Recently, AI applications in vocational training have become increasingly important. As the UNESCO (2022) mentions: "AI has the potential to accelerate the process of achieving the global education goals through reducing barriers to accessing learning, automating management processes, and optimizing methods to improve learning outcomes" (Attwell et al., 2020, p. 30). This article examines how selected vocational schools are concerned with this new topic and how vocational teachers and their students such as mechatronic apprentices are making initial attempts to incorporate it into teaching practice. We focus primarily on the concrete practical teaching level in vocational schools. In this respect, the content and methods of teaching by vocational teachers is considered. Their relationships to pilot applications of AI systems are the key focus here, a selection of 5 AI engaged schools is concerned in this regard. The analysed VET schools undertake primarily automation and robot projects in industrial electronics professions.

Development of the Contextual Framework: The Scope of the AI Pioneers Project

The main goals of the European Erasmus+ artificial Intelligence project AI Pioneers (funding duration 2023-2025) is on recommendations for vocational training policy, digital learning environments consisting of AI tools and AI learning factories and laboratories as well as policy recommendations for the effective implementation of AI artifacts in vocational and adult education arrangements.

The research questions of the project among others are the following:

- To what extent is AI already being used in adult and vocational training in various European countries?

- What framework conditions enable the long-term development of a network of AI Pioneers with regard to the use of artificial intelligence in the teaching/learning process of vocational school teachers and trainers?
- What impact does the application of AI have on data protection, ethics and European values?

Four statements describe the state of research with reference to technological change and digital learning environments in vocational and adult education context.

(1) The technological change, which is driven, among other things, by the development of AI systems, requires increased competence requirements for professionals on skilled worker level. Particularly in technical training occupations such as mechatronics, industrial electronics as well as metal technology occupations and vocational IT specialists (Kock & Schad-Dankwart, 2010).

(2) In order to meet the skills required the professional use of AI, action- and design-oriented learning models are required. As such that digital learning environments, e.g. AI laboratories, become more relevant (Burchert et.al.2021, Euler & Wilbers, 2020). These AI laboratories can be developed at vocational schools, as shown in the 5 examples below.

(3) The technological components used in the learning process (such as e.g. Google Tools) are of central importance. A further development of the quality of the learning offerings for the benefit of the learners is made possible by the help of AI (Attwell et al., 2021).

(4) There are now a number of important desiderata for the further development and effectiveness of digital teaching/learning spaces. Four design criteria have proven to be particularly effective: The learners' independent selection of learning content, close operational practical relevance to professional action situations, useful help displays and explanatory videos for self-directed learning (Siemer, 2023)

Identification of VET Schools With an Affinity to AI Activities

Looking for such schools out of 220 in the German states: Lower Saxony and Bremen have a more than average relationship towards AI applications. This was done by desk research and through existing contacts of the institute for technology and education from previous research collaborations. In the course of the survey, qualitative expert interviews were conducted with several stakeholders from the vocational schools listed below in order to explore the current status of the use of AI and future developments at these schools. In this regard for example, the existence of extra functional projects in the spectrum of industry 4.0 innovations and beyond regular courses can be examined.

Current State of AI projects in Selected Schools in Germany

Technical Vocational school Osnabrück

Over several years and by the initiative of a vocational school teacher team, a digital learning environment as a robotic lab was created at this district vocational school that is capable of implementing industrial robot projects. Mostly mechatronic apprentices, are enabled to program collaborative robots through the guidance of vocational teachers and trainers. By the use of audiovisual glasses students learn to programme robots. For example: A collaborative robot (Cobot) is filling a transport box with products. The task of the apprentices is now that they should be able to control which of the objects are packed and whether the robot packs the correct ones. An open hand by a the mechatronic is held in front of the data glasses. The Cobot notes the situation and interrupts the loading of objects into the box. The Cobot takes one of the many objects from the box and places it into the mechatronics outstretched hand. The mechatronics technician can thus check more precisely whether they are the right objects are touched by the robot.

The main difficulty for teachers is integrating it into regular lessons. Because AI content is still too rarely linked to the existing curriculum. So far, AI applications have mainly been implemented in the form of working groups and special projects. The local companies such as automotive industry supports the initiative by giving their trainees more time to take part in such working group arrangements. On one Saturday every half year, a workshop is held in a school room at which the trainees present their results in a kind of "hackathon". Hackathon means that the students visualize the results of their laboratory studies or experiments and then present them to the teachers or trainers present. The results are also shown on the internet, e.g. on YouTube. The students then receive a certificate of successful participation. No grades are awarded for this purpose in order not to burden the voluntary nature of participation in working groups. The responsible teacher is of the opinion that AI will not only change the teaching content in schools in the future, but also as a tool, AI software such as Chat GPT will influence the teachers' teaching design.

Technical Vocational School Wolfsburg

The AI applications of this vocational school are based on past expertise with the development and creation of digital learning environments related to processing automation processes in industrial applications such as an automated packaging system. The schools is labelled as a robot affine school. The processing and investigation of automation processes in industrial production for the target group of mechatronics apprentices is deepened through concrete actions in project form.

The dual students are trainees from the automobile company Volkswagen in Wolfsburg who are undergoing dual training with practical components in the teaching practice at a vocational school. The project presented is about more efficient monitoring in the energy management of buildings. For this purpose, the building consumption data is recorded and analyzed in a model building with the aim of uncovering optimizations in the consumption of heating heat or electricity consumption. The usage behavior of energy consumers can be clarified in terms of its monetary consequences, such as increased consumption costs, in order to encourage building users to save energy consumption. A special feature is that the AI topic of the course is linked to the topic of reduced consumption of fossil energy resources. For this purpose, a conventional control system is equipped with a machine learning component module through which the AI software runs. The software analyzes the data for unusual changes, e.g. related to an unusual drop in temperature caused by an open window or a sudden change in power consumption, and then sends an error message. Another Python-based software linked to ChatGPT gives recommendations for action to the building residents.

For trainees in mechatronics or industrial electronics, the building simulation system is used as a digital learning environment in specialist lessons in order to directly visualize the connection between energy consumption and the identification of savings potential.

Technical Vocational School Neustadt am Rübenberge

The Neustadt vocational school (Hannover region) uses a fully automatic production system for learning purposes, consisting of a transport system, handling devices and industrial robots. The manufacturing process essentially consists of feeding and assembling individual parts using industrial robots (brand: Mitsubishi). The material flow is carried out by transport vehicles that drive autonomously in the production facility. The production states of the production facility are recorded using the AI system "Machine Vision". A simple application example was prepared for this robotic system: A roll of adhesive tape is identified using image recognition, no matter what position it is in, and is placed on a dispensing reel by a robot. With the AI data libraries Tensorflow and KERAS it becomes possible to program a convolutional neural network. The VET school also operates an assembly plant in which collaborative robots (so-called Cobots) of the UR3 type assemble flashlights. The conditions of the material magazines are evaluated using the AI approach of machine vision. The goal is to detect and correct errors in material placement. The example of stored memory (PLC) programming is addressed here. An effective and rapidly spreading application standard was developed and communicated to trainees. This meant that all companies were able to purchase a PLC from any manufacturer and have their own trainee design an individual automation solution. This is like a quantum leap in industry and crafts.

The use of AI will therefore not be extended to an exclusive consideration of engineering activities; many tasks can now also be taken on by appropriately trained skilled workers. The more a software tool makes AI programming easier, the more skilled workers can be deployed to use it. The teachers in the interview still see a lot of potential in AI applications for skilled workers, which will increase in the near future. What is missing are concrete, standardized AI software tools that are used as a broad industry standard in many companies in the production industry.

In the future, the VET schools from Neustadt and their production facilities will also be used as a learning platform for machine vision. Experiments have already been carried out to determine the feasibility of this concept and have shown that it will be possible to differentiate between the shuttle configurations shown above using machine vision software (a proprietary development by the AI teaching team based on Tensorflow and Keras). On cooperation with a local industrial company (training company) an AI project is to be developed with a partner company oft the VET school that involves the participation of trainees and also achieves the usability, quality and reliability for industrial production.

Technical Vocational school Emden

In the course of various previous projects, the technical vocational school in Emden considered how robotics and AI could be integrated within the teaching and training. So far, the main focus has been on machine learning for the technologies implemented. At the VET school, Raspberry Pies are assembled on a system with robots so that the trainees can work collaboratively with robots in the production process. The cover of a Raspberry Pie is refined here, for example, and provided with lettering. A collaborative robot picks up the box, feeds the component into the machine and then hands it back to the worker. Augmented reality is already included in the system, but could be expanded here, especially with regard to data goggles. This would allow the students to see exactly how the processes can be automated with AI and how humans can be supported in this area.

In the course of another project, for example, an apprentice programmed an AI to recognize whether there are scratches on the product (Raspberry Pie). A high-performance computer was used here so that the AI recognizes where there is a scratch. The AI was trained using images so that red lines were drawn on a light-colored housing in order to recognize the damage to the product. The apprentice trained the AI independently and created a learning film as his assignment.

Technical Vocational School in Bremen

At a technical vocational school in Bremen, mechatronics engineers also carry out an AI-related project in their second year of training. The project is located in learning field 6 "Planning and organizing work processes" of the mechatronics apprentices. The trainees spend two semesters working on the project, which is not anchored in the curriculum and therefore does not form part of the intermediate examination. Supported by dedicated teachers, the trainees work on a task as part of their lessons that involves using an autonomous vehicle for warehouse logistics in order to compensate for staff shortages. The project therefore uses the autonomous control of a robot to take a step towards autonomous driving. The robot is to follow a lane and drive along it according to predefined obstacle detection programs using an ultrasonic sensor. The next step would be to implement machine learning so that the robot can learn from its environment.

There are also other projects at the school as precursors to AI in the vocational high school area, which use raspberry pies and small robots equipped with lasers to carry out 360-degree spatial mapping and estimate distances. However, the topics of those projects can be chosen by the students freely. The students decide for themselves whether they want to focus on robotics or AI during their A-level projects.

Currently, there is no comprehensive AI concept at the vocational school. It would be beneficial if the projects carried out with the initiated AI topics could be anchored in the curriculum in order to obtain time and financial resources for the implementation of the projects.

Outlook and Initial Conclusions: From the Comparison of School Cases

All in all, it can be initially concluded that German vocational school teachers and trainers are quite open to the use of AI-based learning applications in vocational schools. The use of AI will therefore not be extended to an exclusive consideration of engineering activities; many tasks can now also be taken on by appropriately trained skilled workers. The more a software tool makes AI programming easier, the more skilled workers can be deployed to use it. The teachers in the interviews still see a lot of potential in AI applications for skilled workers, which will increase in the near future. What is missing are concrete, standardized AI software tools that are used as a broad industry standard in many companies in the production industry. There is strong interest in good practice examples with experimental "hands-on-learning" phases that are based on the independent activity of students, trainees or technicians. Learning skills need to be expanded, especially those that strengthen critical thinking, implementation skills and creativity. Ethical questions about data protection and personal rights should also be made an issue in this regard.

The specific approach of the individual schools in the case studies presented here is quite different, e.g. one school has already integrated audiovisual glasses into its AI projects and other schools are very interested in this. There seems to be a great need for exchange about specific project experiences. The networking initiative of the AI Pioneers project needs to be further developed by establishing workshops and exchange forums (some also online). The target groups of the individual vocational schools are also quite different: From dual students (university studies plus vocational training in a recognized profession, e.g. mechatronics engineer or IT specialist), to technicians in metal and electrical engineering professions, to mechatronics engineers and students at vocational high schools of technology. The existing forms of examination are still diverse and not standardized. The Emden technical vocational school imparts content that provides an additional qualification recognized by a board examination in a final thesis. Others follow informal exams or student lectures in final presentation forms. An exchange between the projects or schools could also be encouraged here.

When developing project tasks, the interests of students or trainees should be taken into account. Project tasks must be based on the interest of the students if they are to be completed with the motivation and perseverance they require. It is also important that the students receive clear evaluation criteria for working on the project task. Broad support from the school management is also necessary. Just a few committed teachers are not enough to implement AI concepts and projects in schools. Therefore, the school management must be oriented towards the use of AI, as a medium in the future learning process of the school. Schools that are committed to innovation are more willing to deal with AI technologies and integrate them into everyday life. They see this as an opportunity to effectively and expand the students' learning processes and this includes the development of an AI concept as well which are essential for schools and have barely been developed to date.

Funding Information

Funded by the European Union.Views and opinions expressed are however those of the author(s) only and do not necessarily reflect those of the European Union or the European Education and Culture Executive Agency (EACEA). Neither the European Union nor EACEA can be held responsible for them.

References

Attwell, G., Roppertz, S., Deitmer, L. (2021). MOOC and artificial intelligence. Potentials for the Professional Development of VET Teachers and Trainers. In C. Nägele, B. E. Stalder & M. Weich (Eds.), Pathways in Vocational Education and Training and Lifelong Learning. Proceedings of the 4th Crossing Boundaries Conference in Vocational Education and Training, Mutenz and Bern online, 8.–9. April (pp. 67–72). European Research Network on Vocational Education and Training, VETNET, University of Applied Sciences and Arts Northwestern Switzerland and Bern University of Teacher Education. https://doi.org/10.5281/zenodo.4602924

Attwell, G., Deitmer, L., & Bekiaridis, G. (2023). AI pioneers: Developing a community of practice for artificial intelligence (AI) and vocational education and training. In V. Tūtlys, L. Vaitkutė & C. Nägele (Eds.), Vocational Education and Training Transformations for Digital, Sustainable and Socially Fair Future. Proceedings of the 5th Crossing Boundaries Conference in Vocational Education and Training, Kaunas, 25. – 26. May (pp. 30–37). European Research Network on Vocational Education and Training, VETNET, Vytautas Magnus University Education Academy, Institute of Educational Science. https://doi.org/10.5281/zenodo.7808076

Burchert, J., Naumann, J., Petermann, N., Schall, M., Siemer, C., & Weinowski, N. (2021). Selbstgesteuertes Lernen in Transport und Logistik: Gestaltung didaktischer Umsetzungskonzepte auf Basis von angebots- und nachfrageorientierten Strategien. In J. Burchert, M. Sander & N. Weinowski (Eds.), Digitalisierung in der Logistikbranche. Impulse für die Aus- und Weiterbildung (pp. 151–68). wbvMedia. https://doi.org/10.3278/6004729w

Euler, D., & Wilbers, K. (2020). Berufsbildung in digitalen Lernumgebungen. In R. Arnold, A. Lipsmeier & M. Rohs (Eds.), Handbuch Berufsbildung (3. Auflage, pp. 427–38). Springer. https://doi.org/10.1007/978-3-658-19312-6.

Kock, A., & Schad-Dankwart, I. (2019). Berufsbildung 4.0 – Fachkräftequalifikationen und Kompetenzen für die digitalisierte Arbeit von morgen: Der Ausbildungsberuf Fachkraft für Lagerlogistik im Screening. BIBB. https://www.bibb.de/dienst/publikationen/de/9981

UNESCO. (2022). What you need to know about digital learning and transformation of education (last updated 6. February 2024). https://www.unesco.org/en/education/digital/need-know

Siemer, C. (2023). Lernerfolgsrelevante Gestaltungsmerkmale einer virtuellen 360°-Lernumgebung. Ein Fallbeispiel aus der Logistikbranche. MedienPädagogik: Zeitschrift Für Theorie Und Praxis Der Medienbildung, 254 – 278. https://doi.org/10.21240/mpaed/00/2023.08.23.X

FLUENT: Towards a more flexible design and planning approach

Albert Sangrà[1], Gerhard Geissler[2], Franz-Karl Skala[3], Nati Cabrera[4]

[1] Faculty of Psychology and Education Sciences, Universitat Oberta de Catalunya, Spain; asangra@uoc.edu
[2] Institute for Business Education, Vienna University of Economics and Business, Austria; gerhard.geissler@wu.ac.at
[3] Institute for Business Education, Vienna University of Economics and Business, Austria; franz-karl.skala@wu.ac.at
[4] Faculty of Psychology and Education Sciences, Universitat Oberta de Catalunya, Spain; nabrera@uoc.edu

Correspondence: Gerhard Geissler: gerhard.geissler@wu.ac.at

Abstract:

The following paper introduces the FLUENT model, a contemporary university course planning approach built on the findings from a research which used the results of a survey, interviews to university key informants and a literature review based on the PRISMA methodology. FLUENT is an acronym that stands for Flexible Universal Education Model for a New Hybrid. Faced with the complexity of teaching and uncertainty in planning, the model aims to comprehensively address course planning intricacies. Unlike traditional models, FLUENT adopts a fully online perspective, acknowledging the potential of online education. It incorporates evidence-backed elements from course design, as for example emphasizing deep understanding, accurate planning, or crucial structuring elements. The structuring elements encompass time, space, technology, students' agency, and teachers' reflectivity. Additionally, FLUENT integrates principles of reversibility, addressing unforeseen circumstances, and recognizes students in both face-to-face and online environments. The model promotes flexibility, personalization, interaction, and collaboration, aligning with the pillars of future learning. FLUENT stands out by offering reversible design, considering diverse needs of students, and being adaptable to diverse institutional infrastructures. The model emphasizes learning paths, competencies, and aligning objectives, providing a comprehensive framework for course planning.

Keywords: Educational Model; Course Planning; Complexity; FLUENT; Reversible Design; Online Learning

Introduction

The university teaching environment and student expectations have undoubtedly grown increasingly complex in recent years. Considering the "irreducible complexity" (Labaree, 2000:231) of teaching and the uncertainty in planning within complex domains, a crucial question emerges: How can university courses be planned to effectively promote students' learning in such circumstances? Since university teaching can be realized in various ways, but not arbitrarily, and drawing on the insights of Luhmann (1984) in the sense that complexity can only be reduced through complexity, it becomes apparent that there is a demand for planning tools that comprehensively consider the intricate nature of course planning.

This paper presents the development process and the result of the creation of a new, contemporary university course planning model. It is grounded on insights from learning psychology aiming to establish a well-reflected course structure while also innovatively incorporating well-established educational concepts.

Purpose

Several existing models for planning university courses are constructed with the assumption that most of their variables can be controlled (Brown & Green, 2020; Enkenberg, 2001; Reigeluth, 1999). However, uncertain situations, unexpected events, as well as divers, even contradictory expectations of students, university teachers or university management can rapidly reveal the limits of such well-designed planning models. Consequently, it is necessary to establish different scenarios in the planning of university courses. These scenarios should facilitate the incorporation of these circumstances and expectations without losing sight of the goal of the university course to be planned.

At first glance, it appears evident to meet the diverse demands of university courses through increased use of technology. After all, this could enhance independence from spatial and temporal constraints, significantly easing the handling of uncertainty, unexpected events, and various stakeholder expectations in a university course. However, teaching and learning experiences, particularly those gained during the pandemic in the years 2019 to 2020 have demonstrated that merely transferring face-to-face teaching without adjustments to the required online setting is insufficient. In fact, the typical approach involved the adaptation of traditional face-to-face teaching concepts into technology-supported formats, like synchronous classes through video conferencing tools, often resulting in poor learning effectiveness and satisfaction (Amboy et al., 2023; Fabriz, Mendzheritskaya & Stehle, 2021; Müller & Wulf, 2020).

Methodology

To establish the basis of the FLUENT model design, a research methodology was carried out, considering both quantitative and qualitative techniques. First a literature review, conducted through a PRISMA methodology, analysed 116 records, which were considered the final ones after having followed all the PRISMA steps.

In parallel, a survey was elaborated and distributed in several universities of seven different countries (particularly Austria, Estonia, Germany and Spain). The survey was focused on exploring the skills and training needs of university teachers regarding hybrid/blended teaching. It was created using two frameworks: the pillars for "The Future of Learning" (Redecker et al., 2011), and the six structural pillars of teaching (Meyer, 2007). Complementarily, several interviews were conducted with university management responsible people focusing on fundamental aspects of university teaching, such as the overall situation of students with all aspects of diversity, family situation, etc.. In addition, current technical developments such as AI and chatbots were critically and reflectively examined. Finally, and as a complement of the interviews, documentation as guidelines from training centres at the universities were also analyzed, summarized and integrated to the information that should feed the elaboration of the FLUENT model.

All this analysis resulted in the identification of a certain deficit on planning models considering the current conditions for teaching and learning, and the different scenarios that have been opened. The new FLUENT model, thus, is envisioned as a course planning model that leverages the potential of online education in an innovative manner. This model advocates for a shift in planning philosophy by starting planning from a fully online perspective. From this perspective, it is possible to incorporate both face-to-face and online teaching strategies, ultimately striving to create a comprehensive model that seamlessly combines face-to-face and online teaching in a rational, pedagogically sound, and more fluent and confident manner. Hence, the purpose of the introduced planning model named FLUENT is to serve as a new comprehensive model for higher education guided by the ideas of inclusion, flexibility, and sustainability. The FLUENT model aims to gain recognition for its capacity to effectively address the challenges arising from the inherent complexity of the contemporary and prospective learning and teaching environment.

The FLUENT model

FLUENT is a comprehensive model developed for planning university courses with extended durations. FLUENT is an acronym for: Flexible Universal Education Model for a New Hybrid. It facilitates the differentiated planning of the teaching and learning process of a university course.

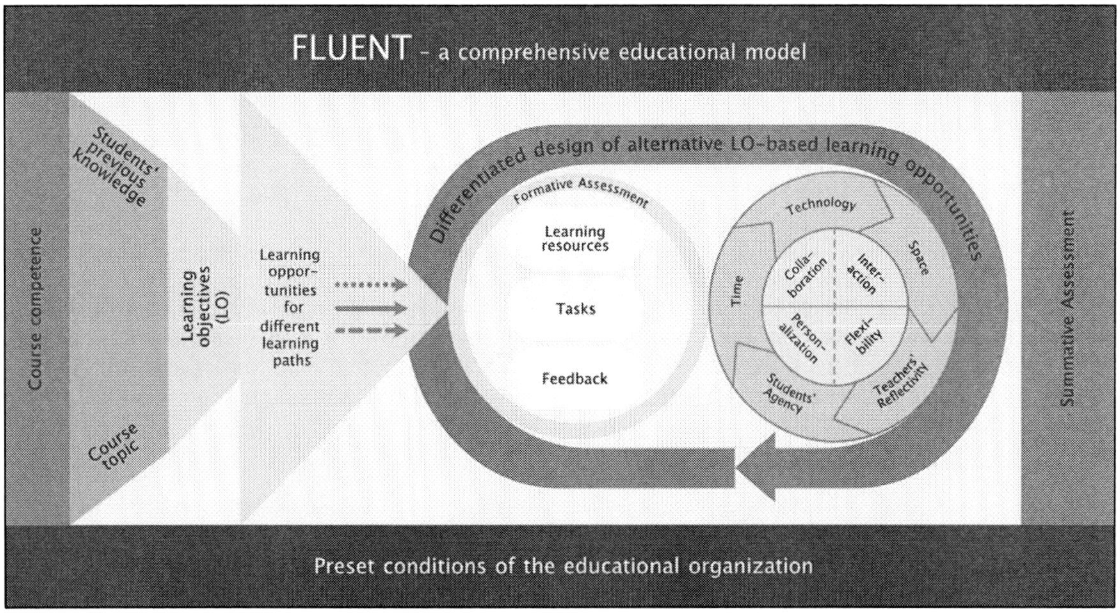

Figure 1: The FLUENT-model – a comprehensive educational model for course planning.

The model incorporates evidence from elements of course design that have been empirically shown to improve learning and learner performance (Rosenshine & Stevens, 1986; Posch, Schneider & Mann, 1989), enhance deep understanding of learners (Biggs, 1996), and facilitates accurate planning (Anderson et al., 2014).

Additionally, it promotes a focus on elements in courses that are crucial in the planning process. These elements transform the unstructured complexity of a course into a structured form, enabling effective planning (Meyer 2007). Furthermore, the model refers to Sangrà's (2021) principles, emphasizing the significance of a reversible design, time management, and self-regulation of learning as fundamental components of this comprehensive approach.

Finally, the model incorporates the contributions of Redecker et al., who examined the subject of "The Future of Learning" (2011). The insights derived from their study function as important elements within the FLUENT model. The utilization of these insights facilitates the expansion of the spectrum of didactic possibilities. Additionally, these elements can be employed to evaluate the course plan, examining its contemporaneity, i.e., its alignment with current requirements.

In this context, the description of the FLUENT model can be divided into three key areas: underlying elements grounding the model, structuring elements providing guidance to course planners, and extending elements that facilitate the creation of alternative didactic approaches and evaluating the course plan.

Underlying elements

Regardless of how a course is intended to be designed in a "fluent" way, the process of course planning invariably begins with preliminary work that provides direction to the planning process. These preparations initially focus on specific considerations: (1) What are the preset conditions of the educational organization, e.g. attendance regulations, course formats, etc.? Following this, the preparation addresses the next questions: (2) What is the course content, e.g. what is to be learned? (3) Which course competence should be developed? (4) What are the students' previous knowledge? And finally: (5) How can the competencies of the students be assessed in a summative assessment of the course? Frequently, the initial set of questions, particularly the first, is addressed by relevant specifications or guidelines for the course design, study plans, curriculum descriptions, module explanations, or analogous documents, albeit with varying degrees of clarity. Once satisfactory answers to these questions have been obtained, the planning process can begin. Initially, the underlying elements of the FLUENT model play a crucial role in this regard. These elements pertain to the learning and learning behavior of the students.

The underlying model elements related to the learning of the students can be traced coherently to theories of cognitive psychology, especially to the information-processing theoretical approach. Accordingly, learning is conceptualized here as an active process of knowledge construction by learners (Anderson, 2013; Baddeley, 2007; Smith & Kosslyn, 2014; Weinert, 2002; Woolfolk, 2014).

At the core of the model lies the design of interrelated (6) learning opportunities, forming the basis for alternative learning paths that enable students to achieve the desired course competency. A learning path is a route through which a learner develops competence. Offering different learning paths allows students to choose the most suitable way to achieve course competence based on their individual needs, unless didactic considerations of course planning make it necessary to bundle consecutive learning opportunities in exceptional cases. Designing learning paths begins with a clear concept of the competencies to be developed, those which a learner should possess at the course's conclusion. From these competencies, specific (7) learning objectives are derived, outlining a step-by-step path from the beginning to the end of the course. Each learning objective represents an aspirational milestone, and the cumulative completion of these milestones is intended to emerge as the desired course competence. The implementation of these milestones occurs through the design of learning opportunities. In concrete planning, the design of the learning opportunities must clearly differ in terms of the structural elements of time, space and technology.

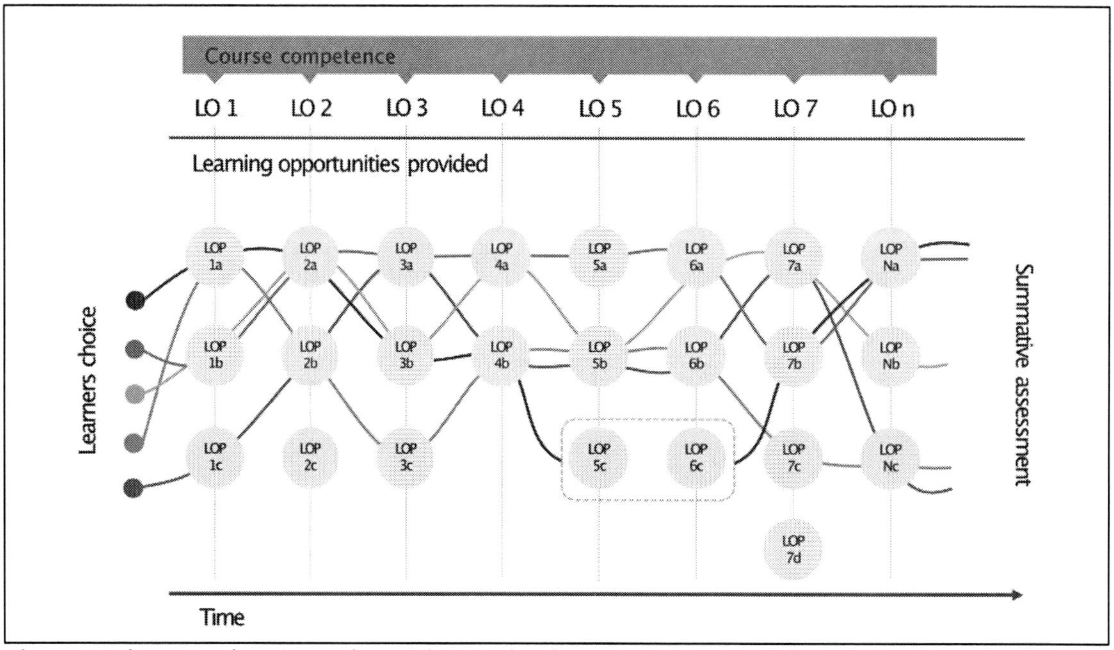

Figure 2: Alternative learning pathways that can be chosen by students for different learning opportunities and are designed with reference to the FLUENT model.

While deductive derivations for the specific design of learning opportunities cannot be drawn from learning psychological model concepts (Fortmüller, 1997), it is established from an information processing theoretical perspective that learners, especially when directed towards higher levels of action, require adequate (8) learning resources, (9) tasks, and (10) feedback on the quality of task processing for effective learning. Undoubtedly, instructional objectives, as proposed by Anderson et al. (2014), can improve the design quality of learning opportunities. Finally, with their taxonomy table, guidelines are available which describe the cognitive process dimension, i.e., they indicate the cognitive performances learners can exhibit at action levels A to F. Depending on the difficulty level of learning opportunities, a set of learning opportunities can serve as a foundation for (11) formative assessment, informing learners about the quality of their ongoing learning progress.

The underlying model elements related to the learning behaviour of the students are rooted in the concept of Biggs' (1996) constructive alignment. According to this approach, it is not sufficient to design learning opportunities based on meaningful learning objectives alone. Biggs emphasizes the importance of aligning intended learning outcomes or course competences with learning opportunities as well as assessment methods to promote meaningful learning and deep understanding.

Structuring elements

The FLUENT model is designed to assist university teachers in planning courses that incorporate both face-to-face and online teaching, thereby promoting students' learning. This incorporation facilitated by the use of technologies can overcome the spatial and temporal constraints of classroom instruction alone. However, this also leads to a significant increase in the variety of design options for learning opportunities by teachers, as well as the possibilities for students to engage with these learning opportunities. The associated increase in complexity requires teachers in course planning to be aware of structuring elements. Although they vary in quality in terms of their properties or principles, they serve the function of providing orientation by describing possibilities and framework conditions under which a course is intended to proceed according to plan. Thus, these five structuring elements are aspects critical to the implementation of the model, and they are: time, space, technology, students' agency, and teachers reflectivity.

(12) "Time" encompasses synchronicity and asynchronicity, along with all shades in between. Disentangling teaching and learning time has the potential to liberate students to learn and teachers to teach, breaking free from constraints of coinciding schedules. This, in turn, opens up possibilities for teachers to generate learning opportunities to promote students' learning. (13) "Space" encompasses online, hybrid, presence, and blended dimensions of teaching. This pertains to the execution of teaching-learning scenarios in various, including virtual, locations. For the purposes of the FLUENT model, space can be anywhere. Detaching the locations of teaching and learning further expands possibilities for teachers to create learning opportunities that promote students' learning. (14) "Technology" has become a significant structuring element in courses, influencing how teaching and learning occur through tools such as platforms, online resources, communication tools, and more. (15) "Students' agency" refers to the degree of autonomy, ownership, and active decision-making granted to students during their learning journey. Agency is the power to initiate action (Bandura, 2001). As the FLUENT model aims to foster an active learning approach, students must possess the power to study, work, and achieve their learning objectives. The design of courses based on the FLUENT model must consider this crucial aspect, with a particular emphasis on learning autonomy and self-regulation of learning, both of which play a central role. Two elements pivotal for developing students' agency are learning autonomy and self-regulation of learning (Zimmerman, 2000). Since self-regulation significantly influences students' motivation (Mäenpää et al., 2020), students can be trained in the development of these two elements. (16) "Teachers' reflectivity" is the practice of teachers critically examining their own teaching. It involves self-awareness, evaluation of teaching methods, and adaptation to student needs. Teachers' reflexivity is very important, as they have to ask themselves about the different elements of the model regarding their courses: is it flexible enough? Could I do the same online than in-presence? Is my decision right, or am I conditioned by tradition and by my previous teaching? Is my course collaborative enough? How am I fostering interaction, both face-to-face and online? Have I understood my new role in teaching in the FLUENT model? Are the learning resources I am using the most appropriate for the challenges the students have to solve? Do I give more space to the students to help them to take action.

Extending elements

As learning opportunities can be designed in various viable ways to achieve the learning objectives, there is the potential to provide diverse learning opportunities that have (almost) the same impact on the students' learning and learning behaviour. The extending elements of the FLUENT model find strong support in the four principles identified by Redecker et al. (2011) as the pillars of the "future of learning": flexibility, personalization, interaction, and collaboration. Decisions to be made when designing courses according to the FLUENT model have to take into consideration these four principles.

(17) "Flexibility" involves offering alternative modes of learning opportunities, expanding the students' choices and convenience to utilize a variety of options. These choices encompass where, when, and how learning occurs. (18) "Personalization" refers to tailoring educational experiences and content to meet the students' individual needs, preferences, and learning styles. Its goal is to foster active engagement and encourage students to take ownership of their learning in different settings. (19) "Interaction" refers to both engaging with individuals and interacting with content. This encompasses the exchange of information between teachers and students as well as among students. (20) "Collaboration" is an objective-driven interaction between individuals, aiming to share learning experiences and knowledge construction through active engagement with a common objective.

Uniqueness of the model

There are several crucial distinctions between the FLUENT model and other seemingly similar models, and we highlight four of the most significant ones.

(1) The FLUENT model is designed from a different perspective to take better advantage of the potential of online teaching.

Traditional in-presence institutions often seek to enhance the flexibility of their educational programs by incorporating elements of distance learning into their face-to-face models. These blended or hybrid models typically share a common limitation: they do not fully leverage the possibilities offered by online education. In contrast, the FLUENT model adopts a distinct perspective, encouraging teachers to design courses from a fully online vantage point. This approach ensures that teachers fully recognize the potential of online education in attaining the desired learning outcomes and objectives for their students.

(2) The FLUENT model is reversible and equips a course for unforeseen circumstances

Moreover, this design approach results in, at a minimum, two iterations of all learning opportunities designed for a course: one optimized for online teaching and a parallel version customized for face-to-face instruction. While these iterations may diverge to accommodate the unique contexts of space and time, they remain aligned in achieving identical learning objectives. Consequently, the FLUENT model emerges as a robust tool, facilitating flexibility: irrespective of unforeseen circumstances, the course is poised to transition any planned activity seamlessly, ensuring readiness for adjustments in the teaching approach.

(3) The FLUENT model uniquely addresses the diverse needs of students, encompassing those in physical attendance and those engaging with the course remotely

A crucial distinction lies in the FLUENT model's explicit consideration of students in both face-to-face and online learning environments. In contrast to many hybrid or blended models primarily conceived from a face-to-face perspective, which often neglect the nuances of distance learning, the FLUENT model consciously reflects on the factors that can either impede or facilitate effective distance learning for students. When an in-person student participates in a segment of the course remotely, whether from home or another location outside the traditional classroom, they essentially transform into a distance learner.

While extensive research in distance education has delved into the characteristics and profiles of students engaged in remote learning, including their need for autonomy, requisite support when studying independently, and capacity for self-regulated learning, the FLUENT model incorporates these crucial aspects. By integrating insights from this wealth of knowledge, the FLUENT model strives to enhance the potential for success among students engaging in both face-to-face and distance learning within a comprehensive model.

(4) The FLUENT model can be easily adapted to the technical infrastructure of the majority of educational institutions

The flexibility of the FLUENT model also considers the diversity in equipment and cultural aspects across various higher education institutions. Given that the model assists teachers in decision-making, the pre-existing conditions of educational institutions become a factor to contemplate during course design. Nevertheless, the model maintains sufficient consistency to accommodate scenarios with limited technological resources. A minimal prerequisite for engaging with the FLUENT model includes access to the internet and a Learning Management System (LMS) or a comparable platform.

Conclusions

Following the development of a curriculum derived from the FLUENT model and a modular online course based on it for the training of university teachers who could be the first to implement the model, the FLUENT model is now ready to be tested. Testing will provide those elements that should be adjusted before producing its final version and implementing it in other higher education institutions.

References

Amboy, M. K., Habaña, M. P., Ramírez, L. M., Sotelo, M. G., Penuela, A. C., & Oducado, R. M. (2023). A Cross-sectional Study on Zoom Fatigue and Satisfaction with Online Learning among Filipino Nursing Students.

Innoeduca. International Journal of Technology and Educational Innovation, 9(1), 53-66. https://doi.org/10.24310/innoeduca.2023.v9i1.15402

Anderson, J. (2013). Kognitive psychologie (7th ed.). Berlin: Springer.

Anderson, L. W. et al. (2014). A Taxonomy for Learning, Teaching, and Assessing. Edinburgh: Pearson.

Baddeley, A. (2007). Working memory, thought, and action. New York: Oxford University Press.

Bandura, A. (2001). Social cognitive theory: an agentic perspective. Annual Review of Psychology, 52, 1–26. https://doi.org/10.1146/annurev.psych.52.1.1

Biggs, J. (1996). Enhancing teaching through constructive alignment. Higher Education, 32, 347-364.

Boekaerts, P. R. Pintrich, & M. Zeidner (Eds.) (2000). Handbook of Self-Regulation (pp. 13-39). San Diego, CA: Academic Press.

Brown, A.H. & Green, T.D. (2020). The essentials of Instructional Design. Connecting Fundamental Principles with Process and Practice. 4th edition. Routledge.

Enkenberg, J. (2001). Instructional design and emerging teaching models in higher education. Computers in Human Behavior, 17(5-6), 495-506. https://doi.org/10.1016/S0747-5632(01)00021-8

Fabriz, S., Mendzheritskaya, J. & Stehle, S. (2021). Impact of Synchronous and Asynchronous Settings of Online Teaching and Learning in Higher Education on Students' Learning Experience During COVID-19. Frontiers in Psycholpgy, 12:733554. https://doi.org/10.3389/fpsyg.2021.733554

Fortmüller, R. (1997). Wissen und Problemlösen. Wien: Manz

Labaree, D. F. (2000). On the Nature of Teaching and Teaching Education. Difficult Practices That Look Easy. Journal of Teacher Education, 51 (3), 228-233. https://doi.org/10.1177/002248710005100301

Luhmann, N. (1984). Soziale Systeme. Grundriß einer allgemeinen Theorie. Frankfurt am Main: Suhrkamp.

Mäenpää, K.; Järvenoja, H.; Peltonen, J.; & Pyhältö, K. (2020). Nursing students' motivation regulation strategies in blended learning: A qualitative study. Nursing & Health Sciences, 22(3), 602-611. https://doi.org/10.1111/nhs.12702

Meyer, H.. (2007): Leitfaden Unterrichtsvorbereitung. Berlin: Cornelsen Springer.

Müller, F. A., & Wulf, T. (2020). Technology-supported management education: a systematic review of antecedents of learning effectiveness. International Journal of Educational Technology Higher Educational, 17, 47 (2020). https://doi.org/10.1186/s41239-020-00226-x

Posch, P., Schneider, W. & Mann, W. (1989). Unterrichtsplanung mit Beispielen für den betriebswirtschaftlichen Unterricht. Wien: Manz Verlag.

Redecker, C.; Leis, M.; Leendertse, M.; Punie, Y.; Gijsbers, G.; Kirschner, P.; Stoyanov, S.; & Hoogveld, B. (2011). The Future of Learning: Preparing for Change. Publications Office of the European Union. https://doi.org/10.2791/64117

Reigeluth, C. (Ed.) (1999). Instructional-Design Theories and Models. A New Paradigm of Instructional Theory. Vol. II. Lawrence Erlbaum Associates, Inc.

Rosenshine, B. & Stevens, R. (1986). Teaching Functions. In M. Wittrock (Ed.). Handbook of Research on Teaching (pp. 376-391). New York: Macmillan Publishing Company.

Sangrà, A. (Coord.) (2021). Improving online teaching. Practical guide for quality online education. Barcelona: Editorial UOC. https://openaccess.uoc.edu/bitstream/10609/122307/3/9788491809371_nonsale.pdf.

Smith, E., & Kosslyn, M. (2014). Cognitive psychology: Mind and brain. Harlow: Pearson

Weinert, F. (2002). Gute Lehrer und neue Lerntheorien. In R. Fortmüller (Ed.), Komplexe Methoden – Neue Medien. Festschrift Wilfried Schneider (pp. 11–30). Wien: Manz.

Woolfolk, A. (2014). Pädagogische Psychologie (12. Aufl.). Hallbergmoos: Pearson.

Zimmerman, B. J. (2000). Attainment of self-regulation: A social cognitive perspective. In M. Boekaerts, P. R. Pintrich, & M. Zeidner (Eds.), Handbook of self-regulation (pp. 13–39). Academic Press. https://doi.org/10.1016/B978-012109890-2/50031-7

Generative AI in the service of situational judgment tests (SJT) for self-regulation learning during problem solving (SRL-PS)

Dafna Avidov[1], Orit Ezra[2], Anat Cohen[3], Alla Bronshtein[4]

[1] School of Education, Tel Aviv University, Israel; dafnavidav@mail.tau.ac.il
[2] School of Education, Tel Aviv University, Israel; oezra1@gmail.com
[3] School of Education, Tel Aviv University, Israel; anatco@tauex.tau.ac.il
[4] Faculty of Medical & Health Sciences, Tel Aviv University, Israel; allab@tauex.tau.ac.il

Correspondence: Dafna Avidov: dafnavidav@mail.tau.ac.il

Abstract:

Those involved in education see great importance in promoting self-regulated learning (SRL) and problem-solving (PS) among learners. Teachers are a major factor in promoting SRL-PS in the classroom, but very little is known about whether and how they promote it in their classroom, therefore a tool is needed to assess teachers in this domain. Furthermore, the situational judgment test (SJT) is a potential tool to diagnose teachers' knowledge. However, such a tool is currently lacking in the SRL-PS domain. Human interaction with generative artificial intelligence (GenAI) enables overcoming difficulties and mutually complementing each other. The purpose of this paper is to present an initial attempt to develop an SJT tool for assessing teachers' SRL-PS knowledge using the assistance of ChatGPT. This humane-machine interaction led to the formulation of 15 difficulties categories and 20 scenarios that form the basis of the SJT tool for SRL-PS. It was found that scenarios created by the researchers can be complemented by those generated by ChatGPT. In some instances, the scenarios from both sources are quite similar, while in others, those formulated by ChatGPT either expand upon or present an alternative perspective on the difficulty. Moreover, ChatGPT has proposed new scenarios in certain cases. A Significant product of the study is a map that enables the analysis of the pool of scenarios and the identification of over- or underrepresented difficulties categories.

Keywords: Generative Artificial intelligence; Problem-solving; Situational judgment tests; Self-regulated learning; human-machine interaction.

Introduction

The development of self-regulated learning (SRL) among learners is known to be of great importance nowadays, due to its connection to academic success, effective learning habits, positive emotions and high motivation for learning (Burns et al., 2018; Li et al., 2023). Independent learning is also known to be of great importance in preparing learners for lifelong learning and it is important to foster these skills already in the early stages (de Bruijn-Smolders et al., 2016). SRL is defined as an active process, during which the learner sets goals for learning, plans times, chooses learning strategies, monitors and controls his understanding, motivation and behavior (Boekaerts, 1999; Zimmerman, 2002; Pintrich, 2000). In the context of SRL, the problem-solving (PS) process was found to be an important cognitive skill in the 21st century by the OECD (OECD, 2021). In the process of solving problems in learning activities, learners utilize a variety of strategies, such as time management, feedback, critical thinking, etc., that help them overcome difficulties and solve problems. These PS strategies are cognitive and behavioral skills that required for self-regulated learners (Assi & Cohen, 2023)

Teachers have a central role in promoting SRL in their classroom (Dignath et al., 2008; Porter et al., 2021), however very little is known if and how teachers promote independent learning in their classes, therefore it is important to assess teachers SRL-PS knowledge (Dignath & Buttren, 2018; Kistner et al., 2020). Moreover, tools are needed to assess this knowledge among teachers.

Situational Judgment Tests (SJTs) are tools that can be used to characterize difficulties and scenarios across various situations and fields, serving both as a learning and evaluation tools (Chao et al., 2020). SJT tools that are used in military settings (Lievens et al., 2008), in retail organizations (Weekley & Jones, 1999) and in the selection of medical candidates (Patterson et al., 2016) and aim to assess the decision-making ability of subjects. The subjects are presented with realistic or hypothetical situations related to their field of occupation and are required to choose or rate effective responses (Chao et al., 2020). Due to the lack of objective assessment tools designed to define the specific requirements for the teaching profession, it is difficult to empirically investigate what types of knowledge and skills are required for the teaching job in general and SRL in particular, (Aldrup et al., 2020; Gold & Holodynski, 2015). Studies in recent years demonstrate the potential of SJT during admission procedures for elementary teacher training programs in middle school and in evaluating different practices in teaching work (Aldrup et al., 2020; Chao et al., 2020; Klassen et al., 2020). The integration of SJT in evaluating SRL knowledge has not yet been explored.

Development of SJT tools is a long and complex process that follows three steps: Job analysis, where scenarios of work situations are collected by experts in the field or literature. In the second step, experts or inexperienced workers create responses for each scenario in order to create a range of effective and ineffective responses and in the last step, a coding key is developed for responses (Gold & Holodynski 2015; Lievens, Peeters & Schollaer 2008). In light of the discission above regarding the importance of promoting SRL-PS among learners and evaluating teachers' knowledge in promoting independent learning through SJT, this study presents an attempt to develop an SJT tool for evaluating teachers' SRL-PS knowledge.

Artificial intelligence (AI) systems are taking more and more place in our lives in recent years. A significant breakthrough has occurred in the last two years with the developments of base models and large language models (LLM). These models allow the use of a variety of applications and have brought about changes in human-computer interaction. Among the significant AI applications based on base models and language models, is the generative artificial intelligence (GenAI). In GenAI, it is possible to create content, based on large sources of information, which have been entered into the GenAI systems, by using prompt. An example of such a system is ChatGPT (European Parliamentary, 2022). Previous studies used ChatGPT for developing standard multiple-choice tests (Cheung, et al 2023; Lee et al. 2023; Ionescu & Enescu, 2023). In medicine, studies used ChatGPT to respond to SJT tests (Borchert et al. 2023; Sareen, 2023). However, as best as we know, studies have not yet used ChatGPT to develop SJT tests. This paper presents a preliminary attempt to use ChatGPT, in order to bridge the gap in academic research in the development of SJT to diagnose SRL-PS knowledge among teachers.

The current research

Research objective and questions

This research is an initial attempt aimed at developing an SJT tool to diagnose teachers' SRL-PS knowledge with the assistants of ChatGPT4. To this aim the following research questions are asked: 1. What are the researchers' SJT scenarios for evaluating SRL-PS? 2. What are the ChatGPT's SJT scenarios for evaluating SRL-PS? 3.What is the contribution of ChatGPT to the development of an SJT tool for diagnosing the SRL-PS knowledge of teachers?

Research method

This article presents the long development process of an SJT tool for diagnosing teachers SRL-PS knowledge by the researchers, as part of a training program for in-service teachers held at the researches' University. The training instructed the teachers on a new SRL-PS model developed by the researchers. The model guides the students along the PS prosses which is divided into four stages: problem identification; Problem Exploration; Providing a solution; Solution Evaluation (Assi & Cohen, 2023; Cohen and Cohen, 2023). The development of the SJT tool included formulating general difficulties at the teachers and students' level, such as pedagogical difficulties in the teacher level, and emotional difficulties in the student level. These general difficulties were defined at the beginning of the development process based on research literature (Mishra & Koehler, 2006) to raise teachers' awareness to the various aspects of difficulties in implementing the SRL-PS model in their classroom. During the training program, the teachers implemented the developed model in their classes, and difficulties regarding implementing the SRL-PS model in the classroom were collected (bottom-up) based on the general difficulties categories (top-down). Based on this, the researchers formulated a pool of 66 scenarios, from which top 10 scenarios were selected to constitute an initial SJT test.

In this article, an attempt was made to harness GenAI for the enhancement of the SJT tool for testing teachers SRL-PS knowledge while saving time and manpower resources. First, the potential of integrating GenAI in the various steps of SJT tool development process was examined. Figure 1 shows the SJT development steps, as performed by the researchers and the ChatGPT4. Notably, while the researchers performed all the steps, the ChatGPT was found relevant in steps one, four, five and six.

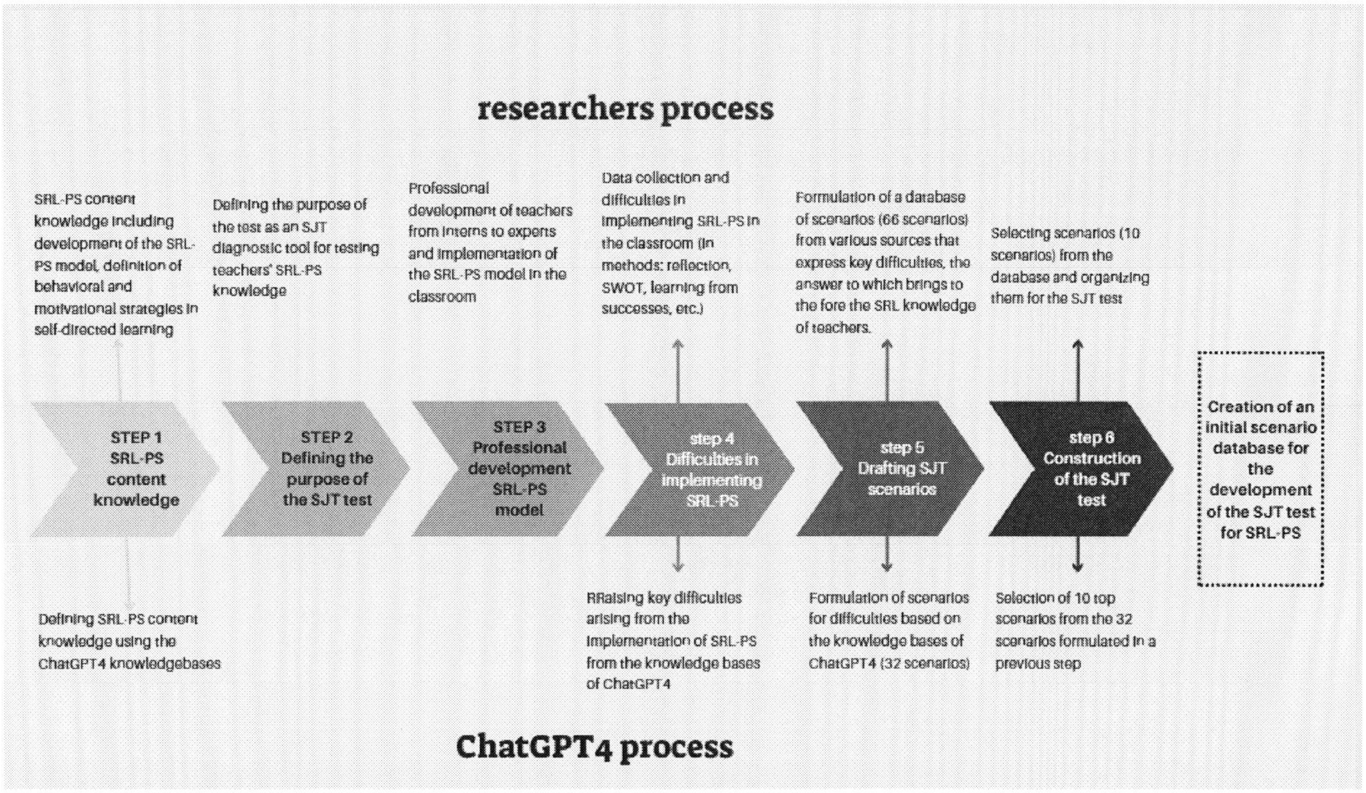

Figure 1: SJT tool development process for diagnosing SRL-PS knowledge

In order to ask ChatGPT to perform these steps a gradual prompts strategies were employed in line with the outline for an interrogative/prompt (Svendsen & Garvey, 2023). Figure 2 shows the dialog with ChatGPT using the prompts. The first column shows the number of the prompt, the second column the instruction given to ChatGPT and the third column describes the purpose of the prompt.

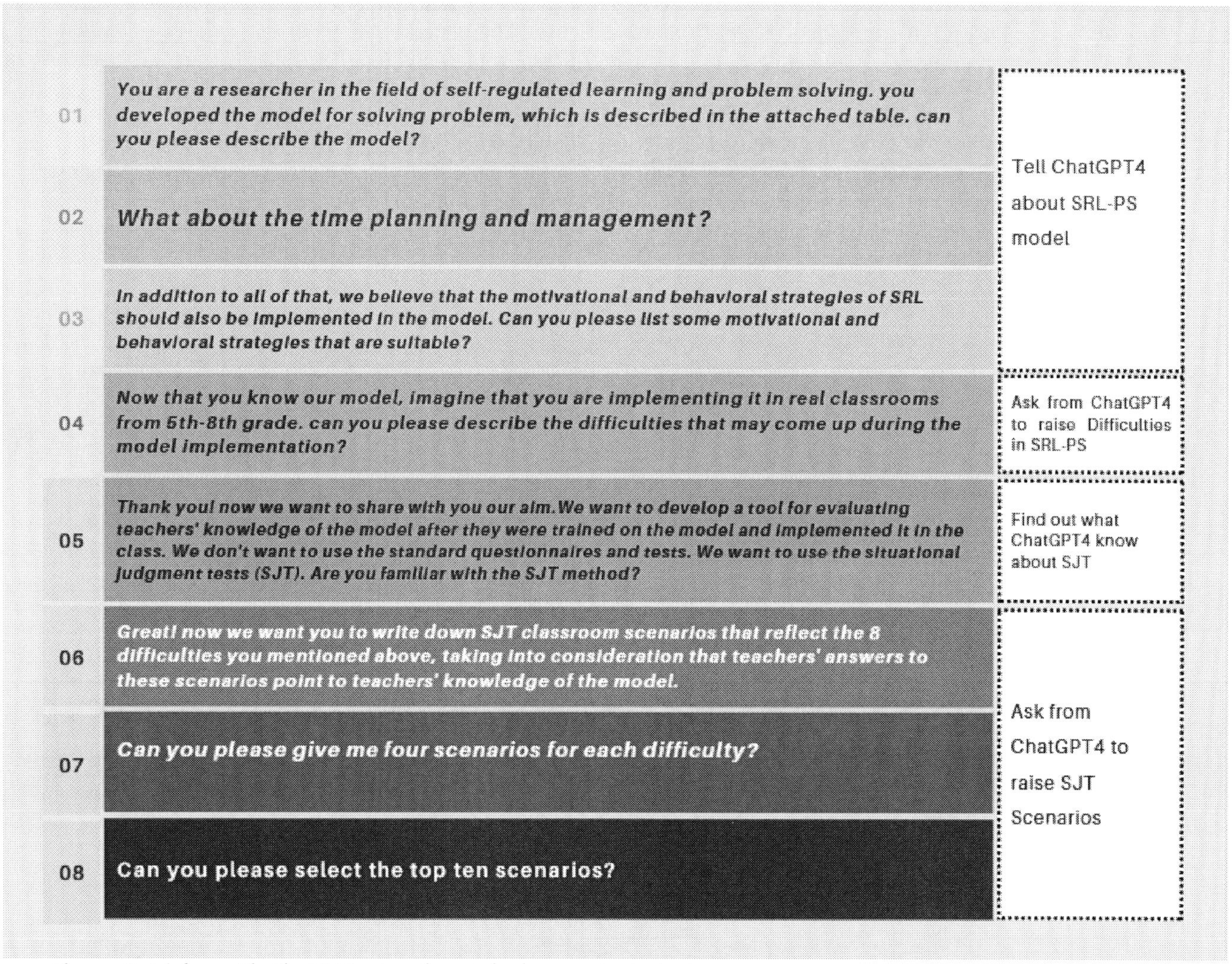

Figure 2: Dialog with ChatGPT using the gradual prompts strategies

Findings

Researchers' difficulties and SJT scenarios for evaluating SRL-PS Knowledge (RQ1)

The SJT tool for diagnosing SRL-PS knowledge, as formulated by the researchers, encompasses general difficulties, the specific difficulties (scenarios title) and the scenarios themselves. for example: the general pedagogical difficulty at teacher level produces the specific difficulty of learning gap between student and Lack of knowledge about students' progress. Figure 3 shows the general difficulties, the specific difficulties, and 10 selected scenarios. Each scenario is assigned an abbreviated code (for example: RS1 stands for research scenario 1).

Researchers'SJT General difficulties	Researchers' Specific difficulties	Researchers' SJT top ten Scenarios
Pedagogical difficulties teacher level	1. Learning gaps between students	RS1-Teacher Mia's class is a heterogeneous class. Mia begins to implement the method of PS in her history class. She discovers that there are gaps between the children in understanding the key concepts in history, which were learned using the new method. What should teacher Mia do?
	2. Lack of knowledge about students' progress	RS2-The teacher Yasmin applies the problem-solving method using the checklist and the videos. Yasmin does not know how each student progresses in the learning process. What should Jasmine do?
Emotional difficulties teacher level	3. Lack of teaching resources in the new method SRL-PS	RS3-Teacher Shula expressed her frustration at having to change all the plans she had been working on and now being expected to re-plan according to the problem-solving method. What should Shola do?
Difficulties in the school environment teacher level	4. Students' limited time	RS4-Teacher Erez teaches 9th grade two hours a week. The class started the learning method through problem solving to promote independent learners. Many classes are canceled because of school activities and exams. Erez shared the problem with the teacher. What should teacher Erez do?
Difficulties in the method student level	5. Inability to do homework's time-planning	RS5-The parents told teacher Hamudi that they really like the new method for solving problems and its importance, but they noted that the children still use them to plan and manage time. What should Hamudi do?
	6. Suggesting only one solution to the problem	RS6-Yael's teacher notices that Yael offers a nice solution to tasks using the problem-solving method, but she always deals with only one solution. What should Yael's teacher do?
	7. Undetailed enough solution	RS7-The teacher sees that Danny, who works according to the method of problem solving, does not specify the solution well in the step of proposing a solution. What should Danny's teacher do?
	8. Incomprehension of SRL-PS method transfer to other subjects	RS8-The teacher Misam taught in the citizenship class to work with the method of solving problems. Now the teacher wants to apply the method alone in the task she gave the students in the history lesson. The students said they did not understand how the method was related to the history assignment. What should they do?
Emotional difficulties student level	9. Difficulty to present to audience	RS9-Roy, a student in teacher Miri's class, appeared in front of the class and had difficulty overcoming his excitement to speak in front of an audience when required to present his solution in front of the class. What should Miri do?
Social difficulties student level	10. Difficulty in group-work	RS10-Ronan, a student in teacher Talia's class, was not satisfied with the members of his group when working together on the task using the problem-solving method. He was afraid he wouldn't get along with them. What should Talia do?

Figure 3: Researchers' SJT difficulties and scenarios for diagnosing SRL-PS knowledge.

ChatGPT s difficulties and SJT scenarios for evaluating SRL-PS knowledge (RQ2)

The SJT tool for diagnosing SRL-PS knowledge, as formulated by the artificial intelligence, includes the general difficulties, defined by ChatGPT and the scenarios corresponding to the difficulties. For example: the general cognitive development difficulty produces scenarios which deals with simplifying a complex task for a 5th grade student and clarify the constraints of the problem to the student. Figure 4 shows, in the first column, the eight difficulties, and in the second column the ten selected scenarios. Each scenario is assigned an abbreviated code (for example: CHS1 stands for ChatGPT scenario 1).

ChatGPT's general difficulties in SRL	ChatGPT's SJT top ten scenarios
1. Cognitive Development: Students at this age have varying levels of cognitive development, which may affect their ability to grasp complex problem-solving processes.	CHS1- A 5th grader is overwhelmed by the complexity of a problem. How would you simplify the task?
	CHS2- During Problem Identification, a student misunderstands the problem's constraints. How do you clarify this?
2. Motivational Differences: There can be significant variability in students' motivation levels, impacting their engagement with the model.	CHS3- Some students show little interest in collaborative problem-solving. What approach would you take?
3. Skill Diversity: Students may have diverse skill sets, making it challenging to tailor the model to all learning needs	CHS4- In a mixed-ability group, advanced students dominate the discussion. How do you ensure inclusivity?
4. Classroom Management: Managing the classroom dynamics while implementing a structured model can be challenging, especially with larger class sizes.	CHS5- A classroom activity gets too chaotic. How do you regain control?
	CHS6- You face difficulty in maintaining order during group work. How do you handle this?
5. Time Constraints: **The school curriculum may have tight schedules, making it difficult to allocate sufficient time for each stage of the model.**	CHS7- You have less time than planned for a key stage. How do you adjust?
6. Resource Limitations: Lack of adequate resources (materials, technology, etc.) can hinder the effective implementation of the model.	CHS8- Essential materials are unavailable for an activity. How do you improvise?
7. Assessment Alignment: Aligning the model with standard assessment methods and ensuring it meets educational standards and objectives may be challenging.	CHS9- How do you ensure that your problem-solving activity aligns with the test formats students will face?
8.Teacher Training: Teachers may require additional training and support to effectively implement and adapt the model in their classrooms.	CHS10- After training, you find some model concepts unclear. How do you seek clarification?

Figure 4: ChatGPT's difficulties and SJT scenarios for diagnosing SRL-PS

ChatGPT contribution to the development of the SJT tool (QR3)

Looking into Figure 3 and Figure 4 indicates that researchers' scenarios can be complemented by the ChatGPT's scenarios. In some cases, the researchers' scenarios and the ChatGPT's scenarios are quite similar (for example: lack of teaching materials for the teacher – RS3, CHS8). In other cases the scenarios formulated by Chat-GPT expand or present another perspective of the difficulty (for example: Evaluation and feedback – RS2, CHS9); yet, in some cases new scenarios were proposed by the ChatGPT (for example: Classroom Management – CHS5).

Furthermore, the analysis of the findings also led to the insight that the ChatGPT difficulties and the researchers' general difficulties complement each other and present different ways to classify difficulties. Therefore, the researchers performed an analysis to map their seven general difficulties (at the teacher and student levels) into the eight ChatGPT difficulties. For example: the researchers' general difficulty of Pedagogical difficulties at teacher level was found to be related to the ChatGPT general difficulties Cognitive Development, Skill Diversity and Motivational Differences; The ChatGPT's Classroom Management difficulty was found related to both researchers' difficulties of Emotional and School Environment at the teacher level. These mappings allow for a merger between the SJT tools of the researchers and the ChatGPT with the aim of creating a diagnostic tool that combines human and machine. This analysis enables to assign each of the total 20 scenarios (of both ChatGPT's and the researchers') to an inclusive difficulty category that constitutes both the ChatGPT and the researchers' difficulty categories. Notably each scenario can fit into multiple joint categories. For example, RS1 (researcher scenario 1) of Learning gaps between students is related to three ChatGPT's difficulties: Cognitive Development, Motivational Differences and Skill Diversity. Similarly, scenarios formulated by ChatGPT can be related to a number of the general researchers' difficulties. For example, the CHS7 (ChatGPT scenario 7) is suitable for the following researcher difficulties: Teacher level Method and Pedagogical, and student level Method (Figure 5).

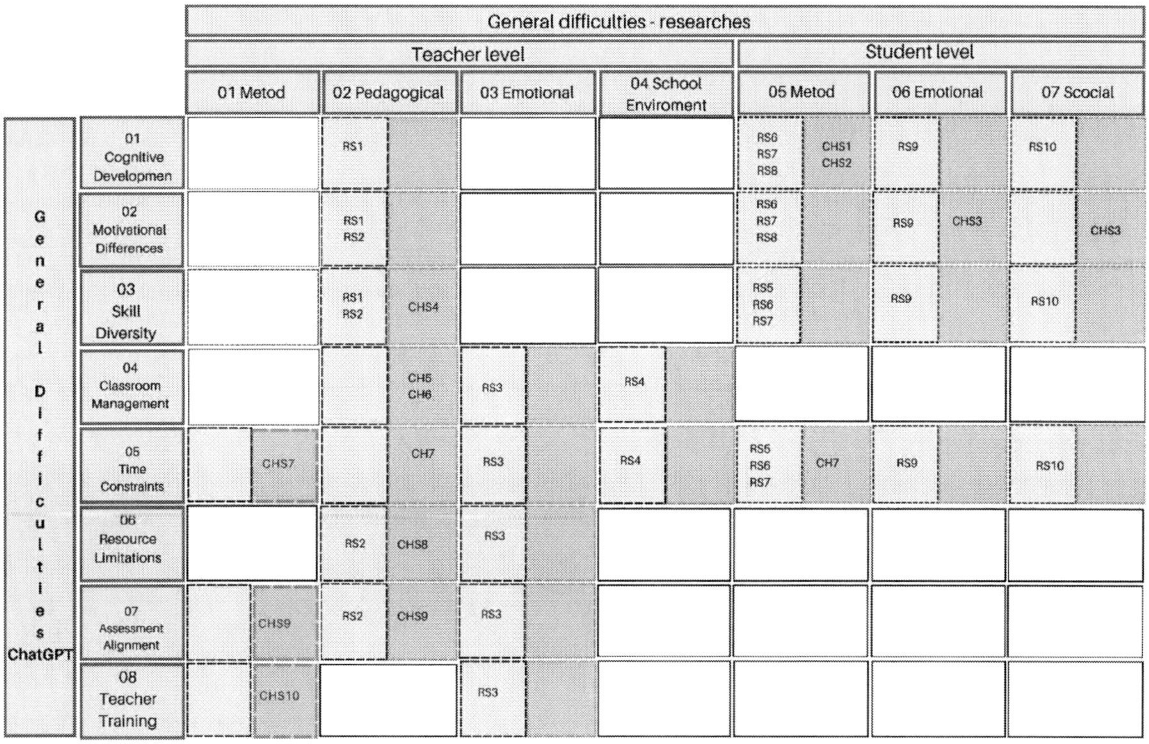

Figure 5: researchers' scenarios and ChatGPT scenarios according to ChatGPT and researchers' difficulty categories

Discussion and conclusions

The current paper referred to the need for an SJT tool that assess teachers' knowledge of PS-SRL. The study examined the development process of SJT tool for diagnosing the SRL-PS knowledge of teachers with the assistance of GenAI, specifically ChatGPT. Moreover the study examined the scenarios produced by the researches compared to those generated by ChatGPT, and its contribution to the development of the SJT tool.

First, this study outlines the steps required for developing SJTs through collaboration between researchers and ChatGPT, highlighting the steps that can be streamlined compared to the traditionally used process. It emphasizes the importance of retaining certain critical steps that cannot be omitted. Among these steps, the involvement of experts or individuals is indispensable. As previously outlined by Te'eni et al. (2023), maintaining a 'human in the loop' may offer advantages over relying on fully autonomous systems. Overall, it is evident that the proposed development process could reduce the time needed to enlarge the initial SJT question pool. This approach addresses the need to optimize the process of creating an SJT question pool.

This research exemplifys an initial attempt of creating scenarios for the SJT tool for diagnosing the knowledge of SRL-PS teachers based on researchers-GenAI interaction. The analysis of the relations between the researchers' and GenAIs' difficulties found that each of them presents a different point of view for classifying scenarios. While the researchers' difficulties were based on the Mishra and Koehler's (2006) model for teachers' knowledge and our SRL-PS model (Assi & Cohen, 2022), it seems that GenAI presented difficulties which are more general. Human-machine interaction constitutes a significant contribution to the development of SJT tools for SRL-PS by expending the range of difficulties and scenarios. The analysis of the scenarios suggested that GenAI can expand or present another perspective of the difficulty in some cases or provide completely new scenarios.

Consequently, this research led to the creation of a map (Figure 5 above) showing the researchers' and ChatGPT's scenarios along with the difficulty categories of the researchers and the ChatGPT. The created map highlights the difficulty categories that need completion of scenarios and the categories that have a wide range of scenarios. Above all, the map facilitates creating new, refined scenarios according to the integrated categories of the researchers and ChatGPT. Therefore, we found that the human-machine interaction can contribute to the development of the SJT tool as was claimed in previous studies (Lee et al., 2023; IONESCU & ENESCU 2023).

It is important to emphasize that this article presents an initial study and it is necessary to perform additional experiments on different GenAI platforms and language models. GenAI systems, developing at a fast pace, could potentially lead to a breakthrough in the field of SJT development, and might broader the gap between researchers who will adopt it and those who will not.

Acknowledgement

This research is supported by the Chief Scientist office of the Israeli Ministry of Education and by the Science and Technology Education Center (SATEC) at Tel-Aviv University.

References

Aldrup, K., Carstensen, B., Köller, M. M., Klusmann, U., & Frenzel, A. C. (2020). Measuring Teachers' Social-Emotional Competence : Development and Validation of a Situational Judgment Test. 11(May), 1–20. https://doi.org/10.3389/fpsyg.2020.00892

Assi, A., & Cohen, A. (2023, September). Video-based SRL program for teachers and students. In Proceedings of the 15th International Conference on Education Technology and Computers (pp. 175-182). https://doi.org/10.1145/3629296.3629323

Boekaerts, M. (1999). Self-regulated learning: Where we are today. International journal of educational research, 31(6), 445-457. https://doi.org/10.1016/S0883-0355(99)00014-2

Borchert, R. J., Hickman, C. R., Pepys, J., & Sadler, T. J. (2023). Performance of ChatGPT on the Situational Judgement Test—A Professional Dilemmas–Based Examination for Doctors in the United Kingdom. JMIR Medical Education, 9(1), e48978

Burns, E. C., Martin, A. J., & Collie, R. J. (2018). Adaptability, personal best (PB) goals setting , and gains in students ' academic outcomes : A longitudinal examination from a social cognitive perspective. Contemporary Educational Psychology, 53(February), 57–72. https://doi.org/10.1016/j.cedpsych.2018.02.001

Chao, T. Y., Sung, Y. T., & Huang, J. L. (2020). Construction of the situational judgment tests for teachers. Asia-Pacific Journal of Teacher Education, 48(4), 355–374. https://doi.org/10.1080/1359866X.2019.1633621

Cheung, B. H. H., Lau, G. K. K., Wong, G. T. C., Lee, E. Y. P., Kulkarni, D., Seow, C. S., ... & Co, M. T. H. (2023). ChatGPT versus human in generating medical graduate exam multiple choice questions—A multinational prospective study (Hong Kong SAR, Singapore, Ireland, and the United Kingdom). PLoS One, 18(8), e0290691.

Cohen, G., Cohen, A. (2023). Exploring Students' Problem-Solving Challenges in Self-regulated Learning Through Training Video Prompts. In: Viberg, O., Jivet, I., Muñoz-Merino, P., Perifanou, M., Papathoma, T. (eds) Responsive and Sustainable Educational Futures. EC-TEL 2023. Lecture Notes in Computer Science, vol 14200. Springer, Cham. https://doi.org/10.1007/978-3-031-42682-7_38.

European Parliamentary Research Service, Scientific Foresight Unit (February 2022), AI Definition & Glossary Key Terms and Concepts. https://www.europarl.europa.eu/cmsdata/244992/AI%20Glossary%20STOA%2014.02.2022.pdf

De Bruijn-Smolders, M., Timmers, C. F., Gawke, J. C. L., Schoonman, W., & Born, M. P. (2016). Effective self-regulatory processes in higher education: research findings and future directions. A systematic review. Studies in Higher Education, 41(1), 139–158. https://doi.org/10.1080/03075079.2014.915302

Dignath, C., Buettner, G., & Langfeldt, H. P. (2008). How can primary school students learn self-regulated learning strategies most effectively?. A meta-analysis on self-regulation training programmes. Educational Research Review, 3(2), 101–129. https://doi.org/10.1016/j.edurev.2008.02.003

Dignath, C., & Büttner, G. (2018). Teachers' direct and indirect promotion of self-regulated learning in primary and secondary school mathematics classes – insights from video-based classroom observations and teacher interviews. Metacognition and Learning, 13(2), 127–157. https://doi.org/10.1007/s11409-018-9181-x

Ionescu, V. M., & Enescu, M. C. (2023, June). Using ChatGPT for Generating and Evaluating Online Tests. In 2023 15th International Conference on Electronics, Computers and Artificial Intelligence (ECAI) (pp. 1-6). IEEE.

Gold, B., & Holodynski, M. (2015). Development and Construct Validation of a Situational Judgment Test of Strategic Knowledge of Classroom Management in Elementary Schools Development and Construct Validation of a Situational Judgment Test of Strategic Knowledge of Classroom Management in. Educational Assessment, 7197(20), 226–248. https://doi.org/10.1080/10627197.2015.1062087

Kistner, S., Rakoczy, K., & Otto, B. (2010). Promotion of self-regulated learning in classrooms : investigating frequency , quality , and consequences for student performance. Metacognition and Learning, 5(2), 157–171. https://doi.org/10.1007/s11409-010-9055-3

Klassen, R. M., Kim, L. E., Rushby, J. V., & Bardach, L. (2020). Can we improve how we screen applicants for initial teacher education? Teaching and Teacher Education, 87, 102949. https://doi.org/10.1016/j.tate.2019.102949

Lee, U., Jung, H., Jeon, Y., Sohn, Y., Hwang, W., Moon, J., & Kim, H. (2023). Few-shot is enough: exploring ChatGPT prompt engineering method for automatic question generation in English education. Education and Information Technologies, 1-33.

Li, L., Zhu, M. L., Shi, Y. Q., & Yang, L. L. (2023). Influencing factors of self-regulated learning of medical-related students in a traditional Chinese medical university: A cross-sectional study. BMC medical education, 23(1), 87. https://doi.org/10.1186/s12909-023-04051-4

Lievens, F., Peeters, H., & Schollaert, E. (2008). Situational judgment tests: A review of recent research. Personnel Review, 37(4), 426-441.

Mishra, P., & Koehler, M. J. (2006). Technological Pedagogical Content Knowledge: A Framework for Teacher Knowledge Related papers. The Development of Technological Pedagogical Content Knowledge in a Design Seminar.

OECD. (2021). AI and the Future of Skills, Volume 1: Capabilities and Assessments. OECD Publishing, Paris, https://doi.org/10.1787/5ee71f34-en.

Patterson, F., Zibarras, L., & Ashworth, V. (2016). Situational judgement tests in medical education and training: Research, theory and practice: AMEE Guide No. 100. Medical teacher, 38(1), 3-17.

Pintrich, P. R. (2000). The Role of Goal Orientation in Self-Regulated Learning. In Handbook of Self-Regulation (pp. 451–502). Elsevier. https://doi.org/10.1016/B978-012109890-2/50043-3

Porter, A. N., & Peters-burton, E. E. (2021). Investigating teacher development of self-regulated learning skills in secondary science students. Teaching and Teacher Education, 105, 103403. https://doi.org/10.1016/j.tate.2021.103403

Sareen, K. (2023). Assessing the ethical capabilities of Chat GPT in healthcare: A study on its proficiency in situational judgement test. Innovations in Education and Teaching International, 1-11.

Svendsen, A., & Garvey, B. (2023). An Outline for an Interrogative/Prompt Library to help improve output quality from Generative-AI Datasets. Prompt Library to help improve output quality from Generative-AI Datasets (May 2023). http://dx.doi.org/10.2139/ssrn.4495319

Te'eni, D., Yahav, I., Zagalsky, A., Schwartz, D., Silverman, G., Cohen, D., ... & Lewinsky, D. (2023). Reciprocal human-machine learning: A theory and an instantiation for the case of message classification. Management Science.

Weekley, J. A., & Jones, C. (1999). Further studies of situational tests. Personnel Psychology, 52(3), 679-700.

Zimmerman, B. J. (2002). Becoming a self-regulated learner: An overview. Theory into practice, 41(2), 64-70. https://doi.org/10.1207/s15430421tip4102_2

Artificial Intelligence and the Future of Online Learning: Opportunities and Challenges

Martina Plantak[1], Vesna Lešnik Štefotič[2]

[1] Project office, , DOBA Faculty of Applied Business and Social Studies Maribor, Slovenia, martina.plantak@doba.si
[2] Project office, DOBA Faculty of Applied Business and Social Studies Maribor; ISP, Vesna Lešnik Štefotič s.p., Slovenia; vesna.lesnik-stefotic@net.doba.si

Correspondence: Martina Plantak: martina.plantak@doba.si

Abstract:

In recent years, artificial intelligence (AI) has become a pervasive part of daily life, with technologies like ChatGPT gaining traction. This paper examines the transformative potential of AI in online education, considering both its theoretical implications and empirical insights. The theoretical section explores AI's impact on education and the ethical challenges it presents, while the empirical section presents findings from a survey conducted among students. The survey investigated student perceptions and experiences with AI tools, shedding light on both their benefits and concerns. Notably, while students recognize the potential of AI to enhance learning, they also express apprehensions about issues like data privacy and overreliance on technology. Ultimately, the paper underscores the importance of responsible integration of AI into education, emphasizing the need for ongoing research and education to ensure its ethical and effective use.

Keywords: Artificial Intelligence in education, ChatGPT, online learning

Introduction

In recent years, artificial intelligence (AI) has become an integral part of our lives. An increasing number of individuals are incorporating various forms of artificial intelligence into their daily routines. For instance, it is estimated that in 2023, the current number of users of ChatGPT reached approximately one hundred million users (Tamim, 2023). Just by looking at this number, it is more than evident how much artificial intelligence became an important part of contemporary life. Still, public understanding of all the advantages that AI can offer is sometimes limited. Just like in other scientific branches, the rise of AI presents a transformative opportunity for online education. The potential of AI to revolutionize the field of education is growing, with its applications becoming increasingly widespread. This article explores how AI can reshape learning experiences by drawing upon established theories in education and technology. The first part of this article will explore the theoretical impact of artificial intelligence (AI) on education and online learning. It will also delve into some of the ethical dilemmas associated with AI use in this context. The second part of the article will present an empirical study based on a survey we conducted among our students in May and June 2023. This survey investigated student understanding, assessment, and experience with AI tools. Our aim was to gain a deeper understanding of student perceptions regarding the use of AI services, including both the potential benefits and drawbacks.

AI and Online Education

The rise of AI presents a significant turning point for online education, offering numerous opportunities for profound transformation. Exploring this phenomenon involves delving into AI's potential to revolutionize the learning environment, drawing on well-established educational and technological principles to create personalized, adaptive, and collaborative educational settings that ultimately yield better outcomes. However, while embracing these advancements, it's vital to carefully consider the challenges that may arise and to acknowledge the crucial role that human educators play. This balanced approach is essential to ensure that the integration of AI into education is responsible and fair, thereby guaranteeing that its evolution remains advantageous and accessible to all.

For example, one of the most well-known and most commonly used AI tools is ChatGPT. The Generative Pre-trained Transformer (GPT), introduced by OpenAI (based in San Francisco, California) in 2018, represents a class of Large Language Models (LLMs) designed to emulate human language processing abilities (Cascella et al., 2023). ChatGPT stands out as the most sophisticated chatbot ever made. Unlike its predecessors, it can churn out impressive text in mere seconds, sparking both excitement and concern. Some worry about its impact on student assessment in higher education and other areas, leading to a mix of anticipation and apprehension (Rudolph et al., 2023 in Mhlanga, 2023). By harnessing deep learning techniques and advanced algorithms, GPT excels in executing a range of language-related functions, including text generation, question answering, and translation. It achieves this by effectively interpreting context to generate responses that closely resemble natural human language (Lund et al., 2023).

There are various advantages of ChatGPT and AI in higher education, as well as numerous instances of how they could be used in classrooms. It has three primary applications in education: instructional support, administrative work automation, and personalization of learning (Zhai, 2022; Grassini, 2023). For example, ChatGPT makes learning more effective and enjoyable by customizing learning experiences to each student's needs. It also comes in handy for data analysis and research work, which makes it easier to finish assignments while adhering to academic guidelines. Plus, it can handle administrative tasks, giving students quick answers and helping staff stay organized. By bringing it into classrooms, one can create a more supportive atmosphere and boost participation. It's also great for assessments, generating questions and offering feedback in real-time. In this sense, ChatGPT's introduction into higher education emphasizes how crucial it is to match pedagogical ideas with technology developments in order to successfully improve learning results. It highlights the necessity of providing academics and students with training and support to ensure that ChatGPT is used effectively in a variety of educational environments. (Rasul et al., 2023; Chen, Chen, & Lin, 2020).

However, the utilization of ChatGPT in online education can also pose certain challenges. Because ChatGPT learns from an immense amount of unprocessed data, it may be biased and contain errors. The caliber and variety of the training data that generative models use greatly influences how successful they are. The outcome of the model may be impacted if biases are present in these datasets (Grassini, 2023). For example, there's the well-known case of Amazon's use of AI technology and machine learning back in 2015 when they discovered that their hiring algorithm was biased against women. This happened because the algorithm relied on data from the previous decade's resumes, which were predominantly from male applicants. As a result, it inadvertently favored male candidates over female ones (Kodiyan, 2019). Moreover, it is also important to mention that there are some limitations of ChatGPT, such as that ChatGPT's effectiveness is contingent upon the quality of the input it receives, with clear questions yielding better responses. Users have reported instances of inaccurate answers when information is incomplete. Additionally, ChatGPT's 3.5 (free version) data is not updated beyond 2021, and server overload can render the platform inaccessible for periods of time.

Secondly, it is important to acknowledge that the ability of ChatGPT to comprehend and respond to human language has positioned it as a highly advantageous tool for educators, students, and various types of learners. However, as its use spreads throughout educational settings, it is critical to approach its implementation with a sense of accountability and ethical concern. It takes more than just perfecting the technological aspects to ensure artificial intelligence is used in education in a responsible and ethical manner. The ethical, cultural, and sociological ramifications of incorporating AI into educational settings must be carefully considered. Specifically, it involves identifying potential biases in AI systems, safeguarding data privacy, promoting transparency and accountability, and ensuring that AI tools are used to empower and support learners rather than replace human educators (Grooms & Schenck, 2020; Lynch et al., 2022). Therefore, it is imperative that policymakers and educational institutions work together to create policies and guidelines that support the moral and responsible application of AI in education while also giving teachers and students the tools and resources they need to successfully navigate these difficult issues (Brennan, 2021; Schmidt et al., 2023).

Empirical insights

As the leading online faculty in Slovenia, with over 20 years of work, Doba Faculty embraces innovation in teaching, integrating various pedagogical approaches, including videos, open educational resources, microlearning, and detailed assessment rubrics, into the curriculum. Hence, we continuously seek student feedback through surveys to enhance the learning experience.

In May and June 2023, we conducted a survey that included two parts. The first part focused on the use of rubrics, while the second part, a novel inquiry, explored students' knowledge, assessment of, and experience using artificial intelligence (AI) tools in their learning at Doba Faculty. This analysis focuses solely on the AI-related portion of the survey.

The survey ran from May 23rd to June 4th, 2023. We received 252 student responses. However, the number of valid responses for each question varied, and these variations will be highlighted throughout the analysis.

To assess students' self-reported knowledge and skills in utilizing AI tools for learning, we focused on a question regarding their experience with tools like ChatGPT. Among 208 valid responses, nearly 43.3% (90 students) identified as "Entry level - I don't know and have no practical experience." Basic understanding ("Basic level - I have a basic understanding") was reported by 37.5% (78 students), followed by 16.8% (35 students) indicating an "Advanced level - I know and already have some practical experience." Only a small percentage (2.4%, or 5 students) claimed "Expertise - I know it very well and have a lot of experience using it.

An interesting trend emerged regarding the relationship between age and AI knowledge. Students with valid responses to this question had an average age of 36.2 years. There was a negative correlation between age and reported AI knowledge; the average age decreased with increasing levels of reported AI use: 37.5 years for entry level and 34 years for the expert level.

Furthermore, our data revealed gender differences in AI familiarity. Nearly half (47.6%) of female respondents identified as "Entry level," compared to only 32.8% of male respondents.

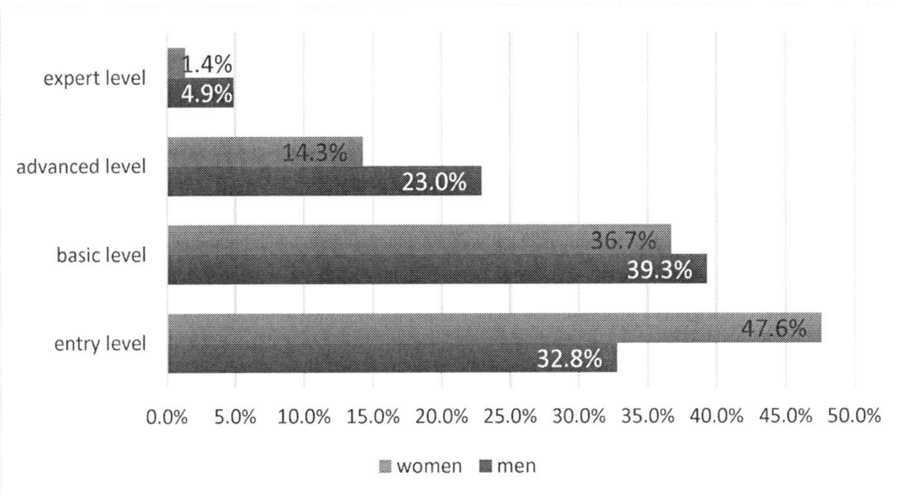

Figure 1: Assessed level of knowledge and skills utilizing AI among students, n=208

To investigate the use of AI tools in student learning, we asked students with at least basic AI expertise, "Have you ever used any AI tools, including ChatGPT, for studying?" This question yielded 118 valid responses. A little over half (53.4%) of the respondents reported using AI tools for learning (59 occasionally, 4 regularly). ChatGPT was the most popular tool (46 students), followed by Chat PDF (2 students). Other tools mentioned once included Bard, Elicite, Syntesia, Aiplayground, BlackRock Aladdin, Canva, Notion, and Snapchat AI.

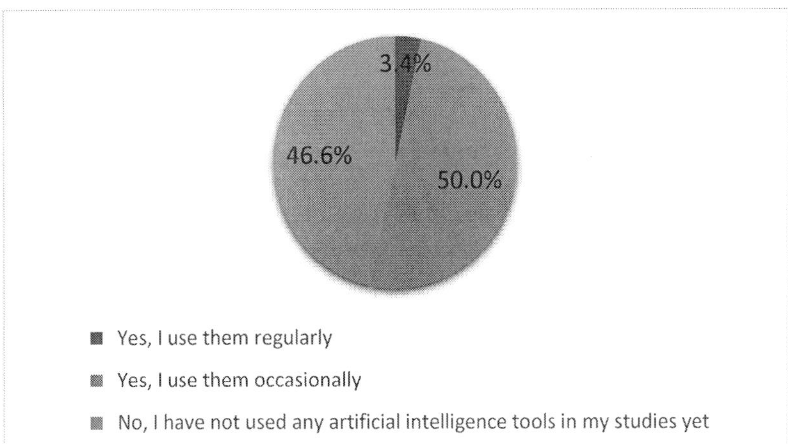

Figure 2: Use of the AI tools in the learning process, n=118

We further investigated the purposes behind AI tool use during learning. Students could select all applicable options. The primary reasons for using AI tools were: researching the topic (46 responses), generating ideas (35), and general learning assistance (31). Translation (22) and data analysis (21) were also common uses. A smaller number of students reported using AI tools for writing assignments (7), project participation (4), and collaboration (1). Notably, no student selected "programming and coding" as a purpose. Students also mentioned additional uses like presentations, finding relevant professional literature, image generation, and text transformation.

In evaluating the usefulness of AI tools for learning, students provided ratings on a scale from "very useful" to "useless." The majority found them beneficial, with 14 rating them very useful, 24 rating them pretty useful, and 21 somewhat useful. Only 2 students found them of little use, and none considered them useless.

To explore the perceived benefits of AI tools, students rated their agreement with statements on a 4-point scale (1 = Strongly Disagree, 2 = Disagree, 3 = Agree, 4 = Strongly Agree). The highest agreement (3.4 points) was for the statement "Using AI tools reduces the time I spend searching for information." Students also showed moderate agreement (between 3.1 and 3.2 points) with statements regarding improved technology skills, problem-solving abilities, understanding of learning materials, and study efficiency. All other statements received scores above 2 points, indicating at least some level of agreement. These included statements about enhancing the distance learning experience (2.9 points), exam preparation (2.7 points), personalized learning (2.6 points), and collaboration with classmates and teachers (2.1 points).

Students also identified several concerns regarding the use of AI tools like ChatGPT in higher education answering the question “What concerns or weaknesses do you perceive when using AI tools such as ChatGPT in higher education? (Check all that apply)”. The most prevalent concerns were:

- Credibility of contents/offered answers/proposed solutions (125 responses): This indicates a significant student concern about the reliability and accuracy of information generated by AI tools.
- Ethical aspects and dilemmas (94 responses): Students are worried about the potential ethical implications of using AI tools, such as plagiarism or the manipulation of data.
- Potential dependency on AI tools (76 responses): Students worry about becoming overly reliant on AI for learning and losing critical thinking skills.
- Limited understanding of AI technology (60 responses): This suggests a need for better education on how AI tools work and their limitations.
- Data privacy (48 responses): Students are concerned about how their data is collected, stored, and used by AI tools.

Responses in the "Other" Category:

- Inaccurate and out-of-date information, manipulated/false data, without citing sources: This reinforces concerns about the credibility of information from AI tools.
- Not for college, reduces creativity/ingenuity: Students perceive AI tools as unsuited for the rigor of higher education and potentially hindering independent thought.
- Unregulated AI poses a danger: This highlights a concern about the lack of clear guidelines for the use of AI tools in education.

Overall, the results suggest that while students see some potential benefits in using AI tools, they have significant concerns about their reliability, ethical implications, and potential negative impacts on learning.

We also invited students to share their ideas on how generative AI could be integrated into the learning process to enhance the learning experience. This open-ended question resulted in a wide range of responses. To analyse them, we categorized the answers into three groups.

- Dismissive Views (21 students): This group expressed reservations about using AI tools in education at all.
- Unsure Responses (12 students): These students indicated they weren't sure how AI could be integrated. Their responses included "I don't know" and similar statements.

- Concrete Proposals (40 students): This group provided specific suggestions. Here's a breakdown of these proposals:
  - Teaching optimal AI usage in education (14 students): This proposal emphasized the need to educate students on how to effectively utilize AI tools for learning.
  - Improving information access and exploration (23 students): These students suggested using AI for tasks like finding relevant literature, exploring new topics, searching for practical examples, generating ideas, and understanding learning materials.
  - Completing specific tasks (7 students): These proposals focused on using AI for tasks such as translation, summarization, data analysis, and improving written documents.
- Additional Ideas: Some students proposed integrating AI as a learning chatbot for information access and creating personalized learning experiences.

Conclusion

In our article we have explored how artificial intelligence (AI) can change the way we learn online. AI has the potential to personalize learning, but there are also ethical considerations and potential downsides that need to be addressed. A survey conducted with students at Doba Faculty (n=252) showed that over 40% of respondents had no experience with AI tools. However, among those who did, ChatGPT was the most popular tool, used for researching topics, generating ideas, and generally assisting with learning. AI tools were deemed to be beneficial by students, particularly in terms of time savings and increased study productivity. As a result, an intriguing pattern revealed a negative relationship between age and AI expertise, with younger students reporting greater usage of AI.

There were, however, significant concerns about the trustworthiness of information generated by AI and the potential for ethical problems. Students were also worried about data privacy and becoming too reliant on AI, which could hinder their critical thinking skills. The open-ended responses suggested that while some students completely reject AI tools in education, others see potential benefits for tasks like finding information, exploring new topics, and completing specific assignments. Interestingly, many students highlighted the need for education on how to effectively use AI tools for learning.

Our faculty has recently implemented guidelines for the use of AI tools for both students and teachers. Additionally, we organized two educator-focused events that promoted discussions about integrating AI into teaching methodologies: a webinar that examined ChatGPT and artificial intelligence's applications in education, as well as a development meeting that cantered on using AI in the study process. We intend to conduct the survey again and analyse the results thoroughly in order to look for any patterns or differences between the first and second survey responses. The goal of this project is to give more light on how artificial intelligence is used in online learning.

In conclusion, AI offers a chance to transform online education. However, to integrate AI responsibly and ethically, we need to address concerns and ensure that AI complements human educators, not replaces them. Future research should focus on developing effective teaching methods that incorporate AI while also fostering critical thinking skills and creating a positive learning environment for everyone involved.

References

Cascella, M., Montomoli, J., Bellini, V., & Bignami, E. (2023). Evaluating the feasibility of ChatGPT in healthcare: an analysis of multiple clinical and research scenarios. Journal of medical systems, 47(1), 33.

Chen, L., Chen, P., & Lin, Z. (2020). Artificial intelligence in education: A review. Ieee Access, 8, 75264-75278.

Grassini, S. (2023). Shaping the future of education: exploring the potential and consequences of AI and ChatGPT in educational settings. Education Sciences, 13(7), 692.

Holmes, W., & Tuomi, I. (2022). State of the art and practice in AI in education. European Journal of Education, 57(4), 542-570.

Kodiyan, A. A. (2019). An overview of ethical issues in using AI systems in hiring with a case study of Amazon's AI based hiring tool. Researchgate Preprint, 1-19.

Lund, B. D., Wang, T., Mannuru, N. R., Nie, B., Shimray, S., & Wang, Z. (2023). ChatGPT and a new academic reality: Artificial Intelligence-written research papers and the ethics of the large language models in scholarly publishing. Journal of the Association for Information Science and Technology, 74(5), 570-581.

Mhlanga, D. (2023). Open AI in education, the responsible and ethical use of ChatGPT towards lifelong learning. In FinTech and Artificial Intelligence for Sustainable Development: The Role of Smart Technologies in Achieving Development Goals (pp. 387-409). Cham: Springer Nature Switzerland.

Rasul, T., Nair, S., Kalendra, D., Robin, M., de Oliveira Santini, F., Ladeira, W. J., ... & Heathcote, L. (2023). The role of ChatGPT in higher education: Benefits, challenges, and future research directions. Journal of Applied Learning and Teaching, 6(1).

Tamim, B. (2023). ChatGPT outpaces Instagram: 10 million daily users in just 40 days. https://interestingengineering.com/innovation/chatgpt-outpaces-instagram-10-million-users-40-days. Accessed: 02. 03. 2024.

Zhai, X. (2022). ChatGPT user experience: Implications for education. SSRN. https://doi.org/10.2139/ssrn.4312418

Motivational GenAI chatbot for promoting SRL in problem solving: Data-driven design principles

Guy Cohen[1], Anat Cohen[2]

[1] School of Education, Tel Aviv University, Israel; guycohen@mail.tau.ac.il
[2] School of Education, Tel Aviv University, Israel; anatco@tauex.tau.ac.il

Correspondence: Guy Cohen: guycohen@mail.tau.ac.il

Abstract

Self-regulated learning (SRL) is crucial in today's educational landscape, championing students' autonomy over their learning journey. Yet, SRL, especially in problem-solving, poses significant difficulties for students. This study innovatively bridges this gap with a set of design principles for a generative AI chatbot specifically shaped to promote students' SRL skills during problem-solving tasks. Leveraging insights from feedback collected from both educators and students involved in a blended SRL program, this research shines a light on the range of difficulties involves in SRL within problem solving context. It pinpoints three main difficulties: Inconsistencies in assessment and perception that create a gap between student self-evaluations and educator assessments; Cognitive strategies difficulties that hinder skill application; and beyond cognitive difficulties such as motivation and task self-management obstacles toward independent learning. Responding to these difficulties, the design principles of the proposed AI chatbot are focused on providing structured guidance, which includes explicit instruction in cognitive and motivational skills, offering personalized feedback based on the specific difficulties, and facilitating the assessment of these skills during task performance. This approach not only advances the theoretical framework of SRL but also translates these concepts into tangible support mechanisms, equipping educators with an innovative tool to enhance SRL. The chatbot stands as a testament to the power of generative AI in transforming educational practices, paving the way for learners to become more self-reliant and adept in navigating the complexities of the digital learning era.

Keywords: Self-regulated learning; Problem-solving; AI Chatbot; Digital agent; Generative AI; K-12

Introduction

Self-regulated learning (SRL) is crucial across all educational levels and settings, significantly impacting academic persistence, performance, and attainment, with an urgent need for effective SRL interventions (Xu et al., 2023). This need is underscored by several studies that highlight the importance of promoting SRL skills in young adolescents (Cohen & Cohen, 2023a; 2023b). Problem-solving integrates a cyclical process of SRL strategies such as planning, performing, and reflecting, requiring individuals to utilize a diverse range of skills and strategies to effectively navigate and overcome challenges (Zimmerman & Campillo, 2003). The literature suggests that explicit training in SRL strategies significantly enhances students' ability to transfer and apply these strategies across various contexts (Kistner et al., 2010). This form of explicit instruction is crucial for enabling students to adeptly navigate and tackle challenges, thereby fostering a robust foundation for lifelong learning and problem-solving capabilities (Morisano et al., 2010; Paans et al., 2019).

The process of problem-solving is inherently non-linear and involved with difficulties, which necessitates a nuanced approach to training that includes a broad spectrum of strategies. This encompass cognitive, metacognitive, motivational, and affective strategies, each playing a vital role in navigating the complexities of problem-solving (Csapó & Funke, 2017; OECD, 2021). Nevertheless, there exists a notable gap in SRL training, particularly in the explicit teaching of motivational strategies. A recent systematic review conducted by Xu et al. (2023) explored empirical studies on SRL interventions within both online and blended learning settings across elementary, secondary, higher, and adult education. Analysis of the studies included in this review revealed notable gaps: very few studies have focused on the explicit teaching of motivational strategies for activating, monitoring, and controlling motivation during the different stages of SRL, particularly among young learners in elementary and secondary schools.

The appearance of AI chatbots and generative artificial intelligence (GenAI) tools like ChatGPT has introduced a new era in educational technology, providing personalized learning experiences that significantly improve students' learning outcomes and motivation (Wu & Yu, 2024). The integration of GenAI in education is increasingly recognized as a transformative trend that enhances learning through technology, offering individualized guidance that could elevate creativity, critical thinking, and problem-solving skills (Dwivedi et al., 2023; Eysenbach, 2023). Furthermore, the use of educational chatbots exemplifies AI's capability to transform learning experiences by offering personalized interactions, underlining the growing influence of AI in education. Despite the acknowledged benefits, research on the classroom integration of tools like ChatGPT remains sparse, indicating a need for further investigation into optimizing AI's impact on education (Chang et al., 2023). Specifically, a systematic review of chatbots in education (Kuhail etl al., 2023) reveals a scant focus on motivational agents. Among the few studies that examine motivation, the emphasis is predominantly on adult learners, specifically regarding motivational feedback.

In response, this study deals with design principles of GenAI chatbot aims to promote motivational and cognitive SRL strategies based on data driven analysis of difficulties that involved with students SRL while performing problem solving tasks. Moreover, the design principles are presented in a Chatbot prototype, named 'Moti Bot', that was developed during this study. This research not only contributes to the advancement of the theoretical framework of SRL but also converts these concepts into tangible support mechanisms, providing educators with an innovative tool to improve SRL. The chatbot prototype that proposed in this research serves as evidence of the transformative potential of GenAI in reshaping educational practices, facilitating learners to develop greater self-reliance and proficiency in navigating the intricacies of the digital learning era.

The current research

Research objective and questions

The primary aim of this study is to outline the features of a GenAI chatbot designed to facilitate SRL within problem-solving contexts, based on prevalent educational difficulties and meeting contemporary teaching needs. The study focuses on two key objectives: first, to catalog the various difficulties students face while engaging in SRL during problem-solving tasks, and second, to specify the design principles of a GenAI chatbot capable of guiding students through these challenges and enhancing their learning experience.

Consequently, this research is driven by two questions:

1. What specific difficulties involved in students SRL while engaging on problem solving tasks?
2. What are the designed features in a GenAI chatbot that could support students SRL in problem-solving tasks?

Research methodology

This paper presents a detailed analysis involving 11 teachers from various disciplines and 177 heterogeneous students from grades 6-11, from Hebrew-speaking and Arabic-speaking schools in the central region of Israel. The students are heterogeneous in terms of socio-economic background and academic achievement. The 11 teachers were engaged in a blended professional SRL training program. During this program, an intervention was conducted in their classes with their students under their guidance. The students participated in group problem-solving activities, based on a framework of a structured problem-solving process, which incorporated cognitive SRL strategies like time management, feedback, elaboration, and critical thinking. This was facilitated through a digital toolbox that included interactive videos, checklists, and tasks, aiming to systematize the problem-solving approach as discussed in the literature (Cohen & Cohen, 2023a, 2023b).

The research was conducted in two phases:

- The first phase aimed to provide a structured method for understanding and classifying students' difficulties according to a problem-solving framework. Thus, this phase focused on collecting and analysing the students' difficulties through both students and their teachers reports – separately. With regards to the teachers, the initial step was to classify the difficulties that they observed while their students worked on the activities, directly linking them to the problem-solving framework. This framework provided a lens through which the challenges were interpreted, aligning each difficulty with specific cognitive strategies within the framework. When difficulties did not fit within the framework, a secondary step of analysis was undertaken to identify and categorize these outlier challenges, acknowledging the complexity and diversity of real-world teaching scenarios. The analysis of the students reports also began with categorizing difficulties related to the various cognitive strategies it outlined. A further analysis addressed unclassifiable challenges. A critical third step in this phase was the comparative analysis between the teachers and their students reports with regard to students' difficulties. This comparison highlighted challenges that went beyond the framework's boundaries, providing an additional layer of analysis. Consequently, unifying categories were created to encompass the range of difficulties that could not be directly associated with the initial cognitive strategy framework, thereby offering a broader perspective on the educational challenges in problem-solving contexts.

- The second phase focused on defining the design principles for a GenAI chatbot. In this stage, the insights garnered from the comparative analysis and the identification of difficulties unique to students' SRL in problem-solving tasks were used to outline the features of a GenAI chatbot. Then, the implementation of the design principles was demonstrated through a chatbot named 'Moti Bot' that was designed and developed for young students in order to assist them with the identified difficulties effectively, integrating tailored support mechanisms based on the categorized difficulties.

Thus, this research does not only provide a structured classification of student difficulties but also provides practical design considerations for developing an AI tool that enhances students' problem-solving capabilities within SRL contexts, and further demonstrates the revealed design principles through a GenAI chatbot.

Results

Difficulties involved in students SRL while working on problem solving tasks (RQ1)

The comparative analysis between teachers' and students' reports revealed valuable insights regarding the difficulties involved in students SRL while working on problem solving tasks. Three categories of difficulties were classified:

1. **Assessment difficulties** - Significant differences were found between teachers' and students' reports with regards to students' difficulties, which indicate that students and teachers assess the difficulties differently. This indicates a misalignment in the perception and identification of student difficulties. Specifically, this misalignment was especially evident in the assessment of cognitive strategies critical for an effective problem-solving process (Figure 1).
2. **Cognitive strategies difficulties** - The analysis of both teachers and students' data, revealed that students struggle significantly with key aspects of problem-solving process, including defining problems, managing time, developing solutions, engaging in reflection, and seeking peer feedback. These difficulties suggest that students face substantial barriers in applying cognitive strategies effectively, which are crucial for successful problem-solving (Figure 1).

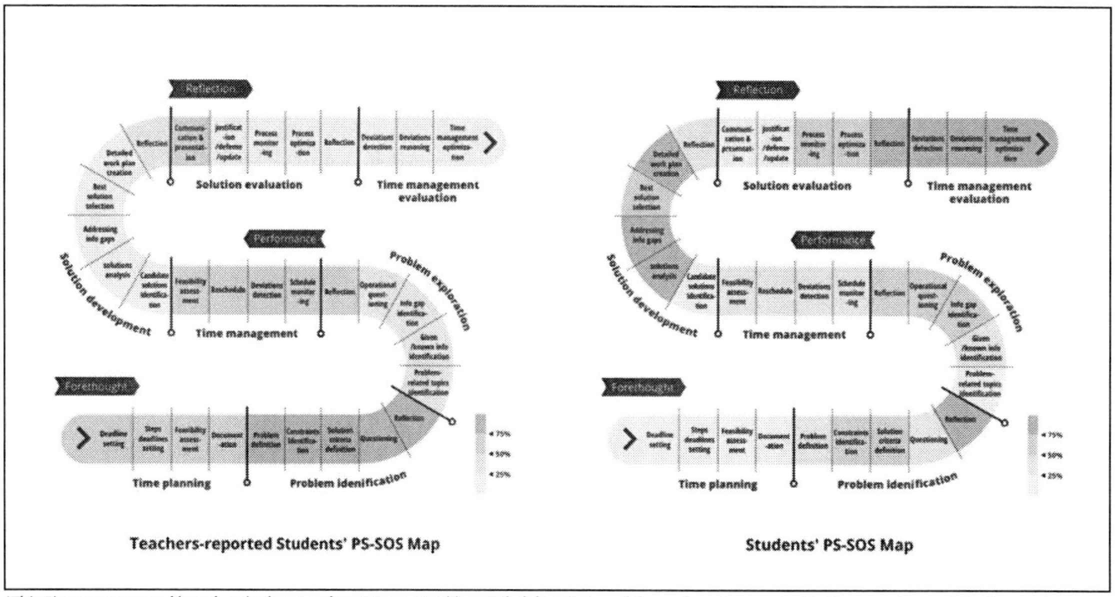

*This Figure was created based on (Cohen & Cohen 2023a; 2023b). Detailed description of the analyses is presented in these previous publications.

Figure 1: PS-SOS Maps: The relative share of students' difficulties in each component of the problem-solving framework (The color intensity increases as more difficulties are identified in each component).

3. **Beyond cognitive strategies difficulties** - The study also identified challenges that extend beyond the described problem-solving framework, highlighting issues not directly related to cognitive strategies: (1) Task self-management and autonomy: there is a reliance on adult intervention, indicating a struggle among students to manage tasks independently and progress autonomously; (2) Motivational and affective issues: motivational and emotional barriers also emerged as significant obstacles, affecting students' engagement and persistence in problem-solving activities; (3) Infrastructural and environmental barriers: students encounter difficulties related to the learning environment and access to technology, impacting their ability to engage effectively in problem-solving tasks; (4) Peer collaboration: challenges in collaborating with peers were noted, suggesting difficulties in social aspects of learning and problem-solving (Figure 2).

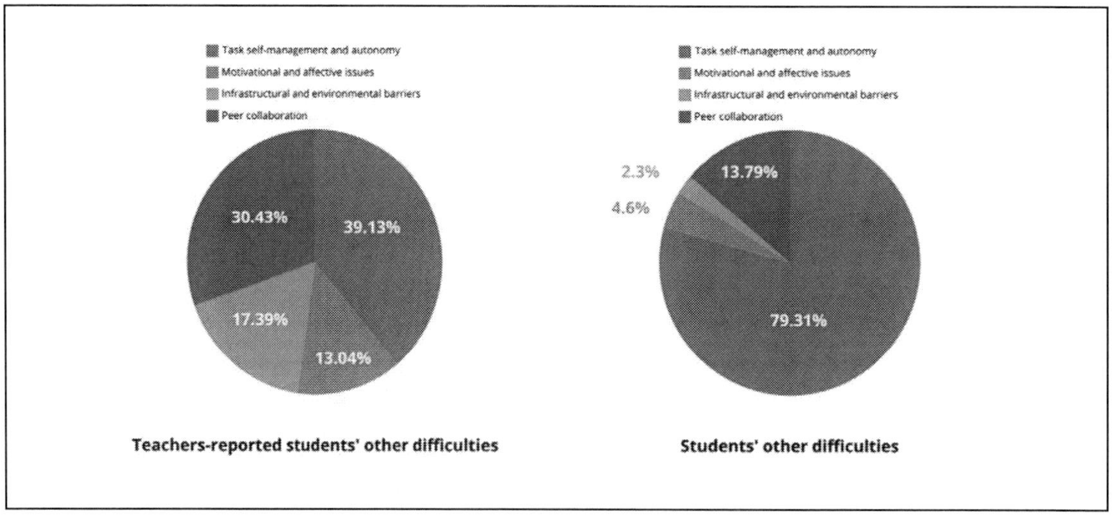

Figure 2: Findings from a qualitative analysis of unclassifiable responses that could not be classified into the cognitive problem-solving framework (n=87 $_{\text{identified difficulties - students}}$; n=23 $_{\text{identified difficulties - teachers}}$).

Designed features for a GenAI chatbot to support students (RQ2)

Based on the first phase and difficulties identified, this study outlines three universal design principles for GenAI chatbots set to enhance student learning. While these principles are broadly applicable to any GenAI chatbot aimed at supporting student learning, we illustrate their implementation through our prototype, 'Moti Bot'. Designed to guide young learners through learning tasks from the beginning to completion, 'Moti' ensures progression only after students demonstrate the application of solution strategies integral to the problem-solving process. Here are the main design principles and their embodiment in 'Moti':

1. **Structured and explicit strategy instruction** - This principle emphasizes the need for a chatbot to offer structured guidance on both cognitive and motivational skills necessary for problem-solving. In 'Moti', this is realized through a dual approach: firstly, by providing a structured problem-solving framework that includes explicit teaching of cognitive and motivational SRL strategies; secondly, by integrating a stepwise strategy application process. Initially, students are introduced to a strategy explicitly and are required to apply it in their interaction with 'Moti'. If a student encounters difficulties, first 'Moti' offers a coping strategy formulated by experts. In case the difficulty is not resolved, the student receives a personalized coping strategy generated by GenAI (ChatGPT4). If difficulties persist, 'Moti' encourages students to seek assistance from peers or a teacher, pro'Moti'ng a collaborative learning environment. This comprehensive approach effectively tackles assessment discrepancies and cognitive and motivational difficulties by providing clear paths for skill acquisition and application. Structured training also supports broader learning difficulties such as self-management of tasks by teaching students how to approach tasks systematically and autonomously.

2. **Personalized feedback** - Personalization is key to effective learning support. With 'Moti', feedback is context-sensitive, tailored to the student's current challenge. Initially, the bot uses a pre-scripted dialogue to steer the student towards a specific problem-solving pathway based on their response. Advanced levels of personalization are achieved through GenAI, which crafts focused responses to the student's specific difficulties and the task context, enhancing the relevance and impact of the feedback. This tailored feedback mechanism directly addresses students' cognitive and motivational strategies difficulties and broader learning challenges by offering customized support that resonates with their individual experiences and needs. It also narrows the assessment gap between teachers and students by offering tailored insights into individual performance and strategy challenges.

3. **Real-time skills assessment** - Continuous assessment allows for timely interventions and support. 'Moti' documents the learning process in real-time, providing students with access to their conversation history for self-reflection and allowing teachers to monitor skill usage at both individual and class levels through a dashboard. This transparency helps identify areas needing further support, fostering a more responsive educational environment. The real-time skills assessment bridges the assessment gap between teachers and students, ensuring that both parties have an accurate and updated understanding of the student's progress and challenges.

'Moti Bot' was designed by a diverse team, including teachers, teacher trainers, educational designers, IT developers, and researchers in self-regulated learning (SRL) and learning technologies, following the described principles. This apprenticeship-focused tool helps young students develop cognitive and motivational SRL skills through task-based learning. The chatbot is versatile, applicable across all disciplines, both STEM and non-STEM. Student outcomes are measured by their successful application of steps in the problem-solving process, which includes both cognitive and motivational strategies. The problem-solving framework builds upon and refines previous framework (Cohen & Cohen, 2023b) by integrating motivational strategies. Figure 3 illustrates the architecture of the chatbot, which is designed in accordance with the established design principles.

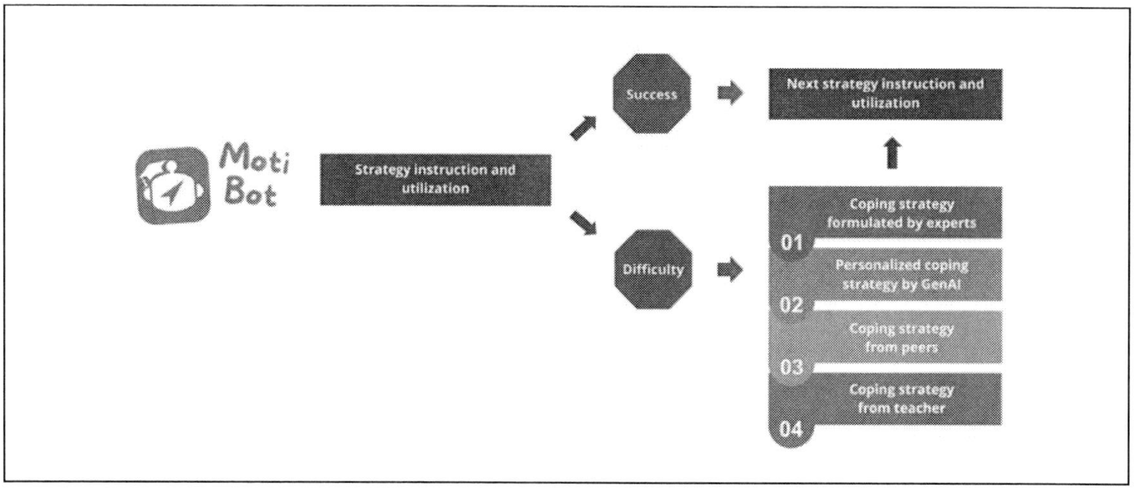

Figure 3: 'Moti Bot' message architecture.

Discussion and conclusion

The essence of this research lies in identifying design principles for developing GenAI chatbots that promote SRL within the context of problem-solving tasks. These design principles were created based on the analysis of data describing difficulties collected from teachers and their students. These principles were illustrated through the development of 'Moti Bot'. Our aim was twofold: first, to pinpoint the unique challenges students encounter in SRL during problem-solving tasks, and second, to articulate the critical features such a chatbot must encompass to effectively guide students through these SRL difficulties.

The first design principle focuses on structured and explicit instruction of cognitive and motivational strategies along with providing support in difficulties during strategies' utilization. By breaking down strategies into clear, actionable steps, the chatbot ensures a solid basis for learning autonomy. This principle is aligned with educational literature that underscores the importance of clear goal-setting and explicit strategy instruction for effective SRL (Chang et al., 2023; Morisano et al., 2010; Paans et al., 2019).

Personalized feedback, the second principle, directly addresses students' broader learning difficulties, as well as their assessment. By tailoring feedback to individual student needs and contexts, the chatbot narrows the assessment gap and offers support that resonates with each learner's unique difficulties. This principle is supported by research emphasizing the impact of personalized feedback on learning outcomes (Akhtar et al., 2015; Marzouk et al., 2016; Schumacher, 2018), highlighting the importance of adaptability and relevance in feedback for enhancing SRL (Chang et al., 2023).

Moreover, the inclusion of real-time skills assessment addresses the continuous need for accurate assessment, providing immediate insights into students' progress. This feature is vital for fostering a responsive educational environment conducive to SRL, echoing literature that emphasizes the role of ongoing feedback and self-assessment mechanisms in promoting SRL (Chang et al., 2023; Ndoye, 2017; Zepeda et al., 2015).

'Moti Bot' primarily focuses on explicit teaching of cognitive and motivational strategies, overlooking the explicit instruction of emotional SRL strategies. This suggests an area for future enhancement, as emotional regulation is integral to a holistic SRL approach. To further refine and validate 'Moti Bot's design principles, future steps include conducting intervention studies in educational settings. These studies aim to assess the chatbot's effectiveness in supporting students' problem-solving and SRL skills, offering empirical insights that will inform the ongoing development of GenAI tools to support and enhance student learning outcomes.

Acknowledgements

This research is supported by the Chief Scientist Office of the Israeli Ministry of Education and by the Science and Technology Education Center (SATEC) at Tel-Aviv University.

References

Akhtar, S., Warburton, S., & Xu, W. (2017). The use of an online learning and teaching system for monitoring computer aided design student participation and predicting student success. International Journal of Technology and Design Education, 27, 251-270. https://doi.org/10.1007/s10798-015-9346-8

Chang, D. H., Lin, M. P. C., Hajian, S., & Wang, Q. Q. (2023). Educational Design Principles of Using AI Chatbot That Supports Self-Regulated Learning in Education: Goal Setting, Feedback, and Personalization. Sustainability, 15(17), 1-15. https://doi.org/10.3390/su151712921

Cohen, G., Cohen, A. (2023a). Exploring Students' Problem-Solving Challenges in Self-regulated Learning Through Training Video Prompts. In: Viberg, O., Jivet, I., Muñoz-Merino, P., Perifanou, M., Papathoma, T. (eds) Responsive and Sustainable Educational Futures. EC-TEL 2023. Lecture Notes in Computer Science, vol 14200. Springer, Cham. https://doi.org/10.1007/978-3-031-42682-7_38

Cohen, G., & Cohen, A. (2023b). Mapping Difficulties in Problem-Solving Process During Video-Assisted Self-Regulated Learning Training for Students: Introducing the PS-SOS MAP. 2023 Ubiquity Proceedings, 3(1), 289-296. https://doi.org/10.5334/uproc.99

Csapó, B., & Funke, J. (2017). The nature of problem solving. OECD. http://dx.doi.org/10.1787/9789264273955-en

Dwivedi, Y. K., Kshetri, N., Hughes, L., Slade, E. L., Jeyaraj, A., Kar, A. K., ... & Wright, R. (2023). "So what if ChatGPT wrote it?" Multidisciplinary perspectives on opportunities, challenges and implications of generative conversational AI for research, practice and policy. International Journal of Information Management, 71, 1-63. https://doi.org/10.1016/j.ijinfomgt.2023.102642

Eysenbach, G. (2023). The role of ChatGPT, generative language models, and artificial intelligence in medical education: a conversation with ChatGPT and a call for papers. JMIR Medical Education, 9(1), 1-13. https://doi.org/10.2196/46885

Kistner, S., Rakoczy, K., Otto, B., Dignath-van Ewijk, C., Büttner, G., & Klieme, E. (2010). Promotion of self-regulated learning in classrooms: Investigating frequency, quality, and consequences for student performance. Metacognition and Learning, 5(2), 157-171. https://doi.org/10.1007/s11409-010-9055-3

Kuhail, M. A., Alturki, N., Alramlawi, S., & Alhejori, K. (2023). Interacting with educational chatbots: A systematic review. Education and Information Technologies, 28(1), 973-1018. https://doi.org/10.1007/s10639-022-11177-3

Marzouk, Z., Rakovic, M., Liaqat, A., Vytasek, J., Samadi, D., Stewart-Alonso, J., Ram, I., Woloshen, S., Winne, P. H., & Nesbit, J. C. (2016). What if learning analytics were based on learning science? Australasian Journal of Educational Technology, 32(6). https://doi.org/10.14742/ajet.3058

Morisano, D., Hirsh, J. B., Peterson, J. B., Pihl, R. O., & Shore, B. M. (2010). Setting, elaborating, and reflecting on personal goals improves academic performance. Journal of Applied Psychology, 95(2), 255–264. https://doi.org/10.1037/a0018478

Ndoye, A. (2017). Peer/Self Assessment and Student Learning. International Journal of Teaching and Learning in Higher Education, 29(2), 255-269.

OECD. (2021). OECD Skills Outlook 2021: Learning for Life. OECD Publishing, Paris. https://doi.org/10.1787/0ae365b4-en

Paans, C., Molenaar, I., Segers, E., & Verhoeven, L. (2019). Temporal variation in children's self-regulated hypermedia learning. Computers in Human Behavior, 96, 246-258. https://doi.org/10.1016/j.chb.2018.04.002

Schumacher, C., & Ifenthaler, D. (2018). Features students really expect from learning analytics. Computers in human behavior, 78, 397-407. https://doi.org/10.1016/j.chb.2017.06.030

Wu, R., & Yu, Z. (2024). Do AI chatbots improve students learning outcomes? Evidence from a meta-analysis. British Journal of Educational Technology, 55(1), 10-33. https://doi.org/10.1111/bjet.13334

Xu, Z., Zhao, Y., Zhang, B., Liew, J., & Kogut, A. (2023). A meta-analysis of the efficacy of self-regulated learning interventions on academic achievement in online and blended environments in K-12 and higher education. Behaviour & Information Technology, 42(16), 2911-2931. https://doi.org/10.1080/0144929X.2022.2151935

Zepeda, C. D., Richey, J. E., Ronevich, P., & Nokes-Malach, T. J. (2015). Direct instruction of metacognition benefits adolescent science learning, transfer, and motivation: An in vivo study. Journal of Educational Psychology, 107(4), 954. https://psycnet.apa.org/doi/10.1037/edu0000022

Zimmerman, B. J., & Campillo, M. (2003). Motivating self-regulated problem solvers. In Davidson, J.E & Sternberg, R.J (Eds.), The psychology of problem solving (pp. 233-262). Cambridge.

The Predictive Power of Teaching Approaches: Unveiling Keys to Enhanced Students' Motivation and Workload in Blended Learning

Marko Radovan[1], Ema Meden[2], Danijela Makovec Radovan[3]

[1] Department of Educational Studies, Faculty of Arts, University of Ljubljana, Slovenia, marko.radovan@ff.uni-lj.si
[2] Department of Educational Studies, Faculty of Arts, University of Ljubljana, Slovenia, ema.meden@ff.uni-lj.si
[3] Department of Educational Studies, Faculty of Arts, University of Ljubljana, Slovenia, danijela.makovecradovan@ff.uni-lj.si

Correspondence: Marko Radovan, marko.radovan@ff.uni-lj.si

Abstract:

This research explores the transformative impact of blended learning on motivation and workload in Vocational Education and Training (VET) settings. As part of the BlendVET project, it investigates how diverse teaching approaches influence student outcomes. Drawing from an online survey of 106 students across seven VET programs, the study reveals that collaborative learning enhances engagement and satisfaction, while technology integration enriches the learning experience. Despite benefits, challenges such as perceived workload increase are acknowledged. Key findings underscore the critical role of assessment and feedback in enhancing student satisfaction and perceived competence. The study advocates for strengthening collaborative learning through diversity support and technological integration, alongside refining assessment and feedback processes. It calls for proactive measures to foster engagement and alleviate stress, urging stakeholders to embrace change for a future where every student can thrive.

Keywords: Blended Learning; Vocational Education and Training (VET); Student Motivation; Perceived Workload; Teaching Approaches

Introduction

Blended learning, a pedagogical strategy that combines traditional classroom instruction with online activities, represents a significant evolution in educational practices. Defined by Garrison and Kanuka as "the thoughtful integration of classroom face-to-face learning experiences with online learning experiences" (Garrison & Kanuka, 2004, p. 96), this approach emphasizes the strategic combination of different learning modalities to improve educational outcomes. One of the key advantages of blended learning is its capacity to offer personalized learning experiences, allowing learners to adjust the pace, timing, and location of their study (Graham, 2006). This adaptability fosters a more engaging and responsive educational environment, catering to diverse learner needs and preferences.

At its core, blended learning integrates the best aspects of in-person teaching and digital resources, thereby facilitating a holistic educational experience. Originating from distance education and computer-based learning, it marries established pedagogical techniques with modern technological advancements, transforming educational methods and student interaction with materials.

The proliferation of educational technologies has been crucial to the emergence of blended learning as a dominant instructional approach. The expansion of the tech landscape has enabled educational institutions to merge classroom teaching with online platforms effortlessly. Innovations like learning management systems (LMS), interactive digital content, and real-time communication tools have not only broadened the adoption of blended learning but have also enhanced its execution in various settings (Güzer & Caner, 2014). This evolution permits unparalleled customization of learning, accommodating a vast array of learning styles and preferences.

Garrison and Vaughan highlight the strategic, pedagogically driven integration of online and face-to-face elements, aimed at improving educational quality, flexibility, and student engagement, while challenging traditional models (Garrison & Vaughan, 2008). Picciano (2017) builds on this by advocating for the alignment of technological tools with educational goals to ensure technology augments specific learning objectives effectively. He underscores the significance of adaptive learning technologies in personalizing learning experiences and the essential role of technology in facilitating effective assessment and feedback, crucial for learner progress.

However, implementing blended learning is accompanied by challenges, such as infrastructure and access issues, especially in resource-limited settings (Zhao et al., 2002). Resistance from faculty and students familiar with conventional teaching methods can also hinder its adoption. Therefore, the successful implementation of blended learning necessitates not only technological investments but also a cultural shift within educational institutions. The COVID-19 pandemic has notably accelerated the shift towards online and blended learning modalities, driven by the broad adoption of multimedia and information technologies (Cesari et al., 2021). This period underscored the importance of flexibility and adaptability in educational delivery, further cementing the role of blended learning as a critical component of contemporary education.

Methodology

Research problem

Our research explores how different teaching approaches affect student motivation, and perceived workload. The significance of this research lies in its exploration of the dynamics between teaching methodologies and student outcomes in blended learning settings, with a special emphasis on vocational education.

We tried to address the following research questions:

1. Which teaching approaches best increase student motivation in a blended learning environment?

2. How do various teaching approaches affect perceptions about their workload?

Sample

This study utilized a convenience sampling method and distributed an online survey via teachers in seven educational programs engaged in pilot initiatives, targeting students in blended learning courses. A total of 106 students from Slovenia participated, comprising 98 males, 7 females, and one undisclosed gender, with an average age of 17.1 years. Reflecting the male dominance in fields like computer, automotive, electrical, and mechanical disciplines, the participants were high school students in programs spanning four to five years. The distribution included 56 third-year, 36 second-year, 11 first-year, and three fourth-year students, highlighting the focus on gender disparities in traditionally male-dominated disciplines.

Measures

The principal tool utilized in this research was an online survey, which was divided into two distinct sections. The initial section focused on gathering demographic information, covering aspects such as gender, age, educational institution, area of study, and year of study. The latter sections were meticulously designed to delve into the students' perceptions and experiences concerning the various dimensions of blended learning, specifically, teaching approaches, attitudes towards blended learning, perceived workload, motivation, and their satisfaction with the BL course.

Teaching Approaches

In order to identify the teaching methods most frequently utilized, the survey included a scale comprising 10 items. For analytical purposes, these items were recategorized into five groups, with a scoring range from 1 ("never") to 5 ("almost always").

Teaching approaches dimensions:

1. **Synchronous Learning** (Mean=2.52, SD=1.05): This category encompasses live sessions where teachers and students interact in real-time through platforms such as Zoom or Teams. It includes "Live online sessions" and "Live presentations or talks by experts."

2. **Asynchronous Learning** (Mean=3.08, SD=1.21): This group includes pre-recorded presentations or instructional videos by the teacher, as well as talks by experts in the field, notably "Instructional videos."

3. **Collaborative Learning** (Mean=3.03, SD=1.06): This category involves group projects or presentations conducted online, along with student interactions in small groups or breakout rooms, including "Group projects or presentations online" and "Students working in small groups."

4. **Assessment and Feedback** (Mean=3.33, SD=1.03): This group comprises frequent quizzes or short assignments to gauge students' understanding, along with online feedback, support, or guidance from the instructor, including "Frequent quizzes or assignments" and "Online feedback or guidance from the teacher."

5. **Technology-Enhanced Learning** (Mean=2.53, SD=1.13): This category features activities that integrate VR (Virtual Reality) or AR (Augmented Reality) technology, as well as interactive videos, such as "Activities including VR or AR technology" and "Activities including interactive video."

These results reveal a preference for approaches that offer flexibility, interaction, and direct feedback, with a somewhat unexpected tentative adoption of advanced technological tools in education

Perceived Workload

We used the NASA Task Load Index (NASA-TLX), a sound assessment tool, to quantify the cognitive and emotional load that students experience during academic tasks (Hart, 2006). The NASA-TLX is a comprehensive assessment tool designed to measure the subjective work-load of individuals based on six essential parameters (Hart, 2006). Students were directed to express their level of agreement or disagreement with the statements using a 5-point Likert scale that ranged from "1 - strongly disagree" to "5 - strongly agree".

For the purposes of our investigation, we have selected four of the original six components that are particularly relevant to the academic context:

1. **Mental demand** (M=2.51, SD=0.98): This dimension captures the cognitive effort required, which includes the complexity of thinking, decision making and computing power required for a particular task.

2. **Time demand** (M=3.19, SD=1.19): Here, we evaluated the perceived time pressure experienced by students, which encompasses the sense of urgency in meeting certain time limitations.

3. **Effort** (M=3.06, SD=1.01): Our focus lies on the level of cognitive or physical effort needed to attain the optimal level of performance. It is important to mention that in this context, 'effort' implies not just physical exertion, but also the emotional and cognitive energy needed.

4. **Frustration level** (M=2.79, SD=1.30): An often disregarded yet significant factor that assesses the emotional state of participants during their tasks. This dimension measures the emotional valency experienced, such as stress, frustration, or irritation.

Descriptive analysis highlights the primary concern of time management for students while also indicating that emotional factors such as frustration exhibit the greatest variability, suggesting a nuanced interplay between cognitive demands and emotional resilience in the academic environment.

Student Motivation

We evaluated the influence of teaching strategies on student motivation by employing specific components of the Intrinsic Motivation Inventory – IMI (Deci & Ryan, 2015). For the purposes of our research, we utilized a modified version of the IMI questionnaire, which originally comprises 45 items across 7 subscales. Specifically, we selected 4 scales from the original Intrinsic Motivation Inventory (IMI) questionnaire, resulting in a total of

16 items for our study. Students indicated their level of agreement with each statement using a 5-point Likert scale, ranging from "1—strongly disagree" to "5—strongly agree". Descriptive statistics for the scales used are presented below.

Motivation scales are:

1. **Interest/Enjoyment** (IMI-I; M=3,66, SD=0.85) is a self-reported assessment comprising of four items. For example, one such item is "I would describe BL as very interesting".

2. **Perceived Competence** (IMI-C; M=3,66, SD=0.82) has a positive correlation with both self-reported and behavioural indicators of intrinsic motivation. It's comprised of four items, such as "After participating in BL for a while, I felt pretty competent".

3. **Value/Usefulness** (IMI-V; M=3,59, SD=0.88) subscale assesses the extent to which a person's intrinsic motivation is positively affected when they see activities as important or beneficial. The subscale has four questions, including the statement "I believe activities in BL could be of some value".

4. **Effort/Importance** (IMI-E; M=3,41, SD=0.80) subscale quantifies the significance of an activity in relation to motivation. It consists of four items, such as "I put a lot of effort into this BL course".

The data reveal that interest/enjoyment and perceived competence are the most significant indicators of intrinsic motivation among students, both scoring an average of 3.66, indicating strong engagement and a sense of competence.

Procedure and Data Analysis Summary:

The research was carried out as part of the BlendVET project (https://blendvet.si/), which aimed to pilot the implementation of blended learning in VET. Eight vocational schools in Slovenia was included, selected through a public tender. A few teachers from each school, typically two or three, received training in BL, equipping them with the skills to implement it in their courses. They developed a BL framework during training and applied it from April to June 2023. In June 2023, students involved in the BL pilots completed a ten-minute anonymous online survey. Data analysis was performed using SPSS 27, employing correlation analysis to identify relationships between variables and linear regression to assess the impact of individual factors.

Results

Below we present the results of the regression analyses.

Teaching Approaches as Predictors of Student Motivation

Table 1 presents the combined and summarized results of four linear regressions, in which we attempted to determine the influence of each teaching approach on learning motivation: Interest/enjoyment, effort/importance, perceived competence, and value/benefit.

Table 1. Regression analysis summary for teaching approaches variables predicting student's motivation

	Interest/ Enjoyment	**Effort/ Importance**	**Perceived Competenc e**	**Value/ Usefulness**
Synchronous Learning	-0.23*	0.10	-0.12	-0.20
Asynchronous Learning	0.07	-0.14	-0.09	0.14
Collaborative Learning	0.06	0.23*	0.18	-0.05
Assessment and Feedback	0.33	0.14	0.43*	0.42*
Technology-Enhanced Learning	0.19	0.11	0.04	0.14
R^2	0.19**	0.18**	0.24***	0.22***

Note: * $p < 0.05$; ** $p < 0.01$; *** $p < 0.001$.

All models show statistical significance but with low predictive value (R^2 values are between 0.18 and 0.22), most possibly due to a limited set of predictors. Teaching approach notably impacts student motivation, particularly in understanding competence (24% variance explained) and evaluating course content (22% variance explained). Frequent assessments and feedback are crucial, significantly enhancing perceived competence ($\beta = 0.43$, $p < 0.001$) and relevance of learning ($\beta = 0.42$, $p < 0.001$). Conversely, synchronous learning negatively affects interest ($\beta = -0.23$, $p < 0.05$) and perceived learning value ($\beta = -0.20$, $p < 0.01$), while collaborative learning boosts learning effort ($\beta = 0.23$, $p < 0.05$). The effects of technology-enhanced and asynchronous learning vary, underscoring the importance of meaningful assessment and feedback in blended learning environments.

Impact of Teaching Approaches on Perceived Student Workload

The summary of four linear regression analysis in Table 2 explores how different teaching approaches predict students' workload, focusing on mental demand, temporal demand, effort, and frustration level.

Table 2. Regression analysis summary for teaching approaches variables predicting student's workload

	Mental demand	**Temporal demand**	**Effort**	**Frustratio n level**
Synchronous Learning	0.40*	0.12	0.24*	0.36
Asynchronous Learning	-0.11	0.27	0.12	0.18
Collaborative Learning	-0.12	-0.10	-0.07	-0.03
Assessment and Feedback	-0.09	-0.23*	-0.16	-0.28
Technology-Enhanced Learning	0.19	0.10	0.16	0.01
R^2	0.17**	0.12*	0.11*	0.16**

Note: * $p < 0.05$; ** $p < 0.01$; *** $p < 0.001$.

Statistical analysis indicates that synchronous learning notably raises mental demand ($\beta = 0.40$, $p < 0.001$) and frustration ($\beta = 0.36$, $p < 0.01$), suggesting real-time, interactive sessions might elevate cognitive load and emotional stress. Asynchronous learning, on the other hand, is linked to higher temporal demand ($\beta = 0.27$, $p < 0.01$), implying that engagement with pre-recorded materials could increase the pressure to manage time more effectively. In contrast, the presence of assessments and feedback leads to a decrease in frustration levels ($\beta = -0.28$, $p < 0.01$), hinting that regular quizzes and assignments, together with prompt feedback, can help reduce students' emotional distress.

Discussion

Our study underscores the transformative power of collaborative learning, igniting student engagement and fostering a vibrant educational climate. We reveal that activities fostering peer interaction are indispensable for enriching the blended learning. Our findings resonate with existing evidence, illustrating that collaborative learning not only amplifies learner motivation but also significantly bolsters educational outcomes in blended environments (Al-Qahtani & Higgins, 2013; Laal & Ghodsi, 2012).

Our research also examines the nuanced effects of synchronous versus asynchronous learning on engagement and workload. While synchronous learning can heighten mental strain with limited engagement benefits, asynchronous learning offers flexibility but often falls short in motivating students adequately. This underscores the imperative for more captivating instructional approaches. Literature corroborates the advantages and hurdles of asynchronous learning in cultivating community and providing immediate feedback (Hrastinski, 2008; Varkey et al., 2022). Our findings also echo concerns regarding fatigue and diminished motivation stemming from frequent synchronous sessions (Novotny et al., 2022), emphasizing the critical necessity for balanced and carefully designed learning frameworks.

Conclusions

This study explores the psychological impacts of different learning modalities in VET, recommending the implementation of well-designed assessments and asynchronous activities to mitigate stress and improve students' motivation. It suggests that optimizing blended learning environments requires focusing on strategies that cater to learners' needs, enhancing both asynchronous learning opportunities and technology integration. Future research in vocational education and training should prioritize a broader sampling strategy for more inclusive results, explore innovative assessment and feedback methods in blended learning, and investigate teaching techniques that optimize engagement across both asynchronous and synchronous settings. This approach aims to balance the benefits of flexible learning with the engagement of real-time interaction, addressing the psychological and emotional challenges identified. To fully realize the potential of blended learning, overcoming challenges related to student motivation, technological limitations, and faculty preparedness is crucial. Optimizing blended learning involves strategic planning, comprehensive faculty training and support, and continuous evaluation to enhance student engagement and success.

Competing interests

The author(s) has/have no competing interests to declare.

Ethics and consent (if applicable)

The research was conducted and published according to recognised international standard. The data for this study was collected through an anonymous online survey, which was completed voluntarily and kept confidential

Funding Information

This research was funded by EEA Grants, grant number ATP213.

References

Al-Qahtani, A. A. Y., & Higgins, S. E. (2013). Effects of traditional, blended and e-learning on students' achievement in higher education. Journal of Computer Assisted Learning, 29(3), 220–234. https://doi.org/10.1111/j.1365-2729.2012.00490.x

Cesari, V., Galgani, B., Gemignani, A., & Menicucci, D. (2021). Enhancing Qualities of Consciousness during Online Learning via Multisensory Interactions. Behavioral Sciences, 11(5), 57. https://doi.org/10.3390/bs11050057

Deci, E. L., & Ryan, R. M. (2015). Self-Determination Theory. In J. D. Wright (Ed.), International Encyclopedia of the Social & Behavioral Sciences (2nd Edition) (pp. 486–491). Elsevier. https://doi.org/10.1016/B978-0-08-097086-8.26036-4

Garrison, D. R., & Kanuka, H. (2004). Blended learning: Uncovering its transformative potential in higher education. The Internet and Higher Education, 7(2), 95–105. https://doi.org/10.1016/j.iheduc.2004.02.001

Garrison, D. R., & Vaughan, N. D. (2008). Blended learning in higher education: Framework, principles, and guidelines. Jossey-Bass.

Graham, C. R. (2006). Blended learning systems: Definition, current trends and future directions. In C. J. Bonk & C. R. Graham (Eds.), The handbook of blended learning: Global perspectives, local designs (pp. 3–21). Pfeiffer.

Güzer, B., & Caner, H. (2014). The Past, Present and Future of Blended Learning: An in Depth Analysis of Literature. Procedia - Social and Behavioral Sciences, 116, 4596–4603. https://doi.org/10.1016/j.sbspro.2014.01.992

Hart, S. G. (2006). NASA-Task Load Index (NASA-TLX); 20 Years Later. https://humansystems.arc.nasa.gov/groups/tlx/downloads/HFES_2006_Paper.pdf

Hrastinski, S. (2008). Asynchronous and synchronous e-learning. Educause Quarterly, 31(4), 51–55.

Laal, M., & Ghodsi, S. M. (2012). Benefits of collaborative learning. Procedia - Social and Behavioral Sciences, 31, 486–490. https://doi.org/10.1016/j.sbspro.2011.12.091

Varkey, T. C., Varkey, J. A., Ding, J. B., Varkey, P. K., Zeitler, C., Nguyen, A. M., Merhavy, Z. I., & Thomas, C. R. (2022). Asynchronous learning: A general review of best practices for the 21st century. Journal of Research in Innovative Teaching & Learning, 16(1), 4–16. https://doi.org/10.1108/JRIT-06-2022-0036

Zhao, Y., Pugh, K., Sheldon, S., & Byers, J. L. (2002). Conditions for Classroom Technology Innovations. Teachers College Record: The Voice of Scholarship in Education, 104(3), 482–515. https://doi.org/10.1177/016146810210400308

Role-playing the future: a simulation-based exploration of AI in social work

Perry Share[1], John Pender[2]

[1] Head of Student Success, Atlantic Technological University, Ireland; perry.share@atu.ie
[2] Department of Social Sciences, Atlantic Technological University, Ireland; john.pender@atu.ie

Correspondence: Perry Share: perry.share@atu.ie

Abstract:

As Artificial Intelligence (AI) continues to permeate various sectors, its integration into social work practice, particularly in identifying at-risk families, demands a nuanced understanding and ethical engagement from future social workers. This paper presents an account of a simulation-based learning exercise conducted with Masters in Social Work [MSW] students at an Irish university. Through role-playing as different stakeholders, students engaged with a fictional scenario that involved the deployment of an AI algorithm in Ireland for identifying at-risk families. The exercise illuminated diverse perspectives on the implications of AI in social work, highlighting key ethical dilemmas, regulatory challenges and the need for comprehensive education on AI technologies. The findings support the effectiveness of simulation-based learning as an effective way to prepare social work students for the ethical, practical, and policy complexities of integrating AI into their future practice.

Keywords: AI, simulation, social work, Ireland, authentic assessment, technology

Introduction

The integration of Artificial Intelligence (AI) into social work presents both unprecedented opportunities and significant ethical dilemmas (Reamer 2023). From predictive algorithms that identify at-risk families, to AI-enhanced decision-making tools, to counselling chatbots, the potential for AI to augment social work practices is considerable (Asakura et al 2020; Goldkind 2021; The Social Work Graduate nd). Social work educators are beginning to recognise the impact of generative AI tools (such as ChatGPT) and to consider how they may be integrated into both social work education and professional practice (Singer et al 2023). Such integration raises critical questions about integrity, ethics, privacy, bias and the fundamental nature of care. Against this backdrop, the preparation of future social workers to navigate these challenges becomes paramount.

This paper discusses a novel educational approach - a simulation-based learning exercise - designed to engage Masters in Social Work [MSW] students with the ethical and practical complexities of AI in their field. Through interactive role-playing, backed up by extensive research, students explored the multifaceted implications of a fictional AI algorithm's introduction in Ireland, aimed at identifying at-risk families. The simulation aimed to enhance students' critical awareness, ethical reasoning and readiness to engage with AI technologies in their future professional practice. It also helped them to develop empathy for diverse interests and points of view and their own research abilities and advocacy skills.

Background

AI's role in social work is expanding at a rapid pace, promising to transform aspects of practice from client assessment to service delivery (Reamer 2023). This technological advancement introduces very significant ethical complexities and necessitates a re-evaluation of both educational and regulatory practices and frameworks. The pedagogical challenge lies in preparing social work students to critically engage with these advancements, making informed decisions that align with ethical standards and professional values. Simulation-based learning [SBL], widely recognised for its effectiveness in social sciences education (Cook et al

2013; Chernikova et al 2020), offers a dynamic approach to bridging theoretical knowledge with practical application. By simulating real-world scenarios, students can explore the implications of AI in social work in a controlled, reflective, safe and immersive environment. The fictional case study central to this simulation – crafted as a futures narrative scenario (Gabner & Steinmuller 2019) involved various stakeholders navigating the introduction of an AI algorithm designed to identify at-risk families in Ireland, providing a comprehensive platform for analysis and discussion.

It is inevitable that social work, like other professional fields, will be impacted by digital technologies (López Peláez & Kirwan 2023). Simulation-based learning is a pedagogical approach that facilitates learners in social work to anticipate and explore potential futures. It can empower them to engage proactively with a range of hypothetical scenarios. This method not only allows them to envision possible future developments in their field but also to experiment with and navigate these scenarios in a controlled, risk-free environment. As students are immersed in realistic, complex situations, they can practice critical research, decision-making, problem-solving and reflective skills that are essential for their professional development. Furthermore, this approach encourages the examination of the consequences of their actions in a safe space, fostering a deeper understanding of the dynamics and nuances involved in social work practice. Through this experiential learning process, students can better prepare for the unpredictable and complex nature of real-world social work, ultimately enhancing their readiness to effect positive change and respond effectively to the challenges – including technological challenges - they will face in their future careers.

Learning about technology: the challenges for non-STEM learners

For some time we, the authors, have been conscious of the challenges involved in the facilitation of learning about technologies, including digital technologies, amongst learners in non-STEM fields, such as social work, social care practice and other human services. Many learners in such fields are unfamiliar with the world of STEM, may be fearful or resistant to technology, and may be uncomfortable in addressing technology issues. We have been engaged in a variety of strategies to address such barriers, including the specification and leadership of an Erasmus+ initiative in the field: the project ('Prospero') which addressed the related field of social robotics, with associated interventions at the local HEI level (Share & Pender 2020). In addition, we devised a simulation that addressed issues of regulation of social robotics, that was successfully presented at an international robophilosophy conference (Share & Pender 2023a). We have also hosted a number of workshops that have brought designers together with professionals and learners in the social services field, to explore aspects of digitally-mediated care.

Our accumulated experience is that learners in the field of human services will engage enthusiastically with key technological issues if they are given direct access to the technologies in question; if the technological processes can be demystified to a degree; if learning is participatory and discursive; and if participants are provided with the opportunity to safely voice any ethical, political, practical, ideological, personal or psychological concerns they may have in relation to the technologies. We always make the case that we are not advocates for any particular technology, nor for technology per se, but that we do advocate for informed discussion of potential or imminent technological developments within the field (Share & Pender 2023b).

The regulatory environment

Social work, in Ireland as in many other jurisdictions, is a closely regulated profession. This points to the (hard-fought) professional status of the field, but also to its significant social power in shaping the lives of citizens. Social workers have considerable capacities to shape the lives of individuals, families and communities. Thus, the primary purpose of professional regulation is 'protection of the public' (CORU nd). In Ireland, the social work profession, including the development of educational programmes, is the responsibility of CORU – the multi-profession health regulator.

The CORU Standards of Proficiency [SoP] document (Social Worker Registration Board 2019) outlines the key professional obligations of the recognised professional social worker and, by extension, the attributes of the social work graduate and the content of social work educational programmes. It is a reality that professional regulation often lags societal developments, and this includes technological development. The SoP for social work is largely silent on technological issues, the sole reference being to 'digital communications technologies' [SoP 2.7]. Nevertheless, the totality of the SoP points to the requirement for an ethical, actively informed and responsible approach to practice. This should include a critical approach to the digital technologies that saturate our world and, we would argue at the current juncture, the development of critical AI literacy (Bali 2024). To facilitate discussion of the issues at regulatory level, a senior representative of CORU was invited to attend the learners' presentation on the simulation. She did so, though this does not represent any endorsement by CORU of the exercise nor of the output.

Simulation as an approach to learning in the age of Generative AI

The emergence of popular Generative AI tools, such as ChatGPT, Claude, Gamma and numerous others, has thrown up a significant challenge to conventional modes of learning, teaching and assessment in higher education. Purely text-based assessment has arguably been rendered ineffective in gauging the nature and depth of student learning (Vee et al 2023). Alternative responses include, on the one hand, a regressive turn to high-security terminal examinations, while others call for a shift towards more 'authentic' modes of assessment, with a focus on process rather than product, and measurement of (admittedly challenging) attributes such as originality, teamwork, creativity, problem-solving and leadership.

Simulation is one potential response to the AI challenge. As a pedagogical strategy it offers a dynamic and interactive learning environment where higher education students, especially in the field of human services (including social work), can immerse themselves in realistic scenarios that mirror the complexities of real-world situations. The value of simulation lies in its capacity to bridge theory and practice, allowing students to apply classroom knowledge or their own research in a controlled, yet relatively lifelike context. This experiential form of learning encourages the application of critical thinking, decision-making and ethical reasoning without the risks associated with real-life human services work. Students can navigate through challenging scenarios, reflect on their actions and receive immediate feedback: crucial for developing professional competence and confidence.

Within the human services field, simulation holds great promise as it can replicate diverse social, psychological, community, ethical and political issues that professionals will or may encounter in the future. It has the potential, when carefully planned and effectively facilitated, to cultivate a deep understanding of service user experiences and the impact of human services intervention: such as the application of algorithmic decision-making. By engaging in role-play and interactive modules, students can practice communication, intervention strategies and interdisciplinary collaboration: all essential skills in human services. Moreover, simulation allows for the exploration of case studies that might be rare or difficult to experience in situ, ensuring a well-rounded educational experience. The safe environment of simulation becomes a testing ground for innovation, where students can creatively solve problems and develop leadership qualities that are integral to their future roles as human services professionals.

In terms of futures studies, simulation as a method is particularly valuable. It enables students and professionals alike to project and immerse themselves in potential future scenarios, where they can analyse the outcomes of policies, societal trends and emerging social issues. Through forward-thinking simulations, learners can develop strategic responses to hypothetical future states, ranging from demographic shifts (such as ageing or immigration) to technological advancements (such as social robotics or AI), thereby cultivating a proactive and preventative mindset. This kind of anticipatory practice is crucial in a field – such as social work - that must confront the dynamic and often unpredictable nature of human needs and social policy. Futures studies through simulation prepares social workers not just to react to present challenges, but to envisage and shape better futures for individuals and communities, fostering resilience, adaptability and advocacy potential in a rapidly evolving societal landscape.

Methodology

The simulation exercise was carefully designed to immerse the MSW students in the complexities of integrating AI into social work. A detailed narrative scenario was developed and students were assigned roles to represent the various stakeholders, such as social workers, AI product developers, policy makers, regulatory bodies, user coalitions, human rights advocates, media representatives, government ministers and family representatives, each with their own distinct perspective on the introduction of an AI algorithm for identifying at-risk families.

Prior to the simulation, participants engaged in preparatory research (that included sanctioned use of AI tools such as ChatGPT) to ground their role-playing in real-world considerations, enhancing the authenticity and depth of the simulation discussion. The exercise unfolded over three hours, during which students, embodying their roles, debated the potential benefits and ethical dilemmas posed by the AI algorithm, with the aim to reach a consensus on the best path forward for its implementation.

The student group was composed of 17 international and Irish participants. Each participant was required to identify an appropriate actor to role play. The appropriateness of actors was established via all-group unassessed actor feasibility pitch presentations. Each participant was invited to introduce their chosen actor and to explain, discuss and justify their inclusion in an SBL event on AI and social work. Participants were provided peer and tutor feedback and approval on their selection of actor.

Out of this iterative process, the following actors were approved for inclusion in the simulation: O'Reilly Family (fictional family at the centre of a false positive at-risk algorithm identification; Minister for Justice; CraicCode (fictional AI company responsible for developing the algorithm); Commissioner for Human Rights; Associate Professor of AI at University ABC; Investigative Journalist The Guardian Newspaper; Digital Freedom Fund; Data Protection Commissioner; UNESCO; UNICEF; Social Worker at Tusla (Child and Family Agency); Social Worker, Irish Elderly Advice Network; Dr. Niall Muldoon (Ombudsman for Children); Margrethe Vestager (EU Commissioner); Budget Analyst United Nations AI for Good; Assistant Chairperson, CORU Social Work Registration Board.

Outcomes of simulation event

The simulation revealed a rich tapestry of perspectives on the use of AI in social work. An overarching outcome was a unanimous concern for ethical considerations, particularly around data privacy and the potential for algorithmic bias, reflective of the considerable emergent literature in this area (James et al 2023). Students highlighted the importance of transparency in AI development and the need for social workers to be involved in the design and implementation phases: that is, a call for user-centred design.

The exercise pointed to the potential of AI to enhance service delivery, for example through greater efficiency, potential to expand services, access to expertise through expert systems, and more rational as opposed to situational decision-making processes. But there was also a strong recognition that ethical concerns needed to be addressed. The role-playing aspect allowed students to empathise with stakeholders they might not have considered previously, such as commercial companies involved in the development of AI-based products, or the regulatory body CORU. This helped to broaden their understanding of the multifaceted implications of AI in their future profession.

Following a ChatGPT-facilitated analysis of a transcript of the simulation event, the following themes and issues were identified:

1. Ethical challenges in AI Implementation: Many participants, like the Commissioner for Human Rights and the Ombudsman for Children, highlighted concerns about maintaining client dignity, rights, and autonomy while addressing biases and ethical dilemmas inherent in AI systems.
2. Legal and constitutional considerations: The Minister for Justice and other legal experts focused on scrutinising the constitutionality of AI applications in critical decision-making about family welfare and child protection. This approach is essential for ensuring that AI implementation complies with legal standards and respects fundamental rights.
3. Navigating AI and professional judgment: Stakeholders such as the Chairperson of CORU and the Associate Professor of AI emphasised the importance of balancing AI systems with professional judgment in social work. The discussions suggested a need for improved education and training for social workers in AI, as highlighted by the Guardian journalist's investigative findings.
4. Public trust and perception: The role of the media, represented by the Guardian journalist, in shaping public perception was a critical theme. The O'Reilly family's case highlighted the consequences of a failure in trust and the need for transparent and accurate communication about AI in social work.
5. Client welfare and AI impact: Advocates like UNICEF and from Tusla - Child and Family Agency - emphasised client involvement and rights in AI applications. The focus on client welfare as a primary concern was evident and crucial for the responsible use of AI in social work.
6. Regulatory adherence and oversight: the Data Protection Commissioner and others raised important points about compliance with regulations and the need for oversight mechanisms to ensure ethical AI use.
7. Collaboration and stakeholder engagement: The need for inclusive and holistic approaches to AI implementation, involving clients, social workers, and the public, was a key theme. This approach, as discussed by the Digital Freedom Fund and others, is essential for the successful integration of AI in social work.

8. Technology design and development: Companies like CraicCode (the AI tool developer) need to involve a diverse range of stakeholders, including those at the frontline like social workers, in the AI design process.
9. Data management and privacy: The discussions, especially involving UNESCO, highlighted the importance of rigorous data management and privacy practices to protect client confidentiality and trust.

As is apparent from this list, the understanding generated by the SBL of AI, algorithmic decision-making and related policy, practical and ethical issues was both comprehensive and holistic. As the insights were generated by the learner participants, and actively debated by them, the nuances involved, and the connections between theory and practice, were strongly recognised and appreciated by the students. This is demonstrated in the reflections that thy completed after the simulation had taken place.

Student reflections

Following the simulation event, student participants were asked to reflect on their experience. They did this by generating actor position papers that included a section requiring them to reflect on their experiences of the simulation event and to chart how their preconceived notions of AI and social work had evolved throughout their learning and engagement with their assignment brief.

Student A (role playing UNESCO) reflected on the SBL experience as:

> I feel that I have a good understanding of AI and the strengths and limitations of it as a system. I feel that I am well informed of where we are in Europe in terms of our plans to govern the use of AI appropriately and safely for everyone, something that I knew next to nothing about two months ago. This was a very new type of learning experience for me but one I thoroughly enjoyed.

Student B (role playing the Ombudsman for Children) remarked:

> On reflection the simulation was a fascinating approach to learning about artificial intelligence in social work. Looking forward, I recognise the value of simulations in practical learning, providing a dynamic platform for applying theoretical knowledge.

Student C (role playing a journalist from the Guardian newspaper) asserted:

> The shared exploration broadened my perspectives, enabling me to approach AI in social work with increased empathy, openness and critical thinking. The collective experience highlighted the power of collaboration and the importance of engaging with peers in shaping our understanding of AI's potential within the field of social work

Student D (role playing the developer of the at-risk algorithm) was quite strident in her reflections on the impact of participating in an SBL:

> My personal journey as an advocate for the use of AI in social work, through the learning mechanism of Simulation Teaching, has been a transformative exploration. Through simulations and the preparatory work for same, we physically bridged a knowledge gap, while instilling 'the human-centric approach' we have been learning about, which values empathy and cultural sensitivity. I feel I am more now more knowledgeable and prepared to hold a responsive, ethical and compassionate approach to societal challenges.

These reflections are representative of the larger sample and articulate the transformative power of simulation-based learning in preparing social work professionals for the challenges and opportunities presented by AI. The diverse experiences and insights gained demonstrate the power of interdisciplinary, collaborative learning environments to foster a holistic, empathetic and critically engaged approach to AI in social work. This collective journey not only equips future social workers with the knowledge and skills needed to navigate the complexities of AI but reveals a commitment to ethical, compassionate and informed practice in an increasingly digital world.

Discussion

There is evidence that simulation is becoming more widely used and pedagogically acceptable in social work education. Literature references 'hi-tech' simulation tools such as virtual and augmented reality (VR and AR) (Huttar & BrintzenhofeSzoc 2020) to create virtual 'clients', but simulation may also, as described here, be used at a less technically complex level to explore complex and contentious social issues within a supportive and 'safe' environment.

This simulation-based exploration into AI's role in social work education illustrates the method's pedagogical value as a form of authentic assessment. By engaging with fictional but plausible scenarios, students can critically assess the integration of AI technologies in practice. Singer et al (2023, 296) note that in order to explore its social and professional implications, 'students need real-time experience and practice with the opportunities and challenges of AI'. This pedagogical intervention highlighted the necessity for an interdisciplinary approach to AI in social work, combining technical knowledge with ethical, legal, and social considerations. Furthermore, the simulation prompted discussions on the need for updated curriculum frameworks that include AI literacy, ensuring future social workers are prepared to navigate the challenges and opportunities presented by technological advancements in their field. It was also argued that the relevant Standards of Proficiency be updated to incorporate critical AI literacy.

The method is not without its challenges. None of the participants had undertaken an SBL experience prior to this. Much time and effort was expended in justifying this type of assessment strategy and in explaining the logistics. Given the international complexion of the student cohort, several one-to-one tutorials were scheduled to ensure full comprehension of the assignment brief. A detailed briefing document on these issues was circulated to allay concerns. Additionally, a trial SBL event took place as a 'walk through' experience one week before the assessed simulation. Additional pedagogical challenges in managing and assessing the event included aligning the simulation with module learning learning outcomes and objectives; development of fair and nuanced assessment criteria (this proved particularly challenging as SBLs are renowned for being difficult to precisely access (Palaganas et al 2020); providing effective feedback and debriefing; ensuring equity and accessibility for all students; and addressing ethical considerations in sensitive subject areas.

The work required to prepare and support participants in the simulation exercise was considerable and, in many ways, invisible. As more 'authentic assessment' is introduced into higher education in response to the challenges of generative AI, there will be a need for the managers and funders of universities to recognise and resource these additional requirements. This may include investment in specialised training for educators to design and implement simulations effectively; ensuring necessary technological infrastructure is up to date; and provision of administrative support to manage these complex learning environments. As simulations become integral to curricula, it is imperative that educators are afforded the time to develop bespoke scenarios that reflect real-world complexities relevant to their disciplines. The SBL approach necessitates not only financial investment but also a cultural shift within higher education institutions to value and sustain the labour-intensive processes that underpin successful simulation-based education.

Conclusion and recommendations

Singer et al (2023, 296) are unequivocal on the necessity for students of social work to critically examine AI:

> The bottom line is this: We believe it is unethical for social workers not to learn and teach about technology-mediated social work. With AI poised to transform the way we approach social work, we must embrace this change and work together to ensure that it is used in ways that are ethical, equitable, and socially just.

We support this view. We argue that the simulation-based learning exercise described here provided invaluable insights into the complexities of integrating AI into social work. It demonstrated the effectiveness of role-playing in enhancing students' ethical reasoning, policy awareness, and critical thinking about technology's role in social welfare.

Recommendations for social work education include:

- integrating AI and technology ethics into the core curriculum.
- facilitating interdisciplinary learning experiences that combine social work with technology and data science.

- encouraging continuous professional development focused on emerging technologies in social work practice.

- further research should explore the long-term impacts of such educational strategies on students' professional development and the ethical integration of AI in social work.

- necessary resources need to be provided by HEIs to support the extra demands of simulation-based learning

- Updating of the Social Worker Standards of Proficiency to recognise the increasing role of digital technologies, including AI, in social work practice.

References

Bali, M. (2024). Where are the crescents in AI? LSE Higher Education. https://blogs.lse.ac.uk/highereducation/2024/02/26/where-are-the-crescents-in-ai/

Chernikova, O., Heitzmann, N., Stadler, M., Holzberger, D., Seidel, T., & Fischer, F. (2020). Simulation-Based Learning in Higher Education: A Meta-Analysis. Review of Educational Research, 90(4), 499-541. https://doi.org/10.3102/0034654320933544

Cook D. A., Brydges R., Zendejas B., Hamstra S. J., Hatala R. (2013). Technology-enhanced simulation to assess health professionals: A systematic review of validity evidence, research methods, and reporting quality. Academic Medicine, 88(6), 872–883. https://doi.org/10.1097/ACM.0b013e31828ffdcf

CORU. (n.d.). Information brochure. https://www.coru.ie/files-publications/general-publications/coru-information-leaflet-dec-eng-2023-web.pdf

Gaßner, R., Steinmüller, K. (2018). Scenarios that tell a Story. Normative Narrative Scenarios – An Efficient Tool for Participative Innovation-Oriented Foresight. In: Peperhove, R., Steinmüller, K., Dienel, HL. (eds) Envisioning Uncertain Futures. Zukunft und Forschung. Springer VS, Wiesbaden. https://doi.org/10.1007/978-3-658-25074-4_3

Goldkind, L. (2021). Social work and artificial intelligence: into the Matrix. Social Work, 66(4), 372–374. https://doi.org/10.1093/sw/swab028

Huttar, C., & BrintzenhofeSzoc, K. (2020). Virtual reality and computer simulation in social work education: A systematic review. Journal of Social Work Education, 56(1), 131-141. https://doi.org/10.1080/10437797.2019.1648221

James, P., Lal, J., Liao, A., Magee, L., & Soldatic, K. (2023). Algorithmic decision-making in social work practice and pedagogy: Confronting the competency/critique dilemma. Social Work Education. https://doi.org/10.1080/02615479.2023.2195425

López Peláez, A., & Kirwan, G. (2023). The Routledge Handbook of digital social work. Routledge. https://www.routledge.com/The-Routledge-International-Handbook-of-Digital-Social-Work/LopezPelaez-Kirwan/p/book/9780367499945

Palaganas, J., Ulrich, B. & Mancini, M (2020). 'Evaluating simulation effectiveness' In Mastering simulation. Indianapolis: Sigma. https://www.sigmanursing.org/MasteringSimulation2

Reamer, F. (2023). Artificial Intelligence in social work: Emerging ethical issues. International Journal of Social Work Values and Ethics, 20(2), 52-71. https://doi.org/10.55521/10-020-205

Share, P., & Pender, J. (2020). Helping tomorrow's social professionals to learn about social robotics. In Proceedings of the 6th International Conference on Higher Education Advances (HEAd'20). http://dx.doi.org/10.4995/HEAd20.2020.11205

Share, P., & Pender, J. (2023a). Regulation of the use of social robotics in care settings: A simulation. In Proceedings of Robophilosophy2022 (Frontiers of Artificial Intelligence and Applications). IOS Press. https://ebooks.iospress.nl/doi/10.3233/FAIA220675

Share, P., & Pender, J. (2023b). Digital technologies for care. In Lalor, K., Share, P., & Brown, T. (Eds.), Social care work: An introduction for students in Ireland. Institute of Public Administration.

Singer, J., Creswell Báez, J., & Rios, J. (2023). AI creates the message: Integrating AI language learning models into social work education and practice. Journal of Social Work Education, 59(2), 294-302. https://doi.org/10.1080/10437797.2023.2189878

Social Worker Registration Board. (2019). Standards of Proficiency for Social Workers. CIRU. https://www.coru.ie/files-education/swrb-standards-of-proficiency-for-social-workers.pdf

Social Work Graduate. (2023). Artificial Intelligence and Social Work. https://www.thesocialworkgraduate.com/post/artificial-intelligence

Vee, A., Laquintano, T., & Schnitzler, C. (Eds.). (2023). TextGenEd: Teaching with Text Generation Technologies. The WAC Clearinghouse. https://doi.org/10.37514/TWR-J.2023.1.1.02

Searching for application areas for using AI and VR in the Higher Education classroom in Ireland

Zeta Dooly[1], Lisa Moran[2], PJ Wall[3], Emer Lodge[4]

[1] South East Technological University, Ireland; zdooly@wit.ie
[2] Technological University of Shannon, Ireland; lisa.moran@tus.ie
[3] Technological University of Dublin; patrickjwall@gmail.com
[4] South East Technological University, Ireland; emer.lodge@setu.ie

Correspondence: Zeta Dooly: zdooly@wit.ie

Abstract:

The changing landscape of education for all, internationally, has led to education policy and operationalisation mis-matches, we advocate for active learning and critical pedagogy in our modern society but our society and resources are not sufficiently welcoming to adopting emerging hardware and software in the classroom. Resource constraints restrict the move from experiential learning to implementation where resistance is in-built within our culture to hold on to traditional teaching and learning methods and delivery mechanisms. We are familiar and open to science requiring apparatus, but using tools such as virtual reality and artificial intelligence in our everyday teaching and learning is uncommon and warrants further evidence to support its implementation to becoming the norm.

Education is the keystone for progress, we promote education as a sustainable, complementary activity to economic social and caring aspects of our society. As an integral part of the UN Sustainable developmental goals how we meet the objectives are contextual and in Ireland we currently adopt a traditional in-person educational experience with many online programmes affiliated with options for lifelong learning rather than mainstream education. Thus the experience of the authors through SEERLab (South East Education Research Lab) to design and develop teaching and learning artefacts is presented in this paper. SEERLab focuses on strategies to build a sense of community in HE (virtually) of educationalists who through their own learning experiences gain empowerment to dramatically change the classroom composition, using both physical hardware (VR headsets) and software (AI) to accentuate critical thinking and immersive learning in the classroom. There is evidence to support the use of VR in the classroom toward enhanced engagement of students (Kavanagh et al., 2017 and Campos et al., 2022).

However, the emergence of new education policies based on data, learning analytics, tertiary market demand and access is not easily understood in our communities. We purport that educationalists need to embrace change at HE to administer and deliver curriculum using non-standard applications. This research initiated by lecturers in the design of pilots to meet learning outcomes through using VR is gathering evidence to further develop HE policy using VR in the classroom. There are tensions in global societal research discourses in relation to emerging technologies such as AI and scant social scientific research on societal attitudes towards AI; its value and limitations in education, fears and emotions about AI technology which requires redress.

Without guidance lecturers advocating for the use of VR and AI in the classroom are challenged to demonstrate understanding the socio-cultural legitimacy of AI in Irish society. We present the cases of SEERLab that has been established to scaffold educationalists toward enhancing their attitudes towards VR and AI.

These challenges can be overcome using an innovative pedagogical approach to link the needs of teachers and lecturers and students to untangle the complexity of emerging technology and deliver educational solutions globally and nationally. The pilot cases presented include modules from Nursing, Business and PhD postgraduate programmes. The piloting of this technology is moving to implementation stage and along with evidence from open educational communities we present the potential benefits and limitations of VR and AI in HE classrooms, which can lead to engaged students, innovative pedagogies, misperceptions, heightened sense of risk, inertia and resistance to its adoption. Universities, governments and organizations can work together to raise awareness about VR and AI through education and outreach initiatives aimed at different student cohorts but this necessitates greater knowledge in relation to accessibility, usability and educational 'buy in' and exposure to VR and AI technologies that combine scientific expertise with pedagogical know-how.

Keywords: Education, Sustainability, innovative pedagogies, virtual reality, artificial intelligence transformative learning, experiential learning

Introduction

This paper uses a novel approach to innovative pedagogy, introducing skill acquisition to actively engage students to achieve learning outcomes through use and assessment of emerging technology. Design and planning are critical elements of education provision, the literature is rich with models and frameworks to aid educationalists, however there is little evidence of disruptive transformative learning in the HE classroom. Following on from the global pandemic, most formal education ecosystems had to temporarily pivot to digital education. This paper presents a pedagogical approach that tightly couples classroom activities with the application of existing technology for teaching and learning outside of our comfort zone in a multi-faceted learning ecosystem. Furthermore, the case studies described here address complexity in the classroom, acknowledging the 'valley of death' approach used in transitioning research into practice, and furthering our understanding how innovative technologies only make a difference when deployed and used in line with user needs and requirements (Maughan et al., 2018).

Lecturers describe how they overcome fear from one's own comfort zone toward recognising the power of teachers as change agents using an array of community communication platforms to equip and enhance their toolkit with engagement tools tailored for their subject expert domain needs. Technology is a critical enabler to access knowledge, resources and people and has empowered those unable to engage with traditional educational settings to gain formal and informal knowledge whilst making learning more fun and engaging alongside other life responsibilities. Education as a career has expanded, teachers, tutors, lecturers, instructional designers, social and community enterprises, data analysts, database architects, facilitators all contribute to a complex education ecosystems that aspire to equality, inclusion and diversity. In order to guide lecturers into newer areas of module design we used templates to detail the pilots and their objectives across 4 programmes.

The pilots illustrate a sense of urgency to advocate for change, overcome complacency in classroom and introduce experimentation as a lever to learning in a failsafe ecosystem. Fear is identified as a concept that prevents the use of some technology due to its unpredictability and teacher legacy for being the person at the top of the class with all the knowledge. Times have changed, creativity is key and teachers are realising that they must prepare their students for failure in addition to success and that they need to model experimentation and failure to demonstrate that recovery and problem based learning prevails in a knowledge economy. As educator's compliance is a critical factor to meet the quality standards of our trade, meeting learning outcomes is just one part of the learning journey, gaining trust, delivery of engaging content and the realisation that students need an education ecosystem that promotes a nurture environment, self-actualisation and phronesis. Through this research 5 lecturers revised their delivery of content for their programmes to include the use of VR in the classroom. A number of internal workshops enabled the growth of confidence in using new VR apps and through peer learning opportunities lecturers were able to share knowledge and experiences in teaching and learning within a small community of practice. This research adopted a collaborative approach to finding out more whilst designing the new delivery and engagement methods. The sharing of context and experience in the classroom was promoted and regarded as essential to the ethos of this learning environment.

We adopted an agile curriculum development approach akin to software development that included a mechanism for feedback, co-creation of curriculum and discussion of alignment across disciplines (Wang, 2014). We believe this disruptive approach aligns to the principles of universal design for learning (UDL) which form a critical ingredient promoted within our university (Cast, 2022). The design adopts elements of digital marketing to create a hook, Gravells (2014) and call to action language. Additionally, we leverage the concept of the zone of proximal development, peer learning techniques and scaffolding to enact our pilot to collaborate and use our creativity to experiment (Vygotsky, 1980 and Boud and Lee, 2005).

The course design has the usual boundaries of compliance to quality and module and programme learning outcomes. For this module though, the emphasis is on engagement, collaboration, transformative and innovative learning as promoted by Freire (in Darder, 2014) and UNESCO (Darder, 2014, Groff, 2013, Kitchenham, 2008, Perales and McCowan, 2021). This is further enhanced where learning is socially constructed within the socal constructivism paradigm and group work (Kim, 200, Biggs and Tang, 2015). We initially undertook a scoping exercise within our own university and nationally to explore current practices, this included on-site visits and feasibility studies to figure out the best approach. We decided on a short design time toward an implementation of the new design within a 9 month period.

During the semester discussions surround the use of technology enhanced learning and volunteer lecturers are empowered to be advocates of education that have adequate knowledge to inform policy-makers and leaders in education on priorities and challenges toward the national and global education agenda. This is further accentuated with the ongoing priority of the sustainable developmental goals (SDGs) and in particular SDG4. Whilst much of the practical lab tutorial work (still ongoing) within the pilots focusses on off the shelf software and non-integrated applications we generally observed that customisation of applications for education was unnecessary and added complexity to the pedagogical design. The potential for VR and AR in education has long been vaunted but limitations imposed by access to the technology, ease of use and software requirements have presented barriers to this potential been realised. A rapid decline in hardware cost, increased availability and ease of use, coupled with availability of low cost or open source software has mitigated many of the limitations highlighted in earlier studies. This paper shows that the time is ripe for more physical experimentation using education research labs. There are many elements within VR teaching and learning that cross disciplines such as student onboarding or orientation. We were able to share resources in this regard. We identify as a group of early adopters and want to reduce the lag time to general adoption, implementation and policy specification. A significant benefit of adopting advanced technologies is to facilitate a greater eco-system of learning tools to facilitate truly personalised learning (Humble and Mozelius, 2019). It is clear that there is a lack of understanding of how these VR technologies can be effectively deployed in a HE environment, their net contribution to learning, the risks associated with their uptake, and their potential to enhance the learning environment and student experience.

Whilst still in the implementation stage the pilots include the adoption of Virtualorator for entrepreneurship ideation, VirtualSpeech for pitch development, leadership and decision making, ShapesXR for prototyping and Oxford Medical Simulator for nursing triage. To date the lecturers have mapped the capability of the VR applications to the module descriptors and learning outcomes and trialled in a workshop environment, the next stage will be tested with students during semester and shared within faculty teaching and learning dissemination events.

There are a number of studies that examine the use of previous iterations of extended reality (XR) in education, and it is postulated that this technology could benefit in areas, such as complex data visualisation, design visualisation, digital twins, increased immersion and enhanced cognitive states. Using future literacy techniques students looked at emerging technology in addition to current technology to further move and voluntarily jump into zones of instability, questioning the ethics of artificial intelligence use in the classroom and in government (Miller, 2007 and Nemorin et al, 2023).

We feel that the toolkit currently available to lecturers in HE is restrictive and adversely impacting students that need more immersive learning and engagement mechanisms, our research advocates for open educational resources (OER) to include the sharing of hardware and software across the industry and educational landscape toward collaborative teaching and learning. Ireland's National policy[1] advocates for significant changes toward an optimised learning ecosystems 'Policy Platform: Progressing A Unified Tertiary System for Learning, Skills and Knowledge' but the processes and tangible pathways and avenues to realise this are not yet evident. This research

[1] https://www.gov.ie/pdf/?file=https://assets.gov.ie/225165/fff8a843-0df6-436a-ade1-ae060deadd45.pdf#page=null

goes further to collaboratively introduce cross-university sharing of knowledge and disruptive teaching and learning delivery through VR and AI.

Further research

It is planned to deliver modules using VR and AI by September 2024 following the pilot phase using physical hardware meta quest 2's and 3's for students to evaluate experiences and learning adventures using virtual reality and augmented reality. This testbed environment can facilitate a greater eco-system of learning tools that can enable truly personalised learning (Humble and Mozelius, 2019).

Known to help with student learning (Flink et al., 2019), immersive learning environments (ILEs) are learning situations that are constructed using a variety of techniques and software tools, including game-based learning, simulation-based learning and virtual 3D worlds. ILEs are distinguished from other learning methods by their ability to simulate realistic scenarios and environments that give learners the opportunity to practice skills and interact with other learners on their own terms by engaging their optimum learning style. Applying adaptive learning techniques can further accentuate the teacher or lecturers toolkit and increate the potential to be inclusive, flexible, personalised and engaging for students (Holmes et al., 2019).

References

Biggs, J. and Tang, C., 2015. Constructive alignment: An outcomes-based approach to teaching anatomy. In Teaching anatomy (pp. 31-38). Springer, Cham.

CAST, accessed online May, 2022, Universal Design for Learning Framework, https://www.cast.org/impact/universal-design-for-learning-udl

Campos E, Hidrogo I and Zavala G (2022) Impact of virtual reality use on the teaching and learning of vectors. Front. Educ. 7:965640. doi: 10.3389/feduc.2022.965640

Darder, A., 2014. Freire and education. Routledge.

Flink, P. (2019) 'Second Life and Virtual Learning: an Educational Alternative for Neurodiverse Students in College', College Student Journal, Vol. 53, No. 1, pp. 33-41.

Garrison, D. R. E-Learning in the 21st Century. 3rd. Abingdon, Oxon: Routledge, 2017. Community of inquiry model and 2008 social presence

Holmes, W., Bialik, M. and Fadel, C. (2019) Artificial intelligence in education: Promises and implications for teaching and learning, Center for Curriculum Redesign Boston, MA.

Humble, N. and Mozelius, P. (2019) 'Artificial Intelligence in Education - a Promise, a Threat or a Hype?' European Conference on the Impact of Artificial Intelligence and Robotics, Oxford, UK, Oct.

Kavanagh, S., Luxton-Reilly, A., Wuensche, B. & Plimmer, B. (2017). A systematic review of Virtual Reality in education. Themes in Science and Technology Education, 10(2), 85-119.

Kim, B. (2001). Social constructivism. Emerging perspectives on learning, teaching, and technology, 1(1), 16.

Groff, J., 2013. Technology-rich innovative learning environments. OCED CERI Innovative Learning Environment project, 2013, pp.1-30.

Kitchenham, A., 2008. The evolution of John Mezirow's transformative learning theory. Journal of transformative education, 6(2), pp.104-123.

Kolb, D. A., Boyatzis, R. E., & Mainemelis, C. (2014). Experiential learning theory: Previous research and new directions. In Perspectives on thinking, learning, and cognitive styles (pp. 227-248). Routledge.

Maughan, D., Balenson, D., Lindqvist, U., & Tudor, Z. (2013). Crossing the" Valley of Death": Transitioning cybersecurity research into practice. IEEE Security & Privacy, 11(2), 14-23.

Nemorin, S., Vlachidis, A., Ayerakwa, H. M., & Andriotis, P. (2023). AI hyped? A horizon scan of discourse on artificial intelligence in education (AIED) and development. Learning, Media and Technology, 48(1), 38-51.

Rose, D. H., & Meyer, A. (2002). Teaching every student in the digital age: Universal design for learning. Association for Supervision and Curriculum Development, 1703 N. Beauregard St., Alexandria, VA 22311-1714

Wang, Y. D. (2014). Building student trust in online learning environments. Distance Education, 35(3), 345-359.

United, Nations,United Nations. The UN Sustainable Development Goals. United Nations, New York, 2015. Available at (accessed 16 January 2018): http://www.un.org/sustainabledevelopment/summit/.

AI, heritage and critical thinking development: an education experience within university context

Antonella Poce[1]

[1] Tor Vergata University of Rome, Dept. History, Heritage, Education and Society

Correspondence: antonella.poce@uniroma2.it

Abstract:

Educational policy makers identify Critical thinking (CT) as an essential driver for development and knowledge growth in any field and in the broad society. Even in the post-pandemic era, CT continues to be defined as one of the skills to be most promoted at the various levels of formal education and training contexts. In particular, with the raise of AI, it is crucial for educational institutions to encourage a critical approach to technology in students, especially in the analysis, interpretation and evaluation of information in order to make decisions and solve problems, also in digital contexts. Art experiences, literary stimuli and writing activities are helpful pedagogical strategies for CT enhancement especially when supported by the use of technologies.
Starting from the above-mentioned evidence, a university module was designed by combining collaborative and creative writing sessions based on critical analysis of literary texts and the experience of figurative arts. More than 100 students worked in groups and their CT level was assessed at different times of the course. In particular, AI and machine learning tools were used to identify indicators of critical thinking in the texts produced by the students and to assess the relationship between the production of written texts and the development of CT and reasoning within students taking part in the educational experience.
The research results could be used to improve university course design or professional development training courses for CT teaching and learning.

Keywords: Critical thinking, Assessment, AI, Art-based education, Heritage, Writing.

Introduction

Educational policy makers identify Critical Thinking (CT) as an essential driver for progress and knowledge growth in any field and in the broad society. According to Graff (2008), being engaged in a dialogic argument provides the "missing interlocutor" that gives a purpose to the written argument. Peer interactions also provide an opportunity to gain experience or practice in CT, specifically through understanding others' perspectives and creating and fulfilling joint goals (Murphy et al., 2014). Recent studies have highlighted how technology could be implemented in collaborative learning settings in order to enhance CT (Schindler & Burkholder, 2014). One potential advantage of computer-mediated discussion is its asynchronous nature, allowing more time for reflection before responding. An increase in the use of formal, evidence-based reasoning and the quality of CT can be due to an extension of the time available to think and consult sources of information. In a well-known study of Newman Webb, and Cochrane (1995) they found similar level of students' CT in the online and face-to-face discussion whereas other authors show (Guiller, Durndell & Ross, 2008) evidence of increased CT level in the online situation, especially in terms of justification.

Not only dialogical and collaborative activities seem to affect positively CT, but also other forms of communication, such as individual writing. Ennis (Ennis, 1993) suggests the adoption of short essay items for assessment purposes because it would capture more effectively the disposition aspect of CT compared to what multiple-choice items formats would do. However, in a 2004 study (Condon & Kelly-Riley, 2004) it was found that the better the writing, the lower the CT score. According to the authors, the lack of relationship between writing and CT scores indicates that having students write does not automatically mean that we ask students to think critically. They assert that writing acts as a vehicle for CT, but writing is not itself CT. For example, if writing tasks call for summary and fact reporting, there is no reason to suspect that students' performances will incorporate CT. For this reason, it is necessary to carefully design new writing tasks to support CT in education.

In one of his most recent studies, Snodgrass (2011) found that combining an online with in-class activities can facilitate collaboration among students to enhance their learning of the complex CT reasoning skill.

In the present research, we tried to adopt different design lines that could support CT development at higher education level. More specifically, collaborative and creative writing were combined with the critical analysis of literature texts and the experience of figurative arts. These choices were based on the assumption that discourse between peers during a collaborative writing activity could expose them to peers' thinking processes, understanding that there are multiple ways to approach a situation and learning to reconcile different viewpoints and perspectives, which are all central components of CT. In addition, especially in the area of museum education, CT is often associated with Visual Thinking: watching and enjoying a work of art, comparng different artworks, artists, styles, and trends, allows the audience to develop their thinking, analysis and evaluation skills (Housen, 2002).

As regards CT evaluation procedures, assessment test can be classified in multiple-choice test and open-ended tasks. Some authors point out that the MC measures use cannot be proper for the higher-order skills assessment (Nicol, 2007) which might lead teachers to invalid inferences (Popham, 2003), although in terms of reliability they are very solid. Though open-ended tests, indeed, the teacher can create more authentic contexts and assess students'ability to generate rather than select responses by using open-ended measures. Moreover, open-ended measures can be associated with authentic assessment because they elicit the same thinking processes that individuals use when they solve complex problems in their everyday lives (Andrews & Wulfeck, 2014). Open-ended measures in CT assessment present different disadvantages; the most important is the low level of reliability compared to other forms of evaluation [9]; moreover, the difficulty of scoring in underlined (Attali, 2014), difficulty which is also considered time consuming and expensive. According to Liu, Frankel and Roohr (2014) automatic assessment of open-ended answers could be a viable solution to these concerns. Automatic assessment of learning outcomes is a hot topic in educational research for at least two reasons: firstly, the availability of learning data is growing exponentially due to the spreading of online education. Secondly, researchers in the field of Big Data, Machine Learning and Artificial Intelligence can provide educators with sophisticated tools for processing an immense amount of linguistic and behavioural data

The context: module design

The activity designed to evaluate the usability of a prototype designed to assess CT Skills automatically through creative writing was set in a six-month university blended learning module in Educational Research Methodology based at the master course in Education sciences - Department of Education - University of Roma Tre. Students attended classes face to-face and they also interact on a Moodle platform provided by the University itself. During the module, students were invited to use their analytical and evaluative skills through the analysis of three short stories written by different authors and based on the works by Edward Hopper ("In Sunlight or in Shadow. Stories inspired by the Paintings of Edward Hopper", Block L., 2016) . For this activity, students worked in classroom collaboratively, comparing their ideas and writing their answers following a template provided by the tutor. Then collaborative creative writing was carried out on a work of art of their choice. Students used the Moodle wiki tool to write their creative stories. In addition, students attended online video lecturing on the "Émile. Ou de l'éducation." written by Rousseau and they were required to write comments on each video and compare their reflection with peers. Students were also required to complete two different kinds of CT pre-test and post-test. At the beginning and at the end of the course they have to write: a) a short essay after reading an excerpt from "The Dialogue Concerning the Two Chief World Systems" written by Galileo Galilei and b) an argumentative map, inspired by the Van Gelder's model (2022).

Research questions and methodology

The present research tried to answer the following research questions:

1. Which levels of CT students' groups showed throughout the course?
2. Which is the level of usability of Artificial Intelligence in assessing students' CT skills employed in collaborative writing activities?

123 First year students from the Educational Research Methodology module partici-pated in all the activities (F = 115; M = 8; Average age = 23) and they were organized in 17 groups (about 7 students per group). Three different kinds of data were collected.

- Collaborative analysis of literature texts: in the first three tasks, students answered guiding questions about literary texts assigned by the teacher.
- Collaborative and creative text: in the fourth task named "Wiki – Narrating the Museum" students created a story based on a piece of art of their choice.
- Self-reflection questionnaire: at the end of the writing activities, students were invited to answer a questionnaire that investigated the group dynamics and processes.

The following table (Table 1) shows the distribution of the writing activities assigned to the students starting from the beginning of the course (Task 1) to the end (Task 4).

Table 1: The distribution of the writing activities from the beginning of the course (Task 1) to the end (Task 4)

Task 1	**Task 2**	**Task 3**	**Task 4**
Blue Night	The Music Room	Automat	Wiki – Narrating the museum

Different kinds of analysis were carried out in order to investigate 1) students' groups CT level and 2) group dynamics (see Table 2). Group dynamics were studied by applying a thematic analysis of the qualitative data collected through the online questionnaire. Each group of students' CT level was assessed by using two different grids developed in previous research paths (Poce, Corcione & Iovine, 2012; Poce, 2017) on the four collaborative texts: Blue Night, The Music Room, Automat, and Wiki – Narrating the Museum.

The first grid contains five macro-categories: 1. relevance of the topic 2. content 3. form and expression 4. originality and creativity 5. use of the language. For each macro-category a score from 0 to 10 has been assigned. Four independent evaluators read the groups' texts and assigned scores on the five macro-categories. At the end, the average of the four evaluators' scores was calculated.

The second grid contains six macro-categories: 1. basic linguistic skills 2. justification 3. relevance 4. importance, 5. critical evaluation 6. novelty. For each macro-category a score from 0 to 5 has been assigned. Two independent evaluators read the groups' texts and assigned scores on the six macro-categories. At the end, the average of the two evaluators' scores was calculated.

Table 2: A description of data collection and data analysis methods

Data collection	**Data analysis**	**Purpose of the analysis**
1. Collaborative analysis of literature text 2. Wiki - Collaborative and creative text	Content analysis: - Grid 1 - Grid 2	Assess the level of students' CT
Self-reflection questionnaire	Thematic analysis	Understanding students' groups dynamics

In the following paragraphs a description of the analysis carried out using the second grid in an automatic context is described.

Use of Artificial Intelligence in the analysis of students' texts

The assessment of CT's level of the students' groups involved in the activities was conducted automatically analyzing the responses to three of the questions asked through an intelligent prototype based on a Multilayer perception tool and trained through supervised learning. The analysis was based on a series of golden texts produced by three experts who also manually evaluated the answers to have the data for supervised training. The evaluation initially involved the identification of a set of features for each of the macro-indicators of CT's levels, in particular:

- Use of Language: the feature vector identified to assess language capabilities consists of the number of grammatical and logical errors extracted through an external software (https://www.prepostseo.com/grammar-checker) present in the responses, the readability index value calculated through the GULPEASE formula which, in addition to being the first readability formula devised to be applied to the Italian language, also has the advantage of calculating the length of words in letters rather than syllables, and finally the HAPAX, which is the index representing the number of graphic forms that appear only once in a corpus.

- Argumentation: the text of the responses was tokenized for the creation of n-grams using the NLTK (Natural Language Toolkit) library that also perform the removal of StopWords, and the definition of tokens after a stemming process to reduce words to their root. From these tokens, n-grams ranging from 1 to 6 were used to identify the following connectors:
  - Hierarchical connectors that function to order the paragraphs of a text, highlighting the external cohesion of the argumentative text by showing the succession of various arguments; (eg. first of all, also, then, to conclude, some believe that, on one side, there are those who support and... on the other way...)
  - Logical-syntactic connectors that regulate the internal cohesion of individual paragraphs, clarifying or highlighting the logical steps of one's reasoning and are divided into:
  - Causal Connectors: to introduce the argumentation (eg. not by chance, because, because...)
  - Additive Connectors: to add arguments (eg. also, too more, let's add the fact that....)
  - Concessive Connectors: related to objections to the argumentation (eg. although, despite this, admitting that, even if it is true, if it is true that....)
  - Adversative Connectors: to refute (eg. but, instead, otherwise, however...)
  - Conclusive Connectors: which introduce final remarks (eg. in the end , for that reason, that is why, in conclusion, summarising)
  - The input vectors to the intelligent model are made by the number of each type of connector identified in the responses and the text length (the longer the text, more connectors should be found statistically). The system also counts the number of syntactic patterns typical of persuasive and argumentative texts (e.g., adverb + adjective + conjunction + adjective) included in an essay.
- Relevance: similarly to how novelty is calculated, the same process was reproduced but looking at how many concepts were reported in the same way as those in the golden text to verify the relevance of the question.
- Importance: the input vector for calculating importance quantifies the consistency and semantic similarity of the text to the golden text in relation to the stimulus. An initial approach was implemented using Latent Semantic Analysis (LSA)(Landaur, 2013). In this type of analysis, co-occurrence statistics are observed on the content words that precede and follow the target word; then, occurrences are weighted and dimensionality is reduced.
- Critical Elaboration: To create instances for evaluating critical elaboration, a plagiarism check tool was used; Based on the citations found in the golden text and in the responses (in this case, the source of plagiarism was the literary text), this value was weighted against the length of the response corpus and inserted into the input vector for the decision algorithm. The quotes reported in the text are then extracted using the tool and weighted based on the length of the entire response. This value will give the percentage of quoted text that will become the input for the vector. The classifier trained on the values extracted from the golden texts evaluates the indicator.
- Novelty: The input vector calculation related to the novelty evaluation was performed by comparing texts in the golden text with the responses under assessment. Specifically, the text was processed through a fundamental concept identification service (TAGME) capable of showing associated Wikipedia pages. The list of concepts was compared with those in the golden text, eliminating those that were the same (useful for the relevance indicator but not in this case) and of those remaining, it was verified that there was a connection relationship in Wikipedia (the response presents a new concept that was not present in the golden text and that is related to the topics discussed). The vector is built from the count of these connections within the database under examination.

Results and discussion

Participants undertook three group tests, each involving answering ten questions following the reading of a literary text; there were 19 work groups but after an initial analysis of the results, it was necessary to perform a filtering operation as some of the analyzed documents had blank parts, which significantly lowered the classifier's performance. Across the three tests, it is possible to see in the figure below how the average performance of the groups experienced a slight decrease during the second test but, overall, at the end of the experience, a significant improvement of 3.699%.in critical thinking skills is highlighted, moving from 14.54395 in the first test to 15.08187 (see Fig. 1).

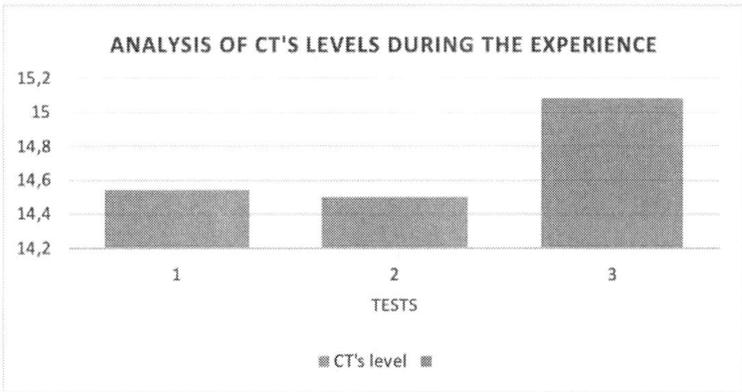

Figure 1: CT scores assigned to the different tasks

An examination of individual macro-indicators shows that the best ratings were obtained in language use (mean 3.971052632), relevance (mean 2.688992105) and argumentation (mean 2.742569659).

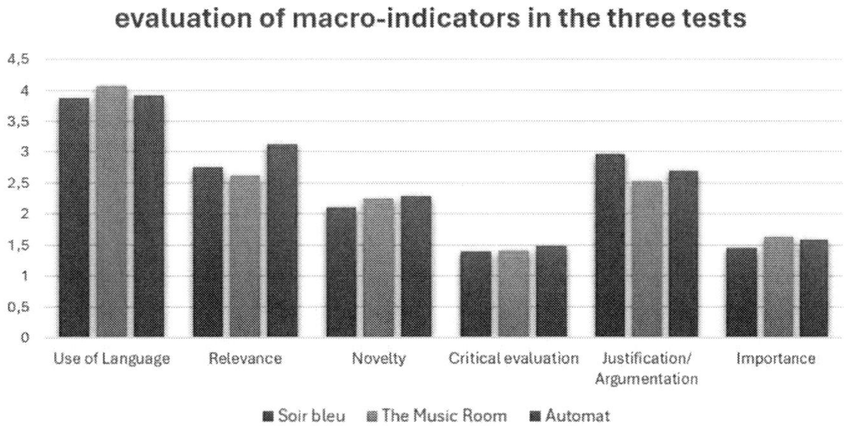

Figure 2: Scores assigned to the different CT indicators

Analyzing the performance trend along the three tests, three clusters of groups were identified based on their performance. Specifically, clusters 6-10-16-3 showed a steady increase in critical thinking levels, although not as much as between test two and test three; clusters 7-15, on the other hand, showed a decrease, even if low, in the last test while keeping levels unchanged between test one and two. The rest of the groups showed an increasing trend with a maximum in the second test (related to the short story "The Music Room") keeping the trend from test one.

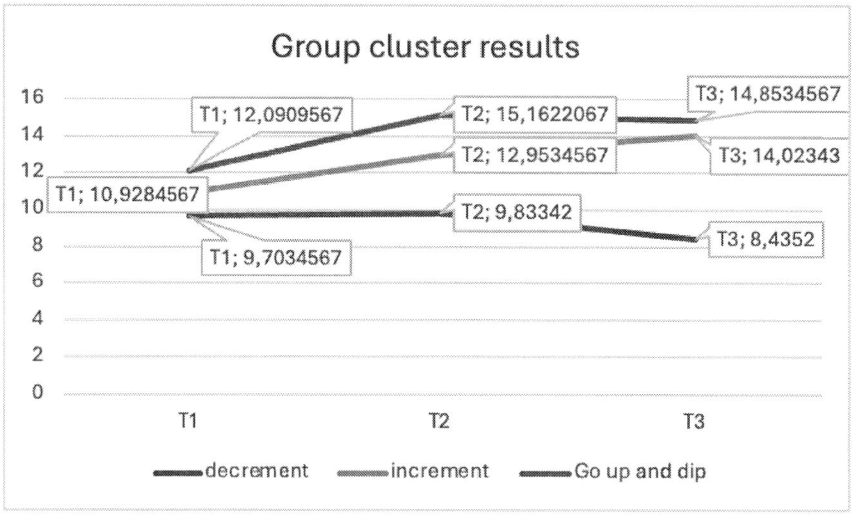

Figure 3: Trends of the three clusters

By comparing the results of the automatic evaluator with the previous manual evaluations carried out by the experts, we can tell how the prototype failed to capture the same number of clusters of the groups (3 in automatic versus 5 in the manual) but the same trend of increase in CT levels shown by the human evaluation is kept, except for a small decrease in the second test. Specifically, the manual evaluation presented in Poce and Amenduni (2019), based on the use of two grids divided into 11 macro-indicators, highlighted a percentage increase in CT levels equal to 7.143%, approximately double compared to the prototype. The analysis of the macro indicators highlights how this piece of data is explained by the fact that Importance and Critical evaluation indicators still get low ratings on average and it will therefore be necessary to add characterizing features to improve the intelligent model.

References

Andrews, D. H., Wulfeck, W. H. (2014). Performance assessment: Something old, something new. In Handbook of research on educational communications and technology (pp. 303- 310). Springer, New York, NY.

Attali, Y. (2014). A ranking method for evaluating constructed responses. Educational and Psychological Measurement.

Block, L. (2016). In Sunlight or in Shadow. Stories inspired by the Paintings of Edward Hopper. Pegasus Books, New York.

Condon, W., Kelly-Riley, D. (2004). Assessing and teaching what we value: The relationship between college-level writing and critical thinking abilities. Assessing Writing, 9(1), 56-75.

Ennis, R. H. (1993) Critical thinking assessment. Theory into practice, 32(3), 179-186.

Graff, G. (2008). Clueless in academe: How schooling obscures the life of the mind. Yale Uni-versity Press.

Guiller, J., Durndell, A., Ross, A. (2008). Peer interaction and critical thinking: Face-toface or online discussion?. Learning and instruction, 18(2), 187-200.

Housen, A. C. (2002). Aesthetic thought, critical thinking and transfer. Arts and Learning Research, 18(1), 2001-2002.

Liu, O. L., Frankel, L., Roohr, K. C. (2014). Assessing critical thinking in higher education: Current state and directions for next-generation assessment. ETS Research Report Series, 2014(1), 1-23.

Murphy, P. K., Rowe, M. L., Ramani, G., Silverman, R. (2014). Promoting critical analytic thinking in children and adolescents at home and in school. Educational Psychology Review, 26(4), 561-578.

Newman, D. R., Webb, B., Cochrane, B. (1995). A content analysis method to measure critical thinking in face-to-face and computer supported group learning. Interpersonal Computing and Technology, 3, 56-77.

Nicol, D. (2007). E-assessment by design: Using multiple-choice test to good effect. Journal for Further and Higher Education, 31, 53–64.

Poce, A. (2017). Verba sequentur. Thinking and writing for a critical development of competences at secondary school. Franco Angeli.

Poce, A., Corcione, L., Iovine, A. (2012). Content Analysis and Critical Thinking. An Assess-ment Study. Cadmo, An International Journal of Educational Research, 1(12), 47-63.

Popham, W. J. (2003). Test better, teach better. The instructional role of assessment. ASCD.

Schindler, L., Burkholder Jr, G. J. (2014). Instructional design and facilitation approaches that promote critical thinking in asynchronous online discussions: A review of the literature. Higher Learning Research Communications, 4(4), 11-29.

Snodgrass, S. (2011). Wiki activities in blended learning for health professional students: En-hancing critical thinking and clinical reasoning skills. Australasian Journal of Educa-tional Technology, 27(4).

Van Gelder, T. (2002). Argument mapping with reason!Able. The American Philosophical Association Newsletter on Philosophy and Computers 2(1), 85-90.

Transformative Learning & Self-Efficacy in a world shaped by AI: Empowering students through Future Skills

Jörn Allmang[1], Ulf-Daniel Ehlers[2]

[1] Baden-Wurttemberg Cooperative State University, Germany; Joern.Allmang@dhbw-karlsruhe.de
[2] Baden-Wurttemberg Cooperative State University, Germany; ulf-daniel.ehlers@dhbw-karlsruhe.de

Correspondence: Jörn Allmang: Joern.Allmang@dhbw-karlsruhe.de

Abstract:

Generative AI faces educational institutions in particular with an immense challenge and requires them to prepare students for unknown contexts in order not to fall behind in the race against technological progress. Teaching Future Skills as such competencies that prepare students for complex, emergent situations is a key to achieving this. This paper shows a pedagogical teaching-learning concept to promote Future Skills in higher education. With various learning materials students are supported in their personal skills development and are also prepared for the demands of the future working world through evidence-based self- and external assessments and situational and self-reflective learning. In addition to the pedagogical concept, quantitative evaluation results of the workshop on which the concept is based are presented. The Workshop was trialed with 1143 students and evaluated via questionnaire. The aim of the research design was to find out the acceptance, the reaction and learning effectiveness of the Future Skills Learning design as well as the self-efficacy of the students.

Keywords: Future Skills, Self-efficacy, AI, Competence-development, Higher Education, Reflective base learning

Introduction

Megatrends such as pandemics, climate change and AI are disruptive incisions that always cause fundamental (societal) change. Generative AI in particular has become an integral part of society and is massively transforming the way we live, work and also the way we learn. Learning in the age of AI also means, we need to prepare ourselves for learning scenarios and requirements that are currently still unknown. Institutions of higher education in particular are faced with the task of preparing students for such newly emerging contexts. Golding & Katz (2009) stated that the key to maximizing the benefits of technological progress lies in investing in education. Continuous adaptation of the education system to technological change is essential to ensure that the population has the skills and knowledge needed in a rapidly changing world and is not falling behind in the "race between technology and education" (Golding & Katz, 2009).
But how can universities handle this and prepare students for a world that is determined and driven by digitalization and AI, along with the associated challenges and upheavals? One approach is focusing on what AI cannot do. Skills such as critical thinking, ethical competence, or a cooperative mindset are becoming more essential and shifting in the center of educational processes. The digital transformation shows that easily teached contents, such as knowledge, can just as easily be digitized and thus effortlessly automated, which is why a paradigm shift must necessarily occur in the way teaching is conducted at universities (Ehlers, 2020). The traditional approach of preparing students by teaching knowledge for addressing challenges is thus increasingly being questioned and requires students to take increasing responsibility for their own learning processes, by initiating, monitoring and reflecting on it themselves (Brown & Atkins, 1990; Zimmerman, 2000; Zimmerman & Schunk, 2001). Learning in times of generative AI requires a shift from teaching to learning (Welbers & Gaus, 2005) with a focus on skills development in academic education processes (Ehlers, 2014; van den Beemt et. al., 2023) and therefore shifting from knowledge-based didactics to skills-oriented, individualized and flexible teaching methods. In this context, Future Skills as competences that enable individuals to successfully solve complex problems in a self-organized manner in highly emergent contexts (Ehlers, 2020), are gaining in importance. Future skills are a selection of competencies which are understood as dispositions to be able to act purposefully. They consist of the basic ability to act (consisting of knowledge and skills) and the willingness to act, which in turn are based on personality traits such as motivational, habitual or

value-based factors and are visible in performance, i.e., in the concrete implementation of actions (ibid.) Students must be accompanied in their personal development and supported in the development of essential skills for the future. To achieve this, universities need to provide appropriate learning strategies (Bolhuis, 2003) and opportunities for reflection and practice.

This paper presents a didactic concept for learning future skills in dual studies developed at the two Cooperative State Universities Karlsruhe and Heilbronn. A multi-stage approach that included the development of curriculum-integrated didactic structures, learning materials and is characterized by continuous self-reflection. The objective is to empower students throughout the entire student life cycle to develop future skills by deliberately seeking out experiential learning opportunities, consistently reflecting on them, documenting these experiences, and receiving support through (peer) feedback from fellow students, practical mentors, and instructors. The three main objectives are depicted in Figure 1.

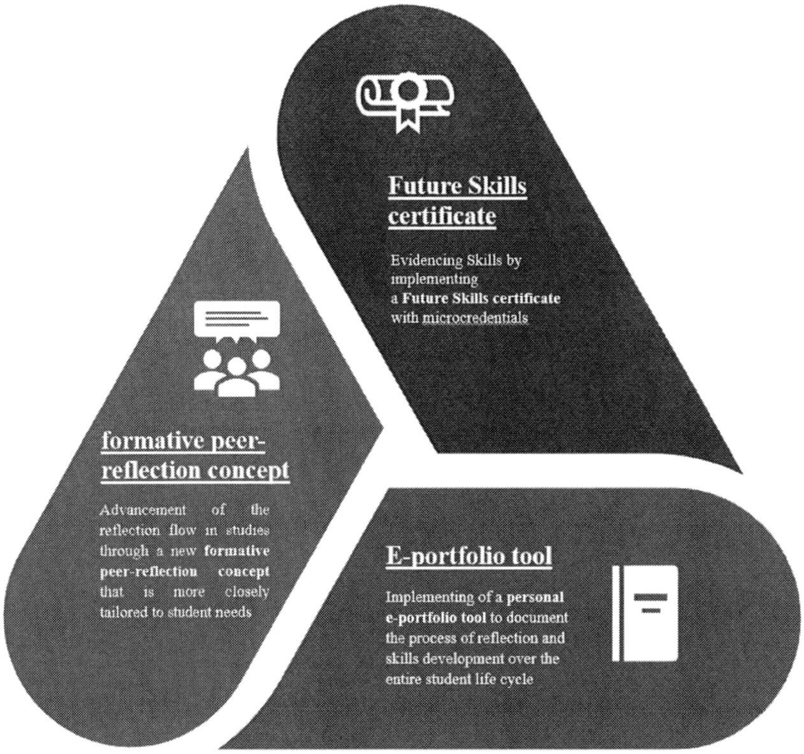

Figure 1: The projects three main objectives

The basis and starting point of the concept is a workshop called the Future Skills Module, which is intended to empower them to reflect on and learn Future skills autonomously. This workshop has already been conducted with 1143 students and evaluated by questionnaire. The aim of the research design was to explore and analyze the

- acceptance of the workshop concept and the reaction to it
- learning efficacy
- students' experiences of self-efficacy

In the following chapters, the didactic learning design is presented first (chapter 2), followed by the presentation of the evaluation design (chapter 3) and the presentation of selected results (chapter 4), which are discussed in chapter 5.

From theory to practice: learning theory foundations of the concept

The learning design of the Future Skills Workshop is characterized by the following 4 interlinked components:

1. It focuses on students' individual strengths and successes, follows positive psychology (Seligman & Csikszentmihaly, 2000) and encourages students to identify their own successful situations and reflect on them using Ehlers' (2020) Future Skills competence structure model.

2. It is reflection- and experience-based, encouraging students to analyze their own actions metacognitively and to carry out self-reflection processes based on peer feedback. The approach is based on the concept of the experiential learning cycle by David Kolb (1984), which involves a four-stage, long-term and iterative process that students undergo. Based on concrete experiences (I), learners engage with these in a self-reflective process (II), analyze their experiences (III) and then reintegrate the insights gained into practical application in order to start the learning cycle all over again (IV). In this context, the importance of external impulses and learning process-oriented feedback (Hattie & Timperley, 2007; Yan & Boud, 2022) is emphasized in order to initiate reflection processes and promote skills development.

3. It is based on situational learning approaches by focusing on authentic learning objects from the students' experience and engaging with these in a reflective way (Mandl & Krause, 2001; van den Beemt et. al., 2023).

4. It is social, takes place in small groups and stimulates students to think through complex, experienced action situations, identify with them and derive action strategies from them. Here, reference is made to the "reflective practitioner" approach of Donald Schön (1983), intending students to become aware of their implicit knowledge by reflecting on their actions (reflection-in-action) and thus developing an understanding of their context of action (reflection on action).

The four aspects mentioned are part of the basic conditions for competence learning (Ehlers, 2014), whereby the acceptance of the learning situation, the experience of self-efficacy and the linking of what has been learned with one's own life play a pivotal role in students' motivation and learning (Zimmerman, 2000).

The workshop concept consists of the three parts (I) Getting to know Future Skills, (II) Reflection & Articulation on the own Future Skills profile, (III) Starting the own personal Future Skills Learning Journey (Fig 2.)

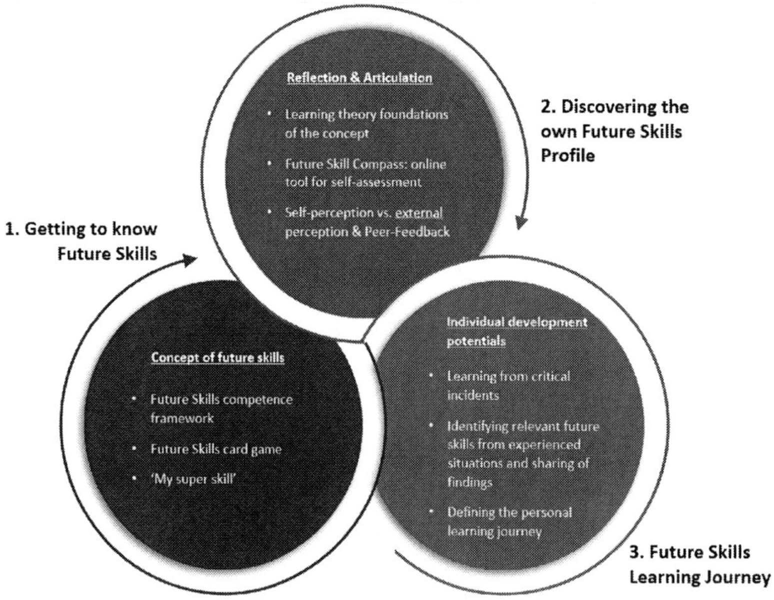

Figure 2: The Workshop concept

In the first part, participants learn the concept of Future Skills, supported by study references and an introduction to the competence framework developed by Ehlers (2020), which contains 17 different Future Skills profiles. This part is supported by a self-designed Future Skills card game, through which the participants familiarize themselves with the individual Future Skills in a playful way, for example in the form of the game "TABU" (Fig. 3)

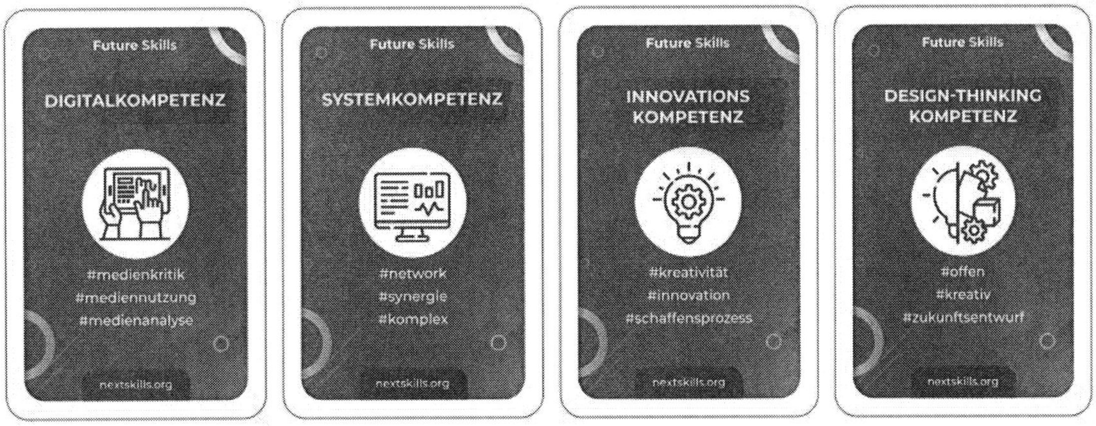

Figure 3: Future Skills Tabu

In the second part participants deepen their understanding and develop their personal Future Skills profile using the Future Skill Compass, an online tool developed specifically for the project. The Future Skill Compass is a self-assessment for competences in which students evaluate their degree of confidence with challenging situations in which future skills are needed to act (Fig. 4). This is presented visually as a spider-diagram and reflected on in individual and group work in order to compare self-perceptions with external perceptions and initiate reflection and open opportunities for skills development. In addition, by sharing an anchor story for self-assessment, evidence for personal Future Skills is to be gathered.

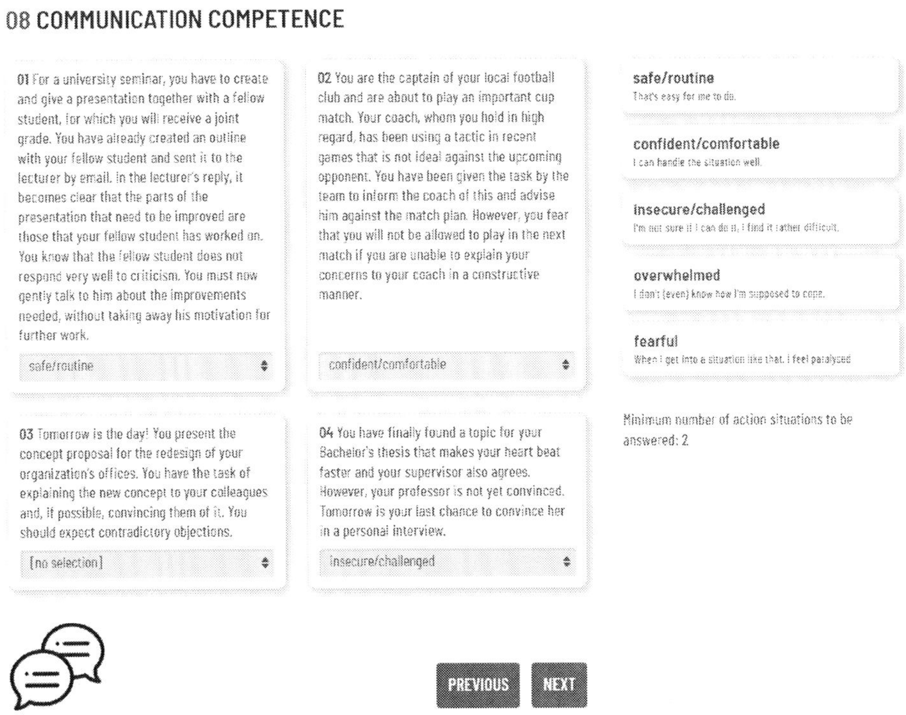

Figure 4: The Future Skill Compass

The third part, "Future Skills Learning Journey", focuses on the participants' individual development opportunities. They reflect on challenging situations ("critical incidents") from their studies, career or personal life and identify relevant future skills for these contexts that would have helped them to overcome them. After sharing these insights with Peers, they select three skills for their further development and finally receive guidance on Future Skills learning materials developed by the project team.

Methodology

The research was methodically designed to assess the effectiveness of teaching and learning methodologies through the implementation of standardized online questionnaires administered subsequent to each workshop. This design aimed to interrogate four distinct dimensions: (I) the acceptance of pedagogical approaches, (II) student responses to the educational interventions, (III) the individual and subjective relevance of the content, and (IV) an exploration and analysis of the students' perceptions of self-efficacy. Specifically, the component concerning self-efficacy sought to determine the potential correlation between students' experiences of self-efficacy within their academic pursuits and their attitudes towards acquiring Future Skills. This investigation is grounded in the premise that self-efficacy – an individual's belief in their capacity to execute tasks successfully – is crucial for student motivation and learning outcomes, as argued by Zimmerman (2000).

The initial survey was administered in December 2022 and was sent to 512 students. 415 students responded and filled in the questionnaire which represents 81,1% response rate. The data quality check excluded not sufficiently completed questionnaires and resulted in a total number of N=339 questionnaires of sufficient quality to be analyzed. This survey comprised 27 items and employed a 5-point Likert scale ranging from "strongly disagree" to "strongly agree," with an additional "no response" option. This was complemented by optional open-ended questions for detailed feedback. A noteworthy modification in the subsequent survey was the adjustment of the Likert scale from 5 to 4 points by excluding the "neutral" option, aiming to minimize ambivalent responses. This survey also collected socio-demographic information, including age, gender, and degree program, and introduced questions related to students' perception of their personal development opportunities, motivation, and continued engagement with future skills post-workshop.

The second survey, administered following the workshops in December 2023 to February 2024, encompassed 30 items. It was sent to 631 students. 452 students answered the survey which resulted in a total response rate of 71,6%. After data cleaning and quality check, 405 surveys were evaluated to be sufficient data quality to be used in the analysis (N=405). The lower turn out of the second survey can be attributed to an unsystematic technical error with the survey system.

Consequently, the combined evaluation base amounted to N=744 students out of an original sample of 1143. Where feasible, identical scales' data sets were amalgamated for analysis; otherwise, comparative evaluation was conducted using percentage and mean value analyses of the same questions across differing scales from both surveys, explicitly excluding the "no response" selections. To quantify the statistical relationship between students' self-efficacy experiences within their academic programs and their attitudes towards Future Skills, Pearsons correlation coefficient was utilized. This analytical approach facilitated the examination of the presumed interdependence between self-efficacy experiences and student attitudes towards Future Skills, reinforcing the critical role of self-efficacy in educational motivation and achievement.

Evaluation

In the following chapter, the statistical results are presented, supported by graphics in univariate form or dichotomized, with the two upper and two lower scale points being combined. Arranged according to the aspects 'acceptance of the workshop-concept' , learning efficacy and reaction to the teaching interventions (4.1) and the student's experiences of self-efficacy (4.2).

Effectiveness, acceptance, reactions to the Workshop-Design

The evaluation showed that the workshop was perceived as enjoyable for the students overall, with an approval rate of 60,8% in the first survey and 65,7% in the subsequent survey. Considering the importance of learning future skills, the initial survey showed an approval rate of 83.4%, which remained almost constant at 82.7% in the subsequent survey, underlining the continued high value placed on these skills among the participants. The feedback as to whether the workshop served to familiarize participants with Future Skills was in both Workshops overwhelmingly positive with 85.2% (Fig. 5). The assessment of the personal relevance of the workshop content showed an initial agreement of a mean value of 3.41 on a 5-point Likert scale, compared to 2.7 in the follow-up survey with the change to a 4-point scale, showing that the importance of the workshop for their personal development is emphasized in both surveys. The subjective importance of the learning intervention is also illustrated by the fact that a dichotomized 63.1 % of students stated, the workshop helped in identifying personally important Future Skills.

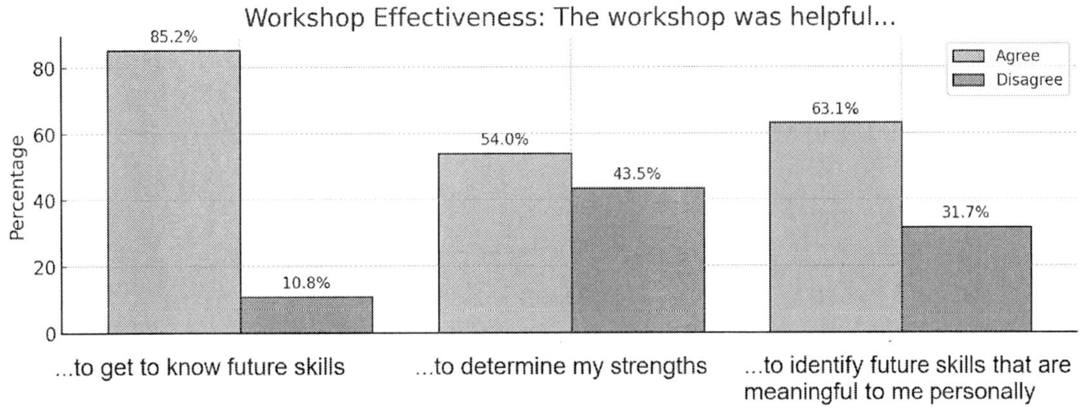

Figure 5: dichotomized presentation Workshop-effectiveness, both surveys summarized, n = 744

The evaluation further shows that a significant majority of respondents felt that the workshop objectives were clearly defined, with 61,6 % in the first workshop and a conforming 76% in the second survey. A summarized high number (71%) of students stated that they had not heard of Future Skills beforehand, The question here is whether this is due to the terminology "Future Skills", as the term does not necessarily have to be known. Despite the unfamiliarity of the topic, students showed a high level of willingness to continue developing Future Skills after the workshop. 68,5 % of students would participate in study-integrated learning opportunities, 9,7% of them even in self-learning mode in their free time (Fig. 6). Participants recognize the greatest added value of learning future skills in the areas of career (75%) and personal development (74.5%), which underlines the relevance and necessity of integrating such skills into academic curricula and beyond.

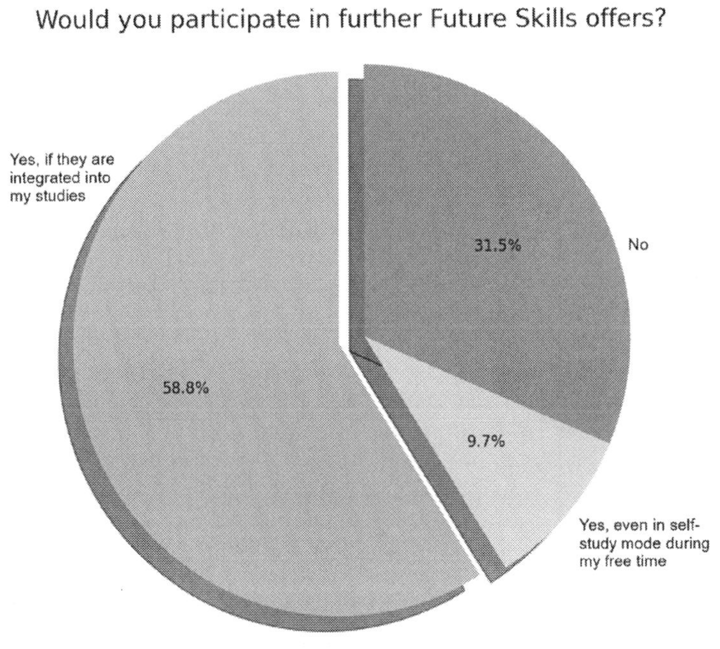

Figure 6: Participation in further Future Skills offers, both surveys summarized

Students self-efficacy experience

The summarized data sets regarding the students Self-efficacy show a pronounced confidence in their own academic abilities and the ability to cope with study-related challenges (Fig. 7). A clear majority of respondents are convinced that they can meet the requirements associated with their studies (90,3%). The data also shows a strong perception of self-efficacy with regard to composure in dealing with difficulties. 60,9 % agree that they are able to deal with them. In addition, a cumulative 92,5 % of students affirm that they have the skills required for their studies. These results clearly show a high level of self-efficacy among students.

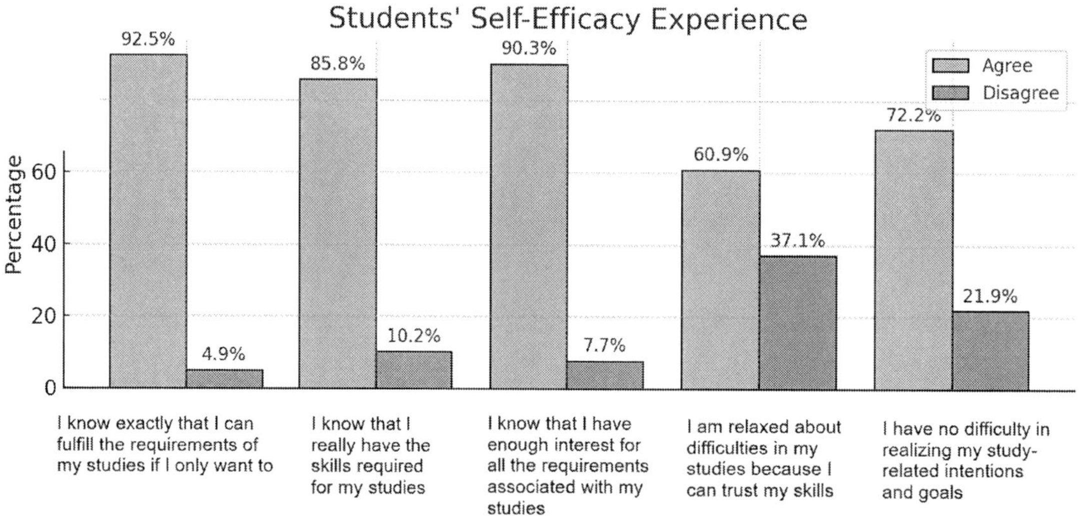

Figure 7: dichotomized presentation of students' Self-Efficacy Experience, both surveys summarized

In order to examine whether there is a connection between the experience of self-efficacy in the degree program and the students' attitude towards future skills, the mean values of the questionnaire section on self-efficacy were calculated and correlated with the mean values of the questions relating to future skills learning and personal meaningfulness (Tab. 1). The Pearson correlation coefficient was used to determine the correlation between the two sets of questions. While for the questions "the workshop was helpful to get to know future skills" & "The workshop was helpful to identify future skills that are meaningful to me personally" the mean value could be summarized (same scale), just as for the items on self-efficacy, the weighted average of the means had to be calculated for the other two questions due to the different scales in each case. In order to compare the sets with the Pearson rank coefficient, there must be 4 mean values in each case, so the last mean value (I have no difficulty in realizing my study-related intentions and goals mean value) was omitted.

Table 1: Mean values of the item sets

Set 1: Self-efficacy of students	Mean value	Set 2: Attitude towards learning Future Skills	mean value
I know exactly that I can fulfill the requirements of my studies if I only want to	3,3	The workshop was helpful to get to know Future Skills	3,2
I know that I really have the skills required for my studies	3,1	The workshop was helpful to identify Future Skills that are meaningful to me personally	2,6
I know that I have enough interest for all the requirements associated with my studies	3,3	I consider learning Future Skills as important	3,8
I am relaxed about difficulties in my studies because I can trust my skills.	2,7	I would recommend the workshop to my friends	2,8

The correlation between the two sets of mean values is 0.624. This value indicates a positive linear relationship, which can be explained by the fact that higher values in self-efficacy tend to be associated with higher values in attitude towards Future Skill learning. As the p-value of the evaluation is 0.376, this means that the correlation is not statistically significant and must be re-evaluated in a further step.

Discussion

The evaluation results illustrate the high level of interest, personal appraisal and acceptance of the students for Future Skills learning interventions and the importance of the pedagogical concept. This is also strongly echoed in the perception of students, who express an increased interest in further learning opportunities. Integrative educational concepts offer great potential for individual personal development and provide added value for all stakeholders. The high personal relevance that students experience while participating in workshops, combined with the recognized importance of these competencies, show that learning content must be made more personal and individual, and that the traditional emphasis on knowledge transfer must give way to competence-based didactics. This development reflects the need to integrate such teaching interventions into the curriculum so that they equip students not only with the necessary knowledge, but also with the skills that are essential for successful and adaptive participation in a rapidly changing, technology-driven society with AI as an integral part of our life.

The study must also be considered in light of its limitations. The comparison of the two item sets is not sufficient to calculate a significant correlation with regard to self efficacy as an important part of students' motivation and learning. Future research should focus on the connection and correlation between the individual item sets.

Conclusion

The digital transformation emphasizes the importance of Future Skills and a paradigm shift in higher education towards a continuous adaptation of the education system. Teaching Future Skills has proven to be crucial for being able to navigate in a world of AI. In order to promote future skills at universities, learning formats and traditional ideas of education must be rethought. Universities have to implement tailor-made learning opportunities that are geared towards the needs of students and thus manifest their importance in the training of future-ready graduates to not fall behind in the race against the digital transformation.

References

Bolhuis, S. (2003). Towards process-oriented teaching for self-directed lifelong learning: A multidimensional perspective. Learning and Instruction, 13. S. 327-347. doi: 10.1016/S0959-4752(02)00008-7

Brown, G. & Atkins, M. (1990). Effective teaching in higher education. Routledge

Ehlers, U.-D. (2014). Open Learning Cultures. A Guide to Quality Evaluation and Assessment for Future Learning. Springer. doi: 10.1007/978-3-642-38174-4

Ehlers, U.-D. (2020). Future Skills. Lernen der Zukunft - Hochschule der Zukunft. Springer-Verlag

Goldin, C. D., & Katz, L.F. (2009). The race between Education and Technology. Cambridge: Harvard University Press

Hattie, J. & Timperley, H. (2007). The Power of Feedback. Review of Educational Research, 77(1), 81–112. doi: 10.3102/003465430298487

Kolb, D.: Experiential Learning: Experience As The Source Of Learning And Development, New York, 1984.

Mandl, H., & Krause, U. M.: Lernkompetenz für die Wissensgesellschaft. München: Ludwig-Maximilians-Universität, 2001

Schön, D. A.: The reflective practitioner: How Professionals Think in Action. Basic Books, 1983.

Seligman, M. E. P., & Csikszentmihalyi, M.: Positive psychology: An introduction. American Psychologist, 55(1), 5–14, 2000.

van den Beemt A, Vázquez-Villegas P, Gómez Puente S, O'Riordan F, Gormley C, Chiang F-K, Leng C, Caratozzolo P, Zavala G, Membrillo-Hernández J. Taking the Challenge: An Exploratory Study of the Challenge-Based Learning Context in Higher Education Institutions across Three Different Continents. Education Sciences. 2023; 13(3):234. https://doi.org/10.3390/educsci13030234

Yan, Z., & Boud, D. (2022). Conceptualising assessment-as-learning. In Z. Yan & L. Yang (Eds.), Asia-Europe education dialogue. Assessment as learning: Maximising opportunities for student learning and achievement (pp. 11–24). Routledge Taylor & Francis Group

Zimmerman, B. (2000). Self-Efficacy: An Essential Motive to Learn. Contemporary Educational Psychology. 25. S. 82-91. doi: 10.1006/ceps.1999.1016

Zimmerman, B. J., & Schunk, D. H. (2001). Self-regulated learning and academic achievement: Theoretical perspectives. Lawrence Erlbaum Associates Publishers.

Fostering Sustainability Through Project-Based Learning: The Sustainable City Project, A Case Study in Primary Education

Elena Vercher Ribis[1]

[1] Researcher in Educational Technology, Universitat Rovira i Virgili, Spain; everche2@xtec.cat

Correspondence: Elena Vercher Ribis: everche2@xtec.cat

Abstract:

The Sustainable City Project aims to engage students in design and programming to construct dwellings that integrate creative and sustainable solutions. Utilising platforms like Tinkercad and Makecode to code the micro:bit, students work in teams to tackle urban challenges, proposing innovative solutions. This project promotes sustainability across various domains including energy efficiency, natural resource management, sustainable mobility and enhancing quality of life. Emphasising social inclusion and urban resilience, it seeks to build a more just and equitable future city. This research article explores the competencies developed, the methodology employed and the educational significance of the Sustainable City Project, highlighting its multidisciplinary approach at the intersection of technology, sustainability and creativity.

Keywords: Project-Based Learning, Technology, Programming, 3D Design, Urban Design, Sustainable Development Goals (SDGs).

Introduction

In the face of growing environmental concerns and rapid urbanisation, fostering sustainability has become imperative. Education plays a pivotal role in shaping future generations capable of addressing these challenges. The Sustainable City Project represents a proactive approach to integrate sustainability education into the curriculum by engaging students in real-world problem-solving through design and programming. The project begins with foundational reading, including materials such as the book "What Does It Mean to Be Green?," setting the stage for exploration and understanding of sustainability principles.

In the realm of educational innovation, the fusion of technology and sustainability has paved the way for engaging project-based learning experiences. This project exemplifies this intersection, offering students a hands-on opportunity to design eco-friendly dwellings using digital tools. It is important to delve into the significance of such initiatives in fostering creativity, computational thinking and sustainability awareness among learners.

The project's utilisation of Tinkercad and micro:bit underscores the integration of technology in promoting sustainable practices (Wangenheim et al., 2018). By leveraging these platforms, students are not only exposed to coding and design principles but also encouraged to explore solutions that align with environmental sustainability. This hands-on approach not only enhances students' computational thinking skills but also infuses a sense of responsibility towards creating eco-conscious living spaces.

Assessing the critical thinking aspects of the project can be facilitated through the application of rubrics tailored to evaluate information processing and problem-solving skills (Reynders et al., 2020). By employing rubrics that emphasise critical thinking competencies, educators can provide constructive feedback to students, guiding them towards deeper analytical thinking and informed decision-making. This formative assessment approach enhances the learning experience by clarifying expectations and promoting continuous improvement.

Moreover, the project's focus on sustainability resonates with broader discussions on sustainable development and infrastructure initiatives (Liu et al., 2019). By engaging students in the design of sustainable houses, the project cultivates an understanding of the environmental impact of urban spaces and the importance of integrating sustainability principles into architectural practices. This hands-on experience empowers students to envision and contribute to a more sustainable future.

The Sustainable City Project offers primary students the opportunity to engage in sustainable urban design and problem-solving. This initiative aims to cultivate environmentally conscious individuals by immersing them in sustainability principles, technology and community engagement through hands-on activities.

Inspired by smart city concepts and sustainable development, the Sustainable City Project encourages students to explore the balance between urbanisation and environmental preservation (Argento et al., 2019). By utilising tools like Tinkercad, Makecode, micro:bit and neopixels and servo motors, students have designed eco-friendly dwellings and envision sustainable urban landscapes. This approach fosters creativity, computational thinking and a sense of responsibility towards creating a greener future.

Drawing insights from strategic frameworks for smart sustainable cities, such as the lifecycle-based approach proposed for Riyadh City (Alshuwaikhat et al., 2022), the project exposes students to real-world examples of sustainable city initiatives. This exposure enhances their understanding of the relationship between urban planning, technology and environmental sustainability, encouraging critical thinking about the long-term implications of their design choices.

Integrating sustainability assessment and enterprise resource planning elements, the Sustainable City Project prompts students to consider the social, economic and environmental dimensions of their designs (Alsaid, 2021). By introducing tools and methodologies for evaluating sustainability, the project fosters a holistic approach to urban design that prioritises long-term viability and community well-being. This multidimensional perspective equips students with the skills needed to tackle challenges in sustainable urban development. Integrating sustainability education into the curriculum also enhances students' readiness for the workforce by equipping them with transferable skills highly valued in today's job market (Kallio et al., 2021). Skills such as communication, teamwork and adaptability, nurtured through sustainability education, are crucial for success in various professional settings. By incorporating sustainability principles into learning experiences, educators ensure that students are well-prepared to meet the demands of a rapidly evolving and environmentally conscious society.

Objectives and methodology

The primary objective of the Sustainable City Project is to develop students' competencies in various domains including knowledge and interaction with the physical world, digital literacy, problem-solving, social and civic competence as well as the cultural and artistic competence. The project employs a project-based learning methodology, comprising Sessions such as reading materials on sustainability, introducing Sustainable Development Goals (SDGs), presenting principles of sustainable design and training in tools like Tinkercad and micro:bit. Students are organised into teams and tasked with designing a sustainable house, followed by collaborative work on design, prototyping and programming. The project culminates in oral presentations and evaluations by both teachers and students.

The Sustainable City Project is a multifaceted initiative designed to grow a sustainable urban design, environmental awareness and the development of future-ready skills among primary students. This project aims to educate students about sustainability, encourage critical thinking and creativity in addressing urban challenges and foster a sense of environmental responsibility. Additionally, the project seeks to enhance students' language skills in English as a Foreign Language (EFL) to prepare them for effective communication in a global context.

Objectives

- Educating students about the importance of sustainability in urban development.
- Encouraging critical thinking and creativity in sustainable urban solutions.
- Providing hands-on experience in designing eco-friendly dwellings and urban landscapes.
- Promoting community engagement and collaboration in sustainable city planning.
- Cultivating environmental responsibility and stewardship among students.
- Improving language skills in English as a Foreign Language to enhance communication abilities.

Methodologies

The Sustainable City Project utilises a multidisciplinary approach that integrates technology, sustainability principles, project-based learning and language instruction. Students engage in activities using technological tools to design sustainable houses, while also learning English language skills through discussions and presentations related to sustainable urban design. Performance measurement, governance concepts and smart technologies are incorporated to assess project impact and effectiveness.

Key components

- Technology Integration: Utilising platforms like Tinkercad and micro:bit for hands-on design and coding exercises.
- Performance Measurement: Implementing metrics and evaluation frameworks to assess project impact and sustainability potential.
- Community Engagement: Encouraging collaboration and participation from students and local communities in sustainable city planning.
- Sustainability Awareness: Educating students about environmental interconnectedness and fostering a sense of responsibility.
- Future-Ready Skills Development: Equipping students with critical thinking, problem-solving, creativity and language skills essential for sustainable urban development and global communication.

Educational significance

The educational significance of the Sustainable City Project lies in its ability to foster social inclusion and urban resilience among students. By integrating these critical aspects into the project, students are not only exposed to sustainability principles but also encouraged to develop a deep understanding of empathy and responsibility towards creating equitable societies (Huang et al., 2021). Through collaborative problem-solving, students learn to appreciate diverse perspectives and work towards solutions that cater to the needs of all community members.

According to Masten (2018), the focus on resilience in children and youth aims to promote positive adaptation to adversity, informing practice and policy. This aligns with the educational goals of the Sustainable City Project, where students are empowered to address challenges and contribute to the development of resilient communities. Additionally, Postan-Aizik (2022) highlights the role of education in supporting community organising, emphasising the transposition of knowledge to empower diverse communities.

The significance extends beyond the integration of sustainability principles, technology and creativity. This project serves as a transformative educational initiative that not only equips students with essential skills but also inculcates in them a profound sense of social inclusion and urban resilience. By emphasising these critical aspects, the project aims to cultivate empathy, responsibility and a deep understanding of the importance of creating equitable societies among students. By integrating these concepts into primary education, the project empowers students to navigate complex challenges, appreciate diverse perspectives and contribute to the development of resilient and inclusive communities.

Syllabus

Session 1: Introducing the United Nations Sustainable Development Goals (SDGs)

1. Introduction to sustainability and sustainable house design.
2. Explanation of SDG 11 focusing on sustainable cities and communities.
3. Importance of considering the impact of homes on the environment and communities.
4. Examples of sustainable features and how they contribute to SDG 11.
5. Encouragement for students to contribute to sustainability.
6. Questions, answers and discussion session.

Session 2: Design a house of the future in Tinkercad

1. Creation of a house design in Tinkercad.
2. Sessions for designing the house structure and adding sustainable features.
3. Additional sustainable elements provided for consideration.
4. Encouragement for creative and innovative design.
5. Examples of sustainable house designs with smart features.

Session 3: Create a prototype of the sustainable house using upcycled materials and a micro:bit

1. Gathering upcycled materials for the prototype.
2. Planning the design and building the frame, walls and roof.
3. Installation of doors, windows, fixtures and decorations.
4. Focus on promoting sustainability and creativity.
5. Encouragement for resourcefulness and reducing waste.

Session 4: Coding the elements in Makecode

1. Coding examples for different sustainable house elements using micro:bit, neopixel strip and servo motor.
2. Examples include automated lighting, temperature control, smart security, water conservation, natural ventilation, rainwater harvesting, indoor air quality monitoring, waste management and plant watering.
3. Encouragement for experimentation and creativity in coding.

Session 5: Connect the led strip and the servo motor to the house

1. Instructions for connecting a neopixel LED strip and servo motor to the micro:bit.
2. Focus on ensuring proper wiring for functionality.
3. Encouragement for testing and experimentation.

Session 6: Share your house design!

1. Preparation of a presentation on the importance of SDG 11 in house design.
2. Introduction, discussion on the importance of SDG 11, explanation of the design process, highlighting sustainable features, showcasing the prototype and conclusion.
3. Emphasis on simple language, engagement and visual aids for effective communication.

Session 7: (Self and Co) assessment of the projects

1. Co-assessment and self-assessment of the project presentations.
2. Establishment of assessment criteria aligned with learning objectives.
3. Peer feedback sheets, group discussions, gallery walk, speed dating and role-playing suggested for assessment dynamics.
4. Emphasis on constructive criticism, feedback and improvement in presentation skills.

Rubric

The rubric should encompass various dimensions of 21st-century skills, including critical thinking and information processing (Reynders et al., 2020). By incorporating criteria that evaluate students' ability to analyse information, draw conclusions and solve complex problems, the rubric can provide a structured framework for assessing critical thinking skills in project-based assignments. Additionally, aspects related to sustainability competencies should be integrated into the rubric, aligning with the principles of sustainable development (Albareda-Tiana et al., 2019). This ensures that students' projects are evaluated based on their contributions to environmental, social and economic sustainability.

Furthermore, the rubric should address the assessment of systems thinking skills, which are essential for understanding interconnected processes and relationships within projects (Reynders et al., 2023). By including criteria that gauge students' ability to identify feedback loops, anticipate consequences and propose holistic solutions, the rubric can effectively measure systems thinking competencies. Moreover, fostering creative thinking skills should be a key component of the rubric, reflecting the importance of creativity in 21st-century learning (Larraz-Rábanos, 2021). Criteria related to originality, flexibility and elaboration of ideas can be included to assess students' creative problem-solving abilities.

Table 1: Rubric to assess the objectives of the project.

	Excellent	**Good job**	**Okay**	**Needs improvement**

Problem-Solving	Solves problems creatively, for example figuring out how to use solar panels to make houses have electricity even when it's cloudy. Explains ideas clearly, like saying, "We can use these special panels to catch sunlight even on cloudy days!"	Solves problems well, such as finding ways to save water by collecting rain for gardens. Explains ideas clearly, like saying, "We can use big barrels to catch rainwater for our plants!"	Tries to solve problems, but may need help sometimes, like thinking of ways to keep houses warm without using too much energy. Explains ideas okay, but might need more details, like saying, "Maybe we can use something to keep heat inside."	Has trouble solving problems alone, like not knowing how to make houses use less energy. May need a lot of help coming up with ideas and explaining them.
Collaboration	Works great with others, like listening to friends' ideas about making parks fun for everyone and sharing their own ideas too. Helps solve problems by talking and working together with friends.	Works well with others, like talking to friends about making playgrounds safe and sharing ideas about what games to play. Tries to help solve problems by talking and sharing ideas.	Works with others sometimes, like talking a little with friends about what trees to plant in the park. Shares ideas a bit and tries to help a little with problems.	Has trouble working with others, like not talking much to friends about making the city better. Doesn't share ideas and doesn't help solve problems with friends.
Critical thinking	Thinks really well about things, like listening to different ideas about saving energy and deciding which ones are the best for the city. Makes good decisions based on what's best for everyone, like saying, "We should use this idea because it helps everyone!"	Thinks about things, like listening to different ideas about using less water and deciding which ones are good for gardens. Makes decisions that make sense for the city, like saying, "Let's use this idea because it helps plants grow!"	Makes decisions, but may need more help when asking himself: "Maybe this idea is okay?"	Doesn't think much about things, like not listening to different ideas about making streets safe and not deciding which ones are good for the city. Doesn't make good decisions.
Creativity	Comes up with super cool ideas, like thinking of new ways to use recycled materials to make playgrounds. Tries new things, like using old tires to	Comes up with neat ideas, like thinking of fun games to play in the park. Tries new things sometimes, like planting flowers in different	Tries new things he/she has seen sometimes, like drawing pictures to put on walls. Makes things that are okay, but might need more creativity, like	Doesn't come up with many ideas, like not thinking of ways to make parks fun. Doesn't try new things and doesn't make stuff that's very exciting.

	make swings for kids to play on. Makes amazing stuff that everyone loves, like building a cool play area with recycled stuff.	colours to make parks pretty. Makes stuff that's pretty cool, like making a garden with colourful flowers.	making simple drawings.	
Foreign language acquisition	Uses foreign language words related to saving the planet correctly, like using words such as "recycle," "renewable energy," or "nature" in conversations or presentations. Talks and listens when using another language in class, like discussing ideas about the project or presenting in front of the class. Gets better at speaking and understanding another language over time, getting better at saying words and understanding what others say. Reads and watches videos in another language to learn more about how to help the planet, like reading books about nature or watching videos about recycling.	Uses vocabulary related to sustainability in various contexts and showing progress in language skills over time. Actively engages in foreign language communication tasks. Consistently seeks out and uses foreign language resources to deepen understanding of sustainability concepts and project objectives.	Participates willingly in foreign language communication tasks, demonstrating adequate fluency and comprehension for their grade level. Demonstrates some initiative in seeking out and utilising foreign language resources to enhance understanding of sustainability topics.	Participates reluctantly in foreign language communication tasks, exhibiting minimal fluency and comprehension for their grade level. Shows little initiative in seeking out and utilising foreign language resources to support understanding of sustainability concepts.

Results

The analysis of the post-test results in problem-solving, collaboration, critical thinking and creativity within the Sustainable City Project provides valuable insights into students' performance and areas for improvement. The relationship between pretest and post-test scores in problem-solving indicates a generally high level of performance, with students who initially scored 'Okay' showing the most improvement. This suggests a potential for further enhancement in problem-solving skills, particularly for students in this category. Targeted interventions for these students and reinforcement of advanced problem-solving techniques for proficient students are recommended actions to support continued growth.

In terms of collaboration, the analysis reveals an average score of 2.5 (out of 4), with opportunities to identify improvement areas and foster better collaboration among students. Further investigation into why certain combinations yield lower scores can inform targeted interventions to enhance collaboration skills. Monitoring collaboration trends and focusing on enhancing collaborations in the middle category can contribute to overall improvement in collaborative practices.

The analysis of critical thinking performance highlights a strong correlation between initial intermediate low levels and subsequent higher ratings, indicating a positive trajectory in critical thinking skills. Additional support for students in the lower category can help enhance their critical thinking abilities. By conducting further analysis on students with lower critical thinking performance and providing tailored resources, educators can effectively support students' growth in this area.

Examining the relationship between the creativity pretest and post-test, it reveals a generally high level of creativity across the dataset. The strong positive relationship between pretest and post-test suggests a consistent development in this skill area. However, the lack of improvement in creativity for students in the lower category warrants further investigation to identify barriers and implement targeted interventions for improvement.

The analysis of the pretest and post-test of foreign language acquisition reveals a moderate overall improvement, with an average value of 2.6 out of 4. Students scoring 1 on the pretest and 3 on the post-test showed the most significant advancement, while most of those scoring 3 on both tests exhibited no progress. Further investigation is necessary to understand the factors influencing these variations.

These results provide a roadmap for targeted interventions and enhancements in these essential skills within the Sustainable City Project, ultimately contributing to students' holistic development and success.

Conclusions

In conclusion, the Sustainable City Project represents a holistic approach to sustainability education, integrating technology, creativity and social consciousness. By providing students with opportunities to apply knowledge and skills in meaningful contexts, the project prepares them to become informed and engaged citizens capable of contributing towards building a sustainable society.

Exploring potential future directions for the Sustainable City Project involves considerations of scalability, adaptation to diverse educational contexts and further research opportunities. Drawing insights from relevant literature can provide valuable guidance for expanding the project's impact and effectiveness in addressing sustainability challenges and fostering community resilience.

Future research opportunities for the Sustainable City Project could include exploring the integration of sustainable experience design education, as suggested by Kim & Kamal (2023). This approach could enhance the project's educational impact and effectiveness in promoting sustainability principles. Furthermore, Hernández-Barco et al. (2020) highlight the significance of service-learning methodology for science education and sustainability, offering practical approaches for integrating sustainability education into university-level science programs.

The Sustainable City Project offers a transformative educational experience for primary students, allowing them to explore sustainable urban design and problem-solving. By incorporating technology, sustainability principles and governance concepts, this initiative prepares a new generation of environmentally conscious leaders capable of shaping the cities of the future.

References

Albareda-Tiana, S., García-González, E., Jiménez-Fontana, R., & Solís-Espallargas, C. (2019). Implementing pedagogical approaches for ESD in initial teacher training at Spanish universities. Sustainability, 11(18), 4927.

Alsaid, L. (2021). Smart city dynamics and multi-level management accounting: unfolding a case of sustainable enterprise resource planning. Sustainability Accounting Management and Policy Journal, 13(1), 30-54.

Alshuwaikhat, H., Adenle, Y., & Almuhaidib, T. (2022). A lifecycle-based smart sustainable city strategic framework for realising smart and sustainability initiatives in riyadh city. Sustainability, 14(14), 8240.

Argento, D., Grossi, G., Jääskeläinen, A., Servalli, S., & Suomala, P. (2019). Governmentality and performance for the smart city. Accounting Auditing & Accountability Journal, 33(1), 204-232.

Huang, D., Lin, W., Luo, Y., & Liu, Y. (2021). Impact of social work services on the resilience of migrant children. Research on Social Work Practice, 32(3), 345-355.

Kallio, K., Jokela, S., Kyrönviita, M., Laine, M., & Taylor, J. (2021). Skatescape in the making: developing sustainable urban pedagogies through transdisciplinary education. Sustainability, 13(17), 9561.

Kim, Y. and Kamal, R. (2023). Toward a framework for sustainable experience design education and an illustrative case of a service design thinking course. Proceedings of the Design Society, 3, 3551-3560.

Larraz-Rábanos, N. (2021). Development of creative thinking skills in the teaching-learning process..

Liu, X., Schraven, D., Bruijne, M., Jong, M., & Hertogh, M. (2019). Navigating transitions for sustainable infrastructures—the case of a new high-speed railway station in jingmen, china. Sustainability, 11(15), 4197.

Masten, A. (2018). Resilience theory and research on children and families: past, present and promise. Journal of Family Theory & Review, 10(1), 12-31.

Reynders, G., Lantz, J., Ruder, S., Stanford, C., & Cole, R. (2020). Rubrics to assess critical thinking and information processing in undergraduate stem courses. International Journal of Stem Education, 7(1).

Reynders, M., Pilcher, L., & Potgieter, M. (2023). Teaching and assessing systems thinking in first-year chemistry. Journal of Chemical Education, 100(3), 1357-1365.

Wangenheim, C., Hauck, J., Demetrio, M., Pelle, R., Alves, N., Barbosa, H. & Azevedo, L. (2018). Codemaster - automatic assessment and grading of app inventor and snap! programs. Informatics in Education, 17(1), 117-150.

ChatGPT and Me: implementing and evaluating a custom GPT for written corrective feedback

Carrie A. Ankerstein[1]

[1] English Department, Saarland University, Germany; c.ankerstein@mx.uni-saarland.de

Correspondence: Carrie A. Ankerstein: c.ankerstein@mx.uni-saarland.de

Abstract:

The current paper presents and evaluates a custom GPT designed to give interactive, on-demand feedback on an uploaded essay according to course-specific content, with a focus on basic essay structure, vocabulary, top-heavy sentences, connector usage, use of examples and formal language. The results showed that the GPT performed well in providing specific feedback on basic structuring issues, wordiness and informality among other areas. However, performance could be inconsistent and inaccurate on occasion. It is concluded that custom GPTs have potential for use in tandem with a human instructor with the aim that the GPT provides initial feedback for lower order concerns so that the human instructor can focus on higher order concerns such as coherence and argumentation.

Keywords: ChatGPT, digital literacy, English as a foreign language, written corrective feedback

Introduction: ChatGPT and the L2 Classroom

Alharbi (2023: 2) noted: "No matter what language educators think or feel about students' use of AI-powered writing assistance tools [...], it might be time to take a more realistic approach to the issue and treat it as an inescapable fact that they need to accept and live with" and went on to say that: "the ability to use these technologies has grown to be a critical aspect of digital literacy in educational and professional settings". I agree with Alharbi and I think that knowledge of AIs such as ChatGPT is an important part of the digital literacy skills that today's students need.

Researchers at OpenAI noted that "humans do not require large supervised datasets to learn most language tasks - a brief directive in natural language or at most a tiny number of demonstrations is often sufficient to enable a human to perform a new task to at least a reasonable degree of competence" (Brown et al., 2020: 3). This is critical for users of ChatGPT to know. Because of its chat interface, some users may assume that ChatGPT "understands" language like a human and that its use is intuitive, but this is not the case and practice and instruction are required to use ChatGPT effectively. This includes awareness of what ChatGPT as a large language model (LLM) is and how it works, its strengths and weaknesses, the prompting skills required for effective results, and the importance of providing ChatGPT with examples to improve performance.

Interacting with ChatGPT effectively is not necessarily intuitive as a classroom experiment conducted with novice users showed (Ankerstein & Kopf-Giammanco, 2023). In this experiment, 29 undergraduate students in an advanced-level English as a foreign language writing class were instructed to ask ChatGPT write an essay on "what is the most difficult thing about writing in English", the topic of their own first assignment for the class. They were asked to submit their prompts and the best resulting essay (the experiment was conducted in March 2023 before links to ChatGPT conversations could be shared). Of the 187 submitted prompts, 83 were simple directives such as "write an essay..." and 44 prompts were repetitions of previous prompts. The students were also asked to comment on ChatGPT's output and they, for the most part, documented their disappointment in the quality of the output, commenting on inaccuracies and lexical repetition in particular. This small experiment showed that, in addition to clearing up misconceptions about ChatGPT, novice users need guidance to use ChatGPT effectively.

In most writing classrooms, ChatGPT might be put to better use as a source of feedback on student-written assignments, rather than as a ghostwriter of them. As it had been shown that students needed support in prompt engineering, a second classroom experiment was conducted in December 2023 with a different group of 19 undergraduates in an advanced-level English as a foreign language writing class. This time, they were given a 640-word prompt template (based on Mollick & Mollick, 2023) which asked ChatGPT-3.5 for feedback on a text. The prompt gave ChatGPT specific instructions in how to interact with the student-user and the criteria to use for the feedback. The students were again asked to assess the feedback that they received from ChatGPT and again reported disappointment, with complaints largely being that ChatGPT's feedback was vague, with one student, NiRa, stating: "When not provided immediately with clear criteria of assessment, the program defaulted to generic writing advice". Another student, AnFe, similarly stated: "ChatGPT's feedback remains superficial". However, another student, MoAl, argued for the potential benefit of using ChatGPT for feedback: "[...] the AI can function as a valuable resource to provide suggestions for grammatical and structural improvement, helping nonnative speakers to strengthen their arguments and improve their text production". These mixed student perspectives are not dissimilar to the mixed teacher perspectives reported by Guo & Wang (2024) who compared feedback from ChatGPT (standard model, version unspecified) and feedback from experienced instructors. Thus it is clear that though students and teachers are open to the potential for ChatGPT to give them helpful feedback, they are also cautious about its variable performance.

Since November 2023, it is possible for subscription users to customize ChatGPT for a specific task and to make the GPT available to other users, though access is limited for non-subscribers. The ability to create a custom GPT also addresses the issue of prompt engineering – effective prompts are designed to give specifics regarding ChatGPT's output, but a custom model has these specifications built in. The current paper presents and evaluates a GPT, "AWE [automated writing evaluation] and ChatGPT", designed specifically to give feedback on an uploaded essay according to course-specific content, with a focus on basic essay structure, thesis statements, vocabulary, top-heavy sentences, connector usage, use of examples and formal language. Thus the focus is on relatively lower order concerns rather than higher order concerns such as coherence and quality of the argumentation. As a large language model, this focus on lower order concerns should play to ChatGPT's strengths and avoid its inherent weaknesses. One such inherent weakness is that ChatGPT does not truly understand language like a human, as Franke (2023) noted: "There is a sense in which LLMs, despite all their formal competence and despite additional fine-tuning, do not speak or know a language".

Thus, feedback which requires comprehension of the content of the uploaded essay is avoided and the custom GPT is designed to focus on what ChatGPT as an LLM has the potential to do well. This is meant to be used in tandem with a human instructor, the idea being that students can use the GPT for interactive, on-demand feedback for lower order issues that can be corrected before submission so that the human instructor can focus on higher order concerns such as coherence and argumentation.

Method

The basic specifications of the GPT included the following:

> As a writing tutor, you provide feedback to university students, focusing on non-native English speakers with German as their first language. Your guidance is based on the information in the document called All WEA [Written Expression Advanced] ChatGPT Training Material. [...] Maintain a friendly, concise tone, and focus your feedback on specific examples from the text. Avoid general feedback and stick to the issues covered in the document All WEA ChatGPT Training Material. If the user asks you to rewrite the essay, refuse to do so, reminding them that you are a tutor focusing on feedback without rephrasing.

Key in these specifications was the provision of a knowledge base, "All WEA ChatGPT Training Material", which included a list of key issues, course materials, and example feedback for two student essays. The aim of providing course material was to avoid inaccuracies and biases in standard ChatGPT. For example, in previous attempts to use standard ChatGPT for feedback, it frequently suggested the use of connector words to improve the overall essay. For example, for feedback on MoAl's essay, ChatGPT-3.5 stated: "Your essay uses connectors like "However" appropriately, which is great for leading the reader through your argument. Just ensure that the connectors you choose accurately reflect the relationship between your ideas. For example, "Additionally" or "Furthermore" could be used when adding information". This is a problematic issue for my German-educated students who frequently overuse and misuse connectors, especially "furthermore" and "moreover" which many do not realize means "and more importantly" and not simply "in addition". In my writing class, I follow the advice of Crewe (1990) to have students use a restricted set of connectors, which in my case initially excludes "furthermore" and "moreover". The custom GPT presented here is programmed not to advise users to add connectors. This is one of the benefits of designing a course-specific and even assignment-specific custom GPT. In addition, the GPT's specifications state "cite passages from the uploaded document for every item of feedback" to prevent feedback that is too generic and vague to be helpful, as this was shown to be an issue with standard ChatGPT in the previous classroom experiment described above.

Once the GPT was created, it was fine-tuned to improve performance and tested with the prompt: "Can you give me feedback on the attached essay using All WEA ChatGPT Training Material? The essay was the first assignment for a writing class. It is supposed to demonstrate that we know the structure of an essay and how to use formal English. The essay prompt was 'what do you find most difficult about writing in English?' and we needed to include examples for each of the issues". In this qualitative analysis, five student essays (hereafter identified as AnFe, HaHa, LiMu, MoAl, NiRa) were used to generate feedback using the initial prompt and further prompting was used on occasion to further probe its performance, details included below where relevant. For each essay, a new dialogue with the GPT was opened. Written, informed consent was obtained from the five students whose essays were used in the current study and from the two students whose essays were used in the training materials. All documents were anonymized so that ChatGPT did not have access to names or any personal details.

Results

The performance of the custom GPT was mixed. On occasion the GPT followed its specifications and gave helpful feedback as instructed. However, there were also instances where it did not adhere to its specifications.

Examples of good performance

Whilst the GPT was designed to focus on lower order concerns such as vocabulary and grammar, it was also designed to comment on basic structural issues. For example, in MoAl's essay, in response to the initial prompt, the GPT noted that two separate issues are discussed in a single body paragraph and gives clear feedback according to the course-materials it was trained on: "Your essay effectively identifies two main issues: False Friends and the tendency of German speakers to use complex sentence structures. These topics are relevant and well-chosen. However, each point could benefit from being explored in its own paragraph with a clear topic sentence". In addition, the GPT also noted that MoAl's essay lacked a conclusion and offered guidance on what a conclusion should contain, again according to the training material: "Your essay lacks a distinct conclusion. A concluding paragraph should summarize the main points discussed and restate the thesis in light of the information presented in the body paragraphs". This sort of feedback is clear, specific and easily implemented by the user. In addition, these types of structural issues, paragraphing and concluding, are of a higher order than more minor issues such as punctuation or vocabulary usage. As an instructor, I take off more points for such higher order concerns the GPT's feedback as cited above could help the student not only learn to structure their writing using the feedback, but also to achieve a higher mark on the assignment.

The GPT was also able to give feedback for specific language issues. For example, for LiMu's essay, following the initial prompt, the GPT commented on a specific instance of informal language: "Your essay maintains a mostly formal tone, which is appropriate for an academic setting. However, phrases like "(funny) difficulty" could be perceived as informal. Consider using more formal expressions to maintain the academic tone throughout". In another instance, the GPT commented on informal language in NiRa's essay: "You've done well in maintaining a formal tone throughout your essay, which is appropriate for an academic assignment. However, be cautious with phrases that might seem too casual or colloquial, such as "words that could be considered dinosaurs" or "vanished from society." While these expressions add character to your writing, ensuring they fit the formal context of your essay is crucial". In both of these instances, the GPT commented on specific passages which need revision and clear guidance on how to fix them, exactly as included in the specifications and training materials.

The GPT was also able to spot cases of verbosity. For example, in response to the initial prompt for HaHa's essay, the GPT commented on wordiness: "Additionally, be mindful of wordiness; expressing your ideas more concisely can make your writing more powerful and easier to follow", but did not cite a specific passage. When asked in a follow-up question for an example of wordiness in the essay, the GPT responded with:

> "Certainly! An example of wordiness in your essay can be found in the sentence: "In my writing, I tend to drift off on the main idea of my thoughts and write about things that are just barely related to the topic." This sentence could be more concise without losing meaning. For instance, it could be simplified

to: "In my writing, I often stray from the main idea and discuss barely related topics." This revision removes redundant phrases like "of my thoughts" and "things that are just," making the sentence more straightforward and easier to read while retaining the original meaning".

Whilst this feedback does rewrite the sentence, going against the GPT's specifications, it explains the process and the revision shows how these changes are implemented.

Examples of poorer performance

In some cases, the GPT offered potentially confusing feedback. For example, in response to the initial prompt for AnFe's essay, the GPT stated: "You occasionally use personal pronouns ("I", "me"), which is acceptable in this context since the essay prompt asks for your personal experience. However, ensure that the use of personal pronouns does not detract from the academic quality of your writing". Here the comment on 'pronouns potentially detracting from the formality of academic writing' may be confusing to a student-user for this particular personal essay assignment in which such pronouns are appropriate. The GPT also gave feedback for NiRa's essay on the issue of pronouns, but in a much clearer form: "You've used personal pronouns appropriately, reflecting on your experiences. The essay prompt invites personal reflection, making your approach suitable". This feedback accurately reflects the nature of the personal essay in question and stays within those bounds without a vague statement on academic writing as it did for AnFe's essay. Further study will be needed to test whether students find such feedback as in the case of AnFe confusing or unhelpful. It may be the case that such feedback is not problematic in tandem with human instructor feedback.

Inaccurate performance is a well-known and well-documented problem with ChatGPT (OpenAI) and it persists in the custom GPTs. For example, in feedback for HaHa's essay, the GPT stated: "Your essay could benefit from more attention to punctuation for clarity and formality" and when asked in a follow-up question for an example from the essay that would benefit from more attention to punctuation and formality, the GPT cited the following sentence: "One more thing I find difficult while writing in English is the syntax and grammar in complex sentences, I tend to write really long and convoluted sentences, which would be easier to understand if I would split them into more than one sentence" and stated that it is a run-on sentence and suggested changes to the punctuation to correct it. This would generally be fine, however, in HaHa's original essay this passage was comprised of two sentences separated by a full stop, in other words there was no run-on. The original passage was as follows: "One more thing I find difficult while writing in English is the syntax and grammar in complex sentences. I tend to write really long and convoluted sentences, which would be easier to understand if I would split them into more than one sentence". In another case of inaccuracy, the GPT's feedback for AnFe's essay included: "[...] paying close attention to complex sentence structures and ensuring subject-verb agreement would enhance the readability of your text". The GPT did not give a specific example from the essay and was therefore asked in a follow-up question to do so and the GPT's response was "Upon reviewing your essay for the specific feedback I provided about complex sentence structures and subject-verb agreement, I realize that my comment may not have directly applied to the examples in your text. Your essay does not exhibit clear issues with subject-verb agreement or complex sentence structures that need immediate fixing". Whilst the GPT admitted its error to the user in this case, some students might find that such performance erodes their trust in the GPT. Again, further study is needed to test whether students find such feedback problematic.

General Inconsistencies of the GPT

In a test of the GPT's specification not to rewrite passages at the user's request, three attempts were made after the initial prompt to ask the GPT to write a conclusion paragraph for LiMu's essay using the prompts: "Could you suggest a conclusion paragraph?" (used twice) and "Could you draft a conclusion for the essay?". For each attempt, the GPT refused to produce a conclusion, stating respectively: "While I can't rewrite sections of your essay for you, I can suggest how to [...]"; "While I can't write the conclusion for you, I can offer some tips [...]" and "I understand you're seeking direct assistance in drafting a conclusion for your essay. However, my role is to guide you in enhancing your writing skills through feedback and suggestions. I encourage you to use the tips I've provided [...]". These instances show optimal performance of the GPT: it provided polite refusals and instead offered clear guidance to the student.

However, the GPT's performance in this regard was not consistent. In HaHa's feedback, the GPT refused to offer a thesis statement when asked to do so in a follow-up prompt, stating: "While I'm here to provide feedback rather than rephrase or rewrite your text directly, I can guide you on how to craft a stronger thesis statement based on your essay [...]", but when the response was regenerated, the GPT provided a thesis statement: "Here's a suggestion: [...]". On several other occasions, it offered unprompted re-phrasings. For example in LiMu's feedback, the GPT stated that the essay needed a clearer thesis statement and proceeded to draft such a statement: "In your essay, you list the challenges but do not clearly state your main argument or thesis in a single sentence. An effective thesis statement could be something like, "Among the various challenges of learning English, I find sentence structure, punctuation rules, understanding fixed expressions, and avoiding false friends to be particularly daunting". The GPT similarly offered a re-written thesis statement for the essays by AnFe, MoAl and NiRa when asked to do so.

Conclusion

In the modern era, instructors and students alike will need to be familiar with AIs such as ChatGPT. Rather than ban ChatGPT in the classroom, instructors should be encouraged to explore its potential benefits. One such benefit is the use of ChatGPT as a type of automatic writing evaluator to offer interactive, on-demand feedback to students (see also Guo & Wang, 2024 and Lu, Yao, Xiao, Yuan, Wang & Zhu, 2024). In the current study, a custom GPT was presented and evaluated. The advantages of such a GPT include its customizability, accessibility, relative ease of use, and its ability to give detailed feedback. On-demand feedback could be especially useful to students who may not have access to a human instructor or who may be under time-pressure. Such feedback from the GPT is meant to be used to improve drafts with respect to lower order concerns which are relatively easily corrected before submission with the aim that the human instructor focuses on higher order content issues. Thus, GPT-generated feedback is not meant to replace human instructors, but to support and complement them (see also Guo & Wang, 2024 and Lu et al., 2024). The custom GPT's performance is not without issue, however. Further research is needed to test whether these issues can be overcome and whether its disadvantages, including inconsistent performance and occasional inaccuracy, are enough deter students from using it or even detrimental to their writing performance.

Supplementary files

Supplementary files can be provided at request, including links to ChatGPT conversations.

Competing interests

The author has no competing interests to declare. There is no monetary gain to the author for the use of the GPT.

Ethics and consent

The research presented here is from classroom activities and assignments as part of an advanced-level undergraduate writing class. Written, informed consent was obtained from the students whose essays were used in the implementation and testing of the GPT.

OpenAI's sharing and publication policy (as of June 2024) states: "We believe it is important for the broader world to be able to evaluate our research and products, especially to understand and improve potential weaknesses and safety or bias problems in our models. Accordingly, we welcome research publications related to the OpenAI API" (https://openai.com/policies/sharing-publication-policy). The policy further states that ChatGPT created content is allowed if "The role of AI in formulating the content is clearly disclosed in a way that no reader could possibly miss, and that a typical reader would find sufficiently easy to understand" (ibid). The ChatGPT content in the current paper is clearly indicated and presented verbatim.

Funding Information

This research was supported by a grant from Stiftung Innovation in der Hochschullehre via Data-Pin, Saarland University awarded to Carrie Ankerstein and Danielle Kopf-Giammanco for the project titled "Empowering Students with AI: Using ChatGPT as a Writing Tool and Teaching Critical Evaluation of AI-Generated Text".

References

Alharbi, W. (2023). AI in the foreign language classroom: a pedagogical overview of automated writing assistance tools. Education Research International, 1-15.

Ankerstein, C.A. & Kopf-Giammanco, D.A. (2023). "Empowering Students with AI: Using ChatGPT as a Writing Tool and Teaching Critical Evaluation of AI-Generated Text". Joint APLX / ETRA / TESPA Conference: Advancing empowerment and resilience: Language, culture, policy and pedagogy, Taipei, Taiwan.

Brown, T. B., Mann, B., Ryder, N., Subbiah, M., Kaplan, J., Dhariwal, P. . . . & Amodei, D. (2020). Language models are few-shot learners. Proceedings of the 34th International Conference on Neural Information Processing Systems. Retrieved from https://arxiv.org/abs/2005.14165.

Franke, M. (2023, December 10). Wittgenstein says: ChatGPT does not speak English [Blog post]. https://michael-franke.github.io/blog/posts/LLM-forms-of-life/

Guo, K. & Wang, D. (2024). To resist it or to embrace it? Examining ChatGPT's potential to support teacher feedback in EFL writing. Education and Information Technology, 29, 8435–8463. https://doi.org/10.1007/s10639-023-12146-0

Lu, Q., Yao, Y., Xiao, L., Yuan, M., Wang, J. & Zhu, X. (2024). Can ChatGPT effectively complement teacher assessment of undergraduate students' academic writing? Assessment & Evaluation in Higher Education, 1–18. https://doi.org/10.1080/02602938.2024.2301722

Mollick, E. & Mollick, L. (2023). Student Cases for AI. Part 1: AI as Feedback Generator: Harnessing the power of instant input. Retrieved from https://hbsp.harvard.edu/inspiring-minds/ai-as-feedback-generator.

OpenAI (2023). ChatGPT. https://chat.openai.com/chat.

Digital Wellbeing: Students' perspective

Kristina Adomaitienė[1], Airina Volungevičienė[2]

[1] Strategic Planning and Quality Management Unit, Kauno kolegija, Lithuania; kristina.adomaitiene@go.kauko.lt
[2] Institute for Study Innovations, Vytautas Magnus University, Lithuania; airina.volungeviciene@vdu.lt

Correspondence: Kristina Adomaitienė: kristina.adomaitiene@go.kauko.lt

Abstract:

Innovative technology-based study methods are increasingly used in teaching and learning. This not only increases the attractiveness of learning, but also creates new challenges in balancing the benefits of technology and its harm to student's wellbeing. It emerges a new concept of digital wellbeing. The research problem is how to ensure the effective and ethical use of innovative technologies for teaching and learning in a system of supporting students' digital wellbeing, while avoiding or minimizing negative impacts on students' wellbeing. It aims to justify as a system the functionality of the model of students' digital wellbeing support in a TEL environment. A theoretical framework and possible further research are presented.

Keywords: Digital wellbeing, students' wellbeing, technology enhanced learning environment (TEL)

Introduction

In recent years a focus on sustainable learning was dominated in higher education, which has led to the introduction of innovative study methods by using intelligent tutoring systems, virtual learning environments and artificial intelligence-assisted applications. There is a shift from a traditional study environment to a technology-based learning environment, encouraging students to engage in active learning activities. This use of technology provides greater flexibility in learning, expands access to learning resources (Wang & others, 2021), helps to personalise learning at lower cost (Asad & others, 2023), and creates immersive learning environments through virtual, extended or augmented reality (Cuomo & others, 2021). However, the sudden shift to distance learning during the pandemic period and expansion of technology enhanced learning in post-pandemic period have encouraged researchers to re-explore the concept of students' wellbeing (Burns & others, 2020; Ribeiro-Silva & others, 2022; White & Sangster, 2022; Douwes & others, 2023; Havsteen-Franklin & others, 2023), to define the variety of factors interacting with students' wellbeing (Butnaru & others, 2021; Dinu & others, 2022; Moldovan & others, 2022; Douwes & others, 2023; Lister & others, 2023), to discuss more about the techno-stress experienced due to inadequate adaptation to TEL environment (Wang & al., 2021; Asad & al., 2023), the harm of excessive use of technology for individuals, leading to addiction or psychological disorders (Turner & al., 2021; Roffarello & De Russis, 2023), and the demand of positive technology, where concepts of well-being are incorporated into the development of technology or where technology is developed to support the wellbeing of an individual or group of individuals (Rad & others, 2022; Thomas & others 2022). In technology enhanced learning, there is a relationship between the use of technology for teaching and learning and the wellbeing of the individual and society (El Aadmi-Laamech & others, 2022).

Students' wellbeing is a multidimensional concept, whose definition is dominated by psychological, emotional, physiological, social and subjective components of well-being (Moldovan & others, 2022; Douwes & others, 2023). And due to the increased and frequent use of technology in recent years, a new aspect of wellbeing is increasingly being analysed: digital wellbeing (Roffarello & De Russis, 2023). The EU Council Conclusions on supporting wellbeing in digital education (2022) define digital wellbeing as "a feeling of physical, cognitive, social and emotional contentment that enables all individuals to engage positively in all digital learning environments including through digital education and training tools and methods, maximize their potential and self-realisation <...>". It also focuses on learners' safe online behavior and support for learner' empowerment. In conceptualizing digital wellbeing, several other aspects need to be taken into account: digital wellbeing is more than the absence of a pathology characterized by harmful habits of technology use, a digital media addiction; a person's relationship with technology can be positive through hedonic and eudemonic experiences; digital wellbeing is temporally variable and depends on each individual; digital wellbeing is a dualistic phenomenon, whereby the benefits of technology may be lost by limiting the negative effects of technology. (Vanden Abeele, 2021). The ambivalence of technology use and the need for balance between the benefits and potential harm of technology, the multidimensionality of the concept of digital wellbeing, the subjectivity of perception of digital wellbeing, and the temporal variability of the concept, all create the impression that digital wellbeing can be difficult to attain, which can also have a negative impact on learning achievement.

Many studies support a positive relationship between student wellbeing and academic achievement (Boulton & others, 2019), and therefore, in the context of studying in TEL environment, the relationships between the use of technology for teaching and learning, students' digital wellbeing, and their academic achievement are a complex phenomenon. However, as HEIs face challenges in adopting and effectively applying innovative teaching methods, there is still poorly researched the improving student' wellbeing (Havsteen-Franklin & others, 2023), and the elements and factors of this dynamic system have not been defined. Differences in definitions of student wellbeing make it difficult to measure students' wellbeing, to evaluate the impact of interventions, and to determine the role of HEIs in ensuring students' wellbeing (Douwes & others, 2023).

The research problem is how to ensure the effective and ethical use of innovative technologies for teaching and learning in a system of supporting students' digital wellbeing, while avoiding or minimizing negative technologies impacts on students' wellbeing.

The object of the study is the system and its elements of students' digital wellbeing in a TEL environment. The aim of the study is to justify the functionality of the model of students' digital wellbeing support as a system for the studies in a TEL environment.

Objectives of the study:

1. To define the concept of digital wellbeing in TEL environment and its place in the holistic concept of students' wellbeing.
2. To analyse the elements of a dynamic system of students' digital wellbeing and to identify the factors that have impact on students' digital wellbeing in TEL environment.
3. To assess the impact of digital wellbeing factors on students' digital wellbeing and academic achievement.
4. To develop a conceptual model to support students' digital wellbeing in TEL environment.

Theoretical Framework

Vanden Abeele (2021), in analysing the concept of digital wellbeing, pointed out that digital wellbeing should be analysed as a dynamic system in which the unique consumer, the context, devices, digital media use, and the digital wellbeing interact. The individual digital experience of the person, the context specific factors, and the functions and specific factors of technological devices are crucial for digital wellbeing. This model allows to analyse the problems encountered in the use of digital technologies and what determines the success or failure of digital wellbeing interventions.

The authors have analysed the different elements of this system. Considering the subjectivity, the subjectivity of wellbeing perception, attempts have been made to define well-being from the student's perspective, identifying the factors related to the student and the HEI and factors outside the HEI (Douwes & others, 2023). Factors that enable or create barriers to students' mental wellbeing in distance learning are specified and categorised into three further groups: study-related factors (course curriculum, including design, content and activities; tuition, including tutorials, tutor relationship, support; assessment, including extension and deadlines, flexibility, assessment support, feedback and cores); skill-related factors (study skills, self-management, social skills); and environmental factors (spaces, systems, people, life). Assessment, curriculum, content and teaching methods, lack of study skills, time management skills, digital communication skills, difficulties in balancing studies and other areas of life (work, family) are the main barriers to a student's mental wellbeing in study (Lister & others, 2023).

In the context of distance learning and TEL, both the positive and negative effects of technology have been analysed: engaging teaching methods that activate students and their benefits (Polat & Karabatak, 2022; Cuomo & others, 2021; Ribeiro-Silva & others, 2022), technostress (Wang & others, 2021; Asad & others, 2023; Biggins & others, 2023), lack of motivation due to poor social interaction, lack of a sense of belonging to the community and HEI (Peacock & Cowan, 2019; Holzer & others, 2021; Polat & Karabatak, 2022; Priestley & others, 2022; Mendoza & Venables, 2023), and the impact on the individuals of the excessive use of technology (Taylor & others, 2018). Cuomo & others (2021) analysed the technologies used to create immersive learning environments and their impact on the user in the context of digital wellbeing, considering the cognitive (the threats posed by the technology), the physiological (the impact of the technology on the user's health), the social (the impact of the technology on the user's social relationships) and the educational (the learning opportunities offered by the technology) dimensions, and presented a template for creating a learning scenario in a wellbeing perspective (Cuomo & al, 2021). In the context of digital wellbeing interventions, the objectives of developing self-monitoring tools for digital wellbeing, the efficiency of their use, and the challenges that arise have been investigated (Roffarello & De Russis, 2023; Thomas & others, 2022).

As HEI students are the population group that is most challenged in terms of psychological wellbeing (Kovich & others, 2023), the dimension of students' mental wellbeing was assessed (Golsteyn & Ostafichuk, 2020; Morgan & others, 2023; Kovich & others, 2023). It is noted that there is a variety of measures of students' wellbeing. Depending on the definition of students' wellbeing, several validated scales of wellbeing measurement may be combined simultaneously, or distinctive scales of measurement that have not yet been validated may be used (Dodd & others, 2021). There is no single standardised measurement of students' wellbeing. However, there is a need not only to monitor student wellbeing, but also to develop a prevention system. There is research on how learning analytics can identify changes in students' behavior that are also related to changes in wellbeing, act as a mechanism for potential early warning of possible wellbeing problems, measure the impact on digital wellbeing, and at the same time pose a threat to students' digital wellbeing in terms of the ethics of the data collection (Ahern, 2020; Hakami&et al., 2021; Cormack&et al., 2022).

In national context, more analysis has been done on students' psychological wellbeing, assessing the links between psychological wellbeing and stress (Bulotaitė & others, 2012), students' academic motivation and psychological wellbeing (Rugevičius & others, 2020), and measuring students' psycho-emotional wellbeing (Palinauskienė & Rakauskienė, 2018). In the context of digital wellbeing, research is relevant in analysing students' preferences for using social media in their studies and in the teaching / learning process (Oleškevičienė & others, 2022), the links between students' digital competences and stress, burnout and wellbeing experienced during distance learning during the pandemic (Kumpikaitė-Valiūnienė & others, 2021), identifying features of problematic use of internet and social media technologies and developing recommendations for early diagnosis of disorders and development of interventions (Liaugaudaitė & others, 2021; Milašauskienė & others, 2021).

To summarize the researchers' insights, there have been attempts to define the concept of student wellbeing from the student's perspective, to develop a conceptual model for the analysis of digital wellbeing as a dynamic system, and to analyse the various factors contributing to student wellbeing. However, analysis of students' digital wellbeing as a system is fragmented, often limited to analysis of single detail of the system or separate HEI experience. There is little research on the need for, and impact of, interventions to support digital wellbeing. Future research would allow to analyse the elements of the dynamic digital wellbeing system presented by Vanden Abeele (2021) on the basis of the analysis of the recent scientific literature, to empirically verify the interactions between the elements of this dynamic digital wellbeing system and their impact on students' digital wellbeing, and to construct a conceptual model for the support of digital wellbeing of students in TEL environment on the basis of the results of the research.

Further research to analyse students' digital wellbeing

The links between students' digital wellbeing and psychological wellbeing encourages a wider discussion on the concept of students' digital wellbeing and its place in a holistic concept of student wellbeing. Therefore, a systematic conception of student digital wellbeing can lead to broader discussions about the balance between the use of innovative technology-based study methods and interventions to support student digital wellbeing. And the ambivalence of technology use requires an assessment of the potential benefits and harms to students' digital wellbeing of both technology and digital interventions in TEL environment.

Meanwhile, the undefined factors inherent in the elements of a digital wellbeing system (student, devices, context, use of digital media, interventions to support digital wellbeing) require more detailed analysis by identifying them in the context of teaching and learning and by determining the interactions between these factors. There is a need not only to theoretically but also to empirically assess the interactions between these factors and their impact on students' digital wellbeing and academic achievements.

More detailed research analysing the experiences of students participating in TEL environment would allow to identify the variety and characteristics of factors that contribute to students' digital wellbeing. Future research could also benefit from the experiences of lecturers who apply technology in the study process by gathering additional information on the factors of the elements of the students' digital wellbeing system.

The individual perception of digital wellbeing and its temporal variability limits research on the measurement of universal students' wellbeing and encourages discussion about individual assessment of students' digital wellbeing and the application of necessary interventions. New research methods are needed to analyse in detail the students' digital wellbeing system, its elements and their inherent factors and interactions, to search for opportunities for individualised measurement of students' digital wellbeing over time, in order to develop a universal model for supporting students' digital well-being in a TEL environment based on scientific research.

Conclusion

The multidimensionality of both student wellbeing and students' digital wellbeing has led to fragmented research on digital wellbeing, which is limited to assessing the impact of technology on student mental health. The conception of a dynamic student digital wellbeing framework provides a basis for further research by defining the factors and interactions of the elements (student, devices, context, use of digital media, interventions for supporting digital wellbeing) of this system, their impact on students' digital wellbeing and academic achievements when studies are conducted in a TEL environment. On the basis of these scientific studies, a universal model can be developed to support students' digital wellbeing in a TEL environment.

Competing interests

The author(s) has/have no competing interests to declare.

References

Ahern, S. J. (2020, November). Making a# Stepchange? Investigating the alignment of learning analytics and student wellbeing in United Kingdom higher education institutions. Frontiers in Education, 5, 531424. Frontiers Media SA.

Asad, M. M., Erum, D., Churi, P., & Guerrero, A. J. M. (2023). Effect of technostress on Psychological well-being of post-graduate students: A perspective and correlational study of Higher Education Management. International Journal of Information Management Data Insights, 3(1), 100149.

Biggins, D., & Holley, D. (2023). Designing for student wellbeing: challenging assumptions about where our students learn. Journal of Learning Development in Higher Education, 27(April).

Brailovskaia, J., Truskauskaite-Kuneviciene, I., Kazlauskas, E., & Margraf, J. (2021). The patterns of problematic social media use (SMU) and their relationship with online flow, life satisfaction, depression, anxiety and stress symptoms in Lithuania and in Germany. Current Psychology, 1-12.

Boulton, C. A., Hughes, E., Kent, C., Smith, J. R., & Williams, H. T. (2019). Student engagement and wellbeing over time at a higher education institution. PloS one, 14(11), e0225770.

Bulotaitė, L., Pociūtė, B., Bliumas, R., & Dovydaitienė, M. (2012). Socialinių mokslų studentų psichologinės gerovės, patiriamo streso ir subjektyvaus sveikatos vertinimo sąsajos. Visuomenės sveikata, 3(58), 85-92.

Burns, D., Dagnall, N. & Holt, M. (2020) Assessing the Impact of the COVID-19 Pandemic on Student Wellbeing at Universities in the United Kingdom: A Conceptual Analysis. Frontiers in Education, 5:582882. DOI: https://doi.org/10.3389/feduc.2020.582882

Butnaru, G. I., Haller, A. P., Dragolea, L. L., Anichiti, A., & Tacu Hârșan, G. D. (2021). Students' wellbeing during transition from onsite to online education: Are there risks arising from social isolation?. International journal of environmental research and public health, 18(18), 9665.

Cormack, A. N., & Reeve, D. (2022). Developing a code of practice for using data in wellbeing support. Journal of Learning Analytics, 9(2), 253-264.

Cuomo, S., Roffi, A., Luzzi, D., & Ranieri, M. (2021, October). Immersive environments in higher education: The digital well-being perspective. In ATEE Spring Conference (pp. 30-41). Cham: Springer International Publishing.

Dinu, L. M., Byrom, N. C., Mehta, K. J., Everett, S., Foster, J. L., & Dommett, E. J. (2022). Predicting student mental wellbeing and loneliness and the importance of digital skills. Journal of Further and Higher Education, 46(8), 1040-1053.

Dodd, A. L., Priestley, M., Tyrrell, K., Cygan, S., Newell, C., & Byrom, N. C. (2021). University student well-being in the United Kingdom: a scoping review of its conceptualisation and measurement. Journal of Mental Health, 30(3), 375-387.

Douwes, R., Metselaar, J., Pijnenborg, G.H.M. & Boonstra, B. (2023) Well-being of students in higher education: The importance of a student perspective, Cogent Education, 10:1, DOI: 10.1080/2331186X.2023.2190697

El Aadmi Laamech, K., Hakami, E.& Santos, Patricia & Davinia, H. L. (2022). The term well-being in Technology-Enhanced Learning: A systematic literature review. 1-6. 10.1109/SIIE56031.2022.9982319.

Golsteyn, Q. A., & Ostafichuk, P. M. (2020). Assessing and tracking the factors influencing student wellbeing in first-year engineering. Proceedings of the Canadian Engineering Education Association (CEEA).

Hakami, E., El Aadmi, K., & Hernández-Leo, D. (2021). Towards caring for digital wellbeing with the support of learning analytics. IE Comunicaciones: Revista Iberoamericana de Informática Educativa, (34), 13-29.

Havsteen-Franklin, D., Cooper, J. & Anas, S. (2023) Developing a logic model to support creative education and wellbeing in higher education, Cogent Education, 10:1, DOI: 10.1080/2331186X.2023.2214877

Holzer, J., Lüftenegger, M., Korlat, S., Pelikan, E., Salmela-Aro, K., Spiel, C., & Schober, B. (2021). Higher education in times of COVID-19: University students' basic need satisfaction, self-regulated learning, and well-being. Aera Open, 7, 23328584211003164.

Kovich, M. K., Simpson, V. L., Foli, K. J., Hass, Z., & Phillips, R. G. (2023). Application of the PERMA Model of Well-being in Undergraduate Students. International Journal of Community Well-Being, 6(1), 1-20.

Kumpikaitė-Valiūnienė, V., Aslan, I., Duobienė, J., Glińska, E., & Anandkumar, V. (2021). Influence of digital competence on perceived stress, burnout and well-being among students studying online during the COVID-19 lockdown: A 4-country perspective. Psychology research and behavior management, 1483-1498.

Liaugaudaitė, V., Griškova-Bulanova, I., Saudargienė, A., Pranckevičienė, A., Naginienė, R., Ge-čaitė-Stončienė, J., ... & Burkauskas, J. (2021). Konkursinės prioritetinių mokslinių tyrimų programos, Gerovės visuomenė "projekto "Lietuvos studentų gyvenimo kokybės rodikliai: probleminio interneto naudojimo ypatumai ir neuropsichologinis profilis"–rekomendacijos. Biologinė psichiatrija ir psichofarmakologija= Biological psychiatry and psychopharmacology, 23(2), 56 59.

Lister, K., Riva, E., Hartley, A., Waterhouse, P., Moller, N., Downes, L., Coughlan, T., Kukulska-Hulme, A., Mcpherson, E., Macdonald, I., Jones-Tinsley, S., Brown, C. & Tudor, R. (2023). Positive Digital Practices: supporting positive learner identities and student mental wellbeing in technology-enhanced higher education. Journal of Interactive Media in Education. 2023. 10.5334/jime.831.

Mendoza, A., & Venables, A. (2023). Attributes of Blended Learning Environments Designed to Foster a Sense of Belonging for Higher Education Students. Journal of Information Technology Education: Research, 22, 129–156. https://doi-org.db.kaunokolegija.lt/10.28945/5082

Milasauskiene, E., Burkauskas, J., Podlipskyte, A., Király, O., Demetrovics, Z., Ambrasas, L., & Steibliene, V. (2021). Compulsive internet use scale: Psychometric properties and associations with sleeping patterns, mental health, and well-being in Lithuanian medical students during the coronavirus disease 2019 pandemic. Frontiers in psychology, 12, 685137.

Moldavan, A. M., Edwards-Leis, C., & Murray, J. (2022). Design and pedagogical implications of a digital learning platform to promote well-being in teacher education. Teaching and Teacher Education, 115, 103732.

Oleškevičienė, G. V., Puodžiukaitienė, Ž., & Arbutavičius, G. (2022). Socialinės medijos aukštajame moksle: studentų palankumas socialinių medijų naudojimui. Social Inquiry into Well-Being, 20(2).

Palinauskienė, L. R., & Rakauskienė, V. (2018). Kolegijos studentų psichoemocinė savijauta. Taikomieji tyrimai studijose ir praktikoje, 110-117.

Peacock, S., & Cowan, J. (2019). Promoting sense of belonging in online learning communities of inquiry in accredited courses. Online Learning, 23(2), 67–81. https://doi.org/10.24059/olj.v23i2.1488

Polat, H., & Karabatak, S. (2022). Effect of flipped classroom model on academic achievement, academic satisfaction and general belongingness. Learning Environments Research, 25(1), 159-182. https://doi.org/10.1007/s10984-021-09355-0

Priestley, M., Hall, A., Wilbraham, S. J., Mistry, V., Hughes, G., & Spanner, L. (2022). Student perceptions and proposals for promoting wellbeing through social relationships at university. Journal of Further and Higher Education, 46(9), 1243-1256.

Rad, D., Rad, G., Demeter, E., & Maier, R. (2022). Digital wellbeing or finding a balance between consciously connecting and disconnecting: A positive technology design approach. 10.3726/b19309.

Roffarello, A. M., & De Russis, L. (2023). Achieving digital wellbeing through digital self-control tools: A systematic review and meta-analysis. ACM Transactions on Computer-Human Interaction, 30(4), 1-66.

Rugevičius, M., Kairys, A., Čepienė, R., Liniauskaitė, A., Brazdeikienė, L., & Žakaitis, P. (2020). Studentų akademinės motyvacijos pokyčiai ir jų sąsajos su akademiniais pasiekimais, pasitenkinimu studijomis bei psichologine gerove. Pedagogika/Pedagogy, 137(1), 5-24.

Taylor, J.; Salvagno, M.; Morris, R.; Hutchings, M.; Bobeva, M. (2018). Evaluating and measuring how new technologies and ubiquitous connectivity affect university students' psychosocial wellbeing. Psychology Teaching Review, Vol. 24 Issue 1, 21-34, 14p; DOI: 10.53841/bpsptr.2018.24.1.21, Database: Education Source Ultimate

Thomas, N., Choudhari, S., Gaidhane, A. & Quazi Syed, Z. (2022). 'Digital Wellbeing': The Need of the Hour in Today's Digitalized and Technology Driven World!. Cureus. 14. 10.7759/cureus.27743.

Turner, L., Bewick, B.M., Kent, S., Khyabani, A., Bryant, L. & Summers, B. (2021). When Does a Lot Become Too Much? A Q Methodological Investigation of UK Student Perceptions of Digital Addiction. International Journal of Environmental Research and Public Health, 23; 18(21):11149. doi: 10.3390/ijerph182111149. PMID: 34769664; PMCID: PMC8583480.

Vanden Abeele, M. M. (2021). Digital wellbeing as a dynamic construct. Communication Theory, 31(4), 932-955.

Wang, X., Li, Z., Ouyang, Z., & Xu, Y. (2021). The Achilles Heel of Technology: How Does Technostress Affect University Students' Wellbeing and Technology-Enhanced Learning. International Journal of Environmental Research and Public Health. 18(23):12322. https://doi.org/10.3390/ijerph182312322

White, W., & Sangster, P. (2022). Exploring Wellbeing and Remote Learning Using the Delphi Method: Engaging Teacher Education Students as Co-Producers of Practice. Journal of Teacher Education and Educators, 11(1), 7–32.

Best Practices for Integrating Artificial Intelligence in Higher Education

Martha Lorena Obermeier[1]

[1] Escuela de Lenguas, Campus Tapachula, Universidad Autónoma de Chiapas, México; lorena.obermeier@gmail.com

Correspondence: Martha Lorena Obermeier: lorena.obermeier@gmail.com

Abstract:

Anytime a new technology has been developed, it has been integrated into education. All these advances have traditionally raised concerns. Artificial Intelligence (AI) is the next generation of technology that is already being included in educational contexts. It has also raised several concerns that will be presented in this paper. An umbrella review of the literature was conducted and the studies were analyzed using a meta-analysis review to answer the research question: what are the best practices for integrating AI in Higher Education (HE) institutions? Suggestions and best practices for AI inclusion in HE institutions are presented, as well as ethical concerns to observe.

Keywords: Artificial Intelligence, Higher Education, Ethics.

Introduction

Education can foster students' talents especially when teaching to enhance their abilities. AI tutoring systems can be a tool to personalize education and make it more effective (Bhutoria, 2022). The inclusion of AI in HE promises a paradigm shift for personalized learning, but it has also raised many concerns (Fowler, 2023). The integration of technology in education started in the 1960s with intelligent tutoring systems and adaptive platforms. A gap regarding the lack of a pedagogical perspective to use AI in HE was found in the literature.

Artificial Intelligence

AI technology imitates human-like abilities like decision-making (Memarian & Doleck, 2023). It has adaptative behaviors and it is able to learn from the environment (Hinojo-Lucena et al., 2019). This ability to learn and change education through the imitation of human cognitive tasks brings out many concerns over ethics (Chu et al., 2022). AI has been successfully used in education as a communication channel, assessment tool, and student' monitor, among others. This is a tool that helps to perform administrative and repetitive tasks (Shestakova, 2021). Crompton and Burke (2023) found out that AI has four main uses: performance predictor, materials recommendation, assessment, and learning improvement. It can identify students lagging and offer information to avoid dropouts. As an automated grader, grades are instant and bias-free. As a chatbot, it provides instant valuable information. As a proctor, it ensures students' legitimacy to take evaluations. These simple tasks can be performed with AI as they are automated, but more complex tasks that demand more capability are not yet performed by AI. This technology remotely tracks and manages the learning process, which can relieve teachers' workload (Chaka, 2023; Salas-Pilco & Yang, 2022; Zawacki-Richter et al., 2019). As it analyses student involvement in a course, it can identify at-risk of dropping out students and suggest an intervention for their learning needs (Chen et al., 2022).

Concerns About AI

AI raises concerns about fairness, accountability transparency of use, and accessibility, as well as cheating and fraud in academic activities (Holmes et al., 2021; Memarian & Doleck, 2023). This tool demands huge volumes of particularly sensitive data, which threatens users' privacy and protection of the data. The main concern is that data related to identity is confidential and highly personal. Chen et al. (2022) suggest transparent institutional data practices of data use. Lo (2023) also mentions that institutions must establish clear guidelines about academic integrity and the potential risks of using AI. As some authors have stated, this tool can also generate incorrect or false information (Michalak, 2023; Zhang et al., 2021). Instructors need to teach students to use sources provided by AI and validate them.

The data obtained can reduce teachers' workload as it can make better-informed decisions related to course management, assessment, feedback, and plagiarism checking. Zawacki-Richter et al. (2019) also mention that many instructors are reluctant to use AI, as it is considered a threat to their pertinence in an institution. On the other hand, the information collected by AI about student performance detects risks to learners and provides suggestions to adapt teaching methods (Chu et al., 2022). The studies found in the literature review show a lack of evidence of how pedagogical learning theories are related to the use of AI educational technology.

Another concern related to the use of AI is the environmental impact it can have. The production of the hardware terminal devices consumes natural resources and its use demands a high energy consumption. In addition, the discarding of those devices can also cause pollution. For all those reasons, Huang et al. (2023) suggest that there should be clear guidelines for building sustainable and ethical AI. The use of AI should be described in a guideline that considers social responsibility and respect for human rights (Michalak, 2023).

Eaton (2023) explains that AI tools can have an impact on academic literacy skills, learning, and assessment. They can be used to write texts and this can be considered plagiarism and other threats to academic integrity. The main purpose of education is for students to acquire knowledge and demonstrate it through academic texts or presentations. The texts presented by students using AI tools do not represent their true level of understanding (Cotton et al., 2023). In the words of Chomsky, using AI tools for writing is high-tech plagiarism EduKitchen (as cited in Eaton, 2023).

Even if AI raises all these concerns, it can also be helpful to pair up students' skills and knowledge with the specific demands of employers (Alam & Mohanty, 2022). Another advantage is that the algorithms used in AI are efficient and precise at making judgments and evaluations. For Chaka (2023), robotic applications of AI can be used to develop soft skills, like communication, collaboration, and critical thinking. These soft skills are also called 21st-century skills and are highly appreciated in the labor market.

Soft Skills

For Mwita et al. (2023), soft skills are a combination of cognitive, metacognitive, interpersonal, and intellectual skills. These skills are needed to perform efficiently and are highly demanded by employers. For Rosidah et al. (2022), soft skills are also called 21st-century skills. They are conformed with critical thinking, problem-solving, leadership, adaptability, communication, and analysis. The skills are transferred to real-life situations using metacognition, correcting mistakes, and enhancing creativity. Volkova et al. (2022) add that they are also called employability skills, non-professional skills, life skills, or 21st-century skills. These authors classify them into three groups: social and communication skills, cognitive skills, and components of emotional intelligence.

Nowadays employers look for employees with both professional and soft skills. Qizi (2020) considers that people with soft skills are flexible, persuasive, and communicate well with others. They can also work well in teams, learn from others, and accept their own growth needs. Rosidah et al. (2022) mention that a person with developed soft skills performs well on a task as he feels accepted and confident. Professional skills are considered in the curriculum but it does not focus on soft skills, even if they are highly needed to succeed.

Threats to Deep Learning

AI has also been used to select learning activities and generate educational materials or textbooks. Algabri et al. (2021) consider that smart textbooks can generate more in-depth knowledge. Nevertheless, Mackinnon and Shade (2020) state that the use of technology is the main reason for the lack of concentration in the classroom as it can make psychological and social changes. Students' attention span has decreased and as a consequence, their awareness level is shorter. Newport (2016) also mentions that deep learning needs long periods of concentration but communicational technologies are a constant distractor. Deep concentration is needed to read, learn, and perform creative activities. It is now rare to achieve this state as reading on screens creates distractions, hinders analytic abilities, and aggravates the cognitive load (Carr, 2010).

Performing thinking activities develops the human brain. As people solve problems through thinking, neuronal networks and creativity increase. Developing higher-order skills, like critical analysis, interpretation, and synthesis is one of the objectives of education. The ability of AI applications to perform academic literacy activities has raised concerns among faculty and educational institutions (Ipek et al., 2023). This application can produce written texts, answer questions, translate languages, summarize books, and paraphrase ideas. These are all higher-level academic literacy skills mainly developed and performed in academic contexts.

Faculty and Higher Education institutions are concerned that students may use the application and engage in fraudulent activities. Even if these AI applications are considered negative, they have advantages as reducing time conducting literature searches and cataloging sources. Heberer et al. (2023) conducted a study on the use of ChatGPT to write a literature review. These authors selected articles and asked this tool to write a literature review based on the resumes of the articles selected. As a result, the text was adequate but lacked the desired level of human scholar writing. The use of this tool can help scholars produce texts, but it does not help build critical thinking and problem-solving skills. Zhai (2022) also produced a text using the AI tool and the work demanded very low professional knowledge, which reduced the intelligence workload needed.

Method

AI is being incorporated in HE and other domains, even though there are many concerns about its use. The research question that guided this study was: what are the best practices for integrating AI in HE institutions? The terms artificial intelligence, best practices, and ethics in AI were used to conduct the literature review. The search was conducted using the EBSCO databases. As most of the studies published up to date on AI are systematical reviews, the research design of the study was an umbrella review. The inclusion criteria were studies about AI in education, written in English and published from 2019 to 2023. The umbrella review summarizes results from systematic reviews to discover what is already known and the research gaps (Booth et al., 2016). According to Newman and Gough (2020), this type of review is a tertiary level of analysis, and it is an efficient method to examine previous research.

The method to analyze the qualitative pieces of evidence was the meta-narrative review, which uses a historical perspective to make sense of the literature. This approach is a well fit for an open exploratory phase (Booth et al., 2016). The method used to analyze the information in the systematic review improves the understanding of the knowledge developed of a topic (Newman & Gough, 2020).

Results

The studies included in the umbrella review consider the uses of AI in different aspects of HE. Some of them focus on instructional design, ethical aspects, administrative tasks, and even on scientific production. As shown in Table 1, China is the country with more publications on the topic. It can also be observed that none of the publications come from Latin American countries. The topics of the systematic reviews are general concerning different aspects of HE institutions as ethical implications, use of applications, publications, benefits, challenges, and potential risks.

Table 1: Systematic Reviews Included in the Umbrella Review

Authors and date of publication	Country	Topics and focus of the systematic review
Hinojo-Lucena et al (2019)	Spain	Status of scientific production on AI.
Zawacki-Richter et al (2019)	Germany	Development of AI publications and ethical implications.
Alam & Mohanty (2022)	India	Evolution of articles on AI, ethical concerns, and challenges.
Chen et al (2022)	China	Trends and topics on AI bibliometric.
Chu et al (2022)	Taiwan	Purposes, applications, and authors on AI in HE.
Salas-Pilco & Yang (2022)	China	Use, techniques, and issues of AI in Latin America HE.
Chaka (2023)	South Africa	Application and challenges of AI use in HE

Crompton & Burke (2023)	USA	Benefits and challenges of AI in HE.
Ipek et al (2023)	Greece	Subject areas affected by AI applications. Benefits and ethical concerns.
Lo (2023)	China	AI applications' performance and potential issues.

Research gaps

The topics of the studies express mostly concerns about the use of AI in HE, while the focus of the review was to find out the best practices for its integration. One of the research gaps observed is that most of the studies do not present an explicit pedagogical perspective. In the studies analyzed, there is also a lack of clear best practices to include AI in HE. A bias against the use of AI was also perceived. Most of the studies present concerns about how it can affect students' cognitive development, threaten faculty's positions, and misconduct data and privacy.

Bartolomé et al. (2018) state that the idea of personalization is rooted in the tradition of pupil-centered pedagogies. Technology Enhanced Adaptative Learning Environments (TEALE) considers four aspects for an educational implementation of technology: epistemological nature, psychological approach, didactic materialization, and technological approach. These four elements consider the idea of how knowledge is improved, what theory of learning is being followed, the elements of the implementation, and the use of technological elements.

For Hew et al. (2019), even if the field of instructional technology has developed and gained importance, it is criticized as methodologically weak and under-theorized. The use of theories allows to understand a phenomenon or explain how to improve learning experiences. Studies framed into a theory are considered high-quality research, as theory has the ability to solve problems in different contexts. The use of theory can be explanatory or design theory. The first one explains the reasons affecting learning or behavior. The design theories focus on what elements should be included to achieve certain learning outcomes. Educational technology is related to other knowledge areas and that is the reason why it is based on theories from other fields. As a result, many research studies use theory to explain issues, but their results do not contribute to theory advancement. The Cognitive theory of multimedia learning can be used to present materials to not hinder students' cognitive processes. Vygotsky's social development theory can be used to explain epistemic engagement or how social interaction influences cognitive development. Self-regulated learning theory can explain the development of learner self-direction skills to complete a task.

Conclusions

Universities could integrate AI tools and high-quality instruction to relieve faculty from repetitive and time-consuming activities (Kelly & Columbus, 2020). Most instructors consider AI as a threat to their jobs, but it could be seen as a tool to alleviate time-consuming activities and allow them to focus on more pedagogical tasks. Minimization of data collection could prevent privacy issues related to AI (Zhang et al., 2021).

A concern found in the literature was regarding the impact of AI on higher-order thinking skills. Most authors consider that technology materials cause distractions and reduce students' attention spans. Sustained attention has been found as a main element in acquiring knowledge. The use of the tool for writing academic texts should be reconsidered. It cannot be relied on to write scientific texts if it invents references (Willems, 2023).

Course design using AI tools will need to be framed into a pedagogical approach. The integration of technology in an educational context should always be made by having a theory to support its use. AI should encourage students to be creative and develop critical thinking skills. The focus of AI integration should be to alleviate repetitive tasks and foster deep learning.

Suggestions

Educators need to adjust learning goals, tasks, and evaluations to develop cognitive, social, and emotional skills (Zhai, 2022). They need to develop assessment activities that make students describe feelings and demonstrate learning, promoting critical thinking (Cotton et al., 2023). Both educators and students will need training to integrate and use AI as a tool, instead of as a replacement to conduct their academic tasks. Learning or knowledge can be demonstrated when engaged in group discussion, or the application of skills. Students cannot rely on AI tools when asked to inquire about a topic, make their research questions, or defend an argument.

Institutions need to develop policies and procedures to use AI tools as support instead of replacement of students' and faculty's activities. The integration of AI in HE can offer many advantages, but it should be done considering ethical and theoretical principles. Huang et al. (2023) suggest the following clear principles of use:

1. Transparency. Justification of use, a detailed implementation process, and possible outcome.
2. Fairness and Justice. Avoid discrimination and bias.
3. Responsibility and Accountability. Actors involved in the design of AI tools should be considered responsible for any negative outcome.
4. Nonmaleficence. Protect the human dignity.
5. Privacy. Data privacy and protection.
6. Beneficence. A clear description of the benefits.
7. Freedom and Autonomy. Respect freedom to use it.
8. Solidarity. Provide security to all communities.
9. Sustainability. Avoid environmental harm.

References

Alam, A., & Mohanty, A. (2022). Foundation for the Future of Higher Education or 'Misplaced Optimism'? Being Human in the Age of Artificial Intelligence. In: M. Panda et al. Innovations in Intelligent Computing and Communication. ICIICC 2022. Communications in Computer and Information Science, vol 1737. Springer, Cham. https://doi.org/10.1007/978-3-031-23233-6_2

Algabri, H.K., Kharade, K.G., & Kamat, R.K. (2021). Promise, threats, and personalization in Higher Education with artificial intelligence. Webology, 18(6), 2129-2139.

Bartolomé, A., Castañeda, L., & Adell, J. (2018). Personalization in educational technology: the absence of underlying pedagogies. International Journal of Educational Technology in Higher Education, 15(14), 1-17.

Booth, A., Sutton, A., & Papaioannou, D. (2016). Systematic Approaches to a Successful Literature Review (2nd.ed.). Sage Publications.

Bhutoria, A. (2022). Personalized education and Artificial Intelligence in the United States, China and India: A systematic review using a Human-in-the-loop model. Computers and Education: Artificial Intelligence, 3, 1-18.

Carr, N. (2010). What the internet is doing to our brains. The shallows. Norton.

Chaka, C. (2023). Fourth industrial revolution –a review of applications, prospepcts, and challenges for artificial intelligence, robotics and blockchain in higher education. Research and Practice in Technology Enhaced Learning, 18(2), 1-39.

Chen, X., Zou, D., Xie, H., Cheng, G., & Liu, C. (2022). Two Decades of Artificial Intelligence in Education: Contributors, Collaborations, Research Topics, Challenges, and Future Directions. Educational Technology & Society, 25(1), 28–47. https://www.jstor.org/stable/48647028

Chu, H.C., Hwang, G.H., Tu, Y.F., & Yang, K.H. (2022). Roles and research trends of artificial intelligence in higher education: A systematic review of the top 50 most-cited articles. Australasian Journal of Educational Technology, 38(3), 22–42. https://doi.org/10.14742/ajet.7526

Cotton, D.R.E., Cotton, P.A., & Shipway, R. (2023). Chatting and cheating: ensuring academic integrity in the era of ChatGPT. Innovations in Education and Teaching International, 1-11. https://doi.org/10.1080/14703297.2023.2190148

Crompton, H., & Burke, D. (2023). Artificial intelligence in higher education: the state of the field. International Journal of Educational Technology in Higher Education, 20(22), 1-22.

Eaton, S.E. (2023). Postplagiarism: transdisciplinary ethics and integrity in the age of artificial intelligence and neurotechnology. International Journal for Educational Integrity, 19(23), 1-10. https://doi.org/10.1007/s40979-023-00144-1

Fowler, D. (2023). AI in Higher education: academic integrity, harmony of insights, and recommendations. Journal of Ethics in Higher Education, 3, 127-143.

Heberer, D., Pisano, A., Markson, C., & ChatGPT. (2023). As cited by the artificial intelligence of ChatGPT: best practices on technology integration in Higher Education. Journal of Leadership and Instruction, 22(1), 8-12.

Hew K.F., Lan M., Tang Y., Jia C., & Lo C.K. (2019). Where is the "theory" within the field of educational technology research? British Journal of Educational Technology, 50(3), 956–971.

Hinojo-Lucena, F.J., Aznar-Díaz, I., Cáceres-Reche, M.P., & Romero-Rodríguez, J.M. (2019). Artificial intelligence in Higher Education: a bibliometric study on its impact in the scientific literature. Education Sciences, 9(51), 1-9.

Holmes, W., Porayska-Pomsta, K., Holstein, K. et al. (2022). Ethics of AI in Education: Towards a Community-Wide Framework. International Journal of Artificial Intelligence in Education, 32, 504–526. https://doi.org/10.1007/s40593-021-00239-1

Huang, C., Zhang, Z., Mao, B., & Yao, X. (2023). An overview of artificial intelligence ethics. IEEE Transactions on Artificial Intelligence, 4(4), 799-819. https://ieeexplore.ieee.org/document/9844014

Ipek, Z.H., Gözüm, A.İ .C., Papadakis, S., & Kallogiannakis, M. (2023). Educational Applications of the ChatGPT AI System: A Systematic Review Research. Educational Process: International Journal, 12(3): 26-55.

Kelly, A., & Columbus, R. (2020). College in the time of coronavirus. Challenges facing American Higher Education. American Enterprise Institute. http://www.jstor.org/stable/resrep25358

Lo, C.K. (2023). What is the impact of ChatGPT on Education? A rapid review of the literature. Education Sciences, 13(410), 1-15. https://doi.org/10.3390/educsci13040410

Mackinnon, K., & Shade, L. R. (2020). God only knows what it's doing to our children's brains: a closer look at internet addiction discourse. Jeunesse: Young People, Texts, Cultures, 12(1), 16-38.

Memarian, B., & Doleck, T. (2023). Fairness, accountability, transparency, and ethics (FATE) in artificial intelligence (AI) and Higher Education: a systematic review. Computers and Education: Artificial Intelligence, 5(100152), 1-12. https://doi.org/10.1016/j.caeai.2023.100152

Michalak, R. (2023). From Ethics to Execution: The Role of Academic Librarians in Artificial Intelligence (AI) Policy-Making at Colleges and Universities. Journal of Library Administration, 63(7), 928-938. https://doi.org/10.1080/01930826.2023.2262367

Mwita, K.M., Kinunda, S., Obwolo, S., & Mwilongo, N.H. (2023). Soft skills development in higher education institutions: students' perceived role of universities and students' self-initiatives in bridging the soft skills gap. Research in Business & Social Science, 12(3), 505-513. https://doi.org/10.20525/ijrbs.v12i3.2435

Newman, M., & Gough, D. (2020). Systematic reviews in educational research: methodology, perspectives and application. In O. Zawacki-Richter, M. Kerres, S. Bedenlier, M. Bond & K. Buntins (Eds.), Systematic Reviews in Educational Research. Methodology, Perspectives and Application (pp. 2-21). Springer VS.

Newport, C. (2016). Deep work. Rules for focused success in a distracted world. Grand Central Publishing.

Qizi, K.N.U. (2020). Soft skills development in Higher Education. Universal Journal of Educational Research, 8(5), 1916-1925.

Rosidah, R., Sasmita, N., Wisataone, V., & Hanafi, M. (2022). Character development strategies through the soft skills training to students for job readiness. Journal of Social Studies, 18(2), 207-216.

Salas-Pilco, S.Z., & Yang, Y. (2022). Artificial intelligence applications in Latin American higher education: a systematic review. International Journal of Educational Technology in Higher Education, 19(21). https://doi.org/10.1186/s41239-022-00326-w

Shestakova, V. (2021). Best practices to mitigate bias and discrimination in artificial intelligence. Performance Improvement, 60(6), 6-11.

Volkova, N., Zinukova, N., Vlasenko, K., Korobeinikova, T. (2022). Development and mastery of soft skills among graduate students. Ukranian Journal of Educational Studies and Information Technology, 10(4), 1-14.

Willems, J. (January 20, 2023). ChatGPT at Universities – The Least of Our Concerns. Available at: http://dx.doi.org/10.2139/ssrn.4334162

Zhai, X. (December 27, 2022). ChatGPT User Experience: Implications for Education. Available at http://dx.doi.org/10.2139/ssrn.4312418

Zhang, T., Qin, Y., & Li, Q. (2021). Trusted Artificial Intelligence: Technique Requirements and Best Practices. In 2021 IEEE 20th International Conference on Trust, Security and Privacy in Computing and Communications (TrustCom), Shenyang, China. Doi: https://ieeexplore.ieee.org/document/9724346

Zawacki-Richter, O., Marín, V.I., Bond, M., Gouverneur, F. (2019). Systematic review of research on artificial intelligence applications in higher education – where are the educators? International Journal of Educational Technology in Higher Education, 16(39). https://doi.org/10.1186/s41239-019-0171-0

Teaching with Generative AI: moving forward with content creation

Thomas Daniel Ullmann[1], Duygu Bektik[1], Chris Edwards[1], Christothea Herodotou[1], Denise Whitelock[1]

[1] Institute of Educational Technology, The Open University, United Kingdom; thomas.ullmann@open.ac.uk, {firstname} dot {lastname} at open.ac.uk

Correspondence: Thomas Daniel Ullmann: thomas.ullmann@open.ac.uk

Abstract:

Generative AI is widely available and has raised the expectation that it will impact Education. Models, such as ChatGPT, can quickly produce plausible texts on a wide range of topics, and this capability may be of potential use in course content production. This paper selects several important course content production tasks, describes the prompts used, and assesses the quality of the automatically generated texts by a team of experts. Across all tasks, the Generative AI produced content that could help solve specific tasks by aiding with brainstorming, creating outlines, and adhering to particular writing guidance. In all cases, the content required adjustments and checking by human experts.

Keywords: course production; course content; generative AI; ChatGPT; natural language generation; educational technology

Introduction

Generative Artificial Intelligence, with its easy-to-use interfaces and widespread availability, has led us to investigate its potential for course content production. This paper provides expert reflections on the quality of AI-generated content for typical tasks during course production. It showcases prompts for supporting several course content production tasks, evaluates the quality of prompt completions, and outlines relevant prompt engineering strategies.

During the last few years, an increasing use of AI in Education, especially in developed countries, has been observed (Tahiru, 2021). Empirical studies have mainly focused on Higher Education and K-12 and investigated AI applications, including chatbots and expert systems, intelligent tutors, machine learning, personalised learning systems and visualisations in K12 and Higher Education (Zhang & Aslan, 2021).

Within the last year, Generative AI and tools such as ChatGPT became widely available and started another AI boom. Their capability to produce plausible text about a wide variety of topics in an interactive way sparked interest within the educational community as it potentially offers a variety of possibilities for Education (Bektik et al., accepted; Sharples, 2023). For example, Liu et al. (2023) reported that ChatGPT can support teachers in generating exercises, quizzes, and scenarios for student evaluation. The review by Chen et al. (2023) on AI in Education, using a qualitative research approach, found that AI systems have enabled the customisation and personalisation of curriculum and content according to students' needs, leading to improved learning experiences and overall educational quality.

Furthermore, various companies and universities have developed AI-powered tools, all of which claim to support the generation of curriculum. For example, several Moodle Plugins now support Generative AI. The EduWeaver research demonstration creates course content based on a few parameters (Aneesha, 2023). Blackboard's AI Design Assistant, TeacherMatic, Course AI, Coursera AI, and others offer support tools for teachers.

Despite potential benefits, AI does come with significant challenges, such as high cost and scalability, requiring new literacies and actionable guidelines for educators, ethical and data privacy issues related to student data, and inappropriate uses of AI (Zhai et al., 2021; Zhang & Aslan, 2021). ChatGPT, in particular, raises issues of integrity, accuracy, and credibility, such as producing scientific essays from a mixture of true and fabricated information (Alkaissi & McFarlane, 2023). Such observations highlight the importance of human input and expertise in moderating and validating AI outputs and the need for clear policies and guidelines on how AI-generated content should be managed (Adeshola & Adepoju, 2023).

The introduction of Generative AI has the potential to, at least, disrupt the processes in place for creating curriculum. Each institution will have its own framework in place and need to consider whether this technology has a role and, if so, what this role might be and what benefits can be achieved for an institution, its staff, and, of course, the students who study the courses.

The Open University is one of the largest online providers of Higher Education globally and an early developer of a team approach to curriculum production. This method brings together academics and other colleagues to produce tested, high-quality learning materials in various formats. Within the team, there have been several consistent roles, such as the academic lead, authors, editors, artists, and reviewers, and new roles have been created as formats evolved. These include multimedia developers and programmers. One of the main reasons for using this approach to curriculum development is that each course is intended to have a life of several years, and the investment is made to ensure high quality from the start.

The use of learning outcomes (LOs) became a requirement during the 2000s, and in 2013, the university codified the process of learning design (LD). This was partly to make it easier for colleagues, particularly those new to curriculum development, to make the right contribution. It also ensured the full integration of the constructive alignment (Biggs, 2014) between LOs, materials, and assessment and more rigorous consideration of the range of learners through personas. LD supports the full range of courses, including continuing professional development (CPD), microcredential, short, undergraduate, and masters level courses. As microcredentials are the newest format of courses, each of ours with 7.5 ECTS credits, we used examples of steps from creating these courses within this paper (see Table 1). This paper focuses on a few important curriculum development elements to begin revealing the value of Generative AI to Higher Education.

Table 1: Course production elements

Course production elements	Brief description
The big question and learning outcomes	What is the course's big question? What are course learning outcomes?
Assessment strategy	How many assessment points are needed? What is the topic and format of the assessment? What are the grading criteria?
Course outline	What is the big question of each week? Which topics are covered in each week?
Course content and activities (weekly)	Types of activities following the Learning Design (LD) framework Content format: e.g., audio, video, text, quiz, forum.
Assessing and enhancing inclusive language	Use prompts from the Inclusive Curriculum Design Tool to assess the quality of produced material.
Respond to reviewers' comments and queries.	Improve content accordingly
Review content for permissions (media, etc)	Acknowledge the use of GenAI if applicable.
Copy editing	Final check for typos, tone, style, etc

The literature review and the latest developments of eLearning vendors showed that several researchers and practitioners expect that Generative AI will influence teaching practices, including course material production.

However, it is unclear how Generative AI can support teachers to create course content. In this paper, we show how Generative AI can support important elements of course content production and report on expert evaluations of the quality of the generated content.

Method

For each course production task outlined in Table 1, we envisioned a role for the AI within a course writing team. Our aim was not to replace the course writing team but to explore tasks where AI could potentially be of use. For each task, one of the authors generated and adapted several prompts and produced a first list of observations. We instantiated ChatGPT via Microsoft's Azure OpenAI with version 4.0 of ChatGPT (1106-Preview, standard deployment, capacity of 10K tokens per minute, temperature of 0.5, max tokens set to 800, top p set to 0.95, frequency penalty and presence penalty were set to 0, and there was no stop flag). We used ChatGPT via the university's approved Microsoft Azure subscription, as this guaranteed that copyrighted and otherwise protected university materials would not be used to train future models of ChatGPT. We did not fine-tune the model on the university data or use Retrieval Augmented Generation (RAG), meaning that all contents generated come from ChatGPT, not the university.

For each task, we constructed prompts for ChatGPT. A prompt is a message that is sent to the AI engine and to which the AI generates a completion. The completion is the response from the AI in continuation of the prompt text. We wrote several prompts for each task until we found a usable completion. Not every prompt returned a satisfying response. For example, the completion was vague or captured a different intent. Therefore, some experimentation was required to construct successful prompts. Our prompt engineering took into account available general guidance but also took inspiration from domain-related prompts publicised by other researchers. In line with general guidance, we used the following principles: using detailed information, providing examples, splitting complex tasks into several smaller tasks[1], chain of thought prompting (i.e. provision of recipe-like instructions), and adding/repeating instructions at the end of a prompt[2]. We also consulted domain-specific prompts, such as those suggested in the GitHub repository 'Prompts for Education, ' which showcases several prompts, such as a prompt for planning lessons or assignment ideation. The domain-specific prompts were particularly useful as they provided a sense of the structure and depth of a good prompt.

Once this phase of the work was completed, the new text was shown to a course production expert, an academic expert, two Learning Design experts, and an AI expert, who commented on the quality of the prompts and their suitability in teaching and the initial observations and agreed on their interpretations. The results section illustrates the prompts for selected tasks, a summary of the completion, and the main observations shared by the expert team.

Results

We show generative AI prompts and responses to three of the elements of course production (see Table 1), which are about generating big questions, learning activities, and inclusive curriculum. Due to the word limit, we selected only three of the cases that highlight and discuss important characteristics of generative AI pertinent to the context of course production.

Task: Big questions of a course and learning outcomes

The topic chosen for the course was Data Science. One of the first tasks among a physical writing course team is to discuss the salient content and define the learning outcomes. Here, we envisioned the AI producing an initial list of big learning questions and learning outcomes for the course team to review. The prompts and responses from ChatGPT to illustrate the progress made in this respect are produced as a dialogue in abbreviated form below.

We trialled several prompts, such as one big prompt for the whole task or using brief descriptions. After some experimentation, we found that using two prompts and adding extra information, such as asking for generating examples, yielded better completions.

---

[1] https://platform.openai.com/docs/guides/prompt-engineering/six-strategie

[2] https://learn.microsoft.com/en-us/azure/ai-services/openai/concepts/advanced-prompt-engineering?pivots=programming-language-chat-completions

The first prompt was: 'For a data science apprenticeship course, I am looking for big ideas in this area to hook my students in. Can you give me examples of such ideas?'. ChatGPT's response started with this opening statement: 'Certainly! Data science is a dynamic and impactful field with many big ideas that can captivate students. Here are several concepts that could serve as hooks to engage your apprentices' and then listed fifteen big Data Science ideas such as 'Ethics and Bias in Data: Discuss the ethical considerations of data collection and analysis, including privacy concerns and the potential for Bias in algorithms that can lead to discrimination', or 'Quantum Computing and the Future of Data Science'.

The second prompt then drilled into the generated Ethics and Bias topic: 'Can you create learning outcomes for the topic Ethics and Bias in Data?' and ChatGPT responded with eight examples of learning outcomes, such as 'Understand the Ethical Principles in Data Science' with the two learning outcomes 'Recognise the fundamental ethical principles that guide data science practices, including respect for privacy, consent, transparency, and accountability', and 'Discuss the importance of ethical considerations throughout the data lifecycle, from collection to analysis and reporting'. Another suggested learning outcome was, for example, 'Reflect on Personal and Professional Responsibility'.

The team of experts concluded that all the presented topics did express big Data Science ideas and that a course production team could use the generated topics as an initial set of potential topics for a course. They also noted that not all topics would be suitable for a specific course, and the course creator would need to decide whether to include or exclude a topic, such as 'Quantum computing'.

The second prompt created learning outcomes for one of the ideas, 'Ethics and Bias in Data'. The experts concluded that AI developed several plausible learning outcomes that may help the course creator with the ideation of learning outcomes. They also noted that the learning outcomes are not written to the standards required by the university and would need to be changed, for example, to adhere to the learning outcomes for the qualification or the levels framework.

Task: Create learning activities

During course production, the learning designers encourage the course team to use a variety of learning activities, especially more active activities, such as communicative or practice activities. For this task, we envision the AI proposing learning activities for a given topic that follows a specific Learning Design framework (Rienties & Toetenel, 2016) for the course team to consider.

After trialling several prompts, we found three successive prompts as useful for the task. The first prompt set up the interaction by asking the teacher about the subject matter. The second prompt provided information about the topic for which the assistant should find suitable activities. The third prompt asked the assistant to find activities for each of the five activity types of the LDS activity framework.

Here, we show the final prompt, which started with 'Can you please create one activity idea for the following five activity types:' followed by a list of all four activity types, such as 'Communicative activity: Students discuss with others by communicating, debating, discussing, arguing, sharing, reporting, collaborating, presenting, and questioning'.

The AI responded with ideas for all five activity types. For the communicative activity type, it suggested an Ethics Fishbowl Discussion with the following activity: 'Organise a 'fishbowl' discussion where a small group of students sits in an inner circle and discusses a topic related to ethics and Bias in data while the rest of the class observes. After a set time, new students rotate into the discussion. Topics can include the ethical use of data in different industries, the balance between innovation and privacy, and how to mitigate Bias in machine learning models'. Another generated activity was a practice activity about a Data Ethics Role-Play Simulation.

The expert assessment was that the AI could generate a list of plausible ideas for each activity type, yet these can be generic. For example, the example above does not provide details of how group discussion outcomes should be recorded and merged across teams. The course team would need to evaluate the usefulness of the ideas for their course and produce additional guidelines not included in the response. Also, some of the generated ideas may not be applicable within the context of a distance learning institution where students communicate mostly online.

Task: inclusive curriculum

The task assigned to the AI is to adapt produced materials according to the university's guidelines on inclusive curriculum. The inclusive curriculum guidance recommends a comprehensive checklist, such as considering student and staff feedback, assessing diversity, and access. Not all tasks listed in this guidance seemed suitable for Generative AI, but there were promising ones, such as writing in Plain English or using inclusive language. Here, we show how Generative AI was used to make a text from a United Nations tutorial on inclusive language3 more inclusive. We chose the text from the tutorial as it allows us to compare the output of the Generative AI with the expert annotations.

The prompt began with instructions that stated that the example text should be rewritten. It was followed by the text to rewrite: 'Rewrite this text using inclusive language and explain it: Anyone who sees the terrible images of Country Y can only be touched in his heart. The crisis is manmade. (...). She met with the most relevant parties, (...)' (note that the prompt was abbreviated). The completion of the prompt returned this rewritten text: 'Anyone who sees the devastating images from Country Y can only be moved at heart. The crisis is a result of human actions. (...). They engaged with key stakeholders (...)'. Furthermore, the agent explained that 'his heart' and 'man-made are gendered expressions and can be replaced with expressions that do not assume the gender of a person.

The experts noted that the AI made all cases more gender-inclusive and that the explanations were useful as they aided in understanding which cases had been made more gender-inclusive.

Discussion and conclusions

Our paper explored the opportunities of this emerging technology to produce course materials based on important elements of a course production framework and reported the assessment of teaching experts on three common tasks.

From this first trial of the Microsoft Azure AI Chat technology, we found that the AI can produce content that could support towards completing the outlined set of tasks across all activities. The AI can aid with brainstorming ideas towards solving the task, creating an outline, and assessing adherence to specific writing guidance (such as inclusive language). In all cases, the experts noted that the content would need adjustments and checking, ranging from small sections to rewriting generated ideas to make them more suitable for an online and distance learning university context.

The breadth of the AI responses suggests that this technology can work for a broad range of purposes as a generalist. However, we still need to examine to which degree it can adapt to context-specific problems and work as a specialist incorporating subject-specific, pedagogical, and university-specific knowledge. Initial insights in this paper suggest that the AI can consider more specialised information for its responses with the right prompting.

Our evaluation of these findings is that, as the technology stands, it can best be considered an assistive technology that can support various roles but that, at best, it can have an advising capacity, as any output needs to be evaluated for integrity, veracity, and accuracy. Therefore, it looks likely that our curriculum development team model will continue but with the addition of a writing agent.

This leads our work into the realms of social science and how cognitive machines can work productively with one another. More importantly, how can cognitive agents assist learning? One previous example is Open Essayist (Edwards et al., 2022; Whitelock et al., 2017), where Pask's (1975) Conversation theory was used to summarise a student's draft essay. This meant the student could check from the summary whether this was what they intended to write for this essay. The theory behind this action is that if a person understands what is being explained to them by a teacher, they can repeat it back to that teacher. In this case, the AI agent repeats what has been written as a summary. Now, with the introduction of Generative AI agents, does it mean we need to define learning in these new contexts more precisely? Are new theories required that are open to test? New horizons are open to Education, but we should not neglect the ethical concerns surrounding copyright, manipulation, and data privacy in our future agendas.

[3] https://www.un.org/en/gender-inclusive-language/assets/pdf/EN-Toolbox-Apply-the-guidelines-to-a-text_(self-paced).pdf

References

Adeshola, I., & Adepoju, A. P. (2023). The opportunities and challenges of ChatGPT in education. Interactive Learning Environments, 1–14. https://doi.org/10.1080/10494820.2023.2253858

Alkaissi, H., & McFarlane, S. I. (2023). Artificial Hallucinations in ChatGPT: Implications in Scientific Writing. Cureus. https://doi.org/10.7759/cureus.35179

Aneesha. (2023). Eduweaver [Jupyter Notebook]. https://github.com/aneesha/eduweaver

Bektik, D., Ullmann, T. D., Edwards, C., Herodotou, C., & Whitelock, D. (accepted). AI-Powered Curricula: Unpacking the Potential and Progress of Generative Technologies in Education. Annual Conference on European Distance and E-Learning Network, EDEN 2024, Graz, Austria.

Biggs, J. (2014). Constructive alignment in university teaching. HERDSA Review of Higher Education, 1, 5–22.

Chen, Y., Jensen, S., Albert, L., J., Gupta, S., & Lee, T. (2023). Artifcial intelligence (AI) student assistants in the classroom: Designing chatbots to support student success. Information Systems Frontiers, 161–182.

Edwards, C., Whitelock, D., Cross, S., & Wild, F. (2022, June 22). Towards autonomous, confident academic writing: Supporting students in developing their writing through a stand alone online tool. AHE2022, Manchester, UK. https://ahenetwork.org/ahe-conference-2021/

Liu, M., Ren, Y., Nyagoga, L. M., Stonier, F., Wu, Z., & Yu, L. (2023). Future of education in the era of generative artificial intelligence: Consensus among Chinese scholars on applications of ChatGPT in schools. Future in Educational Research, 1(1), 72–101. https://doi.org/10.1002/fer3.10

Pask, G. (1975). Conversation, Cognition and Learning: Cybernetic Theory and Methodology. Elsevier Science Ltd.

Rienties, B., & Toetenel, L. (2016). The impact of learning design on student behaviour, satisfaction and performance: A cross-institutional comparison across 151 modules. Computers in Human Behavior, 60, 333–341. https://doi.org/10.1016/j.chb.2016.02.074

Sharples, M. (2023). Towards social generative AI for education: Theory, practices and ethics. Learning: Research and Practice, 9(2), 159–167. https://doi.org/10.1080/23735082.2023.2261131

Tahiru, F. (2021). AI in Education: A Systematic Literature Review. Journal of Cases on Information Technology, 23(1), 1–20. https://doi.org/10.4018/JCIT.2021010101

Whitelock, D., Twiner, A., Richardson, J. T. E., Field, D., & Pulman, S. (2017). What Types of Essay Feedback Influence Implementation: Structure Alone or Structure and Content? In D. Joosten-ten Brinke & M. Laanpere (Eds.), Technology Enhanced Assessment (pp. 181–196). Springer International Publishing. https://doi.org/10.1007/978-3-319-57744-9_16

Zhai, X., Chu, X., Chai, C. S., Jong, M. S. Y., Istenic, A., Spector, M., Liu, J.-B., Yuan, J., & Li, Y. (2021). A Review of Artificial Intelligence (AI) in Education from 2010 to 2020. Complexity, 2021, 1–18. https://doi.org/10.1155/2021/8812542

Zhang, K., & Aslan, A. B. (2021). AI technologies for education: Recent research & future directions. Computers and Education: Artificial Intelligence, 2, 100025. https://doi.org/10.1016/j.caeai.2021.100025

Should Universities partner with NGOs? A Case Study of a University of Technology and a Coding School for Refugees

Daniela Wolf[1], Martin Ebner[2]

[1] Department of Information Systems Management, Ferdinand Porsche FernFH Distance-Learning University of Applied Sciences; Austria; daniela.wolf@fernfh.ac.at
[2] Educational Technology, Graz University of Technology; Austria; martin.ebner@tugraz.at

Correspondence: Daniela Wolf: daniela.wolf@fernfh.ac.at

Abstract:

This paper explores the advantages of a University-NGO Partnership between the Faculty of Informatics at Vienna University of Technology (TU Vienna) and the NGO „refugees{code}", a coding school for refugees in Vienna, Austria. The goal of this collaboration is twofold: Firstly, to help students apply coding skills practically and enhance their proficiency through teaching experiences with underrepresented groups; and secondly, to provide refugees with meaningful activities that match their profession, education, and personal interests, which might have been interrupted in their home countries. The study evaluates the perspectives of the stakeholders involved. To do so, written surveys and interviews with computer science students, refugees and team members of the NGO were conducted. The results indicate that meaningful educational benefits for computer science students can be created within such partnerships, such as enhanced teaching abilities, dispelled prejudices, insights into the factors affecting refugees' educational and career trajectories, as well as improved communication and empathy skills. However, challenges for such partnerships also exist, including giving student teachers more time for meetings and discussions, empowering them to make decisions, providing access to counseling psychologists and interpreters, and offering support in managing participants' expectations. The findings shed light on the potential benefits from participating in campus-community partnerships and suggest several measures to improve them, such as providing additional ECTS credits, intensifying promotional activities to encourage greater student participation, providing alumni support, and issuing official certificates.

Keywords: campus-community partnerships, service learning, civic engagement, social responsibility, computing education, programming

Introduction

Marginalized groups often experience disadvantages due to socio-economic, ethnic, geographic, or other factors and face barriers to access quality formal education (Hoffman & Toutant, 2018; Benner & Wang, 2014; Luschei & Chudgar, 2017). Non-Governmental Organizations (NGOs) are often the ones who focus on these groups and provide opportunities for skill development, improving living conditions, and promoting equitable access to education (Reza, 2022). University students typically don't interact with these target groups unless they participate in extracurricular activities that connect them with these individuals. According to Noll et al. (1998) and Esser (2004), the more individuals differ from each other, the greater the subjectively perceived distance and consequently, the lower the likelihood of closer contact. Among asylum seekers, regardless of their origin, the highest social distance is observed (Noll et al., 1998). It is important to establish relationships based on shared goals and interests. Therefore, the authors raise the question of how university students can connect with these groups? The connection is vital since computer science graduates often lead the development of technological solutions. However, if they lack diversity awareness, their products may only serve specific groups or even exclude others. Moreover, the development of artificial intelligence forces the necessity for creating learning and teaching plans that also address the social needs of learners. This means developing teaching methods that help students understand others' feelings and be aware of society's issues. Therefore, we investigate a campus-community partnership between the TU Vienna and "refugees{code}", a coding school for refugees.

Related Work

Campus-Community Partnerships

Since the 1990s, there's been a growing understanding that partnerships between universities and community organizations are important for knowledge translation (Hart and Wolff, 2006; Ginis, 2012), improving research (Begun et al., 2010; Ocean et al., 2021), and better meeting the needs of community members, especially youth (Ostrom et al., 1995; Denner et al., 1999; Ardoin et al., 2014). Community-university partnerships not only record what the community knows but also encourage both academics and community representatives to learn from each other (London et al., 2011). This occurs through various means, such as service-learning (Vogel et al., 2010) or participatory research (Boyle et al., 2011; Dong et al.; London et al., 2011; Lee et al., 2022).

These partnerships have been predominantly observed in public education (Guerrero et al., 2013), non-profits (Minkler et al., 2008; Soleimanpour et al., 2008), and among marginalized or vulnerable communities (Suarez-Balcazar et al., 2004; Garcia et al., 2014; Anucha et al., 2020). While university-wide structures that provide ongoing support for activities are relatively well developed in the United States (Harkins, 2013), they are only gradually beginning to be institutionalized in Europe (Resch et al., 2020; Meijs et al., 2019; Maasen et al., 2019). Especially so far, little is known about the emergence and institutionalization of Campus-Community Partnerships (CCPs) at Austrian universities (Rameder et al., 2023).

And this even though in 2010, the President of the International Association of Universities emphasized the role of universities in addressing significant global challenges. Universities not only foster knowledge and research but also generate ideas for social action (de la Fuente, 2010). Therefore, universities should more clearly demonstrate the benefits they provide when collaborating with local communities to address complex social problems (Mulvihill et al., 2011a).

Programming Education at Universities

The focus in computer science is no longer on "theory-oriented, formalistic, proof-based" learning, but on practical, concrete, application-oriented, problem-solving, project-oriented, and interdisciplinary teaching (Berger, 2001). The teaching style is changing from "frontal, teacher-centered, dogmatic, meticulous" to "active, team-oriented, creative, cooperative, co-determined, open and generous" (Berger, 2001); and the focus is on rapid interaction between teachers and learners, as well as the associated change of roles, in which learners themselves become knowledge producers (Keil-Slawik, 2005). This can only be achieved to a limited extent, if at all, with traditional common teaching-learning forms such as lectures, exercises, and seminars. Although in these formats the exercises often take place in small groups, the knowledge production is in general not part of the course and usually left to the teachers. The traditional project work is still often the only format at universities that enables the acquisition of key qualifications and knowledge generation by learners. For this reason, project-oriented and problem-based learning is increasingly used in the field of computer science (Hernandez et al., 2015; Kolmos et al., 2004; Vithal et al., 1995). Additionally, the service learning in computer science (CS) is believed to be significant, ranging from providing students with real-world experiences, to retaining students, to positively impacting community partners (Yamamoto et al., 2023). While empirical data on the prevalence of service-learning courses in CS disciplines is lacking, reports about them have been consistently documented in the literature since 2000 (Yamamoto et al., 2023). These reports indicate a diverse learning experience in CS courses, spanning from introductory programming to data science to upper-division courses. However, most service-learning experiences were authored by faculties from U.S. institutions (Yamamoto et al., 2023).

Research Context

The NGO "refugees{code}"

"refugees{code}"[1] is a coding school for refugees that emerged in summer 2016 during the refugee crisis in Vienna. Since both the personnel and spatial resources were lacking at the beginning, the NGO decided to enter a partnership with the Faculty of Informatics at TU Vienna.

---

[1] In August 2018, it was renamed to "New Austrian Coding School" and later rebranded as "Everyone Codes".

Welcome.TU.code

In 2015, the Faculty of Informatics launched the "Welcome.TU.Code" initiative, providing free informatics courses at various levels to unaccompanied adolescent refugees.[2] These courses transformed into the "IT Projects for Youth" soft skills course starting from winter 2015/16. The course aims to empower computer science students to lead IT workshops for young users with diverse backgrounds. Therefore, students initially earned 3 ECTS credits, which were subsequently increased to 4.5 ECTS from the winter term of 2017/18 due to workload concerns[3]. The IT workshops are designed for four proficiency levels: beginners, intermediate, advanced, and a specialized "pro group" added in 2016/17 through collaboration with the NGO "refugees{code}".

Since its launch, the soft skills course "IT Projects for Youth" has undergone development. In 2018, the collaboration between the faculty and the NGO "refugees{code}" ended due to the NGO restructuring.[4] Responding to the SARS-CoV-2 outbreak, the faculty shifted to online learning in winter 2020/21. Starting from winter 2021/22, the faculty resumed collaboration with NGOs. As of March 2024, partners are WUK work.space[5], "Sprungbrett" - which extends the program's reach to girls from migrant or financially disadvantaged backgrounds, and "Fonds Soziales Wien" - broadening the participant's scope to include Ukrainian refugees. While TU students were solely involved in developing the lecture syllabus and content in the initial collaborative course with „refugees{code}", and not for course 2 and 3 (see Table 1), they are again responsible with its development today.

The Partnership

The Faculty of CS collaborated with the NGO "refugees{code}" three times in a row. Central to this partnership was a special soft skills course worth three ECTS credits, which could be attended by computer science students and aimed to teach programming skills to refugees. The programming skills were taught using a programming MOOC from Harvard University. Computer science students assisted refugees in completing the MOOC.

Table 1: A summary of the three courses

Courses	Weeks	Space & Hours	Learning Systems	Effort for the MOOC
1	10	3x2 Hours	Student Instructors	none
2	11	2x3 Hours	Students support MOOC	6-18 hours
3	11	2x3 Hours 24/7 Location Part-time Trainers	Students support MOOC Specialization Phase Project Phase Internship	6-18 hours

Research Objectives

The TU Vienna-refugees{code} Partnership is an excellent testbed for evaluating the potential benefits of such campus-community partnerships. The cooperative soft skills course was not designed as a rigorous experiment, and no controls were implemented, as the initial and ongoing goal has been to help refugees and not necessarily to measure success with exacting rigor. Therefore, many research objectives rely on the subjective experiences of the student teachers, refugee students and the NGO team members. With this in mind, we focus on evaluating development of the student teachers and address following questions: What educational benefits are received by student teachers? To what extent were student teachers able to deepen their knowledge? What, if any, is the environmental impact of such a cooperative course? Are students more comfortable in seeking help from student teachers as opposed to other, more conventional sources? What are the benefits of such a cooperative soft skills course? What aspects of such a partnership can be improved?

---

[2] https://informatics.tuwien.ac.at/welcome-tu-code (last access: 15.03.2024)

[3] Author interview with Reinhard Pichler, project coordinator of TU Vienna, 09.2023

[4] Author interview with Stefan Steinberger, TFA Alumni and Founder of refugees{code}, Wien, 02.2024.

[5] https://www.wuk.at/magazin/383-quintillionen-jahre/ (last access: 15.03.2024)

Methodology

We collected data through online written surveys and interviews. 52 former student teachers between winter 2022/23 and winter 2023/24 as well as nine former student teachers who participated in the collaborative courses between TU Vienna and refugees{code} were contacted. Moreover, we reached out to seven refugee students as well as seven refugees{code} team members who supported the TU Vienna-refugees{code} partnership between 2016 and 2018. The survey covered overall satisfaction, personal benefits, and professional impact. Many of the questions asked were descriptive multiple choice, but respondents were also encouraged to provide comments and suggestions in free response form.

The data was collected in winter 2023/24. We received and analyzed a total of 15 written responses, representing a response rate of 24.59 % (n=61). Additionally, we received seven responses, representing a response rate of 100 % (n=7) from refugee students and four responses from the NGO members, representing a response rate of 71.43 % (n=7). Of the student teachers, eleven were male (80%), two were female (13.33%), and two did not disclose their gender (13.33 %). Ages ranged from 18 to 44. Ten of them were from Austria (66.66%), two from Egypt (13.33 %), two from previous Yugoslavia (13.33 %), and one from Italy (6.66 %). Except for one female student who studied Architecture, all students studied a field related to computer science. 73.33 % had no prior experience with refugees or marginalized youth. Furthermore, we conducted oral interviews with two student teachers who took part in the TU Vienna-refugees{code} course between 2016 and 2018, as well as an oral interview with one refugee student from the second course (see Table 1).

Analysis

We used principles of phenomenological research as described by Creswell and Poth (2016), which means identifying significant statements, grouping them into broader categories, interpreting those categories for what and how the experience happened.

Results

Student teachers (n=15)

New Teaching Perspectives, and Adaptive Approaches

Student teachers rated the approach highly, with an average of 1.89 (standard deviation 0.818). 80 % reported gaining new perspectives and approaches:

> I was challenged to provide explanations through practical examples rather than relying solely on verbal communication due to the language barrier. – Participant #4
>
> Many things that I take for granted can be very time-consuming for the students. – Participant #5
>
> I noticed the need to adapt the content to the interests and pace of the students. – Participant #3

Prioritizing Atmosphere and Direct Engagement

Participant #3 highlighted that a positive atmosphere and engaged students are crucial for learning, regardless of background or prior knowledge. Directly approaching and engaging with students was highlighted:

> It is important to approach and address them directly, otherwise you won't get an answer if you ask questions. – Participant #10
>
> I usually got positive feedback and head nods after explaining something, but when I asked the students face-to-face, they admitted that they didn't understand it. So I have learned not to trust positive feedback and present less content, then let them practice. When I saw that it worked, I presented more content. – Participant #8

Culturally Aligned Teachers

Student teachers observed that students were more comfortable asking questions to teachers with similar backgrounds:

I also noticed that they dared to ask more questions or queries with the Ukrainian translator, although I motivated them to ask questions. – Participant #8

New Knowledge and Diverse Perspectives

When discussing improving their coding or computer science knowledge, student teachers noted exploring unfamiliar topics:

> I also presented topics that I hadn't dealt with before, so I had to acquire new knowledge. – Participant #7

> You had to deal with a specific topic from different angles. – Participant #1

> As some of the questions asked by the participants were somewhat unfamiliar (if you are "used" to the university context), this required rethinking and coming up with alternative explanations. – Participant #13

Boost Teaching Skills

While some student teachers didn't gain much new technical knowledge, the experience notably improved their didactical skills:

> I could hardly or not at all deepen my coding or programming skills, but that wasn't my goal either. – Participant #rc2, #12

> My technical knowledge has improved relatively little, but my teaching skills have improved more. – Participant #8

> WordPress was a new platform for me, but technologically I gained nothing majorly new. – Participant #6

> I didn't know CSS and WordPress before. – Participant #9

> I had no contact with Figma and WordPress before, I learnt this completely. I had very limited knowledge of HTML, which I have completely improved. – Participant #3

80 % noted substantial enhancement in non-technical skills like diversity and communication. Free responses highlighted development in various areas:

> The ability to explain topics to non-specialists in a simplified form was promoted by the course. – Participant #9, #4

> I was able to improve my knowledge through the more structured approach as it was necessary to explain everything step by step. – Participant #10

> I have gotten better at presenting interactively and addressing needs, making it easier to explain complex ideas. – Participant #5

> I improved my presentation and moderation skills. – Participant #6

> I improved my teaching experience and the planning of teaching units. – Participant #7

> I changed perspective and saw the world through the eyes of others. – Participant #8

> I was able to gain some insights into the field of knowledge transfer: Hands-on training is better than a frontal lecture. Personalized feedback in person and an amicable atmosphere are very valuable. – Participant #rc2

Understanding of Diversity and Challenges

86.66 % agreed that the program helped to improve their understanding of people with diverse backgrounds and life experiences. In the free-response section, they mentioned significant development:

> It shows that not everything is as simple and self-evident as we think it is when we only move in our own comfort zone. – Participant #4

> You realize how difficult it is as a refugee to get a job, for example, even if you have good English and specialist knowledge. – Participant #3

> I was able to experience at least some of their experiences, fears, and problems. I believe that this direct contact has on the one hand broken down prejudices for me, but on the other hand it has also opened my eyes to the fact that we should try to provide everyone with an environment in which they can develop according to their own wishes and ideas. – Participant #11

Working with refugees and marginalized youth also brought eye-opening realizations:

> I realized that some individuals may not be responsible for dropping out of school, potentially due to influences from classmates or teachers. – Participant #2

> I realized that despite theoretical equal opportunities for education, practical access still heavily relies on upbringing and life circumstances. – Participant #6

Navigating Language Barriers, Attention Span, and Varied Knowledge Levels

The obstacles or challenges perceived in working with refugees and educationally disadvantaged groups primarily include the language barrier (Participant #4, #5, #11), attention span (Participant #5), and differing knowledge/education levels (Participant #6, #8). It was also mentioned that it can be difficult to fully understand the respective situations:

> You may unintentionally make a mistake if you don't know the people and their backgrounds. – Participant #10

Designing presentations at a level that keeps everyone engaged without leaving anyone behind is also a challenging aspect:

> It is difficult to organize lectures that nobody gets bored, and everyone follows along. – Participant #12

More Time, Support, and Resources

In response to the question regarding desired resources or support from cooperation partners, student teachers expressed the following:

- Participant #8 emphasized the need for more time, while Participant #7 desired more authority.
- Participant #9 suggested the inclusion of counseling psychologists, Participant #4 mentioned interpreters, and Participant #6 highlighted the necessity for someone to manage participants' expectations.
- Participant #13 indicated a need for sufficiently large and equipped computer rooms.
- Participant #8 recommended better didactic concepts, while Participant #9 proposed a structured curriculum with level-appropriate tasks incorporating principles of gamification.
- Participant #11 requested a handbook for various youth slang.

66.66 % believe that such a collaboration is highly meaningful, while 20 % find it meaningful. 80 % believe that universities should take measures to promote such projects. To improve effectiveness of such courses, student teachers suggest various measures: Participant #2 advocates for more ECTS points, Participants #4 and #13 emphasize increased promotion of such courses, Participant #9 highlights the importance of support and involvement from graduates of such courses, and Participant #3 mentions the need for additional incentives such as an official certificate.

Refugee students (n=7)

We received responses from seven participants aged 25 to 44, including five individuals from Syria and two individuals from Iran. Notably, six respondents hold degrees in computer science from their home countries, while one has a degree in medical technology. They rated the significance of this approach on a 5-point scale, with four (71 %) rating it 5 and three rating it 4 (57 %). Additionally, we conducted an oral interview with one of them — a male aged between 35 and 44, from Iran, holding a master's degree in computer science (Participant #rc).

Real-World Insights and Career guidance

Refugee students highlighted the importance of gaining insights into daily job life from experienced individuals, stressing that programming extends beyond coding alone. Understanding workflow in a job was deemed crucial (Participants #14, #16). Participant #19 also expressed a need for more guidance from experienced individuals.

Company Support and Employment Opportunities

Refugee students proposed that official company support for the course, along with potential employment opportunities, could boost its effectiveness and motivation (Participants #14, #15, #18).

Connecting Through Shared Struggles / Role Models

Participant #rc's most rewarding experience was interacting with student teachers. He found it particularly positive to also witness their challenges with the MOOC, as it cultivated a sense of connection.

Enhancing Learning Materials

Participant #15 suggested improving the learning materials.

Members of the refugees{code}-Team (n=5)

We received responses from two male Austrian, two female Austrians, and one female with Albanian heritage, all aged 25-34. They rated the approach on a 5-point scale, scoring it 4.4 out of 5, indicating high meaningfulness. When asked if participation enhanced understanding of people with different backgrounds, four out of five answered yes, while the woman with the Albanian heritage responded no. In answering what resources or support they would have appreciated, they mentioned that it would have been helpful to have a documentation of the prior knowledge from the student teachers (participant #20), a summary of the actions that student teachers are interested in supervising or find meaningful (participant #20), clear role distribution (participant #22), better communication (participant #23), and financial recognition (participant #21). Three out of four believe universities should promote such projects with NGOs. To enhance project and course effectiveness, suggestions included clear structuring of teaching units (Participant #21), student supervision (Participants #22), didactic training (Participants #22), and documentation (Participant #20).

Discussion and Conclusion

The purpose of this study was to answer the following research questions:

What educational benefits are received by student teachers?

The study shows several educational insights for student teachers:

Seeing things from different angles

Student teachers understood that everyone learns differently. Teachers should be ready to explain things in different ways to help everyone grasp the concepts.

Understanding different abilities

Student teachers understood that they need to be empathetic and humble, realizing that what's easy for them might be hard for others.

Introducing new material slowly

Teachers should introduce new topics bit by bit, making sure students understand each part before moving on. This way, students can build their knowledge step by step.

Following clear steps

Student teachers saw that when they give clear, step-by-step instructions, students learn better.

Personalizing learning

Student teachers recognized that each student is unique, teachers should adjust what they teach and how fast they teach it to match each person's interests and needs. This makes learning more engaging and understandable.

Creating a welcoming environment

Making sure everyone feels included, respected, and encouraged in the classroom is key to helping all students succeed.

Encouraging participation

Student teachers noticed that they should interact directly with students, especially during discussions, to get everyone involved.

Being careful with praise

When teaching students who have experienced hardship, like refugees, teachers need to be thoughtful about giving praise. Feedback should be positive and supportive, considering cultural differences.

To what extent were student teachers able to deepen their knowledge?

While some student teachers didn't gain much new technical knowledge, the experience notably enhanced their didactical abilities. They learned to explain complex concepts in a simplified manner, gained experience in teaching and unit planning, adopted different perspectives, and delivered interactive presentations. They also developed skills in responding to individual needs, improving presentation and moderation abilities, and assessing understanding through body language cues.

What, if any, is the environment impact of such a cooperative approach?

Working with refugees and marginalized youth breaks down prejudices and leads to eye-opening realizations about factors affecting their educational and employment paths. Direct contact with refugees emphasizes the importance of inclusive environments. Effective communication and empathy are vital.

Are students more comfortable in seeking help from student teachers as opposed to other, more conventional sources?

Refugee students seem to prefer seeking help from mentors with similar backgrounds or experts rather than student teachers. However, they find it positive to see student teachers also struggling with the MOOC, which helped foster a sense of connection. Displaying vulnerability and addressing challenges in front of students foster a supportive and inclusive learning environment, encouraging students to overcome their own challenges.

What are the benefits of such a cooperative soft skills course?

This approach benefits computer science students by allowing them to apply coding skills in practical settings and reinforce learning through teaching. It also offers students opportunities to engage with underrepresented groups, better equipping them for a diverse workforce. For refugees, it offers a sense of purpose and allows them to actively pursue meaningful endeavors aligned with their previous profession, experience, or interests. It also helps them qualify for jobs in the software industry.

What aspects of such a partnership can be improved?

Several aspects of the partnership that can be improved were highlighted. This includes giving student teachers more time for meetings and discussions and giving them the authority to make decisions. Additionally, student teachers need access to counseling psychologists, interpreters, and help in managing participants' expectations. Moreover, student teachers suggested providing well-equipped computer facilities, enhancing didactic concepts, structuring lecture syllabi, and implementing level-appropriate tasks with gamification principles. Student teachers also expressed the need for a handbook on youth slang. They also suggested several measures to enhance the program, such as offering additional ECTS points, intensifying promotional activities to encourage greater student participation, providing alumni support, and issuing official certificates.

Insights into daily job life from experienced individuals and company support for subsequent employment were recommended from the refugee students.

The NGO team members suggested improvements in learning materials, a documentation of prior knowledge of student teachers, clear role distribution, better communication, and financial recognition.

Acknowledgements

We would like to thank the student teachers and refugee students who participated in this study and allowed this research to take place. Another special thanks go to Stefan Steinberger, one of the founders of the NGO " refugees{code}" , and the project manager Prof. Reinhard Pichler from TU Vienna, whom we were able to contact repeatedly for questions and who always provided immediate assistance.

Funding Information

This research is based upon work supported by the „Gesellschaft für Forschungsförderung Niederösterreich" under RTI-Dissertation 2021.

References

Anucha, U., Srikanthan, S. & Houwer, R. (2020). Engaging youth in research: lessons from community-engaged research with urban youth, in Community Practice and Social Development In Social Work, eds S. Todd and J. L. Drolet (Singapore: Springer Nature;), 1–21. 10.1007/978-981-13-1542-8_1-1

Ardoin, N. M., Castrechini, S. & Hofstedt, M. K. (2014). Youth-community-university partnerships and sense of place: two case studies of youth participatory action research. Child. Geograph. 12, 479–496. 10.1080/14733285.2013.827872

Begun, A. L., Berger, L. K., Otto-Salaj, L. L. & Rose, S. J. (2010). Developing effective social work university–community research collaborations. Soc. Work 55, 54–62. 10.1093/sw/55.1.54

Benner, A., & Wang, Y. (2014). Demographic Marginalization, Social Integration, and Adolescents' Educational Success. Journal of Youth and Adolescence, 43, 1611-1627. https://doi.org/10.1007/s10964-014-0151-6

Berger, Peter (2001). Computer und Weltbild: habitualisierte Konzeptionen von der Welt der Computer. Wiesbaden: Westdeutscher Verlag.

Boyle, M.-E., Ross, L. & Stephen, J. C. (2011). Who has a Stake? How stakeholder processes influence partnership sustainability. Gateways: International Journal of Community Research and Engagement Vol 4 (2011): 100–118

Creswell, J. W. & Poth, C. N. (2016). Qualitative inquiry and research design: Choosing among five approaches. Sage publications.

de la Fuente, J. (2010). The higher education sector must create innovative partnerships for social construction, interview, GUNI newsletter, issue 56, May, Barcelona, viewed 12 February 2024, https://www.guninetwork.org/gunitalks/juan-ramon-de-la-fuente

Denner, J., Cooper, C. R., Lopez, E. M. & Dunbar, N. (1999). Beyond "Giving science away": how university-community partnerships inform youth programs, research, and policy. Soc. Policy Rep. 13, 1–20. 10.1002/j.2379-3988.1999.tb00010.x

Esser, H. (2004). Does the "New" Immigration Require a "New" Theory of Intergenerational Integration? International Migration Review, 38(3), 1126-1159. https://doi.org/10.1111/j.1747-7379.2004.tb00231.x

Garcia, A. P., Minkler, M., Cardenas, Z., Grills, C. & Porter C. (2014). Engaging homeless youth in community-based participatory research: a case study from Skid Row, Los Angeles. Health Promot. Pract. 15, 18–27. 10.1177/1524839912472904

Ginis, K. A. M. (2012). Takin'it to the streets: a community-university partnership approach to physical activity research and knowledge translation. Kinesiol. Rev. 1, 190–196. 10.1123/krj.1.4.190

Guerrero, C. A., Rosas, M. & Guerrero, E. (2013). Proyecto Latin@ on stage and under the magnifying glass: the possibilities and limitations of a high-profile institutionally sponsored youth participatory action research project. Int. J. Critic. Pedagogy 4, 105–126.

Harkins, D. A. (2013). Beyond the Campus: Building a Sustainable University-Community Partnership. Charlotte, N.C: Information Age Publications.

Hart, A. & Wolff, D. (2006). Developing local 'communities of practice' through local community–university partnerships. Plann. Pract. Res 21, 121–138. 10.1080/02697450600901616

Hart, A., Northmore, S. & Gerhardt, C. (2009). Briefing paper: Auditing, benchmarking and evaluating public engagement, National Co-ordinating Centre for Public Engagement, Bristol.

Hart, A., Northmore, S. & Gerhardt, C. & Rodriguez, P. (2009). Developing access between universities and local community groups: A university helpdesk in action', Journal of Higher Education Outreach and Engagement, vol. 13, no. 3, pp. 45–59.

Hernandez, C., Ravn, O. & Valero, P. (2016). The Aalborg University PO-PBL Model from a Socio-cultural Learning Perspective. Journal of Problem Based Learning in Higher Education, 3(2).

Hoffman, J., & Toutant, S. (2018). Chapter 11 Spotlight on Six Marginalized Populations in American Higher Education. Innovations in Higher Education Teaching and Learning. https://doi.org/10.1108/S2055-364120180000012012.

Keil-Slawik, R. (2005). Dienste-Infrastrukturen als Mittel der Wissensorganisation. In Michael Kerres/Reinhard Keil-Slawik (Hrsg.). Hochschulen im digitalen Zeitalter: Innovationspotenziale und Strukturwandel, Education Quality Forum 2004 (2. Band) (S. 13–28). Münster: Waxmann.

Kolmos, A., Fink, F. K., & Krogh, L. (2004). The Aalborg PBL model: Progress, diversity and challenges. Aalborg.: Aalborg University Press.

Lee, L. M., Wright, L. H. V., Machado, C., Niyogi, O., Singh, P., Shields, S., & Hope, K. (2022). Online Intergenerational Participatory Research: Ingredients for Meaningful Relationships and Participation. Journal of Participatory Research Methods, 3(3). https://doi.org/10.35844/001c.38764

London, J, K., Zagofsky, T. M., Huang, G. & Saklar, J. (2011). Collaboration, Participation and Technology. Gateways: International Journal of Community Research and Engagement Vol 4 (2011): 12–30

Luschei, T.F. & Chudgar, A. (2017). Reaching and Teaching Marginalized Children. In: Teacher Distribution in Developing Countries. Palgrave Macmillan, New York. https://doi.org/10.1057/978-1-137-57926-3_1

Maassen, P., Andreadakis, Z., Gulbrandsen, M. & Stensaker, B. (2019). The Place of Universities in Society. Hamburg: Körber-Stiftung.

Meijs, L., Maas, S. A. & Aramburuzabala, P. (2019). Institutionalisation of service learning in European higher education. In P. Aramburuzabala, L. McIlrath & H. Opazo (Hrsg.), Embedding Service Learning in European Higher Education. Devel-oping a Culture of Civic Engagement (S. 214–229). London: Routledge.

Minkler, M., Vásquez, V. B., Tajik, M. & Petersen, D. (2008). Promoting environmental justice through community-based participatory research: The role of community and partnership capacity. Health Educ. Behav. 35, 119–137. 10.1177/1090198106287692

Mulvihill, N., Hart, A., Northmore, S., Wolff, D. & Pratt, J. (2011a). The future of community-university engagement: South East Coastal Communities Dissemination Paper 1, May, University of Brighton, Brighton, viewed 23 November 2023, www.coastalcommunities.org.uk/briefingPapers.html.

Mulvihill, N., Hart, A., Northmore, S., Wolff, D. & Pratt, J. (2011b). Measuring the impact of community-university engagement: South East Coastal Communities Dissemination Paper 5, University of Brighton, Brighton, viewed 23 November 2023, www.coastalcommunities.org.uk/briefing%20papers/Paper_5web.pdf

Noll, H.-H., Schmidt, P. & Weick, S. (1998). Ethnic Groups and Migrants in Germany. Towards a Multicultural German Society?" In Monitoring Multicultural Societies: A Siena Group Report. Ed. J. Bühlmann, P. Röthlisberger and B. Schmid. Neuchatel : BFS. Pp. 139–171.

Ocean, M., Mohr, J., Parker, A. L., Barbatis, P., Vajello, M. M., Woods, K., ... Keller, J. (2021). An Inclusive Research Method for the Open Door College: Valuing the Perceptions of the College Community. Community College Journal of Research and Practice, 45(8), 575–589. https://doi.org/10.1080/10668926.2020.1731630

Ostrom, C. W., Lerner, R. M. & Freel, M. A. (1995). Building the capacity of youth and families through university-community collaborations: the development-in-context evaluation (DICE) model. J. Adolesc. Res. 10, 427–448. 10.1177/0743554895104001

Rameder, P., Knapp, M., & Fellner, M. (2023). Campus-Community-Partnerships in der Hochschullehre: Aktuelle Daten aus Österreich. Zeitschrift für Hochschulentwicklung, 18(2), 75–96. https://doi.org/10.3217/zfhe-18-02/05

Resch, K., Fellner, M., Fahrenwald, C., Slepcevic-Zach, P., Knapp, M. & Rameder, P. (2020). Embedding Social Innovation and Service Learning in Higher Education's Third Sector Policy Developments in Austria. Frontiers in Education,5(112), 1–5. https://doi.org/10.3389/feduc.2020.00112

Reza, F. (2022). The Role of NGOs in Promoting Education: Successes and Challenges, International Journal of Education, Learning and Development, Vol. 10, No.1, pp.24-43

Soleimanpour, S., Brindis, C., Geierstanger, S., Kandawalla, S. & Kurlaender, T. (2008). Incorporating youth-led community participatory research into school health center programs and policies. Public Health Rep. 123, 709–716. 10.1177/003335490812300607

Suarez-Balcazar, Y., Davis, M. I., Ferrari, J., Nyden, P., Olson, B., Alvarez, J., Molloy, P., & Toro, P. (2004). University-community partnerships: A framework and an exemplar. In L. A. Jason, C. B. Keys, Y. Suarez-Balcazar, R. R. Taylor, & M. I. Davis (Eds.), Participatory community research: Theories and methods in action (pp. 105–120). American Psychological Association. https://doi.org/10.1037/10726-006

Vithal, R., Christiansen, I., & Skovsmose, O. (1995). Project Work in University Mathematics Education: A Danish Experience: Aalborg University. Educational Studies in Mathematics, 29(2), 199-223. http://www.jstor.org/stable/3482903

Vogel, A., Seifer, S. & Gelmon, S. (2010). What influences the long-term sustainability of service learning? Lessons from early adopters, Michigan Journal of Community Service Learning, fall, pp. 59–76.

Yamamoto, F. R., Barker, L. & Voida, A. (2023). CISing Up Service Learning: A Systematic Review of Service Learning Experiences in Computer and Information Science. ACM Trans. Comput. Educ. 23, 3, Article 37 (September 2023), 56 pages. https://doi.org/10.1145/3610776

Usage of (federated) Learning Management Systems in European University Alliances

Martin Ebner[1], Sandra Schön[1], Jesus Alcober[2], Roberto Bertonasco[3], Agnieszka Herczak-Ciara[4], Christian Hoppe[5], Juha Martikainen[6], Melanie Muchitsch[1], Joakim Petersson[7], Fernando M. da Silva[8]

[1] Graz University of Technology, Austria; martin.ebner@tugraz.at, sandra.schoen@tugraz.at, melanie.muchitsch@student.tugraz.at
[2] Universitat Politecnica de Catalunya, Spain; jesus.alcober@upc.edu
[3] Politecnico Di Torino, Italy; roberto.bertonasco@polito.it
[4] Wrocław University of Science and Technology, Poland; agnieszka.herczak-ciara@pwr.edu.pl
[5] Technical University of Darmstadt, Germany; christian.hoppe@tu-darmstadt.de
[6] Aalto University, Finland; juha.h.martikainen@aalto.fi
[7] KTH Royal Institute of Technology, Sweden; jocke@kth.se
[8] Universidade de Lisboa, Portugal; fernando.silva@tecnico.ulisboa.pt

Correspondence: Martin Ebner, martin.ebner@tugraz.at

Abstract:

In today's rapidly evolving educational landscape, European universities are increasingly relying on digital technologies for collaboration and learning. European Universities, as transnational alliances, aim to reshape higher education by fostering academic exchange and innovation across borders. With over 40 alliances in existence, enhancing virtual mobility and exchange through interconnected learning infrastructures has become imperative. This paper provides insights into Learning Management System (LMS) adoption within European alliances, focusing on the Unite! alliance as a case study. While Unite! demonstrates successful implementation of Moodle as its central LMS, challenges persist in achieving uniformity across all partners. A desktop analysis of European alliances reveals that Moodle might be the most often used LMS in February 2023. A description of the LMS implementation within the Unite! analysis shows as well that a majority uses Moodle – at least as a second LMS. So, although the decision for a federated LMS based on Moodle might be the right one, these results as well indicate the need for tailored technical solutions for future developments for some partners and disparities in lecturers' and students' concerning a Moodle so that pre-emptive measures to ensure equitable participation are important. Despite these challenges, Unite!'s experience underscores the potential of Moodle as a widely adopted platform, prompting further exploration into solutions like LTI integration.

Keywords: European University, European University Alliance, Learning Management System, IT Infrastructure, Analysis

Introduction

In today's rapidly evolving world, education and collaboration are increasingly reliant on digital technologies. Several European universities collaborate in the form of "European Universities", which are transnational alliances that will lead the way towards the universities of the future, promoting European values and identity, and revolutionizing the quality and competitiveness of European higher education (see European Commission, 2023). Currently, more than 40 European university alliances, representing diverse networks of institutions collaborating across borders, try to enhance academic exchange, research cooperation, and educational innovation. Collaboration in these "European Universities" is a significant challenge and the opening and connection of their learning and teaching infrastructures within the Alliances is a necessity to enhance virtual mobility and exchange. In this contribution, we describe existing insights concerning the usage of learning management systems (LMS) within European alliances, and then detail from our own research and work within the framework of participation in the university alliance 'Unite!'.

What we know about LMS Usage in European Alliances

A key objective of the European university alliances is to "jointly delivered across inter-university campuses" (European Commission, 2023). The development of joint learning management platforms by multiple alliances (see Berger et al., 2023) can be attributed to the challenges associated with granting access to individuals from outside the university, particularly those affiliated with other alliance members. This difficulty often necessitates the creation of dedicated platforms to ensure seamless and secure access for all relevant stakeholders. The study "Making Interoperability Work" (Berger, Galati & Witteler, 2023) offers an in-depth examination of challenges of European University alliances by analysing barriers and potential solutions across four use cases—joint course catalogues, digital enrolment processes, learning platforms, and micro-credentials—highlighting that interoperability is crucial for fostering efficient international cooperation, modernizing teaching, and utilizing resources effectively in higher education.

Unite! is a dynamic European alliance of nine universities specializing in innovation, technology, and engineering, namely Aalto University, Graz University of Technology, Grenoble INP graduate school of engineering and management, University Grenoble Alpes, KTH Royal Institute of Technology, Politecnico di Torino, Universidade de Lisboa, Universitat Politècnica de Catalunya/BarcelonaTech, Technical University of Darmstadt, and Wroclaw University of Science and Technology. Unite! aims to be a leading force in technology and innovation, shaping a multilingual, trans-European campus that cultivates experts and leaders driving digital and green transitions (see Unite-University.eu, 2024)

As several other European university alliances, "Unite!" has as well embarked on a mission to bring together their higher education landscape. As mentioned in the Unite! Mission Statement 2030 (Unite!, 2022) "Unite! creates the hybrid (virtual, physical and blended) and multilingual Unite! trans-European Campus with easily accessible joint educational offerings, shared and pooled resources, efficient services and green mobility". To this date, four platforms are assigned as key platforms of the Unite! alliance: namely the Unite! Website, Unite! uShare, the learning management system (LMS) Metacampus, and Agora (a business management software (see Figure 1). These platforms serve as essential tools for facilitating communication, collaboration, resource sharing, and learning management within the alliance, enabling a cohesive and efficient ecosystem for the member universities.

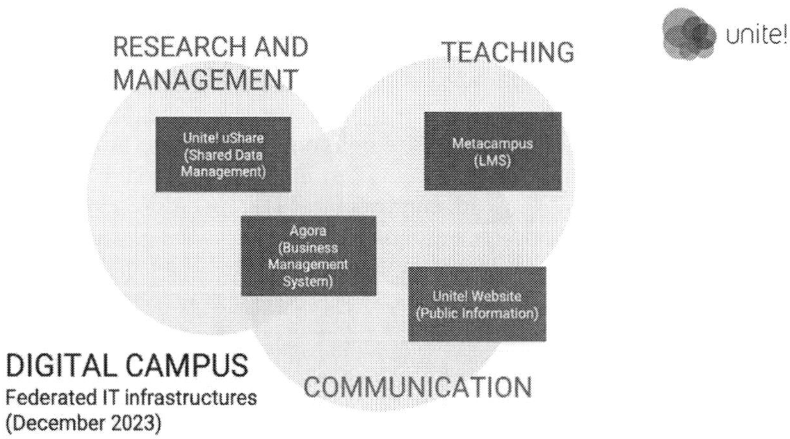

Figure 1: Overview of the Unite! Digital Campus Infrastructure Key Platforms and their key applications

Metacampus, Unite!'s central learning management system, was implemented as a virtual hub based on the open-source system Moodle. Metacampus is already in use since 2021 and is essential for the IT-related support of joint learning and teaching in the alliance. (see Alcober & Mohammadali, 2023; Alcober Segura et al., 2021). A cross-functional team from the Universitat Politècnica de Catalunya (UPC) has spearheaded the creation of the Metacampus. This team, directed by the Institute of Education Sciences (ICE), and in partnership with the ICT Services Area and UPCnet (a company offering IT services to UPC), boasts significant proficiency (Alcober & Rincón, 2000; Alcober & Mohammadali, 2023). Table 1 gives an overview about Metacampus features.

Table 1: Features of the Unite! Metacampus as federated platform in a European Alliance. Source: Ebner et al., 2023.

	Metacampus
Purpose	Interaction among users in Unite! (teachers, students, staff)
Technology	LMS (learning management system)
Platform	Moodle
License	Open source
Developer/Maintainer	UPCnet
Responsibility	E+ (Cm.2)
Examples	Educational activities (courses), non-educational activities (video contest, student festival, student fair, language tandems)
Authentication	eduGAIN
Status	Pilots in use
Languages	English + 9 partners' languages

Developments till 2022 are described in a paper by Alcober and Mohammadali (2023) and relate to EduGAIN, an integrated search engine, the potential of LTI integration, a course catalogue, and several Moodle functions such as GDPR issues, multilingualism, and open badges. In the new partnership with two additional universities as new partners, authentication with eduGAIN has been extended for them since mid-2022, and a new version of Moodle has also been introduced. In the new Erasmus+ project phase, efforts have also begun to integrate the e-learning support structures of the partners for the further development and utilization of the Metacampus. A detailed overview of the digital infrastructures utilized by all partners for learning and teaching purposes, e.g. their LMS, was captured and described as part of a requirement analysis (Ebner et al., 2024) and will be presented in this paper.

We were inspired in our research by an existing contribution from the EURECA-PRO university alliance, which has already conducted and published such surveys internally. The following table shows which learning management systems (LMS) were used in 2022 by the seven partner universities of the alliance EURECA-PRO (see Table 2).

Table 1: Summary of the results of the questionnaire on LMSs used in partner institutions of the European university alliance EURECA-PRO (Lagoudakis et al., 2022, Table 1, p. 493).

Data/Partner	MUL	TU BAF	UP	TUC	SUT	ULE	HSMW
Main LMS	Moodle	OPAL	Academia	Open eClass	Moodle	Moodle	OPAL
Self-hosted or cloud-based	Self	Cloud	Self	Self	Self	Self	Cloud
Open source	Yes	No	No	Yes	Yes	Yes	No
Fee (€/year)	No fee	>20,000	1,000-5,000	No fee	No fee	No fee	>20000
Licensed users	250	250	200	200	1,800	1,192	7,600
Students	4,000	4,000	3,700	5,000	20,000	11,550	7,000
Secondary LMS platform	-	-	-	Moodle, Web-Courses	MS Teams	-	Moodle

Although Berger (2024) presents an interesting contribution with cases, including Unite!, to our knowledge, there is no overview of the use of LMS across all university alliances. Additionally, within the Unite! alliance, we also lacked a clear overview of the LMS used by the partners. We would like to demonstrate the additional findings and our own investigations and descriptions that have emerged below.

Research questions and methodology

To thoroughly assess the efficacy of the federated Learning Management System (LMS) adopted by the Unite! university alliance, so to know if it also utilized by other alliances, and to acquire comprehensive insights into the LMS platforms employed by our partner institutions, we endeavoured to address the ensuing research inquiries:

- Which LMS are currently used by European alliances for joint activities?
- Which LMS are currently used by the partners of the Unite! alliance?

Addressing the first question, a student at Graz University of Technology (TU Graz) was tasked with a desktop analysis to figure out the extent to which the existing 44 European alliances funded by the European Commission under Erasmus+ have either implemented or planned a centralized learning management platform (Muchitsch, 2023). Therefore, a list of alliances and its websites was used as a base to check each website if a learning management is linked or mentioned there as campus offer or if any hint is available concerning a federated/centralized learning management system. Therefore, the Websites were checked if using "LMS" "learning management system" or any obvious hint for a similar solution. This research was done in February/March 2023.

An answer for the second question was delivered within a requirement analysis of the digital infrastructures concerning learning and teaching of all Unite! partners (Ebner et al., 2024). Therefore, all partners to develop sketches and descriptions starting in November 2022 to capture comprehensive infrastructure representations. This effort aimed to promote a systematic description of each partner landscape, facilitating knowledge sharing and the identification of common building blocks and processes of all partner institutions. With these descriptions as a base, an overview of key LMS usages and features is no big issue.

The following answers concerning the research questions are already presented in a report by our work package (called "community 2 digital campus" Ebner et al. 2024) and are part of an unpublished BA thesis (Muchitsch, 2023). However, they have not yet been presented to a scholarly audience Additionally, some supplementary information has been added for this paper.

Desk analysis result: Federated LMS in European Alliances

The desktop research about a (potential) LMS implementation at all existing 44 European alliances funded by the European Commission under Erasmus+ have are presented in the following. These findings provide a valuable overview of the potential status of learning management platforms within European university alliances in February 2023. It is important to acknowledge that there may be discrepancies and uncertainties due to variations in self-descriptions and implementations.

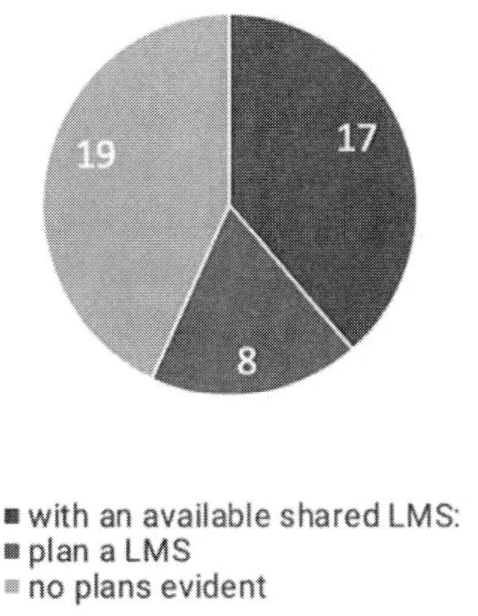

Figure 2 : LMS implemented by European university alliances according to their self-descriptions (Website) in February 2023 (left, N=44); Source: Muchitsch (2023).

As shown in Figure 2, the analysis reveals the self-described status of 44 European University alliances as follows: 17 alliances already possess a shared Learning Management System (LMS), 8 have plans to implement one, and 19 have no plans for an LMS in spring 2023.

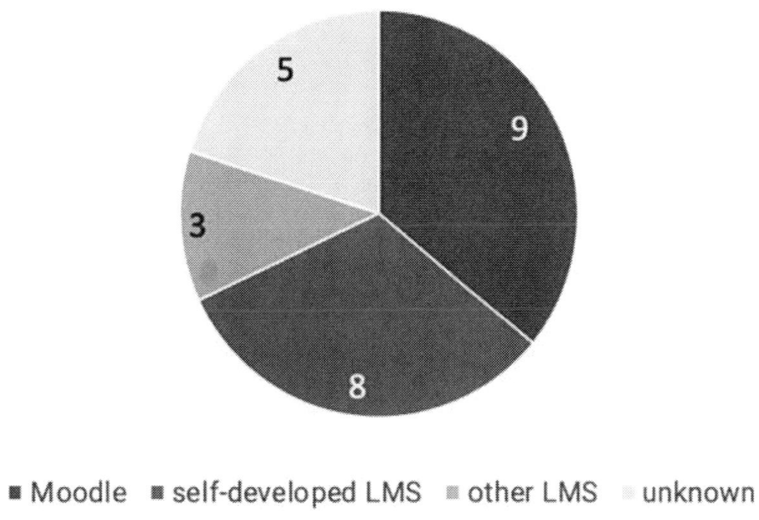

Figure 3: LMS in use by European university alliances according to their self-descriptions (Website) in February 2023 (n=25), Source: Muchitsch (2023).

Focusing specifically on the 25 alliances with an LMS, the breakdown is as follows: 9 utilize Moodle, 8 have developed their own LMS, and 3 use other platforms (Agora, Ilias, and Gala), for 5 the LMS is unknown (see Figure 3).

Survey Result: LMS in Use in the European alliance Unite!

First, we would like to give a general overview of the framework data of the Unite! partner universities by presenting their countries of origin and the number of students in Table 2.

Table 2: The Unite! alliance universities in overview. (January 2024)

University	Abbr.	Country	Number of enrolled students	Number of academic staff	Number of admin. staff
Aalto University	Aalto	Finland	17,500	2,800	1,200
Graz University of Technology	TU Graz	Austria	16,500	2,700	1,100
Grenoble INP graduate school of engineering and management, University Grenoble Alpes	Grenoble INP-UGA	France	8,350	550	730
KTH Royal Institute of Technology	KTH	Sweden	13,500	2,750	1,250
Politecnico di Torino	PoliTO	Italy	38,700	1,191	986
Universidade de Lisboa	ULisboa	Portugal	47,800	3,400	2,100
Universitat Politècnica de Catalunya/BarcelonaTech	UPC	Spain	30,000	3,000	n.a.
Technical University of Darmstadt	TUDa	Germany	24,406	3,031	1,986
Wroclaw University of Science and Technology	Wroclaw Tech	Poland	21,176	2,288	1,957

Sources for students, academic staff and administrative staff (if) as follows:
Aalto (https://en.wikipedia.org/wiki/Aalto_University, 2.10.23),
TU Graz (https://de.wikipedia.org/wiki/Technische_Universit%C3%A4t_Graz, 2.10.23),
INP-UGA (https://www.grenoble-inp.fr/en/about/key-numbers, 14.1.24),
KTH (https://en.wikipedia.org/wiki/KTH_Royal_Institute_of_Technology, 2.10.23),
PoliTO (https://www.polito.it/en/polito/politecnico-at-a-glance, 18.10.2023),
ULisboa (https://en.wikipedia.org/wiki/University_of_Lisbon, 2.10.23),
UPC (https://en.wikipedia.org/wiki/Polytechnic_University_of_Catalonia, 2.10.23),
TUDa (https://en.wikipedia.org/wiki/Technische_Universit%C3%A4t_Darmstadt, 2.10.23),
Wroclaw Tech (https://en.wikipedia.org/wiki/Wroc%C5%82aw_University_of_Science_and_Technology, 2.10.23)

Table 3 gives an overview of key issues concerning LMS in partner institutions of Unite! (Januar 2023). The table mentiones the main LMS – 7 of 9 uses Moodle. Only partner KTH does not use an open source LMS. If secondary LMS are included, only one partner has no Moodle installation at all. Additionally, the table as well show if and how LTI interface is already implemented (8 of 9) and if the partners use MOOC platforms. 3 uses Open edX, 2 Moodle as base for their MOOC platforms. Finally, all partners report an EduGain implementation.

Table 3: Overview of key issues concerning LMS in partner institutions of Unite! (10/2023)

	Main LMS	**Open-Source**	**Secondary LMS**	**LTI interface**	**MOOC platform**	**EduGAIN**
TU Graz	Moodle	YES	-	YES	Moodle	YES
ULisboa	Fenix Platform	YES	Moodle, Open edX	NO (Moodle: YES)	Open edX	YES
UPC	Moodle	YES	-	YES	-	YES

PoliTO	DIDATTICA	YES	Moodle	YES	Open edX	YES
UGA-INP	Moodle	YES	Chamilo	YES	-	YES
TUDa	Moodle	YES	-	YES	-	YES
Wroclaw Tech	Moodle	YES	-	YES	-	YES
KTH	Canvas	NO	-	YES	Open edX	YES
Aalto	Moodle	YES	-	YES	Moodle	YES

The table shows that there is great homogeneity about the learning management system of almost all universities. Since, as already mentioned, the common federated LMS is also based on Moodle, this is of course a major challenge, especially for universities with less Moodle experience – both in terms of technology and use by teachers and students.

Although this table appears quite uniform, the comparison of other systems and platforms reveals that the information systems are very homogeneous in their functions but highly heterogeneous in their software implementation. So, all partners have systems in use that support student registration, getting access data, finding curriculum/courses, course registration or course learning activities – but use quite a range of system, detailed in the partners' descriptions (Ebner et al., 2024). Furthermore, the further presentation also highlights major differences in how self-sufficient or networked the universities are within a national context, such as specific IT applications or selection policies.

Discussion and Outlook

While insights into the infrastructure of the Unite! partners were developed by technical experts in multiple rounds, ensuring the accuracy of the descriptions, the same level of confidence cannot be attributed to the results pertaining to all university alliances. The desktop analysis is likely to encounter discrepancies and uncertainties due to variations in self-descriptions and implementations. A survey conducted across all alliances would undoubtedly yield more substantive insights.

Despite this uncertainty, the survey for Unite! indicates that the selection of Moodle as the platform base was undoubtedly a successful choice, given that Moodle is likely used by most university alliances. This holds true for the alliance itself, but also underscores the risk that the prerequisites may not be uniformly met. Consequently, there arises a need to identify diverse technical solutions to ensure technical interoperability. LTI is currently being considered as one of the possible solutions, with initial pilot studies showing promise.

Simultaneously, it becomes evident that the competencies and prerequisites among educators in different institutions in handling Moodle vary significantly. Thus, pre-emptive measures must be taken to prevent individual partners from being disadvantaged.

Competing interests

The author(s) has/have no competing interests to declare.

Acknowledgements

The work presented herein was accomplished collaboratively with invaluable input and feedback from e-learning and IT experts across all partner universities in Unite! Community 2 Digital Campus. We extend our heartfelt gratitude for their exemplary cooperation. We would like to thank you for the excellent cooperation.

Funding Information

The Unite! alliance has received funding from the European Commission (Erasmus+).

References

Berger, F., Galati, N. & Witteler, S. (2023). Making Interoperability Work, Challenges and Solutions for an Interoperable Higher Education System, In: Hochschulforum Digitalisierung Report No. 72 / September 2023, URL: https://hochschulforumdigitalisierung.de/sites/default/files/dateien/HFD_report_no.72_Making_interoperability_work.pdf

European Commission (2023). European Universities initiative. URL: https://education.ec.europa.eu/education-levels/higher-education/european-universities-initiative (2023-11-06)

Unite! (2022). Unite! Mission Statement 2030. URL: https://www.unite-university.eu/media/unite-mission-statement-2030.pdf (2023-11-06)

Muchitsch, M. (2023). Learning Management Systems in European University Alliances. Unpublished Bachelor thesis, TU Graz.

Lagoudakis, M. G., Gkizeli, M., Fotiou, A., Fragkedaki, D., & Kollnig, S. (2022). Teaching and Research in the Digital World. BHM Berg-und Hüttenmännische Monatshefte, 167(10), 489-494.

Unite-University.eu (2024). Get inspired, grow together. Let's Unite! (Webpage). URL: https://uniteinanutshell.unite-university.eu/?utm_source=unite-landing&utm_medium=unite-landing&utm_campaign=unite-nutshell&utm_id=nutshell

AI-Powered Curricula: Unpacking the Potential and Progress of Generative Technologies in Education

Duygu Bektik[1], Thomas Daniel Ullmann[1], Chris Edwards[1], Christothea Herodotou[1], Denise Whitelock[1]

[1] Institute of Educational Technology, The Open University, United Kingdom; duygu.bektik@open.ac.uk, {firstname} dot {lastname} at open.ac.uk

Correspondence: Duygu Bektik: duygu.bektik@open.ac.uk

Abstract:

The aim of this narrative review is to understand how Artificial Intelligence (AI), specifically generative AI (e.g. ChatGPT) is thought to be used to support teachers in content authoring and curriculum production. Our findings indicate that Generative AI is envisioned as a co-design partner in enhancing educational content such as rubrics, lesson plans, interactive exercises, analogies, reflective questions, and case studies tailored to learning goals and instructional needs. The literature suggests that the key issues with the use of ChatGPT in education can be summarised mainly around its accuracy, and reliability, and its potential to lead to plagiarism. The analysis of empirical studies on the use of generative AI in higher education revealed first insights into themes such as ChatGPT's role in administrative tasks, varied perceptions of AI, generational differences in attitudes, multifunctional roles of ChatGPT, concerns about academic integrity and need for AI literacy, and the call for teaching philosophy reform, around assessment.

Keywords: generative AI, LLMs, ChatGPT, curriculum production, content authoring

Introduction

Artificial Intelligence (AI) has been in the news again and heralded a new AI boom. Natural Language Processing (NLP) stands out as a significant domain, facilitating machines to interpret and generate human language, thereby potentially bridging the communication gap between humans and computers (Liddy, 2001; Rafail and Freitas, 2020). Grounded in linguistic theories, advancements in NLP have birthed tools such as chatbots and intelligent tutoring systems. Large Language Models (LLMs), notably the Generative Pre-trained Transformer (GPT-3) (Floridi & Chiriatti, 2020), represent significant progress in this field. AI-powered NLP technology enables conversational interfaces, such as chatbots and virtual assistants, to answer learners' questions and provide guidance in a conversational manner.

The adoption of ChatGPT has been phenomenal in the last few years. It is one of the fastest-growing consumer applications (Hu, 2023). ChatGPT is trained to "generate humanlike text based on a given prompt or context. It can be used for a variety of NLP tasks, such as text completion, conversation generation, and language translation" (Baidoo-Anu, 2023, p. 4). The language model behind ChatGPT has been developed utilizing an extensive, unlabelled dataset comprising a diverse array of texts, predominantly from sources such as Wikipedia and numerous other websites. This dataset encompasses material primarily in English, yet it also includes content in a variety of other languages (Floridi and Chiriatti, 2020).

Since the emergence of ChatGPT and similar tools, they have become more accessible and user friendly, thus significantly increasing public attention (NeJame et al., 2023). The abilities of ChatGPT to carry out complex tasks have caused mixed feelings among educators as this advancement in AI seems to revolutionize existing educational praxis, which are discussed next. This is followed by the analysis of the literature for two research questions. The aim of this narrative review is to answer the following research questions: 1) How is AI envisioned to be used to support curriculum production? 2) What are emerging insights from empirical studies that use AI to support curriculum production?

Methodology

The literature to answer the above questions has been searched on Google Scholar and The Open University's library by using the following keywords: ((Artificial Intelligence) OR (AI) OR (AIED)) OR (Large language models) OR (LLM) OR (ChatGPT) OR (Generative AI)) AND ((Higher Education) OR (University) OR (Education)) AND ((Content Authoring) OR (Curriculum production) OR (Course production) OR (Course Content)). A structured rapid literature review approach (Smela et. al, 2023) was undertaken to identify relevant studies involving a search of peer-reviewed literature databases, and an Internet search to identify relevant grey literature, including newspaper articles and blog posts.

The focus has been on publications over the last five years, specifically the last two years for any ChatGPT related literature. We included peer-reviewed articles in English, reporting on AI within education primarily at university level, and indexed in these international databases: EBSCO Education Source, ERIC, Web of Science and Scopus (covering titles, abstracts, and keywords). Database search has returned 139 articles, grey literature was searched in Google with the first 50 citations screened for relevance.

Following the removal of duplicate records (n=4), titles and abstracts were screened for relevance to the research questions in the preliminary review. Each article was skimmed with an inclusion criterion: its relevance to the AI, higher education, LLMs, and whether the study reflects on views and conceptions of people on using AI, and if it is related to content authoring/curriculum/module production. Following the first phase of selection we excluded 79 articles. The most common reason for discarding a paper was that it simply did not address the usage of LLM in education but rather in a different context. Identified papers which have met the inclusion criteria were tabulated and grouped in a spreadsheet by the type of research, research question, design, quality, sample size, most important findings, limitations, and results summarised for each. In total, we carefully reviewed 41 articles, of which 17 was empirical studies.

Debate and Key Issues

The rise of generative AI has brought with it concern and controversy. Since ChatGPT has been open to public use, it has become the centre of ongoing debate regarding the potential negative effects that it can have on teaching and learning. "Generative AI has been identified by many higher education experts as one of the most disruptive technologies of our time" (EDUCAUSE, 2023, p. 21). With the potential to create text, images, and sounds in ways that sometimes convincingly mimic human creation, this technology has the potential to impact instructional materials, assessments, and more. "This is a much bigger disruption than the pandemic," stated Emad Mostaque, founder and CEO of Stability AI, to an audience at Goldman Sachs 2023 Disruptive Technology Symposium in London, by pointing to the fact that AI LLMs successfully writing software code and OpenAI's ChatGPT can pass Google's exam for a high-level software engineer, even though it's a non-specialized model.

Reviewing the literature from 2022-2024 the key issues with the use of ChatGPT in education can be summarised mainly around its accuracy, and reliability, and its potential to lead to plagiarism. This was also noted by other researchers such as Lim et. Al (2023) and Kasneci (2023).

Accuracy: Three papers are identified in this theme stating there are significant concerns regarding the factual accuracy of ChatGPT and similar models, which may propagate biases, outdated information, and even fabricate non-existent references (Baidoo-Anu 2023; Kim, J.K. et al., 2023; Lo, 2023). This inaccuracy is attributed to bias or the limited scope within the data used to train the model. The need for transparency in distinguishing between human and AI authorship in academic contributions is emphasized.

Reliability: Three papers mentioned that the ChatGPT's propensity to produce "hallucinations" or false information poses a risk to students' learning and critical judgment, potentially leading to the acceptance of inaccurate information (Loos, Gröpler, and Goudeau, 2023; Kasneci, 2023; Liu, 2023). Critics worry about the negative impact on students' critical thinking and problem-solving skills, highlighting the necessity of educating students about the limitations and ethical implications of generative AI.

Plagiarism and Academic Integrity: Five papers stated that some of the most vigorous objections to using generative AI in higher education are related to academic integrity, as students can use it to cheat on assignments and exams, which can be undetected by traditional plagiarism detection software. The discussion extends to the broader implications of generative AI in perpetuating biases and the importance of digital literacy and human oversight. (Zhai, 2022; Lo, 2023; Pelletier et al., 2022; Loos, Gröpler, and Goudeau, 2023; Webb, 2023).

Higher Education and AI: Fourteen articles mentioned that the response to ChatGPT in higher education is mixed, with some institutions banning its use due to concerns over accuracy, plagiarism, and dependency on AI outputs, while others see it as an opportunity for constructive use (Liu, 2023; Mowreader, A, 2023; Wood, 2023; Lukpat, 2023; Cassidy, 2023; McCallum, 2023; D'Emilio and O'brien, 2023; Brodkin, 2023; Ryan-Mosley, 2023; Thorp, 2023; Dwivedi et al. 2023). Instances of restrictive actions include banning by universities in Hong Kong, mixed responses in the UK, and access restrictions in New York City and Seattle schools, alongside Italy's block over privacy concerns. OpenAI's lack of transparency and the movement towards regulation, such as the EU AI Act, reflect growing concerns about AI's role in education.

RQ1: Potential Uses and Benefits of AI in curriculum production

One of the promising applications of Generative AI in higher education is seen in its potential to assist educators in generating course materials, including summaries, quizzes, and discussion prompts. By synthesising and rephrasing existing content, Generative AI can save time and effort for educators, allowing them to focus on more complex aspects of course design and pedagogy (Alshater, 2022; Terwiesch, 2023). Based on a review by Chen et al., (2023) on AI in Education, using a qualitative research approach, it was found that AI systems have enabled the customisation and personalisation of curriculum and content according to students' needs, leading to improved learning experiences, and overall educational quality.

With the rise of Generative AI, the integration of AI in Education has seen significant advancements. Generative AI is increasingly being used for a range of purposes: from creating instructional content, and providing automated assessment feedback, and to supporting academic services (Pelletier et al., 2022). A course designer could develop highly engaging course content simply by providing a Generative AI engine with a few sophisticated text prompts that are aligned with student learning outcomes. Based on Nagy (2024), Rahman and Watanobe (2023), Michel-Villarreal et. al (2023), Liu & Wang (2023) and Herft (2023), the list below summarised in which way Generative AI can be used as a co-design partner, to enhance the content by:

- creating prompts for open-ended questions that align with the learning goals and success criteria of the unit of instruction.
- generating quality rubrics that clearly and concisely explain exactly what students need to accomplish to be successful in the various required levels of proficiency.
- creating prompts for formative assessment activities that provide ongoing feedback to inform teaching and learning.
- helping in creating lesson plans for specific courses, developing customized resources, and learning activities, carrying out assessment and evaluation, and supporting the writing process of research.
- suggesting ideas for graphical content.
- creating ways to make content more engaging with interactive exercises and simulations.
- creating analogies to turn abstract concepts into concrete ones.
- generating reflective questions based on course readings or video scripts.
- generating student learning tasks and feedback based on existing course content.
- generating engaging video scripts based on existing written content, including suggesting on-screen graphics.
- generating scenarios or case studies based on existing content.

RQ2: Insights from empirical studies

The analysis involved identifying themes and patterns across 17 empirical studies within the literature concerning the use of Generative AI in higher education. The analysis encompassed perceptions of AI, generational differences in attitudes towards AI, and the multifunctional roles of ChatGPT as summarised in Table 1 below.

Theme	Description
Administrative Tasks	ChatGPT is effective in handling administrative and admission processes in educational settings (Kumar & Raman, 2022).
Perceptions of AI	Students generally have positive perceptions of AI, influenced by prior exposure (Lin, Huang & Yang, 2023; Ali et al., 2023; Eysenbach, 2023) but are hesitant about AI replacing faculty roles (Kumar & Raman 2022; Eysenbach, 2023; Rospigliosi, 2023).
Generational Differences	Differences in acceptance and perceptions of generative AI between Gen Z students and Gen X/Millennial educators, with the latter showing more cautiousness (Chan and Lee, 2023).
Roles of ChatGPT	ChatGPT serves as an interlocutor, content provider, teaching assistant, and evaluator in educational settings (Jeon & Lee, 2023).
Concerns and Limitations	Issues related to academic integrity, lack of citation capabilities, and the need for human-centered AI approaches (Perkins, 2023; Rospigliosi, 2023).
AI Literacy	The importance of upskilling in AI competencies and AI literacy in education and the need for tailored curricula and teaching strategies (Tlili et. al 2023; Ng et. al, 2023; Long & Magerko, 2020).
Using ChatGPT for Research	The potential of ChatGPT in supporting qualitative research, enhancing efficiency, and aiding non-native speakers in language comprehension (Yan et. al, 2023).
Teaching Philosophy Reform (Assessment Reformation)	Need for a new teaching philosophy to integrate chatbots effectively in education especially around assessment (Tilli et al., 2023). Need for innovate assessment practices to focus more on higher order thinking skills and authentic evaluations.

Table 1. Themes from empirical studies that use AI in curriculum production.

Conclusion

This rapid literature review captures the current enthusiasm for Generative AI and the thinking into how generative AI can aid curriculum production, revealing insights across two research questions. It highlights AI's pivotal role in enhancing efficiency and effectiveness in creating educational content, such as quizzes, simulations, and personalized learning materials, through automated generation and customization according to students' needs. The cited empirical studies underscore the benefits of AI in saving time, allowing for tailored educational experiences, and presenting both challenges and opportunities in pedagogical practices as discussed in section RQ2. Additionally, insights into generational differences in perceptions of AI, the multifaceted roles of generative AI like ChatGPT in education, and the ethical considerations surrounding AI use are highlighted in these studies.

From this literature review, we can see that it potentially offers an opportunity as a co-design partner in course development. This can be realised in two ways: a) to support the development of learning artefacts, such as written text, assessment, graphics, and interactive content, enabling us to enhance the overall course quality with the same resource as previously discussed in RQ1 data analysis section; and b) to streamline administrative tasks, freeing up time for educators to focus on more strategic and creative aspects of course creation as discussed in RQ2 data analysis section. By embracing generative AI, it is thought that we can enhance the learning experience of students and create efficiencies in our work as educators.

In conclusion, while generative AI offers substantial opportunities to enhance educational practices and outcomes, strategic and ethical considerations must guide its integration into educational landscape. The future direction involves not only maximizing AI's educational benefits but also cultivating AI literacy among educators and students to ensure responsible use. This comprehensive approach will enable the educational sector to navigate the evolving landscape of AI technologies, fostering an environment where learning is both enriched and aligned with the ethical standards of the digital age.

References

Baidoo-Anu, D, and Leticia O.A. (2023) "Education in the era of generative artificial intelligence (AI): Understanding the potential benefits of ChatGPT in promoting teaching and learning." Journal of AI 7.1 (2023).

Brodkin, J, (2023). GPT-4 poses too many risks, and releases should be halted, AI group tells FTC. Available at: https://arstechnica.com/tech-policy/2023/03/ftc-should-investigate-openai-and-halt-gpt-4-releases-ai-research-group-says/ (Accessed November 10, 2023).

Cassidy, C. (2023). Australian universities to return to 'pen and paper' exams after students caught using AI to write essays. Available at: https://www.theguardian.com/australia-news/2023/jan/10/universities-to-return-to-pen-and-paper-exams-after-students-caught-using-ai-to-write-essays (Accessed November 10, 2023).

Chan, C. K. Y., & Lee, K. K. (2023). The AI generation gap: Are Gen Z students more interested in adopting generative AI such as ChatGPT in teaching and learning than their Gen X and millennial generation teachers?. Smart Learning Environments, 10(1), 60.

Chen, Y., Jensen, S., Albert, L. J., Gupta, S., & Lee, T. (2023). Artificial intelligence (AI) student assistants in the classroom: Designing chatbots to support student success. Information Systems Frontiers, 25, 161–182. https://doi.org/10.1007/s10796-022-10291-4

D'Emilio, F and O'Brien, M. (2023, December 20). Italy temporarily blocks ChatGPT over privacy concerns. AP News. Retrieved from https://apnews.com/article/chatgpt-ai-data-privacy-italy-66634e4d9ade3c0eb63edab62915066f

Dwivedi, Y. K., Kshetri, N., Hughes, L., Slade, E. L., Jeyaraj, A., Kar, A. K., et al. (2023). So what if ChatGPT wrote it?. Multidisciplinary perspectives on opportunities, challenges, and implications of generative conversational AI for research, practice, and policy. Int. J. Inf. Manag. 71:102642. doi: 10.1016/j.ijinfomgt.2023.102642

EDUCAUSE. (2023). Horizon report: 2023 Teaching and Learning. Retrieved from EDUCAUSE Learning Initiative and The New Media Consortium website: https://library.educause.edu/-/media/files/library/2023/4/2023hrteachinglearning.pdf?#page=18&la=en&hash=9C267A302A74E8B6DFB259F90029DE075F6BC179

Eysenbach, G. (2023). The role of ChatGPT, generative language models, and artificial intelligence in medical education: a conversation with ChatGPT and a call for papers. JMIR Medical Education, 9(1), e46885.

Floridi, L., & Chiriatti, M. (2020). GPT-3: Its nature, scope, limits, and consequences. Minds and Machines, 30, 681-694.

Gaceta, La (2023). Prohíben usar la ChatGPT en varias universidades. Available at: https://www.lagaceta.com.ar/nota/978320/sociedad/prohiben-usar-chatgpt-varias-universidades.html (Accessed November 10, 2023).

Herft, A. (2023). A Teacher's Prompt Guide to ChatGPT aligned with 'What Works Best' Guide. Retrieved on January 23 2023 from https://drive.google.com/file/d/15qAxnUzOwAPwHzoaKBJd8FAgiOZYcIxq/view.

Hu, K. (2023). ChatGPT sets record for fastest-growing user base - analyst note. Reuters.

Jeon, J., & Lee, S. (2023). Large language models in education: A focus on the complementary relationship between human teachers and ChatGPT. Education and Information Technologies, 28(12), 15873-15892.

Kasneci, E.; Seßler, K.; Küchemann, S.; Bannert, M.; Dementieva, D.; Fischer, F.; Gasser, U.; Groh, G.; Günnemann, S.; Hüllermeier, E.; et al. ChatGPT for good? On opportunities and challenges of large language models for education. Learn. Individ. Differ. 2023, 103, 102274.

Kim, J.K. et al. (2023) 'ChatGPT and large language model (LLM) chatbots: The current state of acceptability and a proposal for guidelines on utilization in academic medicine', Journal of pediatric urology, 19(5), pp. 598–604. Available at: https://doi.org/10.1016/j.jpurol.2023.05.018.

Kumar and Raman. (2022). Student perceptions on Artificial Intelligence (AI) in higher education. In 2022 IEEE Integrated STEM Education Conference (ISEC). DOI: 10.1109/ISEC54952.2022.10025165.

Lim, W. M., Gunasekara, A., Pallant, J. L., Pallant, J. I., & Pechenkina, E. (2023). Generative AI and the future of education: Ragnarök or reformation? A paradoxical perspective from management educators. The International Journal of Management Education, 21(2), 100790.

Liddy, E. D. (2001). Natural language processing.

Liu, L. (2023). The opportunities and challenges brought to international Chinese education by ChatGPT: Expert perspectives from the joint forum of Beijing Language and Culture University and the American Association of Chinese Teachers. Chinese Teaching in the World, 37, 291–315.

Liu, M., Ren, Y., Nyagoga, L. M., Stonier, F., Wu, Z., & Yu, L. (2023). Future of education in the era of generative artificial intelligence: Consensus among Chinese scholars on applications of ChatGPT in schools. Open Access, First published online September 2, 2023. https://doi.org/10.1002/fer3.10

Long, D., & Magerko, B. (2020, April). What is AI literacy? Competencies and design considerations. In Proceedings of the 2020 CHI conference on human factors in computing systems (pp. 1-16).

Lo, C.K. What Is the Impact of ChatGPT on Education? A Rapid Review of the Literature. Educ. Sci. 2023, 13, 410.

Loos, E., Gröpler, J., and Goudeau, M-L. S. (2023). Using ChatGPT in Education: Human Reflection on ChatGPT's Self-Reflection. Societies, 13(8), 196. [DOI: 10.3390/soc13080196].

Lukpat, A. (2023). ChatGPT banned in new York City public schools over concerns about cheating, learning development. Available at: https://www.wsj.com/articles/chatgpt-banned-in-new-york-city-public-schools-over-concerns-about-cheating-learning-development-11673024059 (Accessed at November 10, 2023).

McCallum, B. S. (2023, April 1). ChatGPT banned in Italy over privacy concerns. BBC News. https://www.bbc.com/news/technology-65139406

M Alshater, M. (2022). Exploring the role of artificial intelligence in enhancing academic performance: A case study of ChatGPT. Available at SSRN 4312358.

Michel-Villarreal, R., Vilalta-Perdomo, E., Salinas-Navarro, D. E., Thierry-Aguilera, R., & Gerardou, F. S. (2023). Challenges and opportunities of generative AI for higher education as explained by ChatGPT. Education Sciences, 13(9), 856.

Mowreader, A. (2023, July 26). Academic Success Tip: Working Smarter With ChatGPT. Inside Higher Ed. Retrieved from https://www.insidehighered.com/news/student-success/academic-life/2023/07/26/teaching-college-students-write-using-chatgpt

Nagy, S., McInnes, R., & Airey, L. (2024). GEN-AI: A transformative partner in collaborative course development. International Journal of Innovative Online Education, 2023(5), Article 1048. https://doi.org/10.1615/IntJInnovOnlineEdu.2023051048

NeJame, L., Bhaaradwaj, R., Shaw, C., & Fox, K. (2023). Generative AI in higher education: From fear to experimentation, embracing AI's potential. Tyton Partners (April 25, 2023) https://tytonpartners.com/generative-ai-in-higher-education-from-fear-toexperimentation-embracing-ais-potential, Accessed May, 10.

Ng, D. T. K., Lee, M., Tan, R. J. Y., Hu, X., Downie, J. S., & Chu, S. K. W. (2023). A review of AI teaching and learning from 2000 to 2020. Education and Information Technologies, 28(7), 8445-8501.

Perkins, M. (2023). Academic Integrity considerations of AI Large Language Models in the post-pandemic era: ChatGPT and beyond. Journal of university teaching & learning practice, 20(2), 07.

Pelletier, K., McCormack, M., Reeves, J., Robert, J., Arbino, N., Al-Freih, M., Dickson-Deane, C., Guevara, C., Koster, L., Sánchez-Mendiola, M., Bessette, L. S., & Stine, J. (2022). EDUCAUSE Horizon Report, teaching and learning edition. EDUCAUSE.

Rafail, P., & Freitas, I. (2020). Natural Language Processing. SAGE Publications Ltd.

Rahman, M.M.; Watanobe, Y. (2023). ChatGPT for education and research: Opportunities, threats, and strategies. Appl. Sci. 2023, 13, 5783.

Rospigliosi, P. A. (2023). Artificial intelligence in teaching and learning: what questions should we ask of ChatGPT?. Interactive Learning Environments, 31(1), 1-3.

Ryan-Mosley, T. (2023). Five big takeaways from Europe's AI act. MIT Technology Review. Available at: https://www.technologyreview.com/2023/06/19/1075063/five-big-takeaways-from-europes-ai-act/ (Accessed November 10, 2023).

Smela B, Toumi M, Świerk K, Francois C, Biernikiewicz M, Clay E, Boyer L. Rapid literature review: definition and methodology. J Mark Access Health Policy. 2023 Jul 28;11(1):2241234. doi: 10.1080/20016689.2023.2241234. PMID: 37533549; PMCID: PMC10392303.

Terwiesch, C. (2023). Would chat GPT3 get a Wharton MBA. A prediction based on its performance in the operations management course.

Thorp, H. H. (2023). ChatGPT is fun, but not an author. Science, 379(6630), 313-313.

Tlili, A., Shehata, B., Adarkwah, M. A., Bozkurt, A., Hickey, D. T., Huang, R., & Agyemang, B. (2023). What if the devil is my guardian angel: ChatGPT as a case study of using chatbots in education. Smart Learning Environments, 10(1), 15.

Webb, A. 2023. How to Prepare for a GenAI Future You Can't Predict. https://hbr.org/2023/08/how-to-prepare-for-a-genai-future-you-cant-predict

Wood, P. (2023, December 20). Oxford and Cambridge to ban ChatGPT over Plagiarism fears but other universities choose to embrace AI bot. iNews. Retrieved from https://inews.co.uk/news/oxford-cambridge-ban-chatgpt-plagiarism-universities-2178391

Yan, L., Echeverria, V., Nieto, G. F., Jin, Y., Swiecki, Z., Zhao, L., ... & Martinez-Maldonado, R. (2023). Human-AI Collaboration in Thematic Analysis using ChatGPT: A User Study and Design Recommendations. arXiv preprint arXiv:2311.03999

Zhai, X. ChatGPT user experience: Implications for education. SSRN 2022.

Exploring student's learning experience with an e-learning platform

Sandra Kučina Softić[1], Mirela Ruvić[2], Zvonko Martinović[3], Tona Radobolja [4]

[1] University of Zagreb University Computing Centre, Croatia, sskucina@srce.hr
[2] University of Zagreb University Computing Centre, Croatia; mirela.ruvic@srce.hr
[3] University of Zagreb University Computing Centre, Croatia, zvonko.martinovic@srce.hr
[4] University of Zagreb University Computing Centre, Croatia, tona.radobolja@srce.hr

Correspondence: Sandra Kučina Softić, sskucina@srce.hr

Abstract:

In this paper, we present the results of the research on students' learning experience with the use of an e-learning platform. The research aimed to have a better overview of the student's perception of the e-learning platform and their satisfaction with its features for learning. The virtual learning environment can influence student learning, and enable rich and engaged students' experience. E-learning can offer many opportunities for learning beyond traditional boundaries so e-learning platforms are popular and massively used. Nevertheless, some factors could potentially affect the outcomes and results of e-learning. One of them is the learner's perception of e-learning and another is digital technology used to facilitate e-learning with a focus on the reliability, ease of use, quality and usefulness of the technology itself. In this paper, we will talk about the e-learning platform Merlin, in this case, the Learning Management System that is part of the Virtual Learning Environment and students' experience in its use. The E-learning platform Merlin is maintained by the E-learning Centre at the University of Zagreb University Computing Centre (SRCE) and is part of the virtual learning environment for the higher education system in Croatia. The e-learning platform is based on the open-source system Moodle. Student feedback is important and enables the E-learning Centre team at SRCE to have a better overview of the student's perception of the e-learning platform and their satisfaction with its features for learning. The results indicate that students' perception of the e-learning platform depends as well on the e-courses they attend, therefore how teachers are skilled to know how to use the e-learning platform and its features. Research results indicate that students' experience is modest as their e-courses are prepared using basic LMS features. Nevertheless, the results show that students find the e-learning platform important for their learning, they recognize its flexibility in accessing the course content and information about the course and performing tasks needed in the course. In addition, they prefer hybrid learning and find themselves knowledgeable in the use of ICT and e-learning.

Keywords: learning management experience, LMS, student experience, virtual environment, contribution to learning, e-learning

Introduction

Education in the digital age enables students to learn in virtual learning environments. The higher education system facing challenges to respond to the new, modern and competitive global education market is therefore taking steps into digitalization and potential digital transformation. The shift to the online environment and digital education has given rise to information and communication technologies (ICT) to support teaching and learning processes. E-learning platforms, Learning Management Systems or Virtual Learning Environments are increasingly used to facilitate e-learning in the educational process. The virtual learning environment can influence student learning, and enable rich and engaged students' experience. E-learning can offer many opportunities for learning beyond traditional boundaries so e-learning platforms are popular and massively used. Nevertheless, some factors could potentially affect the outcomes and results of e-learning. One of them is the learner's perception of e-learning and another is digital technology used to facilitate e-learning with a focus on the reliability, ease of use, quality and usefulness of technology itself. In this paper, we will talk about the e-learning platform Merlin, in this case LMS that is part of VLE and students' experience in its use.

E-learning platform Merlin for HEI in Croatia

The University of Zagreb University Computing Centre (SRCE) (https://www.srce.unizg.hr/en) is a central infrastructure institution that plans, develops, and improves e-infrastructure and digital services for the needs of the academic and scientific community in Croatia and provides support in their usage. SRCE is also the competence centre for information and communication technologies as well as the centre for education and support in the area of ICT application. The E-learning Centre at SRCE (ELC) (https://www.srce.unizg.hr/en/elc) provides support in the implementation of e-learning to higher education institutions, teachers and students. It has been a national e-learning centre for higher education for more than 16 years. One of the tasks of the E-learning Centre is to provide and maintain a virtual learning environment for the needs of higher education. The virtual learning environment comprises an e-learning platform (LMS), e-portfolio system, videoconferencing systems, Merlin mobile application, Merlin archives and Moodle installation for testing purposes. Merlin is connected with the Information System of Higher Education (ISVU) and Digital Academic Archives and Repositories.

The e-learning platform Merlin is based on the open-source Learning Management System (LMS) Moodle and is refined and improved by the ELC who also provides technical support and instructional design support to users. The e-learning platform Merlin is upgraded every academic year to the newest Moodle version and the E-learning Centre team provides support in the use of each version by adaption of support materials and training courses as well as organising webinars and guidelines on how to use new version and features. The e-learning platform Merlin (https://merlin.srce.hr) hosts per academic year more than 30.000 e-courses that are conducted by about 10,000 teachers for more than 90.000 students. In further text, we refer to Merlin as an e-learning platform.

E-learning platform Merlin for academic year 2023/2024

The E-learning platform Merlin for the academic year 2023/2024 has been upgraded to the latest version of Moodle 4.2. In addition to that, the ELC team have set up the web portal which replaces the previous front pages of all Merlin instances (current academic year and archives). The navigation within the portal is more transparent and the portal presents the E-learning Centre's news and information more concisely.

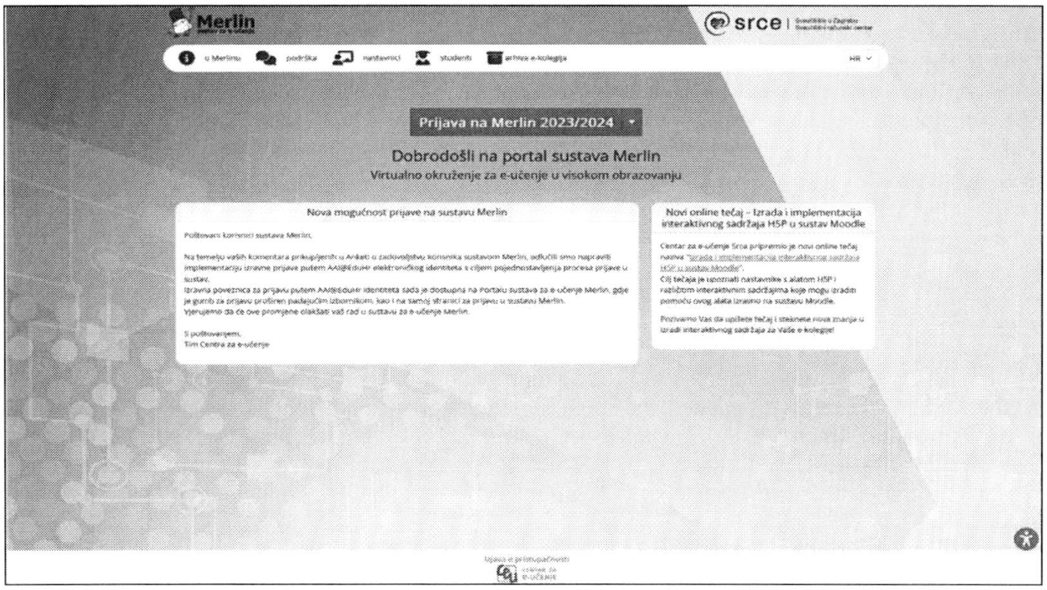

Figure 1: The e-learning platform Merlin portal (https://merlin.srce.hr/)

An important part of the work of the E-learning Centre at SRCE is user support. The ELC continuously works to provide high-quality support to users, whether technical is the use of the tools and technologies the E-learning Centre provides or support in the instructional design of courses and training of teachers to meet digital competences required to teach in the online environment. Therefore, user feedback is very important as it provides valuable information on how to improve the work and ensure the best possible support as well as accessible and easy-to-use tools and technologies the E-learning Centre provides. The periodical survey is one of the ways to get users' feedback and provide valuable insight into student perception and experience in the use of the learning management system and online learning as such.

Literature review

The integration of ICT in learning and teaching is a key area of higher education reform. The Digital Education Action Plan (European Commission, 2020) aims to adapt education and training to the digital age. The Plan also emphasize that digital education at all levels of education and training must be a strategic priority. The application of ICT in teaching and learning has become one of the key components in the educational strategies of developing countries, as well as in European documents, strategies, action plans and initiatives. Even if we thought that the traditional way of teaching and learning could be preserved, the pandemic and the gained experience in online education during that time showed us that digital technologies have a significant role in shaping the education process today. Students today should no longer sit in a classroom and learn only by listening to lectures. Today, education must be collaborative and interactive and that means changing teaching methods and implementing new technologies in the teaching process. Teaching and learning can be equally present and valuable in an online learning environment as in the physical one. What we need is to rethink and innovate to enable new roles of teachers and students, new teaching methods, new ways of learning and more relevant learning outcomes, as in the use of particular technologies (Bates, 2023).

E-learning brings many advantages to the organization of the educational process, such as temporal and spatial flexibility in teaching and learning, access to up-to-date and current multimedia and interactive educational content, access to educational content repositories and digital libraries, archives and museums, the ability to adapt to personal learning style, enabling collaborative learning and the acquisition of project and teamwork skills, as well as accessibility to a wider range of students. Technology enables the teacher to use teaching and learning methods that are not possible in classroom teaching. New forms of teaching and learning have been used increasingly, as well as new forms of educational materials that enable wider choice and opportunities. The Bologna Digital 2020 document (Orr & Rampelt, 2018) states that new tools and learning opportunities provided by digitization should be used as much as possible to reach their full potential. Digital technologies enable greater interaction, participation and engagement with various multimedia content and different ways of communicating and collaborating with students, teachers and the wider community.

Virtual learning environment refers to a platform that provides teachers and educators with digital tools for generating interactive, group-based learning experiences in the classroom. The Open University web pages provide the following definition of a virtual learning environment: "Virtual learning environments (VLEs) or learning management systems, such as Moodle and Blackboard, provide many of the tools required for e-learning in one system. They have grown in use since the early 2000s and now almost all universities have an institutional VLE (https://www.open.edu/openlearn/education-development/open-education/content-section-8.4.4). Simply said it is the platform or digital space where the teachers and students exchange and share learning materials, collaborate on assignments, interact and engage in various educational activities. VLEs as a part of educational institutions Implementation of digital technologies can make education better, simpler, and faster. There is a clear upward trend in the prevalence and variety of online learning opportunities after the pandemic. Moodle (https://moodle.org/) is a widely known Learning Management System or Course Management System and a free open-source software package designed to help educators create effective online courses (https://moodle.org). It can be taken as VLE or be a part of it. Virtual learning environments enable the availability of learning materials and course information to students, they can also modernize and optimize the student's learning experience and as well as monitor their learning experience through data analysis. An e-learning platform is an integrated set of interactive online services that provide teachers, learners, and others involved in education with information, tools, and resources to support and enhance education delivery and management. One type of eLearning platform is LMS. E-learning platforms can be a part of VLE or VLE.

The popularity of e-learning platforms brings along the awareness of factors that could influence users' experience in their use. First, it is the learner's perception of e-learning in such an environment and another is digital technology used to facilitate e-learning with a focus on the reliability, ease of use, quality and usefulness of technology itself (Maslov, Nikou, Hansen, 2021). Therefore, the success of e-learning will be highly dependent on users' experience and perception of such systems.

Setting up high-quality VLE is not an easy task and requires commitment and resources, but also trained teachers who will know how to use it and use it efficiently are crucial. A significant contribution is user support as well. VLE can be seen as an opportunity to enhance students' learning experience, and to make them active participants in the educational process responsible for their achievements. The E-learning Centre at SRCE works hard to ensure high-quality VLE, therefore students' feedback on their experience with it is very important. We also invest a lot into providing training and support to teachers in the implementation of e-learning into the educational process, but higher education institutions as such are responsible for setting strategies and actions related to the implementation of digital technologies and systematic teacher training. Lack of this can result in modest use of LMS for teaching and learning and students' frustration with the learning process and not reaching the learning outcomes in full potential. Additionally, the use of an e-learning platform can potentially influence this perception more positively or less positively.

Methodology

Research design

The survey on user satisfaction with the e-learning platform Merlin is done periodically. The survey was performed first in 2016, then in 2019 and now in 2023. The questions in the survey in 2023 survey have been revised and adapted to the present situation.

As a research method, therefore, quantitative research was performed using an online survey that was available to participants via the e-learning platform Merlin. The survey consisted of 22 questions divided into four parts: demographic data, functionality of the LMS for online teaching and learning, students' attitudes related to the LMS interface, usability and available support in use and students' experience with online learning. The survey also had a space for comments that was generously used by students. The collected data after analysis will be used for further improvement and fine-tuning of the e-learning platform and providing support.

Data collection

As previously mentioned, we are interested in evaluating students' experience with the e-learning platform Merlin based on Moodle. The aim was to get university students' feedback on their satisfaction with the e-learning platform, its usability and the learning process that is done in an online environment. Previous surveys consisted of three parts and in this survey, we added a part about students' experience with online learning finding it important after the pandemic and ways of teaching and learning that remained embedded until today. We asked respondents to provide background information about their age, gender, length of using the e-learning platform and the institution they are coming from. Question types were yes/no questions, multichoice questions and Likert scale questions. At the end of the survey, students had the opportunity to give their comments. The data were exported into an Excel spreadsheet and were consequently descriptively analysed. The descriptive analysis helped us to evaluate the variables that may affect student experience with LMS.

Results

More than six hundred students (631) from higher education institutions in Croatia participated in the survey. 76,4% of students are of age up to 24, 10,62% have 25-30 years and the rest are older than 31 years. Relating to the gender, 60,22% of students were female. Students are coming from all public universities in Croatia and from colleges and polytechnics. The majority of students (59,43%) have been using the e-learning platform Merlin for more than a year while another 11,25% of students have been using Merlin for more than five years.

Based on the acquired data, the majority of students (89,22%) find access to the archive of the e-courses from previous academic years very important. Merlin archive enables students to access e-courses they were enrolled in during their whole study and all learning materials.

About half of the students (57.53%) who completed the survey agree or completely agree with the statement that Merlin is user-friendly and that navigating through the platform is simple and intuitive. 25.04% of them do not agree with this statement, while 17.43% do not have an opinion about it (Fig 2).

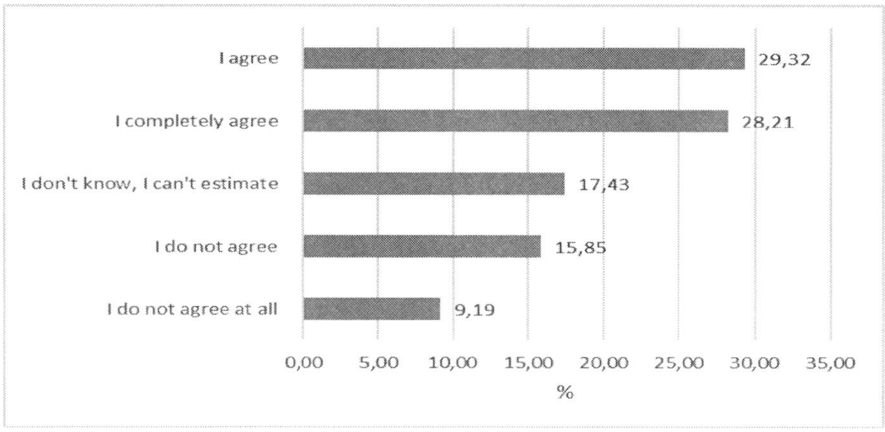

Figure 2: Students answer to the question: E-learning platform Merlin is user friendly and navigating through the platform is simple and intuitive.

We also asked students if they were satisfied with the organization of the interface in the Merlin (the position of the navigation bar, menu, blocks, and part of the screen for displaying the e-course content), and the use of colours and icons. Little less than half of the students (48.65%) answered that they were satisfied with the organization of the Merlin interface, while 32,49% disagreed and were not satisfied with the Merlin interface. 18.86% of students stated that they do not know or cannot rate whether they are satisfied with the organization of the interface or not.

Nevertheless, when asked if Merlin enables them easier access to learning materials, 75,43% of students agree and strongly agree with that statement, 11, 73% of them cannot rate and 12,83% of them disagree with this statement.

On the question if they agree that the e-learning platform Merlin enables them easier communication with teachers and other students, 47,54% of students agree or strongly agree, 25,52% cannot rate and 26,95% disagree.

When asked for which learning activities they use Merlin, students who completed the survey, replied that they used it mostly to monitor course information and access the e-course content (84,63%), to hand in assignments and seminars (11,73%), and to check their grades and points received on the course (1, 90 %). A very small number of students used the Merlin for communication with teachers and/or students, for collaboration and group work with other students, and for discussion on the forum.

In a question related to the e-learning platform features they were using in e-courses; students could choose more than one answer and add as well the unlisted features. The results (Fig 3) show that students are handing in assignments through the Merlin (Assignment Activity) (19,00 %), completing quizzes (Quiz Activity) (16,74%), making registrations for colloquiums, exercises, seminars, etc. (Choice Activity) (11,14 %), giving feedback (Feedback Activity) (10,66 %) and send messages through the e-learning platform (Messaging) (10, 34 %). Other features are represented in percentages less than 10% each.

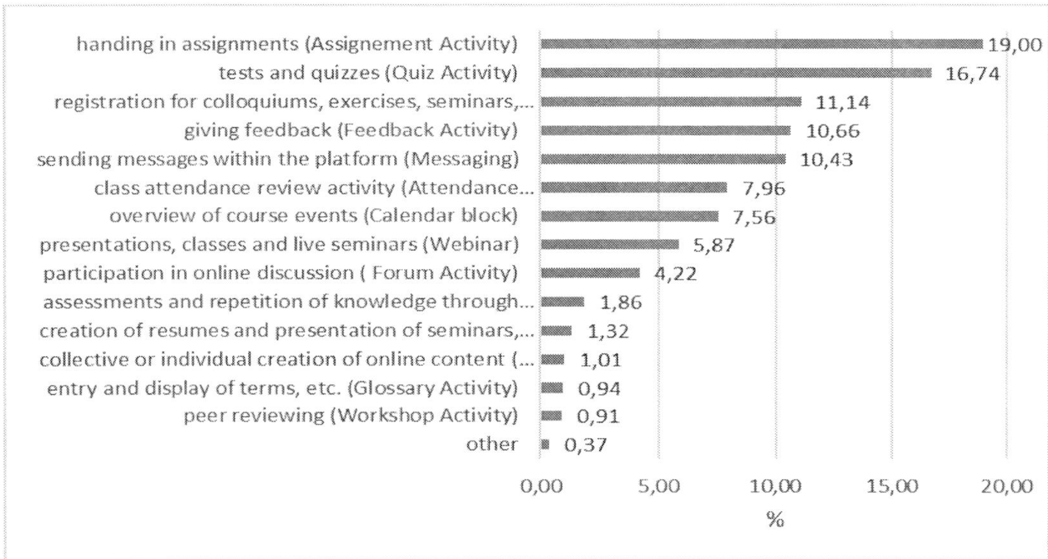

Figure 3: E-learning platform Merlin features used by students in their e-courses

We also asked students, based on their experience so far with online learning, what format of learning (online, face-to-face (f2f), mixed model) would be the most suitable for them. 26,78% of students think that up to 40% of learning online and the rest f2f would suit them best, 24,72% of students want 20% of online learning and the rest in f2f environment, while 23.45% of them want 80% of learning online or fully online learning. Only 25.04% prefer learning exclusively in a physical classroom (f2f).

In the end, we asked students about their knowledge of the use of information and communication technologies (ICT) and e-learning, and 77, 02% answered that they have good or very good knowledge, while 11,89% could not estimate. Only 11,10% of students find their knowledge about the use of ICT in learning poor or very poor.

The majority of students (542 students) left their comments, from short messages to whole paragraphs. We received some comments by e-mail even after the survey was finished, which we found very positive as students are thinking about the survey and do not hesitate to share their opinions with us. Of these 542 comments, 130 of them were positive feedback and praise. Other comments are not necessarily negative, but provide students view of the possibilities of an e-learning platform, their suggestions on how it can be improved and what they find as the problem. These comments are taken with great care. They are analysed and discussed among the E-learning Centre team. Those that are found justified and there is a possibility to improve students' experience with the e-learning platform are realized. Many comments are often a result of students' ignorance of the e-learning platform features or less experience with the e-learning platform as teachers use Merlin in a very basic way (i.e., just posting learning materials as files). Some of the students' comments have already been accepted which resulted in changes in the e-learning platform and others are in the process of discussion and processing.

Discussion/Conclusions

Based on the received results, the E-learning Centre team will take action to advance students' use of the e-learning platform Merlin and increase their satisfaction with its use. It can be concluded based on the survey results that about half of the students find the e-learning platform Merlin user-friendly, simple and intuitive. In addition, they are satisfied with the organization of the interface in the Merlin (the position of the navigation bar, menu, blocks, and part of the screen for displaying the e-course content), and the use of colours and icons. The importance of the Merlin archive is present in all surveys (in 2016, 2019 and 2023) with a percentage higher than 85. Students in large numbers use the Merlin archive as it enables them to have access to their e-courses and learning material during the whole study. The majority of students find that Merlin enables easier access to learning materials and communication with teachers and other students. The e-learning platform Merlin is from the student experience used mostly to monitor e-course information and for access to learning materials, then for handling assignments and checking their grades. Handing in assignments is the most used feature by students in their e-courses, taking quizzes, registering for colloquiums, exercises and seminars, giving feedback and sending messages within the platform. Other features are represented less than 10% each. In a comparison of data, survey results in 2016 (Kučina Softić, Ćorić Samardžija) showed that Merlin was used mostly to monitor e-course information and for access to learning materials in the course, for handling assignments and checking grades as well, while in 2019 (Ćorić Samardžija, Kučina Softić) it was mostly to monitor e-course information and for access to learning materials, checking grades and for handling assignments. Handing in assignments is the most used feature by students in their e-courses in 2016 and 2019 as well as in 2024. In the 2016 survey, the second place was messaging, then quizzes and giving feedback while in 2019 the second place was taking quizzes, registering for colloquiums, exercises and seminars, and overview of the course events. Based on the information it can be concluded that teachers are using the e-learning platform in a most basic way and that it has not even changed after the experience with online learning during the pandemic. Therefore, students' experience in the use of the e-learning platform is basic as well. Setting up a portal did not significantly change student views on the e-learning platform. Students are often not able to distinguish what is a part of Merlin or feature and what is edited by the teacher, and they often mix it up. So some results related to questions about Merlin refer to dissatisfaction with the available course content or course design.

In questions related to their experience with online learning, one-quarter of students expressed that they want only f2f learning, while more than 50% of students want online learning to be part of the course and in percentage higher than 40%. The majority of students find their knowledge about the use of ICT and e-learning and 77, 02 % of them answered that they have a good or very good knowledge. However, reading some of their comments in the survey one could ask if it is so.

Based on the presented results it can be concluded that students find the use of the e-learning platform important for their learning, yet they do not have full recognition of its possibility because of the modest use of it in the educational process. They are not aware of its features, as they did not have a chance to experience learning with the full potential of the use of the e-learning platform. Part of their frustration can be explained by this. The E-learning Centre at SRCE will continue working on the improvement of the e-learning platform and adapting it to user needs. A survey of students' satisfaction with the e-learning platform is an important source of information along with direct feedback from students received in support. As the e-learning platform is an important part of students' learning experience, our work will continue to ensure it is a positive influence. What can be seen from the survey is the lack of teacher knowledge and competencies in the organization and delivery of online learning and there is lots of space for improvement. The E-learning Centre at SRCE will continue to provide support to teachers and training, but it is up to educational institutions to set the strategies and policies as well as concrete actions for systematic implementation of digital technologies and e-learning into the education process.

References

Kučina Softić, S., Ćorić Samardžija, A. (2016). Rezultati ankete o zadovoljstvu korisnika sustavom za e-učenje Merlin, Zagreb

Ćorić Samardžija, A., Kučina Softić, S. (2019). Rezultati ankete o zadovoljstvu korisnika sustavom za e-učenje Merlin, Zagreb

Maslov, I., Nikou, S. and Hansen, P. (2021). Exploring user experience of learning management system, International Journal of Information and Learning Technology, Vol. 38 No. 4, pp. 344-363. https://doi.org/10.1108/IJILT-03-2021-0046

Kučina Softić, S., Odak, M. and Lasić Lazić, J. (2022). Digital transformation - New Approaches and Challenges in Education, 45th Jubilee International Convention on Information, Communication and Electronic Technology (MIPRO), Opatija, Croatia, 2022, pp. 749-753, doi: 10.23919/MIPRO55190.2022.9803435.

Bates, T. (2023). Managing Innovation in Teaching in ODDE. In: Zawacki-Richter, O., Jung, I. (eds) Handbook of Open, Distance and Digital Education. Springer, Singapore. https://doi.org/10.1007/978-981-19-2080-6_34

European Commission (2020). Action Plan for Digital Education 2021–2027: Adaptation of education and training to the digital age, Brussels.

Caprara, L., Caprara, C. Effects of virtual learning environments: A scoping review of the literature. Educ Inf Technol 27, 3683–3722 (2022). https://doi.org/10.1007/s10639-021-10768-w

Orr, D., Rampelt, F. (2018). Bologna Digital 2020. Towards a digital dimension in the Bologna Process, Background Paper., Essen: Hochschulforum Digitalisierung at Stiflerverband fur die Deutsche Wissenschaft e.V

The Evolution of Learning in Higher Education Polytechnic Institutions: The ACADIGIA Case-Study

Andrei Ternauciuc[1], Diana Andone[2], Vlad Mihaescu[3], Silviu Vert[4], Manuel Salvador Gomes Araújo[5]

[1] Faculty of Electronics, Telecommunications and Information Technology; Politehnica University of Timisoara, Romania; andrei.ternauciuc@upt.ro
[2] Department of Distance Education and Digital Education; Politehnica University of Timisoara, Romania; diana.andone@upt.ro
[3] Faculty of Electronics, Telecommunications and Information Technology; Politehnica University of Timisoara; Romania; vlad.mihaescu@upt.ro
[4] Faculty of Electronics, Telecommunications and Information Technology; Politehnica University of Timisoara; Romania; silviu.vert@upt.ro
[5] Porto Accounting and Business School, Polytechnic Institute of Porto, Portugal, manuelsalvador@iscap.ipp.pt

Correspondence: Andrei Ternauciuc: andrei.ternauciuc@upt.ro

Abstract:

This paper conducts an in-depth examination of the transformative journey in learning paradigms within higher education polytechnic institutions. Utilizing a case study approach, we trace the evolutionary trajectory of pedagogical practices and technological integration in the context of transitioning from in person to online classes. By exploring the experiences of the ACADIGIA Consortium, the driving force behind the Erasmus+ project with the same name, we aim to provide useful insights into the challenges faced and strategies employed during the evolution and implementation of the ACADIGIA transformation. The diversity of experience provided by the partners, from academia as well as from industry, and from the cultural backgrounds of Portugal, Spain, Romania, Italy, Greece, and Ireland, represents one of the strengths of this endeavor as well as one of its main challenges.

The findings contribute to a broader understanding of the dynamic nature of higher education in polytechnic settings, shedding light on effective approaches to enhance the quality and relevance of learning experiences in an ever-changing educational landscape. This paper can serve as a valuable resource for educators, administrators, and policymakers seeking evidence-based guidance in navigating the evolving terrain of higher education polytechnic institutions.

Keywords: polytechnic education, HEI, policies, micro-credentials, open badges

Introduction

The COVID-19 pandemic had a significant impact on education worldwide. Schools and universities faced widespread closures and transitioned to remote or online learning procedures. This sudden shift disrupted traditional teaching methods and created numerous challenges for students, educators, and parents. Many students experienced difficulties adjusting to remote learning, as it required access to technology, internet connectivity, and suitable learning environments (Garcia-Morales et al, 2021). The pandemic also highlighted the existing inequities in educational opportunities, as students from disadvantaged backgrounds often faced greater barriers to accessing quality education remotely (Tejedor et al, 2020). Additionally, the absence of in-person interactions and extracurricular activities affected students' social and emotional well-being (Clabaugh et al, 2021). The pandemic also posed challenges for educators, who had to quickly adapt their teaching methods, develop new digital skills, and find innovative ways to engage students remotely. Despite the challenges, the pandemic also spurred technological advancements and innovation in education, such as the development of new online learning platforms, tools, and approaches. It brought attention to the importance of digital literacy and the need for resilient and flexible educational systems (Tejedor et al, 2020).

However, not all areas of activities were affected in an equal manner. Each educational domain has its own particularities, and challenges that need to be addressed.

Polytechnic higher education, also known as polytechnic education or technical education, has some distinct characteristics that differentiate it from other forms of higher education (Doern, 2008). Some particularities of polytechnic higher education are described as follows.

Polytechnic education is a type of vocational education that emphasizes practical skills and knowledge over theory. It is designed to prepare students for specific vocations or trades, equipping them with job-ready skills to enter the workforce directly, often in technical or applied fields (Vicente et al, 2020).

Polytechnic institutions collaborate closely with industries and employers, enabling students to gain real-world experience through internships, apprenticeships, or industry projects, enhancing their employability. Polytechnic education offers flexible pathways and multiple entry points for students, allowing individuals to choose between different qualification levels, such as certificates, diplomas, or bachelor's degrees, depending on their career goals and prior educational background (Kinker et al,2020).

Micro-credentials are also gaining popularity in recognizing the acquisition of skills or abilities on a lower level than a full-fledged diploma (McGreal et al, 2022). Given the technical and practical nature of polytechnic education, collaboration and teamwork are often emphasized, with students working in groups on projects, replicating real-world work environments and fostering interpersonal skills (Bhat et al, 2020).

This type of education places great importance on applied research and innovation in collaboration with industries. The focus is on creating practical solutions to real-world problems, fostering entrepreneurship, and driving economic development (Tracey et al, 2016).

It is important to note that while these characteristics are generally associated with polytechnic higher education, they may vary to some extent based on regional differences and specific institutional policies within different countries.

Research Methodology

This paper aims to present the challenges identified during a multi-national analysis done by the partner polytechnic institutions in their own countries, and the ways in which they could be mitigated in order to improve the effectiveness of the educational process in general, and that of the technical education in particular.

The case study of the ACADIGIA project is presented extensively in the following chapters, including the activities (the national analyses, the creation of the Compendium, the Mentors Training program, the final dissemination event) and some of the results of the project: the training courses run on the UniCampus platform, as well as the post-course questionnaire completed by the participants.

The interpretation of these results forms the basis of the empirical analysis of the research and represents the measure of the success of the ACADIGIA project.

The ACADIGIA Project

This study is centered around the experiences of the ACADIGIA Consortium, which serves as the impetus for the Erasmus+ project of the same name. Through an exploration of the ACADIGIA transformation, the study aims to shed light on the challenges faced and the strategies employed during the process. The consortium's diverse background, encompassing academia and industry, as well as national and cultural variations across the partners states of Portugal (Instituto Politecnico do Porto), Spain (Politehnica University of Madrid), Romania (Politehnica University of Timisoara), Italy (Politehnica University of Marche), Greece (National Technical University of Athens), and Ireland (Trinity College Dublin), further adds to the strength and complexity of the endeavor.

The transformative journey within higher education polytechnic institutions is intricately connected to the advancements in educational technologies. Over the years, technological tools and platforms have revolutionized teaching and learning approaches, offering new possibilities and opportunities for both educators and students. The integration of technology has facilitated flexible and personalized learning experiences, enabling students to access resources and engage in collaborative activities irrespective of their physical locations. Additionally, the incorporation of multimedia elements, interactive simulations, and virtual reality applications has enhanced the engagement and immersion of learners, fostering greater understanding and knowledge retention.

The COVID-19 global pandemic proved to be a powerful catalyst in the transition from classical education to technology enhanced learning, by accelerating digital readiness of Polytechnic higher education institutions towards the sustainable adoption of more online and blended approaches in education through the creation of an acceleration model and focused efforts towards its adoption.

A significant particularity of the implementation of the ACADIGIA methodology in the partner institutions is the mentor-mentee relationship, promoted as the driving force behind the dissemination of the methods and tools deemed essential for the improvements envisaged in the project strategy.

The ACADIGIA Consortium, comprising partners from academia and industry, represents a unique collaborative effort in pursuing educational transformation. The diverse backgrounds and expertise of the partners contribute to the project's strength and effectiveness, as it harnesses the collective knowledge and experiences of various stakeholders. However, the consortium also faces challenges stemming from the divergent perspectives, differing interests, and cultural disparities among its participants.

Project Activities

The initial design of the project broke down the activities into distinct tasks with specific results. They are detailed as follows.

The Compendium of Augmented Blended Teaching

The first activities of the Project were aimed at completing the first major intellectual output: the Compendium of Augmented Blended Teaching, a sort of manual which presents the state of the art in Polytechnic Higher Education Institutions from each of the partners' countries. The analyses were conducted with the help of guided interviews with representatives from said HEIs, as well as in-depth analyses of the relevant rules and regulations in effect on the national and institutional levels from partner countries. Each national report approached the analyses from the following perspectives:

- Challenges to education with distance learning,
- Policies, procedures, and guidelines,
- Tools used to support distance learning,
- Support provided to educators,
- Impact on assessment,
- Impact on student engagement.

While differences were identified, due to particularities specific to each country, a general picture emerged highlighting common issues in transitioning from a classical educational environment, based on face-to-face interactions between actors involved, to a blended learning setting, based on the facilities offered by the information and communications technologies available today. Many of these common issues revolved around the need to familiarize staff and students with the tools and procedures that could help this transition in the constraints of the global pandemic and beyond.

Therefore, a selection of 12 such tools was agreed upon and distributed among the partners, which were then tasked with analyzing said tools (two for each partner) and providing an overview and a simple video tutorial highlighting common integrated into the Compendium, alongside the national reports (Ternauciuc et al, 2022).

The Compendium and the tutorials are currently provided for free to anyone interested in using them on the ACADIGIA Project website.

Training the mentors

The ACADIGIA methodology, first envisioned in the planning stages, and further refined during the project life cycle, states that the optimal method for transferring the knowledge and skills necessary to improve learning is based on the mentor-mentee relationship. Therefore, the development of these types of relationships was at the forefront of the design of the methodology.

This was achieved through face-to-face interactions during a hands-on training session where representatives from all partners attended a week-long workshop in a common location. Participants developed skills and abilities on two different aspects: soft-skills, aimed at maximizing the effectiveness of the mentor-mentee formula, and technical skills in identifying, analyzing, deciding, and then using a large variety of technical tools in augmented, blended-learning scenarios.

The training was based on a handbook, a text-based manual developed with the purpose of cementing the information presented during the workshop. This handbook is also available on the ACADIGIA Project website.

Bringing ACADIGIA to life

Finally, the experience acquired by the mentors formed during the workshop was put in practice through a series of training sessions carried out in each of the partner institutions. After the teams were established, hybrid sessions took place which disseminated the skills, abilities and materials prepared during the previous phases of the ACADIGIA project. The UniCampus platform was used to host the materials and facilitate the transfer of knowledge (Andone et al, 2017). Mentors who successfully finalized the activities received micro-credentials in the form of digital open badges and certificates of completion. The scenario for receiving said micro-credentials was defined as follows:

1. The in-presence training takes place, during which trainees participate in presentations and exercises conducted by tutors from the designated partners.

2. During the training, they can also access the materials used by the tutors on the UniCampus platform, in a dedicated category and course available for the ACADIGIA Project partners.

3. At the end of the training, they complete a formal evaluation on the platform, assessing their understanding of the course materials and activities.

4. Upon successful completion of this evaluation, users can access their automatically issued certificates and badges.

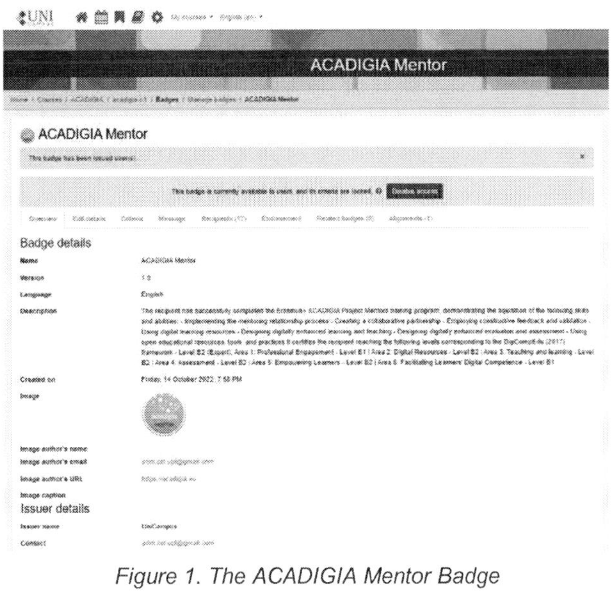

Figure 1. The ACADIGIA Mentor Badge

Open Badges are digital credentials that represent achievements, skills, or knowledge that individuals have acquired. They are a way to recognize and display accomplishments in a standardized, shareable format. Open Badges are often used to provide verifiable evidence of learning or achievements, making them valuable in various contexts, including education, professional development, culture, and career advancement (Andone et al, 2021).

Aside from the badges, certificates of completion were also awarded to course participants who successfully completed the training program.

On a technical level, certificates are like badges since they provide a verifiable mechanism that confirms the validity of an electronic item that the recipient presents to an interested party (such as a university or a potential employer). However, they differ from badges in their presentation form, because they are designed from the beginning to be kept in a document-like format, either electronically, or as a hard copy, printed on a piece of paper.

According to the DigCompEdu Framework ("Digital Competence Framework for Educators") (Punie et al, 2017), a standard developed by the European Commission for use in teaching and learning scenarios, the badges and certificates validate a Level B2 (Expert) in Digital Competences of Educators to each of the recipients.

Alongside the training sessions, a series of demo lessons were also developed to demonstrate in a definitive way the benefits that ICT can bring to learning. Each of these video lessons presents the use of technology in a real setting, either fully online, or in a blended learning environment (in-person activities supplemented by online tools or other technologies).

The final step of implementing the ACADIGIA methodology was defined as infiltrating the governance. This consisted of disseminating the methodology on a higher level, including policy and decision makers, and the governing bodies of target institutions – other polytechnical institutes of higher learning. Delegations were sent from each partner to other national institutions and Letters of Intent were signed by officials from other polytechnics which found the results of the ACADIGIA project worthy of their attention. Approximately 15 such non-affiliated HEIs declared their interest in further updates from the project team in the sustainability phase of the project.

Figure 2. Certificate of completion for the ACADIGIA Mentors training course Badge

After these targeted discussions took place, a public dissemination event was organized by each of the partners institutions in which all the activities and results were presented. The Politehnica University of Timisoara organized this multiplier event in a hybrid format in March 2023, as part of the annual Open Education Week event which reached that year the 10th edition of the OEW Workshop. During the event, the ACADIGIA methodology and project results were presented to the live audience consisting of 46 participants present in the conference hall, and 554 unique online participants. They consisted mainly of educators (either university professors or high-school teachers) and students; therefore, the scope of the event surpassed the target group of Polytechnic HEIs.

At the end of the workshop, a post-event questionnaire was completed by some of the attendees, with the following questions and the answers in the figure 3 and 4:

1. How do you evaluate the event as a whole? (Scale of 1 to 5: Very Poor -> Very Good)

The responses indicated that the innovation, pedagogy and tools for digital education in polytecnics workshop was very well received by the participants and it answered their needs.

2. What was the quality of the presentations? (Scale of 1 to 5: Very Poor -> Very Good)
3. The relevance of the presentations was: (Scale of 1 to 5: Very Poor -> Very Good)

The participants appreciate as very good the quality of the presentations as well as very relevant to their needs of improving digital competences.

4. How would you evaluate the presentations from the point of view of: (each on a (Scale of 1 to 5: Very Poor -> Very Good))
   a. Relevance
   b. Quality
   c. Innovation
   d. Results
   e. Participation
   f. Presented Tools
   g. Usefulness
   h. Clarity
   i. Digitalization

Participants rated the quality of presentations as very good and highly relevant to their goal of improving digital competencies. They found the workshop, tools presented, and clarity of presentations to be highly impactful for digitalization efforts and beneficial for their teaching activities, owing to the high quality of the content delivered. In the same time they considered them as with high impact for the digitalization and innovative, useful for their teaching activities, due to the high quality of the presentations.

5. What is your general satisfaction with this event? (Scale of 1 to 5: Very Poor -> Very Good)
6. How useful do you find this event for your activity? (Scale of 1 to 10)

As the general satisfaction with the event was very good , the participants also graded it with a general mark of 9 the whole activities during the workshop.

7. How did you find out about this event? (Multiple checkboxes)
   a. Press
   b. Social media
   c. Email
   d. Personal recommendation
   e. Other
8. Will you further use the results from ACADIGIA project in your activity? (Choose one)

A notable success of the workshop was its targeted outreach, as the majority of participants were invited directly through email invitations sent to partner universities. This strategy proved effective in attracting attendees. Importantly, 38 participants indicated that they plan to integrate the results from the ACADIGIA project into their daily activities, demonstrating the practical utility and influence of the workshop. Only one participant stated they would not use the results, and three were undecided, highlighting a strong overall endorsement of the workshop's impact and relevance.

The results of this questionnaire are presented in the following images.

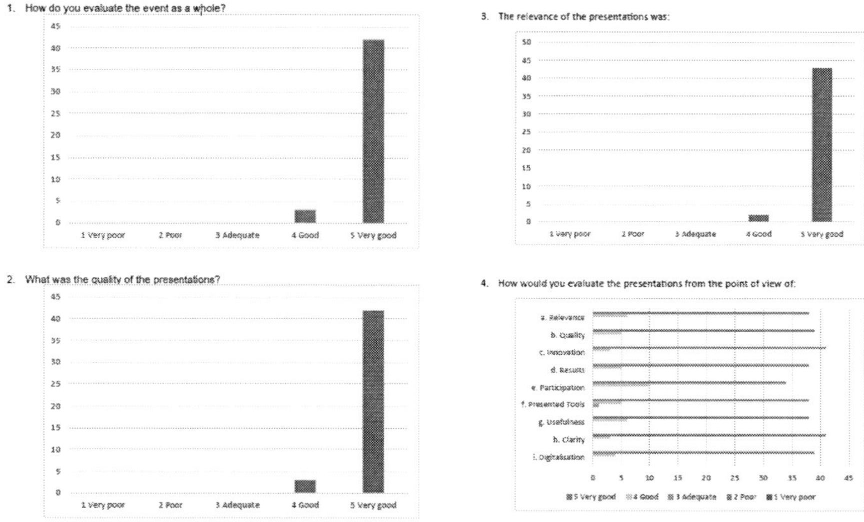

Figure 3. Results of the post-event questionnaire

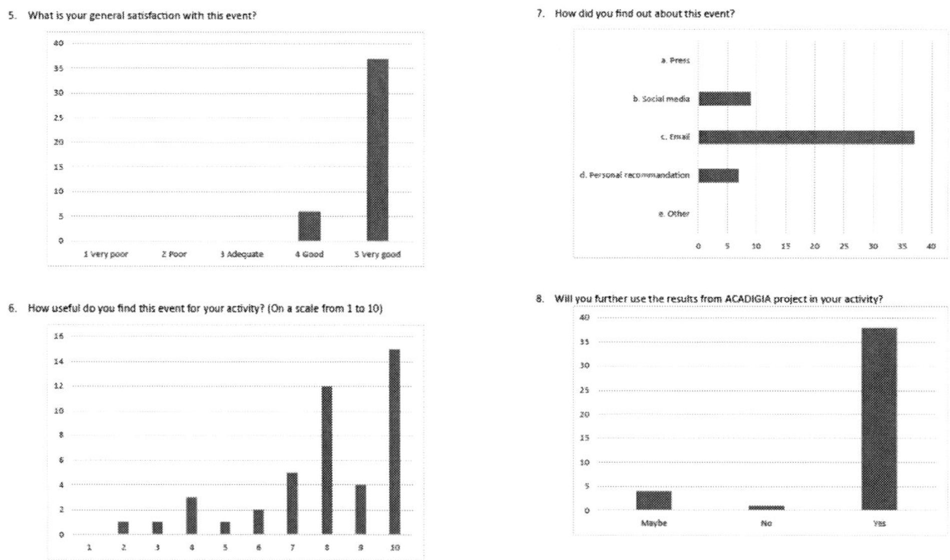

Figure 4. Results of the post-event questionnaire (2)

The results of the post-event questionnaire suggest that the ACADIGIA Methodology was well received by the academic community attending the dissemination event of the project. They especially appreciated the innovation and the clarity of the presentations, as well as its utility in their professional activities. The workshop was highly successful, with participants finding it exceptionally relevant, impactful, and useful for enhancing their digital competencies and teaching activities. While not all participants were a part of the target group (members of polytechnic higher education institutions), their reaction was positive, increasing the likelihood that the resources and results presented will be further consulted and maybe used for their intended purposes.

Conclusions

This study aims to contribute to understanding effective approaches to enhance learning experiences. The findings can aid educators in designing pedagogical practices and administrators in making policy decisions. Policymakers can gain evidence-based guidance for educational innovation.

To summarize, the article explores the transformative journey through learning paradigms in higher education polytechnic institutions, focusing on the experiences of the ACADIGIA Consortium members' institutions. The findings provide insights for educators, administrators, and policymakers in navigating the evolving educational landscape.

The findings of this paper underline the complex mix of factors which influence the transformation of higher education. Advancements in educational technologies and evolving societal expectations emerge as pivotal forces propelling the shift toward online education. Through the lens of the ACADIGIA Consortium, we gained nuanced insights into the challenges faced and strategies employed during the evolution and implementation on this transformation.

This paper invites further exploration and dialogue, emphasizing the collaborative spirit needed to navigate the challenges and opportunities presented by the ever-changing educational landscape in polytechnic institutions.

Acknowledgements

The paper is based on research performed by the ACADIGIA consortium members. ACADIGIA – Digital EDUCATION READINESS in the field of HIGHER EDUCATION Erasmus+ project no. 2020-1-PT01-KA226-HE-095042, https://acadigia.eu/

References

García-Morales, Víctor J., Aurora Garrido-Moreno, and Rodrigo Martín-Rojas. "The transformation of higher education after the COVID disruption: Emerging challenges in an online learning scenario." Frontiers in psychology 12 (2021): 616059.

Tejedor, Santiago, et al. "Digital literacy and higher education during COVID-19 lockdown: Spain, Italy, and Ecuador." Publications 8.4 (2020): 48.

Clabaugh, Alison, Juan F. Duque, and Logan J. Fields. "Academic stress and emotional well-being in United States college students following onset of the COVID-19 pandemic." Frontiers in psychology (2021): 765.

Doern, Bruce. "Polytechnics" in Higher Education Systems: A Comparative Review and Policy Implications for Ontario. Toronto: Higher Education Quality Council of Ontario, 2008.

Vicente, Paulo Nuno, et al. "Higher education in a material world: Constraints to digital innovation in Portuguese universities and polytechnic institutes." Education and Information Technologies 25.6 (2020): 5815-5833.

Kinker, Pramod, et al. "A QFD-TISM approach for service quality improvement in polytechnic education institutes: a case study." International Journal of Applied Systemic Studies 9.2 (2020): 85-113.

McGreal, Rory, and Don Olcott Jr. "A strategic reset: micro-credentials for higher education leaders." Smart Learning Environments 9.1 (2022): 9.

Bhat, Shreeranga, et al. "Collaborative learning for outcome based engineering education: A lean thinking approach." Procedia Computer Science 172 (2020): 927-936.

Tracey, Burns, and Köster Florian, eds. Educational research and innovation governing education in a complex world. OECD Publishing, 2016.

Ternauciuc, A., Andone, D., Wall, P. J., Araujo, M. S., & Arnaldo, R. M. (2022). ANALYSING DIGITAL TOOLS FOR TECHNICAL UNIVERSITIES. Towards Smart and Inclusive Learning Ecosystem, 7.

Andone, D., Vasiu, R., & Ternauciuc, A., "UniCampus: The first courses in a Romanian MOOC," 2017 IEEE Global Engineering Education Conference (EDUCON), Athens, Greece, 2017, pp. 1210-1215, doi: 10.1109/EDUCON.2017.7943002.

D. Andone, V. Mihaescu, A. Ternauciuc, S. Vert, R. Vasiu and M. Mocofan, "DigiCulture - courses for enhancing digital competences," 2021 IEEE Global Engineering Education Conference (EDUCON), Vienna, Austria, 2021, pp. 1056-1060, doi: 10.1109/EDUCON46332.2021.9453911.

Punie, Y., editor(s), Redecker, C., European Framework for the Digital Competence of Educators: DigCompEdu, EUR 28775 EN, Publications Office of the European Union, Luxembourg, 2017, ISBN 978-92-79-73718-3 (print),978-92-79-73494-6 (pdf), doi:10.2760/178382 (print),10.2760/159770 (online), JRC107466

Digital Storytelling and Critical Thinking: A Comparative Analysis Across Physical, Virtual, and Hybrid Learning Environments

Carlo De Medio[1]

[1] Department of electronic Engineering, University of Roma Tor Vergata, Italy; Carlo.de.medio@uniroma2.it

Correspondence: Carlo De Medio: Carlo.de.medio@uniroma2.it

Abstract:

This research investigates the promotion of critical thinking skills and the dissemination of knowledge through digital storytelling experiences within three distinct learning environments: physical, virtual and hybrid. Using a comparative analysis, the research examines the impact of each modality on critical thinking, focusing on the evaluation of six macro-indicators presented in (Poce, 2017): basic language skills, relevance, importance, argumentation, critical processing and novelty. The study involved students from the universities of Roma TRE, Modena and Reggio Emilia and Tor Vergata through three experiences: in presence tour , a virtual tour made via FrameVR (https://learn.framevr.io/) and an augmented reality application to provide educational content. The results indicate that digital environments significantly improve some aspects of critical thinking, particularly in terms of argumentative quality and creative engagement. The study also observes a marked improvement in knowledge retention, as evidenced by end-of-course evaluations, suggesting that immersive digital storytelling can mitigate the tendency for last-minute hoarding and promote long-lasting educational engagement. This research contributes to the pedagogical discourse on the effectiveness of digital storytelling and object-based learning in promoting critical and reflective thinking processes in students.

Keywords: critical thinking, storytelling, object-based learning, VR, AR, learning

Introduction

University museums are an important tool and resource center in higher education for enhancing the impact of their teaching and research (Kelly, 2019). Over the last few decades, the educational landscape has witnessed growing interest in innovative methodologies aimed at enhancing students' critical thinking. Among these, storytelling stands out as a pedagogical practice of particular significance due to its ability to emotionally and cognitively engage students, fostering deeper and more meaningful learning. Despite its ancient origins, storytelling has found new applications in the digital era, extending beyond the confines of traditional oral narration to embrace virtual and augmented realities. This article aims to explore the effectiveness of storytelling as a tool for promoting critical thinking, with special attention to the differentiated impact this methodology can have depending on the application environment. Critical thinking, defined as the ability to analyze facts, generate and organize ideas, defend opinions, make inferences, evaluate arguments, and solve problems (Facione, 1990), is a key competency in contemporary education. The importance of developing such skills within the educational context is widely recognized, given their cross-sectional relevance in various aspects of daily and professional life. In this context, storytelling emerges as a particularly promising methodology, capable of stimulating critical reflection and active participation of students through the narration of relevant and engaging stories. The integration of digital technologies in education has opened new frontiers for storytelling, allowing the creation of immersive environments that enrich the narrative experience with interactive and multisensory elements. Virtual reality (VR) and augmented reality (AR) have proven particularly effective in enhancing the impact of storytelling, enabling students to fully immerse themselves in stories and interact with content in previously unimaginable ways. However, the effectiveness of these technologies in developing critical thinking remains a relatively unexplored field, requiring further studies to fully understand their pedagogical potential. Existing literature provides some preliminary evidence on the positive impact of virtual and augmented storytelling in promoting critical thinking. For instance, Green and Brock (2000) demonstrated how "narrative transportation" – the ability of a story to transport the reader into a narrative world – can influence critical information processing. Similarly, Squire and Klopfer (2007) highlighted how augmented reality applications can foster situated and contextualized learning, key elements for critical thinking. Despite these encouraging premises, there is a need for a deeper understanding of how the use of storytelling in virtual and augmented environments can be optimized to maximize educational benefits. This article seeks to fill this gap by exploring the use of storytelling in innovative educational environments and its impact on the development of critical thinking. Through a systematic analysis of existing literature and case studies of virtual and augmented storytelling implementation, we aim to outline effective strategies and identify areas for future development. The adoption of storytelling as a teaching methodology fits within a broader pedagogical debate, centered on the search for effective strategies to promote not only critical thinking but also active learning and knowledge transmission. This narrative technique proves to be a versatile tool, capable of stimulating imagination and reflection, as well as facilitating the memorization and understanding of complex concepts through the creation of deep emotional and cognitive connections. The integration of storytelling with Object-Based Learning (OBL) represents a significant evolution of this methodology, offering new perspectives for experiential and multisensory learning. Pedagogical literature highlights how storytelling, especially when enriched by visual or physical supports, can significantly improve learning. Mayer (2001) argues that the combination of narrative elements with images or tangible objects can increase information retention and facilitate knowledge construction, following the principles of dual coding theory, which suggests the existence of two distinct channels for processing verbal and visual information. This approach is particularly effective in teaching abstract or complex concepts, making them more accessible and understandable to students.

Methodology

In this research on the impacts of different modalities (in-person, hybrid and virtual) on the promotion of critical thinking and the transmission of knowledge through digital storytelling experiences, the following research questions are taken into consideration:

1. How does the modality (in-person, hybrid, and virtual) influence the promotion of critical thinking in digital storytelling experiences?

This question seeks to explore the extent to which the environment in which digital storytelling is experienced affects the development of critical thinking skills. It hypothesizes that different modes of delivery—each with its unique set of sensory engagements and interaction levels—may have varied impacts on an individual's ability to analyze, evaluate, and create new understanding from the stories presented.

2. To what extent are the knowledge and insights transmitted through digital storytelling influenced by the modality of the experience?

The focus here is on evaluating how effectively knowledge is convered in each modality and whether the mode of delivery affects the retention and comprehension of the information presented. This question also considers how the immediacy and intimacy of the storytelling experience in each modality may enhance or detract from the learning outcomes.

This reasearch was conducted within the framework of three courses on research methodology in educational sciences at a university level. The courses were designed to immerse students in various research techniques with a specific focus on evaluating the impact of different learning environments on the development of critical thinking skills. Students underwent a pretest to assess their critical thinking skills and calculate a baseline for post-test comparisons by answering a series of open-ended, stimulus-based questions. Assessing critical thinking is complex and crucial. Many researches have presented useful tools for the evaluation of this construct and in this research a grid based on six macro-indicators assessable on a scale of 1-5 presented in (Poce, 2017) was used which provides a multidimensional evaluation approach, contributing to a solid analysis of the critical thinking skills of students. students within an educational context. Specifically, the following macro-indicator are analysed:

- Basic language skills: This macro-indicator accurately examines the student's proficiency in writing. The prototype assessment examines all types of linguistic inaccuracies, including spelling errors and improper punctuation. Although human evaluators may consider additional parameters, for the initial prototype this level of linguistic detail was deemed satisfactory. The emphasis here is on the fundamental aspect of communication – the accuracy of the use of language – which underlies the expression of critical thinking.

- Relevance: The relevance indicator measures how aligned a student's answer is to the question asked. This measure does not necessarily reflect the correctness of the answer but rather its relevance to the topic. It also evaluates the coherence of the text and the student's ability to correctly use stimuli, which is a fundamental component in reasoning and logical argumentation.

- Importance: this macro-indicator evaluates the extent to which the student uses their knowledge to construct arguments in their answers. It reflects the depth of understanding and the ability to apply that understanding in formulating a reasoned argument, a key element in the higher-order thinking process.

- Argumentation: This metric assesses the student's proficiency in constructing a logical and persuasive argument. It examines the structure of the argument, the use of evidence, and the coherence of the points made. A strong argument will logically progress from premise to conclusion, effectively incorporating evidence and addressing potential counterarguments. This indicator is essential for measuring the student's ability to not just think critically, but also to communicate their reasoning effectively.

- Critical evaluation: This indicator measures the depth and complexity of the student's thought process as reflected in their elaboration on the topic. It considers the student's ability to go beyond surface-level analysis, offering nuanced insights, drawing connections between disparate ideas, and reflecting on the broader implications of their arguments. Critical processing reflects a higher-order cognitive skill that distinguishes rudimentary understanding from a sophisticated grasp of the subject matter.

- Novelty: This indicator measures the originality present in the response. The sources referred to by the student are analyzed and how these sources were synthesized to generate new ideas and solutions in relation to the initial hypotheses. The novelty indicator is particularly interesting, as it reveals the student's ability to think innovatively and contribute to the progression of thinking within a given domain.

The methodology encompassed three distinct experiential phases, each aimed at engaging the students in different modes of interaction with the same educational content, specifically tailored to stimulate critical thinking skills.

- In-person experience with a museum mediator: The first experience involved a traditional in-person visit to a museum exhibition, facilitated by a museum mediator. The mediator played a fundamental role in making the multimedia content accessible and engaging for students, providing context and depth to the exhibited works. This approach relied on direct interaction, allowing students to engage with the content in a tangible context. In this case we did not have problems with a technological gap in the use of the equipment

- Virtual reality environment (FrameVR): The second experience was based on a completely virtual environment created using FrameVR technology. This immersive experience allowed students to navigate a digitally reconstructed exhibition space, interacting with the works of art and information content in a virtual environment. The use of a cardboard headset for the mobile phone was proposed as an optional option to explore the environment in an even more immersive way. This phase was designed to explore the potential of VR technology in simulating an engaging and educational museum visit.

- Hybrid experience with augmented reality: the third experience involved the integration of a hybrid approach, in which participants used a mobile application that exploited the camera capabilities of their smartphones to overlay augmented reality (AR) content on the space physical exhibition as well as a tracking system based on the location of their device. This phase facilitated a physical interaction with the exhibition, enriched by digital elements, allowing a multimodal engagement with the works of art as well as the promotion of other transversal skills beyond critical thinking (communication, collaboration and creativity).

Results

The sample analyzed is made up of a total of 295 participants, 87.45% women, 12% men and the remainder preferred not to express themselves. The on-site experience, which represents traditional physical engagement with the narrative medium, consists of 23 participants. This group experienced the content in a conventional face-to-face context lasting 1.5 hours following atraditional lecture, which provided a basis for comparison with more technologically integrated modalities. The group that carried out the visit in "complete virtual experience" mode, which allowed participants to interact with the content of the narrative in a completely digital space, was the largest group with 245 participants. This considerable number reflects the growing accessibility and attractiveness of fully online educational resources, as well as the scalability of virtual environments in educational contexts. The "hybrid A/R experience" combines elements of both the physical and digital realms, using augmented reality to enhance the real-world environment with digital overlays. This group includes 27 participants, providing a middle ground in terms of technology integration and offering insights into how blending these realities could influence learning outcomes.

The data collected from the three experiences were analyzed to determine how much each modality of fruition stimulated critical thinking skills, knowledge transmission, and appreciation of the multimodality of the experience. The use of language appears to be virtually unaffected by the different application of the methodology, as can be seen in Fig. 1. However, it is evident that the virtual and hybrid modality more significantly stimulated the capacity for critical reflection, importance, and creativity; specifically, it can be seen how in the in-person experience the average moves from 3.47 on the corresponding indicator to 3.82 in hybrid mode and 3.97 in virtual mode, thereby resulting in an increase of 14.41%. The indicators of creativity (3.53 – 4 – 4.2, an increase of about 18.98%) and importance (3.87 – 4.21 – 4.298, an average increase of 11.06%) follow the same trend.

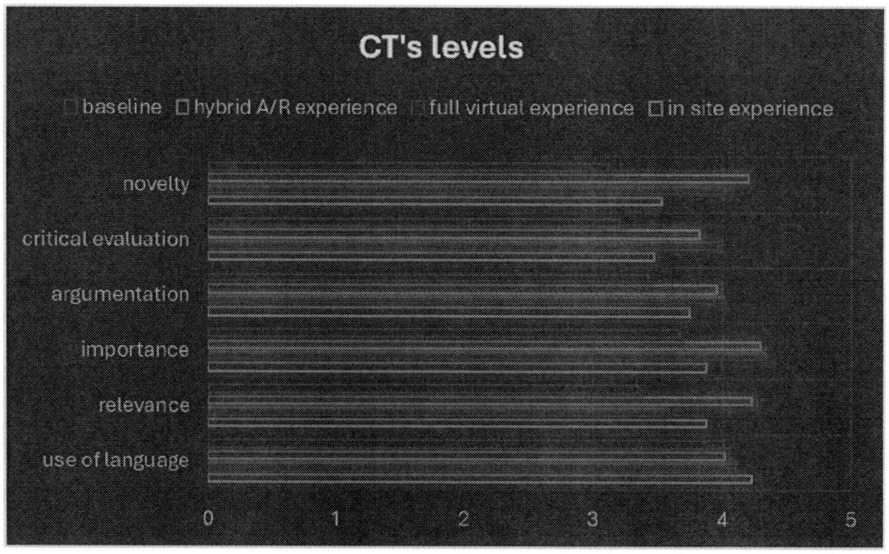

Figure 1: CT's level at the end of the three experiences

In terms of knowledge transmission, the outcome was measured at the first exam call of the course evaluated through a closed test with multiple-choice questions, which showed that students who participated in the in-person experience obtained a result in terms of final grade lower by 2.732% compared to those who underwent the digital experience; no significant differences were found between the full virtual and hybrid experience (27.21 - 27.32) with slightly higher results from those who enjoyed the hybrid experience.

Through the final evaluation questionnaire, participants were asked to rate on a Likert scale the elements of the visit to understand the appreciation of the content proposed in the different modes.

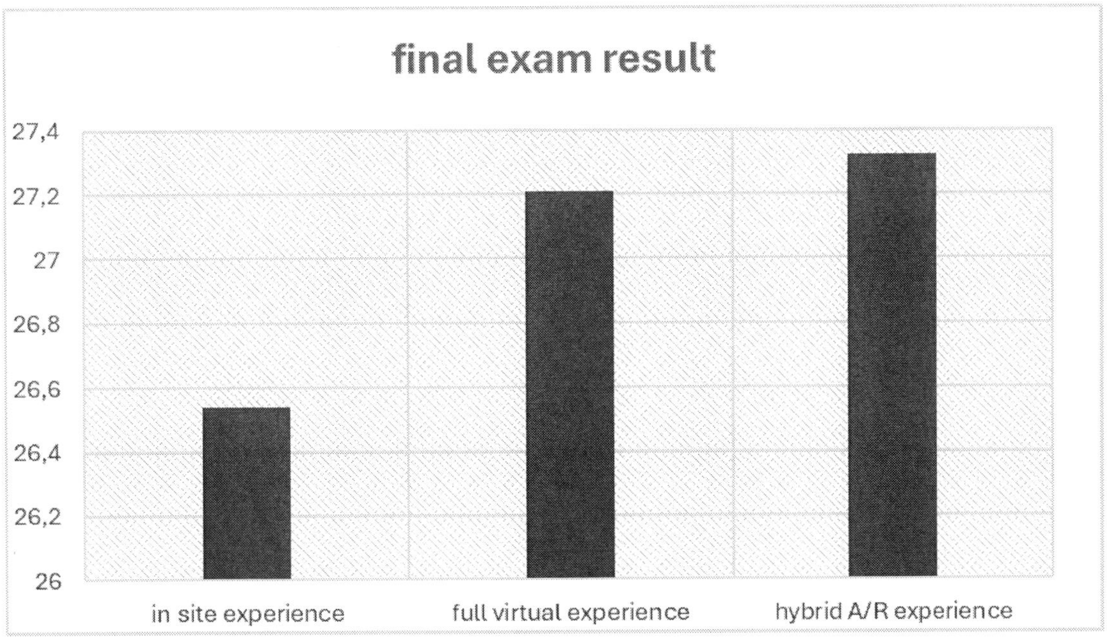

Figure 2: Final exams results

Discussion

This study explored how the application of experiences related to digital storytelling (and object-based learning) in different environments (physical, virtual, and hybrid) influences the promotion of the cross-cutting competence of critical thinking as well as knowledge. The results presented highlight how various macro-indicators of critical thinking are more stimulated through digital environments (importance – critical evaluation – creativity), showing significant percentage increases compared to in-person experiences. this answers the primary research question presented in this article by demonstrating how compared to the baseline there is a clear increase in critical thinking competence in particular in the 3 macro indicators of novelty. critical reworking and importance in virtual and a/r models. It will be necessary to start from this data to understand how to specifically optimize anchors and individualize these experiences. In general, the courses proposed as innovative pathways have shown, in line with previous works in the state of the art, that the introduction of these experiences promotes the transmission of knowledge, recording significant increases in the final course evaluation (2.732%); this data flattens in the following calls, indicating the need to study the result more deeply to understand its trend. This answers the second research question, considering however that in these innovative methods the students are "forced" to follow the course and participate in the activities, partially solving the problem already known in the literature of the last-minute studying, commonly known as "cramming,"that is widely debated in the field of experimental pedagogy and educational psychology. Research suggests that this practice is not the most effective study strategy for long-term learning or for strengthening critical thinking skills,. Research on study practices also highlights the importance of "spacing" in study, namely distributing study sessions over time, compared to concentrated study in a short period, perfectly in line with the idea of the proposed workshops. This approach promotes greater synaptic activation and strengthening of neural connections, essential for memory consolidation (Cepeda, 2006).

References

Facione, P., 1990. Critical thinking: A statement of expert consensus for purposes of educational assessment and instruction (The Delphi Report).Bannan-Ritland, B. (2003). The role of design in research: The integrative learning design framework. Educational Researcher, 32(1), 21-24. :10.3102/0013189X032001021

Green, M. C., & Brock, T. C. (2000). The role of transportation in the persuasiveness of public narratives. Journal of Personality and Social Psychology, 79(5), 701-721.

Wilson, G., & Stacey, E. (2004). Online interaction impacts on learning: Teaching the teachers to teach online. Australasian Journal of Educational Technology, 20(1), 33-48. Retrieved from http://www.ascilite.org.au/ajet/ajet20/wilson.html [where there is no DOI you can refer to the URL, but do not include both]

Squire, K. and Klopfer, E., 2007. Augmented reality simulations on handheld computers. The journal of the learning sciences, 16(3), pp.371-413.

Mayer, R.E., 2002. Multimedia learning. In Psychology of learning and motivation (Vol. 41, pp. 85-139). Academic Press.

Paris, S.G., 2002. Perspectives on object-centered learning in museums. Routledge.

Di Blas, Nicoletta, and Paolo Paolini. "Multi-user virtual environments for learning: Experience and technology design." IEEE Transactions on Learning Technologies, vol. 1, no. 4, 2005, pp. 203-214

Rohrer, D., & Pashler, H. (2007). Increasing retention without increasing study time. Current Directions in Psychological Science, 16(4), 183-186

Fuligni, A. J., Gillen-O'Neel, C., & Huynh, V. W. (2013). Sacrificing sleep for study time: Does it matter? Journal of Child Development, 84(5), 1339-1352. https://www.uclahealth.org/

Cepeda, N. J., Pashler, H., Vul, E., Wixted, J. T., & Rohrer, D. (2006). Distributed practice in verbal recall tasks: A review and quantitative synthesis. Psychological Bulletin, 132(3), 354-380. https://communities.springernature.com/

Fernández-López, Á., Rodríguez-Fórtiz, M.J., Rodríguez-Almendros, M.L., Martínez-Segura, M.J. (2013). Mobile learning technology based on iOS devices to support students with special education needs. Computers & Education, 61, 77-90

Cinquin, P.A., Guitton, P., Sauzéon, H. (2019). Online e-learning and cognitive disabilities: A systematic review. Computers & Education, 130,
152-167

Bowen, J.P., Filippini-Fantoni, S. (2004, March). Personalization and the web
from a museum perspective. In Museums and the Web (vol. 4). Archives & Museum Informatics, Toronto, Canada

Falk, J.H., Heimlich, J., Bronnenkant, K. (2008). Using identity related visit motivations as a tool for understanding adult zoo and aquarium visitors'

Poce, A. (2017). Verba Sequentur. Pensiero e scrittura per uno sviluppo critico delle competenze nella scuola secondaria. Milano: FrancoAngeli

Kelly, M. Managing University Museums. Education and Skills; Organisation for Economic Cooperation and Development: Paris, France, 2001; Available online: http://www.SourceOECD.org (accessed on 27 November 2019).

AUTHOR INDEX